Researching New Reli Movements

'The most important "first" that this book achieves is its bold questioning of the whole intellectual apparatus of the sociology of religion as it has been applied to the understanding of the new religious movements. I am confident that Elisabeth Arweck's study will quickly become required reading in the sociology of new religious movements.'

Professor David Martin, Emeritus Professor of Sociology,
London School of Economics, University of London

'Powerful and original . . . it succeeds triumphantly in being at the same time an important, high-quality academic study and a book for our times.'

Professor David Marsland, Professorial Research Fellow in Sociology,
University of Buckingham

New religious movements such as Scientology, Jehovah's Witnesses and the Unification Church (Moonies) are now well established in mainstream cultural consciousness. However, responses to these 'cult' groups still tend to be overwhelmingly negative, characterized by the furious reactions that they evoke from majority interests. Modern societies need to learn how to respond to such movements and how to interpret their benefits and dangers.

Researching New Religious Movements provides a fresh look at the history and development of 'anti-cult' groups and the response of mainstream churches to these new movements. In this unique reception study, Elisabeth Arweck traces the path of scholarship of new religious movements, exploring the development of research in this growing field. She considers academic and media interventions on both sides, with special emphasis on the problems of objectivity inherent in terminologies of 'sects', 'cults', and 'brainwashing'. Ideal for students and researchers, this much-needed book takes the debate over new religious movements to a more sophisticated level.

Elisabeth Arweck is a Research Fellow at the University of Warwick's Religions and Education Research Unit and CEDAR (Centre for Educational Development, Appraisal and Research). She is an editor of the *Journal of Contemporary Religion*, co-author of *New Religious Movements in Western Europe* (1997) and co-editor of *Theorizing Faith* (2002).

Researching New Religious Movements

Responses and redefinitions

Elisabeth Arweck

LONDON AND NEW YORK

First published 2006
by Routledge
2 Park Square, Milton Park, Abingdon, Oxon OX14 4RN

Simultaneously published in the USA and Canada
by Routledge
270 Madison Avenue, New York, NY 10016

Routledge is an imprint of the Taylor & Francis Group

Typeset by RefineCatch Limited, Bungay, Suffolk
Printed and bound in Great Britain by Antony Rowe Ltd,
Chippenham, Wiltshire

British Library Cataloguing in Publication Data
A catalogue record for this book is available from the British Library

Library of Congress Cataloging in Publication Data
Arweck, Elisabeth.
    Researching new religious movements : responses and redefinitions /
Elisabeth Arweck.—1st ed.
        p. cm.
    English and German.
    Includes bibliographical references.
    ISBN 0–415–27754–X (hardback : alk. paper)—ISBN 0–415–
27755–8 (pbk. : alk. paper)—ISBN 0–203–64237–6 (e-book)
1. Cults—Germany.   2. Religion and sociology—
Germany.   3. Cults—Great Britain.   4. Religion and sociology—
Great Britain.   I. Title.
    BL980.G3A79   2005
    200′.7′041—dc22   2005017222

ISBN10: 0–415–27754–X (hbk)
ISBN10: 0–415–27755–8 (pbk)

ISBN13: 9–78–0–415–27754–9 (hbk)
ISBN13: 9–78–0–415–27755–6 (pbk)

Contents

Foreword

For the last decade Elisabeth Arweck has been an unobtrusive but increasingly valued presence in the international sociology of religion. She is editor, alongside Peter Clarke, of the *Journal of Contemporary Religion*. As a member of Peter Clarke's research institute at King's College, London, she accumulated an unrivalled archive of materials on New Religious Movements (NRMs) and her linguistic skills enabled her to make the bibliography on NRMs that she published jointly with Peter Clarke a genuinely European as well as Anglophone research resource for the discipline. Now in this book we see the fruits of many years of scholarship and reflection on the problems in the field of NRM studies.

The book is a 'first' in a number of senses. It is the first systematic comparison of the situation of NRMs in two European societies and thus adds a valuable extra dimension to a field which American sociology has pioneered. It is also the first full-length study that I am aware of which is to NRMs what musicologists call a 'reception study'; that is, it is concerned with how the emergence of New Religious Movements from the 1960s onwards was understood and responded to by other interested parties, conducted by someone who is linguistically and culturally at home in Europe. These include the mainstream churches to which, in interestingly different ways, the British and German states passed the hot political potato that the new movements soon came to represent, a move which would have been inconceivable in the US with its strict separation of state and church. Another important interest group that was galvanised into action by the new movements was what quickly came to be popularly known as 'the anti-cult movement', a number of voluntary organizations, mostly made up of the concerned relatives of converts to NRMs. The experience of losing a member of the family to a communitarian religious group about which little was initially known, by a process that often seemed incomprehensible and even sinister, drew parents in particular into one or other of the 'anti-cult' organizations. As the book shows, some of the new religious groups were more likely than others to meet with a hostile or fearful response from the families of converts. The book examines the reasons why the concept of 'brainwashing' became the standard explanation the 'anti-cult' organizations and the mass media offered to explain why educated and intelligent young people were joining the new religious groups. Dr Arweck traces the changing policies of the 'anti-cult movement' and the moves that the NRMs in turn took to counter its activities and charges. The part the mass media played in inventing the now-stereotyped popular images of these religious movements and their opponents is an integral part of the story. So, too, is the role of the academic researchers who found in the NRMs a new focus for the study of religion in a supposedly 'secular' era, and a topic that could constitute a lifetime's work and the making of many a career. The tension between the academic research community and the 'anti-cult' organizations is a persistent thread in the weave.

Perhaps the most important 'first' that this book achieves is its bold questioning of the whole intellectual apparatus of the Sociology of Religion as it has been applied to the understanding of the New Religious Movements. For the first time this has not been used as the source of an 'objective', or, at least, disinterested framework for the research but has itself been held up for interrogation as the *product* of a complex set of interactions with the other interested parties in what, as the story unfolds, looks more and more like a developing dance, not so much choreographed as improvised, in which all the interested parties move among shifting alliances and hostilities, until it settles into an increasingly predictable pattern.

I am confident that Elisabeth Arweck's study will quickly become required reading in the sociology of new religious movements and will move the debate on to new and important ground, not least by its reformulation of what is at stake in the ethics of research in this and related fields.

David Martin
Woking, April, 2005

Acknowledgements

A book written without the help and support of others is a rarity. This book is no such rarity. I am indebted to many who have contributed in various ways, by providing information, assistance, and encouragement at different stages of this project. Mrs Bernice Martin, now Emeritus Reader in Sociology at Royal Holloway College, not only encouraged and guided this project in its initial stages by helping it germinate and grow, but also accompanied it throughout, not least with countless invaluable acts of friendship. Peter B. Clarke, now Professor Emeritus of History and Sociology at King's College London, contributed by supervising my PhD thesis and involving me in the work of the Centre for New Religions at King's. This experience shaped ideas and led to joint projects, such as the annotated bibliography on new religious movements and editorship of the *Journal of Contemporary Religion*, founded by Professor Clarke as *Religion Today* in the early 1980s. Practical and moral support at various stages during this project came from Rudolf Muller, Dr Joanna Savory, Chris and Rainhild Wells, Michael York, now Professor Emeritus at Bath Spa University College, Dr Athena Leoussi, Professor David Martin, Ann Henderson, and lastly, because most especially, Andrew Stewart-Brown.

A number of people in Germany contributed to my research, among them Hans Liebl, *Sektenbeauftragter* of the Roman Catholic Church in Munich, staff at the *Evangelische Zentralstelle für Weltanschauungsfragen* in Stuttgart, especially Dr Reinhart Hummel, Professor Rainer Flasche at the University of Marburg, members of REMID, namely Thomas Schweer and Steffen Rink, and Professor Martin Baumann at the University of Lucerne. A number of interviewees in Britain graciously answered many a probing question, among them Eileen Barker, now Professor Emeritus at the London School of Economics, University of London, Professor Jim Beckford at the University of Warwick, Dr Judith Coney, Professor Paul Heelas at the University of Lancaster, and (the late) Dr Bryan R. Wilson, Fellow (Emeritus) of All Soul's College Oxford. Their views and observations formed an important background to my thinking and argument.

Mrs Audrey Chaytor, now former chairperson of FAIR, Lady Daphne Vane, now former member of the FAIR Committee, Mrs Ursula MacKenzie, now retired Secretary of FAIR, Miss Joy Caton, formerly at the Deo Gloria Trust in Bromley, Kent, Christian Szurko of Dialog Center International, and Paul Rose, former MP for Manchester Blackley, all generously made time for meetings and conversations.

I am grateful to the archivist at the Church of England Archives, Dr Brenda Hough, to Canon Martin Reardon of Churches Together in England, Dr Anne Richards and Colin Podmore, both at Church House, and the Church of England Enquiry Centre. Dr Teresa Gonçalves of the Pontifical Council for Interreligious Dialogue and Professor Michael Fuss at the Università Gregoriana kindly assisted with information. I greatly appreciated conversations with members of staff at the Home Office.

The Central Research Fund Committee of the University of London provided a grant from the Irwin Fund in 1991 and King's College London granted a travel award from the Sargeaunt Fund.

1 What this book is about

Minority or non-mainstream religions and religious groups keep appearing in the limelight of the media's attention, usually in connection with a 'scandalous' affair of some kind or seemingly incomprehensible 'bizarre' or 'lunatic' behaviour. Recent events which have made the headlines include the suicide of Ricky Rodriguez, a former member of the Children of God (now The Family). A 'product' of 'flirty fishing', Rodriguez – nicknamed 'Davidito', the young 'prophet' – was the son of David Berg's consort Maria and had been held up as an exemplar for child rearing in the group, destined to be the future leader. Before committing suicide Rodriguez recorded a somewhat theatrical indictment against his upbringing on video and then killed Angela Smith, his erstwhile nanny, as a dramatic act of revenge. The incident had wider implications, leading to the examination of the connection between Family Care Foundation, a charitable organization, and The Family International. Another recent 'story' is that of Tim Guest who grew up in the Rajneesh (Osho) movement, the experience of which he recounts in *My Life in Orange* (2004) as well as in international newspaper articles. The violence of the Jonestown tragedy of 1978, the demise of David Koresh's Branch Davidians in the Waco compound in 1993, the sarin gas attack in the Tokyo underground perpetrated by Aum Shinrikyo or Aum Supreme Truth (now Aleph) in 1995, the voluntary death of the Heaven's Gate members in 1997, and the deaths of the members of the Movement for the Restoration of the Ten Commandments of God in 2000 remain live issues, thanks to continuous media coverage. With regular reports about such dramatic and sensational 'stories' in the press as well as the fictional dramatization of some of these in feature-length films and novels, the 'man and woman in the street' are reminded of the subject of 'cults' again and again and attracted to reading about and watching 'weird' and 'outlandish' occurrences unfolding, only to have all the stereotypical perceptions about such groups continually reinforced and confirmed. 'Cults' and any (religious) group or community that might fit the category provide media-effective material, especially when there is a connection with stars or 'famous' personalities, such as John Travolta and Tom Cruise's membership of Scientology; often, they present volatile combinations of the very ingredients in which the media are interested:

religion, money, sexual misdemeanour, children, exploitation, 'bizarre' rituals, exotic locations, and so on.

Looking at media coverage over the years, we can chart the progression and expansion of the 'cult' category: the 'cults' of the 1960s and 1970s (such as the Children of God/The Family, Rajneeshism/Osho movement, Scientology, the Unification Church or 'Moonies', ISKCON, etc.) have been kept alive by issues which arise from the maturation of these movements, including the second generation of members and former members raising their voices, issues of succession (once charismatic leaders have died), movements adapting their teachings, especially in cases where millennial/apocalyptic predictions have failed to materialize, as, for example, in the Church Universal and Triumphant (CUT), and surviving members and/or family members holding annual memorial events, as, for example, in the case of the Jonestown tragedy, or the media reminding the public of recurring anniversaries. In the case of groups, such as the Branch Davidians and Aum Shinrikyo, legal issues and other processes are ongoing, ranging from property rights to trials, restriction orders on existing members, and compensation of victims.

However, the media have also seized moral panics over issues, such as the 'satanic ritual abuse', a strand of the 'cult scare' which reported of subversive satanic activities and large-scale satanic conspiracy (see Richardson, Best and Bromley, 1991; La Fontaine, 1994), involving a fusion of satanism with witchcraft and child abuse. This theme has resurfaced recently with Pentecostal practices being related to exorcism and reports of violence against children occurring in the process of exorcizing demons. The death of Victoria Climbié, the eight-year-old girl who suffered cruel abuse and neglect by her aunt and her aunt's partner, has been connected with such practices. The couple visited the Universal Church of the Kingdom of God in Finsbury Park in London at least once with Victoria (BBC Newsnight, March 2005). Sexual abuse allegations also surfaced in 'cults', such as The Family and ISKCON (Hare Krishna movement), and extended to more 'mainstream' religious groups (e.g. Buddhist groups) culminating in the controversy about false memory syndrome. In the early 1990s, authorities in Spain, Argentina, France, and Australia organized raids on communes of The Family, removing hundreds of children and, in some cases, arresting the adults.

In addition, 'older' groups, which one might consider the 'new religious movements' of the nineteenth century, such as Mormonism or the Jehovah's Witnesses, are often lumped into the 'cult' category. The abduction and subsequent liberation of Elizabeth Smart in 2002, together with the later trial of her abductors and the fictionalization of her 'story', have received a great deal of media attention, as have polygamous Mormon groups. Any religious or ideological group which appears to be out of the ordinary or causing a public stir runs the risk of being portrayed as a 'cult', including groups like Falun Gong, Colonia Dignidad, and the Kabballah Centre (in the news because of the membership of celebrities, such as Madonna), and groupings within the mainstream churches, 'cults within the Church', such as the Nine O'Clock service (Howard, 1996), the *Engelwerk* (Angels' Work), and Opus Dei, with suspicions about the last having been revived with the appointment of the current Minister for Education in the UK, Ruth Kelly, who is a lay member.

The turn of the millennium provided another opportunity to highlight 'wayward' groups and movements whose teachings include apocalyptic and millennial ideas, but this was quickly superseded by the dramatic events of 9/11 and the emerging debate about sectarian Islamic groups waging 'holy war' against the West. While the destruction of the Twin Towers in New York showed unprecedented levels of violence ostensibly motivated by religious conviction, it added a new dimension to the debate about violent religion and especially violent 'cults', a theme which had also played some part in the trial of the Oklahoma City bomber, Timothy McVeigh, a white supremacist, who had detonated a truck bomb in front of a federal building in Oklahoma City in April 1995. The events of 9/11 have had a major impact on the way the 'cult' category is used in the media, as political motives are bound in tightly with religious beliefs which are depicted in media-typical fashion, namely with minimal differentiation and stereotypical categories.

Interestingly, the expansion of the 'cult' category has also found its way into the academic/social scientific study of 'new religious movements', with some papers and articles drawing parallels between 'cults' and Al-Qaeda (see e.g. Melton, 2003; 2004: 238–239; Introvigne, 2004; Lucas and Robbins, 2004). However, the expansion of the 'cult' category entails a muddying of this very category, thus adding further confusion and lack of clarity to a concept which is already contested and controverted – a point which this volume argues.

Readers of this book looking for a compendium of groups and movements which the media and some social scientists variously subsume under the 'cult' heading will look in vain. This volume is not about individual groups or movements and their particular developments, even if these are the 'stories' which attract the media, the public, and the academic community as well as those who fund their research. Readers who are looking for up-to-date accounts between the covers of this book will therefore be disappointed, because what this book is about is to show the *processes* involved in bringing about the constellation of the 'players' in this field – the movements themselves, the media, the parents, the 'anti-cult' movement, the churches, and the academic community. This book provides the tools for 'reading' these (ostensibly) disparate media 'stories' and gaining an understanding of the various strands of 'discourses' that have evolved since 'cults' became topical in the late 1960s and early 1970s and how these strands have interacted and influenced one another over time. The fact that, historically, certain groups tended to be the main stimuli to these processes – for example, the Unification Church coming to be viewed as the cult *par excellence* – explains why they appear in the text disproportionately.

In essence, this volume offers three new things: first, no other work has looked at the history and development of 'anti-cult' groups and the response of the mainstream churches to these new movements as systematically as it is done here. Second, no other work has attempted to draw as in-depth a comparison of the 'anti-cult movement' (ACM) and the churches between the UK and Germany, a comparison which illustrates at the same time the wider context of the Anglo-Saxon countries and Continental Europe and highlights the cultural and historical factors which have been at work to shape the respective (and very different) responses. This comparison demonstrates that the American model is not the only one and that cultural and historical differences matter. These differences continue to matter, both on a national and international level. At the national level, the presence of the Jehovah's Witnesses, for example, in the UK or the US causes no major political problems and only raises legal issues in connection with their refusal to have blood transfusions. However, in Germany, the position of the Jehovah's Witnesses vis-à-vis the State during the Third Reich continues to be a matter of public debate and their application for legal recognition as a 'body under public law' (*Körperschaft des öffentlichen Rechts*), a legal status which is not automatically bestowed on religious organizations, has required the German courts to take into account political and legal considerations and has been exercising them for over a decade. The most recent court decision on 24 March 2005 resulted from the *Land* of Berlin rejecting the compromise proposed by the fifth Senate of the Upper Administrative Court (*Oberverwaltungsgericht*) of Berlin. Before the recent decision in March, it was anticipated that whichever side lost the case could appeal to the highest tribunal, the federal administrative court (*Bundesverwaltungsgericht*). However, the court ruled not only that the Jehovah's Witnesses should be granted the status of 'body under public law' in Berlin, but also that the *Land* of Berlin should not be given leave to appeal against this verdict. This status grants religious organizations a number of rights, among them raising taxes, establishing charitable organizations, and providing religious education in state schools. The implications are currently under discussion, with the director of the Hannah Arendt Institute for Research into Totalitarianism at the University of Dresden, Professor Gerhard Besier, commenting on the case in *Die Welt* (26 March 2005). Professor Besier is a voice which had raised contention in connection with Scientology after he had published critically on Germany's 'sect hysteria' and the 'faith envy' of the two main churches and spoke passionately about Scientology's 'battle for tolerance and religious pluralism' at the opening of its European headquarters in Brussels in September 2003. Thus, despite an ostensible settlement by the court, the case of the Jehovah's Witnesses continues to reverberate in German juridical and political life. They may now seek to gain similar recognition in other *Länder*.

At the international level, Scientology is a case in point. Again, Scientology does not raise any major political issues in the US or the UK, but it does in Germany where its 'anti-constitutional objectives' have placed it (since 1997) under observation from the federal office of *Verfassungsschutz* (a decision upheld by the court in 2004, after an appeal by Scientology, but the Upper Administrative Court of the *Land* of Saarland ruled in late April 2005 that Scientology should not be observed by the *Verfassungsschutz* of this *Land*) and where Scientology members cannot (easily) hold public office. From an American point of view, the way Germany treats Scientology and its members is perceived to be in contravention of the bill of human rights – hence the censure in the US Department of State's annual Human Rights Reports (see e.g. http://www.state.gov/g/drl/rls/hrrpt/2004/) and representations by high-ranking US politicians on behalf of Scientology. Other examples where cultural and historical factors have proved to matter include the occasion when Tom Cruise, while co-hosting a Nobel Peace Prize Concert in Oslo in late 2004 with Oprah Winfrey, used the platform to plug Scientology, and instances when Scientology volunteer ministers have offered their 'Assists' as part of relief efforts around the world, ranging from earthquakes to the Oklahoma City bombing, 'Ground Zero', the 2002 Moscow theatre hostage crisis, the hurricane-struck areas of Florida, the floods in eastern Germany in 2002, and most recently, Tsunami affected areas. New religious movements (NRMs) operate on the international level like global organizations and businesses, but as Jim Beckford has pointed out in his *Cult Controversies* (1985), the way in which they insert themselves into the respective host societies depends on the particular *modus operandi* available to them, given particular cultural and historical circumstances. Further, a number of NRMs have formed, sometimes in conjunction with religious leaders and human rights advocates, pan-European and transnational associations to combat 'religious discrimination' and other 'human rights violations', for example, the 'European Foundation for Human Rights and Tolerance' which was formed in March 2005 and hosted by Scientology's European headquarters.

Third, this book does not accord unique privilege to the voice of the academics/social scientists in this field of study or the academic discourse and does not consider the body of academic knowledge as automatically standing above the body of knowledge which the other contenders in the debate have accumulated. For this reason, academics working in this field may find this book unsatisfactory or in disagreement with their own positions, because it seeks to show that academics/social scientists/sociologists of religion are similar to the other interest groups involved in the debate of NRMs in that they, too, have brought different sets of agendas into play. These are partly related to pressures to which the academic community itself has been subjected, such as obtaining funding, raising institutional profiles, and the need to produce publications, arising partly from the desire to build personal reputations, and partly from the particular stances which academics have adopted with regard to new religious movements, some of which are driven by personal motives. Some or all of this has induced some academics to go where the current news story is and thus 'jump on a band-wagon', such as linking NRMs and Al-Qaeda and related groups. Such factors are of particular pertinence with regard to the comparison of the academic communities in the Anglo-Saxon countries and in Germany, with the influence of the former on the latter having a significant impact on the relationship between the academic community on the one hand and the churches and the ACM on the other hand.

This book accordingly seeks to provide a map of the discourses which the different interested parties have developed since the inception of the debate and to show the processes and interactions between these various parties, as they have shaped and moulded the respective standpoints over time. This volume is thus a piece of intellectual history, which is why its intention is not to bring the reader up to date with recent developments, but to elucidate where it all originated and to delineate the ground rules on which the inter-actions have come to operate. The book's concern is therefore to convey a sense of the *generic* nature of the processes involved (which are replicated again and again) and the uniqueness of the cultural context from which the generic forms arise. Hence the differences in approaches and responses in Germany, as compared to the UK and as compared to the US.

Issues regarding 'cults' or new religious movements become even more complicated when human rights issues are invoked in global or pan-European structures and when different national legal structures clash with one another, as happens, for example, in the case of the US and Germany. The overriding principle of the First Amendment in the US collides with Germany's overriding commitment not to tolerate any conditions which may harbour fascist tendencies and Germany's concomitant sense of obliga-tion towards eternal vigilance. Thus, international and transnational links may be in tension with local and national situations.

There is a running theme in the 'story' of the discourses, which is the way in which academics have found themselves on the opposite end of the spec-trum to the ACM (and also the churches) and the way in which the ACM has felt 'let down' by the academics. The reason for this has been the differ-ence between their respective purposes and approaches, with the perspective of the ACM located within a paradigm largely shaped by psychology and the perspective of the academics located within a paradigm shaped by social science and the sociology of religion. The disparity between the two has led to very different ways of tackling the topic and formulating research ques-tions, while at the same time spurring modification of their respective posi-tions, as the various parties involved sought to conduct some dialogue with one another, to the point of having found areas where sections of the ACM and the academic community converge.

In the light of earlier remarks about the way the academic discourse is treated in this volume, I therefore do not start with a ready-made tool kit from the sociology of religion, because, when I embarked on my research journey, I found that it could not be taken for granted. Thus, I could not start with definitions of the concepts of 'cult', 'sect' or 'new religious movement', nor could I come to any definitive judgement about which term was the 'right' one to use. However, I have come to a *pragmatic* judgement about the use of the terms, settling for 'new religious movement' as the least 'contaminated', albeit not an entirely 'objective' term. Similarly, theories about recruitment to NRMs and processes inside the different groups have all been all up for question and are thus not treated as unassailable 'objective' knowledge. To a considerable extent, this problem arises from issues concerning the ethics of academic investigation, which involves the various discourses which have been formulated and is intimately bound up with the seriousness and integrity which individual academics have ascribed to 'rules' of ethical conduct in research.

The book reflects the notion of *process* in two senses: first, it records the processes by which knowledge is acquired and the pitfalls which revealed themselves to me as a relatively inexperienced researcher in this field with regard to what could or could not be said. Therefore, the book does not start with the 'findings' at which my investigation arrived, but takes the reader on the very research journey on which I embarked. This involved careful examination of available sources *before* drawing any conclusions. It also involved careful disentangling of parallel strands and then interweaving them in the respective accounts. Second, it was the processes in the field that my research tried to uncover in order to show how the discourses emerged and how they relate to one another. This book is thus not a textbook for methodological tool kits and findings either – it interrogates both and throws both into question. Those interested in the relationships between the various parties – without which they cannot understand the moral context – will get something valuable from this book, but it does not provide a set of pigeon-holes which would accommodate all the different groups. All of this is in question because I have been interested in the way in which the existing pigeon-holes were constructed and in whether existing tool kits have relevance for the discussion of Islamic terrorist groups. This may be so, but it cannot be assumed to be the case. If one were to draw out the commonalities between the current headlines and disregard the history of the discourses, one would arrive at a set of peculiar conclusions, because one would not compare like with like and simply feed into existing media stereotypes. Readers of this book will need to suspend any desire for easy answers and 'neat' categories and be prepared for ambiguities and paradoxes.

For those who do not want to follow the detailed unfolding of the various processes, here is the map of the chapters. For anyone interested in the substantive material about the ACM and the churches, see Chapters 5 and 6. Chapters 3 and 4 show how the various aspects and factors evolved over time and set out the respective parameters. The Conclusions present the findings in pulling together what we *can* say about the processes in the two countries (Britain and Germany) and give an indication of how the more up-to-date material can be slotted in. Chapter 2 takes the reader on the research journey such as I experienced it from the outset of my project. Chapter 3 outlines what made the emergence of NRMs a *new* phenomenon and how it elicited a range of responses on the institutional level. It also looks at the impact of this new phenomenon on the sociology of religion in Britain and on *Religionswissenschaft* in Germany. Chapter 4 points out the relevant cultural differences between Britain and Germany, in particular the respective roles of the churches and the academic community. Chapter 5 looks at the origins and development of FAIR in Britain and *Elterninitiative* in Germany. Chapter 6 describes the responses formulated by the Church of England, the Lutheran Church in Germany, and the Roman Catholic Church, and finally, Chapter 7 presents my conclusions.

2 Milestones in a research itinerary

This book grew out of a bibliographic project and the accumulation of comparative documentary data on new religious movements (NRMs) and the responses to them in Britain and Germany. My aim was to gain an overview of the existing material and to find out who was involved in the debate. I also wanted to know whether there were major strands in the arguments around which the debate revolved and whether there were any differences between the two countries, differences in the chronological unfolding of the debate, in the emphasis placed on arguments and aspects, and in the approaches which the different parties involved had taken. Explanations to account for such differences also needed to be explored.

Blazing the research trail

I had previously examined the situation of NRMs in France and presented the findings in an MA thesis in Germany (Arweck, 1985). The path of this research might have alerted me to the level of academic interest in the subject in Germany, had I not been relatively inexperienced in this field. However, examining the state of academic research of NRMs at that time proved an important component of my enterprise.

The MA thesis left me with the feeling that I had not really got to the bottom of the issue, especially regarding the literature available to me within the allotted time. The provenance of some works and their political agenda often revealed themselves only after careful scrutiny of the text and examination of the context from which they arose. I became sensitive to questions asking: Who are the publishers? What is the background of the author? Does the author have an axe to grind? What is the author's agenda? Is the author affiliated with some organization? etc. I realized that there was what can be called 'contaminated writing' – writing with a hidden agenda. The implication is that texts and documents need to be looked at in the particular context in which they are embedded. This also entails the necessity to examine and assess the importance of the documents in that context or, to use a theological expression, their *Sitz im Leben*, the reasons for which they are created, the response they elicit, etc.

The material I gathered and assessed for the MA thesis consisted largely of literature by NRMs themselves – pamphlets, brochures, newsletters, hand-outs, posters, books, etc. (which I collected at meetings or requested by mail – an exercise which in itself provided valuable data), literature by various 'anti-cult' groups and church organizations, and journalistic accounts in newspapers, magazines, and books. Most of this secondary literature largely agreed on the underlying causes and consequences of the *phénomène sectaire* (the general heading of the NRM phenomenon in France) and the measures to remedy the situation. Overall, the arguments could be attrib-uted to the 'anti-cult' perspective. Hardly any literature seemed to provide analysis from within an academic (social scientific) framework: that at my disposal either took a psychological approach, for example Pavlos's *The Cult Experience* (Pavlos, 1982), or examined 'traditional sects' from a socio-logical perspective, such as Wilson's *Religious Sects* (1970a). The former were helpful, but seemed to confirm the 'anti-cult' stance rather than coun-ter-balance it – a consequence inherent in psychological studies as they tend to look for the (latent) pathology in NRM members or leaders. However, studies exist which do not present a negative picture of NRMs or NRM membership[1] and others which point to both positive and negative effects of membership (Levine, 1981; 1978). Yet neither psychological nor 'sect' approach seemed to yield a theoretical framework for the study of NRMs.

While completing fieldwork and collection of materials I discovered the American and British literature – a substantial body of writings taking an analytical, academic approach. However, access to this material was very difficult; for example, the only available copy of Wilson's book (1970b) was the French translation. Together with the time constraint, I could not study this material sufficiently to include it in the MA thesis.

During my fieldwork I discovered that some parents' organizations (in Germany and France) seemed somewhat reluctant to grant access to infor-mation, if not altogether suspicious of my project. I was asked to provide confirmation from university authorities and my supervisor. Even after I had complied with such requests, the information sent by one organization was disappointingly sparse – an experience, I later discovered, shared by other researchers (Scheffler, 1989: 51–52). Another organization still did not seem quite convinced of my *bona fides* (good faith) when I consulted its archives, the documents I was allowed to see were carefully selected and I felt a watchful eye on me while reading the files. Although this seemed 'strange' at the time, I accepted it, because I was grateful for access to (at least some) information and because it seemed plausible that confidential material should need careful handling. However, with increasing experience, I real-ized that the supervision was to preclude theft or destruction of documents. Due to 'bad' experiences (NRM members posing as students or willing help-ers as a ploy to 'infiltrate' organizations known to be hostile towards them), parents' organizations had 'learnt' to be wary of would-be students. Later, various people told me about such incidents, often pointing out that there was not sufficient proof to make a case against individuals or groups, yet emphasizing that circumstantial evidence gave rise to very strong suspicions. Yet, at the time, no-one explained such precautions.

Continuing the trail

After the MA degree, I decided to explore the recently discovered Anglo-Saxon literature by embarking on a doctoral thesis. Although the initial intention was to examine the role of the media in the NRM debate, I soon realized that the very fact of carrying out research and engaging with those involved in the debate affected my research and the way I went about it. The need to address methodological and ethical questions became more and more urgent. The further I progressed, the more pressing such questions became and this finally changed the research focus. While the compilation of primary and secondary materials continued, the emphasis was on existing *academic* literature, particularly literature published in Britain, with various sources informing the overview of the literature (Arweck and Clarke, 1997).

I began with the material available at the (then) Centre for New Religions at King's College London where I worked with the Director, Professor Peter Clarke, as a voluntary research assistant. Further materials were collected during a research trip to Germany in 1992, when I visited a number of institutions and their representatives, among them *Evangelische Zentralstelle für Weltanschauungsfragen* (then located) in Stuttgart, the *Sektenbeauftragte* for the Roman Catholic Church in Munich (Hans Liebl), Professor Rainer Flasche at the University of Marburg, and a (then) newly formed organization called REMID (*Religionswissenschaftlicher Medien-und Informationsdienst e.V.*) in Marburg. At the same time, the (albeit unsystematic) collection continued of newspaper cuttings, newsletters, and other primary and secondary writings, including government reports, church reports, conference proceedings, etc. These sources referred to groups and movements across Western Europe, although my focus remained on the UK and Western Germany.

Some insight into the situation of NRMs in Britain and Germany allowed the formulation of hypotheses about the way in which NRMs and the debate surrounding them had developed in the two countries. My general supposition was that there would be both parallels and significant differences. My first assumption was that NRMs had appeared slightly later in Germany, having on the whole originated in the United States and spread from there to the UK and then to Continental Europe. As in the US and UK, NRMs in Germany were not immediately perceived as problematic or controversial; in some cases, such as the Children of God (now The Family), there was some collaboration with local churches or groups on account of their seemingly Christian beliefs. (Deo Gloria Outreach, one of the first 'anti-cult' groups in Britain, resulted from such a collaboration, after it had gone sour.) In the US, NRMs were perceived as a new and to some extent problematic phenomenon in the late 1960s; in the UK, the first cases of controversial NRM membership were reported in the early to mid-1970s, when the stories of parents who had 'lost' children to NRMs appeared in the media;[2] and in Germany, the controversy over NRM membership surfaced slightly later, towards the mid- and late 1970s, with the first parents' group forming in the late 1970s. My theory envisioned a 'ripple' effect of this new wave spreading in stages across the Atlantic to the UK and from the UK across the Channel to the Continent. However, the first 'anti-cult' group in Britain, FAIR (then 'Family Action and Information Rescue', now 'Family Action and Information Resource'), was founded in 1976 and the first parents' organization in Germany, *Elterninitiative zur Hilfe gegen seelische Abhängigkeit und religiösen Extremismus*, was founded in 1975.

FAIR arose from the concern of parents and relatives who had gathered around a Member of Parliament, Paul Rose. In 1974, his secretary – whose friend's son had joined the UC (Rose, 1981a: 186) – told him about the consequences of 'cult' involvement, which prompted him to raise questions about 'cults' in Parliament;[3] these attracted the interest of concerned parents and relatives. The German organization, *Elterninitiative*, also arose from the concern of parents and relatives, but these had gathered around a representative of the Protestant–Lutheran Church, Pastor Friedrich–Wilhelm Haack, the first specialist in the Church on this matter (*Sektenbeauftragte*). Haack was both instrumental and influential in shaping the aims and perspective of the *Elterninitiative*.

Haack had been appointed *Sektenbeauftragter* as early as 1969, after the post had been especially created for him. It arose from Haack's personal concern with the 'competition' to the Lutheran Church from 'other faith communities'.[4] Haack became aware of these well before the arrival of NRMs in Germany: in the 1960s, he examined 'traditional sects' or the 'NRMs of the nineteenth century' – Jehovah's Witnesses, Mormons, spiritualists, etc.[5] Haack was also interested in 'folk' or marginal religion, local or regional manifestations of belief and spirituality or healers and clairvoyants offering paths to salvation. Underlying Haack's study of such phenomena was an apologetic agenda, although he never fully explained its theological basis. His papers on apologetics (Haack, 1988f) provide some insight, but not a systematic presentation of his views. Even after NRMs or *Jugendreligionen* (youth religions), as Haack came to call them, had become the particular focus of his work, his interest in religious groups and movements outside the mainstream continued. As early as 1965 Haack had founded the *Arbeitsgemeinschaft für Religions- und Weltanschauungsfragen* or ARW (Association for the Study of Questions of Religion and *Weltanschauung*), initially with the intention of acting as an intermediary between the Church and other faith communities and to provide information for the Church (Ach, 1995b). It became his private collection and its publishing arm (*Verlag der ARW*) printed his numerous books.

In their formative years, both FAIR and *Elterninitiative* were – like CERF

(Citizens Engaged in Reuniting Families)[6] in the US and ADFI (*Association pour la Défense de la Famille and de l'Individu*)[7] in France – primarily concerned with the Unification Church (UC), with others focusing on different 'cults', for example FREECOG which concentrated on the Children of God.[8] Both widened their remit, as parents with children in other movements gradually joined their ranks. Both emphasized their concern for the *family* in dealing with the effects of 'cult' membership, an aspect reflected in their names.

The models for Haack and the parents' groups in Germany were American and French groups, such as CERF and ADFI – both in organizational terms and in terms of key ideas and concepts to explain 'cult' membership and its effects (for example, the notion of 'brainwashing'); these were adjusted to the German context and complemented with other ideas, such as Haack's own perspective. The *Elterninitiative* in Munich in turn served as a model for organizations set up subsequently in other parts of Germany (Haack, 1986c: 58) in the late 1970s and early 1980s.[9]

My second assumption was that in Germany, the mainstream Churches – particularly the Lutheran Church – were involved in the 'cult' debate almost from the very beginning. Haack was the first specialist on marginal religions in the Lutheran Church of Bavaria. When *Elterninitiative* in Munich was set up, the Roman Catholic Church, too, had installed such a specialist (Hans Löffelmann) in its Munich diocese and became one of the founding members of *Elterninitiative* (Haack *et al.*, 1986: 112; Schuster 1986: 6). More such specialists (*Sektenbeauftragte*) were appointed over time, in both the Protestant and Roman Catholic Church, so that each *Landeskirche* or diocese had at least one.[10] Together they form a network of information, expertise, and co-operation, including colleagues in Austria and Switzerland.

In Germany, ministers and priests – the grassroots level of the church hierarchies – became involved from the beginning, because parents saw them as their first port of call, when 'cult' membership caused problems in their families. To begin with, parents saw the problem as a *religious* one. In Britain on the other hand, parents first consulted their MPs on this matter, perceiving it as a *political* matter. Whatever involvement the Anglican Church had on the grassroots level (local vicars) remained at that level, as the Church did not feel called upon to set any mechanisms in place; it only did so much later. Vicars did not call for concerted action or seek co-operation from colleagues so that the Anglican Church did not grasp this nettle until the mid-1980s, when a question was put before the General Synod by a delegate who had encountered the 'cult' problem in his own parish. Even then it took some time before the Church formulated a response, because the Anglican Church did not have any committees or other mechanisms in place to deal with the issue.

By contrast, the Roman Catholic Church (RCC) did have structures in place for dealing with the 'cult' issue. However, it took pressure from the grassroots for the Vatican to put NRMs on its agenda. The Vatican secretariats did not feel compelled to address this issue, because NRMs fell into the category of 'other faiths' for which various bodies were set up to examine whether and what kind of dialogue there should be. Thus the RCC, too, entered the debate about NRMs at a late stage: the first document on the subject – the Vatican Report – was made public in 1986.

In Germany, the Lutheran Church had gradually installed *Sekten-beauftragte* in every *Landeskirche* (province) and created, as early as 1960, a national church institution, the *Evangelische Zentralstelle für Weltanschauungsfragen* (EZW). In some ways a re-creation of its historic precursor, the *Apologetische Centrale* – established in 1919, but closed under the Nazi regime in 1937 (Pöhlmann, 1998; 2000) – the EZW was given a wide remit: to monitor 'religious currents and *Weltanschauungen*' outside the Church. The EZW was not specifically designed to deal with NRMs, as its purpose was to watch other religions and spiritual currents of the time and to assess the way in which they were relevant for the Church.[11] Given the broad formulation of this brief, NRMs naturally fell within the EZW's remit, once their presence was felt in Germany. Thus, by the time NRMs became a hot issue in Germany, the Lutheran Church had structures and institutions in place which could address pastoral and theological issues.

The Roman Catholic Church in Germany, too, ensured the presence of a *Sektenbeauftragter* in each diocese and thus dealt with the issue at the grassroots level where it had arisen. The immediate pastoral concerns were taken care of, although it was left to local priests to tackle the nitty-gritty. As an international institution, the Vatican did not deal with the NRM question until much later, when mounting pressure from the grass-roots called for a general debate within the church and the formulation of official policy. These calls coincided with developments in Latin America (and other parts of the world) where new religious, particularly Pentecostal, groups became serious competitors and forced the Church to address the consequent pastoral and theological problems.

My third assumption concerned the role of the academics: in both countries, sociologists and other social scientists joined the debate last. In Britain, academics started looking at NRMs in the late 1970s and early 1980s. In her introduction to *New Religious Movements: A Perspective of Understanding Society*, Eileen Barker remarked on the growing interest in the study of new religions, but pointed out that 'little has been done in the way of systematic-ally comparing or assessing the various hypotheses' (Barker, 1982b: ix). Likewise, while conceding that 'a great deal of research into new religions has already been carried out', Peter Clarke stated during a lecture in 1985, that 'without further in-depth research, comment and observation will continue to be based on intuition rather than hard fact'. In the early 1980s, the first institutional bases for academic research in this area were created, among them the Centre for New Religions at King's College London and the Centre for New Religious Movements at Selly Oak Colleges in Birmingham.[12]

In Germany, academic concern with new religions emerged very slowly, with only a handful of academics taking an interest. The first handful of essays date from the late 1970s: NRMs as a subject for research in *Religionswissenschaft* (Flasche, 1978), UC theology (Flasche, 1981), an unpublished report for the (then) Ministry of Youth, Family, and Health (Hardin and Kehrer, 1978a), a short paper in an educational journal (Hardin and Kehrer, 1978b), 'non-church religious groups' (Kehrer, 1980a) in a collection on the history of religions (Kehrer, 1980b), an unpublished MA thesis (University of Tübingen) on the Children of God (Kuner, 1979), a published PhD thesis (submitted in 1982, University of Tübingen) on membership in the Children of God, the UC, and Ananda Marga (Kuner, 1983a), and UC history in Germany (Hardin and Kuner, 1981) in an edited volume on the UC (Kehrer, 1981a). According to Günter Kehrer (Kehrer, 1980a), research on NRMs by sociologists and religious studies scholars in the US and Britain did not have any impact on the debate in Germany at that time. This remark illustrates (and supports) my argument that the academic community in Germany neither received nor debated, let alone communicated, the findings of their Anglo-Saxon counterparts. The first major publication was Kehrer's collection on the UC (Kehrer, 1981a). More material appeared in the mid- to late 1980s, but overall, the academic community in Germany did not show the same amount of interest in new religions as their American or British counterparts. Also, when German academics did, they looked towards their Anglo-Saxon colleagues for theoretical frameworks, just as the 'anti-cult' groups had looked towards their Anglo-Saxon counterparts for organizational and explanatory frameworks. Kuner, for example, used Wuthnow (1982) to explain the surge of NRMs in the late 1960s and early 1970s (Kuner, 1983c); Eiben used Stark and Bainbridge's notions of 'sect', 'cult', and 'cult movement', Wallis's typology of world-affirming and world-rejecting NRMs, and Stark and Bainbridge's 'audience' and 'client cults' (Eiben, 1992).

Academic concern with NRMs in Germany has approached the subject from two disciplines: *Religionswissenschaft* and sociology of religion. Traditionally, *Religionswissenschaft* describes religions, their historical development, geographical spread, belief systems, etc. This approach favours detailed accounts of beliefs and organizational structures rather than social aspects or interaction between members, movements, and society. It is – or at least has been – a textually based discipline grounded in written documents and data, obvious sources for the study of historical religions. My own research was shaped by this tradition and therefore – at least initially – largely based on written material. Only recently have practitioners of *Religionswissenschaft* begun to exchange their 'armchair' approach for fieldwork. For example, REMID's statutes explicitly state empirical research methods as an integral part of its approach (REMID Annual Report 1989–90: 15). This, too, may be due to Anglo-Saxon influence.

There is more material from the perspective of *Religionswissenschaft* than from that of sociology of religion; while Flasche has been writing on the subject and supervising a number of doctoral theses (Scheffler, 1989), Kehrer has turned away from the subject after publishing the UC volume (Kehrer, 1981a) and some articles; there is no record of publications on NRMs after the mid-1980s. In 1986, Kehrer contributed 'critical periods in the history of new religions' (Kehrer, 1986) to *The Disappearance of Religions* (Zinser, 1986), and, in 1983, the public perception of 'youth religions' (Kehrer, 1983) to *The History of Religion in Public* (Falaturi *et al.*, 1983). Kehrer's main publications on NRMs cluster around the early 1980s (Kehrer, 1980a; 1981a; 1981b; 1982; Hardin and Kehrer, 1982). In the early 1990s, he was to have been co-editor of a collection on the 20-year-old NRM debate in Germany, but this volume was ultimately not published. His co-author, Bert Hardin, indicated to me that he – like Kehrer – had left this topic behind. Available evidence suggests that Kehrer did not want to become embroiled in the heated debate and controversies surrounding NRMs. An article in *Der Spiegel* in 1980 quotes him saying that, after having studied NRMs for two years, their activities sometimes really got to him and that a society which considers anything reversible *would* find it difficult to understand people taking religion so seriously (*Der Spiegel*, 1980: 71). Kehrer probably felt entangled in conflicting interests and did not want to be caught between NRMs and public perception.

Kehrer's reluctance to get too involved in the NRM debate illustrates the traditional attitude of German academics, namely to stand aloof from the subject(s) of one's study. Hence also the 'armchair' approach. Academics do not normally become enmeshed in causes or campaigns, because being an academic means pursuing ideas, theories, knowledge, not putting academic results or credentials in the service of a cause. This also explains vociferous objections, as expressed by Pastor Haack, to academics taking part in NRM-sponsored conferences. The German or Continental idea of academia is the pursuit of knowledge for its own sake, for no other purpose save the exploration and enhancement of knowledge. Thus, for someone like Kehrer to find himself caught between two fronts – NRMs and 'anti-cult' groups/the public – must have felt very uncomfortable. My studies at a German university communicated this attitude and induced some of this aloofness – hence my initial *documentary* research. Jürgen Eiben is one of the few academics in Germany writing from a sociological perspective, although it is unclear how much fieldwork is involved in his work. His publications are also informed by the Anglo-Saxon literature (Eiben, 1992; 1996).

In early 1989, a group of *Religionswissenschaft* graduates some of whom had studied under Professor Flasche, set up the *Religionswissenschaftlicher Medien- und Informationsdienst e.V.* (REMID) to meet the perceived lack of academic voices in the German NRM debate. REMID's stated aim is to bring the voice of academia to the fore and to introduce 'scientific' findings (informed by *Religionswissenschaft*) into the debate by communicating research results independently of religious beliefs and convictions to the wider public, which promotes peaceful and tolerant coexistence of different religions and facilitates mutual understanding and respect (REMID Annual Report 1989–1990: 15).[13] In November 1990, REMID had its baptism of fire, when it issued a statement on Scientology in Germany (REMID, 1990), intended for information on request (Thiede, 1992b). The Scientology debate had become especially topical in the wake of German reunification in 1989 and the first wave of NRM activities in former East Germany. REMID argued that, given the constitutionally guaranteed freedom of religion and the principle of tolerance in pluralistic society, Scientology had to be granted as much religious freedom as any other religious organization or church (REMID Annual Report 1989–1990: 12–14). Scientology quickly appropriated the statement as evidence that it *was* a religion – a focal question of the debate – even a *bona fide* religion deserving of protection under national law.

The incident showed that REMID had ventured into territory where others, such as Kehrer, feared to tread: having identified a 'gap' in the market, REMID thought – perhaps somewhat naively (Thiede, 1992b) – that academic credentials and expertise could fill this gap. It had, however, not reckoned with the politics, the fine mesh (or lack) of interaction between the parties involved. It had not pondered the reasons for the apparent 'gap in the market' and became caught in the mesh. This must have done REMID a disservice, not least by raising the suspicion that it was a 'front organization' for Scientology, as enquiries to that effect were received by the EZW (Thiede, 1992b: 151). Conversely, an enquiry directed to REMID's office suspected it to be a 'front' organization for the Churches (*spirita* 6 (1), 1992: 86). These contrary suspicions illustrate that REMID had surfaced as a new 'player' in the field and that existing players tried to locate its position. The incident situated (even if only temporarily) REMID where it had not intended to be, as people 'judged' according to their *own* position: some put REMID in the penumbra of Scientology, others in that of the churches.

Apart from gathering material, I attended meetings, seminars, conferences, and other events to discover issues and make contacts. From the early 1990s, I attended conferences run by organizations such as the Centre for Studies on New Religions (CESNUR),[14] seminars such as the six-monthly INFORM seminars,[15] the annual conference on 'Contemporary and New Age Religions in the British Isles',[16] and the annual conference at King's College London,[17] 'New Religious Movements: Challenge and Response', organized in 1995 by Dr B. R. Wilson and Soka Gakkai UK at the latter's headquarters at Taplow, Berkshire, and lectures at Taplow.

The Taplow conference revived for me the debate over whether academics should take part in NRM-sponsored conferences. This debate goes back to the 1980s, when the UC sponsored multi-disciplinary conferences for academics. This led to an entire issue of *Sociological Analysis* (44 (3), 1983) being dedicated to this debate. Scholars responded to an introductory summary of the main arguments against participation (Horowitz, 1983).

While three contributors (Barker, 1983a; Wallis, 1983; Wilson, 1983) stated their respective positions, one (Beckford, 1983c) examined wider implications for the academic community. When I later presented one of two seminar papers on the debate (Arweck, 1994a; 1994b), someone asked why I concerned myself with it, as he considered it over and done with – to some extent a valid point, as no-one talked about such issues, but precisely the reason why I raised them. As some academics had stopped attending sponsored conferences, the question was why, if – as had been argued – there was nothing to it. However, others still accepted such invitations. The methodological questions raised – such as how close academics should be to the subjects they study – had not really been addressed or solved. Therefore, I attended the Taplow conference with mixed feelings. Sponsored conferences may no longer be topical in that the debate about how close researchers should get to the groups they study has abated, but other forms of association between NRM members and scholars studying them still are, such as the Taplow lecture series, which invites academics to give or attend papers, with members of the movement present. In my view, photos in internal publications which do not clearly state the identity of the audience raise issues. NRM members attending academic conferences as speakers and audience also raise issues. The London conference in 1993 was the first in my experience which included a whole session by NRM representatives. As long as speakers and participants adhered to the 'rules' of academic exchange, the boundaries between insiders and outsiders were clear, but the representative of one organization violated the 'rules' by imposing his agenda. Also, should academics declare sympathies towards spiritual currents or practices or even membership, for example NRM members who have undergone academic programmes? If so, should all academics declare their religious affiliation or allegiance? Is it possible to be a 'good' academic and a 'good' religionist? Where should one draw the line? What about the closeness between research object/subject and researcher? Some of these questions surfaced during the 1988 conference on 'Work and Business', when a speaker was severely criticized for disclosing personal affinity with an organization (Binning, 1988).

Among non-academic meetings were conferences organized by FAIR, for example, 'Cultism – A Case for Treatment' (1990, Cambridge) and 'Influence and Stress Related Issues' (FAIR, 1993); FAIR's annual open meeting, the themes and speakers of which have ranged widely, from the impact of 'cults' (Singer, 1989), mind control (Hassan, 1990), 'cults' in the New Europe (Gandow, 1992), false memory syndrome (Ofshe, 1994), 'cults in Japan' (1995), to new religions in Russia (Dvorkin, 1997), and the meeting of 'anti-cult' groups in the UK to form an umbrella organization, in November 1989, with Lord Rodney, then chairman of FAIR, presiding – a milestone in my research. I had assumed that everyone present approved of my attendance. However, while some did, others were neutral, and yet others clearly objected. The meeting taught me several things: the 'anti-cult' movement is not a uniform entity – differences between and within individual groups need to be identified; my attendance as observer had an impact – participants seemed to behave differently and to choose words more carefully; attending as the representative of the Centre for New Religions afforded some 'protection', because its director was respected and trusted by some of those present; some wanted me to be party to their brief, not an observer.

Trailing politics and ethics

Encountering the range of concepts and ideas in these settings and connecting with an information network was very useful. However, I learnt that information is not necessarily and not always free-flowing or contact made easily. Obtaining information and meeting people involved political aspects: who I am, what I am doing, what I know, and whom I know. While researching I could not always preserve the status of 'neutral' observer: I felt either increasingly involved or pushed towards becoming so. My initial unquestioned assumption that I should remain an 'academic observer' became an issue. When it was difficult to uphold this status, I reminded myself of the ideals of social scientific research: objectivity, neutrality, detachment, value-free judgement, bracketing personal preconceptions and prejudices, etc., while also wondering whether it was too idealistic to maintain them.

Enquiries addressed to the Centre of New Religions provided insights into some social responses to NRMs: concerned families, relatives, and friends pointed to problematic aspects of NRM membership; journalists conveyed the approach of the media; students in search of material for theses and projects demonstrated the extent to which NRMs had become a topic for research; public authorities highlighted 'political' aspects involved in day-to-day decision-making. Family members affected by NRM membership hoped to obtain information from institutions like the Centre. They often needed to talk to someone who was knowledgeable about the particular movement and took seriously the difficulties and anxieties with which they struggled. People in public offices expected practical advice from academic 'experts' to deal with a range of everyday and complex matters – Should a hall be rented to an organization (which may not be an NRM at all)? Should an organization have or retain charitable status?[18] Can an NRM leader enter the country?[19] Can an NRM place advertisements on television?[20] In some cases, the notion of an 'expert' can be problematic, for example in adversarial contexts, such as in court or in certain media programmes.

There are political aspects in the relationships between organizations concerned with the study of NRMs, aspects also related to access to information, which may not necessarily be confidential. Sometimes, being an academic seemed to be an advantage, at other times, the opposite seemed to be the case: with 'anti-cult' groups and parents, I sometimes felt welcome as an academic and rejected because of it at other times. While some appreciated my 'objective' approach to NRMs, others resented my reluctance, if not refusal, to condemn NRMs and NRM practices outright. Such attitudes indicate the opinion of academics in general: academic researchers are 'lumped' together in one group, just as 'cults' and 'anti-cult' groups have been. Individual academics are thus not necessarily judged on their own merits, but on the basis what impression the academic community as a whole has created.

At least some NRMs have formed certain expectations towards academics, such as legitimation (for example, participation at NRM-sponsored conferences or lecture series, teaching NRM members enrolled in religious studies courses, links through NRM-funded projects, visiting professorships at NRM-founded universities, such as Soka University in Tokyo), support in court cases (academics have acted as expert witnesses for NRMs), or advice on how to obtain or safeguard charitable status (academics have written affidavits on behalf of NRMs in cases where charitable status was reviewed or investigated, as happened, for example, in the UC's libel case in 1980).

Being in a certain place at a particular time can carry significance: while I considered attending an (often) non-academic event as part of my job (participant observation, etc.), the organizers interpreted my presence as support.

I detected political structures within the academic community: some seemed careful (ethical?) about the way they carried out research and used data, while others did not seem to see the need for addressing some of the questions that became increasingly important to me. Citing examples here would be invidious, but some of my interviews with academics reinforce this point. In discussing the question of 'objectivity' in the research process, one of my interviewees commented that researchers can minimize the impact of prejudice and preconceptions, which a researcher is likely to bring along, by using certain 'techniques', such as 'bracketing off'. However, he conceded that different researchers produce research accounts of differing quality and that the variation depends on the *ability* of the researcher to use appropriate methods and to interpret the research findings. The variation in ability, he said, was influenced by a range of factors, such as training, experience, access to data, facilities, criticism from peers, guidance, supervision, etc. Another interviewee said that he did not know of any devices which would enhance awareness of preconceived ideas or assumptions and that this had to be largely left to the sensitivity of the investigator, adding that the personal quality of the investigator mattered. However, he commented that it was not easy to formulate just what that personal quality was, pointing out that sociology sometimes lacks terms for phenomena which are quite well known socially, although not always articulated.

My questions included the following: how close can/should academics be to their subjects? How much hospitality should academics accept from NRMs? Should academics attend NRM-sponsored conferences? If yes, should expenses be accepted? If yes, how much? Should academics attend conferences organized jointly by academics and NRMs? Should participant observation be overt or covert – which or what combination of the two will ensure 'authentic' data? If covert participant observation is ruled out as unethical, how do we avoid only seeing the group's 'shop window displays'? How much time is needed to investigate a group? How much and what kind of participation should there be in participant observation?

Further questions preoccupied me: should academics stand up for NRMs, for example, by defending their activities at press conferences? Should academics sign petitions on behalf of NRMs? Should academics appear as expert witnesses for NRMs? Should they write affidavits for NRMs? What about the quality of research based on 'flying' field visits? Should NRMs impose their agenda on academic conferences, as happened at the 1993 conference in London? What about academics with sympathies or even allegiances to a particular *Weltanschauung*? What about the increasing number of NRM members enrolled in university programmes? What about NRM graduates in academic posts? Are they any different from theologians or other committed religionists? Should research projects be funded by NRMs? How do academics preserve a 'healthy' distance between themselves and their 'subjects' to avoid 'going native' or adopting a particular group as *their* tribe or *their* area of expertise or being adopted in turn by a group as *their* expert? What about academics 'with a mission', who use their academic standing to support and defend a particular position? Commenting on 'subjects' and the researcher's attitude, Pepinsky uses advice quoted from L. T. Wilkin: 'Kings and queens have subjects, researchers should not!' (Pepinsky, 1980: 232). Sometimes, academics create the impression that they represent the group they study, simply by using the group-specific vocabulary.

On the whole, establishing contact and receiving information from academics was fairly straightforward. On the whole, the academic community was willing to provide information or findings, especially factual information, theoretical approaches, and conceptual frameworks. However, there has been a gap in social scientific discussion on the very questions mentioned above, especially attendance at NRM-sponsored conferences and the relationship between researcher and group – *open* discussion in seminars or at conferences, not private or informal conversations among colleagues.

At times, I felt discomfort in accepting the (sometimes lavish) hospitality of NRMs, for example the invitation to the Taplow conference required some soul-searching. I also wondered whether academic work should be published by publishing houses linked with NRMs[21] or in journals edited by NRM members.[22] In what way do NRM imprints differ from Christian publishing houses, such as SPCK whose foundation in 1698 was driven by Thomas Bray, a Church of England priest, who set out to extend the knowledge of the Christian faith through education and publishing (SPCK, n.d.)? I wondered whether academics should accept research funding from NRMs, whether academics should do anything which would or could be construed to support NRMs.

In 1993, The Family launched an appeal to members of the International Society for the Study of Religion (ISSR/SISR) for affidavits on their behalf. At this time, The Family faced allegations of child abuse, with a substantial number of children having been taken into custody in Spain, France, Australia and Argentina. Some academics had indeed supplied *To Whom It May Concern* statements for circulars (dated 21 August, 1993; 20 September, 1993), declaring their data showed clear evidence that the allegations were unfounded. Regardless of whether the allegations against The Family were actually true (in fact, the charges were dropped in all cases and the children returned to their parents), the question in my mind was whether academics' remit included supplying such statements and becoming what one might consider an apologist for the movement.[23] Such support seemed to me un-academic, an act of taking sides, ostensibly incompatible with the academic 'objectivity' and 'value neutrality', a political act which turns the supposedly detached observer into an involved and active party. Such instances make academics part of their data.

The trail in the field

In semi-structured interviews with British academics, I explored some of these burning methodological questions, an exercise which illustrated the point about the quality of the researcher and becoming part of one's data. The interviews yielded qualitative data which are comparable in some instances, but not in all. Although the sample was by no means representative, it nonetheless gave insight into the way academics have coped with methodological questions and showed whether there is a consensus regarding these questions. The interviews could not be matched with a sample of German scholars, not least because of the different academic cultures, the topic of Chapter 4.

It took time to develop links with representatives of the 'anti-cult' movement. The previously mentioned meeting to create an 'anti-cult' umbrella organization proved very instructive about 'anti-cult' organizations and the significance of being an academic. Some groups did not communicate or talk with me at all. With others, a friendly, albeit loose link developed. The group I followed and made contact with more closely was FAIR; I attended its annual lecture, maintained contact with Lady Daphne Vane, one of its founding members and international representative, and Mrs Audrey Chaytor, who succeeded Lord Rodney as chairman in 1992. My association with the Centre at King's College London helped me build some trust and goodwill. Before FAIR's London office closed in 1994, Mrs Ursula MacKenzie, until then in charge of the office, was very helpful in providing material and information.

The difficulty with researching groups such as FAIR and *Elterninitiative* is that little has been written about or by them. Unlike *Elterninitiative*, FAIR publishes a newsletter, *FAIR NEWS*, which started in the late 1970s as a couple of A4 sheets. When Ursula MacKenzie became the editor in the early 1980s, information and reports on movements was supplemented by an editorial and regular updates about FAIR itself. The format of *FAIR NEWS* changed in 1994, when Mrs MacKenzie retired, restricting information about FAIR to reports of its annual meeting and international activities. I extracted information about FAIR's origins and development from the newsletters, conversations with, for instance, Audrey Chaytor, Daphne Vane, Ursula MacKenzie, Christian Szurko, and Paul Rose, and various other sources.

Research on the Anglican Church's response to NRMs also started with gathering written material, including relevant passages in *Hansard* on questions raised or statements made about NRMs in Parliament or the House of Lords. (*Hansard* also proved valuable for occasions when members of both Houses addressed the question of 'cults' in general, for example regarding reform of the charity laws.) References (British Council of Churches, 1978; 1985; Bennett, 1988) pointed me to the British Council of Churches (BCC, now Churches Together in England). Although the archives of the Church of England include relevant documentation, it could not be consulted, as it was not catalogued and was marked 'confidential'. Access to some documents was possible through Canon Martin Reardon, General Secretary of Churches Together in England at Inter Church House. As he had been General Secretary of the Board for Mission and Unity at the time when the Anglican Church developed its formal response to NRMs, he was an important 'source' of information, as was Mr Colin Podmore, who took over from Canon Reardon in 1989, and Dr Anne Richards who succeeded Mr Podmore in 1991, when the Board for Mission and Unity was split into the Board for Mission and the Council for Christian Unity. Dr Richards represents the Board at INFORM's Board of Governors meetings.

Regarding the Roman Catholic Church's response to NRMs, I contacted one of the Vatican Councils, the *Pontificium Consilium Pro Dialogo Inter Religiones* (Pontifical Council for Interreligious Dialogue). A new post, held by Dr Teresa Gonçalves, had been created there in the early 1990s consisting in responsibility for NRMs. Other sources included the Council's *Bulletin* and various papers and articles written by representatives of Vatican Secretariats. The latter are examined in Chapter 6.

From trail to framework

As mentioned at the beginning, my research was largely based on written documents and material, complemented by fieldwork. Primary research was thus outside my brief and resources. The observations which I gathered during my research – the political aspects, the varying degrees to which academics can be (and have been) involved with their area of study, the range of institutions and organizations involved – led me to realize that the debate of NRMs involves a variety of voices. These can be put in chronological order (which voice appeared at which moment in time), they can be placed in a range of camps (which voices are arguing for what views/perspectives), they can be assessed according to their political weight (which voices are heard over and above others). The last question is closely linked to the *context* in which the voices are heard. It is determined by the 'agenda' of those who set the context. For example, a journalist is likely to give more weight to the voice of a parent affected by NRM membership, to the voice of a former member, and/or the voice of someone speaking out against NRMs. The journalist's 'agenda' is likely to be a 'good' story. A public authority is likely to give more weight to the voice of 'expert' opinion, as it would wish to have all the relevant 'facts' for considering general issues and wider social implications. The weight of the voices is also bound up with the reputation of those representing them: the voice of a pressure group will carry less weight than the voice of a well-established academic; the former is a voluntary self-help organization, the latter is part of a professional discipline and institution. Consequently, there is a *contest* between the different voices: they are jostling for legitimation, they are competing with and among one another, they are forming alliances with and fronts against one another. Where there is contest, there are vested interests; thus, the voices involved in this contest have something to lose. This book seeks to show why this is so.

At some point I realized that I was about to become such a 'voice' myself, ready to compete with other voices and tempted to form alliances. Yet, I felt strongly about upholding 'academic ideals', striving to maintain adequate fairness towards and distance from all parties concerned. In trying to balance professional ideals with ethical and methodological difficulties, I lost my voice completely, to the point of not daring to assess anything, for fear of making 'value' judgements. Yet, on the 'sub-professional' level, I was aware of strong feelings and opinions about my research. I reached the point where I could not say anything that others had not said before. My idea of meticulous, 'objective' scholarship forbade me to comment in any way – it would have meant giving up my 'objective', scholarly distance and falling into a camp. The very fact of selecting from the accumulated data implied indirect comment. In attempting to give equal space to the voices in the debate, I not only failed, but became paralysed. This brought me up sharp against the fact that I am indeed part of my own data. I found myself 'defending' NRMs in informal conversations, even when I did not have any sympathies or even respect for a group. The effort to make the '(wo)man in the street' understand the internally consistent nature of a particular belief system pushed me into the role of devil's advocate and I became, unintentionally, an advocate of the devil.

It was not possible to practise the ideal of the objective stance which the social sciences still seem to uphold nor could this ideal be anywhere near research reality. The interviews with scholars allowed me to consult 'experts', who write about research in a pluralistic social setting where participants have a claim on loyalty and fairness (and that includes my interviewees!), about my dilemma; I could explore whether this double-bind is distinctive of the social scientists, compared with the other voices: the 'anti-cult' movement, the churches, the state, the media.

As it is not possible to cover all the voices in the space available, the focus of this book is on the response of the 'anti-cult' groups and the mainstream churches in Britain and Germany, although the positions of other voices are included where relevant. The next chapter outlines what made the emergence of NRMs a *new* phenomenon and how it elicited a range of responses on the institutional level. It also shows the impact of this new phenomenon on the sociology of religion in Britain and *Religionswissenschaft* in Germany.

Notes

1   See Kuner, 1982; 1983b; Galanter *at al.*, 1979; Galanter, 1989; Kilbourne, 1983; Levine and Slater, 1976; Ungerleider and Wellisch, 1979; Judah, 1974a; Anthony and Robbins, 1974; Bromley and Shupe, 1981a.

2   For example, the case of Rosalind Mitchell (née Masters) who had joined and left the Unification Church (UC) in the early 1970s. Her story was of interest to the media, because by the time she left, her parents, brother, and sister had joined the UC, with Mr Masters making a substantial donation of money and property to the movement (Beale and Mitchell, 1978). There was also the case of Judy and Jane Salter: Judy Salter joined the UC in 1978 during a visit to America. However, she returned to her parents, only to re-join some months later. Her sister Jane followed suit some months later. The *Daily Mail* covered this case in 1978 and 1979. Both 'stories' became topical again during the libel suit brought against the *Daily Mail* by the UC in 1980/81, when Rosalind Mitchell, her father Henry Masters, and Jane Salter appeared as witnesses in the trial. Other individual cases followed: Kevin Fisher joined the UC in 1978. His mother, Mrs Margaret Fisher, died in early 1980 without having seen her son again (*Daily Express*, 6 February 1980). Francis Vaugham joined the UC in 1979. His father, David Vaugham, tried to get him out (the *Sunday Express*, 2 March 1980; *The Times*, 1 March, 1980). Matthew Smalley's mother, Mrs Robina Smalley, tried to win her son back from the UC in America (the *Daily Mail*, 6 March 1980; *The Sunday Times*, 28 September 1980). What these 'stories' have in common is that these young people tended to come from a middle-class background with educational opportunities, including public school, university, and trips abroad where most of the UC members were recruited. Most of them had articulate parents who would not accept their children's choice; they tried to bring them back home, which often involved trips to the US. The combination of individual hardship and heartbreak has been newsworthy, especially when set against the 'sinister' and 'bizarre' practices of the movements and their leaders.

3   On 22 October 1975, Mr Rose addressed the House of Commons on the UC (*Hansard*, Vol. 898: 678–684), followed by a response from Michael Meacher, then Under-Secretary of State for Health and Social Security (*Hansard*, Vol. 898: 684–688). Mr Rose addressed the House again on 23 February 1997 (*Hansard*, Vol. 926: 1586–1594) and submitted questions on various occasions:

11 March 1976 (*Hansard*, Vol. 907: 297), 23 March 1976 (*Hansard*, Vol. 908: 103), 28 April 1976 (*Hansard*, Vol. 910: 107), 14 June 1976 (*Hansard*, Vol. 913: 46), 15 June 1976 (*Hansard*, Vol. 913: 89), 20th October 1976 (*Hansard*, Vol. 917: 480), and 26 October 1976 (*Hansard*, Vol. 918: 138–139).

4   Haack could be called a 'moral entrepreneur' with a dog collar, who threw his allegiance to the Church and its support behind his cause. The term 'moral entrepreneur' or 'moral crusader' describes (groups of) individuals who generate public concern and mobilize public opinion or the opinion of legislators and law enforcers that 'something needs to be done' about the object of concern (Becker, 1963, cited in Wallis, 1976a). The object of concern can generate a 'moral panic', 'a condition, episode, person or groups of persons [which] emerges to become defined as a threat to societal values and interests' (Cohen, 1972). The debate surrounding Scientology approached the level of moral panic; Wallis demonstrates the role of moral entrepreneurs in the deviance amplification model (Wallis, 1975a; 1976a: 205–212). Any number of individuals or agencies can be(come) moral entrepreneurs; important for our context is that they may also have a variety of interests and motivations (Wallis, 1976a: 211–212).

5   A number of studies draw historical parallels between allegations levelled against the NRMs of the past and those levelled against the NRMs of the present (Shupe and Bromley, 1980a; Mayer, 1985; Walsh, 1993).

6   CERF was founded by Rabbi Maurice Davis (Haack, 1986b) in August 1975 (Hauth, 1981: 36). The sources somewhat disagree on FREECOG: Haack refers to FREECOG as 'Free of Children of God' and as *probably* the first parents' organization in the US, created towards the end of the 1960s at the instigation of Ted Patrick whom Governor Reagan appointed, in 1971, 'Special Representative for Community Relations in San Diego and Imperial Counties in Southern California' and to whom parents whose children had joined the Children of God had turned for help (Haack, 1986b: 106–107; Patrick and Dulak, 1976). Enroth refers to FREECOG as 'The Parents' Committee to Free our Sons and Daughters from the Children of God Organization' and as the first parents' group in the US, founded in 1971 in San Diego, with similar organizations following: Citizen Freedom Foundation (CFF), Individual Freedom Foundation, Citizen Engaged in Reuniting Families, etc. (Enroth, 1977: 190). Hauth gives 1972 as FREECOG's founding date and states that CFF resulted from the association of 31 parents' groups in 26 states in 1979, with headquarters in Los Angeles (Hauth, 1981: 36).

7   ADFI was founded in 1974 by Mr and Mrs Champollion in Rennes after their son had joined the UC. Since 1982, ADFI operates as UNADFI (*Union Nationale des Associations de Défense de la Famille et des Individus*), an association of ADFI organizations in different parts of France (*Famille Magazine*, 12 Novembre 1988: 33). M. Champollion died in 1975 and Mme Champollion died in 2003 (*BULLES 79*, 3e trimestre 2003: 1–2).

8   The early parents' or 'anti-cult' groups can be considered single-issue campaign groups or *Bürgerinitiativen* which started forming at that time.

9   *Aktion für geistige und psychische Freiheit – Arbeitsgemeinschaft der Elterninitiativen e.V.* (AGPF) was founded in 1977 as an umbrella organization for parents' groups and 'committed individuals' (Flöther, 1985: 133). Its activities only became prominent in the early to mid-1980s with its first conference (1984) and published proceedings (Flöther, 1985). Not all parents' organizations in Germany joined AGPF; for example, the *Elterninitiative* in Munich did not. *Elterninitiative zur Wahrung der Geistigen Freiheit e.V. Leverkusen* was founded in 1984 by Ursula Zöpel whose son became involved with ISKCON in 1979 (*EL-Mitteilungen 5–6*, 1990: 4). *Sekten-Info Essen e.V.* was founded in

1984. *Elterninitiative gegen psychische Abhängigkeit und religiösen Extremismus Berlin e.V.* was founded in early 1980, registered as an association (*eingetragener Verein*) in early 1981, and in early 1985 changed its name to *Eltern- und Betroffeneninitiative gegen psychische Abhängigkeit – für geistige Freiheit Berlin e.V.*, EBI. In the mid-1980s, EBI set up a rehabilitation project for ex-members, *Fluchtpunkt* (Lemke *et al.*, 1985). The group was set up under the auspices of Pastor Gandow, *Sektenbeauftragter* in Berlin since 1978 (Gandow, 1985: 37). In the wake of the 1977 youth synod on 'youth sects', the then bishop Kruse set up an *Arbeitsgruppe Jugendreligionen* in 1978, after the self-immolation of Ananda Marga members in Berlin (ibid.). Another early organization is ABI (*Aktion Bildungsinformation e.V.*) in Stuttgart, a consumer protection organization, which focuses on educational matters. It began examining Scientology in 1975, after ABI staff were offered courses in the street. Since the early 1980s, ABI's work has included other NRMs. *Aktion Psychokultgefahren e.V.* (APG) is not a parents' group either; created in 1981 by R.-D. Mucha and U. Müller in Düsseldorf and institutionalized in 1983, it takes a multi-disciplinary approach and is dedicated to collecting information, disseminating and undertaking research, and providing counselling. In 1985, the *Arbeitskreis Jugendreligionen*, concerned with the welfare of youth, was founded in Hamburg, as a sub-section of *Aktion Jugendschutz*, to offer counselling and help in cases of problematic NRM membership (*EL-Mitteilungen* 12, 1988: 13–14). Hauth (1981: 35–36) states that after the creation of *Elterninitiative*, other such groups, described as 'regional organizations', followed in Northrhine-Westphalia (late 1976) and Lower Saxony (early 1979).

10 Rüdiger Hauth has been *Beauftragter für Sekten und Weltanschauungsfragen im Volksmissionarischem Amt* (Office for Mission) in Witten in North-rhine-Westphalia since 1971 (Hauth, 1979; 1981). Pastor Gandow became *Sektenbeauftragter* in Berlin in 1978 (Gandow, 1985: 37). By 1979, there were eight *Sektenbeauftragte* in the Lutheran Church (Hauth, 1979: 117) and one in the Roman Catholic Church (ibid.: 118).

11 Counterparts to the EZW exist in France and Denmark: *Centre de Documentation sur les Eglises et les Sectes*, set up by the late Dominican Friar Chéry, and Dialog Center in Aarhus, Denmark, set up by theologian Johannes Aagaard (Arweck, 1985: 157). Friar Chéry published the second edition of his *L'Offensive des Sectes* as early as 1954 (Chéry, 1954). The Dialog Center has been operative on a national level since 1974 and on an international level since 1975, with Associate members forming the Dialog Center International (*Update & Dialog*, 1992: 5).

12 'The Study Centre for New Religious Movements in Primal Societies' was founded in 1981 by Harold Turner who carried out research into PRINERMS, new religious movements arising from the interaction between universal religions and primal culture (Turner, 1977a; 1978; 1979; 1989a). In 1984, it became 'The Centre for New Religious Movements', when Turner looked at NRMs in the West (Turner, 1989b). Turner took part in the World Council of Churches' consultation on NRMs in Amsterdam in 1986 (Brockway and Rajashekar, 1987), where he applied the PRINERMS concept to NRMs in the West (Turner, 1987). The renamed Centre continued research into the interaction of biblical and primal cultures and its relevance for pastoral concerns in relation to NRMs (Woodhall, 1992) and contributed to the F.I.U.C. Symposium in Vienna in 1991 (Woodhall, 1991). In 1996, another renaming created 'The Centre for the Study of New Religious Movements', and in 1999, 'The Research Unit for New Religions and Churches' (RUNERC).

13 A centre in Marburg which gathers documents is one way in which REMID pursues its aims and an 'institutionalization' of knowledge and expertise. Two

REMID members run a publishing house (diagonal-Verlag) and a periodical (*spirita*).

14   CESNUR was founded in 1988 in Italy during a seminar on new religions organized by Massimo Introvigne, Jean-François Mayer, and Ernesto Zucchini. The headquarters are in Turin, Italy (Introvigne, 1992: 5–12). CESNUR holds an annual conference with varying venues and co-organizers, for example: 'New Religious Movements: The European Situation' (in 1990, Lugano); 'The Challenge of Magic: Spiritualism, Satanism and Occultism in Contemporary Society' (1992, Lyon) with *Centre de Recherche et d'Études Anthropologiques*, University of Lyon; 'New Religions and the New Europe' (in 1993, London) with INFORM (Information Network Focus on Religious Movements, founded in 1988 by Professor Eileen Barker (Barker, 1989a: 141–144) and ISAR (Institute for the Study of American Religion, founded by Gordon Melton in 1969 and based in Santa Barbara, California; Melton, 1992: ix).

15   Topics have ranged from the media and NRMs (November 1997), the New Age (April 1990), leaving NRMs (November 1991), children in NRMs (March 1992), Humanistic Psychology and Human Potential Movement (November 1992), NRMs and mental health (December 1994), to NRMs and money (December 1996).

16   Organized by Marion Bowman at Bath Spa University College (until 1997, Bath College of Higher Education) and now at the Open University at Milton Keynes. In May 1992, the Ilkley Group organized 'The Sociology of the New Age' in Glastonbury.

17   These were organized by the Centre for New Religions, e.g. NRMs: Work and Business (1988), New Age Dimensions of Goddess Spirituality (1990; York and Arweck, n.y.), Women, Discipleship, and Spiritual Power (1991; Puttick and Clarke, 1993), Japanese New Religions (1992; Clarke and Somers, 1994a), and Buddhism in Modern Contexts (1995).

18   After the libel case which the Unification Church brought against the *Daily Mail* in 1980, the jury attached a rider to its verdict for the review of UC's charitable status. The Charity Commission undertook this task, but after consideration of the charity laws and expert opinion, decided that the UC could not be denied charitable status.

19   For example, the UC's leader, Sun Myung Moon cancelled his visit to Britain in November 1995, after the (then) Home Secretary Michael Howard refused to lift a ban on his entry (the *Independent*, 3 November, 1995: 5). Mr Howard's German counterpart, Manfred Kanther, followed suit (*Berliner Dialog 3*, 1995: 29).

20   After the law regulating advertising changed, Scientology advertised on a satellite channel. Complaints led the ITC (Independent Television Commission) to investigate and, on the basis of available information, to decide that Scientology should not be allowed to advertise on TV. Scientology appealed and the ITC turned to academic 'expert' opinion. Mr A. Wilson, Senior Advertising Standards Officer with the ITC, talked on this matter at the Winter 1997 INFORM Seminar (Wilson, 1997).

21   Rose of Sharon Press and Paragon House are UC imprints which published some academic collections, for example, *The Social Impact of New Religious Movements* (Wilson, 1981), which incidentally resulted from a UC-sponsored conference; *The Family and the Unification Church* (James, 1983); *Alternatives to Mainline Churches in America* (Fichter, 1983); *Religious Movements: Genesis, Exodus, and Numbers* (Stark, 1985); *Spiritual Choices* (Anthony *et al.*, 1987). There have been concerns about the possible links between the UC and Edwin Mellen Press (interview with Professor J. Beckford; St John, 1993).

22   For example, *ISKCON Communications* which was mainly intended for

internal use, but also circulated to interested academics. Since late 1997, the journal is available on subscription. It includes articles by academic researchers and ISKCON members, some of whom have academic degrees.

23   In 1984, ISKCON (Hare Krishna movement) in Ireland faced the loss of its charitable status. It assembled a set of documents as corroborating evidence for the justification of its charitable status. Apart from germane organizations in the Hindu community and religionists, academics were invited to declare it a *bona fide* religion. Roy Wallis and John Hinnells – among others – provided supporting affidavits (ISKCON, 1984).

3 Institutions and institutional knowledge

This chapter comprises two parts: the first outlines what made the emergence of NRMs a *new* phenomenon and how this elicited a range of institutional responses and competing forms of institutional knowledge. The second part looks at the emergence of academic discourses in the sociology of religion in Britain and *Religionswissenschaft* in Germany.

INSTITUTIONS

A vexed question of consequence

When the new religious movements (NRMs) emerged in the late 1960s and early 1970s, they presented a *new* phenomenon in Western societies. Peter Clarke's definition takes a chronological view, identifying as 'new' religious groups which have emerged in North America and Europe since 1945 (e.g. Clarke, 1992: 58; 1997: xxvii–xxviii). Others, such as James Beckford and Eileen Barker, agree with this broad definition, stating that 'it was only in the 1950s and 1960s that these distinctly new movements came to light in Western Europe (Beckford and Levasseur, 1986: 31) and that "... one might say that the groups which are currently referred to as new religious movements have, in most cases, appeared since the Second World War ..." (Barker, 1985a: 37). It is true that the foundation of some movements occurred earlier. For example, Soka Gakkai[1] and Divine Light Mission (DLM, now Elan Vital/Prem Rawat Foundation),[2] were founded in the 1930s. Rastafarianism started at the beginning of the twentieth century,[3] and the New Age movement's spiritual roots lie in the late nineteenth century, in Transcendentalism (Baker, 1996), Theosophy (Ruppert, 1993; Washington, 1993) and New Thought (Larson, 1985).[4] However, the important point about NRMs is that they have only come to prominence in the West since the Second World War.

The term 'NRMs' is widely used by academics as part of their institutional language. The use of language and terminology reaches beyond personal preferences and reveals the position of the speaker. In his work on the 'secularization of religious language', Richard Fenn sees language as both bridge and boundary between individual and society and argues that where language is constrained by social rank or institutional boundary, it is derivative from forces located beyond the individual speaker (Fenn, 1982: xxxi–xxxii). Dillon and Richardson highlight the 'politics of representation' in tracing the construction of the 'cult' concept (Dillon and Richardson, 1995). A contributor to the now defunct nurel-l list (Cowan, 2000) – an internet (Hadden and Cowan, 2000) discussion group on NRMs set up by Irving Hexham in 1993 – spoke about the 'distinction in language worlds', pointing out that 'politicians, journalists, [and] scholars all pursue language for different motivations' (nurel-l list, January 1998). The term 'NRMs' is the preferred and generally accepted term for academics, because, first, it is considered neutral and value-free – unlike 'cult' or 'sect', which have negative connotations, especially when qualified with pejorative adjectives, such as 'destructive' or 'bizarre'. The media, the 'anti-cult movement', and popular works generally use 'destructive cults' or 'pseudo-religions'. Second, 'cult' and 'sect' are technical terms in the sociology of religion to describe types of groups distinctly different from NRMs[5] so 'NRM' serves to maintain precision and avoid confusion.[6] Third, scholars want a language which reflects *their* understanding of the phenomenon and in this sense, language has 'political' implications, as Dillon and Richardson (1995) argue. However, some have used 'cult', for example Beckford in his *Cult Controversies*, to 'preserve the character and feel of popular sentiment' which considers 'cults' 'small, insignificant, inward-looking, unorthodox, wild, and possibly threatening' (Beckford, 1985: 12, 13). Although this would normally be indicated by inverted commas, he considers this tedious in a book. Beckford's use of 'cult' is similar to mine, but I retain the inverted commas as a reminder of the connotations.

The problem of well-defined terms is reflected in NRMs' self-definitions (they reject the 'cult label') and Continental designations which often refer to 'sects' and treat them with earlier groups, such as Jehovah's Witnesses or Mormons. Had NRMs appeared before the Second World War, they would have been classified as 'cults' or 'sects' (Barker, 1985a: 37) and an early article about the UC indeed categorizes it as 'sect' (Beckford, 1976). The persistence of 'sect' in Continental Europe is due to the Roman Catholic Church's strong influence there. As 'sect' was used for any non-mainstream form of religion, the NRMs of the nineteenth century are subsumed in the same category as those of the twentieth century, an illustration of Fenn's institutional boundaries constraining language (Fenn, 1982). However, lumping together sets of groups implies that groups like Jehovah's Witnesses are like NRMs. One reason for this fusion is the view from the mainstream churches: their obvious interest in following schismatic and sectarian trends within Christianity drives the study of unorthodox religions. In Germany, Kurt Hutten's classic *Seher, Grübler, Enthusiasten* (first edition 1958, updated 1984) is widely used among clergy. Another reason for treating NRMs and 'traditional sects' together is the recent success of groups like

Jehovah's Witnesses (Stark and Iannaccone, 1997). Their strictness – one of Stark's criteria for success or failure (Stark, 1996b) – led to numerous enquiries with organizations dedicated to 'cult' affected families. For three consecutive years, Jehovah's Witnesses occupied place five in FAIR's list of groups engendering most enquiries, preceded, in 1990, by Scientology, UC, Central London Church of Christ, and Children of God (*FAIR NEWS*, Autumn 1991: 3; Autumn 1992: 2; Winter 1993/4: 2). INFORM listed them in sixth place in its 1992 list (INFORM Annual Report, 1992: 4) and, despite a slight decline, they still ranked among the top ten in 1994 (INFORM Annual Report, 1994).

In Germany, the term *Jugendreligionen* was coined by Pastor Haack, used interchangeably with *Jugendsekten* (youth sects) and *destruktive Kulte*, a literal translation of 'destructive cults'. *Jugendreligionen* also appears in academic writings, often with 'so-called' (*sogenannte Jugendreligionen*) or in quotes (*'Jugendreligionen'*). In France, *sectes* is commonly used for NRMs, as is the more general *phénomène sectaire*. In Italy, *sette* (sects) or *i nuovi culti* (the new cults) are used. Similar terminology is current in other European countries.

Government agencies and public authorities have struggled with appropriate terminology, especially regarding attempts to find legal instruments to prevent abuses in religious guise, yet safeguard religious freedom and the rights of established religions and churches. The Cottrell Report's (1983; 1984) use of 'NRMs' raised objections in the European Parliament, which deemed it too all-embracing, too unclear about 'new' or 'old', too suggestive of restricting religious freedom. Fearing restriction, most established religions received the report with caution, even rejection. The threat to religious freedom also exercised the Council of Europe's Committee of Ministers in February 1994, which resorted to 'certain sects and religious movements of a non-traditional character'.

The vexed question of definitions and language in academic and other institutions illustrates how much of an epistemological minefield the source material is. The phenomenon has different labels, depending on the speakers and their purpose. I am using academic language, because I am writing as an academic, but language is contested, even within academia, where there is no consensus either about which movements should be regarded as NRMs. Some include the People's Temple, others do not (Richardson, 1980). Some consider Scientology an NRM, others treat it as a form of magic (Stark and Bainbridge, 1985), a 'manipulationist sect' (Wilson, 1970b: 197), and a form of modern, secular religion (Wilson, 1990). Some NRMs began as therapeutic groups, such as Dianetics which preceded Scientology (Wallis, 1976b) and *est* (Bry, 1976; Fenwick, 1976; Greene, 1976; Hoffman, 1977; Hann, 1982; Heelas, 1987). Stark's initial theory of religious groups' success or failure relates specifically to NRMs (Stark, 1987), but his revised model relates to *all* movements (Stark, 1996b), and his test cases are two 'sects': Jehovah's Witnesses (Stark and Iannaccone, 1997) and Christian Science

(Stark, 1998). Wilson's *Social Dimensions of Sectarianism* (1990) also aims for one framework for NRMs and 'sects'. However, Barker warns against placing a large number of movements under one single umbrella term, as this implies that they must share certain characteristics, although 'It is arguably the case that the only characteristic these movements share is to have been referred to at some time as new religious movements' (Barker, 1985a: 37). This statement also reveals a certain circularity in the discussion. While the contest over defining and using terms may be literally 'academic' as long as it involves scholarly circles, it is not when it involves legal consequences. In Germany, some *Länder* authorities categorize Scientology as a commercial enterprise, which deprives it of charitable status and causes 'official' definition, the movement's self-representation, and public perception to clash.

What *is* new about new religious movements?

In describing the 'new' aspects of NRMs, I am drawing on sociological findings which were established *after* the phenomenon had established itself and *after* institutions had been established. Thus, in order to untangle the relationship between institutions and their involvement in the debate, I am anticipating data from later research.

That new forms of religion should appear was not new – the history of religion is full of foundations of new religious groups, communities, orders, heresies, orthodoxies, and religions. Innovation in religion *per se* is nothing new, as comparative studies of historic and contemporary religions testify. That NRMs were forming in *Western* societies was not really new either: possibly due to the impact of rapid social change (Beckford, 1986). Latin America and Africa have seen the proliferation of 'new' groups, with Pentecostalism – incidentally another contested label (D. Martin, 1990; Corten, 1997) – making significant inroads and combining syncretic elements through in- and acculturation.

The teachings of NRMs were not completely new either. Some deliberately invoke venerable traditions or teachers: ISKCON (International Society for Krishna Consciousness), better known as the Hare Krishna movement, locates itself within Vaishnava Hinduism, in the line of the sixteenth-century Bengali monk Chaitanya Mahaprabhu (Judah, 1974b; Daner, 1976; Rochford, 1985; Knott, 1986; 1993; Shinn, 1987; Rochford, 1995; Nye, 1996; 2001) and Soka Gakkai associates itself with Nichiren Shoshu, a Nichiren sect professing the teachings of the thirteenth-century Japanese monk Nichiren Daishonin. Sociologists have long observed that innovative groups typically appeal to tradition (Hill, 1973). This makes the relationship between 'old' and 'new' ambiguous, as recognized by the European Parliament, which replaced 'NRMs' by 'new organizations operating under the protection afforded to religious bodies'. Students of Japanese religious movements distinguish between 'new' and 'new, new' movements (Clarke and Somers, 1994b; Clarke, 1997: xxxi). Some even question whether 'religion' applies to (some) NRMs and thus evoke the difficulty of defining 'religion' (Byrne and Clarke, 1992). Some NRMs – for example Scientology (Black, n.d.; Flinn, n.d.) – claim to be, and want recognition as, religions, while others – for example TM (Spiritual Counterfeits Project, 1978) – claim to be secular.

NRMs have not been new either regarding their modes of congregating members or organizing collectives. Historical predecessors exemplify forms of communal living, ascetic behaviour, ritual practices, and attitudes towards non-members, which NRMs adopted.

Nevertheless, there *are* aspects which mark NRMs as distinctly *new*: first, the way in which they have *combined* ideas and practices for their teachings and applied them in developing their organizations. Barker (1985a: 37–38) speaks of new 'idiosyncratic *structures* of both the belief systems and the practices', 'the particular combinations of items that are selected, and the rhetoric in which they are packaged'. The teachings of (at least some) NRMs have been described as syncretic, combining various elements from different traditions (Chryssides, 1992; Cornille, 1994) and NRMs have adapted these in specific ways to different cultural contexts, as Cornille (1991) shows for Mahikari, a Japanese movement, in Europe. The syncretic aspect could locate NRMs in postmodernity: Wilson and Dobbelaere (1994) consider Soka Gakkai 'in tune with the times' and students of New Age thought ponder its possible postmodern quality (Partridge, 1999; Heelas, 1993; 1994; 1995), which Heelas (1996: 216–218) ultimately rejects.

Durkheim realized the importance of the *content* of religion in that different belief systems and sacred values are related to different patterns and degrees of social solidarity and Weber attended to the *content* of religious knowledge systems to analyse their social logic, the 'elective affinity' between patterns of social action and idea systems. It is not surprising that doctrine and creed partly determine how movements behave towards or insert themselves in host societies (Wallis, 1984; 1979b; Beckford, 1985: 76–92) including expansion beyond the initial host countries. In some ways, NRMs operate like transnational or multinational companies and use national boundaries for administrative divisions, but transfer resources as needed. However, different sociocultural and legal frameworks require different modes of insertion (Beckford, 1983a; 1983b) and these account for differences in NRMs' behaviour and practices in different geographical locations.

Early social scientific study of this 'new' phenomenon showed that, despite similarities, NRMs significantly differed from one another. This made it difficult to generalize about them, for example by developing general typologies, as each movement presents distinctive doctrines and tenets. Sweeping generalizations have been a point of friction between academics and the 'anti-cult movement' (ACM). Where the ACM might talk about 'cults' engaging in a set of activities – itemized in checklists as the 'marks of a cult' (see e.g. Pavlos, 1982: 4; Hounan and Hogg, 1985: Chapter 6), academics might speak of a *particular* movement engaging in a *particular* activity comparable to, although not the same as, another movement's activity. Conflict of context and purpose regarding their construction explain the 'gap' between such statements. Academics construct 'ideal types' – grounded in *both* theory *and* empirical findings – whose purpose and language differ from those required for political or legal contexts. Such typologies accommodate general tendencies in NRMs rather than identical movements: NRMs in a particular category share some, but not *all*, features. If, for example, asked in court whether *all* NRMs engage in 'brainwashing' or 'breaking up families', academics would find it difficult to answer, because academic motives and purpose for NRM categorization differ greatly from those of the ACM, which subsumes them under one heading: 'movements which take away our children'. Academics also find it difficult to answer, because – as Fenn (1982) suggests – some institutions 'impose' their language on those dealing with them and some settings, especially court and classroom, specialize in raising doubts about the trustworthiness, credibility, and authority of 'serious speech'.

Typologies illustrate the intellectual efforts involved in identifying common features and general traits of NRMs. They display a range of new elements, as they have drawn on non-Christian and esoteric sources available in the 'global village', with globalization (Beyer, 1994; Kurtz, 1995; Featherstone, Lash, and Robertson, 1995; Hexham and Poewe, 1997) facilitating the movement of people and ideas and locations, such as Goa (India) or Cusco (Peru), magnetizing spiritual seekers. Academics did not start with the premise that NRMs alienate children from their parents; they started with questions: What are these movements? What are their boundaries? Who joins them? What are their beliefs? etc. The answers revealed complexity, not easy labels. However, the ACM has used whatever leverage it can in legal and political processes or moral crusades to check 'cults'. When it draws on academic findings, the 'gap' between its and academics' approach becomes obvious. It tends to be *selective* in its use of academic writings, choosing what is closest to its view and what best serves its purpose, rejecting what it perceives as biased research resulting from too close a connection between academic and subject.

Second, NRMs are 'new' for the kind of people attracted to them. There is substantial evidence that members have tended to be relatively young, well educated, idealistically minded, mostly middle-class, receptive to religious or spiritual matters.[7] Before NRMs emerged, 'unorthodox' or 'deviant' groups had been associated with membership considered to be deprived in some way, especially of social status or economic means.

Third, NRMs are new because of their visibility, due to their effective use of modern means of communication and transport – the printed and broadcast media and systems for storing, retrieving and transmitting information (Beckford and Levasseur, 1986: 31–32; Beckford, 1985: 24). Media attention has also made NRMs highly visible, although the amount of attention has been disproportionate in relation to the number of active NRM members.

Membership is another vexed question – it is difficult, if not impossible, to indicate or estimate figures (Beckford and Levasseur, 1986: 30; Barker, 1983b; 1989a: 149–155; Clarke, 1997). There is first the question of who to count as a member. Generally, NRMs have core or full-time members and part-time or affiliated members. Some – Bainbridge and Stark's (1979; 1980) 'audience' and 'client cults' – have no formal membership, some – such as New Age groups – a fluctuating membership, some dual or multiple membership. NRM membership can be described as a set of concentric circles, with core members forming the innermost circle as the most committed. The outer circles illustrate increasingly weaker commitment for part-time and affiliated members, friends or sympathizers. Barker (1989a: 150–151) speaks of different membership 'layers'. Clarke's survey (1987b: 11–15) distinguishes between full- and part-members and sympathizers. The telephone survey commissioned by the German *Enquête-Kommission* in 1997 distinguished between actual members or sympathizers and course participants or clients (Hemminger, 1997). Second, there is the discrepancy between claimed membership and 'guestimates' by 'experts'. For obvious reasons, NRMs tend to quote inflated figures, sometimes including even enquirers. Researchers agree that both NRMs' and non-academic observers' estimates are highly optimistic, if not exaggerated, and that full-time membership is actually quite modest, a view supported by the *Enquête-Kommission*'s survey. Researchers also agree about the high turnover, with few of those interested actually becoming fully committed members (Barker, 1984; Beckford, 1986; Beckford and Levasseur, 1986: 30).

Fourth, NRMs have been 'new' regarding the opposition they have encountered: a movement in its own right emerged to counteract them. The 'anti-cult' movement arose as a single-issue campaign, shortly after NRMs had started to recruit, with the first groups forming in the US in the early 1970s and in Britain and Germany in the mid-1970s. The initiative largely came from 'cult'-affected parents and those sympathetic to their plight. In time, local groups gradually linked up and formed a national and international network. With increasing organization and awareness, the ACM has taken on the role of 'moral entrepreneur' and has – to some extent – succeeded in mobilizing concern and action in the churches, public authorities, and government agencies.

Fifth, NRMs have been 'new' regarding the attention they received from the academic community. When they began to emerge, recruiting from the 'cultic milieu' of the counter-culture (Roszak, 1968; Tipton, 1984; B. Martin, 1981b), it was not the socially or economically deprived who joined them, but bright young people. The children of the *Daily Telegraph* readers – typically resident in the Home Counties, the 'English bible belt' – tended to join the UC in the mid-1970s (Rose, 1981b: 63), just as in the US where members 'tend[ed] to be from intact, idealistic, believing families with some religious background', mainly middle-class, their average age between 19 and 20 (Clark, 1976: 2; 1977: 3; 1978a: 1–2). Some social scientists became directly involved, when their students or even their own children joined. The help of British academics was enlisted in 1980 by Casey McCann (FAIR's co-chairman in the mid-1980s) to return students from the US where they had joined the UC while on holiday (Cheal, 1985).

For academics, the NRM phenomenon questioned received theories about joining 'sects' or 'unorthodox' groups. Such membership had been explained in terms of deprivation, but this did not apply to NRMs. Sociologists realized that NRMs' teachings were 'new' and that NRMs differed markedly from 'traditional sects'. Therefore, sociologists needed to examine NRM teachings carefully and revise 'old' theories. Beckford (1981a), for example, rejected the functional approach to NRMs, because it was reductionist and condescending and because it distracted from the *content* of teachings, beliefs, and practices. Sociologists further realized that they had to take NRMs seriously by engaging with them on their own terms, the very approach considered unnecessary for the views of those labelled 'deviant' or 'mentally ill'. However, setting aside such labels and received opinion allows access to meaning and internal consistency in such views (Lindner, 1954). This is the leap which the public has not taken (or cannot take) in relation to 'cults', so labels like 'bizarre' and 'weird' persist. Academics *made* the leap by entering NRMs' thought worlds. Thus, when they use NRM language to explain beliefs, they 'sound' like NRM members and appear sympathetic or to have 'crossed over into the other camp'. When they 'translate' NRM language, they 'sound' like NRM spokespersons. Yet, 'translating' and interpreting NRM language is part of academic work. Academics who act as expert witnesses interpret a group which cannot interpret for itself or is not believed. Yet there is a fine balance between seeking to understand, interpreting for non-members, and speaking as if part of a group. Academics speak as outsiders who understand. In my view, the balance is not always maintained, academic pursuit is not always understood by non-academics, and does not always fit the agenda of other agencies. 'Anti-cult' groups are not concerned with *beliefs*, but with *behaviour*, and thus consider teachings only in this light.

NRMs thus challenged sociologists in several respects. First, they needed to test hitherto accepted theories and concepts. Realizing that these did not apply, they needed to develop new theoretical frameworks to account for NRMs' emergence and apparent success. Second, they were confronted with ACM notions accounting for conversion and recruitment, especially 'brainwashing'. The ACM was ahead of academics in explaining NRM membership, because parents had been affected first and were the most anxious to account for seemingly inexplicable behaviour. Interestingly, the ACM's framework itself derives from *academic* sources: it is based on studies of American prisoners of war in 1950s China (Schein *et al.*, 1961; Lifton,

1961) and on clinical psychiatry (Clark, 1976; 1979a). By their very nature, these psychological studies took a negative view of recruitment and membership.

An overview of the academic literature shows that early writings applied traditional theories to NRMs, with a gradual move towards their adaptation and replacement. This was coupled with examining ACM concepts, such as 'brainwashing', 'coercive persuasion', etc., which demonstrates the ACM's impact on scholarly studies (Hargrove, 1982a). On the whole, they sought to refute, even discredit, ACM concepts. While the number of sociological publications in Britain was fairly modest until the early 1980s (the larger academic community in the US had, of course, begun sooner), a consider-able amount and range of literature has appeared since then, including general and specialized bibliographies (Choquette, 1985; Saliba, 1990c; Arweck and Clarke, 1997; Bjorling, 1990; Littler, 1991; Lewis, 1989; Blasi and Cuneo, 1986; Pritchett, 1985; Shupe *et al.*, 1984; Melton, 1982). Also, research institutes for NRM study and research and discrete university courses developed. In Britain, the Centre for New Religious Movements at Selly Oak Colleges, Birmingham, was founded in 1981 by Harold Turner, followed by the Centre for New Religions at King's College London under Peter Clarke's directorship. INFORM was set up by Eileen Barker in 1988. BACRA (Bath Archive for Contemporary Religious Affairs) was started by Michael York at Bath Spa University College in 1997. In Germany, *Forschungsinstitut Neureligionen* was created in Marburg under Rainer Flasche and REMID began in early 1989.

Finally, NRMs have been 'new' in that their members did not act like 'subjects' who could be studied like a 'tribe' or a menagerie of curios. They put in place mechanisms for communicating with the outside world and for presenting *their* views on what was said about them: 'especially among their official spokesmen they were made up of an articulate bourgeoisie which was in every obvious sense on a parity with the status and intellectual competence of the sociological researchers' (B. Martin, 1981a: 99). Just as parents were articulate and organized in setting up ACM groups, NRM members proved equally articulate and organized, both in representing themselves and in joining the debate about them; they disputed, for example, that they were 'brainwashed' or 'exploited'. This brought a new aspect to research: findings came under the scrutiny of the researched and this 'inhibited any tendency to dismiss the challenge of facing their alternative knowledge paradigms' (ibid.).

This new aspect has to be seen in a wider context, namely the paradigm clash in sociology of religion and anthropology, largely brought about by a 'subtle shift in the relative power and status of the scientific observer and of his subject matter' (ibid.: 98). Western scholars became sensitive to the fact that they could no longer treat people in the Third World as 'subject matter'. They realized that their disciplines were a kind of 'intellectual colonialism' and they sought to remedy this by according some 'ontological parity to the knowledge paradigm of those they studied' (ibid.: 98–99). This shift has affected both the researcher's status and research methodology. It has questioned the idea of 'objectivity' and has made data gathering an *interactive, negotiated* process – of crucial consequence in NRM research, as NRMs can stipulate conditions before allowing access and control knowledge about them. Researchers can thus not produce reliable accounts when faced with short periods of participant observation and/or limited information. The issue of access and control is illustrated by Gordon Melton and John Lewis's visit to Aum Shinrikyo just after the poison attack in the Tokyo underground and the government raids. At this point, Aum's responsibility was not established. The two researchers expressed concern for religious rights and fear of government repression. Also, Melton had commented earlier that alleged scandals normally turn out to have been exaggerated (Reader, 1995; *Religion Watch*, September/October, 1995), only to find himself contradicted later when more knowledge was available.

The idea of 'objectivity' is also questioned by New Agers for whom objective thinking is an *ignis fatuus* and observation and communication are always informed by personal interests and presuppositions. Truths cannot be communicated without being in some way interpreted and therefore 'contaminated'. Personal experience is the *locus* of, and access to, truth (Partridge, 1999). Here, New Age thinking engages with postmodern thinking: not only are our epistemic judgements affected by our worldviews, our worldviews are all there is; we have no access to reality apart from the conceptually constructed reality of our worldviews and discourse. This matches Kantian thinking, according to which we can perceive the world only through our senses, but we cannot be sure that things *are* the way we perceive them, that we perceive *das Ding an sich*.

Since the mid-1980s, NRM members have become schooled in academic discourse, with increasing numbers involved in university programmes, PhDs, and academic projects. This may count as proof that they are neither 'zombies' nor unable to think for themselves. However, this has added another ingredient to the NRM debate: 'subjects' are talking back and questioning, if not disputing, academic theories and views about them, an experience already encountered by social scientists in women's studies and studies of blacks (the *Independent*, 8 December 1997). That NRM members (can) challenge statements about them is one reason why studying documentation is not sufficient in itself. This links with the difficulties of my initial approach: it is not enough to ask where texts come from, as some are heavily contested and different parties draw on each other's work. Just as the ACM uses academic work for its purposes, so do NRMs – to make representations to authorities, for example, to refute allegations – the reason for the Children of God's appeal for academic affidavits – or to provide evidence to the Charity Commission.[8]

The chronology of knowledge paradigms

The main question arising from these considerations is this: why did the NRM phenomenon stir and receive so much attention, despite not reaching large-scale proportions? I see the explanation of this question in terms of the institutions which accumulated NRM knowledge, their vested interests, the contest of explanatory models, and the views on what action should be taken.

In tracing the history and chronology of institutions and their theoretical frameworks, one needs to bear in mind that things did not develop in a straight line or in 'neat' succession. Developments occurred in an *interactive process*, in which the behaviour and adaptive reactions of NRMs played as much a part as those of the other 'players in the field' (parents, churches, academics, etc.). These can be compared to actors who gradually appear on a stage; their roles develop as they enter, requiring a certain amount of improvisation and depending on 'cues' from the other actors; no-one takes centre-stage all the time; some recede into the background, when others take the limelight. More than one scene can be played at any one time, with roles having to be negotiated and adjusted, changing circumstances permitting. There has been continuous interaction, reaction, and adaptation between NRMs, parents, public authorities, churches, media, academics, and other agencies. The contemporaneous aspect of this process can, of course, only be recorded in linear description. The adaptive processes in institutions and thought have to be seen as the contest of voices mentioned earlier, with evolutionary changes related to the 'balance of power' between the voices.

The parental paradigm

The chronology of social responses to NRMs starts with the parents directly affected by 'cult' membership. They were supported by individuals who felt involved, some by virtue of their profession. Together, they started as loosely connected groups, which became more organized over time, just like 'cults' (in the sociological sense) start with informal meetings and slowly evolve towards formal structures, as numbers increase, theologies consolidate, and the process of institutionalization takes its course. 'Cult-like' features have incidentally been ascribed to the ACM (Introvigne, 1995).

Parents' groups were motivated by the need to exchange experience and information, the promise to draw support, and the hope of solving the problem which had suddenly overshadowed their lives. Parental self-help groups formed at a time when information about NRMs was scarce and little help was forthcoming from church or public authorities. They often focused on one particular NRM, but extended their remit as the number of parents and awareness of other movements increased. Connections with similar groups were established (inter)nationally to extend the network of information and practical help across borders. As it was common for NRM members to be recruited or re-located abroad, geographical distance compounded the problem of maintaining contact.

Thus, the 'anti-cult movement' had mobilized. Apart from supporting parents, it has aimed to make the public, churches, and public authorities aware of the 'cult' problem. It has considered the churches and media as 'natural allies' (the media more so than the churches) and sought to press for existing law to be enforced or complemented where necessary, by lobbying Parliament and government agencies.

The concerted action of parents led to the first knowledge paradigm and knowledge bases about 'cults'. Their networks compiled information and case histories of personal experiences (by parents, friends, ex-members) and legal matters, such as unlicensed street collections, etc. Paul Rose, for example, accumulated extensive files, including correspondence, affidavits from former members, UC literature, etc. The parents' explanatory framework or knowledge paradigm focuses on the *individual*, as parents are concerned with *their particular child*. This explains why *psychology* and *psychiatry*, rather than *sociology*, informed this paradigm, with two ostensibly unrelated areas of psychological study providing the structure: (1) the clinical study of cases negatively affected by 'cult' membership; the first 'cult casualties' were treated by psychiatrists, who then became the first 'experts', and (2) psychiatric studies of prisoners of war (POWs) and re-education programmes in Communist China. These two areas were brought together by the co-operation of three people: Dr John G. Clark, Dr Louis J. West, and Dr Margaret Singer.

Regarding the first area, Clark dealt with clinical cases of problematic 'cult' membership in the mid-1970s, when he was Assistant Professor of Psychiatry at Harvard Medical School and Massachusetts General Hospital. Based on his sample,[9] Clark found that no existing model explained the symptoms[10] and that the *quality* of the conversion experience was the decisive factor, not its conceptual content. The central phenomenon of 'cult membership' was a 'massive dissociation'[11] and its 'systematic maintenance' (Clark, 1977; 1978a). Conversion resulted in a personality shift or – in psychiatric terms – 'depersonalization' ('imposed' personality occluding the 'original' personality, Clark, 1976: 3), with symptoms of classic schizophrenia and acute psychosis, which could not be counteracted by any customary drugs or treatments. However, 'deprogramming' brought about 're-personalization', although it left individuals 'vulnerable' for about a year, during which they experienced 'strong impulses' to return (ibid.). Clark also refers to conversion as 'thought reform' and the induction period as 'coercive persuasion' (Clark, 1976: 4; 1977: 4; 1978a: 5).[12]

Clark's model had a significant influence on the ACM perspective both in the US and Europe. In 1977 or 1978, Clark addressed a FAIR meeting in the House of Commons (Rose, 1981b: 46ff) and in February 1978, he attended a conference organized by the German Society of Child and Adolescent Psychiatry (Clark, 1978a; 1979a). The published proceedings

(Müller-Küppers and Specht, 1979) further disseminated his work and that of Singer (1979b) and Lifton (1979).

Studies of POWs had been conducted in the 1950s by Hunter (1953; 1956), Lifton (1961 [1989]; 1956; 1967; 1979), and Schein (Schein *et al.*, 1961; Schein, 1956; 1957; 1959). Hunter introduced the term 'brainwashing' (Lifton, 1961: 15; Bromley and Shupe, 1981a; Borenstein, 1995), but neither Lifton nor Schein adopted it, preferring 'thought reform' and 'coercive persuasion', respectively.[13] Lifton and Schein saw ideological reform or conversion as a sequence of three stages.[14] It is important that parallels were drawn between these processes and conversion to 'cults',[15] which led the ACM to adopt the 'brainwashing thesis' as the explanation for 'cult' recruitment. One of the proponents of this thesis, Dr Margaret Singer, had worked with Schein on POW responses following repatriation (Singer and Schein, 1958).[16] West, too, had worked on the subject (Farber *et al.*, 1966 [1956]) and later collated his expertise with Singer's (West and Singer, 1980).

The insights from Lifton's 'thought reform', Schein's 'coercive persuasion', and Clark's clinical cases form the basis of the ACM knowledge paradigm. The 'brainwashing thesis' provided a *plausible* explanation, sociologically speaking, a structure of meaning (Berger, 1970: 71; 1969: 54–56). Its implications relieved parents of feeling guilty and inadequate, because converts are 'victims'. Conversion is inevitable given conducive circumstances. This is the *passivist* model of conversion, which posits the individual as *determined* by social or psychological factors, in contrast to the *activist* model, which sees conversion as a *negotiated* process (Strauss, 1979; Richardson, 1985a). The brainwashing thesis exonerates parents *and* recruits (also retrospectively),[17] because the blame lies squarely with the 'cult's' sophisticated techniques. (Considering that Clark's sample included cases showing signs of mental disorder before conversion, this aspect appears somewhat two-edged.) The exoneration has a moral agenda, but is coated in (sometimes highly technical) scientific language mediated through an 'authority', literally one 'in a white coat'. Such language makes the conversion process mechanical and inevitable, yet also reversible, justifying parents' hope to have their children restored.

Clark's theory also indicated what made people vulnerable to 'cult' membership and explained mental and physiological mechanisms of conversion and apparent personality change. Actual or likely casualties gave parents reason to mobilize public authorities and health care professionals[18] and resulted in the 'medicalization' of the issue (Robbins and Anthony, 1982). Singer's work with former members who experienced problems after leaving (Singer, 1979a; 1979b) 'confirmed' Clark's theory of post-membership 'vulnerability'.

Interestingly, both Clark and Singer related 'cult' membership and its consequences to theoretical frameworks familiar *to them*. Singer (and others) integrated it with 'thought reform' in China, Clark with existing psychiatric models. This suggests that shifts in knowledge paradigms do not occur as long as they can accommodate 'new' data (Kuhn, 1962). In the early and mid-1970s, 'cults' were explained within *existing* paradigms in psychology and psychiatry, although these did not quite fit, just as sociologists also began studying NRMs within their existing paradigm, until they realized its limitations.

Only a handful of people consistently appear as proponents of the ACM paradigm. Clark and Singer have been influential from the very beginning, but their paths developed in different directions. While Clark's voice was important in the late 1970s, it receded in the background from the early 1980s.[19] In contrast, Margaret Singer's voice became stronger, to the point of turning into a 'career' voice, despite her relatively low-key academic profile.[20] West's voice was heard occasionally in the 1980s and 1990s (West, 1982; 1987; 1990; 1993; West and Langone, 1986; West and Martin, 1996).[21]

However, those who adopted the brainwashing thesis ignored the fact that this type of conversion was actually not very effective. Of over 3,500 American POWs captured during the Korean War, only 50 made pro-Communist statements and only 25 refused repatriation (Scheflin and Opton, 1978: 89, cited in Bromley and Shupe, 1981a: 99). The majority simply put this experience behind them. Schein concluded that the Chinese conversion efforts were a failure (Schein, 1959: 332, cited in Bromley and Shupe, 1981a: 99). In fact, the psychiatric literature on brainwashing makes no claims about terrifyingly effective methods of subverting human reason and qualified statements undermine the stereotypes promoted by 'anti-cultists' (Bromley and Shupe, 1981a: 99–100). Yet other literature seemed to support such stereotypes, such as *The Manchurian Candidate* (Condon, 1958) or *Operation Mind Control* (Bowart, 1978). Bowart claimed that brainwashing was part of the psychological warfare of the American 'cryptocracy', perhaps not too far-fetched given CIA experiments in the 1950s (the *Independent*, 14 October 1988). Yet in Pattie Hearst's trial, the court did not accept the brainwashing defence (Hearst and Moscov, 1983; Boulton, 1975) – despite Louis West's attestation. The idea of brainwashing has resurfaced in cases of apparently inexplicable transformation, for example in 'converts' to Al-Qaeda and the Washington 'sniper' (Lee Malvo).

The brainwashing thesis ignores the *voluntary* participation of those involved. This may explain why the ACM did not draw parallels between 'cult' membership and monastic orders (Bromley and Shupe, 1979) or training in military academies (Dornbusch, 1955). Processes in these settings are known to social psychologists and sociologists studying group dynamics and interpersonal behaviour (Lewin, 1973; Lieberman, 1956; Bromley and Shupe, 1981a: 97) as well as obedience to authority (Milgram, 1974) and group pressure (Asch, 1952).

Nevertheless, the brainwashing thesis gave parents not only a knowledge paradigm, but also allies for their cause. This helped them to articulate their problem and legitimate their campaign. FAIR in Britain emerged from the alliance of a politician, parents, former members, journalists, and local clergy – an alliance of mutual benefit: the politician acted on behalf of constituents and public interest, with evidence supplied by parents; parents and former members received help and support; journalists supplied and received information to raise public awareness; individual clergy had pastoral concerns and theological interests (Rose, 1981b). In Germany, parents initially rallied around Pastor Haack who had a long-standing personal interest. The knowledge paradigm there was initially a combination of theological and pastoral concerns and elements of the brainwashing thesis adapted to the German context.

In recent years, the thesis has become refined. Steven Hassan argues that 'brainwashing' is used too loosely in the media (when he had been a UC member, he *knew* he had *not* been brainwashed), but it is a coercive technique effective in producing compliance. Its effect dissipates once the context within which it occurred is gone. 'Mind control' or 'thought reform' is more subtle in achieving unwitting co-operation and soliciting private information, involving little or no overt abuse and combining hypnotic processes with group dynamics to create indoctrination. This is what deceives and manipulates individuals. Hassan adds a component – control of information – to the three in Festinger's 'cognitive dissonance theory' – control of behaviour, thoughts, and emotions. He uses Schein *et al.*'s three steps to explain how control of the mind occurs. However, he also includes hypnotism, which he relates to trance-inducing techniques (meditation, repetition or forced attention), manipulation and deception (Hassan, 1988: 55–72). Hassan's thinking has been influential in Britain: he addressed the FAIR meeting in 1990 (Hassan, 1990) and FAIR circulated his ideas (*FAIR NEWS*, Spring 1990: 2–4). A British edition of his book was published in 1990 and a German translation in 1993.

Despite having the 'brainwashing thesis' as a common denominator, the ACM is neither a uniform block of opinion nor speaks with one voice. Therefore, although there is scope for alliance and co-operation, there is no over-arching principle for concerted action. Nothing ever came of efforts (in the late 1980s) to create an ACM umbrella organization in the UK, precisely because of differences between groups. With hindsight, it seems likely that the idea of the umbrella organization was a response to the establishment of INFORM.

Reactive processes

In the formative stages, the lines between 'anti-cultists' and 'cultists' were not as sharply drawn – these resulted from reactive processes. For example, the UC only appointed official spokespersons in *reaction* to the parents' mobilization. According to Paul Rose, to begin with, grassroots members – not spokespersons – dealt with telephone enquiries. The UC only placed guards outside its London headquarters after FAIR members had entered to remove a member. It also created an association for parents sympathetic to their children's membership, evidently to counterbalance 'anti-cult' groups. It used litigation through libel action as a 'strategy' to deal with (perceived) critics. Paul Rose fought such an action (Rose, 1981b), as did James Beckford and the *Daily Mail*, regarding respective articles in *Time Out*, *Psychology Today* (Beckford, 1976), and the *Daily Mail*. Despite protracted proceedings, the first two actions did not go to court, but caused tremendous upset and worry. The third went to court in 1980/81 and ended in failure for the UC. Libel action is an 'effective' strategy because of the high stakes involved – for both parties: immense costs in terms of time, finances, reputation, and career. As libel is a personalized matter (only *individuals* can be libelled), such actions are hard to fight, also because they are extremely newsworthy. Both Rose and Beckford felt their careers and livelihoods threatened. As a consequence of the UC's defeat in the *Daily Mail* trial, Dennis Orme, then UC leader in Britain, was relieved of his post. Strangely, although libel actions are personalized, individuals may not necessarily have legal responsibility for costs. Organizations can step in, as happened in the *Daily Mail* case. When the High Court ordered Orme to provide security or face the dismissal of the case (*The Times*, 4 November 1980; *Daily Mail*, 4 November 1980), the money was ultimately provided by the UC (*Daily Mail*, 11 November 1980; 28 November 1980; 4 December 1980; 29 January 1981). This instance involved two organizations of financial parity, but in the other two actions, the balance of financial power was tilted in UC's favour.

In the early days, NRMs also sought to create links: first, between themselves – informally to begin with, more formally later, as, for example, in the wake of the European Parliament's resolution in 1984. Second, with the academic community: since the early 1970s (*Unification Movement Newsletter*, April 1988: 3), the UC has sponsored all-expenses-paid conferences under the auspices of its various foundations, such as New ERA (New Ecumenical Research Association) and International Cultural Foundation (Fleming and Schuler, 1990: 14), with other NRMs following suit, including ISKCON (Barker, 1986a; Subhananda dasa, 1986a; D'Costa, 1996) and Soka Gakkai (e.g. the Taplow conference). Third, with political and religious leaders: in late 1973, the UC's leader, Sun Myung Moon, launched an extensive 'Day of Hope' campaign in the US (*Time*, 13 October 1973, cited in Rose, 1981b: 25–31). In September 1974, Moon spoke to thousands in Madison Square Garden (Rose, 1981b: 28). In early 1975, the UC claimed that Moon had received honorary citizenship from 73 cities and addressed 180 Congress leaders and that 153 governors and mayors had proclaimed 'Day of Hope and Unification' – among them Jimmy Carter and Ronald Reagan (ibid.: 30–31). All this illustrates how fluid the situation and how untroubled public perception was at the time regarding NRMs and their activities. Neither politicians nor academics saw any reason to shun dealings with the UC and probably took counsel from each other: if the UC can be received by politicians, academics can attend its conferences and vice versa.

However, the first *critical* reports about the UC also emerged at that time. An article by Jonathan Marshall on 'Korean Evangelism' appeared in the September/October 1974 edition of the Californian magazine *Pacific Research and World Empire Telegram*. It focused on alleged links between the UC and political organizations in Korea and Japan (Rose, 1981b: 26–28). In the UK, the first critical article appeared in *Time Out* (11–17 April 1975). While criticism in America focused on UC's *political* involvement, criticism in the UK focused on its *recruitment* strategies and *religious* practices as well as political connections.

Academic interest in NRMs had several causes: (1) this new and fascinating phenomenon questioned, even invalidated, existing theories; (2) it raised controversy; (3) it offered the opportunity of a new field of study and thus opened new career avenues, in an area which – according to some – had run out of research matter. Graduates in the late 1950s were dissuaded from research in the sociology of religion, because there was apparently nothing worthwhile left to study (B. Martin, 1981a: 94). However, as we have seen, sociologists did not enter a *terra nova*, they found the territory already occupied.

The perspective of the Church of England

While the mainstream churches in Germany became involved in the NRM debate right from the start, the churches in Britain did not develop a *formalized* response until the late 1980s. Whatever support parents received from clergy occurred on the grassroots level, not as part of a general strategy. Apart from a six-page pamphlet on the UC in 1978, the British Council of Churches (BCC) did not comment. In his report for 1985, the Revd Kenneth Cracknell, a Methodist minister, then Secretary of BCC's Committee for Relations with People of Other Faiths, stated his commitment to dialogue with NRMs and defended his address at a Scientology conference in London. His successor, the Revd Clinton Bennett, spoke at the 'Interfaith Thanksgiving' at the UC's headquarters, held after the case against UC's charitable status had been withdrawn (Bennett, 1988). The commitment to dialogue fits into the wider context of ecumenism and interfaith dialogue in the Church of England and World Council of Churches. Groups like the UC were welcomed by church organizations specializing in ecumenical links, because ecumenism was considered the way forward for a declining church and work in these agencies offered career structures. The Roman Catholic Church, too, looked towards ecumenical links in dealing with NRMs.

The Church of England was 'nudged' into action by a question in the General Synod, submitted in November 1983 by the (then) Dean of St. Albans. The matter was referred to the (then) Board for Mission and

Unity which, after due consultation and deliberation, presented in 1984 suggestions and considerations to the House of Bishops. The Church faced a dilemma: information on NRMs was desirable, but allegations levelled at NRMs – especially regarding proselytism – could also be levelled at orthodox Christian groups. The need for pastoral guidance was acknowledged, but direct criticism of NRM teachings was questioned. Therefore, the Church proceeded with extreme caution, to avoid undesirable publicity and possible litigation. It was mindful of the power of the press and of the NRMs. It was also aware of the consequences of possible legislation by government or European agencies, which could threaten religious freedom – the reason why the BCC's Executive Committee did not endorse the Cottrell resolution, which it had communicated to the British MEPs in May 1984. In the wake of the Cottrell Report, 'anti-anti-cult' groups formed to promote religious freedom – the very area of common ground with established churches.

By 1984, the Board for Mission and Unity had proposed a three-pronged approach: information, pastoral guidelines, legal provisions. It suggested an approach to an independent agency for the provision of information (consultations to that effect had been going on with the Centre at King's College London), to draw up general pastoral guidelines and to examine the law's adequacy to safeguard against abuses. In the light of the Cottrell proposals, the House of Bishops opted against exploring *new* legislation, preferring instead to see existing legislation tightened.

In the meantime, the BCC held a conference in April 1986 assembling representatives of various churches and denominations, with Harold Turner among the speakers. As individual cases were discussed during this general consultation about NRMs, the proceedings were only distributed to participants. The BCC's Executive Committee then asked Canon Reardon to represent them, because it considered the Anglican Church's approach to NRMs to be in full agreement with its own. A parallel development was the emerging idea for INFORM – minuted meetings took place from late 1986 (General Synod, 1989: 2)[22] – and INFORM was to become the Church's information centre. In the House of Lords, the Bishop of Chelmsford declared the Church's co-operation with INFORM in February 1988 (*Hansard*, 10.02.1988: cols. 247–275), as did the 1989 Synod Report and the Bishop of Chester's speech in the House of Lords in November 1989 (*Hansard*, 30.11.1989: cols. 542–546).

However, the creation of INFORM added to the NRM controversy, raising a range of issues, as stated by Alan Meale MP in March 1989 (*Hansard*, 13.03.1989: cols. 188–191), to which the (then) Home Office Minister John Patten replied (ibid.: cols. 191–196), and by Radio 4's *Face the Facts* (25 May 1989) and *Sunday* programmes (22 October 1995). The underlying issue was that the ACM groups did not trust INFORM's founder, Professor Eileen Barker who had researched the UC. This is an example of academics finding the field occupied: INFORM was to combine academic research with providing information and referring cases for counselling. The latter took it into territory which had so far been the reserve of the 'anti-cult' groups.

Further, in early 1988, the (then) Attorney General, Sir Patrick Mayhew, announced in the House of Commons that the investigation into the UC's charitable status would be abandoned (*Hansard*, 03.02.1988: cols. 974–978). This investigation had been one of the outcomes of the *Daily Mail* libel case. The announcement had two effects: first, the Home Office embarked on a general reform of the charity law, with a White Paper issued (HMSO, 1989) and debated in the House of Lords in 1989 (*Hansard*, 21.11–14.12.1989: cols. 499–690). Second, John Saxby (then Prebendary in Exeter) submitted a private member's motion to the General Synod in February 1988, arguing for the Church to take legal action against the UC's charitable status. The motion was, however, not discussed before November 1989 (*Report of Proceedings* in General Synod, 1990), together with an amendment by the Archdeacon of Croydon, but led to the Synod Report of June 1989 (General Synod, 1989). This report consisted of three sections: the House of Bishops' recommendations,[23] the Church's general attitude,[24] and a draft code of practice,[25] with an Appendix including extracts from the Government's White Paper on charities.[26]

The Church's cautious approach suggests it did not want to 'go it alone' and explains the wide consultation and slow progress in formulating its stance. The Church found collaboration from the BCC, from some academic institutions, and finally from INFORM which had made a 'timely' appearance. The Government's review of the charity law was also convenient, because it did not involve *new* legislation. Also, the Church wanted its theological response informed by academic knowledge. The Synod Report's code of practice suggests that the Church wanted neither a chummy nor an antagonistic relationship with NRMs. Therefore, INFORM suited the Church – no other institution offered academic research combined with information and counselling, but the Church's perspective also suited INFORM, because its creation had Church support. The (then) Archbishop of Canterbury Robert Runcie became one of its patrons and Canon Reardon its vice-chairman. Other churches were represented, including the Free Church Federal Council, Baptist Union, Methodist Church, and Roman Catholic Church. INFORM also gained a ready-made network of church-appointed advisors as (re)sources for information and help.

The perspective of the Roman Catholic Church

Roman Catholic priests – like Anglican clergy – initially dealt with the issue on the local parish level. Like the Anglican Church, the RCC joined the NRM debate late. However, its response needs to be seen in the light of its respective position in Britain and Germany. While a minority church in Britain, it is in Germany – alongside the Protestant Church – an established church and forms a pillar of social and public life. It followed the Protestant

Church in establishing a national network of *Sektenbeauftragte*, which took care of NRM issues. In Britain, however, there was no burning need for action: Fr Hans Wjngaards had set up Housetop Centre in the early 1980s, a Catholic charity providing information, advice, and pastoral care, whose brief included NRMs, and once INFORM was set up, the matter was effectively dealt with, especially as Fr Wjngaards collaborated with INFORM as a Governor.

However, an assessment of the Roman Catholic Church's (RCC's) response to NRMs also needs to consider the Church's international dimension and global perspective as well as its hierarchical and unwieldy structure – it took time to co-ordinate the Vatican dicasteries and to activate its administrative and doctrinal apparatus. Seen from Vatican eyes, the emergence of the NRMs indicated manifestations of 'non-Christian' faith, a category for which the Secretariat for Non-Christians (Secretariatus pro non Christianis) had existed since 1964, with the task of exploring how to relate to, and conduct dialogue with, other faiths (Secretariatus pro non Christianis, 1984; Arinze and Tomko, 1991). Previously, RC doctrine had not allowed acknowledgement of 'truth' in other religions, to see them as 'alternative', yet valid 'paths up the mountain'. It took Vatican Two to usher in a process of softening its stance. Rapid social changes in the modern world forced the Church to take note of other religions, in ways which went beyond ecumenical channels (see also Saliba, 1992). Liberation theology and popular Pentecostalism greatly challenged the Church in Latin America. The Fourth Extraordinary Consistory, convened by Pope John Paul II in April 1991, addressed the Latin-American bishops' concern about the 'alarming proliferation' of 'sects'. Cardinal Tomko, Prefect of the Congregation for the Evangelization of Peoples, approached this topic from the encyclical *Redemptoris Missio* (Tomko, 1991), while Cardinal Arinze, Prefect of the Pontifical Council for Interreligious Dialogue, reported on the pastoral approach to the NRM challenge (Arinze, 1991) and regional summaries described specific local variations (Corripio Ahumada *et al.*, 1991). Although a central text regarding the Church's missionary mandate and dialogue with other religions, *Redemptoris Missio* makes no reference to NRMs. Therefore, its relevance needs interpretative extrapolation by Vatican theologians – a parish priest facing parents with a 'cult' problem could derive no pastoral guidance from it.

The Vatican was 'nudged' into action by the concern about 'sects, new religious movements, and cults' expressed by Episcopal Conferences throughout the world. It conducted a survey and then compiled a report – the Vatican Report (Secretariat for Promoting Christian Unity *et al.*, 1986) – based on questionnaire responses and documents from 75 Episcopal Conferences and regional episcopal bodies. The Report was published under the aegis of *four* Vatican offices which had co-operated in this project: Secretariat for Promoting Christian Unity, Secretariat for Non-Christians, Secretariat for Non-Believers, and Pontifical Council for Culture. None of these included NRMs in their remit. This suggests that the Church was somewhat slow in asking the 'right' questions and explains why the Church has treated NRMs as a separate category – NRMs did not figure in its dialogue with 'other' religions.

The Vatican Report revealed that NRMs were perceived as a threat – a 'pastoral challenge' – and that information, education, and 'a renewed pastoral approach' were needed. It addressed terminology and the reasons for NRMs' success and set them against the context of modernity. It included respondents' suggestions of pastoral approaches, an outline of the Church's attitude towards NRMs, extracts from the Extraordinary Synod's final report of 1985, and questions for further study. The Report showed overlap in the perceptions of NRMs among RC clergy and parents' groups – what they are, what they do, and why they are successful. It used language of the ACM paradigm, such as 'deception', 'mind control', 'behaviour modification technique', etc. This is most likely due to the way the information was gathered, as those most knowledgeable would have completed the questionnaires, namely local priests with pastoral experience (see also Saliba, 1992). Another overlap with parents' groups was the Church's wish for the State to take measures against NRMs, although these were not specified (Secretariat for Promoting Christian Unity *et al.*, 1986: 16). Such statements offered scope for co-operation between priests and parents, particularly on the parish level where care for *individuals* was paramount.

However, the Report rejected the practice of 'deprogramming' – on grounds of religious freedom and individual rights – and stated that the Church's principles and beliefs neither allowed it to condemn or combat nor see NRMs outlawed or expelled. The Church saw their emergence largely in terms of the mainstream churches' failure and looked inward for diagnosis and remedy. This perceived failure provided a strong reason for seeking allies through ecumenical channels. Therefore, the RCC welcomed the World Council of Churches' 1986 conference (Brockway and Rajashekar, 1987), which again illustrates how theological perspectives were complemented and informed by academic findings. Vatican officials, such as Teresa Gonçalves (1990; 1993: 83–84) of the *Pontificium Pro Dialogo Inter Religiones* and Elisabeth Peter (1990) and Michael-Paul Gallagher (1993) of the Pontifical Council for Dialogue with Non-Believers, attended academic conferences.

Interestingly, the Vatican Report saw few openings for dialogue with NRMs, despite the Church's commitment to dialogue with other faiths. This suggests that the Church was in the process of formulating the basis on which to conduct dialogue with NRMs. At the same time, NRMs like ISKCON sought to open channels within the Vatican's framework of *inter-religious* dialogue. ISKCON's response to the Report (Subhananda dasa, 1986b) welcomed the Church's call for increased understanding. Gonçalves (1990: 5–6) conceded in 1990 that the Church had not taken an official position on dialogue with NRMs, but affirmed general willingness.

Yet, the 1992 Plenary Assembly of the *Pontificium* (*Bulletin* 82, 1993) clearly saw dialogue with NRMs *separate* from dialogue with other world religions. Despite this, some new Buddhist groups, such as Rissho-Koseikai, were *included* in the dialogue with Buddhists (Shirieda, 1993: 46; 60–62). In her report to the Plenary, Gonçalves (1993: 84–86) set out the specific problems involved in dialogue with NRMs, as does Fitzgerald (1991; 1992). Fuss (1992a) encloses dialogue with NRMs within ecumenical dialogue.

The Vatican Report's stated need for continued study of NRMs resulted in further research by F.I.U.C. (*Fédération Internationale des Universités Catholiques*). Its research plan comprised various phases, the first producing a dossier of papers by around 30 members of Catholic Universities (Fuss, 1990a) and the next consisting of seminars in Europe, the United States, Latin America, and Asia organized in 1991 and 1992 with the collaboration of the *Pontificium*. The last seminar's proceedings are published (Salazar, 1994). While the Vatican Report focused on pastoral concerns, the F.I.U.C. project pursued academic and inter-disciplinary perspectives to inform these concerns. This project underlines two aspects: first, the complementary role of academic research and theoretical findings regarding the theological/pastoral perspective; second, the Church's international and global viewpoint regarding the NRMs challenging its position in different parts of the world. Involving the network of Catholic universities and organizing symposiums on different continents ensured the international dimensions.

Cardinal Arinze's report (1991) to the Fourth Extraordinary Consistory followed the Vatican Report's perception of NRMs and reasons for their success. However, it goes further concerning the Church's pastoral response: it identifies *particular* failures and suggests measures, such as creating base communities and teaching the gospel in a meaningful way. Yet overall, Arinze's report underlines the Church's *reactive* stance in asking how it can match what NRMs offer.

Since 1992, Teresa Gonçalves has held a new post in the *Pontificium*, especially created to deal with NRMs. It involves collating primary and secondary information to build a *resource centre*, a task to which various Vatican offices had been assigned before. Both the F.I.U.C. project and the special NRM post indicate a process of institutionalization regarding knowledge about NRMs. They are efforts to claim knowledge and set up a knowledge base – knowledge which is largely created *by* the Church itself – somewhat derivatively – and *for* itself. The Vatican has as yet to define the NRM phenomenon so that it can decide how to deal with NRMs within inter-religious dialogue. The inclusion of some Japanese new religions in inter-religious dialogue with Buddhism shows that the process of definition is ongoing. Saliba concludes that the Church cannot respond to NRMs in the traditional way, but is not quite ready to develop a universal policy towards them. Hence the *informal* dialogue with some NRMs (Saliba, 1992: 35–36). However, the initiative for dialogue has come from NRMs, not from the Church, and this, too, accords with its *reactive* stance.

INSTITUTIONAL KNOWLEDGE

Although this book mainly focuses on the development and response of institutions, particularly the 'anti-cult movement' and established churches, the role of sociologists and the media also need to be considered. Their involvement has already been indicated, but the background against which the social sciences developed since the Second World War is important. This section sketches the chronology of sociology of religion in Britain and *Religionswissenschaft* in Germany and outlines the media's role in the NRM controversy.

Sociology of religion after the War

In order to understand why research on NRMs provided new avenues for sociologists regarding research material and careers, one needs to appreciate the background against which sociology of religion had developed in the decades preceding the counter-culture and NRMs. Classical sociology of religion, as pursued by Weber and Durkheim, was concerned with the macro-social level (Berger and Luckmann, [1963] 1969.)[27] Since the end of the Second World War, it had tended to work on less global, but empirically more verifiable, issues. However, sociological studies were mainly carried out by Protestant and Catholic theologians:

> In the period since the Second World War there has been a remarkable development of sociologically oriented research carried on under ecclesiastical auspices, to the point where today a sizeable body of literature has been produced by this enterprise.
>
> (Berger and Luckmann, 1969: 62)

'Sizeable body of literature' refers to an extensive international bibliography in Goldschmidt and Matthes (1962). This kind of research mainly dealt with issues regarding church attendance, religious commitment, political attitudes, etc., which served agencies in churches, administration, and politics. Research by French Catholics – Le Bras and the group *Economie et Humanisme* – was particularly notable, as were numerous, predominantly sociographic studies in the Netherlands. Sociography deals with society's 'material substrata' and falls under 'social morphology', a term coined by Durkheim in 1898 (König, 1960: 257–268). More sociological studies used theoretical terms to 'dress up' a collection of factual data, for example formal and informal social organization of parishes, relation of parishes to community, role of clergy, etc. (ibid.: 243–244). Many Catholic-sponsored institutes undertook such research using headings, such as 'religious sociology', 'parish sociology' or 'pastoral sociology' (Berger and Luckmann, 1969: 62). This was 'a religious variety of market research' and 'employer oriented in its motivations'; the focus was church-affiliated religiosity and the methodology was technically and ideologically functional (ibid.: 63).

A principal periodical, published under Catholic auspices, was *Social Compass*, a descendant of the International Conference for the Sociology of Religion (ICSR), organized in 1948 by Catholic social scientists from France, Belgium, and the Netherlands. ICSR is now ISSR – International Society for the Sociology of Religion.[28] *Review of Religious Research* began in the late 1950s under the auspices of the Religious Research Association (RRA), an association of Protestant sociologists in the US dating from the mid-1940s. Its Catholic counterpart, the American Catholic Sociological Society (ACSS) had started in the late 1930s and published *The American Catholic Sociological Review*. By the mid-1960s, members' interests focused more on sociology of religion and the journal became *Sociological Analysis*. In 1971, ACSS changed to Association for the Sociology of Religion to reflect an increasingly 'secular' membership and in 1993, *Sociological Analysis* became *Sociology of Religion*. The Society for the Scientific Study of Religion (SSSR) was formed in the mid-1950s, but the *Journal for the Scientific Study of Religion* did not appear before 1961 (Stark, 1999).

Yet there were researchers who continued with classical sociological approaches, among them Howard Becker, Gerhard Lenski, Milton Yinger, Talcott Parsons. Their work was, however, not enough to make sociology of religion a *mainstream* discipline:

> the sociology of religion is marginal in terms of the sociological enterprise proper (as distinguished from the ecclesiastical research enterprise discussed before), both in terms of its practice and in terms of its thought . . . the implication is quite clear: religion is not a central concern for sociological theory or for sociological analysis of contemporary society. Religion can, therefore, be left in the main to the social historians, to the ethnologists or to those few sociologists with an antiquarian interest in 'the classics' – and, of course, to that fairly alienated group of colleagues employed by religious institutions.
>
> (Berger and Luckmann, 1969: 64)

Other scholars who did not entirely fit the mould of sociographic methodology included Peter Berger, Thomas Luckmann, Charles Glock, Robert Bellah, Rodney Stark, Bryan Wilson, David Martin, Roy Wallis, and James Beckford.[29]

The impact of counter-culture and NRMs

In the US, religion has always been a live issue, because religion and religious innovation have thrived in that pluralistic setting. Thus, there has always been considerable academic interest in, and a sizeable academic system to study, religious phenomena. When first the counter-culture and then NRMs emerged, sociologists of religion examined them, addressing, for example, the role of deprivation (Glock, 1964), religion and society in tension (Glock and Stark, 1965), the origin of religious groups (Glock, 1973), the new religious consciousness (Glock and Bellah, 1976), the broken covenant (Bellah, 1975), conversion to a deviant perspective (Lofland and Stark, 1965). It should therefore not be surprising that the beginnings of NRM studies are found where religion flourished. Interest in, and awareness of, the new phenomena spawned further studies and furnished sociology of religion in the US with 'new' research matter. The discipline was revitalized (Robbins, 1988a): it attracted more students and scholarly output increased steadily during the 1970s and 1980s.

The advent of the counter-culture coincided with the expansion of the academic system throughout Britain and Europe. Historically, departments of divinity had dominated. Their prominence dated from a period when universities trained clergy. Theology, considered the 'queen of sciences', was the knowledge paradigm with which the social sciences initially competed (B. Martin, 1981a: 92). By the late 1960s, when the churches were in decline and church employment no longer had social cachet, the star of divinity departments was in the descendant. Therefore, following the American lead, social sciences – not divinity – concerned themselves with the counter-culture and NRMs and *sociology* became the major source of academic NRM study in Britain, not *theology*.

Themes in the study of NRMs

The early studies in Anglo-Saxon countries worked within theoretical frameworks so far applied to non-mainstream religions or 'sects'. This basically involved a functionalist or Marxist approach: deprivation accounted for conversion to, and membership in, such groups. Initially, deprivation was seen in materialistic terms, then in terms of class or status, then extended to deprivation generally. The application of this theory illustrates that paradigms do not shift as long as they can accommodate new data. Both functionalist and Marxist approaches worked with the concept of deprivation, but they differed in language. Marxist interpretations stressed how religious responses 'mask' properly and overtly political or revolutionary responses to deprivation, while functionalist interpretations stressed the positive value of religious responses for society as a whole. Despite the Weberian tradition (and apart from studies of charisma), these were the predominant frameworks for analysing 'sects', frameworks which were deterministic and oriented towards *macro*-social structures.

Deprivation was employed to account for NRMs' emergence, attraction, and development. The theory sees NRMs as religious revivals which satisfy un-met human needs, help people cope with problems otherwise not addressed, and act as catalysts for religious change. According to Saliba (following Talcott Parsons), religion and NRMs have served five major functions: (1) explanatory: religion offers explanations, interpretations, and rationalizations of all aspects of human existence; (2) emotional: religion offers identity, security, and courage, which reduces anxiety, stress, and tension; (3) social: religion creates social solidarity; (4) validating: religion establishes cultural values and inculcates social and ethical norms; (5) adaptive: religious beliefs and rituals are tools for ecological survival (Saliba, 1990a: xxxi–xxxiii). Galanter (1989) applies socio-biological theory to NRMs, such as the UC. Glock (1964) argues that deprivation theory explains the rise of new religions, their development, and 'potentiality' for survival. Greeley (1970) argues that occult beliefs and behaviour have several functions, such as providing meaning. Stark and Bainbridge (1980a) consider the theory incomplete and suggest a negative association between religious compensators and actual rewards in 'sects', to which Wallis and Bruce (1984) respond critically. Wallis (1975c) questions the validity of deprivation to account for NRM membership. Barker (1986b) questions deprivation in economic terms and relates it instead to spirituality and human relations. Earlier, she suggested five positive functional aspects which accounted for UC members' spiritual well-being (Barker, 1979). Hargrove (1980) considers religious needs left un-met by major social changes in the postwar period as accounting for the rise of NRMs. Beckford (1981a) rejects functional analyses of NRMs because they distract from the content of teachings and practices. Heelas and Heelas (1988) question whether deprivation can adequately account for conversion.

However, while working with these models, sociologists found that they did not quite fit: the concept of (economic) deprivation did not agree with NRM members' middle-class background. The misfit made the phenomenon fascinating and challenging and stimulated sociological debate about the theories' applicability and refinement. Saliba (1990a: xxxiv–xxxvi) identifies seven, somewhat overlapping approaches which bypass or reformulate deprivation: (1) NRMs are genuine religious revivals; (2) NRMs confirm the secularization thesis; (3) NRMs are forms of experimental religion; (4) NRMs result from disenchantment with 'the establishment'; (5) NRMs result from rapid social change and its concomitant erosion of values and norms; (6) NRMs are indicators of an emerging new humanism; (7) NRMs result from the breakdown of 'civil religion'.

However, taking a sociological approach – functionalist or Marxist – put social scientists in opposition to the 'anti-cult' perspective. Seeing NRMs and NRM membership in terms of fulfilling needs assigns NRMs a *positive*, beneficial role in society and recognizes them as genuine, legitimate alternatives. Further, attending to social *macro*-structures rather than individuals is offensive to those concerned with (and about) a *particular individual*: 'The functional viewpoint is in direct conflict with the anticult [sic] conception of a cult as a spurious religious organization that can be better likened to a cancerous growth in an otherwise healthy organism' (ibid.: xxxiii). For NRM opponents, statements about NRMs' beneficial effects suggest sympathy, if not support for them: a 'number of sociologists and religious studies scholars have explicitly or *implicitly* evinced sympathy with embattled cults *through their analyses*, through testimony as "expert witnesses" in courts and legislative chambers and through their participation in conferences sponsored by religious movements' (Robbins, 1988b: 161; emphasis added). Therefore, (at least) one reason why social scientists have been *perceived* as sympathetic lies in their theoretical perspectives and methodological approaches. One of my academic interviewees commented that such perceptions are likely in a *contentious* field, but this was not necessarily a bad thing, as long as the basis of one's sympathy *and* detachment is understood. Another said that it was by default almost that social scientific work comes across as sympathetic. Two others thought that the perceived sympathy is a combination of things, which includes social scientific research techniques. Another stated that it was related to the focus of sociological study, the way religion is understood and defined, and the methods rather than sociologists' innate desire to defend or be sympathetic to movements. Saliba (1990b: ix) points out that the very fact of refraining from condemning or using negative language about 'cults' makes social scientists appear sympathetic: 'a scholar who does not state clearly in public talks and printed word that the cults are evil institutions whose activities should at least be curtailed ... finds himself or herself accused of being a cult sympathizer or suspected of being a secret member of one of the cults themselves!'

Sociologists also applied 'classical' sociological concepts to the definition of 'sect' and 'cult'. Definitions are closely linked with devising typologies for the wide range of NRMs. Such attempts overlap greatly with the question of NRMs' newness or distinctiveness compared to previous non-mainstream groups. The ACM and churches have addressed this question, albeit in different forms. The debate is ongoing and it has proved extremely difficult to arrive at a consensus, both about the precise boundary of the NRM category and the best tool for analysing NRMs. The debate largely revolves around the use to which analysis is put, not only in academia, but also in the interaction between academics and other participants.

Typologies

Troeltsch's tripartite typology – church, sect, and mysticism, with church and sect in opposition (Troeltsch, 1931; Scharf, 1970; Wilson, 1970b) – served as the basis for subsequent typologies. Wilson's (1970b) detailed critique of Troeltsch's model points to weaknesses. Niebuhr (1954) developed Troeltsch's typology further, establishing a developmental connection between church and sect: sects either die or change into denominations. However, Wilson argues that not all sects go through the denominalization process and David Martin argues that religious groups do not have to undergo the sect stage to become denominations (Scharf, 1970: 106).

Adapting von Wiese's classification, Becker (1932: 621–628) suggests a four-part typology – ecclesia, denomination, sect, cult – and establishes a continuum from cult to ecclesia. Yinger (1957; 1970) also builds on Troeltsch in distinguishing five types of religious organization: universal church, ecclesia, denomination or class church, established sect, and transient sect. His typology is based on sects' attitude towards the predominating order: they accept, oppose or ignore it. A later, sixth category is the cult. Yinger's typology is more refined because religious groups can move in either direction along the classificatory range. Clark's (1937; Simmel and Stählin, 1957: 286–287) criteria are cultural aspects (belief contents, rituals, organization), which suggests seven types of sects: pessimistic or adventist (millenarian), perfectionist/subjectivist, charismatic and pentecostal, communist, legalistic or objectivistic, New Thought, and esoteric.

Wilson (1969: 363–364) questions the theological bias in the church–sect dichotomy and argues for a sociologically based typology. His central criterion is the sect's response to the world, which is one of greater or lesser rejection. His typology of 1959 proposes four types: conversionist, adventist or revolutionist, introversionist or pietist, and gnostic sects. Wilson (1959) is also concerned with the circumstances leading to the emergence of sects and group commitment. His refined typology comprises seven types: conversionist, revolutionary, introversionist, manipulationist, thaumaturgical, reformist, and utopian (Wilson, 1963, reprinted as Wilson, 1969: 364–371; also 1970b: 36–47). David Martin's (1962) examination of the denomination stresses its distinction from both church and sect. The church–sect typology's utility for sociological research has been called into question: in 1967, the *Journal for the Scientific Study of Religion* presented a symposium, including Goode (1967a; 1967b), Demerath (1967a; 1967b), Eister (1967), and Gustafson (1967). Other critical voices are Dittes (1971), Johnson (1957; 1963; 1971), Swatos (1976), and Robertson (1970).

While Wilson accommodated mainly 'established sects', Wallis – following Weber – applied the criterion of response to the world to his typology of NRMs, the first to analyse NRMs specifically. He refined his initial dichotomy of world-affirming and world-rejecting (Wallis, 1978c) to a tripartite typology by adding world-accommodating (Wallis, 1979b; 1982a; 1984; 1985). Bird's (1979a) typology is designed to demonstrate typical variations regarding NRM members' 'moral accountability'. The relationship between followers and masters can be of three types: devotee, disciple, or apprentice. Moral questions are also central to Robbins and Anthony's (1979a) typology. NRMs are classified according to their responses to 'the present climate of moral ambiguity': dualistic and monistic movements, the latter sub-divided into technical and charismatic movements, one-level monistic and two-level monistic systems. Bainbridge and Stark (1980) distinguish three types of 'cults', according to the tension with their sociocultural environment: cult movements which maintain high tension, client cults which provide 'magical services', such as TM

(Transcendental Meditation), and audience cults in which followers participate through the media, such as astrology.

Lofland and Richardson's (1984) typology accommodates NRMs and non-religious social movements: the 'religious movement organization's (RMO)' degree of 'corporateness' determines five types: clinics, congregations, collectives, corps, and colonies. Beckford's typology is based on the mode of NRMs' insertion into their host societies and combines internal social relationships with external ones. Different insertion modes are arranged along two intersecting axes: internal and external; the co-ordinates are, respectively, devotee, adept, client, patron, apostate and retreat, revitalization, release. This framework also seeks to 'emphasize the association between NRMs' profiles of internal relationships and their differential susceptibility to controversy' (Beckford, 1985: 76–93).

Theoretical approaches

Sociologists' studies 'tested' theories and propositions proffered by the ACM (Hargrove, 1982a), mainly the 'brainwashing' thesis. They found NRMs had a high turnover in membership, that those who joined were 'normal', and the reasons why members were likely to join. The issue of 'brainwashing' is, of course, closely connected with conversion: if NRM members are not 'brainwashed', how are they converted?[30] Numerous studies revolved around the UC, initially the main focus of 'anti-cult' groups.[31] While sound academic reasons motivated testing ACM-constructed propositions,[32] the endeavour included an element of 'career opportunity'. Examining social processes in NRM membership turned academics into 'experts' and contestants of the ACM paradigm. This proved important in the media context where the opposition of voices has often encouraged, if not forced, academics to take the more partisan position. They found themselves slipping into the role of devil's advocate, but in doing so, *appeared* as advocates of the devil.

Subsequent research examined the emergence of NRMs in the wake of the counter-culture,[33] the validity of the secularization thesis,[34] parallels between NRMs and novel religions in the past, NRMs and rapid social change,[35] deviance,[36] the applicability to NRMs of Weberian concepts, such as charisma[37] and modern capitalism (Heelas, 1991; 1992; Roberts, 1995), comparative studies of NRMs in different countries (Beckford, 1981b; 1983b; 1983d), leaving NRMs (Beckford, 1978b; Richardson *et al.*, 1986; Wright, 1984; 1987; Bromley, 1988a) and the role of apostates (Shupe and Bromley, 1981; Hall, 1988), the 'anti-cult' movement,[38] the media,[39] NRMs' finances (Bromley and Shupe, 1980; Richardson, 1983; 1988; Bird and Westley, 1985; Heelas, 1990b), how the State has dealt with NRMs (Kehrer, 1981b; Beckford, 1983d; 1993; Robbins, 1987; Barker, 1989b), and recently, NRMs' millenarian aspects (Bowie, 1997; Kaplan, 1997; Robbins and Palmer, 1997; Hargrove, 1982b). There is overlap in these areas, which makes categorizing social scientific works a formidable task.[40] More comprehensive overviews can be found in Beckford and Richardson's (1983) bibliography for the US and Europe, Robbins's (1983) selective review of sociological studies, and Beckford's (1988) survey of literature outside the UK and the US.

Religionswissenschaft

In Germany, the situation has been different: *Religionswissenschaft* did not really break out of the mould of sociographic, anthropological, apologetic, and historic study of religion until the early 1980s, when it entered the NRM debate. Sociology of religion, such as existed, mainly concentrated on the established churches, not only because of church sponsorship, as Berger and Luckmann pointed out, but also because of the churches' social role. The Roman Catholic and Lutheran Protestant Church have formed pillars in German society, with the status of *Volkskirche*, which affords them state protection. A 'gentleman's agreement' regarding proselytization did not pit them against one another (one is born into either), nor was there serious competition. However, Germany is becoming a pluralist, multicultural society, a process which is challenging the churches' 'monopoly' (see Hummel, 1994b). Since the Second World War, the non-conformist tradition has not been highly visible. One of the reasons may be that under National Socialism, 'established sects' were – although numerically insignificant – subject to harassment, despite their willingness to co-operate with the regime (see King, 1982). Non-mainstream religions were studied in church institutions, such as the *Evangelische Zentralstelle für Weltanschauungsfragen* (EZW), created in the 1960s. These had apologetic interests and motives, while *Religionswissenschaft* examined the history of religions and historic religions – hence its study of (ancient) texts and documents.

Academics in the UK found the field occupied, when they began researching NRMs and their attention was – at least initially – directed to ACM arguments and theories, which they tested in empirical studies. Both ACM (and NRMs) used academic findings, when it served their purpose. Given different approaches, academics and ACM have stood in some tension to one another, even in downright opposition, as in the case of INFORM.[41] Academic research was also used by the churches in Britain to complement theological and pastoral perspectives.

In Germany, by contrast, academic research independent of the churches did not inform theological perspectives. There has been resistance to taking on board academic findings. For example, Pastor Haack criticized the edited volume on the UC (Kehrer, 1981a) for allowing a UC member (Feige, 1981) to contribute and Berger and Hexel's (1981a) study was criticized for its approach (EZW, 1982a; 1982b). Several reasons account for this, comparable to the differences between British academics and ACM. First, German academics entered the debate quite late. The ACM's knowledge paradigm was firmly in place by then, as were links with public authorities and the media. Second, research in *Religionswissenschaft* and sociology created the perception that academics were too close to their subjects and their findings not relevant to parents, because they 'minimized' the 'cult' problem. Here, too, academically framed questions put phenomena in perspective, which entails some relativization. For parents, their particular case counts, not *general* statistics or perspectives.

Therefore lack of understanding regarding the academic enterprise mingled with hostility towards newcomers to the field. *Academic* (abstract) consideration was not wanted, but *practical* advice and intervention. In my view, suspicion towards academics has been more pronounced in Germany. Also the public expect authorities to act, for example by closing legal loopholes. There was 'no demand' for academic findings, either from the churches (they had in-house expertise) or from the State (ACM thinking informed public authorities, as their reports on *Jugendreligionen* show), while academic perspectives found *some* receptivity in Anglo-Saxon countries. Another important aspect is that in Germany, neither *Religionswissenschaft* nor sociology had any groundwork in this field. They had little theory and few explanatory concepts and therefore worked on texts and the history of NRMs, until they 'borrowed' Anglo-Saxon approaches.

The number of German academics engaged in this research has been (and still is) small. Thus, the subject has been marginal and the pressure greater on those working in it. The topic has not been adopted in university programmes, because there are no career openings. REMID's purpose is to open new professional channels for *Religionswissenschaft* and to make academic voices heard, but its members cover the wider spectrum of non-mainstream religions. The Government's *Enquête-Kommission* in 1996 brought some progress, in that one of its twelve 'experts' was a professor of *Religionswissenschaft*, although one without NRM expertise.

The few academics have not covered the range of aspects and approaches of their Anglo-Saxon counterparts. Just comparing output gives an idea of scale: Saliba's bibliography (1990c) of literature in English includes *c.*2,200 entries, while my database of German publications includes just over 100 entries. Despite covering similar ground, research also dealt with topics specific to the German context. Academics focused on specific movements: the UC (Flasche, 1981; 1982a; Kehrer, 1981a), New Age (Bochinger, 1995; Stenger, 1993), Rajneeshism (Süss, 1994), and neo-Germanic paganism (von Schnurbein, 1992). They sought to refute the claim that NRM members were 'brainwashed' or different from the general population or harmed by membership (Kuner, 1982; 1983a; 1983b). They studied the emergence and success of NRMs in terms of deprivation or *anomie* (although they used neither term) – for example, the loss of meaning in modern society (Mikos, 1982), modern society's impact on identity (Wittmann, 1982), the failure of the mainstream churches (Schubert, 1982). Some went one step further and examined NRMs as groups with political motives, drawing parallels with

extreme right- and left-wing movements (Hardin and Kehrer, 1978b), interpreting NRMs as protest movements against the malaise of modernity
(Berger and Hexel, 1981a) – although Waßner (1991) disputes this – or
even as germinating terrorist groups (van Delden, 1988).[42] Academics examined how the media portrayed NRMs (Usarski, 1988; Scheffler, 1989),
recorded religious communities in a given locality (Meier-Hüsing, 1990;
Ruttmann, 1993; Gantzel *et al.*, 1994), continued the history-of-religions
approach (Flasche, 1985; 1987a; 1988a; Usarski, 1989), reflected on the
role of sociology of religion and *Religionswissenschaft* in the study of
NRMs,[43] and studied social responses to NRMs[44] and motives for joining
NRMs.[45]

Methodology and ethics

Developments in a period of changing perspectives and paradigms in academic studies of NRMs have been seriously compounded by the way knowledge has been contested. Therefore, the issue of methodology and ethics is
most intriguing – a highly contentious area neither explained by theories
nor widely discussed nor even properly addressed. There is awareness that
researchers have become part of their data (Barker, 1986b; Robertson,
1985; Robbins, 1988b: 161), that objectivity is but an ideal[46] and often
not even desirable (Barker, 1987b). There is something curious about
'methodological agnosticism': the erosion of boundaries between researcher
and subjects has had significant consequences for legitimization strategies.
One needs to indicate in what capacity one speaks and there are no
'uncontaminated' sources – in the sense of Berger's 'cultural contamination'.

However, methodology and ethics have been addressed in the debate
about covert participant observation. Homan's discussion arose from an
exchange with Bulmer on this topic. Homan (1991: viii) had used surrepti-
tious methods 'innocently', but became concerned when challenged by
American colleagues and became aware of objections to deception and disguise in the literature. Homan (1980) initially defended these methods and
Bulmer (1980) commented critically. Both expanded on the issues: Bulmer
(1982) on the merits of covert participation, Homan (1991) on *The Ethics of
Social Research*. However, despite occasional references to NRMs, Homan
does *not* address ethical questions specifically relating to the study of
NRMs.

One of the dangers of covert methods is that researchers might be found
out and face 'persecution' from subjects, damage their reputation, and cause
repercussions for their colleagues. Homan (1991: 125) discusses Barker's
(1984) work on the UC regarding the reputation of social research *in
general*: although her research methods were 'exemplary', her credibility
was challenged because close consultation and acceptance of hospitality at
sponsored conferences were interpreted as collusion with, and manipulation
by, subjects. This is but *one* aspect, however valid, of a far wider issue.

Homan's discussion of privacy, informed consent, and ethical conduct focuses on the viewpoints and perspectives of researchers and research associations. The underlying assumption is that there should be codes of conduct and guidelines for ethical research, safeguarded by appropriate mechanisms. Another underlying assumption is that research subjects have indisputable rights (privacy, informed consent, etc.). However, the onus is on the researcher to ensure these, as Homan sees subjects only as informants or persons to be observed. He does not address the *reactive* aspect of research beyond noting possible effects of observation, as for example in Festinger *et al.*'s (1956) research. Homan's subjects *do not talk back*, except when they are unhappy about the way academic accounts represent them.

Homan's discussion of ethical issues is thus tangential to NRMs: it does not confront the *politics* involved or the contest of truth claims. Covert methods actually evade or postpone the negotiation of truth claims. Here, Wallis's experience of studying Scientology is highly pertinent – his initial attempt to conduct research covertly and the later 'harassment'. Further, when he published an account of his 'research career' (Wallis, 1977), Scientology requested the right to reply, arguing that researchers (and by implication the public) would then get the full picture. Thus a rejoinder by a Scientology representative (Gaiman, 1977) was added. Homan (1991: 125) refers to the rejoinder in the context of credibility and raises an issue which *is* important for NRM study, although he does not explore it: do research findings improve or diminish in value, when controlled by subjects – by manipulating access or screening reports before publication?

Wallis's negotiation with Scientology regarding the publication of his book is another illustration of competing truth claims. Wallis submitted the manuscript of *The Road to Total Freedom* (Wallis, 1976a) to Scientology leaders for comment; this shows he was mindful of their right to have a say. He was also mindful of potential legal suits, but found himself between a rock and a hard place: exercising academic freedom and perhaps incurring prosecution or consulting the movement and perhaps sacrificing some findings. In the end, through compromise and negotiation passages were edited to mutual satisfaction (Wallis, 1977). Homan (1991: 167ff) mentions these negotiations as an example of the 'strains of research'.

The methodological and ethical problems raised by studying NRMs are in theory nothing new, but the political aspect and its potential consequences make these problems highly acute. One consequence of the way sociology and *Religionswissenschaft* have studied NRMs has arisen from the context of institutionalized knowledge. Research has become an inextricably political act, given the involvement of NRMs, churches, ACM, and the media. While not all that much is new on the abstract/theoretical level, in practice, everything is different, because of the political dimension, because of the use to which research is or can be put. There is *both* sensitivity towards NRM-sponsored conferences *and* formal discussion in academic forums; the extreme political situation is bracketed off, because confronting it would be to recognize the quagmire.

Barker's (1995) paper on 'The Scientific Study of Religion? You Must be Joking!' explores accounts of NRMs constructed by the parties involved (ACM, the media, legal representatives, therapists, social scientists, etc.). Barker distinguishes between primary and secondary constructions, with social scientific accounts in the second category. These obviously are, and have to be, different from primary constructions, which makes the categories (self-) evident and useful. However, Barker does not address how different constructions relate to one another in the research process and how truth claims are mediated – where the boundaries lie between 'primary' and 'secondary'. This is important in the light of previous statements about blurred boundaries and negotiated accounts.

An exchange during the INFORM seminar in November 1997 illustrates issues involved in the mediation of truth claims: Madeleine Bunting, then the *Guardian*'s Religious Affairs Editor, discussed an article about the Friends of the Western Buddhist Order (FWBO) in conversation with Guhyapati, FWBO's Communications Officer. (The article had appeared on 27 October 1997, followed by the response of a senior FWBO member on 8 November 1997.) Despite FWBO's involvement in the preparation of the article, Guhyapati's comments conveyed FWBO's dissatisfaction with the published version. Yet, it was clear that both journalist and FWBO officer felt strongly about their positions and thought they had given as much ground to the other as possible.

Barker's paper illustrates two things: first, we get only so far with field immersion and method: 'insider' accounts are still considered inferior to sociological accounts, as they are primary constructions.[47] Second, it is much less easy to distinguish between primary and secondary constructions, given that subjects have a voice, are given a voice, and demand to be given a voice – as Wallis's work shows. When research involves negotiation, because the researcher involves subjects and gives them a voice, secondary and primary constructions blur and secondary constructions may be contested, as the *Guardian* article on FWBO shows. Further, the distinction between insider and outsider accounts is muddied. Readers cannot know how much researchers were lobbied before writing up their data: the process of negotiating truth claims tends to be invisible. In Wallis's case, we know that his subjects had a say in the final draft, but we do not know *where in the text* amendments were made. Negotiation, in itself potentially political, can be compounded by political motives: Wallis was mindful of possible legal action, if he did not give his subjects a say. Such mindfulness may thwart the publication of academic material altogether, as occurred recently regarding an entry which I had prepared for an encyclopaedia. Political motives can also entail political battles between 'actors' and this aspect is also invisible to the public eye, unless incidents or people bring it into the open.

The blurring of primary and secondary constructions also occurs between different groups. Some NRMs present their views and positions at academic conferences, such as the presentations at the 1993 conference in London. A conference in Marburg, held in January 1995, also included representatives from religious groups. This was hotly debated among participants, some questioning the benefit of such presentations in an academic forum (Frick, 1995). Rituals have been performed at academic conferences, for example at the Nature Religion Conference at Lancaster in 1996 and the conference on shamanism in Newcastle in 1998. Academic conferences attract controversy when participants are dissuaded from attending or withdraw because of a perceived 'political' agenda.[48] The Bruderhof's action in reaction to a contribution in *Harmful Religion* (Osborn and Walker, 1997) again illustrates contested knowledge and related political and financial aspects.[49]

These examples show that contest affects various contexts and venues. Any representation of NRMs in public can involve contest, with the rules evolving as events unfold. While the Bruderhof might have opted for legal litigation ten years ago, it simply dealt with 'disagreement' by effectively withdrawing the contested knowledge from circulation.

Wallis, like Barker, divides 'constructions' of NRMs into two categories: externalist and internalist; the former are based on observations from outside, while the latter seek understanding through the movements' own worldview and close association with members. Two further categories, hostile and non-hostile, lead to hostile externalist/internalist accounts and non-hostile externalist/internalist accounts (Wallis, 1980; 1984).[50]

These parameters were included in my interviews with social scientists in Britain and one German theologian to find out where they might position themselves. While some simply considered their approach 'externalist' and 'non-hostile', others qualified their understanding of the terms in locating their work in the model. Regarding the question of (non-)hostility, the German theologian commented that the answer was not a foregone conclusion, but the result of a *process* which evolved in dealings with particular groups, implying that his initially neutral or open attitude could be 'overruled' by a group's behaviour.

Wallis's categories are as problematic as Barker's: they reflect the history of the NRM controversy and implicitly acknowledge the politics involved in the academic study of NRMs. The categories 'hostile' and 'non-hostile' collude with categories used by the media and with their agenda, rather than present academically constructed categories. Neither Barker's nor Wallis's model takes into account the politics of interaction which have become embedded in social science, as some NRM members are treated as members and then as social scientists, and as some social scientists have (often unpublicized) personal affinities with groups or beliefs or practices.[51] Barker's categories are shattered by the practice of contested knowledge; Wallis's model tries to merge ethical with methodological concerns. Both Homan and Barker show how hard sociology is hanging on to the idea of an enlightened social science striving towards 'objective' truth. If researchers are backed by the authority of an institution, it may be possible to practise Bryan Wilson's 'sympathetic detachment' or Berger's 'methodological atheism'. However, if authority is called into question, the sand is shifting and shifting further than either Homan or Barker intimate.

The role of the media

The media, too, have played an important role in the NRM debate and contributed significantly to the controversy. Social scientific studies show that the media have tended to portray NRMs in predominantly negative terms and taken a stereotypical approach (van Driel and Richardson, 1985; 1988a; Beckford and Cole, 1988; Scheffler, 1989). The media tend to lump NRMs together and make sweeping generalizations about members, leaders, beliefs, and practices. Gillian Lindt (1981–1982) analysed media coverage of the People's Temple in the six weeks following the Jonestown events and reviewed selected literature published soon after. She concluded that Jonestown deepened the public's uneasiness or suspicion about most NRMs, despite significant differences between the People's Temple and other NRMs.[52]

NRMs have been a very attractive subject for the media, because they offer all the ingredients for 'a good story': power, money, sexuality, religion, controversy – in any combination. The stories are highly personalized, with media items focusing on individual cases (hence the media's 'natural alliance' with the ACM), (allegedly) scandalous behaviour of leaders (who can be shown to have feet of clay), 'atrocity stories', the 'exploitation' of hapless victims – in short, copy with a strong 'human element'. Other aspects – the idea of the enemy in our midst, 'infiltration' of the corridors of power, possible political ramifications, the idea of hidden conspiracies, etc. – have made NRMs a gift to investigative journalism (Coulter, 1984; Hounan and Hogg, 1985; Rodríguez, 1988; Kaplan and Marshall, 1996), novelists,[53] playwrights, and scriptwriters for television, radio, and cinema. The media have paid remarkably little attention to social scientific work (van Driel and Richardson, 1986; 1988b) and have not really understood the questions and methods in academic study.[54]

However, the media have used academics to produce 'good' copy or programmes – 'good' for business or audience ratings. Again, this is related to what is media effective. For Peter Evans (1994: 155–159), topicality, opportunism, and timing make for 'newsworthy' stories, but controversy is the main ingredient for audience participation programmes on television, as some academics discovered at painful cost (Ussher, 1994). Journalists and the media work in ways which are diametrically opposed to academics: tight deadlines, unequivocal arguments and opinions, succinctly expressed, preferably in sound bites (see S. Evans, 1997; P. Evans, 1994) contrasting with carefully considered conclusions drawn from carefully collated data. The media's agenda and interests differ significantly from those of academics who often feel they have to make compromises which compromise them and/or their work.[55]

The media attention of NRMs may be random and driven by 'news-worthy' events – the deaths in Jonestown, Waco, of Solar Temple members, and in the Tokyo underground after Aum Shinrikyo's sarin attack, but media coverage also provokes responses. Fortuitous reports have played a crucial part in the chronology: negatively in fuelling controversy and stereotypical images, positively in uncovering information, reaching a wider audience, and investigating NRMs. In FAIR's early stage, the media helped parents get attention and obtain information. Recently, media publicity supported the rights of those affected by NRM membership, as in the case of the French grandparents who objected – for reasons of access – to their grandson attending the Sahaja Yoga boarding-school in India.

Social scientists are drawn into interaction with churches, 'anti-cult' groups, and the media. What they do and what they say may attract media spotlight – potentially advantageous for furthering a career, especially when university management wishes to raise the institution's profile, and potentially dangerous, especially when the media turn the tables, as, for example, in the controversy about INFORM.

Notes

1 The founders were Tsunesaburo Makiguchi and Josei Toda. Causton (1988), Chairman of Soka Gakkai UK until his death in 1995 (the *Daily Telegraph*, 25 January 1995), presents an 'insider's' introduction to beliefs and practices, while Snow (1976) examines Soka Gakkai in the US, Wilson (1985a) its aims and visions, Wilson and Dobbelaere (1994) Soka Gakkai in the UK, Morgan (1986) its evangelization strategies, and Nakano (1992) its emphasis on peace.

2 DLM was founded in the 1930s in India by Shri Hans Ji Maharaj (Downton, 1979; 1980; Pakleppa, 1975).

3 It is connected with Marcus Garvey's Back-to-Africa movement (Cashmore, 1983; 1984; Clarke, 1986; Loth, 1991; 1992).

4 The literature on the New Age movement has become almost impossible to survey. General works include Sutcliffe, 2002; Heelas, 1996; Hanegraaff, 1996; York, 1995; Bochinger, 1995; Lewis and Melton, 1992; Bloom, 1991.

5 Wallis (1975b; 1974) sees 'sect' and 'cult' in a continuum: a sect's followers perceive its ideology as offering unique access to truth and sects tend to isolate themselves from wider society, while cults are individualistic, without a source of authority, and informally organized. Changes can lead to the transformation of a cult to a sect in a process of 'sectarianization', as Wallis (1979a) describes in his analysis of Christian Science and Scientology. His concepts are consonant with Troeltsch's (1931) tripartite typology (church, sect, mystical movement) and Campbell's (1972) 'cultic milieu'. Richardson *et al.* (1986) follow Wallis in their 'typology of disaffiliation modes'. Stark and Bainbridge (1981) define 'sects' as high-tension, schismatic religious movements which remain within an established religious tradition, while 'cults' are deviant groups, because they depart from conventional religions. The definitions of 'cult' and 'sect' are closely linked with efforts to develop typologies of NRMs.

6 Some argue that 'cult' has become unusable for social scientists, because it

has become lumbered with 'baggage'. Lofland and Richardson (1984) consider the terms 'imprecise, overgeneralized and burdened with historical associations' and instead use 'religious movement organization' (RMO). Dillon and Richardson (1995) argue that 'cult' has become politicized and suggest ways in which scholars can avoid using the term. Definitions continue to exercise researchers and students in this field. In October 1997, the nurel-l list discussed NRMs – what should be considered new, a religion, a religious group, a movement – and suggested more precise terms, such as 'invented religions', 'contemporary religious movements', 'alternative religious movements'.

7   See Barker, 1984; 1980a; 1981a; 1983b; Greeley, 1970; Levine, 1980; Kuner 1983c; Piryns, 1984; Hardacre, 1985; Hargrove, 1985; Beckford, 1986; Waßner, 1991; Stenger, 1993; Wilson and Dobbelaere, 1994.

8   The Church of Scientology distributed essays by academics which discuss whether it is a *bona fide* religion. It was impossible to tell whether the essays were commissioned or drawn from authors' existing work. One of these had originally been written as an affidavit for the Charity Commissioners, but its subsequent publication had not been agreed with the author.

9   Clark's testimony to the Vermont Senate's Special Investigating Committee of 1976 refers to two and a half years of research which involved examination of 27 subjects at all stages of association in six 'cults', and interviews with interested and informed observers (Clark, 1976: 1, 5). Clark's paper to the Association of Psychology in New Jersey in May 1977 mentions over 40 cases of various stages of membership and their families, but states particular interest in the cases with medical conditions (Clark, 1977). Clark's paper to the German Society for Child and Adolescent Psychiatry in 1978 speaks of a clinical study over four years involving 50 individuals and 75 sets of parents, examined by himself, and 150 individuals examined by his colleagues, with complementary information received from Margaret Singer (Clark, 1978a). Clark (1977: 8; 1979a) further drew on an article (Bear and Fedio, 1977) which establishes a neurological link with mental problems.

10 Clark (1977: 1–2) refers to the psychoanalytical model, the sociological model presented by Lofland (1980 [1966]), and the 'purely psycho-physiological model'.

11 The concept of dissociation was first introduced by Janet (1929). Dissociative phenomena occur in all mental activities, pathological or not (West, 1967, cited in Clark, 1978a: 9). Clark saw significant similarity between mental and behavioural changes provoked by continual dissociation (a state which he claims converts to 'cults') and those caused by chronic temporal lobe epilepsy. Bear and Fedio (1977) studied patients who suffered from this epilepsy and recorded a list of personality changes in them. These similarities led Clark to argue that information is processed in the limbic and mid-brain structures, the very location of perception and consciousness, and that dissociation is an important mechanism of processing information (Clark, 1979a: 100–101).

12 Clark distinguishes three categories of potential recruits: the first, 40 per cent of the sample, had no history of mental or emotional problems, but comprised young people who experienced fear and depression, typical for those leaving home for the first time. Their conversion was an adaptive response to social and psychological pressure. The second included young people who experienced emotional problems and a kind of *malaise* during adolescence. They followed the seeker pattern; some had been diagnosed as mentally ill. They were easy to recruit, because they welcomed the chance to leave their old selves behind. The third 'seemed' to consist of 'delinquent and socio-pathic personalities' who legitimate deviant behaviour with the cloak of religion. They did not experience 'dissociation' and tended to occupy positions of power within the 'cult', which

elicited in them feelings of security and total commitment (Clark, 1977: 5–6; 1978a: 6–7). Others identify potential recruits through motives (Woodrow, 1977: 170; Pavlos, 1982: 5) or see membership resulting from combined social and personal factors (Pavlos, 1982: 20, 55).

13   According to Bromley and Shupe, 'brainwashing' is a misleading translation of the Chinese 'hsi nao', which means 'to cleanse the mind'. Lifton (1961: 4) rejects the term,' because its 'loose usage makes the word a rallying point for fear, resentment, urges toward submission, justification for failure, irresponsible accusation, and for a wide gamut of emotional extremism'. Schein also rejects Hunter's sensationalist translation and speaks of the more extreme (and infrequent) attempts at 'hsi nao' as 'coercive persuasion' (Schein *et al.*, 1961; Bromley and Shupe, 1981a: 230). Hunter's job as a journalist may explain his leaning towards sensationalism.

14   Lifton identified these in Chinese 'revolutionary colleges' designed to disseminate Maoist communist ideology as group identification, emotional conflict, submission, and rebirth (Lifton, 1967; also Bromley and Shupe, 1981a: 96–97; and Schein *et al.*, 1961: 261) in the 'ritualization of belief' or adoption of new beliefs and behaviour in a 'total institution' as unfreezing, changing, refreezing (ibid.: 270–282). Lifton (1979: 75–79) points to features connected with 'thought reform': milieu control, mystical manipulation, the request for purity, the cult of confession, sacred science, loading of the language, doctrine over person, dispensing of existence.

15   Sargant (1957) notes parallels between 'brainwashing' in POWs and religious conversion in evangelical contexts and Bromley and Shupe (1981a: 98) make a similar point without referring to Sargant.

16   The way in which Singer incorporated the phenomena observed in cases of problematic 'cult' membership in the findings about POWs illustrates how new phenomena are integrated into a familiar paradigm, *before* existing paradigms are questioned and revised – a process which fits in with Kuhn's (1962) theory on how paradigm shifts occur. It may be argued that Singer saw no need to revise her paradigm in the light of new insights.

17   In the case of former members, guilt or blame for having joined are eliminated retrospectively. For 'deprogrammed' ex-members, the necessity for this drastic action is explained, because without it, they could not have left; they can 'forgive' their parents for intervening and therefore generally justify and defend the practice (Edwards, 1979; von Hammerstein, 1980; Swatland and Swatland, 1982). Ex-members' accounts have been important for vindicating the 'brainwashing thesis', but academics have pointed to problematic aspects of such accounts, sometimes constructed as 'atrocity stories' (Beckford, 1985; Bromley, Shupe and Ventimiglia, 1979; Shupe and Bromley, 1981). Some former members turned their experience into a career and have thus vested interests in maintaining the thesis, for example Ian Haworth (Cult Information Centre, London) and Steven Hassan, now an 'exit counsellor' (Hassan, 1988; 2000).

18   The question of casualties again illustrates the different approaches in ACM and social scientific thinking, although neither would dispute that NRM membership entails casualties. However, while the ACM looks at *individual* cases and considers each a tragedy in itself (and one too many) which must be prevented, social scientists compare with national averages or similar groups. This highlights again that ACM and academics ask different kinds of questions. In the ACM view, to say that 90 per cent of ex-members experience no problems still leaves 10 per cent *with* a problem and citing such statistics belittles the issue.

19   There are no major publications on NRMs by Clark, apart from some articles and papers (Clark, 1978b; 1978c; 1979a; 1979b). From the late 1970s, he

published jointly with others (Clark *et al.*, 1981; Langone and Clark, 1984; 1985). He was listed as Assistant Clinical Professor of Psychiatry at Harvard Medical School in the Editorial Advisory Board of *Cultic Studies Journal*, published by the American Family Foundation (AFF). He died in October 1999 (*FAIR News*, Autumn 1999: 18–19).

20   Singer continued to publish, mostly papers and jointly authored works (Singer, 1978; 1979a; 1979b; 1985; Ofshe and Singer, 1986; Singer *et al.*, 1990; Singer and Lalich, 1995; 1997). She appeared as expert witness in a number of cases, for example in the *Daily Mail* trial in 1980/81, and she addressed ACM audiences, for example the FAIR meeting in 1989. She was listed on the Editorial Advisory Board of *Cultic Studies Journal* as Adjunct Professor of Psychology at the University of California, Berkeley. Singer was apparently excluded from the American Psychological Association (APA) and filed suit against the APA (with Richard Ofshe) for discrediting the theory of 'coercive persuasion'. She died in November 2003 (Rubenstein, 2003).

21   West also served on the Editorial Advisory Board of *Cultic Studies Journal*, which listed him as Professor of Psychiatry, Neuropsychiatric Institute, University of California, Los Angeles. He died in January 1999.

22   First discussions took place during 1986 between the Home Office and Eileen Barker. In 1986, the (then) Voluntary Services Unit (VSU) included charities and NRMs in its remit after a reorganization in the Home Office. This entailed a review of the approach to NRMs and related correspondence, which became connected with Barker's idea – then at the point of germination – of an information centre. The idea combined with a government grant then created INFORM. In the course of the discussions, representatives of the Anglican Church – for example, Canon Reardon – were brought into the project. Barker (1990) recounts INFORM's development from the founder's perspective.

23   Recommendations regarding the need for an independent agency for 'objective information' – this was to be INFORM which had begun work in January 1988 – and the need for pastoral guidelines; the latter had been addressed by BCC's Day Consultation in 1986, but written guidelines were to be complemented by diocesan advisors who would form part of INFORM's network (General Synod, 1989: 1–6).

24   This consisted of comments on NRM teachings and practices from a theological perspective (General Synod, 1989: 6–9).

25   The code had two parts: the first addresses grievances associated with NRMs, the second addresses practices associated with the ACM (General Synod, 1989: 9–11).

26   The review of the charity law was consonant with the Church's view that *existing* legislation should be carefully examined and, if necessary, amended. The Church did not want a particular religious movement singled out, as this would have been arbitrary and discriminating, as indicated by the Archdeacon of Croydon (General Synod, 1990: 1279–1280).

27   The date in brackets is the original publication, reprinted in Robertson, 1969.

28   More details about ISSR's history are in Dobbelaere, 1989.

29   In a recent article, Berger (2002) states that sociology has fallen victim to two deformations and is therefore in decline: the first, beginning in the 1950s, is 'methodological fetishism', the second, part of the 'cultural revolution' of the late 1960s, is 'ideological advocacy'. The first is the dominance of method over content leading to invariable use of quantitative methods. The reason why these are favoured is twofold: sociologists want to be on a level with natural scientists and funding goes to 'scientific' projects. The second deformation involving a 'marxisant' ideology, ignores the principle of objectivity, and engages in the defence of 'victims'.

30 There are numerous studies of conversion (Daner, 1975; Downton, 1979; Barker, 1978; 1985b; Strauss, 1979; Balch, 1980; Long and Hadden, 1983; Snow and Machalek, 1984; Gartrell and Shannon, 1985; Richardson, 1985a; Morgan, 1986; Heelas, 1990a). General models of conversion have been applied to conversion to NRMs (Lofland and Stark, 1965; Greil, 1977; Heirich, 1977; Beckford, 1978a; Bankstone, Forsyth and Floyd, 1981; Bruce, 1982; Lofland and Skonovd, 1983; Greil and Rudy, 1984). For an overview of the literature, see Rambo, 1982 and 1993.

31 Barker (1982b) points out that the UC receives more attention, which is due to the controversy about the movement and the fact that it is more studied.

32 These are related to sociological questions: How many are involved in NRMs? How typical is a phenomenon compared with others? The question why particular people are more attracted to NRMs is not really a sociological one – it involves too many variables – but one for social psychology. Given sociology's concern, there is nothing 'sinister' in questioning the 'brainwashing' thesis. As sociology does not start with NRM 'casualties', its findings would lead academics to a different position. However, given the media's tendency to push 'experts' towards the role of devil's advocate, academics might present their hypotheses differently from what they intended. Due to media influence, the ACM sets the agenda: academic 'experts' are asked whether NRMs are harmful. This leads back to Fenn's discussion of language use in institutions.

33 See Roszak, 1968; Tipton, 1984; Carroll, 1973; Conover, 1973; Leech, 1973; Musgrove, 1974; Shepherd, 1974; Glock, 1976; Glock and Bellah, 1976; Hartman, 1976; Mildenberger, 1976; Holroyd, 1977; Foss and Larkin, 1979; Ahlstrom, 1980; Sundback, 1980.

34 Wilson (1975; 1976; 1979; 1985b; 1988) sees NRMs as confirming the secularization thesis. Hammond (1987) thinks they contribute to the secularization process. Wallis (1984) explains the rise of new religions in reference to rationalization and secularization. Stark and Bainbridge (1980b) see secularization as the primary cause for the renewal of religiosity. Several authors contest or challenge the secularization thesis (Bell, 1977; Anthony, Robbins and Schwartz, 1983; most contributors to Hammond, 1985; Hadden, 1987; contributors to Beckford and Luckmann, 1989 and to Bruce, 1992, except Wilson, 1992). Campbell (1978) sees secularization and increased religiosity as part of the same development. David Martin (1978) outlines patterns of secularization. Hanson (1997) maintains that some theorists argue at cross purposes.

35 Hargrove (1980) examines how major social changes since the Second World War relate to the emergence of NRMs. Beckford's edited volume (1986; also 1987) examines how rapid social change gives rise to novel religious interpretations and how NRMs in turn influence processes of change.

36 Three models describe the relationship between NRMs and the response of state and society: (1) deviance resulting from processes within the individual, (2) 'labelling model': deviant behaviour is behaviour which is labelled as such – scapegoat theory, studies of mental illness (Goffman, 1968), and stigmatization of 'cults' in the media (Usarski, 1988; Wallis, 1976a: 210–211) are relevant here, (3) 'deviance amplification model': it explains the interactive processes between deviant behaviour and societal reaction (Wallis, 1976a: 205–211). Wallis (1975a; 1976a) applies the third model to Scientology. Hampshire and Beckford (1983) compare a past NRM (Mormonism) with a contemporary NRM (UC) regarding deviance amplification.

37 See Cozin, 1973; Barnes, 1978; Bird, 1979b; Johnson, 1979; Léger, 1982; Wallis, 1982b; 1986; Dupertius, 1986; Barker, 1987a; 1993; Palmer, 1988; Carter, 1990; Gatto Trocchi, 1993.

38 See Beckford, 1979; 1981b; 1982; 1983e; Shupe and Bromley, 1979; 1980b;

1994; Bromley, Busching and Shupe, 1982; Shupe, Hardin and Bromley, 1983; Shupe, Bromley and Oliver, 1984; Bromley, 1988b; Bromley and Shupe, 1995.

39 See van Driel and Richardson, 1985; 1988a; Beckford and Cole, 1988; Scheffler, 1989; Beckford, 1994; Borenstein, 1995; Richardson, 1996; Campiche, 1997; Richardson and van Driel, 1997.

40 Choquette's (1985) bibliography arranges the material by discipline: historical, sociological and anthropological, psychological and psychiatric, theological and religious, and legal, with 'mixed' works under 'interdisciplinary collected essays'. Saliba (1990c) lists entries under four headings: (1) sources for the social scientific study of NRMs (reference works), (2) the historical background (theoretical and general studies, studies on particular groups), (3) general, theoretical, and methodological studies, (4) contemporary studies on specific groups. Arweck and Clarke's (1997) bibliography lists entries alphabetically.

41 The antagonism was bound up with several factors. Groups like FAIR would have liked more support and co-operation from both Anglican Church and State, but the Church took a very cautious approach and avoided taking any sides and the State did not grant charitable status or funding. Further, the ACM perceived INFORM's founder as too close to the UC and therefore considered her work unacceptable.

42 *Jugendreligionen* as protest movements is a current theme in non-academic literature. The question of (potential) political engagement or terrorist threat may be connected with the Baader-Meinhoff group whose members had a 'respectable' 'middle-class' background. The group evolved from the 1968 student protests and officially disbanded in April 1998.

43 Kuner (1983c) outlines questions which sociology should address to grasp the NRM phenomenon; Flasche (1987b) asks whether the New Age movement is a topic for *Religionswissenschaft*; Rink and Schweer (1993) discuss the approach of *Religionswissenschaft* with Flasche; Usarski (1990a) and Baumann (1995) point out that *Religionswissenschaft* was not prepared for the NRM debate in the 1970s, which was therefore dominated by theologians; Eiben (1996) examines how academic research can contribute to the debate; and Bochinger (1996) records a debate about the remit and role of *Religionswissenschaft*.

44 Kehrer (1981b) looks at tolerance regarding State, churches, and 'sects'; Flasche (1982b) looks at 'persecution', using the UC as an example; Hardin and Kehrer (1982) offer a model of how society rejects new belief systems which demand commitment; Kehrer (1983) looks at the campaign against *Jugendreligionen*; Neumann and Fischer's (1987) volume looks at tolerance and persecution regarding religious minorities; Flasche (1988b) examines responses to NRMs; Usarski (1990b; 1995) applies 'labelling' to the NRM debate and analyses the role of church officials.

45 Hardin and Kehrer (1978c) analyse commitment and personal identity in the UC; Klosinski (1985) examines why members of the Rajneesh movement joined; Karow (1990) explains membership in the UC and Rajneesh movement as a response to meaninglessness and dissolving social structures.

46 One of my interviewees commented that she could not see how sociologists can 'bracket off' personal values or attitudes and be 'value-free'.

47 Some primary constructions may be considered valid by social scientists, such as the description of rituals and the explanations of why rituals are performed, while others may not, such as stories of miracle healings or legends about leaders, irrespective of whether there may be 'scientific' proof for these. Primary constructions which involve value clashes may be more complex.

48 REMID commented that Pastor Gandow was trying to prevent his colleagues from participating at 'academic conferences held by scholars of religious studies' (nurel-l list, 4 April 1998). This prompted two Church representatives to

withdraw from the conference organized jointly by REMID and CESNUR in March 1998, on the grounds that it anticipated conclusions and thus had a political agenda.

49   The Bruderhof threatened to sue, but then apparently withdrew the book from circulation by buying the entire print run (Wroe, 1998).

50   Wallis's review article of 1980 was first published in *The Zetetic*, a slightly edited version is in the appendix of his book (Wallis, 1984).

51   In his book on the New Age, Heelas (1996: last chapter) offers a personal (and favourable) view of some beliefs and practices. There should be room in a book on a particular movement for academics to pass more personal judgements, as they are informed, not purely personal or subjective, and balanced with negative things (personal communication). Graham Harvey remarks in his review of Lewis (1996) that increased interest in paganism is 'related to the number of academically trained Pagans and of academics sympathetic to Paganism' (*Journal of Contemporary Religion 13* (1), 1998: 131). Alan Williams detects affection for the Zoroastrian religion in general and the British community in particular in Hinnells's (1996) book (*Journal of Contemporary Religion* 13 (2), 1998: 275).

52   Lindt (1981–1982: 160–162) identifies five recurring themes: (1) the portrayal of Jim Jones as 'demonic', 'fraudulent', a 'psychopath', (2) the portrayal of members as 'zombies' or 'programmed robots', who have undergone 'brainwashing', 'mind control', 'mental seduction', 'oppression', (3) violence as a defining characteristic of the movement, (4) the use of 'cult' as a label, (5) references to other 'cults' or 'sects' for comparison. Although the press used a wide range of source materials, it had little consideration for assessing the meaning of available information or informants' credibility. The press relied mostly on the stories of defectors, distraught relatives, and friends.

53   For example, Ehrlich's (1978) fictional story of 'the cult'; Spinrad's (1981) novel on the totalitarian mechanisms of religious groups; Kirchner's (1981) fictional account of 'cult' membership; Harold Robbins's (1982) novel on televangelism; Brooks's (1985) book based on the UC; Updike's (1988) novel on a spiritual journey; Bahre's (1995) novel on an imaginary 'sect', the Children of the Light. Some pursue an 'educational' agenda, such as Kirchner and Brooks. A precursor is, of course, *Elmer Gantry*.

54   In my experience, journalists who consult academics do not want to look too closely at questions which academics address; paradoxically, they nevertheless want to feature the voice of an 'expert', often for 'balance' and 'legitimation'. More recently, journalists have used academic 'discourse' and sound *as if* they understand.

55   Haslam and Bryman (1994) gathered academics' accounts of their media experiences and offer valuable insight into differences in approach and agenda.

4   Sketching in the cultural background

THE CONTOURS OF RELIGIOUS CULTURES

Since I am seeking to show the responses of particular institutions in Britain and Germany, it is necessary to provide some background by locating the institutions in their wider cultural contexts. Comparing the religious and academic cultures in Britain and Germany allows the salient differences between the two countries to become evident. This will promote understanding the responses of churches and academic communities to NRMs and explain the interlinking threads between them.

An outline of the historical setting

The differences between the religious cultures in Britain and Germany have their origins in the Reformation. Britain was already a nation state then, while Germany was not, and this – the existence (or absence) of the nation state – is significant for the relationship between secular and spiritual powers. The Reformation took a different course in the two countries. In Britain, the forces which carried it never gained full control, but they succeeded in assuming dominance for a period during the Commonwealth after the Civil War. The Established Church arose partly from the upheaval of the Reformation and partly from political processes following Henry VIII's break with Rome. Its position as the national church was strengthened, first by the Elizabethan Settlement under Elizabeth I and later during the Restoration under Charles II. Therefore, compared with the rest of Europe, the English state church is unusual: the Settlement rejected servility to Rome and Geneva and offered a *via media* which was to create a church designed to meet the English people's spiritual needs and then developed in its own specific ways. The distinctiveness of the Church of England is the combination of conservative and reformed traditions; its essence is conveyed in the phrase 'a largely Catholic church within a predominantly Protestant country' (Davie, 1994: 158). The course of the Reformation indicates the way in which religious tolerance was ultimately established: after the violent conflicts of the Civil War and the brief triumph of Puritanism during the

Commonwealth, the Restoration brought a measure of tolerance, although non-conformists did not have equal access to political power until the nineteenth century. The particular relationship between establishment and religious pluralism is the point in which Britain differs most significantly from Germany.

The Restoration brought a backlash against Puritanism and united Church and monarchy, with countervailing forces – both political and religious – in Parliament and the country as a whole. An accommodation was necessary between the two sides. This led to incipient pluralism (which was exported to America) and to manifest pluralism in the twentieth century. The tensions between religion and nationhood are important for historical differences between European countries: 'The patterns of European religion derive from the tension and the partnership between Caesar and God, and from the relationship between religion and the search for national integrity and identity' (D. Martin, 1978: 100). In England, there has never been a political split within society which coincided with major religious division, unlike, for example, in France (Davie, 1994: 15). A greater degree of pluralism existed at an earlier stage, especially in the presence of dissent in various forms (D. Martin, 1967). Thus, between the mid-sixteenth and late eighteenth centuries, 'the very plurality and diversity of religious groups prevented British politics from being dominated by a single, major confrontation between church and State, politics and religion, or church and church. The consolidation of the British State did not therefore cast politics into a mould which necessarily polarized or amalgamated religion and politics' (Beckford, 1991: 179). Yet, in England, a limited monopoly emerged, with a state church partially counterbalanced by a bloc of dissent in the population at large (D. Martin, 1978: 20). However, in Germany, an amalgamation of religion and politics essentially happened in the wake of the Reformation, given the regents' power to dictate the religion of their territories and expel those who did not accept it.

In Britain, the developments culminating in the Glorious Revolution (1688–1689) conferred a dual role on the monarch: first, the royal powers were transferred to Parliament, with the monarch largely as a figurehead with nominal powers. Second, given Charles II's sympathy towards the Catholic Church and James II's overt Catholicism, the principle was established that the monarch, as supreme governor of the church, should be a Protestant. The coronation oath requires the head of state to uphold 'the Protestant reformed religion established by law' and to 'maintain and preserve inviolably the settlement of the Church of England, and the doctrine, worship, discipline and government thereof, as by law established in England' (Davie, 1994: 144–145).

After 1688, Britain developed into a naval-based imperial power which pitted itself against Catholic France (Colley, 1994). The culture of imperialism – closely linked to Protestantism – held at bay the disunity which existed at sub-national level, and formed the overarching canopy which held the

United Kingdom together.[1] The monarchy was closely associated with a Protestantism vague enough to be compatible with the expansion of incipient pluralism. Non-conformist forces built structures outside the established ones from which they were barred: for example, exclusion from Oxford and Cambridge, where clergy were trained, compelled them to found Dissenting Academies. From the Restoration onwards, Church, monarchy, and tradition – all three defined as Protestant – formed an arch over incipient pluralism. At the same time, the ascending importance of dissenting forces increasingly hollowed out 'established' institutions. By the middle of the nineteenth century, the two were roughly equal, with a very small Roman Catholic sector (4 per cent), largely formed by Irish migrants, which increased to around 10 per cent by the late twentieth century.

In Germany, course and outcome of the Reformation were very different. Germany was then a collective of independent principalities gathered under the wide umbrella of the Holy Roman Empire. Therefore, from the very beginning, secular power was closely linked with religion – thanks to his *Landesherr* (sovereign) Luther was protected and could answer for his theses at the *Reichstag* of Augsburg, rather than before a spiritual court in Rome. This close link continued throughout the religious wars of the seventeenth century, until the Treaty of Westphalia (1648), when the patchwork of virtually sovereign states was legalized and the principle of *eius regio, cuius religio* (first brokered in the *Augsburger Friede* of 1555) was reaffirmed. Established churches were thus formed under the aegis of particular regents, with secular powers favouring Protestantism being of equal strength to those fighting to preserve Catholicism, a balance which the religious wars could not offset. Consequently, from the late seventeenth to the nineteenth century, established churches and regions which adhered to either faith were fairly neatly divided. This left little room for dissident religion or tolerance of religious dissidence. After the unification of Germany in the nineteenth century, the relationship between church and State was negotiated – during the *Kulturkampf* in Prussia, when the State sought preponderance over spiritual power. This relationship was again negotiated in the process of establishing the Weimar Republic, when the *Staatskirchenrecht* (the laws regulating the relationship) became part of the constitution. It was re-negotiated after the Second World War, when the *Staatskirchenrecht* was reviewed. However, such negotiations never abandoned the principle of co-operation and distribution of tasks between State and churches. They concerned the *degree* of co-operation and particular assignments.

Therefore, Germany is divided into Protestant and Catholic regions of virtually equal strength in membership. Given the historical links between secular and spiritual powers, the State has come to a particular accommodation with the churches and the churches have regarded the State as the proper partner for particular responsibilities.[2] The cultural establishment is thus of a dual and mutual nature: church tax is the mechanism by which Church and State achieve certain, mutually beneficial aims. In Britain, private initiative, not the State, supplies funds for the religious establishment. The Church of England owns considerable property, for example.

In Britain, the introduction of state education after 1870 brought a compromise in that non-denominational Christian teachings were instituted in state schools, whereas religious specialists continued to teach in the church schools. By the mid-nineteenth century, the Church of England and the non-conformist churches had reached more or less equal strength. The churches were the pioneers of welfare provision, but by the twentieth century, they were no longer the primary providers, as state and secular institutions had taken over. In Germany, the Church had a long tradition of providing religious education and welfare, a tradition reaching far back to times before Germany was a nation state, and this provision continued after the state system was established.

In Britain, the incipient pluralism of the previous centuries unfolded into explicit pluralism in the nineteenth century, without however abolishing the Established Church. In Germany, once the assorted principalities had united in one dominion, negotiations about the specific obligations of secular and spiritual institutions resulted in the churches becoming licensed agents. Such negotiations were particularly visible in Prussia under Bismarck. The *Kulturkampf* set conservative forces, allied with the Catholic Church, against the State which assumed rights for functions hitherto the Church's sole prerogatives, such as contracting marriages. With the establishment of the Weimar Republic, the separation of Church and State became enshrined in the Constitution: although *de facto* separate, they agreed on a mutually beneficial distribution of tasks. This co-operation continued after the Second World War, but the memory of the churches' equivocal role in the Nazi period left an acute sensitivity to the dangers of automatic acceptance of state requirements. In Britain, neither Established Church nor other churches are direct agents of the State.

Religious culture in Britain

Although the established nature of the Church in England suggests a prominent role in society, the data on religious practice (D. Martin, 1967; Davie, 1994) paint a different picture. The Church's social importance does not match its implicit status: there is evidence of comparative indifference to religious practice, but also evidence of the opposite (D. Martin, 1967: 15). Davie's shorthand phrase 'believing without belonging' expresses this conflicting evidence, which points to both the decline in religious practice and the persistence of religion. In postwar Britain, most people continue to believe, but see no need to participate with even minimal regularity in religious institutions. Yet, relatively few people have opted out of religion altogether. The churches' profile contrasts with the fact that only a minority are members. These are disproportionately elderly and female, with largely Conservative voting habits (Davie, 1994: 2; D. Martin, 1967: 58).[3]

The central theme in Davie's *Religion in Britain since 1945* is the 'increasingly evident mismatch between statistics relating to religious practice and those which indicate levels of religious belief': relatively high levels of belief match low levels of practice, the latter demonstrating an undeniable degree of secularization (Davie, 1994: 4–5).[4] Despite various developments in the postwar period, there is an underlying trend which has remained unchanged: the failure of the mainline (mostly Christian) churches to maintain regular contact with the majority of people. At the same time, less conventional forms of religiosity have increased, even within the mainstream churches (ibid.: 30–43).

The 1960s and 1970s are the most relevant for the context of NRMs – they are decades of sharply falling religious practice and growth of religion outside the mainstream churches (see Brown, 2001). The 1960s are marked by significant social changes, regarding general attitudes and significant immigration. Traditional, largely Christian, values were no longer taken for granted and generally questioned. The decline in church membership reached alarming levels (Hastings, 1986). The churches were first thrown into confusion and then provoked into radical reaction. To present themselves as 'modern' and 'relevant', they borrowed ideas and forms of expression from the secular world, a process which brought secularization into the churches themselves. A series of reforms occurred: intellectually in the theological and moral debates; organizationally in the re-arrangement of parishes; liturgically in modernizing scripture and worship, and ecumenically in various endeavours towards greater ecclesiastical collaboration. For the Roman Catholic Church, Vatican II brought about the great transformation.

The 1970s saw the beginning of the reversal of this trend, with a reaffirmation of the sacred, although this process occurred in unexpected ways. The 1970s also saw the emergence of religion outside the churches, with the appearance of NRMs and 'house churches' and the formation of minority religions among immigrant communities. There was widespread indifference regarding established religion, although this tended to take the form of Christian nominalism – in the sense of non-active, but self-ascribed church members (Davie, 1994: 72), while significant minorities – Christian and non-Christian – were developing. For the latter, membership is sought and chosen, instead of assumed and taken for granted. This included the Church of England's evangelical wing. Thus, while membership of the principal Christian denominations was declining,[5] there was considerable proportional growth in non-Christian religions, even if the overall figures remained relatively small. Considerable diversity characterizes non-Christian religions, which illustrates the unfolding of pluralism in Britain mentioned above. Davie (1994: 51, 63) speaks of a 'limited pluralism'.[6]

Two further points are important regarding this period. First, the process of secularization – outside and inside the churches – created a vacuum: many young people who, given their social background, would 'normally' have gravitated towards the Church did not become committed members. They formed the 'pool' from which NRM members were drawn in the 1970s, the children of the *Daily Telegraph* readers from the English 'bible belt', as Paul Rose put it. Second, because of the tradition of tolerance towards non-conformist religion, the Church did not immediately perceive the new forms of religion and new religious communities arising during the 1970s as a threat or as rivals and therefore saw no immediate need for action.

Regarding the question of establishment, the essential link between Church and State has remained intact, despite considerable changes in the postwar period. Due to the decline in active Anglican membership, the connection is taken much less for granted now than it was immediately after the war. In the 1960s, two-thirds of the population identified them-selves as Church of England – less, if Scotland and Wales are taken into account (D. Martin, 1967: 36). However, the Church's occasional offices continue to play an important part in the lives of individuals and com-munities in performing *rites de passage*, especially at the end of people's lives (Davie, 1994: 56; 81; D. Martin, 1967: 92) or when secular festivals overlap with ecclesiastical ones (D. Martin, 1967: 92).

As relatively few people either belong to a church or attend religious services with any regularity, taking faith or religion seriously has increas-ingly become the exception in British society; not only the data point to this, but also incomprehension regarding contemporary debates about religious pluralism, highlighted by the debates about the *Satanic Verses* and (espe-cially Muslim) 'fundamentalism'. Being British seems to include a low-key approach to religiosity (Davie, 1994: 69; D. Martin, 1967: 67ff). This implies that those who migrate to Britain should – at least in public – adopt this approach. Few people are hostile to religion, even if bewildered by 'extreme' religious expressions. Regarding belief, nominalism, rather than secularism, is the residual category; regarding institutions, the Established Church remains an integral part of the State (Davie, 1994: 68–70).

This also explains why church schools are still popular. A disproportion-ate number of parents are opting for them, although, given the provision of religious education,[7] they may do this for reasons other than religion, namely 'uniform, discipline, traditional education, and manners'.[8] Research suggests that for children who attend church schools, there does not seem any measurable effect on their attitudes towards Christianity.[9] Church schools may be popular precisely because they are ineffective in encouraging a positive attitude to religion: parents perceive them as good because they fit the general perception of accepted religiosity (Davie, 1994: 130, 134–135).[10]

Regarding religion's social or public aspect – civic religion, as opposed to its individual or personal aspect – common religion, its function is in the foreground. The Church of England and Other Faiths Project at the Uni-versity of Warwick (1994–1996) defined civic religion as taking place on 'occasions on which members of the public participate in activities intended to place the life of villages, towns and cities in a religious setting . . . [which] includes such things as annual services for the local emergency services and judiciary, the recital of prayers before council meetings, the decoration of public places at times of religious festival' (Gilliat, 1999). Civic religion borrows legitimacy from Christianity, although it is in the process of incorporating elements from other world religions, especially in cities with mayors from non-Christian backgrounds (ibid.). Rituals surrounding the royal family exemplify the essence of this relationship. Constructed primarily to represent the nation, to convey a sense of Britishness, such rituals embody national feeling rather than Christian doctrine. The monarch is, however, both Head of State and Supreme Governor of the Church. Public events reinforce this duality so that the monarchy appears sacred and national, with a deliberate confusion between the two (Davie, 1994: 86).

Among examples of civic religion are the coronation (as a powerful act of sacralization), the Jubilee celebrations, Remembrance Sunday, royal funerals, such as those of the Princess of Wales and the Queen Mother. They all include a significant Church presence to provide a sacred dimension, a presence which is rarely controversial, but its lack would be.[11] Religion on the public level is far more effective, for it remains a symbol, a marker of history, a reminder of the past, and a powerful source of identity (Davie, 1994: 86–88; D. Martin, 1967: 57, 89f.).

The fact of 'establishment'[12] is bequeathed by history, a legacy with advantages and disadvantages, but not a static state of affairs. The Church is not identified with the State, but has a special relationship with the political order. This relationship is two-sided: establishment confers upon one church rights and privileges. These are to some extent restricted and limited: for example, the right of some bishops to sit in the House of Lords includes the State's right to influence episcopal appointments. There is a balancing of rights and restrictions and how rights and privileges are used (Davie, 1994: 140–142).

Links between Church and State are not just about connections at the centre of government, but include links with individuals and the community in the parishes through offices and civic events. Anyone who resides in an Anglican parish has the right to be baptized, married, and buried in their parish church, whether Anglican or not. However, unlike Germany, there is no default mechanism for church membership, as baptism and regular contact with the church are not necessarily integral to socialization. The right to access exists as part of the Church's universal claim and its duty to bring the ordinances of religion within the reach of anyone desiring them, but this is more theory than practice, given low attendance and lack of commitment. Nevertheless, the territorial structure of parishes is a shadow expression of the claim to universality and still has consequences.

The Church's established nature requires that some, even if no longer all, the General Synod's decisions are subject to Parliamentary approval.[13] Although the Synod takes *de facto* responsibility for Church affairs, the ultimate authority lies with the Crown: the monarch, through Parliament, not only gives royal assent, but has the ultimate say over the Synod. The monarch thus represents the apogee of the Church–State relationship. Despite questions about the royal family's role in the established Church, few voices have called for disestablishment. If establishment were indeed to be abolished, something would have to replace it, and this poses big questions (Davie, 1994: 144–149).

The Church–State relationship weighs in the controversy over the Church's involvement in secular matters. The question is whether the established Church should combine its pastoral role vis-à-vis the government of the day with an effective critical voice. Although some negate this, others see the established status as a strength for the Church to speak out, as in debates about capital punishment and homosexuality in the postwar period (Davies, 1989) and during the Thatcher era (D. Martin, 1989).

Tightening the frame

The particular relationship between the State and Anglican Church allows the Established Church to enjoy status and visibility, despite the presence of other Christian and non-Christian churches and religions; at the same time, the Church is hollowed out in terms of adherence and practice. The Church of England has the monarch as its figurehead and functions as a civic religion. Therefore, bishops and local clergy regard themselves as spokespersons for the country in religious matters, including ethnic minority religions and NRMs. The Church takes for granted that it acts on behalf of other religions. Its co-operation with INFORM can be seen in the light of this role. INFORM's creation can be considered as an illustration of the alliance between State and Church and a residue of the Church's universal claim, status, and belonging.

The Church is at the fringes of welfare and education structures, but as civic religion it is at the centre of society. Given its representation in the House of Lords and the monarch's role as its 'Supreme Governor', the Church is not only established, but continues to be part of 'the establishment' – in Davie's other sense. However, although the established church has the trappings of power, it has *de facto* less power than these might suggest.

No political party has considered itself affiliated with any one religion or church, although evidence suggests affinities, reflected in the voting behaviour of church members and the choice of Conservative candidates in particular constituencies. No party distinctly or explicitly professes allegiance to Christianity or any other religion (the formation of the Islamic Party is a fairly recent development), unlike Germany, where two conservative parties include the term 'Christian' in their names. Therefore, compared with the rest of Europe and the United States, the Church of England's role is rather unusual. It is a half-way house between Scandinavia and the United States. The situation in Britain is characterized by an established church within a secularized system.

In Britain, the situation of semi-pluralism or restricted pluralism (the presence of other-faith communities) makes it imperative for the Church to proceed with caution. The tradition of dissent and tolerance forbids it to speak out against other faith groups, while its role as the over-arching religious body dictates an attitude of dialogue and integration. The emergence of ethnic minorities practising their own religions has turned Britain into a more pluralistic and multicultural society, albeit a society with a predominantly Christian heritage. Germany has been experiencing this process since the last decade or so, with the emergence of a sizeable Islamic community. The formation of other-faith communities has been an important development for the Anglican Church, as has the emergence of NRMs. Regarding other faiths, the Church proceeded along ecumenical lines, at a time when ecumenism was considered the way forward in inter-religious relations. Regarding NRMs, the Church was faced with a new phenomenon, so that it started with a wait-and-see approach while relying on parochial clergy to deal with immediate problems; eventually, grassroots pressure urged the Church to tackle the issue. Following 'systemic procedures' one of its committees, the (then) Board for Mission and Unity, was charged with NRM matters. However, when the issue came to the Synod's agenda, the Church's attention was on more pressing matters: liturgical changes and women's ordination. This last momentous question coincided with the Saxby motion in 1989. Thus, the Church first categorized NRMs as an ecumenical and multicultural concern and treated them like other-faith religions. However, the questions tabled in the Synod called upon the Church to react in a more specific way. They called for an official stance towards NRMs and specific pastoral guidelines.

The Catholic presence in Britain – largely Irish in origin, but now with a strong middle class – was for some time exempt from secularization processes, but has experienced serious decline since the 1960s, although not nearly as acutely as the Church of England and non-conformists (Free Churches).

Religious culture in Germany

The historical developments in Germany forged a close relationship between State and Church, despite their separation in the Weimar constitution. This relationship is guided by the idea of a partnership (Stammler, 1986: 585). There is neither strict separation – as in France – nor the privileged position of State or established church – as in Scandinavia or Britain.[14] However, Germany *has* something akin to 'established religion' as it treats some religious communities, the churches included, differently from others.

The two main Christian churches (*Großkirchen*) – the Protestant Church[15] and the Roman Catholic Church[16] – consider themselves as *Volkskirchen* (Daiber, 1996; Huber, 1996) and as sharing in the overall welfare and responsibility of the whole nation. They are *Großinstitutionen* (large institutions), similar to political parties and national associations, and play an important part in the nation's social life. They have a say in many public institutions and influence opinion-forming and decision-making processes. They are appreciated as important pillars of society in that they uphold religious tradition and provide stability (Stammler, 1986: 579).

Like the Church of England, the churches ensure universal provision through the parochial system and assume universal membership. Baptism is the habitual way to membership, with most children baptized in the church where their parents became members (Rohde, 1981). Membership is an 'accident' of residence and family, normally determined by geographical region and family tradition, so that affiliation is mostly Roman Catholic or Protestant. Thus membership is part of most young people's lives, at least until they are old enough to decide for themselves. Due to low mobility, congregations tended to remain stable with most people growing up and staying in their parish. In 1950, 96 per cent belonged to one or other church (Stern, 1998: 4). In the mid-1980s, this figure was about 85 per cent, with an almost equal share between the churches: in 1986, 42 per cent Protestant and 43 per cent Catholic (Stammler, 1986: 579). Recent figures show a decline, but 69 per cent still belong to one or other church, with the ratio virtually unchanged (Stern, 1998: 4).[17] Almost 70 million out of a population of about 82 million are self-declared Christian, even if they do not practise.[18]

The legal framework

The legal relationship between State and religious communities, as delimited in the *Staatskirchenrecht*, is characterized by three principles: neutrality, tolerance, and parity. Neutrality implies three things: first, the State is not identified with any one religious confession – hence the absence of a state church, as stipulated in the Weimar constitution (Art. 137, para 1). Second, the law treats religious communities and groups of a particular *Weltanschauung* equally, and they thus enjoy constitutional rights and guarantees. Third, the State must respect the principle of non-intervention (*Gebot der Nichtintervention*), which gives every religious community – including its subsidiary (e.g. charitable) organizations – the right to organize and manage its own affairs, as long as it does so within the confines of generally applicable laws. Both the Weimar constitution (Art. 137, para 3) and *Grundgesetz* (Art. 140) stipulate this (Robbers, 1986: 470).

The principle of tolerance is closely linked with religious freedom. It allows religions and *Weltanschauungen* to develop freely and requires the State to promote the development of religions within the constitutional framework. The principle of parity requires the State to treat all religious communities equally (ibid.).

Differential treatment nevertheless arises from the churches' legal status (*Rechtsstatus*). They are *Körperschaften des öffentlichen Rechts* (corporations under public law), a status conferred by the *Staatskirchen-recht*, which includes a number of privileges. Other religious communities can obtain this status (Weimar constitution, Art. 137, para 5; *Grundgesetz*, Art. 140). Some free churches and the Jewish community have it, but others, for example Jehovah's Witnesses (JW), did not until very recently. In 1997, the Federal Administrative Court (*Bundesverwaltungsgericht*) in Berlin ruled that the JW should not be recognized (AZ: BverwG 7C 11.96 of 26 June 1997). The court's reasons are complex, but they refer to the JW not agreeing with essential constitutional principles relating to democracy and tolerance and having a structurally negative understanding of the State. *Körperschaft* status is not commonly conferred, a convincing legal case must be made to obtain it. By contrast, religions in Britain are tolerated as long as they do not break the law.

Despite the clear legal separation of Church and State and the principle of neutrality, there is a complicated network of relations between State and churches, regulated by the *staatliche Kirchenrecht*. This set of concordats and agreements not only ensures continued historical privileges, but consolidates some of these in granting state subsidies, giving churches a say (*Mitwirkungsrechte*) in public institutions, and affirming the idea of the churches' *Öffentlichkeitsauftrag* or public mandate (Stammler, 1986: 585; Wilkens, 1981: 595). Due to privileges and considerable shared interest, particularly public welfare, there is close co-operation between State and churches. This also accords with the constitutional principle of subsidiarity, which allows the State actively to support the churches and their auxiliary organizations (Stern 1998: 2; Stammler, 1986: 582; 583).

The partnership principle

Art. 140 of the *Grundgesetz* gives *Körperschaften des öffentlichen Rechts* the right to raise membership fees (*Pflichtbeiträge*) or 'church tax' (even non-Christian communities call it thus) by using the *bürgerlichen Steuerlisten* or tax lists. The State collects this tax for the churches (in return of a fee) by deducting it at source like income tax. However, the recognized free churches choose not to avail themselves of this privilege (Stammler, 1986: 583). Church tax is a clear indicator of membership and fluctuations in revenue are an obvious gauge of affiliation. Taxpayers must officially disaffiliate to avoid church tax, which they do in a formal act of withdrawal in a registry office. Between 1968 and 1977, tax income for both churches showed a steady increase until 1974, a significant fall in 1975, and a steady increase after 1976. The fall documents the unusual number of church leavers in 1974 (Rohde, 1981: 600).

In the second half of the 1960s and in 1974, the number of church leavers reached alarming proportions. While in 1966, 38,213 (0.13 per cent) left the Protestant Church, this figure rose steadily to 216,217 (0.79 per cent) in 1974. By 1978, the number had fallen to 109,797 (0.41 per cent)

(*Statistisches Jahrbuch für die Bundesrepublik Deutschland*, 1969, 1972–1980). In 1979, the number had fallen further: 99,653 (0.4 per cent) (Rohde, 1981: 605). Those leaving the Roman Catholic Church in 1966 were 22,043 (0.08 per cent). This figure rose to 83,172 (0.3 per cent) in 1974. By 1978, it had fallen to 52,273 (0.2 per cent) (ibid.). These statistics attest that Germany has had (and still has) a high proportion of church members. The impact of leavers in 1974 was therefore far more dramatic for the churches than membership decline was for the Church of England at that time, because Anglican membership had started at a far lower level. It had been *declining* continually since the end of the last century, despite a slight upward blip in the decade after 1945 (Brown, 2001), but in Germany, membership had been *increasing* in the postwar period (Rohde, 1981: 600): in 1950, 96 per cent were 'churched'. Decline was therefore not so novel a phenomenon for the Church of England as it was for the German churches. Disaffiliation in Germany was undoubtedly connected with the repercussions of Vatican II and the 'student revolt' of 1968. The latter combined protest against 'the establishment' with the quest for alternative spirituality. Reunification (after the fall of the Berlin Wall in 1989) brought a new tax, the solidarity supplement (*Solidaritätszuschlag*), to defray the cost of rebuilding the new provinces (*die neuen deutschen Bundesländer*). Many left the church to reduce their taxes. In 1992, disaffiliation reached another high point with almost 200,000 leaving the Catholic Church alone – the annual average is at *c.*155,000 (Stern, 1998: 7).

Apart from raising 'church tax', 'established religions' can offer religious education in state schools (most schools are state run and financed),[19] are exempt from some taxes (e.g. land tax), have a say in the public media (*öffentliches Rundfunkwesen*)[20] and state universities,[21] and provide pastoral care in hospitals, prisons, and the armed forces. The state retains the exclusive right to marry people (*Ziviltrauung*) and jurisdiction in all legal matters (*Ausübung der Rechtssprechung in allen Angelegenheiten des Rechts*).

The State benefits considerably from the churches: their charitable activities and contributions to public welfare exonerate it from obligations which it would otherwise have to fulfil. Those in need can turn to church-run childcare facilities, hospitals, old people's and nursing homes, rehabilitation centres, home care schemes, advice centres for refugees and foreigners, family planning centres, care for the disabled, telephone helplines, youth care, etc. The well-being of young people is promoted through *Jugendhilfe* (help for young people) which includes looking after the neglected or damaged and general care. *Jugendhilfe* is provided by institutions created by authorities or charitable associations and (religious) youth associations. Such organizations have close financial and legal links with the state. Other areas where the churches supplant the state include work in developing countries and disaster relief (Stern, 1998: 3–4; Stammler, 1986: 581; 586). The public tends to take co-operation and distribution of tasks between

State and churches for granted and may not even be aware of the precise arrangements. In Britain, social needs are shared by state agencies (the National Health Service, Citizens Advice Bureaux, etc.) and independent charitable organizations (the Samaritans, Scope, Age Concern, etc.), although currently the crisis in the welfare state is resulting in an increasing role for voluntary agencies, including those of the churches, for example, in provision of homes for the elderly.

Churches and politics

As in the Netherlands, State and churches in Germany are linked politically: after the Second World War, members of both churches created the Christian-Democratic Union (*Christlich-Demokratische Union* or CDU). It formed the government under Konrad Adenauer in 1949 when the Federal Republic of Germany was founded. Except for a 13-year spell, the CDU managed the affairs of the country until the elections in late 1998. Its Bavarian sister party, the Christian-Social Union (*Christlich-Soziale Union* or CSU) is even closer to the Catholic Church (Stern, 1998: 6). The churches' influence (*Mitwirkung*) in legislation and state administration is also manifest in their presence in the capital where they maintain offices (Stammler, 1986: 586).

Since the War, both churches have actively addressed questions they consider to be of public concern. In (at times joint) statements, such as the *Denkschriften der EKD*, they have commented on current affairs and political matters, to facilitate 'rational debate', reduce social tensions, and help prepare for political action (ibid.). Protestant churches also created discussion forums or academies (*Evangelische Akademien*) where seminars and conferences address current questions. The annual *Kirchentag*, which each church organizes in turn for grassroots members, pursues similar aims.

Although the churches are aware of their waning monopoly, Germany is still a country in which the Christian faith, Christian values, and the Christian churches play an integral role in society (Stern, 1998: 6). The churches are characterized by a remarkable stability (*Festigkeit*) in their position in State, politics, and society (Wilkens, 1981: 598). The great majority of members are not regular churchgoers, but they – like their British counterparts – turn to the churches for *rites de passages*,[22] special feast days[23] and occasions when Christian symbols (crucifixes in public places) or practices (school prayers) are disputed.[24]

The compressed view

In Germany, the symbiotic relationship between State and 'established' religions functions well. The separation of State and church – in a legal and organizational sense, as the constitution requires – is not always obvious nor is the separation between political parties and churches, despite the law relating to State and church. The primary objective is consensus. At times, the more conservative Catholic provinces (*Bundesländer*) launch campaigns against 'moral abuses', such as abortion or the removal of crosses from class-rooms, but overall, religion supports fundamental values which are widely shared by Western civilization. As they are not particularly bound to any church, such values are hardly controversial. However, the churches do not have the role which the Church of England plays in public life. For Germans, civil religion or religion tinged with nationality are unfamiliar notions.

Drawing conclusions

The different roles of the churches in Britain and Germany go some way towards explaining the difference in their respective responses to NRMs, especially regarding the question of who deals with them first. The Church of England's somewhat cumbersome machinery needs to be set in motion before anything can happen. Also, the Church looks towards the State as ally and partner and is restrained by the tradition of tolerance and its estab-lished nature. The churches in Germany are assumed to have responsibility for the general public, a public mandate, and a role in society which requires active participation in debating major social issues. They are also so closely woven into the fabric of institutional and social life that they can tackle issues in concerted action with other institutions. They perceived the emer-ging NRMs as a threat, not least because NRMs' active proselytism risked breaking the traditional chain of religious affiliation. Given prevailing religious culture, the churches had no experience of 'losing' members, especially the young, to non-mainstream religions.

   The Church of England, too, feels responsible for people, but its concern is different. Britain is far more accustomed to dissident religion and thus more tolerant. Therefore, the Church did not immediately perceive NRMs as rivals. It had anyway previous experience of rivals. Britain has been a pluralist society for longer, with a long-standing non-conformist tradition. Throughout most of the twentieth century, the religious establishment has been weak and religious practice low. The emergence of NRMs was thus less intensely felt. Voluntarism and the Church's assumption to speak for *all* religions would constrain overtly prescriptive or hostile statements regard-ing other religions. Voluntarism and tolerance have produced the English low-key approach to religion, which shies away from, is even suspicious of, fanaticism. This approach does not take religion too seriously or welcome overt proselytism. Level of commitment and proselytism would have raised the Church's objections to NRMs rather than NRM beliefs. Further, despite its status as the established church, the Anglican Church has *de facto* little power. Compared with the churches in Germany, it is not as integrated into the network of social institutions. This accounts for the distinct differ-ences in the way the churches in Germany and England articulate issues and interact with society.

However, the Church of England's role in 'civic religion' gives it a political dimension. Hence one's first thought is to consult the constituency MP rather than local clergy, who might refer one to the MP anyway, with the argument that such 'matters need to be raised in the House of Commons'. Indeed, this is the place where 'such matters' are generally aired. In Germany, the principle of subsidiarity means dealing with matters at the lowest possible institutional level and therefore one would approach the local priest or pastor in the sure knowledge of receiving advice and having the matter taken further, if necessary.

The Anglican Church's response consisted in first mobilizing its internal system and then looking towards assistance from outside agencies. It sought advice from the State and the academic community. Once this process was begun, Church, State, and academic community coalesced in the creation of INFORM. In Germany, the Protestant Church had mechanisms in place to tackle the NRM issue: the remit of institutions where theologians were researching non-mainstream religious movements was expanded to include NRMs. The Roman Catholic Church (RCC) approached the issue in two ways: on the national level, in Germany (in Britain, its minority situation muted action), it took a pragmatic course: it 'fell in' with the Protestant Church's strategy of installing theological specialists in each diocese and participating in the information network. As an international body with a centralized system, the RCC became aware of global dimensions and concerns. The NRMs in Western countries were negligible compared with the RCC's problems world-wide, with liberation theology, inculturation, implementation and repercussions of Vatican II, etc. The emergence of Pentecostalism in Latin-America, the Pacific Rim, and Africa alerted it to the global dimension of NRMs: Pentecostal 'sects' seriously challenged the Church because it lost members. The grassroots clergy pressed for addressing the 'sect' problem and guiding pastoral care. They expected such guidance from the Vatican, but none of the then existing Vatican documents included any. Thus, these issues were assigned to Vatican Secretariats, some of which had been created only recently by Vatican II decree. As this decree also commanded modern science to be taken seriously, the recently instituted Secretariat for Non-Believers invited a delegation of social scientists (Peter Berger, Robert Bellah, David Martin, Harvey Cox, Talcott Parsons, Bryan Wilson) in 1968. Given the Vatican's centralized, hierarchical, and bureaucratic organization, the secretariats – removed from grassroots 'reality' – consider issues in the light of dogma, interfaith matters, proselytization, ecumenism, etc., with international implications in mind. The Vatican 'machinery' slowly cranked into action: first by gathering information in a survey, then by engaging in an international consultation process. This included academic research and involved F.I.U.C., the association of Catholic Universities. The work of four Vatican Secretariats contracted to one secretariat and was then placed in the hands of one person. The RCC continually built up its own body of information and research, which allowed it to (slowly) 'find its feet' and develop its own paradigm, in accordance with existing tradition and knowledge. While it generally considered NRMs a separate category (despite some NRMs wishing to be treated as parts of existing world religions), it was exploring interfaith dialogue.

THE CONTOURS OF ACADEMIC CULTURES

The previous section compared the religious cultures in Britain and Germany as essential background to the churches' response. This section looks at the academic cultures as essential background to academic responses and paradigms.

Academic culture in Britain

Sociology of religion did not really take root as a mainstream discipline in British academia until the mid-1960s. Donald MacRae's comments in his introduction to David Martin's *A Sociology of English Religion* (1967) reinforce this point:

> The sociology of religion has developed late in Britain. Theology, the history of religions, comparative religion, ethnographic studies of religion, are all fields which the British have vigorously and successfully cultivated. But while, for example, political sociology has thoroughly established itself, it is only recently that sociologists have sympathetically concerned themselves with the investigation of religion, both belief and practice, in our society.
>
> (Martin, 1967: 7)

While Bryan Wilson and John Highet were 'lonely pioneers' in the 1950s, 'some of the best students in British sociology concern themselves with the subject' in the 1960s (ibid.). However, in exploring the question of how the past neglect can be explained, MacRae points to an ideological factor: religion was considered a 'dead' subject and thus without future:

> Religion has been thought of as a dying factor in an increasingly secular society. So future-directed a subject as sociology should not, therefore, be concerned with it. (Or religion has been dismissed as epiphenomenal: the surface appearance of harsh reality – a Freudian or Marxist illusion.) And in sociology there is always – as both virtue and vice – ... the curious persistence of positivism; and positivism has either in its Comteam form offered a new religion, or more usually despised the non-natural and not thought it worth attention.
>
> (ibid.: 7–8)

MacRae further comments that British sociologists looked towards American sociology, which was 'immensely rich and creative' in the 1940s and 1950s. However, at the same time, 'Unfortunately with few exceptions ... American sociology of religion has been small in quantity and often sickly in quality' (ibid.: 8). Another reason for the neglect of sociology in Britain is of a more practical nature: 'sociology – and funds for social research – has a bias towards the immediate and publicly accredited areas of social problems' and 'Religion has not been seen as a field for applied socio-logical virtue' (ibid.), a point reiterated in Berger's recent (2002) diagnosis of sociology's 'deformations'. Funding issues were highly topical for the social sciences during the Thatcher era, when expenditure for academic purposes was severely curtailed, as they have been recently regarding university 'top-up fees'.

However, in the late 1960s, sociology of religion became a flourishing subject for undergraduate courses. Sociologists became interested in alterna-tive religion and spirituality, but this interest did not bear academic fruit – in terms of graduates, PhD theses, and lecturers – until the late 1970s and early 1980s, after undergraduates had filtered through the system.

The 1960s saw institutional changes in higher education: divinity/theology faculties were transformed and denominational teacher-training colleges were structurally reformed, while the number of universities was itself increased. This reorganization involved a shift in academic 'power bases'. The emergence of the new NRM phenomenon also entailed a paradigm shift in that theories about marginal and non-mainstream religious groups provoked a review. Sociologists progressed from earlier deterministic and functional models of relative deprivation and class dif-ferences to new explanations and classifications for NRMs. They exam-ined why social changes should bring about the NRM phenomenon. Empirical studies of membership found a revolving-door syndrome or pattern of seeker careers. Initially at least, such research was 'ACM-led', in the sense that social scientists wanted to 'test' theories, especially 'brain-washing', developed by the ACM as explanations for 'cult' membership. Sociologists 'disproved' these and pointed to the element of 'choice' in the decision to join NRMs.

In Britain, departments of divinity/theology saw a decline in student numbers, with fewer and fewer potential ordinands feeding into this system (just as the classics departments were facing an intake crisis). The divinity/theology departments moved with the trend: they widened their remit (diversified) and offered religious studies courses. While before, they might have had the odd 'specialist' in sociology of religion or a non-Christian world religion, the shrinking of their traditional student constituency made them realize that they could harness the new interest in the social sciences to their advantage. In terms of market forces, they joined the dynamic of sup-ply and demand. Similarly, courses in media studies were offered later within religious studies sections to attract a different student clientèle.

The department of Religious Studies at Lancaster, for example, was set up in 1967. In the following 25 years, about a dozen such departments were created all over Britain and some traditional theological faculties turned into departments of theology and religious studies. The reverse also happened: in 1993, the Department of Religious Studies of the University of Wales in Cardiff became the Department of Religious and Theological Studies, to emphasize the strength of its theological teaching and research (Trevett, 1993: 23). The department at Lancaster produced several hundred graduates who now teach religious studies in schools, in the UK, and overseas; about 80 have taken up lectureships and chairs in colleges and universities around the world, over half of them in the UK (Clayton, 1995). Another example is the School of Oriental and African Studies (SOAS) where religious studies courses started in the late 1970s and the first degrees were awarded in 1981. The programme gradually extended and enrolment increased steadily (Hawting, 1992: 19; Fisher, 1993: 16). A residential course in a convent was added in 1983 as an opportunity to read and talk within a religious setting (Fisher, 1993). In 1992, a separate Religious Studies Department was set up (Hawting, 1992: 19). The Department of Theology in Lampeter appended a religious studies programme in 1981 (Badham, 1996: 23).

While in the late 1950s and early to mid-1960s, the number of sociologists of religion had been small, interest in the new spirituality and institutional changes from the late 1960s onwards increased graduate numbers from some of the restructured/hybrid departments. From the 1970s onwards, these graduates had to be absorbed. Although the emergence of NRMs gave sociology of religion a new lease of life, it took time for career structures to develop in existing and new departments.

Another structural change occurred in the denominational colleges, which trained teachers for church schools. New regulations required them to get attached to fully fledged universities and be accredited by the Council for National Academic Awards (CNAA) which regulated the non-university sector. In order to comply, some colleges amalgamated with universities or polytechnics and were thus transformed into university departments. During the 1960s, with teaching becoming a graduate profession, the two-year college courses were replaced by three-year degree courses, as the CNAA required. Therefore, colleges needed university attachment or affiliation. Their institutional arrangements varied, but what used to be their nucleus – the religion department – was sometimes converted to a religious studies or sociology of religion department or sector. These departments absorbed graduates from recently established sociology of religion departments and most of them maintained interest in, and connections with, religious education. Another factor affected the former colleges: the decline in denominational schools, as, for example, in the case of Methodism; decreasing membership meant fewer Methodist schools. Therefore, the colleges looked for new areas of study – Dr Harold Turner at Selly Oak Colleges

(Birmingham), for example, turned his attention further afield by studying new Christian groups in Africa.

The Walsall campus of the University of Wolverhampton may serve as an example of a teacher-training college's transformation: it started as the West Midlands College of Education, with the principal purpose of training school teachers. It became a religious studies department within the School of Education. Both teacher education and services to the teaching profession remained high priorities for school and department (Chryssides, 1997: 10). Another example was West Sussex Institute of Higher Education: its religious studies department offered various options in the BA Combined Studies degree, focusing on Christianity and world religions from the perspectives of philosophy, psychology, and sociology of religion. These were covered by multiple teaching methods, including field trips and visiting speakers. At this institution, too, religious education was still an important element, both regarding some staff members' research interests and in-service courses for teachers (Potter, 1993: 25).[25]

Some of the new generation of sociologists of religion started their careers in the new hybrid departments, where divinity/theology and religious studies co-existed, while others – including Roy Wallis, Eileen Barker, James Beckford – were in mainstream sociology departments. Apart from sociology, history and anthropology also became growth areas.

The former divinity/theology departments were fighting a kind of rear-guard action against being squeezed out altogether. King's College London, for example, an Anglican foundation, produced some of the country's cler-ical elite, among them several bishops. Losing ground was serious. Recruits for the priesthood increasingly came from mature vocations. Thus, in an effort to diversify, the department offered other subjects, including NRMs. In 1982, the Centre for New Religions was set up in the Department of Theology under the directorship of Peter Clarke. In 1989, the departments of the History and Philosophy of Religions, Christian Doctrine and History, and Biblical Studies merged to form the Department of Theology and Religious Studies. Course unit (modular) degrees in theology, religious studies, and biblical studies were introduced in 1990, together with joint degrees involving other departments. In 1993, MA courses started in anthropology, sociology of religion, Indian religions, Islamic studies, women and religion, and philosophy of religion (Nye, 1993: 17).[26]

From the early 1980s, universities came under increasing financial pres-sure under the Thatcher government. Securing funds became a ruthless enterprise. Universities and departments competed with one another – a situation no doubt compounded by the Research Assessment Exercise (Hastings, 1995) – and undoubtedly strained institutional relationships. Departments had to show that there was a viable 'market' for their academic 'products'. Concepts borrowed from industry and business were also intro-duced, such as management structures, assessment schemes (for students and academic staff), mechanisms for quality assurance,[27] and the creation of 'internal markets' so that departments 'bought' services from one another – just as in the NHS. This development was, of course, modified again later. These changes have contributed to a highly competitive atmosphere in which prestige and status are measured in terms of obtaining funds for particular projects and attracting students.

Academics' attendance at NRM-sponsored conferences needs to be seen against the background of increasing curtailment of funds in the 1980s. It coincided with British academics' taking up invitations to (often all-expenses-paid) conferences sponsored by NRMs – especially the Unification Church – and agreeing to publish their papers under the imprint of NRM-owned publishing houses. In the early 1990s, the idea of setting up research projects jointly with NRMs began to take shape. The 1980s are also the period when ethical questions permeated NRM research and the 'politics of survival' led to the creation of 'research centres' and 'research projects' to attract students and status.[28]

In Britain, the distinction between *Religionswissenschaft* and sociology does not exist.[29] While *Religionswissenschaft* is concerned with historical and theoretical aspects of religion, academic work in Britain is typically grounded in empirical methodology. The empiricist tradition goes back to the nineteenth century, when a major purpose of universities consisted in preparing the administrative elite for service to country and empire – hence research into Middle-Eastern religions and languages. Social science in particular was pragmatic and empirical because of the flow from the academic to the practical, for example in welfare and poverty-related research. In the pursuit of 'truth', fieldwork – immersion in the subject, a technique used in anthropology, involving interviews, questionnaires, and participant observation – is combined with textual analysis and observance of academic 'objectivity' (positivism).

These methodological tools were applied to the study of NRMs, but there was growing awareness of methodological problems specific to studying NRMs: academics were not used to subjects 'talking back' and contesting their findings. When they adopted a group as 'their tribe', they risked being adopted or even appropriated by the group. The issues involved questioned the idea of academic 'objectivity' and the degree to which it could be observed. Academics' attendance at NRM-sponsored conferences questioned it further. Contact with (some) groups had an unexpected side effect: they developed expectations towards academics studying them. They wanted academics to speak for, and sometimes speak out for, them; they also asked for advice in dealing with the outside world. This raised the question of how close the association between academics and 'subjects' should be. Once academics were established, they rated as 'experts' and were treated accordingly. The notion of 'expert' underlies the NRM debate and is particularly relevant in court contexts when academics serve as 'expert witnesses'.[30]

At the same time, it became evident that NRMs have some control over information and insight regarding their beliefs, practices, and everyday activities: they negotiate what they give and they (want to) have a say in interpreting information. 'Shop window' presentations are what researchers risk to capture when they visit NRMs for a limited amount of time, as happened to Gordon Melton and John Lewis when visiting Aum Shinrikyo. In Bryan Wilson's view, researchers must find ways around the 'PR' version, for example, by checking information in various ways. Such contact with NRMs raises the question of who controls or 'owns' the meaning and/or interpretation of data. This question entails sociologists' inability to 'warn' against particular NRMs or predict which might develop in such a way that they become a danger to the wider society. NRM members also started becoming academics in their own right by completing university courses and joining those studying them. NRMs set up separate infrastructures of academic debate, such as educational programmes for schools, scholarly journals, publishing houses, academic conferences, etc. NRM members' participation in academic forums illustrates how demarcation lines blur and how difficult it is to uphold the ideal of 'objectivity'. Interestingly, an introduction to *Religionswissenschaft* states that scholars in this discipline look for informants among believers who bear witness to their faith, not for believers who *analyse* their faith (Greschat, 1988: 73; emphasis added).

The question of data interpretation is also relevant for the Anglican and Roman Catholic Churches in that they, too, resort to the sociological framework. The ACM has, however, proved resistant to sociological findings and adhered to its own paradigm, a paradigm based on psychology and psychiatry. The ACM's problem is insufficient academic validation to reinforce its paradigm. It has no resources for studies which would earn credibility and 'kudos', despite attempts to secure funds for projects under the umbrella of FECRIS.[31] The ACM employs the psychological paradigm, because psychology – like parents and the media – is interested in *individual* cases, in contrast to sociological studies which examine *groups*, social aspects, and group dynamics. Therefore, the paradigm within which data are interpreted depends on perspective, selection, and selectivity. The selection of some aspects necessarily involves the de-selection of others and this implies a certain degree of subjectivity (Wolfe, 1990; Greschat, 1988: 24; 79).

While the Roman Catholic and Anglican Churches have used sociological findings in developing their respective responses to NRMs, the differences should be noted regarding state and public authorities' use of academic work. In Britain, the State initially only took action regarding NRMs by reference to existing laws. In the latter part of the 1980s, however, the State's approach changed: it was involved in creating INFORM (in 1988), with discussions and the first draft proposal developing in late 1986. With INFORM, the State effectively launched into a 'joint venture' with an academic. This implies that the academic perspective must have been perceived as appropriate – in fact, *more* appropriate than existing options. Yet in Germany, the academic paradigm found it consistently hard to make its voice heard by state agencies, until the *Enquête-Kommission*'s final report signalled a turning-point with the inclusion of academic findings (see also Deutscher Bundestag, 1998b). In the United States, authorities were criticized for not 'listening' to academic expertise before the Waco tragedy unfolded. In response, the authorities commissioned Nancy Ammerman to investigate academics' role in situations, such as the stand-off at Waco, and submit a report (Ammerman, 1993).[32] It remains to be seen to what extent Ammerman's recommendations have been taken on board. It is possible that academics' status as 'experts' was used to build a smoke-screen, just as Royal Commissions have been used for such purposes.

Academic culture in Germany

While NRMs became important for academic study in Britain, in terms of the number of academics working in this area, expanding institutional structures, and the enhanced profile of the particular academic discipline (sociology) within which NRMs are studied, this was not the case for academic NRM study in Germany. This difference needs to be explained.

Religionswissenschaft

One main reason for this difference concerns the academic culture in Germany, in particular the discipline within which NRMs have been studied, namely *Religionswissenschaft*. Like sociology, it is relatively young (Zinser, 1988b: 1), arising in the nineteenth century from liberal Protestant theology (Kehrer, 1998) and philological interest in ancient texts. *Religionswissenschaft* thus owes a great deal to theology, but is also indebted to philosophy, philology, and ethnology. The connection with theology and philology raises the question about the place of *Religionswissenschaft*: within which discipline should its history be traced and should it be considered part of cultural and social studies or part of theology (Zinser, 1988b: 1). It also raises the question of its roots: do they lie in the Enlightenment or the Romantic period (Kippenberg, 1991)? Von Stietencron (1989: 87, 90) links *Religionswissenschaft* with two major developments in the nineteenth century: first, the rapidly growing interest in philology and oriental studies in the early nineteenth century, stimulated by unprecedented quantities of original sources from Egypt, the Near East, Persia, India, and China. While ethnology and anthropology gained importance in Anglo-American and French research, the study of religion in Germany was dominated by philological concern with oriental and classical texts, which lasted well into the twentieth century. Sociology and social anthropology gained significance in *Religionswissenschaft* only after the Second World War. Second, theologians adopted text-based methods to research the history of religion and used textual analysis for exegesis.

The concern with philology obviously focused *Religionswissenschaft* primarily on textual sources and documents. The discovery of the

Indo-European languages towards the end of the eighteenth century gave the study of languages and comparative linguistics a new impetus (von Stietencron, 1989: 88). This was also important in attempts, started during the Enlightenment, to reconstruct the 'natural' and 'pure' religion of mankind (universal religion), which, it was thought, would be found by delving deep into history where the earliest religious documents would be rediscovered. These would reveal primeval religion, *Urreligion* (ibid.; Greschat, 1988: 100). (There are parallels in sociology's early assumptions that the origins of institutions could be traced, through history or anthropology, within an evolutionary framework.) Voltaire and Herder believed that 'the infancy of mankind' would be found in India, the very country whose culture became more accessible through the discovery of the Indo-European languages. Language was conceived as the fundamental medium for the expression of human thought so that the idea of a language held in common with the ancient Aryans conveyed the possibility that other things could be held in common, such as thought, worldviews, religion, etc. Comparison of languages led to comparison of myths, rituals, religious concepts, etc. (von Stietencron, 1989: 88–89; Nanko, 1991: 22).

The Indo-European languages were regarded as textbooks from which the early stages of religion and society could be deciphered. Scholars devoted their lives to the transcription and translation of ancient texts, among them Max Müller, generally considered as the *Vater der* (father of) *Religionswissenschaft* and thus as having laid its foundations. He was also influential in sociology of religion in its endeavour to trace the origins of institutions. Müller joined the general trend of the time which was to find the origins (*Ursprünge*) in languages and he devoted himself to the study of the oldest of the four Vedas, the Rig-Veda.[33] Since then, texts – sacred texts and documents (Greschat, 1988: 38ff., 45ff.) – are considered the raw material *par excellence* for the work of *Religionswissenschaft*. Thus, *Religionswissenschaft* started as the 'science' of texts and has to a considerable extent remained so (ibid.: 40; Pilger, 1988: 18; Rudolph, 1988; von Stietencron, 1989: 89), especially for those engaged in studying the history of religion (Rudolph, 1988). The chair of Indology and Comparative *Religionswissenschaft* at the University of Tübingen illustrates the close link between linguistics and religion. It was inaugurated in 1848, when Rudolph von Roth, a Sanskrit scholar, introduced lectures on the general history of religion, which then became compulsory for theological students (von Stietencron, 1989: 89). Nanko (1991) describes von Roth's influence on the development of *Religionswissenschaft* in Tübingen.

For Rudolph, the study of texts is 'the foundation and backbone' of *Religionswissenschaft* in its concern with religions, religious traditions and concepts. Any study of *Religionswissenschaft* – whether comparative, sociological, psychological or geographical – is predicated on historical work (Rudolph, 1988: 40). The distinctiveness of the discipline's method consists in the complementary use of historical (data collection) and systematic approaches (development of concepts, classifications, theory building) (Baumann, 1993: 28). The philological concern was detrimental to research on religious artefacts (implements, tombs, images, temples) and religious expression (ritual, dance, music, etc.), although these are now included in the study of *Religionswissenschaft* (Greschat, 1988: 50–62; Lang, 1988; Stolz, 1988a).

Theology's influence on *Religionswissenschaft* is closely linked to the study of languages and texts: some (Catholic and Protestant) theologians adopted textual study for exploring the history of religion, thereby introducing theological concepts to *Religionswissenschaft*. This approach was practised by the *Göttinger religionshistorische Schule*, a school of Protestant theology, with whom theologians, such as W. Wrede, W. Bousset, H. Gunkel, and E. Troeltsch, were associated. It established the critical appraisal of texts as an essential method for exegesis (von Stietencron, 1989: 90). However, theologians of this school resisted the inclusion of history of religion in theology courses, as Adolf von Harnack's speech of 1901 in Berlin documents (ibid.; Waardenburg, 1991b). Yet, despite objections, theology departments began to create chairs at the beginning of twentieth century.[34]

Apart from introducing theological concepts to *Religionswissenschaft*, the *Göttinger Schule* had another lasting influence: it introduced Schleiermacher's idea of religion, posited on the personal experience of God's awe-inspiring power, an idea considered a 'romantic' reaction to the Enlightenment emphasis on reason and religion's rational content (von Stietencron, 1989: 90). This led to a branch of *Religionswissenschaft* associated with Rudolf Otto and Friedrich Heiler, namely phenomenology (ibid.: 90–91; Rudolph, 1991: 152).

Greschat comments that from its early development, *Religionswissenschaft* bifurcated into history of religion (*Religionsgeschichte*) and comparative history of religion (*Vergleichende Religiongeschichte*).[35] The latter includes phenomenology of religion (*Religionphänomenologie*) and *systematische Religionswissenschaft* (systematic study of religion). Most scholars work in both branches (Greschat, 1988: 35). While historians of religion research individual religions, the comparative branch uses results from history of religion to establish systems or general categories which fit various aspects of different religions.[36] History of religion is interested in the *orthodox* character of beliefs and the tension between what a religion should be (ideal state) and what it really is (actual state) (Greschat, 1988: 35, 94, 96). In its early stages, history of religion thus looked for the unchangeable and orthodox in religion so that anything perceived as unorthodox or marginal was not worthy of attention. *Religionswissenschaft* still looks askance at what developed as a significant area of study in ethnology, namely new religions and new religious movements. (ibid.: 19).

Systematische Religionswissenschaft deals with three areas: religious theory, comparison of religions, and phenomenology of religion. Religious theory is interested in the development of a religion and in the essence or nature (*Wesen*) of religion. Greschat (1988: 100, 112) maintains that *Religionswissenschaft* is not suited to developing theories and Frick (1997: 16) comments that some scholars shy away from theory-building. Students of *Religionswissenschaft* make systematic use of historical material by drawing comparisons, hence *Vergleichende Religionsgeschichte*. Phenomenology seeks to relate different phenomena (mysticism, sect, myth, etc.) with one another, to classify and describe them, according to their 'essential nature' (*eigentliches Wesen*). Phenomenology, too, uses examples from history of religion in order to proceed from the particular to the general and vice versa. Van der Leeuw's work is considered as pioneering, with Heiler and Widengren cited as other important phenomenologists (Greschat, 1988: 87–115).[37] Phenomenology developed theories by way of intuition and speculation. Existing religions were ignored, unless they were needed to illustrate theory (Flasche, 1989: 203). The concern with phenomena and the 'nature' of religion effectively blocked sociological interpretations (Gladigow, 1991: 192).

Religionswissenschaft *and institutional structures*

Von Stietencron (1989: 91) lists 14 universities in Germany which offer courses in *Religionswissenschaft* or history of religion. Between them, they have 18 departments where *Religionswissenschaft* is taught – in some universities, more than one department is involved (ibid.: 7). Waardenburg (1998: 22) counts over 30 chairs related to *Religionswissenschaft*, most of them outside theology departments. There is, however, no chair in the sociology of religion. The degree in *Religionswissenschaft* is awarded either within philosophy (13 universities) or theology (10 universities), with a choice of either at some universities. However, it seems there is no general consensus about what should be taught: there are neither agreed schemes for degree courses nor general regulations for examinations. What is taught at one university is not taught at another (Greschat, 1988: 7), which Waardenburg (1991a: 87) considers an advantage: 'thank heaven, we have no institution, doctrine or person to lay down what *Religionswissenschaft* should be. There is and should be pluriformity in both practice and principle'.

This picture of pluriformity is borne out by a survey of university courses, which Frick (1997) undertook over six years (1991–1997).[38] His findings show significant differences between the courses and document a wide spectrum in the way *Religionswissenschaft* is conceived as a subject. This heterogeneity stretches from philological and psycho-analytical orientations – combining antiquity with literature and addressing political questions with methods of *Religionswissenschaft* – to more 'traditional' orientations – approaching contemporary religions with historical methods and assigning philosophical questions a secondary role (Frick, 1997: 14). Zinser (1988b: 2) notes that scarce resources do not allow one department to cover all areas.

Regarding historical religions, method, and theoretical approaches, departments may represent totally different positions, but they complement one another. In Zinser's view, these differences should be turned to advantage for research and study. His introduction to *Religionswissenschaft* (Zinser, 1988a) addresses the main issues in the light of the discipline's disputed history and lack of a recognized 'canon' of foundations (Zinser, 1988b: 1, 2).

As a relatively recent discipline, *Religionswissenschaft*'s profile within university structures and viable career paths outside academia is a problem. Von Stietencron (1989: 92) argues that it needs to secure adequate representation in the range of university subjects to preserve its independence and ensure greater continuity. The *Deutsche Forschungsgemeinschaft* or DFG (German Research Association), for example,[39] a major funding body, does not include *Religionswissenschaft* in its list of academic disciplines.[40] Attempts to have it included have so far not succeeded. In the 1970s and 1980s, new faculties have been created as departments of *Religionswissenschaften*. These are actually theology departments by a different name (ibid.: 93). There is general agreement among scholars of *Religionswissenschaft* that this designation is a misnomer, bound to undermine the discipline's independence. The reason for the 'misnomer' is a pragmatic one: the laws regulating the affairs of church and state require theology departments to be tied to one of the major religions (*konfessionsgebunden*) (Rudolph, 1988: 38–39), a requirement which these new departments circumvent. Some universities have dissolved theology departments and placed theology in philosophy departments. *Religionswissenschaft* is also in jeopardy when chairs become defunct on holders' retirement (von Stietencron, 1989: 93).[41]

Frick concludes that *Religionswissenschaft* lacks a clear and recognizable profile as an academic discipline. He attributes this to two closely related issues. First, many departments apparently do not offer foundation courses, indispensable for the study of *Religionswissenschaft*. This means that students cannot build their main courses on these and that there is no agreed basic knowledge students are expected to acquire. Second, there is the question of methodological foundations (Frick, 1997: 15), which is widely debated and on which opinions range widely. Indeed, even the *Gegenstand* of *Religionswissenschaft* – the very matter with which it should be concerned – is at dispute, a topic which Gladigow (1988) discusses in detail. This issue is important because *Gegenstand* and methods are closely linked (Zinser, 1988b: 1–2). Some scholars, such as Michael Pye (1982) and Jacques Waardenburg (1986), consider *Religionswissenschaft* an autonomous discipline, others think it lacks its own approach (Pilger, 1988: 19; Baumann, 1993: 28). Zinser (1988b: 2) states that *Religionswissenschaft* still faces the task of constituting itself as an 'autonomous cultural and social science' by determining subject matter and methods. A concomitant of this process is lack of clarity in terminology: Pilger (1988: 20) notes the interchangeability of 'historian of religion', 'anthropologist of religion', 'phenomenologist of religion', etc. Despite *Religionswissenschaft*'s mainly text-based orientation, its students consider it an 'empirical science' (Baumann, 1993: 29). For Hultkrantz (1972: 365), the common denominator in *Religionswissenschaft* is the perspective, the classification of the material from the religions' viewpoint, but the methods used belong to other disciplines: 'it is an interesting, albeit disappointing fact that the history of religion does not really have methods of its own. It is simply the fact that our subject has borrowed its technical apparatus from neighbouring disciplines.' (my translation) Among the 'neighbouring disciplines' are sociology and sociology of religion. However, the current debate about methods in *Religionswissenschaft* has pushed the phenomenological approach to the background and brought empirical methods to the foreground (Pilger, 1988: 19).

The methodological chapter of Baumann's (1993) *Buddhism in Germany* may serve as an illustration for the transition between the traditional approach which relies on historical method and the more recent trend which looks towards empirical methods (field research, interviews, participant observation). Baumann drew most of his data from publications and other written documents, but borrowed qualitative empirical methods from the social sciences (Baumann, 1993: 25–42). The debate about methodology continues, as the report of the Marburg conference in November 1995 illustrates (Bochinger, 1996). It reveals some ambiguity: the traditional approach does not qualify *Religionswissenschaft* as a social science, but the modern approach brings it closer to social science. Sociology and sociology of religion are, however, considered auxiliary or sub-disciplines from which *Religionswissenschaft* can draw. The range of views and the ongoing debate make it difficult to say which trend *Religionswissenschaft* is following. Those embracing the modern approach are likely to be of the younger generation and to be influenced by Anglo-Saxon methods.

Frick's survey also found that concepts regarding method in *Religionswissenschaft* were rather vague: a combination of methods borrowed from sciences are considered complementary to the historical approach. The controversy about methods revolves around the question of whether there is a method particular to *Religionswissenschaft* or whether appropriate methods are adopted from related disciplines. Baumann (1993: 27) states that since the 1960s, general opinion has been leaning towards the latter. The debate does not address potentially problematic implications of 'borrowing' methods, such as 'objectivity' or researching one's own religion. Greschat (1988: 13–14, 24, 79) postulates 'objectivity' as the appropriate method for *Religionswissenschaft*, but also points to the need for selection. He argues for the 'personalization' of *Religionswissenschaft* as proposed by W. Cantwell Smith in the late 1950s (ibid.: 64, 133f). Borrowed methods are not readily adoptable or adaptable for *Religionswissenschaft* (Frick, 1997: 15), precisely the point which Pilger (1988: 18–19) deplores: *Religionswissenschaft* is steeped in the history of religions and produces textual analyses,[42] but neglects the study of contemporary religious communities and undergraduate courses fail to discuss appropriate methods.[43] Baumann's (1989: 19) response to Pilger questions *Religionswissenschaft*'s need for specific methods and argues that a discipline can establish itself on the basis of the particularity of its subject matter and use appropriate methods from related sciences where necessary. For Pilger, borrowing methods is a weakness, for Baumann, it is a strength, and for Rudolph, it is a virtue. It is also a particular feature of *Religionswissenschaft*, which makes it special among academic disciplines. *Religionswissenschaft* may appear to lack autonomy and clarity, but it would be unjustified to turn this into a reproach (Rudolph, 1973: 177f). Baumann (1989: 20–21) draws attention to numerous empirical studies of contemporary religion, some of which are carried out in Britain rather than Germany. This reference underlines the point that some students of *Religionswissenschaft* have looked towards Anglo-Saxon research and methods.

While *Religionswissenschaft* is fighting to preserve and raise its profile in the academic world, it lacks profile outside academic structures. Von Stietencron points to a rather peculiar situation: student numbers in *Religionswissenschaft* have been rising, but very few career or job prospects exist for graduates. Employment at universities is difficult, with only a few posts available and posts in theology departments involving the confessional tie.[44] There is no employment in teaching either (von Stietencron, 1989: 94–96).[45] Rink (1997: 17–22) found that only about one in ten graduates of *Religionswissenschaft* finds related professional occupation. His examination of possible career paths sees job prospects in terms of market rules regulating supply and demand and concludes that demand is low for practitioners of *Religionswissenschaft*.

Conclusions

In Germany, NRMs have not been as important an issue in the study of *Religionswissenschaft* as they have been for the social sciences in Britain nor have they contributed to a growth of the discipline. The number of academics has been and remains small; institutional structures have not expanded, the profile of *Religionswissenschaft* has not risen significantly, and overall, academics have not been involved in constructing an explanatory paradigm for NRMs beyond the academic sphere nor have they had significant impact on the wider debate. The *Enquête-Kommission*'s report, however, suggested some change in the reception of academic knowledge. In cases where academics sought to contribute to the debate, they – like their British counterparts – found the field already occupied and experienced the pitfalls of controversy. As only a few worked in this field, most of them chose not to get too deeply involved.

The reasons why NRMs did not become an important academic subject are mainly related to *Religionswissenschaft*, a discipline which has been struggling to emancipate itself from theology (Waardenburg, 1991b: 44ff.), regarding both methods and institutional structures. Further, *Religionswissenschaft*'s close link with philology and philosophy has encouraged the study of texts in foreign languages, classification of 'phenomena', the (re-) construction of 'ideal' religion, and the quest for religion's 'true nature'. This entailed an 'armchair' approach to religion(s) or anthropological research in far-flung places and the neglect of religion as lived and practised in everyday life. The focus on the orthodox and ideal in religion(s) overlooked the unorthodox, deviant or marginal. The concept of religion as a phenomenon *sui generis* excluded the examination of social or economic parameters. Therefore, new religions were – at least initially – not deemed worthy of investigation. The deeply rooted belief that religion cannot be trivial was the greatest barrier to *Religionswissenschaft* adopting new religions as a study object (see also Kehrer, 1998). Flasche (1978) therefore discussed whether NRMs could or should be a subject matter (*Gegenstand*).

Given its prevalent concern with textual sources, *Religionswissenschaft*'s treatment of religion has tended to be descriptive and abstract, a feature of academic endeavour in general. Nanko (1991: 22) quite rightly points out that Germany had no need to look at foreign cultures, because it was not a colonial power. The close connection with theology brought some overlap: theology adopted methods of *Religionswissenschaft* for its exegetical work (see also Rudolph, 1988: 38–39) and made use of *Religionswissenschaft*, for example, in apologetics and missiology. Hence combined professorships for missiology and *Religionswissenschaft* (Rudolph, 1991: 154). In Greschat's (1988: 103) view, *Religionswissenschaft* can indeed be useful for theology, but its work should not be used as ammunition against other religions. Although *Religionswissenschaft* could help clarify beliefs on both sides, inter-faith dialogue has a theological agenda (ibid.: 70) and is thus not part of *Religionswissenschaft*. Ever since it emerged, *Religionswissenschaft* has been engaged in emancipating itself from theology. This has involved highlighting differences in method, while acknowledging areas of overlap. In his introduction to *Religionswissenschaft*, Greschat (1988) repeatedly points out the differences and appends a section on the distinctions between the two disciplines (also Rudolph, 1988: 46–47).

The close connection between *Religionswissenschaft* and theology meant that the churches did not look towards the academic community to derive an explanatory paradigm for the emergence and success of NRMs. Theologians were methodologically equipped to carry out work which students of *Religionswissenschaft* might have undertaken, such as the study of NRMs' historical predecessors or NRMs' origins and writings. In some ways, theologians were *better* equipped than *Religionswissenschaftler* because their apologetic concerns unequivocally placed NRMs within their remit. Since the 1920s, the churches – the Protestant Church in particular – had taken up the study of unorthodox/non-mainstream religions as a way of engaging with, and answering to, contemporary issues, while *Religionswissenschaft* had to go some way towards making NRMs its business. It had to revise its view of religion's 'ideal' state and develop an interest in religion's unorthodox and marginal state.

The close link with theology and philology has left *Religionswissenschaft* without a distinct methodology. Hence the ongoing *Methodenstreit* (debate about methods). It calls for a clear line between *Religionswissenschaft* and theology, a demand to which introductions to *Religionswissenschaft* in the late 1980s (Stolz, 1988b; Zinser, 1988a; Greschat, 1988; Waardenburg, 1986; Kehrer, 1988) may have responded. It also calls for adopting appropriate methods from other disciplines. Therefore, the social sciences are considered auxiliary disciplines and sociology of religion is considered a sub-section of *Religionswissenschaft*, not a discipline in its own right. This is reflected in the absence of professorships in sociology of religion and the consequent lack of an institutional base in Germany.[46]

Institutionally, *Religionswissenschaft* may be an established academic discipline in that it is a recognized and taught subject. Yet, within university structures, *Religionswissenschaft* is part of either theology departments (and subject to the concomitant confessional tie) or other departments. Further, the use of the term *Religionswissenschaften* for theological departments by a different name undermines efforts to demarcate (proper) *Religionswissenschaft* clearly from theology. As a taught subject, *Religionswissenschaft* apparently has no agreed curriculum or foundation courses, so that the contents of undergraduate courses vary greatly, as do definitions of *Religionswissenschaft*.

Finally, career prospects for graduates are not promising: only a handful can be absorbed in existing academic structures and viable openings in the job market. The low demand for qualified *Religionswissenschaftler* prompted some graduates to create REMID to promote professional prospects and work towards empirical approaches (Bochinger, 1996). REMID stood the law of supply and demand on its head: instead of allowing supply (availability of scholars and their work in the study of religion and NRMs) to meet demand (need for academic paradigm in NRM debate), they ignored the absence of demand and provided the supply, hoping that demand would follow supply (see Rink, 1997). REMID focused on the NRM debate in particular, because it perceived the deficit in academic contributions. This has, however, meant involvement of a kind which is unusual, as German academics prefer to pursue their studies in the safety of their institutions (the 'ivory-tower approach') to the rough and tumble of public debate. REMID experienced some 'rough reality' when its first press statement was appropriated by the Church of Scientology, just as Günter Kehrer did when he had become caught between the fronts.

Notes

1 At times, deliberate cultivation of a British identity based on ecclesiastical allegiance was fostered and the Church did not hesitate to claim that it embodied 'the Englishness of English Religion', referring to it as 'Our National Church' – claims based on the intertwining of church and state at many levels (Robbins, 1982).

2 Since the Reformation, Christians of different confessions denied each other the right to religious freedom and sought to use worldly powers for dealing with 'heretics' and keeping order. It was inconceivable that 'orthodoxy' and 'heresy' should co-exist and any possible means was justified to punish those abjuring 'true faith' and to restore unity; 'true religion' was regarded an essential foundation of political order (Böckenförde, 1990: 34–35). This also explains the absence of tolerance for non-conformist religion. The Roman Catholic Church preserved this principle until Vatican II, when religious freedom was finally affirmed as a personal right (*Recht der Person*) instead of the right of truth (*Recht der Wahrheit*) (ibid.: 41–54).

3 Links between Conservative Party and Church are reflected in the description of the Church as 'the Tory Party at prayer'. The distribution of religious allegiance among politicians provides an index of the alignment of religious forces in the overall structure of class, status, and power. The Liberal Party's historical connections with non-conformity and Anglicans' connections with the traditional ruling class are documented. Politicians from the land-owning class or educated at the elite public schools have been overwhelmingly Anglican (D. Martin, 1967: 49).

4 The relationship between belief and practice is linked with geographical factors (differences between Scotland, Wales, and Northern Ireland and between urban and rural areas) and sociological factors (variations of religious behaviour according to class, race, and gender). Davie (1994: Ch. 6) provides details of differences and variations of belief in the UK and regional patterns, a combination of parameters characteristic of religion in Britain for quite some time (D. Martin, 1967: 18ff.).

5 Membership in the Church of England has been on a downward trend, independent of the indicators used, although it occurs at varying rates regarding time and place. However, varying indicators show varying patterns of decline (Davie, 1994: 52; D. Martin, 1967: 37). Religious practice in England has not really undergone any major alteration since the end of the last century (D. Martin, 1967: 37).

6 This paragraph is indebted to Davie, 1994: 33–51.

7 The 1944 Education Act provided non-denominational Religious Instruction (RI) in county (fully State-funded) schools, which was non-denominational Christian, mainly biblical, instruction, with each Local Education Authority (LEA) producing its own syllabus. By the mid-1970s, some LEA syllabuses had become multi-faith, effectively ceasing to instruct children in faith, although the law had not changed. The term 'RI' was replaced by 'Religious Education' (RE). The 1988 Education Act confirmed this practice. RE consisted of Christianity and 'the other principal religions represented in Great Britain', leaving it to the LEAs to interpret this for their own syllabuses. In 1994, two model syllabuses (naming six religions) were produced for national guidance, superseded in 2004 with non-statutory national guidelines for RE (which are multi-faith) and indication of how RE might contribute to citizenship and social cohesion (see Jackson, 2004).

8 The decline in Anglican practice was mirrored in diminishing support for

Sunday Schools, although support for the *notion* of Sunday School remained strong. Religious education was also strongly supported: four out of five felt that religion should be passed on in religious education and children should be taught prayers (D. Martin, 1967: 41– 42, 57).

9   However, there is a more positive effect regarding pupils attending Catholic schools (Davie, 1994: 134).

10   In Levitt's (1992) study, mothers had no problem with religious education as such or with some form of collective worship in school, but they openly criticized any expression of fervent or over-demonstrative religion and those who tried to influence others' beliefs (Davie, 1994: 135).

11   However, the thanksgiving service for the Falklands victory was a powerful example of the Church challenging, rather than legitimating, the State (Davie, 1994: 87).

12   Davie (1994: 139ff.) emphasizes the need to use terminology appropriately and distinguishes carefully between matters relating to the constitutional framework and the initiatives within it. 'Establishment' is used in two ways: first, the links between the Church of England and the State, second, pervasive, if somewhat elusive, links in certain circles of society. The two are related in that senior Church members are part of both.

13   This can be seen from two viewpoints: the need for approval could be questioned as not all Members of Parliament may have much interest in the Church, but affirmed as a mechanism for providing 'breathing space', as, for example, in the case of women's ordination (Davie, 1994: 144).

14   Robbers (1986: 469) distinguishes three types of countries: with strict separation – the United States, France, Portugal, the Netherlands; with a state church – Scandinavia, Great Britain, Greece; with different degrees of separation and co-operation – Belgium, Spain, Italy, Germany.

15   It is a union of 17 autonomous *Landeskirchen* (provincial or regional churches), the boundaries of which refer to historically grown territories and do not coincide with political boundaries. History also explains the three Protestant *Konfessionen* (creeds): *lutherisch* (Lutheran), *reformiert* (Calvinist), and *uniert* (unified). The *Landeskirchen*, affiliated as the *Evangelische Kirche Deutschland* or EKD (Protestant Church of Germany), see themselves as an association rather than as one church. *Landeskirchen* of the same *Konfession* also form associations (Stammler, 1986: 580–581). In 1991, the *Landeskirchen* in eastern and western Germany united retaining the name 'EKD' (Stern 1998: 6).

16   It comprises 21 territorial dioceses (*Bistümer*), five of which are archdioceses. The territorial structure developed historically and boundaries are not identical with state boundaries. A national body, *Deutsche Bischofskonferenz* (conference of German bishops), meets twice yearly for consultation and co-ordination. Vatican II led to the *Gemeinsame Synode der Bistümer in der BRD* (joint synod of German dioceses) in 1971; half its members are clergy and lay people. The synod takes place once a decade, but has no legislative powers; it aims to promote the Church's faith (Stammler, 1986: 582).

17   28 million are Roman Catholic and just over 28 million Protestant. 1.5 million belong to other Christian communities; 1 million of these belong to the orthodox churches, 87,000 are Methodists and 68,000 Baptists (Stern, 1998: 4). Numerically, the free churches and other religious communities play a very minor role (Stammler, 1986: 583). Islam is the exception, but its growth is a recent development.

18   The reunification of Germany in 1990 added 17 million with no religious affiliation. Immigration in the 1960s (*Gastarbeiter*) added 7 million who are not German citizens. Muslims form the third biggest religious community (Stern 1998: 10–12). In 1991, *perestroika* and the dissolution of the Soviet Union

increased the Jewish community to *c.*66,000, compared to 28,000 in 1989 (ibid.: 7, 9).

19 Although Islam does not have *Körperschaft* status, state schools with a high proportion of Muslim pupils offer Islamic religious education as part of the curriculum (Stern, 1998: 11). Plans for religious education for Muslim pupils started in the 1980s (Scotland, 1987). According to Stern (1998: 11), the problems Muslims have encountered have more to do with immigration and employment than with religious intolerance – for example, there has been little protest regarding traditional Muslim dress, unlike in France. Stern seems to suggest that socio-economic questions are far more important to Germans than religion *per se*. This ties in with Hardin and Kehrer's (1982) exploration of the strong opposition against NRMs: Germans seemed more concerned with social security, health insurance, and pension rights than religious beliefs. However, recent developments, such as the current headscarf debate, may point to changes.

20 Public institutions follow the *Proporz-System*: proportional representation of political parties, creeds, regions, interest and minority groups, etc.

21 Clergy are trained in theological faculties at state universities. Both churches have universities, but the state only recognizes up to two years of study there.

22 Rohde's figures for the Protestant Church (he compares 1963 with 1979) show that the decline in baptisms accounts far more for the decline in births than churchleavers. Also, in 1979, *c.*96 per cent of those baptized were confirmed, but church weddings had halved and only 6 per cent of members had attended church, while up until 1968, attendance had remained steady. The (significant) decline in attendance occurred between 1969 and 1973 and has remained steady since 1974. In 1979, *c.*94 per cent had a church funeral, a percentage which has been unchanged for quite some time (Rohde, 1981: 603–604). The 1990 European Values Study (EVS) provides more recent figures on items such as church attendance (Barker *et al.*, 1993).

23 For the Protestant Church, attendance is considerably higher for church festivals, with an upward trend for services at Christmas (Rohde, 1981: 604).

24 When the *Bundesverfassungsgericht* (the highest constitutional court) decided in 1995 that crucifixes in the classroom were illegal, politicians and the public took to the streets in protest (Stern, 1998: 7). This issue is a recurring one and also features in the present headscarf debate.

25 Staff in the 'new' universities and 'university sector colleges' form the membership of NATFHE Religious Studies Section, a body within the National Association of Teachers in Higher Education, which represents lecturers in Further and Higher Education working in Religious Studies, Religious Education, and Theology (Cush, 1995: 2).

26 The second half of the 1990s augured reverse processes: the department at Lancaster underwent major restructuring in the mid-1990s (Clayton, 1995), as has Wolverhampton. In the late 1990s, the closure of some Religious Studies departments was announced, for example University College Chichester (formerly West Sussex Institutes of Higher Education) and Sunderland; others have reduced the number of courses, partly by not (immediately) replacing retired staff, notably at LSE and King's College London.

27 The University of Wolverhampton has the distinction of being the first British university to gain BS5750 and IS9001 [sic], the internationally recognized hallmark of quality (Chryssides, 1997). Apart from British Standard 5750 and ISO9000, there is a procedure to measure 'graduateness' (Roberts, 1998: 107–108).

28 In September 1994, the London School of Economics introduced an MSc in

Sociology, with the possibility of specializing in the Sociology of New Religious Movements (*BASR Bulletin*, November 1994: 26–27).

29   In Britain, the social sciences have infiltrated other disciplines, with distinctions becoming less easy to draw. Postmodernist theorizing is basically the incorporation of the sociology of knowledge into other disciplines.

30   INFORM's role straddles academic institutions and 'player in the NRM field'. It is academic in that its creation is due to the work and motivation of an academic engaged in the study of NRMs; in that it relies heavily on academic findings; and in that it pursues research interests. INFORM is thus under academic tutelage and confers academic standing on those working for it. Yet, INFORM's work challenges what it calls 'the ivory tower perspective' of social science; it realizes that it is politically involved and that the nature of its work does not allow it to be 100 per cent objective.

31   FECRIS stands for *Fédération Européene des Centres de Recherche et d'Information sur le Sectarisme* or *European Federation of Centres for Research and Information on Sectarianism*. It is an umbrella organization which brings together cult monitoring groups on the European-wide level. FECRIS's inaugural meeting took place in Paris in October 1994 (*FAIR NEWS*, January 1995: 13).

32   In her report, Ammerman (1993: 1) 'attempts to assess the nature and quality of the expert advice available to the agencies involved in this situation and to make some suggestions about how that advice might better be utilized in the future'. Substantial parts of the report are included in a published article (Ammerman, 1995). Put crudely, the report addresses the question of what kind of 'experts' state authorities should listen to: academic or ACM 'experts'. In the Waco case, it seems the agencies found ACM 'experts' more credible.

33   Müller spent most of his life copying the Rig-Veda and commentaries from manuscripts which had come from India to England, France, and Germany (Greschat, 1988: 37). Another linguist, Thomas W. Rhys Davids, who had studied Sanskrit in Breslau and served in the British Colonial Service in Sri Lanka, collected and translated ancient Pali texts. However, unlike Müller, he was in direct contact with the people and country of the texts he collected and studied, while Müller remained an 'armchair' philologist and, as Greschat (1988: 49) notes, built up an image of an 'ideal India', the India of the 'classics', like scholars of Greek did regarding Homer's Greece.

34   In 1910, the first chair for *Allgemeine Religionsgeschichte und Religionsphilosophie* (General History and Philosophy of Religion) was created in Berlin for the Danish theologian E. Lehmann, with another following in Leipzig in 1912 for N. Söderblum. In 1920, a chair for *Vergleichende Religionsgeschichte and Religionsphilosophie* (Comparative History of Religion and Philosophy of Religion) was set up in Marburg for F. Heiler (von Stietencron, 1989: 90). In Bonn and Leipzig, chairs for *Religionswissenschaft* were created in the Faculty of Arts (Waardenburg, 1991b: 46).

35   This twofold structure was postulated by Joachim Wach (1924), who considered sociology of religion and psychology of religion as complementary to *Religionswissenschaft* and excluded philosophy of religion (Rudolph, 1988: 39). Flasche (1989: 204) comments that Wach's work has virtually been ignored by students of *Religionswissenschaft*, but it has, of course, been used by sociologists. Flasche (1989: 203) further states that given its dual orientation – philological/ethnological and origins/religion *per se* – the subject is Janus-faced. The bifurcation occurred because *Religionswissenschaft* was not put on a sound footing regarding theory and method specific to its concerns.

36   Joachim Wach explained the two branches as two different approaches: history of religion provides a longitudinal section of one particular religion by

following it from its beginning to a later stage (evolutionary development), while comparative study of religion provides a cross-section of a variety of religions by following one particular aspect in all of them. Conceiving religion in evolutionary terms led to the view of tribal religions as 'primitive' and Western religion (Christianity) as 'highly developed' religion (*Hochreligion*) (Greschat, 1988: 64). In sociology, the most developed stage would be reached when humanity grew out of religion altogether.

37 Kippenberg and Luchesi's (1991) edited volume includes a number of contributions on van der Leeuw and his predecessors (see also Colpe, 1988; Flasche, 1989).

38 Frick (1997: 8–9) provides details about the survey method. Although he looked at all the universities, Frick restricts his comments to the seven major ones: (Free University of) Berlin, Bonn, Bremen, Hanover, Leipzig, Marburg, and Tübingen.

39 DFG is a charitable organization founded in 1951 to promote scientific research in Germany and international co-operation between the sciences. It receives (substantial) funds mainly from national and regional public sources and distributes these as grants to research projects or institutions. DFG is also involved in planning and co-ordinating new projects, developing special programmes, and establishing special research areas in universities.

40 For disciplines listed, two 'experts' are nominated (every two years) to decide on the merit of applications. Those relating to *Religionswissenschaft* are assessed by theologians.

41 Three chairs were lost to *Religionswissenschaft* in this way (von Stietencron, 1989: 93). Financial pressure on universities, due to restrictive government policies, played a role, but there are theologians whose teaching licences are withdrawn by the church, when their teaching is, for example, considered incompatible. Such theologians retain their professorship, but cannot remain in the theology department. Further complications arise when they leave or retire (von Stietencron, 1989: 94; Rink, 1997: 22).

42 According to a long-standing maxim at the University of Marburg, *Religionswissenschaft* can only be concerned with religions or religious phenomena which are at least 100 years old and/or located outside Europe (Pilger, 1988: 18).

43 Pilger looked towards sociology for appropriate methods (participant observation, interviews, group discussions, questionnaires) regarding his project, the study of the *Bund Freireligiöser Gemeinden Deutschlands*, an association of self-ascribed pantheists, a-religious or anti-religious. His fieldwork experience makes him advise undergraduates against such projects, but he argues strongly for empirical studies of contemporary religious communities in Western societies, provided university courses cover the groundwork (Pilger, 1988: 18, 20).

44 The church has the final say for posts in *Religionswissenschaft* attached to theology departments and posts related to theology, even if these are not in theology departments (von Stietencron, 1989: 95). In about a third of departments, the confessional tie almost precludes successful applications from *Religionswissenschaftler*. In Marburg, for example, the occupant of the chair for history of religion was expected to be a Protestant, because the chair is in the department of Protestant Theology (Rink, 1997: 22).

45 Unlike in Britain, graduates are expected to seek employment for jobs and posts closely related to their university courses, otherwise job applications are (usually) not considered. Teacher training involves a relevant university degree.

46 Günter Kehrer in the Department of Cultural Studies at Tübingen is one of the
    very few scholars in *Religionswissenschaft* who has been working in sociology
    of religion. He is variously described as Professor for *Religionswissenschaft* and
    Professor for the Sociology of Religion. He undertook the first sociologically
    oriented studies on NRMs, but distanced himself from the subject after the early
    1980s. His paper at the Marburg conference did not change that.

5 The 'anti-cult' movement's response

THE ACM RESPONSE IN BRITAIN: THE CASE OF FAIR

This section deals with FAIR (Family, Action, Information and Resource), the first 'anti-cult group' in the UK. It documents FAIR's establishment and development since its beginnings in the mid-1970s, together with FAIR's aims and attitudes towards 'cults'. It describes FAIR's remit: the groups which have been central to FAIR's campaigns and the 'cult' activities members have been most concerned about. The term 'anti-cult group' is examined and its perception of organizations like FAIR. FAIR's position on 'brainwashing' and 'deprogramming', concepts closely linked with 'anti-cult' thinking, is outlined. FAIR's connections with the wider 'anti-cult' network are described. FAIR's newsletter and other publications are surveyed, as are FAIR's activities. An important aspect is FAIR's view of the academic approach and the State's handling of the 'cult' issue.

Introduction

FAIR is the first 'anti-cult' organization which was established in Britain. To date, no history of the 'anti-cult movement' (ACM) in Britain or elsewhere has been attempted, although there are typologies which distinguish between secular anti-cult and religious counter-cult groups (Introvigne, 1995; Cowan, 2002; 2003). The information here is based on FAIR's publications,[1] information from staff and members, and some media reports (e.g. Victor, 1994). Casey McCann's (1986) article provides useful information, as does Paul Rose's (1981a) account of his political career and his unpublished book (Rose, 1981b) on the Unification Church (UC). There are some references in scholarly works, such as Beckford's *Cult Controversies* (1985: 224–225) and Chryssides's 'Britain's Anti-Cult Movement' (1999).

FAIR was conceived as a organization to support parents and relatives who face difficulties in coping with 'cult' membership. In this respect, FAIR resembles organizations across Europe, such as *Elterninitiative* in Munich or ADFI (*Association pour la Défense de la Famille et de l'Individu*) in Paris. Until 1994, 'FAIR' stood for 'Family Action Information and Rescue', with each word carefully chosen (*FAIR NEWS*, Summer 1993: 1–2). Suggestions to change, for example, to 'Family Advice Information and Rehabilitation' (*FAIR NEWS*, April 1984: 2), finally led to a majority vote for 'Family Action Information and Resource' (*FAIR NEWS*, October 1994: 4).

FAIR's history

FAIR describes itself as 'a voluntary organisation established in 1976 to support relatives and friends affected by Cults [sic]. It believes in Human Rights'. FAIR is the main 'anti-cult' organization in Britain, founded in 1976 by Paul Rose, then MP for Manchester Blackley. He fought an unsuccessful defence of a libel action against the UC, while acting as FAIR's first chairman. He did not stand for re-election in 1979, retiring from political life and FAIR in 1978. The last chapter of his book (Rose, 1981a) records his involvement with the 'cult' problem. His (commissioned) book on the UC was ultimately not published, because the publishers feared a libel case. The *Daily Mail* trial had just concluded at the time. Rose returned to his former profession (solicitor, now coroner) and is still active in 'cult' matters at a local level.

In his message to FAIR's 1996 Annual Open Meeting,[2] Rose explained how he became involved:

> my involvement with the problem of destructive cults came about for-tuitously. In taking up a single case, I became unwittingly the focus of heart rending letters and complaints from parents and relatives of mainly young people who had joined various cults, and one in particular. . . . I was merely the vehicle for the expression of deep seated feelings and concerns common to so many people in various walks of life which needed a channel . . . through which to express themselves.

Rose had raised the issue in Parliament and received a flood of letters. This led to a meeting of people who shared his concern and eventually to the formation of FAIR. Further questions and debates in Parliament ensued, with correspondence, media coverage and support increasing. Individual members supplied informal counselling and assistance on request, as no other programmes existed at that time. Rose described this period as follows:

> Gradually a coalition of concerned politicians, journalists, relatives of members and many former members, together with a number of clergy-men working together with the Deo Gloria Trust[3] was at last able to help relatives come to terms with a situation that had arisen which they could not understand, on occasion persuade members or would-be members of the truth about the organisations that they had joined or were about to join, inform the general public of the methods and aims of various cults, and those activities were reflected in the name of FAIR.

FAIR and journalists then co-operated closely in supplying and receiving information. Those who initially gathered around Rose were a 'mixed bunch': parents and relatives formed the backbone, with involvement from participants in UC workshops, former members, interested clergy, and journalists. From this group, a FAIR committee was elected. The new organization ran on donations, mainly from parents. However, FAIR also faced difficulties with 'disinformation, forged documents, vilification', even 'cult' infiltration, and constant threat of libel, made real in Rose's case.

After Rose's chairmanship, Barry Morrison, then Anglican chaplain at the Polytechnic of Central London and member of the team ministry of All Souls Church, Langham Place, and Tony Freeland, a UC member's twin brother, became joint chairs. Both had been on FAIR's committee since 1977. They were succeeded by Pete Broadbent, then Assistant Chaplain at the North London Polytechnic and curate of Emmanuel, Holloway, later Archdeacon of Northolt. He had experience with 'cults', having worked with students in Durham and Cambridge. In late 1984, the chairmanship was shared by Casey McCann and Daphne Vane. McCann was then a staff member of Sevenoaks School, a large independent school for boys. He had become involved with FAIR in 1980, when two former sixth-form students joined the UC in the US while on holiday. After his attempts to talk to them in San Francisco failed, he turned to academics who had connections through UC-sponsored conferences and UC-related publications (Cheal, 1985). McCann's campaign received important media coverage in *The Times* and the *Daily Mail* in June 1981. McCann had also served as FAIR's treasurer. Daphne Vane is one of FAIR's founding members and its International Representative.

The Revd Neil Dawson from Kennington, South London, became Acting Chairman in 1986 and served for three years, because no other chair could be found. In late 1988, Lord Rodney, a Conservative peer, was elected. He had first-hand experience of cult involvement in his family and led a parliamentary group on cult activities. Due to his unexpected death in October 1992, Audrey Chaytor, another long-standing (since 1980) FAIR member, succeeded him. In 2000, Tom Sackville, former MP for Bolton West, became chair.

After FAIR had been 'freed from the preoccupation with supporting Rose's libel action' (Beckford, 1985: 225), there was room for expansion and change. Four developments occurred in the late 1970s and early 1980s. First, FAIR encouraged the creation of regional branches, which built a federal structure. Second, FAIR was brought closer to evangelical Christian groups, because its chairs were clergymen when Deo Gloria Trust came to prominence.[4] Third, FAIR established closer links with 'anti-cult' groups in other parts of the world. Finally, FAIR extended its remit to include all 'destructive cults' (ibid.). FAIR's federal structure is similar to that of ADFI in France, which operates nationwide as UNADFI (*Union National des Associations pour la Défense de la Famille et de l'Individu*). In Germany, parents' groups operate independently, but can join a national association, AGPF (*Aktion für Geistige und Psychische Freiheit*), located in Bonn.

In 1983, Broadbent pointed to the extended range of groups and movements in FAIR's work, including not only the UC, but the 'whole gamut of mystical philosophies, diverse Messiahs, political surrogates and self-exploratory therapies' (*FAIR NEWS*, April 1983: 1). This was reflected in the newsletter's contents: while the UC still dominated in May 1979, other movements – Beshara, Bhagwan Rajneesh, Divine Light Mission (DLM), School of Economic Science (SES) – appeared in September 1979. In 1985, McCann referred to FAIR's expanded compass which included 'problems arising from COG, Scientologists, Hare Krishna, and Bhagwan Shree Rajneesh' (Cheal, 1985). However, coverage in *FAIR NEWS* suggests that the UC was still FAIR's priority.[5]

FAIR's wider remit meant more work. The establishment of an office in May 1983 replaced part-time secretarial arrangements (started in 1980). This allowed FAIR to operate as an organization and re-evaluate its aims and *raison d'être*. For Broadbent, 1982 was the year of consolidation and 1983 the year of reappraisal, an exercise in stock-taking and reflecting about FAIR's principles. Five areas needed improvement: support for families, information about 'cults', counselling facilities, government taking the 'cult' problem seriously, FAIR's style in dealing with the public and media (*FAIR NEWS*, October 1983: 1). In 1989, Lord Rodney's appraisal prompted him to urge FAIR to make the most of its resources, co-operate effectively and liaise with other organizations (*FAIR NEWS*, Autumn 1989: 1).

There were other difficulties for FAIR: in 1987, Cyril Vosper, a committee member, was convicted in Germany of kidnapping and causing bodily harm to Barbara Schwarz, a 32-year-old Scientologist. Vosper had allegedly tried to 'deprogramme' her (Victor, 1994: 9). Also, FAIR's newsletter pointed to criticism and smear campaigns by 'cults'; for example, an article in the Spring 1987 edition of *Freedom* (a Scientology publication), which 'lashes out against FAIR, Cultists Anonymous, and psychiatrists', and an item in the January 1988 edition of *Unification Briefing*. Thus 'cults' sought to undermine FAIR's credibility in its initial stages.

In her address to FAIR's 1991 AGM, Audrey Chaytor, then vice-chairman, spoke of that year as 'a specially difficult one' in which she 'had some bizarre things happen to me', although she provides no specific details. She also stated that she was not alone in this. These difficulties are also reflected in *FAIR NEWS* of Autumn 1991, which mentions 'views allegedly expressed in the name of FAIR (or about FAIR) . . . by persons who have not consulted us prior to expressing their opinions'.

FAIR and 'cults'

FAIR had meetings with 'cult' representatives, for example, in 1979 after the performance of a play, *Freefall*, staged at the ICA Theatre in London and based on the COG. FAIR's newsletter commented on this discussion in positive terms. In 1983, FAIR met with members of Lifewave who tried to 'persuade FAIR to stop publicizing our disquiet about the activities of this group'. A Lifewave member 'had posed as a concerned parent' and the telephone conversation had been transcribed. FAIR recognized parts of the transcript, but felt others must have been inserted. From then on, enquirers were directed to FAIR's box number and members' personal details were no longer passed on (*FAIR NEWS*, April 1983: 5).

In 1982, FAIR representatives visited the Emin headquarters in Putney. Emin had enquired whether FAIR had any complaints about it, apparently prompted by the group's intention to apply for charitable status. Although the reception was 'courteous', Emin's managing director and his wife insisted that the complaints by worried relatives – heavy financial commitment, family estrangement, and fear of leaving – had no foundation. FAIR was not convinced of Emin's sole concern with a 'scientific approach to esoteric research'. In November 1982, FAIR discussed its reports in the newsletters with Scientology. The meeting was 'conducted in a friendly tone throughout' and addressed FAIR's main objections – deceptive recruitment, exorbitant costs of courses, and harsh disciplinary measures.

However, overall, relations with 'cults' were strained: some repeatedly attacked 'anti-cult' groups in their publications and 'cult' members contacted FAIR's office posing as concerned relatives. For example, 'Anti-Cult is a Cult' in ISKCON Report (No. 1) commented that critics dwelt on misunderstandings, mistakes or individuals' behaviour and that ISKCON should not be lumped in with 'true cult movements'. ACM groups were also accused of avoiding 'honest and open dialogue'. Subhananda das's (1978) booklet *Please Don't Lump Us In: A Request to the Media* compares negative 'cult' hallmarks with ISKCON's positive stance.

McCann (1986: 7) explains that contact with 'cults' were attempts to influence their practices in a positive way and therefore 'positive and purposeful'. Broadbent, too, pointed this out to FAIR's 1983 AGM:

> We are rather concerned to keep the channels of communications between FAIR and the cults, frustrating though such contact can sometimes be. We have met several representatives of the cults over the past year, and have used the opportunity to urge greater freedom of access to families and to press them on some of their more outrageous practices.

Despite the benefits, McCann (1986: 7) admits difficulties, both in view of the attitudes displayed by both sides:

> efforts have been concentrating on moderating or reforming ... practices. This sometimes takes the form of day to day dealing with leaders and senior figures in the organisation structures of New Religions to see if issues of concern, especially individual ones, might be resolved. This

has not always had the greatest support. Indeed one senior figure in the 'anti cult movement' recently delivered herself of the view that 'negotiating with the Unification Church was akin to and as valuable as trying to negotiate with Hitler'. It was matched, however, by a senior official in the Unification Church suggesting that 'dealing with FAIR was like suggesting that Israel should negotiate with the PLO'.

FAIR's membership and structure

FAIR is run by a committee which discusses important policy questions and issues suggested by members. According to Broadbent, FAIR is run in this way because 'tricky issues' require a collective view and committee membership is subject to vetting, unlike FAIR membership (*FAIR NEWS*, April 1983: 1). Formally constituted membership was rejected on account of cumbersome procedures (*FAIR NEWS*, April 1984: 1). However, two categories of newsletter subscribers have existed since FAIR started applying for charitable status: subscribers 'only' and FAIR members, the latter known to FAIR, often members of 'cult affected' families, in agreement with FAIR's aims. They can vote in the AGM business meeting which elects the committee and agrees policy. They also assist at the committee's request. New members need to be proposed and seconded by existing members and accepted by the committee. FAIR had 120 members in the late 1990s. The committee consists of chairman, secretary, treasurer, and up to five elected and three co-opted members.

FAIR's branches outside London operate independently. They have considerable freedom of manoeuvre and can therefore make the most of local resources (Beckford, 1985: 225). Some have their own membership and constitution. The need for counsellors and information points in various geographical locations, close to enquirers, prompted the FAIR committee to call on members to build a strong regional network. The first branches appeared in the late 1970s, with others following in the early and mid-1980s. They submitted regional reports to the AGM and items of branch news were included in the newsletter. The branches' activities were no different from those of the London office: answering enquiries, distributing literature, collecting information, warning about 'cult' activity on a local level, giving educational talks, keeping contact with the media, alerting local authorities, counselling, passing on information.

FAIR and its regional branches are funded by voluntary donations from members and parents. Costs include office overheads, travel expenses and support of regional branches, contact with international cult monitoring groups, counselling, and preventative education. There is no funding from public sources. Over the years, FAIR's financial situation seems to have often been precarious. Appeals for donations appeared in *FAIR NEWS* to cover running costs or make particular purchases. Subscribers are reminded to maintain their newsletter subscriptions, as these are FAIR's only regular income. FAIR's efforts to obtain charitable status have remained unsuccessful. Two factors have made recognition difficult: FAIR's lobbying activities and the Home Office's way of handling applications in the 1980s, when it screened more rigorously than in the late 1970s.

McCann (1986: 6–7) points to considerable shared membership and differences in emphasis among 'anti-cult groups' in Britain:

> The overlap in membership is almost complete in that members of CA [Cultists Anonymous] may often be FAIR 'supporters' . . ., and some FAIR supporters may subscribe to the Evangelical stances of the Deo Gloria Trust. Whilst in general terms there will be sympathy with the overall view that by and large people are better off out of Cults than in them, it is the practical expression of this view which differentiates between them.

FAIR's close association with Deo Gloria Trust and the religious profile of its early chairmen created the impression that FAIR had a strong Christian orientation. However, although membership included many committed Christians, it also included members of other faiths or no faith. FAIR regards itself as non-religious in outlook and liberal regarding members' beliefs, while Deo Gloria had a very distinct evangelical Christian commitment. Parents' attachment may have floated between them and tensions existed, but parents supported FAIR because they perceived its stance as more realistic (McCann, 1986: 7). With some 500 supporters and about 1,000 newsletter subscribers McCann considered FAIR the best supported, organized, and influential 'anti-cult' group in the UK, although it speaks for a minority of parents. In his message to the 1996 FAIR meeting, Rose referred to FAIR as a pressure group with an essential part to play in the democratic process.

Until October 1994, FAIR maintained its London office, where Ursula MacKenzie, supported by part-time secretarial help, responded to enquiries and edited the newsletter for 14 years. The work was initially taken over by Carole Tyrrell, but since late 1995, FAIR's day-to-day business was in the hands of Audrey Chaytor and Daphne Vane. In 2002, the latter retired from the committee. In 1994, FAIR introduced an advisory body, a group of 'professional people who are good friends of FAIR' (*FAIR NEWS*, Autumn/Winter 1995/6: 2).

FAIR's aims

FAIR's support for parents and relatives not only consists in moral support and solidarity, but also in providing information, advice, and counselling. Counselling is also for 'cult' members willing to discuss membership and for former members. In early 1982, FAIR's committee identified support for parents and counselling as an area to improve. In her AGM address in 1985, Daphne Vane underlined the importance of care for families. This and education of the public were confirmed as FAIR's main aims in late 1986. Parents are shocked and amazed that someone could join a 'bizarre' group and that this 'someone' should be their 'normal' son or daughter. Parents often keep their children's 'cult' membership from friends and neighbours and desperately search for advice and help, which they find in FAIR.

Demand for information kept growing, as Broadbent indicated in 1983: 'The correspondence load is growing . . . and [so do] telephone enquiries . . . Many of them were requests for information, and we continue to try to provide accurate and up-to-date advice on the practice of specific cults' (*FAIR NEWS*, October 1983: 1). The accent on information continues, as Audrey Chaytor emphasized in 1995: 'The commitment to give speedy and correct information is still our priority' (*FAIR NEWS*, Autumn/Winter 1995/6: 2).

However, FAIR acknowledges that it has neither patent solutions nor the ability to keep families together at any cost. Although it tries to keep lines of communications open between members and their families, in some cases the family itself may be the problem. While FAIR sympathizes, supports, and advises parents, it does not interfere with their decisions. The advice intends parents to come to informed decisions. The editorial of April 1987 *FAIR NEWS* argued, for example, that condoning cult membership might greatly delay departure in that 'the young cult member is less likely to take a critical look at his group than if he knew his family had strong reservations.' In the editorial of *FAIR NEWS*, July 1985, a FAIR committee member, himself an affected parent, affirmed that action needed to come from within the family itself: 'real help . . . lies in that family's own approach. . . . There are no miracle cures. . . . If one idea fails there is another one to be tried. Those parents who adopt this approach usually succeed. This is the benefit a parent receives from good counselling'.

FAIR shares its aim to educate the wider public about problems of existing and potential 'cult' membership with similar organizations in the UK, Europe, and worldwide. Broadbent considered the publicity created by the *Daily Mail* libel case an opportunity to pursue this very aim. This case (tried in late 1980) concerned a series of *Daily Mail* articles alleging (among other things) that the UC was 'the cult that breaks up families'. The trial was the longest in the history of libel cases and went against the UC, even after appeal.

FAIR's aim to raise public awareness includes targeting public figures and academics to 'prevent them . . . from accepting innocent sounding invitations and therewith inadvertently lending support to organisations like the Unification Church' (*FAIR NEWS*, October 1986: 2). FAIR believes that particular preventative education is needed for students, especially in their first year and those from overseas, because they are more vulnerable. The editorial in the January 1987 newsletter counts raising public awareness and helping those 'harmed' as major components of FAIR's existence. Eventually, organizations such as FAIR should be redundant. Statistics of 'cult' membership in the UK would look different 'were it not for the ceaseless efforts' by FAIR and similar groups, although there is no reason for complacency or slackening (*FAIR NEWS*, April 1988: 1). Therefore, educating the public also means raising awareness of FAIR and its work – to correct the sometimes distorted picture projected by the media and make FAIR more widely known.

FAIR has repeatedly pointed out that it is not 'anti-religious', but opposes practices detrimental to the well-being of the individual. The June 1981 newsletter stated, for example, that

> FAIR . . . does not approve of 'Moonie bashing'. Our aim is to challenge the influence of those whose ideas and principles might endanger the freedom of the individual and family life, to prevent the growth and expansion of a social menace. But we are not opposed to the individual cult members.
>
> Fighting deception and exploitation does not mean fighting the deceived and exploited! This might be compared with a medical situation in which doctors and researchers combat germs and viruses but not the patients affected by them.

FAIR's concerns are thus not so much related to teachings, but to the way teachings translate into practice and affect individual freedom and choice:

> it is being assumed that cult opposition has been built on doctrinal objections, while in reality the methods and practices of extremist groups are under fire, not their beliefs, provided of course that these are not being used to justify controversial practices. (For example the UC's doctrine of 'heavenly deception' and COG's flirty fishing.)
>
> (*FAIR NEWS*, April 1983: 9)

In 1985, McCann outlined FAIR's general position: affirmation of freedom of belief and respect for existing legislation:

a) We respect the right of everyone to choose their God and their form of worship within the framework of accepted legal conventions.
b) We do not believe that legislation should be introduced to remedy the more unacceptable practices and procedures adopted by some cults.

> (*FAIR NEWS*, October 1985: 1)

As FAIR progressed, its aims expanded to include better links with government agencies, strengthening the network, keeping the media informed, and regular meetings with 'cults'. However, family support, counselling, and raising public awareness have continued as its core aims.

FAIR's remit

FAIR's remit expanded with the number of movements operating in the UK, increasing in the late 1970s and early 1980s, as Broadbent pointed out to the AGM in 1982:

> Cult activity has shown a worrying increase over the year . . . the sheer diversity of cults operating in this country is becoming a real cause for concern. We have over 100 groups on file, ranging from minuscule local sub-Christian deviations, through a multitude of pseudo-scientific and marginally Eastern-based philosophies, to the more monolithic and well-known such as the Moonies, Children of God, etc.
>
> (*FAIR NEWS*, October 1982)

Broadbent also outlined the common traits:

> What is common to all . . . is their increasingly sophisticated method of deception and plausibility. Many of them *seem* harmless and will actually try to differentiate themselves from cults with such disclaimers as 'We're not like the Moonies, you know' – but underneath lurk the same tragic stories of personality disruption, family break-up, and unquestioning obedience to a leader whose claims, to any rational person, would seem utterly laughable.
>
> (*FAIR NEWS*, October 1982)

'Family break-up' refers to the UC libel case and the *Daily Mail* articles about 'the cult that breaks up families'. The comments on 'cult' beliefs somewhat contradict FAIR's professed concern with behaviour and practices (rather than belief content) and its principle of supporting freedom of belief. However, as a clergyman, Broadbent would naturally have considered beliefs important.

His comments offered broad criteria for identifying a 'cult'. Morrison drew up a list of ten characteristics: (1) secrecy, evasion, and deceit; (2) indifference to morality; (3) extreme authoritarianism and a strong leader; (4) extreme sensitivity to outside criticism; (5) intensive indoctrination; (6) demand for total commitment; (7) community living; (8) wealth; (9) political connections; (10) faith based on guilt and fear. Regarding the first point, FAIR was mindful that it, too, could be accused of secrecy and therefore opened the AGM to everyone (*FAIR NEWS*, October 1983: 1). Regarding point 5, Rose sees parallels between totalitarian political parties and 'cults', given hierarchical structures, pressures on members, fear of leaving, and indoctrination methods, parallels also frequently drawn in the German literature.

There are other lists of 'cult' characteristics. In October 1994, *FAIR NEWS* included a '10 Point Guide' drawn up by 'a consultant psychiatrist': (1) two major 'cult' types: self-improvement/counselling and new religious movements; (2) charismatic guru/leader, usually male; (3) use of words/ phrases out of context, with meanings differing from general use; (4) rigid set of rules, some contrary to laws; (5) hierarchical structure; stages can be passed through rapidly with reward of becoming elite: hence obscure pass-words, etc., rites of passage, ceremonies; (6) rigid obedience enforced with punitive action; (7) strong peer pressure; (8) control over sexual behaviour, different from outside social norms; (9) use of apparently philosophical and religious concepts, actually distorted and skewed; (10) pooling of finances/ tithing. Pastor Haack also devised a checklist. 'Anti-cult' groups generally use and disseminate such lists, with some characteristics cited more than others. Deception and exploitation have ranked high and are therefore examined more closely.

Deception and exploitation

Deception surfaced in various guises, during fundraising when 'cult' members solicited money under false pretences. This occurred mainly in the late 1970s and early 1980s, although *FAIR NEWS* reported such incidents up to the early 1990s. Deceptive recruitment, one of the main and long-standing parental complaints, was recognized as a distinctive 'cult' feature from the very beginning, as Rose stated in his address to the 1996 meeting:

> the method of inveigling people into joining through front organisa-tions, apparently innocuous invitations to meetings seemingly uncon-nected with a cult, was another side of the dishonesty which was revealed as a common factor.

For parents, this was compounded by 'cults' approaching young people away from home, for example, while travelling or in their first term at uni-versity or during critical periods. In 1989, the California Supreme Court ruled that two former members could sue the UC for fraud regarding decep-tive recruitment (and 'brainwashing'). David Molko and Tracy Leal were given leave to go to trial with claims that they were tricked by recruiters who denied UC membership. While religious *beliefs* were entitled to full protec-tion, the court stated, religiously motivated *conduct* was subject to state restriction.[6] The case stirred controversy among established churches and denominations: some feared the ruling might lead to judicial regulation of religious recruitment and conversion, others applauded the decision, arguing that this did not concern religion, but informed consent of those proselytized.
Another form of deception occurs in contests for young people, in which 'front organizations' or misleading names conceal 'cult' connections. The International Cultural Foundation (ICF) and Festival of World Culture, both linked with the UC, have launched essay, song, or painting contests. The Church of Scientology has run essay contests for young science-fiction writers. The Church Universal and Triumphant reportedly used 'Montessori'

for one of its enterprises. In some cases, this is done to improve public image: 'well organised propaganda campaigns . . . are often financed and directed by obscure front organisations of well-known cults. Participants may have no idea of the true identity of the sponsors' (*FAIR NEWS*, January 1986: 1).

Parental complaints about recruitment practices also related to what happened to members after joining. New members tended to distance themselves from their families in order to devote themselves fully to the movement. For parents, this meant severe disruption of their families and destruction of their children's lives: instead of pursuing promising careers, they fulfilled menial duties and sacrificed personal comforts. Some members donated their savings, even their inheritances.

Parents said they did not recognize their children after they had joined, describing their state as trance-like. They must have been 'brainwashed', parents reasoned. They also felt that grassroots members were exploited: while these toiled and lived extremely frugally, leaders amassed fortunes and wealth, enjoyed a very comfortable, if not opulent lifestyle,[7] and pursued doubtful aims. Even charitable or public-spirited actions are seen in this light: 'Furthering of the movement and, in many cases, its leaders appears to be the main aim. Society does not really benefit from their presence, because even seemingly outreaching projects are mainly designed to promote the cult, often exploiting the altruism of its young members in the process' (*FAIR NEWS*, April 1987: 1). Leaders are believed to be motivated by power and money, by the desire to impose their belief system on society, because it needs cleansing or saving. Unquestioning obedience to leaders ultimately ends in tragedy, as in the cases of People's Temple, Branch Davidians, Solar Temple, and Aum Shinrikyo – tragedies whose reoccurrence must be prevented. In this respect, 'cults' are a threat to democratic society. In his 1996 address, Rose stated that 'fundamentalism whether of a religious or political nature is the greatest danger to our open society that we in the democratic world now face'. After his first committee meeting in 1981, he concurred with FAIR's perception that 'cults' conned people, were dangerous and inimical to the family, and that the general public were unaware of their activities.

What makes a 'cult'?

Despite the checklists for the 'marks of a cult', the boundary between *bona fide* religions and 'cults' or 'cult-like' groups has not always been clear-cut. *FAIR NEWS* pointed to the limitations of checklists, especially regarding small localized groups. The difficulty applies especially to groups within Christianity – old or new. When *FAIR NEWS* reported on Opus Dei and charismatic groups, readers questioned whether they should be ranked with groups like the UC or Rajneeshism. In 1983, Broadbent clarified:

> FAIR's position is that wherever any group begins to exhibit some of
> the characteristics of a cult – authoritarian leadership, hierarchical

structures, 'guru' dependency, etc. – then that group, whether religious or political, is open to criticism, and its adherents need to be warned of the dangerous course being embarked on.

(*FAIR NEWS*, January 1983: 8)

Further, he argued, any newly emerging groups – including small Christian fellowships – might develop into, or result in, new 'cults' if doctrinal differences produce schisms. In 1989, *FAIR NEWS* (Spring: 2) set out FAIR's brief regarding Christian groups and pointed out how fine the dividing line could be:

> we often have to decide whether or not a group enquirers want us to investigate fits into FAIR's brief. We do have some firm guidelines. For example, orthodox world religions ... are clearly outside our brief, as are mainstream Christian denominations. When it comes to break-away groups of either of these the situation is not quite so straightforward. Splinter groups may have been created because of shortcomings within the main religions, and they may gradually develop into independent denominations. Others, however, are formed by ambitious persons of power ... Under these circumstances there is a strong possibility that the group will take on cultist features. But the dividing line between both categories is not always clearly defined.

FAIR readers have apparently been divided, with criticism for the mention of groups perceived as *bona fide* by some and 'suspect' by others. Therefore, until such groups were better known, 'FAIR may come in for criticism both for mentioning or for ignoring a group which is in this kind of no-man's-land' (ibid.).

As to new religions, FAIR's rule of thumb directed it to concentrate on groups 'most of which developed and became known in the 1960s and 70s or even later'. However, 'traditional' or 'established sects' ('established cults' in FAIR's terminology), such as Mormonism and Jehovah's Witnesses, were also covered, because of similarities with 'cults' and readers' requests for information (*FAIR NEWS*, July 1983: 6). For this reason, Opus Dei was included in *FAIR NEWS*.[8]

As FAIR's concern focuses on 'cult' *practices* rather than beliefs, the newsletter introduced 'borderline cases', groups new to its files and not known long enough to warrant classification as 'cults'. When *FAIR NEWS* reported on such groups, an introductory sentence explained their status, judged on account of available information: 'We need a minimum of reliable and factual information before we can give any opinion on the groups in question' (ibid.: 5).

The terms 'cult' and 'new religious movement' have also been debated; the latter is rejected as too general and neutral:

Criticism has been expressed regarding our use of the word 'cults'. The fashionable alternative is 'New Religious Movement'; but we feel that this term is too all-embracing, that it does not differentiate between acceptable and harmful organisations.

(*FAIR NEWS*, January 1983: 5)

It ['NRMs'] would inevitably include groups which have developed within mainstream religions and are not really our concern.

(*FAIR NEWS*, April 1983: 2)

FAIR's working definition is derived from Longman's New Universal Dictionary (1982): 'cult' is 'religion regarded as unorthodox or spurious' and 'spurious' means 'having a superficial deceptive resemblance' or 'based on mistaken ideas'. This seemed a suitable description for the groups on FAIR's files, including 'the bizarre but relatively harmless to the extremist and dangerous' (ibid.).

However, featuring in a report does not automatically classify a group as a 'cult', as disclaimers indicate: 'A mention in our newsletter does not necessarily mean the seal of condemnation' (ibid.). The intention of such reports is to share or solicit available information, especially regarding borderline cases. Often, enquiries, complaints or media attention prompted FAIR's concern with a group. Some readers wanted FAIR's remit broadened to include occultism and spiritualism, others wanted it to stick to 'cults proper'. However, FAIR tended to cover 'problematic' groups. When reports of 'devil worship and magic' increased and 'satanic ritual abuse' became topical in the late 1980s, the newsletter covered such topics, although they had initially been considered beyond FAIR's brief. Borderline cases came to be listed under 'miscellaneous', separated from the 'cult news section'.[9] The complaint-led reporting resulted in the inclusion of a wide variety of groups, ranging from Aum Shinrikyo and Amway to Smith's Friends and the Raëlians. Yet, despite explanations and clarifications, questions of boundary and definition continued to spark enquiries. In 1985, a query about Friends of the Western Buddhist Order was answered with 'The movement is a branch of genuine, mainstream Buddhism' (*FAIR NEWS*, January 1985: 16), a local paper's reference to the Baha'i faith as a 'cult' was deemed 'mistaken', and *Cursillos* were explained as courses on the basics of Christian faith, with no cause for concern (*FAIR NEWS*, October 1985: 15).

FAIR's strong commitment to raise 'cult' awareness was tempered by repeated warnings against witchhunts. Rose cautioned against them and argued for balanced appraisal, given FAIR's commitment to freedom of speech and religion, 'since it is the very antithesis of freedom of thought that is induced by the methods, practices and outright dishonesty of the cults that are deserving of criticism'. In connection with the *Daily Mail* libel case, the June 1981 newsletter stated that witchhunts may overstate the case against 'cults', incur loss of credibility and fuel sympathy for 'cults'. It was necessary to be clear and firm about the dangers, but also balanced in recognizing that not all 'cult' members are, for example, held against their will. FAIR also disapproved of a smoke bomb being dropped through the letter box of a UC member after the libel case, because this amounted to 'persecution in a witchhunt style'.

FAIR an 'anti-cult' group?

At the 1996 Meeting, a question from the floor referred to FAIR as an 'anti-cult group'. Immediately, someone objected: 'We are not an *anti-cult* group!' FAIR does not like this label, because it is perceived as derogatory, and prefers more neutral terms, such as 'cult-monitoring', 'cult-watching' or 'cult-observing' group. The latter may sow confusion, because academic centres are sometimes subsumed under 'cult-watching groups'.

Initially, those radically opposed to 'cult' activities used 'anti-cult' in a *positive* way to describe their stance, but 'cults' used it in a *negative* way, to attack groups like FAIR for being 'anti-religious'. Media reports reinforced the negative image. FAIR had to steer a course between two extremes:

> FAIR is constantly forced to walk a tight-rope. There are those who want us to be an 'anti-cult' organisation, with a 'hatchet' view of all cults and their activities. This stance we repudiate entirely (although the media often misleadingly characterise FAIR as an anti-cult group). We occasionally disappoint parents who want us to be more 'hard line'.[10] On the other side there is the pressure from cults and their allies to give them a clean bill of health and to underplay the complaints we receive. Of late this pressure has manifested itself in the shape of ill-informed attacks[11] . . . and the occasional bit of 'dirty' publicity.
>
> (*FAIR NEWS*, July 1983: 1)

Broadbent rejected the 'anti-cult' label, because FAIR supports and counsels friends and relatives of 'cult' members, goes by practices, not beliefs, is a non-sectarian, non-religious organization, and does not influence 'cult' members to join other religious organizations (ibid.: 7). For FAIR, 'anti-cult' is associated with 'cult-bashing', 'heresy-hunting', even 'witch-hunting' – attributes which do not reflect its aims and purpose, as there is nothing rabid or persecutory about its focus on malpractices and parental support. McCann spoke of a 'reasoned' response to help those 'who face considerable sadness when a family member joins a new religious movement' (*FAIR NEWS*, January 1984: 13). Some members argued that if FAIR was not *for* 'cults', it surely must be *anti* 'cults', an implication rejected by the newsletter editor. In fact, the use of 'anti-cult' was attributed to academics:

> The word 'anti-cult' is a catch phrase, coined by academics, which conjurs [sic] up the image of medieval witch hunters or – in more modern

terms – those who consider everything connected with cults as evil and want to see every cult member proscribed by law. We are anti-deception, anti-exploitation and against the splitting of families. But we have no religious axe to grind, and cult members are not enemies but somebody's children, people in great need of caring concern.

(*FAIR NEWS*, April 1984: 2)

There are thus various stances between and within groups commonly designated as 'anti-cult movement', but McCann (1986: 6) points to lack of discrimination:

> The term 'anti cult movement' is the creation of commentators seeking to find a set of words to describe and convey . . . a sense of the activities of those groups, [which are] less than enamoured of the behaviour of some New Religions. . . . many of the same commentators have been critical of the 'anti cult movement'. They have accused it, maybe rightly, of seeing the world of Cults as a homogenous one, of failing to recognise different patterns of development in cultic structures . . . In response, protest could be made at the lack of discrimination on the part of these very commentators when describing the 'Anti Cult Movement'. There are as many differences in motives and varieties of response there too, and many who labour within it take issue with the negative tones implicit in 'anti cult'. They see their task being in the long British tradition of seeking compromise, and maybe doing more for religious freedom than their critics often appreciate.

'Brainwashing' and 'deprogramming'

Parents cited 'trance-like states', 'glazed eyes', and unwillingness to discuss anything but their new beliefs to describe their convert children. The 'brainwashing' thesis provided the explanation as a method of conversion and indoctrination which effects radical change in individuals' thought and behaviour. The thesis assumes that conversion is imposed and induced, that the converted are not actively involved in the process and therefore victims. It also assumes that this happens without individuals' intention or will (precisely the opposite of what the theory of 'blaming the victim' assumes, another theory invoked to explain membership). Conversion is thus not the result of individuals' active and conscious striving. Academic research contradicted such assumptions in showing that conversion neither happens overnight nor without active co-operation on the part of would-be converts (Beckford, 1978a).

Further, techniques, such as 'love bombing',[12] sleep deprivation, poor diet, continuous activity (lectures, chanting, praying) combined with intense group pressure and (requested) suspension of rational thinking create a state of suggestibility which heightens converts' willingness to abandon hitherto held beliefs and adopt the worldview presented by the group. Conditions described as sensory deprivation[13] are conducive to conversion, because they lower resistance towards change in attitude and belief and make individuals sensitive to social influence (Pavlos, 1982: 24).

The work of Lifton (1961) and Schein *et al.* (1961) on 'thought reform' in 1950s China provided a theory of understanding 'cult' conversion. Chinese Communists used the technique to indoctrinate political prisoners.[14] Lifton and Schein also spoke of 'coercive persuasion', because prisoners were treated with rewards and punishments, which were not related to Pavlov's conditioning techniques. Many 'anti-cult' groups believe that thought control is closely associated with 'mind control' as practised by 'cults': both work on group pressure and group dynamics to induce desired behaviour and thinking. William Sergant (1957) and John Clark (1977; 1979a; 1979c) provide explanations of the *physiological* processes involved. Sergant notes parallels between 'brainwashing' in POWs and conversion in evangelical contexts. Regarding the careful preparation of 'spontaneous' conversion, evangelists have intuitively grasped the principles which soften the mind for indoctrination. In Clark's (1979c) view, 'cults' aim at changing 'the very fabric of the surrounding society' and imposing totalitarian controls. 'Cultist' indoctrination 'employs excessive stress to break down the mind's ability to carry out' complex processes and 'substitutes a rigid and dull simplicity in which the adaptive function, at least in its higher intellectual form, has atrophied'. Schein *et al.* (1961: 261) describe the adoption of new beliefs and behaviour as 'ritualization of belief', which occurs in 'total institutions' – environments in which a leader is in control of formal doctrine and its expression.

While the 'brainwashing' thesis and concomitant ideas are common currency in everyday 'anti-cult' parlance, there is little, if any mention in FAIR's newsletter. One might think it is taken for granted, but not discussed. Successful court cases which have hinged on the 'brainwashing' argument reinforce this supposition: in the case of Robin George, a jury ordered ISKCON to pay substantial damages for kidnapping and 'brainwashing'. McCann indicated that many parents adhered to the brainwashing thesis, but that he had considerable doubts about it. The theory admittedly suited both sides: it explains to parents why their child has joined this 'nasty sect' and allows ex-members to say 'I was brainwashed' (Cheal, 1985). It is therefore a plausible explanation for parents and former members to understand a process outside their range of experience. In this sense it is a metaphor (Beckford, 1985).

However, McCann (1986: 7) explains that not all parents adopted the 'brainwashing model':

> Deo Gloria Trust and CA do, in the main, subscribe to the brainwashing and mind control thesis as explanations of the pertinent factors that obtain when people join New Religions. FAIR views it, at best, as only

one in a range of possible explanations. It is true that there are some who subscribe to the view that techniques of brainwashing or questionable processes of mind control best explain what obtains when people join New Religions. . . . However, the vast majority of parents remain uncertain about . . . this, recognising that it is doubtful whether concepts appropriate to prisoner of war camps can be transferred to the context of New Religions. Also the fact that recruitment into Cults is low, and turnover rates so high makes the whole issue even more questionable. Besides this, some parents have recognised aspects of the same process, without coercive elements, as being present in many management development programmes[15] . . . Further evidence for the uncertainty about the brainwashing hypothesis has been the low incidence rate of kidnapping and deprogramming . . . in the UK.

However, there is a good turnout when speakers like Margaret Singer address FAIR's Annual Meeting – speakers well known for subscribing to the notion of 'mind control' in the 'cult' context. Yet, a parent whose son had joined ISKCON for just three months, contradicted the idea of instant conversion:

> Although it may appear as if a normal young person instantly changed into a cult member, that is not usually the case. It more often happens that a gradual change took place, starting with a vague dissatisfaction with life itself or with some part of it.
>
> (*FAIR NEWS*, July 1985: 1)

Lord Rodney stated that 'The concern is the anguish they ["cults"] cause. Breaking members away from their families is their secret, because by changing someone's environment utterly you can change the way they think.' This, he said, was similar to 'brainwashing' and interrogation techniques familiar to intelligence networks (Doyle, 1989). *FAIR NEWS* (Spring 1990: 2–4) also described Steven Hassan's understanding of 'mind control' in detail. In his view, the controversy about 'brainwashing' largely arises from a misconception of basic terms. His *Combatting Cult Mind Control* (1988) distinguishes 'brainwashing' and 'mind control' as two different processes.

Deprogramming is an equally controversial and coercive practice which aims to reverse indoctrination or 'brainwashing'. The term is used in data processing as the opposite of 'programming', namely erasing a programme. Used in the 'cult' context, deprogramming assumes that individuals can be influenced so as to 'automatically' (without self-reflection) take on thought and behaviour patterns. In practical terms, deprogramming involves – often forceful – physical removal (kidnapping), followed by 'de-conversion' or 'de-indoctrination'. Kidnapping entails criminal acts for which deprogrammers and parents have been convicted.

The first deprogrammings became known in the mid-1970s, especially when Patricia Hearst's parents resorted to this measure after she was freed from the Symbionese Liberation Army (SLA).[16] Ted Patrick is generally credited with introducing deprogramming as a means to 'fight cults'. His autobiography, *Let Our Children Go*, written with Tom Dulak (1976), justifies and describes the techniques used (also Patrick, 1979). Edward Levine (1981) makes 'the case for deprogramming religious cult members', as does Enroth in *Youth, Brainwashing and Extremist Cults* (1977).

In the mid-1970s, an organization called POWER (People's Organized Workshop on Ersatz Religions) issued a 'Handbook for Deprogrammers' (Leduc and de Plaige, 1978: 345–356). POWER turned out to be run by a young man 'whose motivation and intentions were never clearly revealed'. Occasional newsletters took a radical position towards 'cults' and included the promotion of deprogramming. The 'Handbook' was a brochure entitled 'Deprogramming: The Constructive Destruction of Belief. A Manual of Technique' and circulated in 1976. (Leduc and de Plaige claim that the manual – of which they make extensive use in their appendix – was obtained during a secret conference of 50 deprogrammers in 1977 and distributed in France by Scientology.) POWER was suspected to be a 'front organization', created to discredit the emerging 'anti-cult' movement. Although it had disappeared by 1977, it had attracted considerable publicity (hence Leduc and de Plaige's investigative journalism) and tarnished FAIR's image (Beckford, 1985: 228–230), as the 'manual' indicated several groups in Britain allegedly practising deprogramming (Leduc and le Plaige, 1978: 356).

Some 'cults' used deprogramming as a bogey to members, which justified the need for, or reinforced, barriers to the outside. The UC reportedly circulated a document which described the alleged methods in graphic detail and listed FAIR, EMERGE, and Deo Gloria Trust as 'main agencies'. Ironically, in 1983, the *Rajneesh Times* offered a course in deprogramming 'to help people who want to free themselves from the adverse effects of cult membership'.

However, FAIR has consistently distanced itself from deprogramming,[17] as its May 1979 newsletter (p. 1) stated:

> to comment on reports . . . that Moonies are being warned to expect 'deprogramming' if they come in contact with FAIR. The word 'deprogramming' has come to be associated with certain illicit and violent methods of reversing so-called 'brainwashing'. We wish to make it absolutely clear that the counselling FAIR offers has nothing in common with this. We neither approve of, use, or recommend any coercive methods of persuading youngsters out of the cults. Nor do we recommend kidnapping . . . That these things have happened in the US does not mean that they happen, or should happen, here.

An AFF study (Langone, 1984) apparently endorsed FAIR's stance. In 1982, AFF's *The Advisor* included a questionnaire, to which 94 parents responded. The findings showed various ways 'cult' members' potential departure can be viewed (may never leave; may leave, if forcibly deprogrammed; may leave, if counselled; may leave voluntarily), but there was no way of *predicting* how members might leave. The data suggested that: a high percentage leave *without* forced deprogramming, many deprogrammings fail, a number of deprogrammings end up in court. Thus, FAIR concluded, parents should consider carefully before taking the decision in favour of deprogramming (*FAIR NEWS*, January 1985: 3–4).

In his address to the 1996 Meeting, Rose declared deprogramming to be 'worse than brainwashing' and therefore to be rejected. Freeland rejected it because it uses the same means as 'cults', namely deception, and plays into their hands in reinforcing and justifying their propaganda; counselling should happen with individuals' consent, although many ex-members would not agree. Indeed, accounts of successful deprogrammings express former members' gratitude and relief for the intervention (Swatland and Swatland, 1982; von Hammerstein, 1980; Edwards, 1979).[18]

In connection with his attempts to return pupils from America McCann was asked why he did not just find out where they were, bundle them into a waiting car, and whisk them off to the airport (reportedly the procedure used in kidnapping and subsequent deprogramming cases, as shown on BBC1's *Heart of the Matter* of June 1997). He rejected such action as 'a ludicrous way to go about things' and on the grounds that 'If people want to believe that their god is an omelette, then they've got to be allowed to get on with it, as long as they don't interfere with the rest of us' (Cheal, 1985).

FAIR NEWS reported on (un)successful cases of deprogramming.[19] *FAIR NEWS* sympathized with parents who tried such action, but drew attention to possible consequences:

> failure may result in a far greater gulf between parents and cult member than ever before. Parental desperation is very understandable, but desperate *methods* are often inadvisable and should be given very careful consideration, lest they might lead to a worsening of the situation.
>
> (*FAIR NEWS*, October 1982: 8)

However, the perception that FAIR was in favour of deprogramming persisted. In 1983, the section on deprogramming in Channel 4's booklet, *Whatever Else You Want No 4*, stated that 'There are only a few deprogrammers in this country, and you may be able to make contact with them via FAIR'. *FAIR NEWS* (April 1983: 13) felt that the statement was 'unfortunate and misleading', because 'FAIR does, of course, not support deprogramming, nor does it recommend commercial practitioners'.[20]

Nevertheless, FAIR faced calls for more radical action from its own ranks, reflected in members' suggestions of what FAIR's acronym should stand for. In 1984, some wanted 'Rehabilitation', because 'Rescue' might imply that FAIR practised or recommended coercive deprogramming; others wanted more 'action' and 'rescue' from FAIR, even proposing an 'SAS style troop for extricating youngsters from cults', which FAIR rejected as too extreme. This was the point when the 'hardliners' broke away to form Cultists Anonymous.

At the 1985 AGM, McCann reaffirmed that FAIR did not recommend, support, or encourage coercive deprogramming and disapproved of organizations and persons who practised it. The reasons cited were: high failure rate, damage caused to family relationships, heightened commitment on members' part in case of failure, offences against civil liberty, attributing membership to a single cause ('brainwashing'), leaving only negative memories of 'cult' involvement. McCann 'considered coercive deprogramming a money-making racket which encouraged preying on the misery of families with cult involvement' (FAIR NEWS, October 1985: 1). Similar objections were cited by Elizabeth Tylden, a consultant psychiatrist working closely with FAIR (FAIR NEWS, June 1986: 3).

FAIR within the wider network

FAIR is part of the wider national and international network of 'cult-monitoring' groups. The need for co-operation between them arose from parents' difficulties with 'cult' membership across geographical and political boundaries. Parents' found it hard to keep contact when their children were recruited abroad or relocated without notice. They complained that 'cults' did not provide information about their children's whereabouts, even on request. Thus, just as 'cults' developed into multinational organizations, 'cult-monitoring' groups established transnational structures to improve effectiveness and maximize use of resources.

This was important for FAIR's work, as Rose stressed in his message to the 1996 meeting:

> Another enormous leap forward has been the interchange of ideas and connections with similar organisations in other countries as one of the well known features of a number of these cults is their targeting of persons who are away from home, separated from their families, lonely and undergoing stressful situations.

Overseas contacts began in 1981 and over time the necessity to co-operate closely with 'like-minded workers in the field', in Britain and abroad, was reiterated. FAIR NEWS also reminded other groups that they were all fighting for the same cause and this could only be achieved when everyone worked together 'instead of squabbling and/or working mainly for their own satisfaction' (FAIR NEWS, January 1987: 1).

The late 1980s saw an attempt to bring 'cult-observing' groups in Britain under a nationwide umbrella organization. A meeting in March 1988 explored various aspects of closer collaboration regarding experience and resources. Further meetings in May and November 1989[21] discussed coun-selling, training, ex-members' rehabilitation, research, and the media. As to organizational structures, Lord Rodney was to be chair; organizations, rather than individuals, were to be members. The stated aims were 'to fur-ther co-operation and co-ordination between the groups concerned with the detrimental effect of cults within society'. However, no name could be agreed on. Although a date was set for another next meeting, the initiative for the new organization fizzled out.

Co-operation with other organizations

FAIR has built connections with other 'cult monitoring' groups on the national and international level. In Britain, these groups are (or were) either similar to FAIR, such as Deo Gloria Outreach, Cultists Anonymous, Cult Information Centre,[22] Reachout Trust,[23] CONCERN,[24] Housetop,[25] the Dialogue Centre in Dublin,[26] the Irish Family Foundation (IFF),[27] or ex-members' groups, such as EMERGE (Ex-Members of Extremist Religious Groups),[28] the Ex-Cult Members Support Group, T.O.L.C. (Triumphing Over London Cults),[29] or rehabilitation programmes, such as Catalyst.[30]

FAIR forged connections in Europe and other countries. First contacts were made in the late 1970s, when FAIR met with organizations in the United States, Europe, and Australia. As with the British groups, the pur-pose of such contacts is exchange of information and mutual help. Among the European contacts, those with Germany and France have perhaps been closest, as Ursula MacKenzie and Daphne Vane speak the respective languages. In Germany, FAIR has had contact with Pastor Haack and *Elterninitiative* (*Ei*) in Munich (Haack was *Ei*'s chairman), Pastor Thomas Gandow and *Eltern- und Betroffeneninitiative* (EBI) in Berlin, *Evangelische Zentralstelle für Weltanschauungsfragen* (EZW), and AGPF in Bonn. In France, FAIR has links with ADFI in Paris.

Other groups in Europe with which FAIR has (had) connections include Panhellenic Parents Union (PPU) in Athens,[31] Asociación Pro Juventud (APJ) in Spain, the Dialog Center in Aarhus, Denmark, and the parents' initiative in Austria. By the late 1980s, FAIR claimed about 100 contacts worldwide (*FAIR NEWS*, April 1988: 2).

A European umbrella organization

FAIR is a member of the umbrella organization for 'cult monitoring' groups in Europe, which had its inaugural meeting in Paris in October 1994. Known by its acronym, FECRIS, the *Fédération Européene des Centres de Recherche et d'Information sur le Sectarisme* or *European Federation of Centres for Research and Information on Sectarianism*, arose from an initia-tive to mark the International Year of the Family. The impulse came from an associate of UNADFI in Paris, Dr Jacques Richard, who became FECRIS's first president, and this explains the use of 'sect' in the name. FECRIS's aim is 'to generate funds for research on sectarianism. It is intended that the research will concentrate on the cultural and social patterns of development of sects'. FECRIS is conceived as 'a catalyst for research work, which we hope will be done by organisations whose mandate it is to protect the rights of individuals to live an unfettered life in ways of their choice, without pain or prejudice "to themselves or others" '. Membership consists of representatives from *bona fide* support groups; groups outside Europe can become Associate Members (*FAIR NEWS*, January 1995: 13).

FECRIS could be considered a counter initiative to FIREPHIM, *Fédération Internationale des Religions et Philosophies Minoritaires*, which formed in late 1992, with Danièle Gounord, Scientology's spokesperson for France and Europe, as chairperson; Bernard Mitjavile, UC leader in France, as treasurer; and Jacques Aizac, a Raëlian, as general secretary. FIREPHIM chose Strasbourg as its seat in order to be heard by the European Parliament and Court for Human Rights. It aimed to 'destroy' ADFI which it considered a 'hate group, an intolerant and anti-religious association whose mere existence endangered human rights'. Other founding organizations included Sri Chinmoy, Wicca, Jehovah's Witnesses, and COG.

FECRIS's second meeting in April 1995, attended by representatives from six countries, decided that 'the legal aspects of family/cult relationships should be the first subject for research by an appropriate university or professional department' (*FAIR NEWS*, Spring 1995: 13). Existing legal decisions should be explored among member associations to form the basis of, and provide direction for, research. This suggests that FECRIS aims to establish new structures of institutional knowledge, located in university law departments. The European Citizens Action Service (ECAS) was to help prepare funding applications to EC sources. The meeting was also concerned with communications technology and data storage. By late 1995, FECRIS's statutes and internal rules were drafted and a grant application was under way. A meeting in early 1996 in Germany suggested extracting from a list of court cases details which could benefit affected individuals. In April 1999, FECRIS (now with representatives from 10 countries) organized a conference in Paris to focus on problems of 'cult' activity in European countries. It included a presentation by Alain Vivien, chair for the (then) recently formed French Interministerial Mission on Action against Cults (MILS) and a unanimously adopted Common Declaration on measures to be taken. By late 1999, FECRIS had a web site (modified in 2001: www.fecris.org). FECRIS also requested advisory status with the Council of Europe after the legal affairs committee had proposed a European observatory on 'cults'. The Council's Standing Committee of the Parliamentary Assembly granted the status in March 2005 (FECRIS Press Statement of 21st March 2005). In April 2000, Daphne Vane (Vice-president) and Jean Nokin (President), reported on the European situation at the AFF conference on 'Cults and the Millennium'. FECRIS also applied for NGO status with the UN. In June 2001, a meeting in Paris focused on the plight of victims, problems connected with legal action against cults, health, and the protection of children. FECRIS welcomed the About–Picard Law which the French Assembly had adopted in May 2001. By then, FECRIS had an office in Paris, 36 associations, representing 24 countries (17 members, 19 correspondents), funding from the French government, and an (internal) electronic newsletter, 'Quid Novi?'. FECRIS's meetings concentrated on legal aspects, with a questionnaire about cults and the law being sent to lawyers. In May 2002, FECRIS held a conference on 'Children and Cults' in Barcelona.

International connections

FAIR has continuously built international connections and used conferences as opportunities to promote such links. A worldwide network and the location of FAIR's work in an international context have been important ways of underlining the need for international action and support routes.

In America, FAIR has been in contact with Citizen Freedom Foundation (CFF), Cult Awareness Network (CAN),[32] and American Family Foundation (AFF).[33] Information from them and conference reports[34] appeared in FAIR's newsletter and FAIR used some of their literature, such as CFF's 'warning leaflet' and AFF published articles by M. Langone, L. West, M. Singer, J. Clark, S. Hassan, etc. In Canada, FAIR has had links with the Cult Project,[35] Info-Culte Inc.,[36] and No Longer Children.[37] A long-standing contact in Australia has been Adrian van Leen's CCG Ministries[38] and in New Zealand, Free Mind Foundation, a parents' group set up in 1982.

FAIR's publications

FAIR's main publication is its newsletter, *FAIR NEWS*. It started in the late 1970s with a few A4 pages published three times a year. The contents revolved largely around the UC, with information about other movements added from September 1979 onwards. The newsletter expanded, as the volume of news increased. After various changes, *FAIR NEWS* found its format with the June 1982 edition, which was retained until the editor, Ursula MacKenzie, retired in late 1994.

A typical edition consisted of around 18 typed pages, with the table of contents on the cover page, news from the FAIR Committee, general news, items about 'cults', media reports, new publications, and last-minute news. From 1983 *FAIR NEWS* became a quarterly in order to pass on more information more quickly. Editorials came to be included, which discussed particular 'cult'-related aspects or topical issues, such as ex-members and the job market, average length of membership, the anniversary of the Jonestown tragedy, the fall of the Berlin Wall, etc. Contributions from parents and former members featured at times, including testimonies and accounts of personal 'cult' experience. Reports on activities of cult-monitoring groups in Britain and elsewhere were included – press releases, conferences, political and legal matters. From April 1985, *FAIR NEWS* included the disclaimer that 'We have made every effort to ensure that the information in this News-letter is correct, but we welcome notification of inaccuracies', and occasional corrections.

After Ursula MacKenzie's retirement, Carole Tyrrell became editor, with Audrey Chaytor as Managing Editor and two people on the editorial board, of whom Daphne Vane was one. The format changed to a more 'professional' layout and style. Although the structure largely remained, new features were introduced, such as articles, FAIR's 'mission statement' on the front page, and the focus on particular issues in some editions. However, since the 1995/6 Autumn/Winter issue, the editorial team's composition has varied, although Audrey Chaytor and Daphne Vane have remained.

The readership of *FAIR NEWS* ranges from concerned parents and relatives to those people interested in the subject and even 'cult' members:

> Many people [. . .] on the FAIR mailing list [. . .] want to stay in touch with cults in general and [. . .] want up-to-date information on the group with which their own friends/relatives are involved. Some merely want to know what the latest emergent groups are. Others are members of new religious movements who want to know what FAIR is saying.
>
> (*FAIR NEWS*, January 1984: 1)

Among those who want to be kept informed are clergy, youth leaders, politicians, university staff, journalists, etc. Having 'cult' members among the readership precluded the inclusion of confidential information, such as case histories or counselling experience.

FAIR has also published occasional papers, for example, the proceedings of its Seminar on *Influence and Stress Related Issues* (FAIR, 1993). Trans-cripts of talks at the annual meetings are available, for example Margaret Singer's address in 1989 and Pastor Gandow's in 1992 (Gandow, 1992). FAIR has also distributed ex-members' testimonies.

FAIR prepared information or fact sheets on some 'cults' for 'reliable and authoritative comment on beliefs and practices'. The sheets outline leader-ship, history, teaching, lifestyle, main activities, attractions, and dangers and indicate addresses, publications, and further reading. FAIR devised a guide to 'cults' in Britain, with brief descriptions of *c.*20 groups, intended for those looking for basic information about active groups. FAIR produced leaflets, on its aims and practices, to warn young people and students (10,000 were distributed in 1993), and practical advice for parents. FAIR provides infor-mation packs on some groups and has compiled a booklist. This literature has to be updated from time to time to take account of new developments.

FAIR's activities

As FAIR's aims and activities are closely intertwined, it is difficult to draw a clear line between the two. This section therefore deals with activities not mentioned earlier. The provision of information and counselling requires the management of information: it needs to be collected, processed, and distributed. Collection occurs through the network of members, branches, and international contacts; distribution occurs through FAIR's literature, media contacts, and speaking engagements in schools and seminars. FAIR acts as a referral agency by putting those requiring counselling in touch with appropriate advisers (professionals or parents). FAIR has worked with other 'caring' organizations and continued to improve its referral network. No statistics of this aspect of FAIR's work are available, except for a reference in *FAIR NEWS* (October 1985: 1) to over 100 families having received counselling in 1985. Until late 1994, FAIR's office in London dealt with enquiries, over 50 per cent of which required support and counselling (ibid.: 1–2), with a helpline operating outside office hours.

Responding to enquiries

There was a continuous increase in the number of enquiries from concerned individuals, MPs, libraries, authorities, and social workers. For example, a steep increase occurred during 1989, but it was difficult to know whether this reflected an increase in problems or whether more people found their way to FAIR. Topical events, such as the events in Waco in 1993, multiplied enquiries noticeably.

FAIR's statistics indicate that in the early to mid-1980s, the average volume of correspondence consisted of 1,500 letters, in addition to telephone calls (1,000 in 1985), which increased to 1,700 in the late 1980s and early 1990s.[39] Requests for information from students increased: over 60 students who prepared dissertations or theses requested information packs in 1993. For 1992/3 (the year of the Waco events), 1,000 additional (compared to 1991/2) enquiries were received – a trend which continued in the following year. For 1993/4, *FAIR NEWS* reported 3,025 communications, but no further statistics appeared after 1994. Occasional editorial comments suggest that enquiries have decreased in recent years.

FAIR recorded which movements attracted most enquiries; these were listed, first in a 'top ten' and then in a 'top fifteen' chart. In 1981/82, the UC topped the list, followed by DLM, Rajneesh, Scientology, COG, and Emin. In 1989/90, the UC was still at the top, followed by Scientology, CLCC, COG, est,[40] Sahaja Yoga, New Age, ISKCON, Rajneesh, and the Jesus Army. In 1990/91, Scientology topped the list, followed by UC, CLCC, COG, Jehovah's Witnesses (JW), Emin, Sahaja Yoga, fundamentalist groups, Transcendental Meditation (TM), and the Jesus Army. In 1991/92, Scientology was still at the top, followed by the UC, CLCC, COG, JW, TM,

Sahaja Yoga, and the Jesus Army. For 1992/93, the chart did not change significantly, except that places 8–10 were taken by the Branch Davidians, ISKCON, and Tvind (Humana). In 1993/94, Scientology was still at the top, followed by CLCC, the UC, COG, JW, the Jesus Army, Amway, Sahaja Yoga, Emin, and the SES. No further charts were drawn up after 1994.

Conferences and annual meetings

Among FAIR's conferences and seminars was 'Influence and Stress Related Issues' (March 1993) and 'Families and New Religions' (June 1985). FAIR co-organized 'Cultism – A Case for Treatment' in Cambridge (November 1990), (with Dr Barry Hart), 'Cults and Counselling' at the University of Hull (1994), and (with *British Journal of Hospital Medicine* and *British Journal of Nursing*) 'Post Traumatic Stress, Dissociative Disorders and the Influence of Cult' in London (February 1995). Two FAIR branches (Greater Manchester, Merseyside) organized 'Cults – A Cause for Concern' (November 1985).

FAIR usually holds its annual meeting in London (except in 1982 when the venue was Birmingham), normally combined with FAIR's committee meeting. These meetings started as AGMs with chairperson's address, treasurer's and regional branch reports, and an Open Forum to discuss problems, share news, and air opinions. Occasional guest speakers were invited, for example in 1985, Peter Hounan, co-author of *Secret Cult*. Attendance ranged between 80 and 120, often depending on speaker and topic, with known speakers attracting sizeable audiences. In the late 1980s, the AGM included Annual Open Meetings with invited speakers, among them J. West (1987), F.-W. Haack (1988), M. Singer (1989), S. Hassan (1990), P. Ryan (1991), T. Gandow (1992), B. Tully (1993). Since 1994, these have been replaced by 'The FAIR Lecture', given that year by R. Ofshe.

Lobbying

Since its inception, FAIR has sought to bring 'cult'-related problems to the attention of Members of Parliament (MPs) and government, in the hope that awareness would spawn action. Paul Rose had raised the issue in the House of Commons to attract attention to 'cult' activities. Therefore, lobbying MPs has been one of FAIR's main activities:

> FAIR is pleased to know that the cult situation is being taken very seriously by a certain prominent member of Parliament who may soon be in a position to put pressure where it would be most effective.
>
> An increasing number of MP's [sic] have been lobbied by parents and FAIR. Parents seem to be particularly concerned about the charitable status of the cults in this country.
>
> (*F.A.I.R. NEWSLETTER*, May 1979: 2)

Whenever Parliament or government departments consider 'cult'-related issues, FAIR members and supporters are encouraged to write to their constituency MPs and MEPs (a strategy also used by NRMs). When the Home Office reconsidered its ban on Scientology (non-British members were barred from entering the UK), FAIR made representations and advised members to write to their MPs, the Home and Foreign Secretaries, and the Attorney General. Some FAIR members have kept MPs up to date, among them Tom Sackville. When an influx of UC members from the US was expected in 1980, parents were encouraged to write to the Select Committee on Home Affairs and local MPs to express concern and request an official enquiry into the 'unacceptable' activities of 'cults', especially fundraising, charitable status, coercive methods of indoctrination, and destruction of families.

Under Broadbent's chairmanship, lobbying was identified as an area requiring improvement: the government needed to be convinced 'that the precious values of freedom of thought and freedom of religious belief are not incompatible with concerted action against groups in which the former is denied in the name of the latter' (*FAIR NEWS*, January 1983: 2). At that time, Richard Cottrell MEP had begun his report to the European Parliament (Cottrell, 1984).[41] As FAIR was hopeful that Cottrell's fact-finding and reporting would result in action, it was important to contribute information:

> Approaches have already been made to MPs and others, and we hope that MEP Richard Cottrell's evidence to the European Parliament will stir our own legislators into action. You can help. Does your MP know about your child's case? If not, please make sure that he/she does. The more constituency MPs who are badgered by their voters on this subject, the better.
>
> (*FAIR NEWS*, January 1983: 2)

Prior to the European Parliament elections, chairperson Audrey Chaytor encouraged members to write to MEPs, particularly to urge action regarding children in 'cults', as 1994 was the International Year of the Family.

In April 1984, about 100 parents and grandparents lobbied MPs to draw the government's attention to the problem of 'cult' involvement. The lobbyists, who wanted to remain anonymous to avoid repercussions for their 'cult' involved relatives, declared their initiative independent of FAIR, although most of them supported FAIR.[42] FAIR was seeking charitable status and could therefore not engage in lobbying. The lobbyists called for more media publicity, regular questions in Parliament, government funding, an official inquiry, inquiry into 'cult' finances, and instruction about 'cults' in RE lessons.[43] FAIR kept the parliamentary group on 'cults' informed and parliamentary debates provided opportunities to supply briefing material to members of both houses, for example to Lord Rodney before a debate in the House of Lords in February 1988, hence his association with FAIR.

Through him, FAIR had a spokesperson in the Lords and in Europe and thus a vital link with the world of politics:

> Lord Rodney never stopped tackling parliamentarians on our behalf, including the Prime Minister. He set up a parliamentary group on cults, made up of MPs and Peers, and spread the message in the Council of Europe to which he was a delegate.
>
> (*FAIR NEWS*, Autumn 1992: 1)

FAIR and academia

The nature of academic work

FAIR's stance towards academic perspectives has on the whole been ambivalent. Studies which support its view of 'cults' or fit the ACM paradigm are welcomed and deemed 'correct' or 'applicable' and those which do not are dismissed, ignored, or criticized. Groups like FAIR conflict with the very approach and methods academics take, which – even if they are ideals applied with varying degrees of success – tend to strive for an objective, value-free, unbiased view and follow Weber's concept of *verstehen*. Cult-monitoring groups often interpret academic results as minimizing families' problems and disregarding human suffering caused by 'cults'. Academics have been perceived as 'sitting on the fence', unwilling to side with those who criticize or condemn 'cults' for malpractices. Thus, often by default, academics have appeared to support or speak out in favour of 'cults', when they have, in fact, just done their work. Simply using 'insider' vocabulary at times implies academics' sympathy, even membership. Yet, academics have also been criticized for not applying their methods rigorously enough and lacking objectivity when presenting the arguments involved.

In his review of Eileen Barker's (1984) *The Making of a Moonie*, McCann points to 'inherent inadequacies' of the sociological approach:

> Sociology is . . . about groups and the generalities of group behaviour. . . . Seldom, if ever, can it descend to examine individual examples. But individual cases need to be examined if only to act as a counter to hectic conclusions. Given the deterministic role that Mrs Barker attributes to converts and non-converts alike, this is vital.
>
> To be fair, she does produce snippets of individual cases, but what is lacking is a sustained and detailed analysis of these. I think we should recognise the necessary limitations of a sociological approach and should shift the discussion to what constitutes reasonable pressure and influence – in short, *values* have to be brought into the argument.
>
> (*FAIR NEWS*, October 1984: 17; emphasis added)

Yet, despite reservations and criticism, McCann considered the volume 'a most stimulating and interesting book', 'provocative', 'essential reading for parents, counsellors, Moonies and ex-Moonies alike' (ibid.: 16, 17). A *FAIR NEWS* reader's comment illustrates how the very nature of academic work lends itself to perceptions of supporting 'cults':

> The book is scrupulously fair and objective but makes no moral judgment. No doubt, as an academic the author feels she should not judge, but as a result of the great publicity given to this subject, the effect of the book is unfortunately to whitewash the UC. Already the media are concluding that the Moonies are not so dangerous after all and that they should be tolerated like other religious organisations.
>
> (*FAIR NEWS*, January 1986: 13)[44]

The view that academics' efforts towards neutrality project a positive view of 'cults' and lead to complacency is reflected in comments on Barker's (1980a) article in *Clergy Review*:

> As it [the article] tries to present an impartial view of the cult scene it is useful to counteract over-sensational press reports, but the altogether too positive and rose-coloured picture created might lead to dangerous complacency and to the opinion that after a close and sober look there is really not all that much cause for concern. Mrs Barker does not mention anything about deception and exploitation experienced by so many, and one wonders whether she saw the Unification Church only in its 'Sunday best'.
>
> (*NEWSLETTER*, February 1981: 6)

Participation at 'cult' sponsored conferences is seen as playing into the hands of 'cults': presence and attendance alone count as support and lending credibility.

There may be a lack of understanding of academic work. There may even be a lack of willingness to understand it in its own terms, as this would undermine the 'anti-cult' stance considerably. Some academics' campaigns in favour of 'cults' and their occasional use of academic findings to disprove 'anti-cult' arguments reinforce these suspicions. Often, academic work is not understood in its own terms, but judged from the 'ideological' perspective of the 'anti-cult' stance – resulting in a clash of paradigms. As the ACM stance is as of necessity negative, anything that does not reinforce it must be dismissed or criticized.

Those in the 'cult-monitoring' field may not 'recognize' aspects of the phenomenon when seen from a different perspective. What is not recognized is contested or not believed. Therefore, what 'anti-cultists' recognize in academic writings as familiar or part of their experience, they agree with; if they do not, they reject, often 'rationalizing' rejection. This accounts for the ambivalence. An example is Barker's statement that 'cult' membership does, on average, not last beyond two years. The editorial of FAIR NEWS October 1987 (p. 1) commented:

> this opinion . . . has become almost a pet hate for those parents whose offspring have practically turned into permanent fixtures in some cult or other. . . . If cult involvement were really a short-term affair for the majority, counsellors might advise parents to sit back and wait with patience for junior to outgrow this fad which was merely part of his/her maturing process.

Further, FAIR had many parents on file whose children had been members for ten years or more (ibid.). Barker's statement was seen to belittle and minimize 'cult' involvement. However, it could be argued that an organization like FAIR is likely to attract those for whom 'cult' membership is of long standing and *not* those for whom it is of 'average' length.

Theory vs practice

'Anti-cultists' perceive a gap between academic theory and their day-to-day practical reality:

> Ever since the Jonestown tragedy and the *Daily Mail* trial made head-lines, people have been interested in cults, but for the majority . . . the interest is abstract and theoretical. . . . the theorists fall into two categories: the collectors and the debaters. In general the involve-ment of the collectors is fairly short-lived. They gather information for specific purposes, but their interest dies once their aims have been achieved. . . . The debaters are often academics whose involvement with the subject ranges from in-depth research to very superficial study. Many hold strong views which they defend . . . and much hairsplitting takes place.
>
> (*FAIR NEWS*, April 1985: 1)

The editorial of FAIR NEWS, June 1986, speaks of researchers in 'ivory towers'. Hence the complaint that the academic approach knows little, if anything, about human suffering and hence the comment that academics would 'change their tune' if one of their family joined. This aspect relates to the difference in interest between sociological research and 'anti-cult' con-cern, between wider social implications and focus on the individual. Thus statements about small proportions being affected by 'cult'-related problems are perforce rejected.

At the 1990 Annual Open Meeting, Lord Rodney did not attack the academic approach, but regarded it as questionable, because it disregards human suffering and damage to families, sits on the fence, and lends credibility to 'cults':

There are those – mostly academics – who set out to examine these cults in a cool and logical way: What motivates people to join them? Are they free agents? How long does the average member remain in a cult? and so forth. I have nothing against this approach, but I do not think those adopting it can quantify the human suffering involved. I do not wish ill on anyone, but let them have a loved one duped into joining a cult, and I wonder how detached they would remain. The other objection I have is that their association with these cults helps the groups in their search for credibility. Otherwise why are they welcomed at their meetings and featured in their newsletters? . . . I believe in the end you either consider the activities of cults anti-social, deceptive and destructive of family life – or you don't. I do not think we can sit on the fence.

(*FAIR NEWS*, Autumn 1990: 1)

In 1995, Audrey Chaytor expressed, albeit less sharply, concern for human suffering and the academic approach's inadequacy in dealing with it:

While acknowledging that much necessary and academic research has been done, these studies address the belief systems and not the suffering of relatives and close friends of cult members. Only we – and I do not mean only FAIR – are able to do that with compassion. I am convinced that the stance we have taken over the years, and which is echoed throughout Europe, is the right one for us.

(*FAIR NEWS*, Spring 1995: 2)

The editorial of *FAIR NEWS*, January 1987, also pointed to the duality of academic research: its rightful place and usefulness for counsellors, but its lop-sidedness if it disregards practical effects and implications. This view is echoed in the editorial of Winter 1992/93, which commented that academic research into beliefs and practices was useful and informative, but did not provide practical help for those involved.

FAIR's 1985 conference on 'Families and New Religions' made salient the differences in perspective between academics and FAIR supporters. The purpose was to hear from and question academics about their work.[45] The divisive topics revolved around three areas: (1) terminology regarding 'cults' vs. 'new religions': parents thought 'cults' did not deserve to be called 'religions', as this would afford them respectability and legal protection, although they did not behave like 'proper' religions; (2) parents' felt that academics were 'sitting on the fence' and did not appreciate their plight, as some academics had failed to consider the full effect of 'cult' practice on human relationships; (3) 'brainwashing'. The second topic reverberates in McCann's review of Kim Knott's (1986) *My Sweet Lord*. While welcomed as 'a slender yet valuable book' and a 'valuable addition to the growing British output of works on New Religions in the U.K.', it is 'a very uncritical work', because there is 'no serious treatment of all the worries of parents with sons or daughters in the Movement'. Also, 'F.A.I.R. and Deo Gloria are wheeled out as anti-cult organisations pursuing campaigns "against new religious groups like Hare Krishna" ' (*FAIR NEWS*, June 1986: 12–13).

Critiques of academic work

An example of academic findings being appraised in a neutral, if not positive, way is the critique of Barker's (1983c) paper on participants of UC workshops – here, findings chimed with FAIR's experience (*FAIR NEWS*, October 1982: 16). Also, at FAIR's AGM in 1985, McCann expressed thanks to British academics who made their knowledge and insight accessible and stated that, for the first time, FAIR felt less need to depend on American material (*FAIR NEWS*, October 1985: 1; McCann, 1986: 8). Yet, his review of Bob Mullan's *Life as Laughter* (1983) is rather unfavourable, because, first, Mullan's methods lack academic rigour, and second, his description of the 'anti-cult' groups in the UK and US is inaccurate.[46] The book appealed to Rajneesh followers, which raised questions about the author's impartiality. McCann finds the case studies on the followers wanting and criticizes the section on 'anti-cult' groups as dated and untrue.[47] Although the book is 'rushed, under-researched and poorly thought-out', McCann nevertheless recommends FAIR members to read it, as it has 'some worthwhile things to say' (*FAIR NEWS*, January 1984: 13).

McCann's review of Roy Wallis's *The Elementary Forms of the New Religious Life* (1984) is more balanced: although he finds fault, he draws attention to the aspects useful to FAIR and recommends openness towards academic work:

> Wallis's new book . . . will be of considerable use to members of FAIR, and it will force us to evaluate the quality and the variety of our responses. . . . It will also help us to evaluate material and publications on New Religious Movements. Wallis's book is not without its faults. It is expensive, in places well-written, and very often the assertions are cogently argued and stimulatingly presented. But I did detect more than a hint of intolerance towards opposing views (the work of Margaret Singer, for example, is much too cavalierly written off). . . . I would suggest that we in FAIR are working with more commitment and less self-interest than many academics in this field, but we should be open to exchanging views, ideas and information with them.
>
> (*FAIR NEWS*, July 1984: 16)

McCann deems James Beckford's *Cult Controversies* (1985) of limited use: apart from 'some rather good cameos' of the movements described and 'a crisp, extremely helpful and valuable progress through "The Moral Career of the Ex-Moonie" ', a 'realistic account of how Moonies leave the

Unification Movement', McCann judges it to be of 'scarce help' to those in FAIR. Again, the author failed to 'bring a touch of realism to a study of this kind', digressed into theoretical concerns by considering the term 'cult', and presents 'very jagged rather than clear thinking' in the chapter on 'cult' classification. The section on the 'anti-cult' campaign and FAIR is criticized: 'I did not recognise FAIR as Dr. Beckford described it which makes me worried about the quality of the rest of the commentary' (*FAIR NEWS*, October 1985: 18).

'Cult' associations

Academics who are or are seen to be close to 'cults' lend them credibility. For example, when *Unification News* of October 1985 featured *The Making of a Moonie* on its in-house publications page, this was considered proof of closeness.[48] Academics and public figures who take part in 'cult' organized conferences lose respectability and credibility in 'anti-cultist' eyes. Conferences organized by the UC and UC-affiliated organizations have featured most prominently. In many cases, especially to begin with, prospective participants were not aware of UC connections. The controversy arose particularly about participants who *knowingly* attended and accepted all-expenses-paid invitations. For example, after the ICUS (International Conference on the Unity of the Sciences, a UC branch) conference of November 1981, attended by 800 scholars, FAIR's newsletter (February 1982: 6) listed British participants.[49] Thus, when McCann reviewed Barker's (1982a) collection of conference papers, her close association with the UC was at issue:

> Mrs Barker ... is one of a group of academics whose name causes exasperation to some parents. ... This is partly due to a genuine worry about the extent to which in pursuing her research interests she may have compromised her academic impartiality by an overly close relationship with the Moonies. Eileen Barker is the best guardian of her conscience in this matter, but I ... remain convinced that her scholarly endeavours are honourable, helpful and ultimately worthwhile. ... There is cause for concern, however, over the question whether she is as wise and prudent as she might be in allowing herself to become so closely associated with the U.C. As the main academic and public commentator on the Unification Church, her academic respectability is tarnished by some of the less honourable pursuits of that group.
>
> (*FAIR NEWS*, October 1984: 16)

Although McCann accepts that the volume is 'of scholarly interest' and 'should be judged on that basis', it is of 'limited use' for those associated with FAIR. There is also a sideswipe regarding the contributors:

Most of the writers belong to that new Cult 'The Mutual Adoration Society' made up of 'Cult' academics whose central activity seems to be writing papers for each other, sponsoring conferences (however financed?) for each other, and reviewing each others' books and papers. Like all cults they have a leader. Whether she [Eileen Barker] has charisma or not, depends on whether or not you belong to the 'elect'. They also have a particular line on how their affairs and concerns should be viewed. They seem to be an inordinately complacent and self-satisfied lot of mystagogues.

(ibid.)

Other comments suggested that academics should apply their methods rigorously to lend credence to their findings, as Daphne Vane's reference to *The Making of a Moonie* indicates:

of those in research we ask that your objectivity remains paramount. The value of a recent sociological study on the Moonies was reduced because of its subjectivity. In my view this virtually nullified the results, thus undermining the intellectual credibility of the work.

(*FAIR NEWS*, January 1985: 1)

The review of Barker's (1989a) practical introduction to NRMs reinforces this point: if academics claim to be objective in their work, objectivity requires both sides of the argument:

there are . . . sections on which opinions are bound to be sharply divided, for example the chapter on brainwashing. Dr. Barker quotes freely from sources which back her own theory, namely that thought reform does not exist in the cult context, but she does not refer to the research of others, such as Dr. Margaret Singer, whose findings differ. Since the book is meant to be highly objective, both sides of the argument should have been given consideration.

(*FAIR NEWS*, Winter 1989/90: 15)

The same criticism goes for the chapter on atrocity tales, where ex-members accounts are dismissed, but reports about failed deprogrammings given full credit. However, there are sections 'which are useful, particularly . . . factual information, and . . . paragraphs . . . which correspond with findings by other authors and which can be endorsed'. Therefore, 'As an introduction to the topic Dr Barker's book is a useful addition to the literature already available'. Yet, there are no warnings about 'cult' membership, which could 'be considered as encouraging complacency' (ibid.: 14–15).

Another point of friction is the view that academics are taken in and used, when they conduct field research in 'cult' centres, take students to centres or invite 'cult' representatives to speak to students. They are shown what the 'cult' wants them to see, not the reality of grassroots members, and exposing students to 'blatant propaganda' may be considered 'irresponsible' (*FAIR NEWS*, June 1986: 10). Information gathered in 'showpiece situations' (which 'cult' organized conferences are) inevitably results in academics minimizing problems and adopting the view that parents exaggerate the situation:

> Many a theorist has fallen victim to clever PR promotions, accepting shows laid on at cult headquarters as a true picture of the group. . . . This almost inevitably leads to a condescending attitude towards worried parents. They are labelled 'clinging' and 'overreacting' and are advised in a patronising manner 'to accept that young people do leave home to do their own thing'. . . . The theorist underestimates the cults . . . and does not realise that they will exploit anybody (including the theorists themselves) and anything that might further their own ends.
>
> (*FAIR NEWS*, April 1985: 1)

An extreme case of academics being taken in by 'cults' is when they work for 'cult' owned academic institutions, as in the case of the University of Bridgeport, Connecticut, which was effectively taken over by a UC branch, Professors World Peace Academy (PWPA) in the early 1990s.[50]

Academic treatment of FAIR

Feeling misrepresented in academic writings may also account for FAIR's (and other groups') ambivalence towards academics. McCann stated that he did not recognize FAIR as described in *Cult Controversies* or *Life as Laughter*. Some academics have undoubtedly lumped 'anti-cult' groups into one category – 'the anti-cult movement' – while insisting that NRMs should *not* be lumped together, but examined individually in their specific chronological and geographical contexts. According to McCann (1986: 6), academics did not differentiate enough:

> It may be true sometimes that . . . people give utterance to views about Cults which whilst often very colourfully expressed are certainly condemnatory in tone. It would be wrong, however, to deduce from these isolated instances that this is all that is being said or done in the British 'Anti Cult Movement', so called. Many British academics have failed to note this, ignoring its reasonable reservations, and have sometimes adopted the standards of the tabloid press in their commentaries on it.

There are differences not only *between* various cult-monitoring groups, but also between voices and strands of thinking *within* them. They tend to support, and co-operate with, one another, because – despite actual and potential differences in approach – they see themselves in the same 'camp'. Thus, when necessary and expedient, 'political' alliances form.

McCann also accused academics of having judged British 'anti-cult' groups on the basis of their American counterparts: they 'have been guilty of borrowing models of "anti cult behaviour", more appropriate to America and Canada . . . and using them to attempt explanations of what they mistakenly believe is the same phenomena in the UK' (ibid.). This comment 'forgets' that American ACM groups had served as models for European groups and that these slowly developed their own style. It also 'forgets' that – at least in their formative years – British cult-monitoring groups judged 'cults' by reports and information received from the US.

FAIR and INFORM

When INFORM was officially launched in late 1987, FAIR declared that it would not co-operate closely, thus correcting a misrepresentation in the *Guardian* (16 September 1987):

> Though FAIR will watch developments with interest and an open mind, it has NOT been 'won over' by INFORM since that would amount to buying the proverbial pig in a poke. Furthermore, though we are willing to answer enquiries concerning factual information there is no question of 'opening our files' to INFORM or anybody else because of the confidential nature of our work. We would like to offer this assurance to our readers some of whom have already expressed concern.
>
> (*FAIR NEWS*, October 1987: 3–4)

One of the objections related to INFORM's claim to be the first organization to offer objective information:

> the researcher who ought to have been given credit for his undisputedly objective information is Dr. Peter Clarke of King's College . . . He has also given opportunity to other academics to publish articles and to give talks on the subject of New Religions. So INFORM's claim to being the first organisation to offer objective information is not altogether justified.
>
> (ibid.: 4)

FAIR NEWS, April 1988, reflected on enquiries received about INFORM and addressed some concerns. There was annoyance that INFORM should have received financial support from the government, when FAIR had been working in the field for twelve years *without* such support, despite providing government with advice and dealing with cases referred to FAIR. There was annoyance about INFORM's claim that advice given so far had been biased, sensational, and frightening. However, there was no evidence to substantiate rumours about INFORM receiving funding from 'cults'.

INFORM's professional approach was 'unaffected by . . . [religion's] emotional and spiritual power' and therefore, 'Dr. Barker is not aware of how powerful and dangerous and corrupting perverted religion can be, or what hold it can have over followers'. Further, as FAIR was still learning after years 'in the cult field', INFORM's relative inexperience, short-term assured funding (the initial grant covered three years), and ambitious projects made its future uncertain. However, existing cult-monitoring groups might hopefully co-operate successfully in the end (ibid.: 3).[51]

The report of the November 1989 INFORM Seminar again referred to its theoretical approach and the minimizing of risks and dangers of 'cult involvement':

> the overall impression . . . was that the whole cult topic was treated in a theoretical-abstract manner, with risks and dangers tuned down. For example, Dr. Barker stated . . . that while cults might pose problems for some, involvement in such groups was 'a positive experience for vast numbers of members'. 'Some have given thousands real benefits.'. . . There was little mention of such casualties during the seminar, nor was the plight of families taken up much. One was left with the impression that the cult problem was a molehill rather than a mountain.
>
> (FAIR NEWS, Winter 1989/90: 4, 5)

INFORM's claim about objective information accounted for strained relations:

> It was also pointed out . . . that the organisation came into being because information available up to then was 'grossly inaccurate' [and] 'causing unnecessary suffering'. Since INFORM claims to be highly objective, it seems strange that these sweeping statements are repeated again and again. . . . *This self-claim to high superiority has done much to create a barrier between INFORM and those who deal with the numerous casualties of cult involvement.*
>
> (FAIR NEWS, Winter 1989/90: 4–5; emphasis added)

Despite some rapprochement in recent years, relations between INFORM and FAIR have remained somewhat strained.

A difference in roles

McCann rightly drew attention to the different roles of academics and FAIR: although they work the same ground, they work for different reasons, use different tools, and pursue different aims. McCann (1986: 8) employs the metaphor of botanist and gardener:

> If some academics, viewing some of the exotic new plants in the Kew

Gardens of religious development have been concerned with growth patterns, seeding etc., then FAIR's role has been that of the gardener trying to ensure that the new plants grow in an orderly way (and that may mean some pruning too!), and do not like ivy stifle the growth of other valuable plants.

While, in McCann's view, the gardener's role is not an 'ignoble task', one might add, the botanist's isn't either. However, gardeners and botanists may be in competition with, and antagonistic towards, one another in the pursuit of their aims and choice of methods. This would explain disagreements and conflicts between them.

FAIR and the State

From its very beginnings, FAIR wanted government and public authorities to support its aims. Rose was convinced that State action was required to remedy the situation and therefore raised the question in Parliament. By lobbying constituency MPs, peers, and MEPs, FAIR has sought to bring the matter to politicians' attention. In 1983, FAIR met with civil servants in the Home Office, DHSS, and Department of Education and Science to discuss immigration law, charitable status, children's education in 'cults', National Insurance contributions, and illegal street collections. FAIR's efforts have had mixed results: 'cult' concerns on the agenda of both Houses alternated with apparent lack of interest.

With Lord Rodney as chair, FAIR had a spokesperson in the very agencies where it wanted to be heard, for example, in the House of Lords which debated the issue in February 1988, thanks to his initiative. However, Lord Rodney's death weakened this link, leaving FAIR with the impression that interest in its concerns is meagre, as Audrey Chaytor declared:

> the All Party Committee of the House of Commons appears to have waned. Lord Rodney worked so hard to keep that Committee together . . . with one or two exceptions only, I usually find a very poor response from the House of Commons. I know how busy they can be, but there is a very good reason that they should support FAIR, and that is that we are the organisation which cares for their constituents when they have serious problems and when others would have given up. I am aware that other organisations supply information but none give the family back up which we give.
>
> (*FAIR NEWS*, October 1994: 3–4)

FAIR's disappointment dates back to Rose's time as an MP; he 'had very little support or even understanding and sympathy when he sought to alert Government and other officials to the dangers of cults' (*NEWSLETTER*, June 1981: 1).

FAIR feels that most of its 'sister organizations' in Europe receive at least some government backing, while its applications for funding and charitable status have been unsuccessful. In 1988, the Home Office turned down an application for a grant, because it already supported work in this field by funding INFORM. FAIR's intense pursuit of charitable status in the early 1980s proved fruitless. In FAIR's view, governments in other countries have taken 'cult' issues more seriously, not only in supporting 'cult-monitoring' groups financially, but also in taking direct action. In Austria and Germany, government ministries have issued publications for information and prevention and notified youth advice centres, when the British government seemingly ignored the problem. Recent measures in France, such as the Interministerial Mission and the About-Picard Law have reinforced this view.

The Cottrell Report

The Cottrell Report promised to address the 'cult' issue across Europe and initiate concerted action across national borders. FAIR met (in late 1982) and co-operated with Richard Cottrell and *FAIR NEWS* followed the progress from preliminary to full report and the responses it elicited. Although FAIR welcomed the document as a basis for debate in the European Parliament, it did not entirely concur:

> We have been concerned that *government* needs to take the cult problem seriously. In this . . . area, we have contributed to the Cottrell investigations and report to the European Parliament by making submissions, and by encouraging parents to do the same. We have not agreed with all Mr Cottrell's conclusions, but we are grateful that cults have now become a matter of international concern.
>
> (*FAIR NEWS*, October 1983: 1)

FAIR NEWS expressed appreciation of the adoption of Cottrell's resolution (in May 1984) and considered its code of practice an important step forward, although it was to be voluntary and its implementation thus depended on 'cults'. The code sought to remedy some of the relatives' grievances (Cottrell, 1984; Wilshire, 1984: 10–11), but sparked a heated debate about religious freedom. Pete Broadbent considered the code a major achievement:

> Perhaps the most significant feature of the past year has been the resolution by the European Parliament . . . There is now an important battle to be won to ensure that the code of practice . . . is implemented and negotiated with the cults, so that they are seen to be accountable and able to be called into question for any corrupt and despicable practices.
>
> (*FAIR NEWS*, October 1984: 1)[52]

In the wake of the Report, both Houses of Parliament gave the 'cult' issue some attention. This was encouraging to groups like FAIR, although no direct measures resulted from the debates.

In May 1984, Richard Needham, then MP for Wiltshire North, raised a constituent's case in the House of Commons (he died after having become schizophrenic in the aftermath of an Exegesis training[53]), calling on the government to help prevent such cases. In his response, David Mellor, then Parliamentary Under-Secretary of State in the Home Office, stated that 'the sinister activities of some of the groups must be exposed by every means possible and most vigorously discouraged', while pointing out that individual freedom tied the hands of government (*Hansard*, 14.5.1984: 124–127). This is a typical example of ministerial statements regarding 'cults': any problems which contravene existing law will result in appropriate action, but government is bound by that very law and committed to upholding individual freedoms. Mellor also paid tribute to FAIR and Deo Gloria and referred to the Attorney General's efforts to remove two UC-connected charities from the register of charities.

When the House of Lords debated 'cults' on 11 July 1984, Lady Elliot of Harwood enquired about government action to monitor the activities of 'religious cults'. Lord Elton, then Parliamentary Under-Secretary of State in the Home Office, stated that 'cults' were under scrutiny and allegations of illegality were fully investigated. Again, the right to charitable status was challenged, but the debate ended without firm conclusions.

In October 1984, David Alton, a Liberal MP,[54] introduced a Private Member's bill, which had 'one simple aim and provision – to allow parents and next of kin rights of access to relatives who have joined religious cults'. He quoted from two sample letters from parents and raised the issues of charitable status and deception (*Hansard*, 24.10.1984: 707–709). Lack of time prevented the bill from proceeding past its second reading. Alton had, however, gained support from MPs whose constituents had approached them about 'cults'; their interest and concern again encouraged FAIR. While it hoped for further research on the matter, it anticipated that legislation would create tension and criticism from those concerned about religious freedom. David Alton also asked the Secretary of State for the Home Office about the latter's response to Cottrell's resolution. David Mellor's written answer stalled: nothing could be said before the reactions of various parties and other member governments had been evaluated (*Hansard*, 31.10.1984: 979).

Legislation and religious freedom

FAIR was aware that government action against 'cults' had to be balanced against individual rights and freedoms:

> In this country, we have lobbied MPs to see that existing laws are

properly enforced, but we are loath to press for the kind of measures of intolerance and curtailment of religious and political liberties which are often advocated by parents in the USA.

(*FAIR NEWS*, October 1983: 1)

Cottrell's resolution emphasized that the validity of religious beliefs was not in question, but the lawfulness of recruitment practices and members' treatment was – precisely FAIR's view. FAIR concurred with the reference to Article 9 of the European Convention for the Protection of Human Rights, which the European Parliament's legal affairs committee had endorsed in February 1984. The 'cult' problem should thus be embedded in the context of human rights – a view reflected in FAIR's 'mission statement'.

FAIR concluded from the Cottrell Report that 'cult'-related problems would be solved by implementing existing laws and the report's recommendations, not by *new* legislation:

We already have the legislation we need. What is required is implementation. Calling the cults into question when they break street trading law, when they interfere with the rights of minors, when they flout immigration laws, when they interfere with families' access to each other. It would be a mistake for FAIR to become involved with the strident call of the intolerant who would seek to have cults proscribed and banned.

(*FAIR NEWS*, October 1984: 1)

Chairman Dawson reinforced this view in 1986 (*FAIR NEWS*, October 1986: 1): it had also been the conclusion of Alain Vivien's report to the French Assembly in 1983, although that report had suggested new legal proposals (Vivien, 1985).[55] At the 1996 FAIR Meeting, Tom Sackville, then Home Office minister with – as he stated – 'nominal responsibility for cults', affirmed the need to respect existing law and the difficulty of framing new legislation – the very reasons why, as Rose had pointed out, government had so far not had the courage to tackle the problem. Sackville personally wished for action, but ministerial duty bound him. The government's excessive neutrality to date was now replaced by opposition to, and willingness to fight, 'cults'. This could, however, not proceed further, as Sackville lost his seat in the following elections.

Europe after the Cottrell report

After Cottrell's resolution was adopted, the matter was referred to the Council of Europe to achieve a common approach within that context. The Council's legal affairs committee received the matter as late as 1987, when the Council members were asked about the legal status of 'cults' in their countries. The British response was that religious associations may set up tax-exempt charitable trusts if they match the classifications defined in law and that public authorities supported INFORM. Meanwhile, in late November 1988, Richard Cottrell called for a Royal Commission to investigate 'cults' and 'religious sects' in Britain, as the government had failed to understand the significance of the problem. In February 1992, the Council of Europe's Parliamentary Assembly considered how abuse in the name of religion could be regulated without violating religious freedom. The Assembly did not see the need for new laws, but deliberated the official registration of religious movements, an idea suggested by Sir John Hunt, MP for Ravensbourne, who delivered a report on sects and new religious movements on behalf of the Committee on Legal Affairs and Human Rights. The Committee of Ministers favoured information, but rejected registration, because states should not be invited to take steps 'based on a value judgment concerning cults and beliefs . . . it being understood that members of sects should respect the law of the country'. This went against Cottrell's proposed harmonization of tax exemption and charity status across Europe and thus against a statute creating a Europe-wide legal structure for charities and voluntary organizations.

The policy was reaffirmed in February 1996, when the European Parliament adopted another 'Resolution on Cults in Europe'. It refers to the Convention on Human Rights, the Charter on the Rights of the Child, and to the Council of Europe's recommendations. It reaffirms the basic principles of democracy and law, including freedom of conscience and religion, and calls on member states to ensure that legal authorities and police make effective use of existing legal provisions, to co-operate actively and more closely, to ascertain whether their judicial, fiscal, and penal provisions are adequate to prevent unlawful actions, not to grant legal status automatically, and to accelerate exchange of information.

In November 1996, the European Parliament's Civil Liberties and Internal Affairs Committee met representatives of the corresponding committees of the member states, with a full report announced for 1997. Again, the importance of religious freedom was underlined, as was the differentiation between (legitimate) 'sects' and groups under the guise of 'religion', for which criteria were outlined. Differences between member states regarding the 'sect' phenomenon were pointed out. On 15 April 1998, the Committee passed Resolution 134, which invites member states to 'take measures, in compliance with the principles of legality, with a view to fighting abuses caused to people by certain sects which should be denied the status of cult or religious organisation endowing them with certain tax advantages and legal protection'.

Charitable status

The areas in which FAIR has most wanted government to be proactive are charitable status and education of the public, as Rose emphasized in his address to the 1996 meeting:

The continued benefits given by charitable status and the archaic libel laws that allow them to silence criticism, together with the lack of education afforded to the general public through Government agencies, are all matters that should be pressed by FAIR in the coming months before a General Election.

There had been reason to hope for action regarding charitable status since the judge's verdict of the *Daily Mail* libel case. In May 1982, Mrs Thatcher was asked to speed up this process, but the Charity Commission required more information. There was concern that no action would be taken before the appeal in the libel case judgement in November 1983. After the Charity Commissioners had refused twice to hold an inquiry under the 1980 Charities Act, Sir Michael Havers, (then) Attorney General, called on them again in early 1983 to remove the two UC-associated trusts and began proceedings for an inquiry through the High Court. However, in April 1983, the idea of fighting a test case against the Charity Commission was abandoned, because it would have given the UC a reprieve. Yet, in June 1983, Treasury solicitors were instructed to prepare the High Court challenge and in January 1985, the Attorney General issued a summons against the UC. In February 1985, the (then) Home Secretary, Leon Brittan, indicated he would welcome a parliamentary investigation into 'cult' activities in the light of the Attorney General's proceedings regarding the UC's charitable status and willingness to look at other groups.

In his reply to Tom Sackville, the Attorney General, now Sir Patrick Mayhew, stated on 3 February 1988 that proceedings had been discontinued, because 'the totality of evidence now available to me is insufficient to enable me to substantiate any of those particular allegations to the extent needed to rebut the strong legal presumption of charitable status that English law gives to any religion' (*Hansard*, 3.2.1988: 978). On 15 February 1988, Sir Patrick confirmed this in response to David Wilshire's question whether any new evidence was likely to reverse the decision. Thus, the debate in the House of Lords on 10 February 1988, initiated by Lord Rodney, had had no impact on the government's position. Lord Rodney had voiced concern about lack of government intervention, disappointment about the Attorney General's decision, and reservations about INFORM and its government funding (*Hansard*, 10.2.1988).[56] Nor was the meeting which Lord Rodney, Tom Sackville, and John Hunt had with the Home Secretary to air similar concerns in March 1988 of any avail. In early 1989, Alan Meale, MP for Mansfield, called for an Inland Revenue investigation into a printing firm whose manager was director of a UC business and into the UC's businesses. He asked the minister for the Home Office, (then) John Patten, whether he would accept a delegation on this matter.

The controversy about the Attorney General's decision had also resulted in calls to change charity law. This led to a White Paper in 1989, 'Charities: A Framework for the Future' (HMSO, 1989), expected 'with great interest' by 'cult-monitoring' groups because of possible effects on 'extremist religious cults'. The chapter on 'Charitable Status' included a three-page section on religion and references to 'cults'. In November 1989, the debate on the White Paper in the House of Lords did mention 'religious cults' (*Hansard*, 30.11.1989). In a *Guardian* article (9 January 1991), which argued that existing law was not sufficient to protect the public against 'cult' activities, David Wilshire, then chairman of the all-party parliamentary group on 'cults', expressed his disappointment about the government's intention not to change the law, although he spoke of the 'creative use' of existing legislation, by strengthening trade description and consumer protection.

Overall, in FAIR's view, the government has not done enough to combat 'cults' and their activities, despite the commitment of some MPs and MEPs. Rose explains why:

> We also faced, and still face, the fact that neither Government . . . nor the Charity Commissioners have ever had the courage to confront this problem. Part of the reason is the difficulty in differentiating quite benign groups from those that are dangerous, and another difficulty is our total commitment to freedom of speech and religious belief. . . . successive governments have failed to come to grips with the reality of the misery caused by various cults, notwithstanding the efforts . . . [of some] Parliamentarians and persons outside Parliament who have brought to their attention these activities.

FAIR's endeavour to involve government and public authorities in its campaign against 'cults' has thus had mixed results: FAIR has been able to catch the attention of ministers and both Houses of Parliament, but has also experienced disappointment about apparent lack of concern. FAIR's hopes that charity law would be used against 'cults' were dashed, despite changes to this law in the late 1980s. On the European level, FAIR co-operated with Richard Cottrell and welcomed the European Parliament's resolution, especially the recommended code of conduct. However, due to concerns about individual and religious freedoms (strongly voiced by established churches and denominations), the Cottrell Report did not lead to any major measures in Britain or Europe. The activities of FECRIS and its links with the French government suggest an alternative approach to activate Europe's political institutions.

Conclusions

Just as 'cults' have changed and adapted to the prevailing situation in their host societies over time, 'cult monitoring' groups have undergone change. While they have sustained their messages and aims, they have adapted in presenting and pursuing these. Initially, FAIR – like other 'cult-monitoring' groups – looked towards the United States for an explanation of the emerging 'cult' phenomenon and its attraction for young people. This was because 'cults' appeared there first, before making an impact in the UK and Continental Europe. Groups like FAIR assumed that experiences accumulated in the US would automatically apply to the European context. Thus, explanatory models proposed by John Clark, Margaret Singer, Robert Lifton, and Edgar Schein, some of whom had collaborated (Singer and Schein, 1958), were taken on board. Clark and Singer produced their first papers in 1977 (Clark, 1977; Singer, 1977), when cult-monitoring groups were beginning to form in Europe. Only slowly have other models been considered, after academics in Britain became interested in NRMs, began field research, and developed an alternative explanatory framework. As Casey McCann mentioned, with the growth of academic work in the UK, FAIR relied less on material from the US. Another aspect of change is reflected in FAIR's replacement of 'rescue' with 'resource' as the last term in its acronym.

Further, FAIR has sought to involve a range of professionals in its work to broaden its horizons and place the 'cult' issue into wider social contexts. One of these has been medicine and psychiatry, where conversion and membership are treated as mental health problems. Robbins and Anthony (1982) speak of the 'medicalization' of deviant religious groups, arguing that this is a conceptualization which has consolidated the 'anti-cult' coalition. The medical framework has remained, even if it has been broadened, as FAIR conferences on 'post-traumatic stress disorders' and 'influence and stress related issues' illustrate. FAIR has engaged political processes, such as lobbying, and media contacts to keep awareness of its campaign fresh, although the media have been a somewhat mixed blessing in that FAIR has at times been subjected to a distorting 'media treatment'.

FAIR originally set out as a small group of people sharing a common interest. From this evolved an established organization with national and international connections, which Rose considers an important pressure group. Two of its chairmen, Pete Broadbent and Lord Rodney, initiated a process of reflection and re-evaluation of how FAIR worked, used its resources, and should shape its future. *FAIR NEWS* repeatedly stated that FAIR's ultimate aim was to become redundant, yet while 'cults' existed, FAIR had an important role to play. While the closure of its office suggests shrinking structures and demand for its services, FAIR's presence (since 2000) on the internet (www.fair-cult-concern.co.uk) suggests a new stage, one in which 'modern' technology assists with resources and dissemination.

THE ACM RESPONSE IN GERMANY: THE CASE OF ELTERNINITIATIVE

This section deals with *Elterninitiative zur Hilfe gegen seelische Abhängigkeit und religiösen Extremismus e.V.* (Parents' Initiative for Help against Mental Dependency and Religious Extremism), a parents' organization in

Munich, the first to form in Germany in the mid-1970s. Being the first of its kind makes this association important, as does the significant role which Pastor Friedrich-Wilhelm Haack played in founding it and shaping its understanding of 'cult' membership. This section describes how *Elterninitiative* was created, what aims it pursues, and how it perceives its campaign in relation to 'cults' and wider society. The place of *Elterninitiative*'s work within 'anti-cult' or 'cult-monitoring' activity in Germany is assessed, with reference to its links with similar organizations, government, public authorities, political parties, and institutions concerned with the protection of youth. Areas of common concern and difference between FAIR and *Elterninitiative* are explored and evaluated.

Ei's history

Elterninitiative zur Hilfe gegen seelische Abhängigkeit und religiösen Extremismus e.V. (EI e.V., Ei, or *Münchener Elterninitiative*) is a direct counterpart to FAIR in Britain in that it is the first parents' organization in Germany. As with FAIR, little is written about *Ei* so that information has to be extracted from its publications, such as the proceedings of its tenth anniversary conference (Haack *et al.*, 1986) and two volumes published on the occasion of its twentieth anniversary (Elterninitiative, 1995; 1996); the first is a collection of essays written by close collaborators, the second includes proceedings of the conference held in 1995. Unlike FAIR, *Elterninitiative* does not publish a newsletter.[57] Like FAIR, it was founded to provide advice and support for those affected by 'cult' membership in their families.

Elterninitiative's founding date is September 1975 (Dürholt and Kroll, 1994: 54; Haack *et al.*, 1986: 57; Schuster, 1986: 6). It claims to be the oldest and biggest organization of its kind (Haack, 1984b: 44), with a nationwide membership of around 500 (Elterninitiative, 1996: appendix). The impetus for its creation came from relatives who kept asking the *Sektenbeauftragte* (designated clergy specializing in gathering and disseminating information about 'sects' and in pastoral care for affected relatives) where parents and relatives could meet, exchange information, and offer help to each other. As in FAIR's case, there was then no provision for counselling affected parents (Schneider, 1995: 187).

Pastor Haack suggested the name of the new association. The 'novel elements' were 'parents' initiative' and 'religious extremism'. The first term was to indicate the concern of parents, regardless of whether their children were involved in 'cults'[58] and to emphasize that it was *parents* who were affected when their children joined. The second term was to indicate that *Ei* was not opposed to religion or religious groups, but to organizations which considered themselves and their teachings in absolute and exclusive terms, namely those which did not feel bound by generally accepted norms of behaviour and used methods which undermined individuals as responsible and mature social beings (Haack *et al.*, 1986: 88–89).

Ei's aims

At its constituent meeting, Ei's aims and purpose were outlined as follows:

> The Association aims to assist parents and young people to become free of the patronising pupilage of extremist religious groups. In the first instance, the work of the Association is directed to those who are affected by the 'new youth religions'. Further, the Association will take preventative measures by informing the public and the authorities [about the activities of 'youth religions']. Co-operation with similar associations on an international level shall provide help in cases where the activities of the 'new youth religions' go beyond state boundaries and are thus placed in a different legal context.
>
> (ibid.: 88)[59]

One of Ei's main activities thus consists in gathering and providing information about 'sects' (Sekten), Jugendreligionen (youth religions), 'guru movements', and 'therapy cults' (Psychokulte) – all terms coined by Pastor Haack. Ei also offers parents and relatives the opportunity to meet others like them so that they can compare notes, give each other advice, and share each other's experiences (Dürholt and Kroll, 1994: 54).

As indicated in its statutes, Ei is also engaged in Aufklärungsarbeit – disseminating information, warning the public against 'cult' membership, and providing information about consequences of membership for families and members. Schuster (1986: 7), an Ei committee member, also emphasizes the importance of informing the public and raising public awareness about Jugendreligionen. This includes consultation with politicians and public officials and support for political or legal action against 'cults'. Ei refutes the accusation by some Jugendreligionen that its work violates religious freedom. It argues (as does Haack) that although this freedom is enshrined in the Grundgesetz (constitution), this does not rule out critical discussion of ideologies, religions, or the behaviour of those who represent these. It points out that the constitution also guarantees freedom of expression, which is as fundamental a right as religious freedom.

Haack (1990a: 77) describes 'parents' initiatives' as an umbrella term for organizations whose members' relatives are in 'youth religions', 'guru movements', 'therapy cults' or 'destructive cults'. Members of parents' initiatives do not consider their children's new religious orientation as an enrichment. The term 'parents' initiatives' also refers to organizations which are not strictly speaking parents' associations, but information centres or 'anti-cult' groups.[60] All these organizations pursue the following aims: mutual assistance for members and informing the public about 'cults', problems they cause, and consequences of membership. Mucha (1988: 69–71) of Aktion Psychokultgefahren e. V. in Düsseldorf shows how parents' initiatives advise and support parents.

Pastor Haack's role

Pastor Haack had been instrumental in setting up and shaping *Ei*: he was one of the key founding members and served as *Ei*'s chairman or committee member until his death in 1991 (Dürholt and Kroll, 1994: 56). At this point, *Ei* needed to review its work (Westhoven, 1995: 212). Ach (1995a: 31) hints at internal dissension, apparently related to a faction which wanted to dispense with Haack altogether. However, some people had joined *Ei* because of their acquaintance with Haack. In the late 1990s, board members included Bernd Dürholt, Ilse Kroll, Ursula Höft, and Karl H. Schneider, and Willi Röder (chair). Udo Schuster (1988), another long-standing member, has been politically active in the federal committee of *Junge Union*.

The close co-operation with Pastor Haack provided *Ei* with a publishing outlet, as his *Arbeitsgemeinschaft für Religions- und Weltanschauungsfragen* (ARW) provided the facilities. The volume edited by Dürholt and Kroll (1994)[61] and the two anniversary volumes (Elterninitiative, 1995; 1996) are ARW publications. Also, some of Haack's books (e.g. 1984b) include brief descriptions of *Ei*.

Ei's self-perception

Elterninitiative describes itself as group of 'concerned' people – the German word is *betroffen*, which can mean 'concerned' in the sense of 'affected'/ 'concerned' or 'worried'/'troubled'. Both meanings are implied in this context: parents whose children are members of a *Jugendreligion*, young people who were (would-be) members or have friends who joined, and 'concerned citizens' who consider such religious groups dangerous for adherents and society (Haack, 1984b: 45). Schuster (1995: 198) speaks of a 'challenge' for society, a term often used in this context (e.g. Behnk, 1996a) – a bibliographic search reveals in some 40 publications using 'challenge' in the title alone.

Ei has on the whole adopted Haack's terminology: it speaks of *Jugend-religionen*, but also of *destruktive Kulte* (destructive cults) – the latter a direct translation from the English – as an umbrella term for various types of movements and, when used by parents, to stress the 'destructive' aspect (Haack *et al.*, 1986: 57, 60). In this sense it is intended as a value judgement, the very reason why *Elterninitiative* (1985: 1) thinks it should not be used, because this precludes change and correction in the groups thus described. *Ei* points out that Haack's *Jugendreligionen* (a term coined in the mid-1970s) was intended to be neutral and replace 'destructive cults', but it, too, turned into a value judgement over time, an observation also made by Haack. However, *Elterninitiative zur Wahrung der Geistigen Freiheit e.V. in Leverkusen* uses the term in the title of its newsletter and *Sekten-Info Essen e.V.* (n.d.: 4) considers the term 'appropriate'.

Some of *Ei*'s supporters are clergy or people working for the churches or for other religious communities. They feel 'concerned' because, in their view, 'extremist groups' distort religion's fundamental purpose, which is to serve humankind, an idea upheld by the churches. *Ei* supporters consider it 'wrong' and 'dangerous', when 'good' or 'bad' are judged solely by 'religious' groups' own standards, and regard it as 'extremely dubious', when 'good' equates to 'useful for the group' and 'bad' equates to 'harmful for the group' (Haack, 1984b: 45; Haack *et al.*, 1986: 61).

However, despite co-operation and support from clergy and churches, *Ei* has never considered itself an extension of the churches. It wants to help 'victims of businesses disguised as religion', and offer help and advice to relatives so that they can cope. It does not campaign against other faiths (Schuster, 1986: 6). Pastor Wolfgang Behnk, Haack's successor, comments that *Ei* is inter-denominational and not formally connected with either mainstream church. There has, however, been a bond of solidarity with the churches and their 'sect experts' (Behnk himself is an *Ei* member), but *Ei* is neither an affiliated branch of, nor a combat troop for, the churches, but an independent body which co-operates with the churches in matters of concern to every citizen. The churches' solidarity with parents is connected with their view of apologetics: this involves not just theoretical discussion of non-Christian theologies, but pastoral care and service for others (Behnk, 1995: 61, 64). Schuster (1995: 198) is critical of those in the church who do not interpret apologetics in this sense and practise 'misunderstood dialogue and liberality' by allowing 'cults' to serve their purposes.

Wolfgang Götzer, a member of the *Bundestag* (Parliament) and its Committee for Youth, Family and Health, who contributed to the conference marking *Ei*'s tenth anniversary, also refers to this kind of criticism: parents are accused of being the churches' menials in their campaign against any religious minorities considered to be outside the constitutional order. Some within the churches take such criticism on board and, guided by misunderstood liberality, call for less action in this matter. However, this accusation is inapplicable and careful evidence is needed to document in each case that criticism is well founded and does not stem from blanket condemnation (Götzer, 1986: 35). However, in Schneider's (1995: 187) view, *Ei*'s association with a church organization was necessary at the beginning, but turned into an Achilles' heel for its cause. For some time, public authorities simply referred enquiries about 'cults' to church institutions. This delayed the wider discussion of this 'social-psychological phenomenon'.[62]

Some *Ei* members are volunteers, some are full-time workers (Elterninitiative, 1995). Manfred Ach, a volunteer, was one of the earliest members. He juggled a full-time job, family, and the tasks of an *Ei* committee member and *Ei Referent*, a public speaker for 'cult'-related issues, as the personal account of his 15 years' membership describes (Ach, 1995a). Ach was one of the members whose involvement resulted from close co-operation with Haack: together they set up the publishing arm, *Arbeitsgemeinschaft für Religions- und Weltanschauungsfragen*.

Ei and its members see their work as a service to society, because 'religious radicals who wish to bring about their aims by using political and economic means are not an asset to society'. *Ei* rejects the idea that 'total freedom' can be effected by 'total discipline' and that a 'democracy of the heart where everyone directs their heart towards God's will' should make people uniform. Many families have experienced the consequences of such extreme forms of religion: young people leave their careers, hand over their possessions, break contact with family and friends, and change totally. Those who cannot share such concerns should imagine someone close to them involved with such religious groups, turning away from them after undergoing 'soul-washing' (another term coined by Haack to replace 'brainwashing'), and unreceptive to any critical discussion. However, *Ei* does, of course, not wish this on anyone.

Ei believes that 'cults' exploit a growing tendency in society which is to avoid social problems and tensions. It believes that 'cults' use manipulative techniques and close-knit organizational structures to exert influence over members. The destructive effect of this can lead to what *Ei* considers an 'irreversible psycho-pathological change of personality'. Society will have to deal with people damaged by 'cult' membership and they will be a social burden.

There is also concern about children in 'cults' and their socialization in institutions outside established social contexts. They will grow up having little, if anything, in common with wider culture. *Ei* does not offer patent or blanket solutions, only thoughts and suggestions based on personal experience (Haack, 1984b: 45–46; Schuster, 1986: 7–8). Children in 'cults' is a recurrent theme in *Ei*'s (e.g. Nußbaum, 1996) publications (and FAIR's). One of the *Sektenexperten* published a book about the topic (Eimuth, 1996a; 1992c) and the German media have also taken up the subject (*Der Spiegel* 18, 1997: 86–99).

Ei's models

In his contribution to *Ei*'s tenth anniversary volume (Haack *et al.*, 1986), Haack states that the concept of *Ei* was without precedent, although its foundation had been inspired by similar groups in the US and France. He refers in particular to CERF (Citizens Engaged in Reuniting Families), which arose from Rabbi Maurice Davis's pastoral concerns, and quotes CERF's aims as representing the overall aims of parents' initiatives. ADFI was an inspirational mentor for *Ei*'s foundation (it had set out to protect parents and young people against the destructive activities of 'politico-religious sects') and Haack's personal contacts with ADFI were a major factor in *Ei*'s foundation process. *Ei* in turn served as a blueprint for similar groups in Germany. Just as FAIR was, initially, primarily concerned with the UC's activities, *Ei*'s early work also focused on this movement. Its remit widened, as parents with children in other movements joined (Haack, 1986b: 88, 108–109, 112; 1986c: 57–58; 1990a: 77–78).

Haack stresses that all parents' initiatives share the concern for the *family*, an aspect reflected in their names and aims and in their rejection of unlawful acts, including the practice of deprogramming. The prime motive for parents' groups was to do their work 'with the greatest care and responsibility', not to embark on a crusade against 'cults' (Haack, 1986c: 58–59).

The role of parents

Elterninitiative had seven founding members: a concerned couple (whose daughter had been involved with the UC),[63] a lawyer, two clergymen (Haack and another clergyman with experience in UC matters), the wife of a clergyman (Haack's wife), and the then *Sektenbeauftragte* of the Roman Catholic Church (Hans Löffelmann). Other parents present at the foundational meeting did not want their names included in the list of founding members, although they became members (Haack, 1986b: 88, 90, 101, 112; 1986c: 60; Schuster, 1986: 6). As parents constituted a *minority* in the founding process, the role of parents in the creation and operation of parents' initiatives across Germany has been an issue. Often, as Haack concedes, individuals not immediately affected by 'cults' provided the initial impetus for creating parents' groups: those 'concerned' about the issue, some 'concerned Christians', some 'concerned citizens'. 'Cults' and occasionally members of parents' groups raised this issue. Scientology, for example, spoke of fraudulent labels (*Etikettenschwindel*), suggesting that parents' initiatives were 'instruments' of the *Sektenbeauftragten*. Haack points out that 'cults' attacked parents' initiatives, because the latter's criticism interfered with their aims.[64]

Parents with children in 'cults' tended not get too involved and avoided, for example, committee membership. The reasons are the same as for the British parents associated with FAIR: parents shun publicity, because they fear detrimental consequences for the relationship with their child and/or negative repercussions for their child. Haack explains that, from the beginning, *Ei*'s committee was to include individuals who could not be blackmailed on account of their children's membership, were well-informed about the issue, and had relatively secure jobs. With regard to the latter, Haack refers to Scientology's attempts to undermine critics to the point of jeopardizing their livelihoods. There were attempts to sow discord in parents' initiatives and heated debates took place internally about aims and methods (Haack, 1986b: 89–91, 91–99, 101; 1986c: 60, 61).

Haack points to *Ei*'s beneficial effect in that its existence changed the attitude of officials and public authorities. Parents found that these began to take their concerns more seriously, while they had often felt 'blamed' for their children's membership before (Haack, 1986b: 101). Karbe (1980: 33), whose daughter got involved with the UC in the mid-1970s, also refers to parents feeling 'blamed'. He became AGPF's deputy chairman and had been, according to Thiel (1986: 86–91), one of the main driving forces for setting it up.

The idea of self-help

Parents' organizations consider their work as a service to society, alongside their primary aim of supporting affected families. They see themselves as organizations which help people to help themselves (*Selbsthilfe-Organisationen*) – hence the term *Selbsthilfe* in some names, such as *Baden-Württembergische Eltern- und Betroffeneninitiative zur Selbsthilfe gegen destruktive Kulte* (EBIS e.V.) – organizations within a society based on democracy and tolerance, consisting of people who recognized social peril and wish to do something about it. This work has humanitarian and political aims. *Selbsthilfe* includes regular meetings for parents – often attended by those who cannot or do not wish to join formally – to discuss matters which concern them and offer advice (Haack, 1986b: 114). Schuster, co-editor of *Ei*'s tenth anniversary volume (Haack *et al.*, 1986), chose *Hilfe zur Selbsthilfe* (Helping People to Help Themselves) as the title of his preface (Schuster, 1986). He uses John F. Kennedy's well-known slogan to describe *Ei*'s motto: 'Don't ask what the State can do for you, but what you can do for the State.' Those who have faced 'cult' membership in the family are able to assist others in this situation by offering advice and sharing experience. The motives for getting involved with a parents' initiative vary: 'cult' membership in the family, a wish to warn others against the hazards of membership, a perception (by Christians and members of other religions) of 'cults' endangering society (Haack, 1986c: 62).

The work of parents' initiatives has been effective in alerting public and government agencies about 'cult' activities. They were, for instance, instrumental in bringing about the European Parliament's resolution, just as parents in Britain contributed to the Cottrell Report. Institutions and companies have been warned about 'front' organizations so that management and training courses connected with them were cancelled, just as FAIR has alerted 'unsuspecting' people to such activities. *Ei* published a directory (Elterninitiative, 1985) to help enquirers identify 'front' organizations, a list later incorporated in Haack's (1990a) *Findungshilfe* (register).

Parents' initiatives have offered care for former members, but there is still a perceived need for a comprehensive project.[65] In Haack's (1986c: 78–79) view, groups like *Ei* could give an impetus to 'research' by identifying suitable scientists and use results for its work. Haack does, however, not mean *social scientific* research. He (1986c: 79) rejects as 'irrelevant' the research in Kehrer's (1981a) edited volume, the 'Tübinger Studie', as he calls it. He rejects the 'Vienna Study' (Berger and Hexel, 1981a) as an 'ideological tract'. Given his influence on *Ei*, it is highly likely that *Ei* members subscribe to Haack's views on this topic. These chime with the aim of FECRIS, which consists in identifying suitable areas of research and commissioning appropriate researchers.

According to Haack (1986b: 113–114), *Ei* members played a leading role in creating AGPF, although *Ei* did in fact not join. AGPF was incorporated as an association in December 1978. Its constituent meeting was attended by 26 people, 11 of whom were founding members, but none of the founding members were associations. In 1985, nine parents' organizations were AGPF members (Kempcke, 1985). The first AGPF chairman was a member of the *Bundestag* (Dr Friedrich Vogel), later a minister. AGPF sees its task in representing the concerns of parents' organizations vis-à-vis the State and society, to warn against the dangers of *Jugendreligionen*, and to establish contact with organizations similar to itself in other countries.

Ei's significance

In his contribution to *Ei*'s twentieth anniversary volume, Behnk (1995: 64) points to three aspects which make the work of parents' initiatives relevant: (1) they offer a 'strategy for survival' to individuals affected by 'cult' membership, (2) they provide community processes for coping with parents' problems, (3) they act as social and political catalysts. Behnk (1995: 64–75) comments on these points in greater detail.

First, individuals directly affected by 'cult' membership in the family find help in parents' groups where analysis and reflection improve understanding of their case. Information and counselling contribute towards an 'objective' and differentiated evaluation of the situation. There is space to work through emotions and find appropriate ways of dealing with the problem, especially maintaining contact with 'cult' members. Parents' emotions are associated with Freud's *Trauerarbeit* (mourning) and feelings of guilt, emotional processes echoed in FAIR members' comments. In Behnk's view, spiritual matters also need to be considered and, speaking as a pastor, he argues that being grounded in the Christian faith helps people cope.

Second, parents' initiatives offer a community where shared experiences and mutual support help individuals to devise survival strategies. Identifying recognizable patterns and similarities benefits both the group and members. Information and perspectives from non-affected third parties widen the network and exchange of information.

Third, social institutions and politicians need to be included to increase the effectiveness of opposition against 'cults', especially in the face of 'cult coalitions', such as the *Konferenz für Religionsfreiheit und Menschenrechte* (Conference for Religious Freedom and Human Rights) of 1991. The experience of parents and relatives complements the 'critical assessment of sect experts' and thus convinces social institutions that urgent action is needed. Groups like *Ei* can disprove the supposition that parents are 'subjective' and 'over-emotional': if their experiences are described in reflective and emotionally controlled ways, they are vital for the wider debate and instructive for society. Co-operation with the media and public authorities will reduce sensationalism and indifference. Parents' groups want society to recognize the 'cult' problem and take appropriate measures.

Ei's future tasks

In his contribution, Willi Röder (1995) looks at Ei's present and future tasks. Its 20 years of existence have provided Ei with a 'rich stock of experience', consisting of archives and personal knowledge. Counselling and information have been two of Ei's most important and indispensable tasks and would continue to be Ei's core work. Ei's local discussion groups have kept their ears to the ground and reported locally organized 'cult' events. The discussion groups are similar to FAIR's branches, with a two-way flow of information.

While in Ei's early years, parents applied mainly for information about the movements which their children had joined, in recent years, an increasing number of young people have asked for information. Röder attributes this partly to their fascination with occultism, which includes experiments with ouija boards and black masses. Young people are reported to be especially curious about the supernatural and occult matters (Zinser, 1990; 1991; Mischo, 1991; Hemminger, 1988; Helsper, 1992) – findings which are reflected in enquiries with parents' groups. Also, Röder states, more and more young people have become active in Ei. However, the increasing number of groups and movements has become another challenge for Ei, as the range of 'products' in the 'supermarket of salvation' continues to expand, with some 'old products being repackaged'. Thus, some of Ei's work consists in 'consumer protection' (Verbraucherschutz), in telling people about 'false promises of one-sided advertising', a task on which Aktion Bildungsinformation e.V. (1979; Heinemann, 1981) in Stuttgart concentrates, especially regarding Scientology.

Röder further points out that the way 'cults' have treated their members and members' relatives has been an important criterion for Ei. 'Cult' promises are often contradicted by the experiences of relatives and former members and this needs pointing out. If 'cults' claim to save souls and to take a holistic approach, victims need be considered. For 'cults' to say that mistakes were made is simply a 'crass minimization' of damage caused to affected families and ex-members (especially regarding the abuse of children in COG) and an attempt to appease critics. In Röder's view, the way 'cults' treat members and relatives has remained unchanged,[66] because concerned parents do not fit into a 'cult' concept which suggests to followers that it offers a 'saving formula', a 'divine leader', the 'saved family' – notions developed by Haack as characteristics of Jugendreligionen. This worldview does not admit alternative perspectives and considers critics as instruments of 'the other world', the world outside.

Commenting on the media coverage of 'cults', Röder thinks it has not been thorough enough, despite the plethora of new TV channels, and Behnk (1996a: 75) points to the lack of differentiation between 'sects'. Despite their dialogue format, talkshows, for example, seldom touch on the actual problems, because 'cult' spokespersons are well prepared and manage to come across well, while proper dialogue requires thorough information.

Light-entertainment programmes also miss the point, because 'cults' are a serious matter, especially in view of the events in Waco and Guyana.

Given the political activities of some 'cults' or *Politsekten* (political sects), such as *Europäische Arbeiterpartei* (EAP, European Workers' Party, now known as *Bürgerrechtsbewegung Solidarität*, Civil Movement Solidarity)[67] and Transcendental Meditation, *Ei* needs greater co-operation with the established democratic parties. Candidates of TM's Natural Law Party (now officially dissolved) gained 20 per cent of the votes in one Bavarian town and stood in French and British general elections. *Ei* already works successfully with other parents' groups in Germany and the churches' 'sect experts'.

Ei's 'cult' concept

Elterninitiative has largely adopted Haack's terminology and concepts. This is obviously due to their close co-operation. *Ei* thus speaks of *Jugendreligionen* or *Jugendsekten* (often *Sekten* for short), *Psychomutation, Seelenwäsche*, etc. However, Haack's influence has reached further in that *most* parents' organizations have adopted his terminology. Another term coined by Haack is *Psychokulte* (therapy cults), of which he distinguished two kinds: those with techniques which promise self-discovery or self-realization and establishments with therapies (*Therapie-Institutionen*) – Heelas's 'self-religions'. The followers of both types show the effects of *Psychomutation*, a distinct personality change (Haack, 1990a: 191). Schneider (1995: 189–190) lists organizations, such as Landmark Education, *Verein zur Förderung der Psychologischen Menschenkenntnis* (VPM), Scientology/Dianetics, *Ontologische Einweihungsschule* (Hannes Scholl), EAP, and *Die Bewegung* (Silo) as examples of 'therapy cults'. These groups do not immediately suggest religion or *Weltanschauung*, but reveal ideological and religious elements on closer inspection. Their slogans are 'We have the saving principle' or 'We enable those who are able' and they offer *Lebenshilfe* (advice on how to live). Such advice is a commodity which is sold in very expensive seminars. The ideologies involved often lie in the grey areas between the humanities, psychotherapies, *Lebenshilfe*, 'mental hygiene' (*Psychohygiene*), and religion. The groups claim to be genuine religions and wish to be treated accordingly.[68] Schuster (1995: 200–202) distinguishes between *Jugendreligionen*, in Haack's sense (e.g. Scientology, ISKCON, Rajneeshism), groups which offer new revelations (*Neuoffenbarungsbewegungen*), e.g. *Universelles Leben*, Fiat Lux, political 'sects' (e.g. Lyndon LaRouche, also known as EAP, or *Patrioten für Deutschland*, TM – because of the Natural Law Party, VPM), pagan groups (*völkisch-heidnische Gruppen*) with links to the extreme political left and right, occultism/spiritism, and small groups offering therapy, meditation, and esotericism. The precise definition of terms varies between authors and there is overlap between categories. Scientology can be found under *Jugendreligionen* or *Psychokulte*. There is, however, agreement on the movements' harmful methods and aims.

In his paper to *Ei*'s 1995 conference, Behnk (1996a: 77–78) considers the categories of 'dangerous' and 'harmless' 'sects' a 'fatal simplification' and argues that Scientology has become the 'dangerous sect' *par excellence* in Germany, although it is certainly not the only 'dangerous sect', a view also expressed by Nüchtern (1997: 65). Branding one group as 'dangerous' means minimizing the effects of other groups, such as Jehovah's Witnesses and *Universelles Leben*, and leaving the problems they create unaddressed.

Regarding the term 'sect', Behnk (1996a: 80–83) speaks of a 'semantic confusion'. Since the 1970s, a 'secularized sect notion' has been in use: any group perceived to have the characteristics of a religious sect – ideological exclusivity and hierarchical totality – is called a 'sect'. People refer to psychological, political or commercial 'sects' to indicate that they deserve social disapprobation. Behnk doubts, however, that 'sect' could be replaced with 'cult' (*Kult*) or 'destructive cult' (*destruktiver Kult*), because it would be difficult to make these terms acceptable for popular usage. Also, the notion of 'sect' in the sense used in *Religionswissenschaft* is indispensable. Behnk rejects the term 'new religious movements', because it is neutral and thus does not signal problems regarding groups designated as such. (Its neutrality is, of course, the very reason why it is used in social science.) Yet, in Behnk's view, it is counterproductive to call an organization, such as Scientology, a 'sect', because it should not be recognized as a religion. Non-religious problematic groups require a different term (although Behnk does not offer one). This would allow the State to take action, because such groups would not be protected by the constitution or require the state to be neutral.

Ei, 'brainwashing' and deprogramming

Ei's position on 'brainwashing' accords with Haack's concepts of 'soulwashing' and *Psychomutation*. These and his notion of indoctrination are described in the section on Haack.

Just like FAIR, parents' initiatives in Germany were associated with deprogramming which discredited them and their work. However, just like FAIR, *Ei* (and other parents' groups) have distanced themselves from this practice, although there is no condemnation of parents who resort to it. In response to media reports, enquiries from members, and offers of deprogramming services, *Ei*'s committee issued a statement in 1982[69] (Haack, 1986b: 101, 103–105, 111–112). Information about *Ei*'s (and other parents' groups') stance prior to 1982 was not available to me. Thiel (1986: 90–91) claims that Karbe had great sympathies for deprogramming. *Ei*'s statement declares categorical rejection of deprogramming, because it employs kidnapping and emotional pressure. Parents are warned against inflicting this procedure, considered to be similar to 'brainwashing', on their children. They should decline the proffered services of professional deprogrammers and report to *Ei*'s committee when they are approached. Deprogramming may lead to even greater commitment to 'sects' and therefore be counterproductive. Other reasons against this practice include cost and doubtful success in cases where ex-members are not able to re-adapt to society, where deprogramming may in fact prevent full rehabilitation. If it is carried out by former members, they may not have sufficient expertise which relates to a specific group and new developments in groups may have superseded former members' knowledge. Also, unlawful measures may involve parents and relatives in law suits (Haack, 1986b: 105, 109–111). These are also the reasons why FAIR repudiated deprogramming.

At the same time, *Ei*'s committee rejected attempts to discredit and reproach parents who resorted to deprogramming, an option often born out of concern for their child and 'bad advice'. No-one, except legal institutions, should try or judge such parents, least of all 'sects' and 'youth religions', as they themselves practise a 'dangerous form' of deprogramming and 'soul-washing' and thus create the very situation which impels parents to take such action. Groups with methods of indoctrination which violate individuals' rights have no right to set themselves up as guardians of religious freedom. However, 'wrong actions' committed by 'youth religions' do not justify unlawful measures. *Ei*'s statement emphasizes that only 'decisive' and 'clear' information can counteract the actions of 'youth religions' and 'extreme sects' in the long run. Haack reaffirmed this position in the 1980s (ibid.: 105–106).[70]

The wider network

The national network

Ei's discussion groups form a local network of help and information, with a two-way flow of information between main office and local groups, just like that between FAIR and its branches. Other parents' organizations operate similar networks. For example, from late 1988, regular meetings of *Arbeitskreis Klassische und Fundamentalistische Sekten* (Working Group on Classical and Fundamentalist Sects) for former 'cult' members and anyone concerned were announced in *EL-Mitteilungen*, the newsletter of a parents' group.

Ei also networks nationally with other parents' groups and related organizations, such as *Eltern- und Betroffeneninitiative gegen psychische Abhängigkeit – für geistige Freiheit Berlin e.V.* (EBI), a group working closely with Pastor Gandow, *SINUS-Sekteninformation und Selbsthilfe Hessen und Thüringen e.V.* in Frankfurt, *Eltern- und Betroffeneninitiative gegen psychische Abhängigkeit Sachsen e.V.* in Leipzig,[71] and *Elterninitiative in Hamburg und Schleswig-Holstein zur Hilfe gegen seelische Abhängigkeit und Mißbrauch der Religion e.V.* in Lübeck (Dürholt and Kroll, 1994: 55). There is also *Niedersächsische Elterninitiative gegen Mißbrauch der Religion e.V.* whose chairperson, Hildegard Nußbaum, contributed to *Ei*'s twentieth anniversary conference (Nußbaum, 1996).[72] After the fall of the

Berlin Wall in 1989, parents' organizations formed in eastern Germany, among them EBI Leipzig. Usarski (1995) argues that *Sektenexperten* were influential in creating these groups, just as they had been in western Germany.

Ei and other parents' initiatives have worked closely with the *Sektenbeauftragte* of both churches, among them Rüdiger Hauth (one of *Ei*'s conference volumes – Elterninitiative, 1996 – is dedicated to his 25 years in office) and with *Konsultation Landeskirchlicher Beauftragter* (KLB) in Kassel (Elterninitiative, 1995: 21–22). There are links with state authorities, establishments and associations dedicated to the protection of youth (*Jugendschutzverbände*) – *Aktion Psychokultgefahren e.V.* in Düsseldorf, for example, supplies information to the *Jugendamt* (youth office) (Mucha, 1988: 72; 74) – and with political parties, such as *Junge Union*.

International network

Since its inception, *Ei* has forged connections with organizations outside Germany, facilitated by Pastor Haack's links. The inspiration which organizations in the US, UK, and France lent to *Ei*'s foundation translated into exchange and co-operation with these and others in Europe and worldwide. The volume commemorating *Ei*'s twentieth anniversary (Elterninitiative, 1995) includes letters of congratulations from AFF, FAIR, and UNADFI. *Ei* established links with the Panhellenic Parents Union (PPU) in Greece – which also has links with FAIR – during two international seminars in September 1984 and 1987 (Alevisopoulos, 1995). Both provided opportunities for parents' groups to get to know each other and improve exchange of information about the 'real aims' and recruitment methods of *Jugendreligionen*. They were also opportunities for parents to exchange personal experiences and gather information. Given PPU's Greek Orthodox patronage and participants' different denominations, the seminars also had an ecumenical aspect. A third seminar in November 1993 on 'Human rights and social problems caused by psychological dependency on totalitarian sects and *Jugendreligionen* in Europe' included – for the first time – representatives from former Eastern Bloc countries. Therefore, the conference resolution stressed the need to intensify co-operation between parents' organizations across Europe and announced the creation of the 'Pan-Orthodox Association of Parents' Initiatives' to promote this aim. A designated committee was to organize another conference in an 'orthodox country'. The findings of the seminar's legal committee almost match FECRIS's programme.

Ei's activities

Like FAIR, *Ei* holds an annual conference with invited speakers (*Sektenexperten*, politicians, legal experts, members of other parents' initiatives), which is an occasion for members to meet. *Ei* has also organized seminars jointly with other organizations, for example with *Junge Union* in 1984 (Junge Union Bayern, 1985) and *Arbeitsgemeinschaft Demokratischer Kreise* and *Europäische Akademie Bayerns* (Schuster, 1988). *Elterninitiative* was involved in one of the earliest conferences (or 'consultation of experts') on *Jugendreligionen*, organized in 1979 by *Evangelische Akademie Tutzing*. It assembled a range of 'experts' – theologians, teachers, doctors, parents – who consulted with officials of the Federal Ministry for Youth, Family and Health (*Bundesministerium für Jugend, Familie und Gesundheit*). Some contributions were published (Evangelische Akademie Tutzing, 1980).[73] The conference was not so much concerned with the teachings of *Jugendreligionen* as with social effects, health problems, and damage to individuals and society – a view shared by FAIR. Behnk (1996a: 81) states that the criticism of 'sects' is not aimed at members, but at the 'sectarian' mode of organizations which victimize members. Individual members' beliefs are not at issue, but the social consequences of 'sect' ideology and practice are. The groups which caused concern during the conference in Tutzing included Ananda Marga, DLM, ISKCON, COG, the UC, Scientology, and TM – groups which Haack's early (e.g. 1974) publications had identified as *Jugendreligionen*. The conference resolution affirmed the following:

> It is with concern that they [conference participants] observe how especially young people and young adults can be damaged by the practices of these groups regarding health and social skills. Group pressures can lead to extreme psychological dependencies, interference with personal development, loss of ability to judge, loss of taking initiative, and social isolation. The conference led to the conviction that concrete financial and/or power-wielding interests are behind these groups. They are not beneficial to the commonweal. Given this worrying development, it is important to understand the effects as socio-political problems and authorities, institutions and private organisations ... should therefore continue to inform the public more effectively and strengthen their assistance. In particular, existing legal provision should be used better.
>
> (Evangelische Akademie Tutzing, 1980: 42)

Ei and the State

As in FAIR's case, one of the main objectives of German parents' organizations consists in taking their concerns to public authorities, government agencies, and political parties. Unlike FAIR, parents' groups have been more successful in this endeavour: they established contact with such agencies much earlier and more effectively, on the local, national, and European level. A member of the *Bundestag* (Parliament) became AGPF's first president. AGPF's first letter to the Federal Ministries for the Interior, Justice, and

Youth, Family and Health in late 1977 made authorities aware of concerns about *Jugendreligionen* by pointing out how young people join them and leave everything behind to dedicate themselves wholly to religious leaders or gurus. Membership entails a drastic change in personality, which eventually destroys individuals. The letter urges ministers to take up this issue, because State and society will have to find the causes for this phenomenon and make clear to young people that joining 'extremist religious groups' does not solve personal or social problems. (Haack, 1986b: 113–114)

The State represented at conferences

Since the late 1970s (starting with the *Expertenkonsultation* in 1979), representatives of State and government have participated in conferences organized by parents' groups to gain insights and provide input. Another milestone was the international conference on the 'Consequences for society and health of new totalitarian religious and pseudo-religious movements' in November 1981, organized jointly in Bonn by AGPF, the federal government, the Federal Medical Association (*Bundesärztekammer*), the Federal Association for Health Education (*Bundesvereinigung für Gesundheitserziehung*), and the German Society for Child and Youth Psychiatry (*Deutsche Gesellschaft für Kinder- und Jugendpsychiatrie*). Norbert Blüm, then Senator in Berlin for federal affairs and acting chairman of CDU's social committees (he was later federal minister for labour), was one of the speakers, as were former UC members (among them Allan Wood), medical professors and health educationists (J. Clark, L. West, M. Galper), and theologians (J. Aagaard, P. Zulehner) (Schulze-Berndt, 1981a).

Members of the *Bundestag* and *Landtag* (provincial parliaments) and the European Parliament contributed to *Ei* conferences and seminars, for example to its tenth anniversary conference in 1985, the International Year of Youth. Participants included Wolfgang Bötsch, (then) leader of the parliamentary party of the conservative parties (*Parlamentarischer Geschäftsführer der CDU/CSU-Bundestagsfraktion*),[74] Gebhard Glück, (then) member of the Bavarian *Landtag* and under-secretary in the ministry for work and social order (*Staatssekretär im Bayrischen Staatsministerium für Arbeit und Sozialordnung*),[75] Reinhold Bocklet, (then) a member of the European Parliament,[76] and Wolfgang Götzer, (then) a member of the *Bundestag* and the Committee for Youth, Family and Health.[77] These speakers acknowledged the importance of *Elterninitiative* and its 'sister' organizations and expressed appreciation of their commitment and expertise.

Politicians and parliamentarians also showed support at *Ei*'s twentieth anniversary conference: messages were received from Edmund Stoiber, then Bavaria's minister president, Norbert Blüm, Renate Rennebach, member of the *Bundestag* (until 2002) and spokesperson of the Social Democratic Party's (SPD's) political party for questions regarding religious groups, including 'destructive cults' (she also served on the *Enquête-Kommission* when it was set up in May 1996), Markus Sackman, (then) a member of the Bavarian *Landtag* and chairman of the youth wing of the conservative party in Bavaria, *Junge Union Bayern*, and Ursula Caberta, an official in Hamburg's authority for interior affairs.[78] Bernd Kränzle, (then) member of the Bavarian *Landtag* and under-secretary in the ministry of justice, attended the conference.[79]

The duties of the State: religious freedom

In Germany, as in the UK and other countries, religious freedom is a constitutionally guaranteed right (Art. 4 of the *Grundgesetz*). New religious communities can invoke this right and the protection it affords. Religious freedom is twinned with the State's duty of neutrality regarding religion and religious communities. The constitution requires the State to abstain from taking sides in questions of *Weltanschauung* and not to distinguish between 'genuine' and 'false' religion. This duty restrains State action. Therefore, Glück (1986: 21) points out, parents' initiatives have more room for manoeuvre.

Generally speaking, parents' organizations and *Sektenexperten* believe that *Jugendreligionen* and *Psychokulte* claim to be religions as described in the constitution, but actually just use religion as a 'front' for political power, financial gain, and influence. Some authors therefore speak of 'industrial' (e.g. Haack, 1991a) or 'political' 'sects' (e.g. Schuster, 1995: 200–202) to highlight what they see as the principal interest. One of the widely debated questions is therefore whether such groups are genuine religions and deserve the protection of the law. In some instances, this question has involved the courts, often in cases regarding Scientology's recognition as a *Religions- und Weltanschauungsgemeinschaft* (religious organization) in the constitutional sense or classification as a commercial enterprise, on the grounds that the sale of its goods and services is not an integral part of practising its religious beliefs. In Behnk's (1996a: 79) view, the State must examine whether religious freedom is used as an excuse for commercial and political interests. Religious groups should not be able to claim the protection of religious freedom beyond the boundaries of society's general laws and norms. The State should be able to intervene when the rights of the child are involved, for example in cases where Jehovah's Witnesses parents refuse blood transfusions (Behnk, 1996a: 79, 83).[80]

The protection of human dignity and youth

Although the constitution requires the State's neutrality in religious matters, it also stipulates the State's duty to protect the human dignity and health of its citizens. The State also has responsibilities for the care of young people (*Jugendschutz*). Court rulings have given these duties precedence over the requirement of neutrality so that the State *can* take a position vis-à-vis religious teachings, *provided* there is evidence to justify warnings against such teachings (for example if they are perceived to be dangerous) or *provided* that such teachings go against the values (*Wertordnung*) which the constitution seeks to protect. The State must, however, respect the principle of balance (*Grundsatz der Verhältnismäßigkeit*), which means that it must take into account aspects of individual and public concern and keep within the boundaries set by necessity and reason. The State must also still be guided by its duty of neutrality. Therefore, it needs to tread a very fine line between these two requirements. While the constitutional right to religious freedom is upheld without prejudice, this freedom has limits (Kränzle, 1996: 61–62).

Glück (1986: 21, 33, 34; 1985: 121) also stresses the aspect of limits: the State can require religious communities to respect 'indispensable and generally recognized values' of the free democratic order. The Federal Ministry for Youth, Family and Health commissioned experts to examine how Art. 4 relates to problems caused by *Jugendreligionen*. Exercising basic rights may not violate the highest constitutional value – human dignity. Thus, any activities of *Jugendreligionen* which violate human dignity do not come under constitutional protection, especially psychological or physical influence which aims to change individuals' personality and reduce or destroy their autonomy and self-determination.

Bocklet (1986: 17–18) points out that members of the European Community have similar obligations: according to Article 220 of the Treaty of Rome, member states have a duty to preserve the rights of their citizens and should, if necessary, negotiate with one another to ensure the protection of persons and personal rights in commensurate conditions.

Trade regulations and consumer protection

The question of *Jugendreligionen* and religious freedom is coupled with the question of how existing legal instruments can be used against 'cults'. Effective use of trade regulations is a recurrent theme, regarding, for example, registration of businesses. In Kränzle's (1996: 61) view, such regulations are of limited use, despite important court decisions: although businesses need to be registered, no details have to be provided about those who run the business. State action is also restricted by the fact that most 'cult' members are adults who joined of their own free will, even if they were exposed to techniques of persuasion.

An area where the State could use existing legislation more effectively and introduce new legislation is consumer protection. In fact, Keltsch's (1996) contribution to *Ei*'s twentieth anniversary conference discusses both areas. His proposals amount to a sophisticated set of regulations for consumer protection. This is particularly pertinent for groups which offer therapies of any kind, because although *Naturheilpraktiker* (naturopaths) are regulated, healers and 'alternative' practitioners are not.

In November 1994, the sixty-seventh conference of the health ministers of the *Länder* passed a unanimous vote that consumers of commercial therapies should be protected against abusive techniques, namely those which manipulate consciousness, psyche, and personality. The conference appealed to the Federal Health Minister to set up a task force which should explore possible legal provision (Kränzle, 1996: 65). Consumer protection includes regulation of unfair competition, which – some argue – could be used against deceptive recruiting practices (Götzer, 1986: 40–41).

In early 1998, the *Bundesrat*[81] passed draft legislation to the government. After consideration by the government, it should have gone to the *Bundestag* and then to relevant committees. The *Enquête-Kommission*'s interim report of 1997 (Deutscher Bundestag, 1997: 37–38) had included recommendations regarding this legislation and in January 1998, the *Enquête-Kommission* had deliberated it and welcomed legal provision in this area, although its remit did not allow for any decision. The draft legislation proposed to regulate the contractual agreements between commercial therapists and their clients, but did not intend to jeopardize the livelihood of *bona fide* therapists. In early February 2004, Antje Blumenthal, member of the *Bundestag*, announced in a press release that the government commissioned 'model project' did not offer sufficient preventive measures and that legal provision would be put in place this year to ensure consumer protection in this area. In September 2004 (Drucksache 683/04), the *Bundesrat*'s committee for legal affairs recommended that the *Bundesrat* should *not* introduce the draft legislation (Drucksache 690/03) in Parliament, although the *Bundesrat*'s committee for health matters *had* backed it. The Bundesrat followed the recommendation in late September 2004 (Drucksache 683/04), which effectively obliterated the initiative.

Criminal law and other legal instruments

The ministers of justice in the *Länder* have also concerned themselves with problems caused by *Jugendreligionen*. Thanks to the initiative of Baden-Württemberg's ministry of justice, the sixty-third conference of ministers in early 1992 examined Scientology's behaviour in the light of criminal law and decided to tighten measures. That year, the minister presidents' conference called for Scientology to be placed under the observation of the *Verfassungsschutz* (the body in charge of protecting the constitution), although it was uncertain at the time whether this was legally admissible. The *Verfassungsschutz* of the province of Saarland also examined Scientology's compatibility with the constitution (*Verfassungstreue*) at that time. *Jugendreligionen* featured again on the agenda of sixty-sixth conference of justice ministers (Kränzle, 1996: 59).

Other areas where existing laws can be used more effectively or tightened include registration of individuals. Bavaria, for example, reformed its law so that 'cult' members cannot be moved from centre to centre without any possibility of tracing them. Glück (1986: 22–24, 38–40) sees three areas where the State could apply existing law: first, monitoring social security arrangements for 'cult' members to ensure provision for sickness and old age; second, consistent application of regulations relating to working conditions; third, prevention of abuse of tax exemption and charitable status.

State and youth

The duty of State and public authorities to protect young people is one reason why they have taken up the issue of *Jugendreligionen*. *Jugendschutz* describes any measures which protect children and young people from influences arising in social contexts (work environment, mass media, public events), which might affect their mental and physical health. *Jugendschutz* consists of laws regulating young people's rights at work and in public life (restaurants, gambling arcades, sale of alcohol) and publications for which they are the target audience.

Young people's well-being (*Jugendwohlfahrt*) is promoted through *Jugendhilfe* (literally: help for young people) as laid down in relevant laws (*Jugendwohlfahrtgesetz*). *Jugendhilfe* has three aspects: *Jugendfürsorge* (guardianship), *Jugendpflege* (care) and *Jugendschutz* (protection). *Jugendfürsorge* pertains to neglected or damaged young people, *Jugendpflege* comprises measures which promote young people's social skills and education. These (*Jugendhilfe*) are provided by dedicated institutions created by public authorities (*Jugendwohlfahrtsbehörden; Jugendamt*) and by independent organizations, including charitable associations and (religious) youth associations. The latter are mainly engaged in *Jugendpflege* offering leisure activities and holidays, political education, international meetings, etc. (*Jugendarbeit*). The public sector should support, promote, and co-operate with the non-public sector and only close gaps left by the non-public sector.

Federal and provincial governments take *Jugendschutz* seriously, with a separate federal ministry for youth and provision stipulated in the Bavarian constitution.[82] Germany's political parties are equally committed to protecting young people against undue influences. The conservative party in Bavaria, for example, included this in its manifesto (Bötsch, 1986: 13). Various *Jugendschutz* organizations have dealt with 'cults' and published information. These often have *Aktion Jugendschutz* in their names (Aktion Jugendschutz, n.d.; Aktion Jugendschutz Nordrhein-Westfalen, 1980), with some organized by the churches, such as *Aktion Jugendschutz, Katholische Landesarbeitsstelle Rheinland-Pfalz e.V.* (Aktion Jugendschutz, 1978; 1983[83]) and *Arbeitsgemeinschaft der Evangelischen Jugend in der BRD und Berlin West e.V.* (Arbeitsgemeinschaft, 1978a; 1978b; 1978c), some independent (Landesarbeitsgemeinschaft der Freien Wohlfahrtspflege in Niedersachsen, 1979; Landesstelle Jugendschutz Niedersachsen *et al.*, 1995; Arbeitsgemeinschaft Kinder- und Jugendschutz, 1993).

Funding

The State has come under fire from *Jugendreligionen* regarding funding. Until the mid-1980s, Federal and *Länder* authorities supported parents' organizations financially to cover running costs, conference organization, and production of publications. AGPF received such support (DM 140,000 annually, according to Kempcke, 1985), as did *Sekten-Info Essen e.V.*[84] AGPF received sponsorship from the Federal Ministry for Youth, Family and Health to organize its 1984 conference on 'Family and Destructive Cults' and publish proceedings. *Ei* received financial help for some publications (Glück, 1986: 25; Evangelische Akademie Tutzing, 1980: 2). *Aktion Bildungsinformation e.V.* in Stuttgart received funding from Baden-Württemberg's government in 1991 and 1992 (reportedly an annual sum of DM 100,000). *Aktion Psychokultgefahren e.V.* received funds from the province of Westphalia and the city of Düsseldorf (Mucha, 1988: 68). The State lent such support because of its duty to inform the public and contribute towards research.[85]

In 1985, the Rajneesh group in Cologne (Wioska Rajneesh Neo-Sannyas Commune e.V.) challenged the Federal Government's support of AGPF in court. The administrative court in Cologne ruled that such subsidies went against the law and proscribed further grants. This action proved a landmark case, because it questioned to what extent State and public authorities should be involved in the work of parents' groups. It questioned whether the State had overstepped the very line it must tread between neutrality and protection of its citizens. The court ruling's interpretation of the constitutional principle of the State's neutrality precluded public funds for organizations which are not neutral themselves. The court declared both annual subsidies and funds for particular projects as unlawful. The ruling also implied recognition of Rajneeshism under Art. 4, although it did not address the question of defining religion (Kempcke, 1985). In 1988, the same Rajneesh group challenged public funds for *Sekten-Info Essen e.V.*, on which the administrative court in Gelsenkirchen gave its verdict in October 1988. The city of Essen was not to subsidise *Sekten-Info Essen e.V.* by any means (both city and group appealed) and Rajneeshism was to be recognized under Art. 4 (Sekten-Info Essen e.V., [1989]: 4–6). The federal administrative court confirmed these judgements in March 1992, when it pronounced that the Federal Government may not subsidize any associations fighting so-called 'youth religions' or 'youth sects', including the Rajneesh movement, because it does not have legal authority to do so. AGPF lodged a constitutional complaint and *Sekten-Info Essen e.V.* announced that it would exclude the Rajneesh movement from its remit.

In 1992, the Scientology associations in Stuttgart and Munich challenged the province of Baden-Württemberg's subsidy to ABI e.V. in Stuttgart and obtained an injunction by referring to the federal administrative court's verdict of March 1992. The administrative court in Mannheim later reversed the injunction, because it considered it doubtful that the plaintiffs should be recognized as religious groups under Art. 4. The case was, however, referred to the next instance.

The State's duty to issue warnings

In 1987, TM brought a case against the Federal Government as to whether the State can or should warn against *Jugendreligionen*. In 1989, the federal administrative court ruled that the State *may* issue warnings and indeed *needs* to do so, irrespective of the right to religious freedom, when there is good reason for such warnings. This is part of the Federal Government's constitutional authority to inform the public. The court further ruled that the activities of a religion or religious community can justify such warnings, if they adversely affect the dignity, life or health of other citizens. Even well-founded suspicion of danger can justify the issue of warnings. The government is not restricted to inform only about facts which harbour danger, but can draw judicious conclusions, as long as these cohere with factual evidence.

Thus State funding for parents' groups and information, even the provision of information by the State itself, are linked with the State's constitutional duty of neutrality. The *Bundesverfassungsgericht*, the court which settles matters of constitutional import in the last instance, ruled in 1989 that the Federal Government may indeed warn against *Jugendreligionen* and thus confirmed previous rulings. Also, the highest administrative court (*Bundesverwaltungsgericht*) pronounced that the State may subsidize a private organization whose purpose is to warn against *Jugendreligionen*, although the organization needs to be neutral in questions of *Weltanschauung*. The Federal Court in Switzerland reached a similar verdict in rejecting complaints by Scientology and the UC about public funds for Info-Sekta, a non-public association (Keltsch, 1996: 31).

These judgements indicate that the State (Federal Government, public authorities) may publish and distribute material designed to inform about, even warn against, *Jugendreligionen*. However, the State can no longer grant subsidies to parents' organizations. There were fears – unfounded, as it turned out – that the State might stop publishing information altogether (EZW, 1995e: 216). The *Enquête-Kommission* also addressed the question whether the State should fund advice and information centres.

State information

In his contribution to *Ei*'s tenth anniversary conference, Götzer (1986: 37) called for regular reports from Federal and *Länder* ministries about new developments regarding 'cults'. Like the *Verfassungsschutz*, authorities responsible for 'cults' should produce annual reports, without parliaments having to request these. In fact, both Federal and *Länder* governments do publish reports and information about *Jugendreligionen*, although not on a regular basis.

One of the earliest publications of this kind is that by the Federal Ministry for Youth, Family and Health published in 1980 (Bundesminister für Jugend, Famile und Gesundheit, 1980), to which AGPF (1980) responded in an eight-page statement. In 1996, the Federal Ministry for Family, Senior Citizens, Women and Youth published a brochure on Scientology (Bundesministerium für Familie, Senioren, Frauen und Jugend, 1996).

The first provincial government to issue a report was Rhineland-Palatinate, which dealt with 'young people in destructive religious groups' as early as 1979 (Landesregierung Rheinland-Pfalz, 1979). In the same year, North-Rhine-Westphalia published its first report on 'youth sects' in the region, followed by a second report in 1983 (Minister für Arbeit, Gesundheit und Soziales des Landes NRW, 1979; 1983). In 1993, Westphalia's ministry for work, health and social affairs published (in conjunction with a *Jugend-schutz* authority) a report on 'communities with new religious beliefs' which focuses on Scientology and legal matters (Arbeitsgemeinschaft Kinder- und Jugendschutz, 1993). In 1996, Westphalia's ministry for interior affairs published a document which explored whether Scientology was a threat to democracy and whether the *Verfassungsschutz* should observe its activities (Innenministerium des Landes Nordrhein-Westfalen, 1996), a live issue since the early 1990s.

In 1983, Berlin's Senator for schools, youth, and sport issued a report about 'youth sects' and 'therapy cults' (Senator für Schulwesen, Jugend und Sport, Berlin, 1983), followed in 1994 by a brochure about 'new religious movements and so-called therapy cults' (Schipmann, 1994), which provoked dispute from three of the groups mentioned. They objected to being included and sought an injunction against further distribution. However, the courts ruled that the province of Berlin was within its constitutional rights and obligations to inform the public (EZW, 1995e). At the request of the *Landtag*, Bavaria's ministry for culture produced a report in February 1985. In Götzer's (1986: 38) view, the report was largely superficial and dealt in commonplaces, which indicated that the ministry avoided taking responsibility. It was either incompetent or intent on minimizing the problem. Alfred Sauter of *Junge Union Bayern* protested sharply against the dismissive presentation of the work of parents' initiatives.

In 1988, Baden-Württemberg reported on the structure and activities of 'youth religions' (Ministerium für Kultus und Sport Baden-Württemberg, 1988). Again, some movements severely criticized statements about themselves and the Rajneesh group contested them in court. Although the case had a successful outcome in the first instance, the appeal went against the group. In the same year, Berlin's authority for women, youth and family published information about 'religious movements' and 'therapy cults' (Senatsverwaltung für Frauen, Jugend und Familie (Berlin), 1988).

In 1994, Baden-Württemberg's *Interministerielle Arbeitsgruppe für Fragen sog. Jugendsekten und Psychogruppen* (Inter-Ministerial Working Party for Questions of So-Called Youth Sects and Therapy Cults) submitted its first report (Landtag von Baden-Württemberg, 1994). The working party arose from the *Landtag*'s request in early 1992 that the government take legal measures against Scientology, with a decision by the ministerial council following in June 1993. The working party's task was to 'inform, advise and – if necessary – warn state and society about the activities of the so-called youth sects and therapy cults'. The report describes its remit and aims, the situation of 'youth sects' and 'therapy cults' in Baden-Württemberg, and measures taken by relevant ministries. Two further reports were submitted in 1995 and 1997 (Landtag von Baden-Württemberg, 1995; 1997); a fourth report was to cover 1997–1998.

In 1995, the province of Schleswig-Holstein published two reports: the first describes activities of 'sects' in the province (Schleswig-Holsteinischer Landtag, 1995); the second focuses on legal aspects, especially possible measures by public authorities (Ministerpräsidentin des Landes Schleswig-Holstein, 1995).

State information centres

In his contribution to the *Ei*'s tenth anniversary conference, Götzer (1986: 35–36) calls for national and provincial information centres on 'cults', which should be attached to the Federal Ministry for Youth, Family and Health and relevant ministries in the *Länder*. These should gather all legal cases involving 'cults' inside and outside courts, such as verdicts, judicial enquiries, criminal and civil cases, cases in administrative and industrial courts, and violations of regulations. Centralizing such archives does not go against existing legislation and the material could be accessible to any authority in need of information or involved in legal proceedings.

Götzer's idea was not entirely new. As early as 1979, the Hanns Seidel Foundation had surveyed legal aspects relating to 'cults' and published the results (Engstfeld and Hanns-Seidel-Stiftung, 1981). In 1984, Westphalia had set up a centre of documentation and information (*Dokumentations- und Informationszentrum Jugendsekten/Psychokulte*) in Düsseldorf (attached to a *Jugendschutz* organization, *Arbeitsgemeinschaft Kinder- und Jugend-schutz*), which helped compile a survey of legal cases and jurisdiction (Abel *et al.*, 1991).

According to Glück (1986: 22), a 'sect centre' was created in the Bavarian youth office (*Landesjugendamt*) to collect up-to-date information about 'cults'. It, too, hoped to amass reliable archive material to inform future action by authorities. The centre co-operates with *Ei*, the churches, and other public authorities. Schleswig-Holstein set up a centre (*Dokumentationsstelle 'Sekten und sektenähnliche Vereinigungen'*) in Kiel, which published a report (Ministerpräsidentin des Landes Schleswig-Holstein, 1995).

In February 1992, a discussion group for federal and provincial author-ities (*Bund-Länder-Gesprächskreis*) was created to keep abreast of 'sect' problems, exchange information, and suggest measures to national and provincial authorities. In November 1993, this body commissioned the federal office of administration (*Bundesverwaltungsamt*) to set up a centre and since 1 January, 1994, the *zentrale Dokumentationsstelle* in Cologne has been operative as part of the *Bundesverwaltungsamt*. Its purpose is to collect legal cases and documents regarding 'youth sects' and 'therapy cults'.

Conflicting court rulings

State and public authorities have been encumbered by conflicting court rulings on questions relating to *Jugendreligionen*. A lower court may give way to the case brought by a movement, which the higher court then disallows. This happened, for example, in the case of the Rajneesh group's objections to Baden-Württemberg's report. Another example concerns groups which have applied for licences to run private schools, as Scientology and *Universelles Leben* have in Bavaria. While the administrative court (*Verwaltungsgericht*) in Würzburg ruled in 1991 that *Universelles Leben* could run a primary school, the federal administrative court (*Bundesverwaltungsgericht*) in Berlin ruled in 1992 that Scientology could not run an inter-denominational school in Munich.[86]

Another issue concerns how religions organize their financial affairs. Art. 4 leaves this to their discretion. In 1992, the *Bundesverwaltungsgericht* passed a *Grundsatzurteil* (fundamental ruling) stating that even if a group's business interests outweigh its other activities, the group should not lose constitutional protection. The court confirmed its ruling in 1997 declaring that commercial activities which supply financial means for religious groups fall in principle under the protection of Art. 4. Only when religious groups are shown to pursue exclusively commercial interests and use religious teachings as a pretext for commercial objectives, are they excluded from protection.

Although this ruling stands, other courts have come to different views. While the upper administrative court (*Oberverwaltungsgericht*) in Hamburg and the administrative court (*Verwaltungsgericht*) in Munich ruled, respectively, that Scientology and Universelles Leben should be recognized as *bona fide* religious groups, the federal industrial court (*Bundesarbeitsgericht*) in Kassel ruled in March 1995 that Scientology should not be considered a church, but a commercial enterprise (*Wirtschaftsunternehmen*).[87] Another ruling of the court in Hamburg stated that Scientology has the character of a business. Although the question of constitutional protection was not addressed, the court did not accept Scientology's argument that the sale of goods (books, e-meters, etc.) and services (courses) was part of exercising its religion and ruled that Scientology had to pay taxes. In December 2003, the *Verwaltungsgerichtshof* (administrative tribunal) of Baden-Württemberg in Mannheim ruled that the Scientology group in Baden-Württemberg should retain its legal status as an association, because it does not pursue any commercial activities. The *Regierungsprädium* (government) in Stuttgart had deprived Scientology of this status, a decision which the administrative court in Stuttgart had reversed. The tribunal tried the appeal and followed the ruling of the *Bundesverwaltungsgericht* of 1997.

These examples show the State's legal difficulties. Kränzle (1996: 63) points out that the activities of 'dubious' religious groups are under the watchful eye of public authorities in charge of security and criminal offences. However, prosecution can only proceed if based on sufficient evidence. This requirement rules out an outright ban: religious groups are protected by the freedom to assemble and freedom of association. Only if there is incontrovertible proof that their purpose or activities go against the law, can associations be banned. Such proof has so far not been adduced. Behnk (1996a: 77) points out that banning Scientology, for example, would drive it underground and would make it even harder to exert any control over it. Therefore, a ban can only be the last resort. The Federal Ministry's report of 1980 had also ruled out a general ban of *Jugendsekten* (Bundesminister für Jugend, Famile und Gesundheit, 1980) and Schuster (1985: 101) thinks that a ban is probably not possible or even appropriate. For Kränzle (1996: 63–64) and Behnk (1996a: 77), informing the public and raising public awareness are indispensable. For Kränzle, information is not just about facts (structures, aims) regarding 'cults', but also about the meaning of life and values and both require the co-operation of parents, public and private institutions of *Jugendhilfe*, and the churches. For Behnk, information and democratic opposition are more effective in counteracting groups, such as Scientology, and society must not allow sectarian extremism to gain too much of a foothold.

Ei and politics

Ei *and Junge Union*

In *Ei*'s view, *Jugendreligionen* are a social problem and all social institutions need to address it – churches, public authorities, government, and political parties. The Conservative Party's youth wing, *Junge Union*, was one of the first political parties to incorporate the issue in its manifesto. From the mid-1970s, its federal chairmen[88] organized lecture series for the public and documentation for the series was published as the *Sektenreport* (Frank *et al.*, 1993).[89] Special seminars took place in all provincial associations of the party at least once a year; for example, 'Jugendsekten – Die Freiheit des einzelnen schützen' (Youth Sects: Protecting Personal Freedom) was organized in late 1984, jointly with *Ei*, with proceedings (Junge Union Bayern, 1985), including a contribution from the then Federal Minister for the Family, H. Geißler. In June 1992, *Junge Union* organized a conference in Hamburg on 'Scientology – Macht, Kommerz und Psychoterror' (Scientology: Power, Business, and Psychological Terror), with speakers including representatives from federal ministries and committees, party activists, clergy, and members of parents' initiatives. The conference's press release called for Scientology to be observed by the *Verfassungsschutz*.

Junge Union also asked questions in the provincial parliaments[90] which resulted in some provincial governments' reports being publicly distributed. Political foundations, such as Konrad Adenauer and Hanns Seidel Foundation, held special seminars regarding legal matters and published outcomes (Hanns-Seidel-Stiftung 1979; Engstfeld and Hanns-Seidel-Stiftung, 1981). *Junge Union* published information about 'cults' and their activities (Schuster and Sackmann, n.d.), including Scientology (Junge Union Bayern, n.d.; Junge Union Deutschlands, 1993; Junge Union Nordwürttemberg, 1992; 1995) and Rajneeshism (Schuster, 1984).

Other parties

Other political parties have taken up the 'cult' issue. As early as 1983, the conference of the conservative party in Bavaria (CSU) debated a motion from *Junge Union Bayern* regarding nationwide regulations for charitable status. The motion referred to 'youth religions' in particular and called on the Federal Government to introduce such regulations, clarify the limits of Art. 4, support parents' organizations and other self-help groups, contribute actively to the debate by involving social institutions (schools, youth organizations, institutions for political education, media), strengthen the family, and offer people values and meaning to prevent them from joining 'youth sects'.

In the *Landtag* of Baden-Württemberg, an all-party motion of early 1992 called for an investigation into, even a ban on, Scientology's controversial practices. In particular, it called for improved information about Scientology, more help for people who had become 'victims', and clarification of whether Scientology's activities (auditing, purification rundown, etc.) fall under 'pastoral care' or treatments subject to professional control. Scientology's status as a 'church' should also be carefully examined and a centre put in place to provide legal advice for those affected. Co-operation between political parties, trade unions, and trade associations should counteract the influence of 'sects' in business and a centralized system of information should be created to record 'front' organizations.

In Autumn 1995, the Social Democratic Party's (SPD) parliamentary party created a working party on 'sects', and in March 1996, it held a discussion on 'cults' in Bonn.[91] The working party's spokesperson, Renate Rennebach, maintained links with parents' groups, as indicated by her message to Ei's *Festschrift* and her presentation at EBI Leipzig's conference in March 1996. SPD's parliamentary party also applied for an *Enquête-Kommission*,[92] whose task was summarized in four points: (1) to undertake a 'fundamental, comprehensive analysis and appraisal of so-called sects and therapy cults' active in Germany, including their national and international networks, the dangers they present to individuals and society, existing jurisdiction, and the scope of religious freedom (Art. 4), and to assemble and assess information gathered by private, public, and church institutions; (2) to examine the reasons for membership and (3) the problems arising from membership and leaving; (4) to review socio-political discussions conducted to date and make recommendations for action (Deutscher Bundestag, Drucksache 13/3867, 27.2.96). The *Bundestag* debated this application in March 1996: the conservative parties questioned whether the *Kommission* could report within the proposed timetable (two years); the Liberal Democratic Party (FDP) argued against the State dealing with (pseudo-)religious groups, and the Green Party pointed out that the groups' religious character was not at issue, but their totalitarian claims (Eimuth, 1996b: 188).[93] The *Enquête-Kommission 'Sogenannte Sekten und Psychogruppen'* consisting of 12 parliamentarians and 12 experts was instated in 1996.

The *Kommission*'s interim report in July 1997 (Deutscher Bundestag, 1997) – adopted by majority vote, but the parliamentary party of *Bündnis 90/Die Grünen* (The Greens) abstained, as did one 'expert (ibid.: 4, 39–42) – gives an account of the first year of its work. In her preface, chairperson Ortrun Schätzle points to the *Kommission*'s 'problem-oriented approach' and its aim to objectify or de-emotionalize the discussion and thus steer clear of condemnation *and* minimization. The final report was published in June 1998 (Deutscher Bundestag, 1998), with the *Kommission* pointing out that its task did not consist in examining individual groups or their beliefs. Its work was guided by the State's obligations, while the potential for conflict and problems in religious and ideological communities was examined. As the *Kommission* found only some groups to be potentially problematic (*konfliktträchtig*), this precluded generalizations about the wide range of new religious and ideological communities and therapy groups. The *Kommission* desisted from using the term 'sect', precisely because it denotes generalization and stigmatization. The *Kommission* found that the greatest conflicts arise in the social environment of involved individuals and that these are not 'passive victims', but active agents in the joining process. This does, however, not relieve the State of its responsibilities: it needs to intervene when laws and basic rights are violated or criminal acts are committed in the guise of religion. The State should support individuals by providing information and raising awareness – measures which are reflected in the *Kommission*'s recommendations, which also include: the establishment of a federal foundation (*Bundesstiftung*) to centralize various aspects; legal provision for State funding of private advice and information centres; increased national and international co-operation to close considerable research gaps. The *Kommission* took the view that Scientology is not a religious community, but a political-extremist enterprise and therefore called for its continued observation by the *Verfassungsschutz*. However, it did not deem constitutional changes regarding new religious groups necessary, as complementing existing legislation and providing information would form a framework for the State to deal with such groups, as would society's tolerance of unproblematic groups.

Questions in parliament

Just like British MPs, members of the national and provincial parliaments have raised questions about 'cults' to put the subject on the agenda of governments and ministries. As early as October 1978, MP Meinecke asked the Federal Government which 'youth religions' had charitable status and whether it had evidence that most groups pursued political rather than religious-ideological objectives (Deutscher Bundestag, 8. Wahlperiode, Drucksache 8/2186: 9, 13.10.1978). In his question to the Federal Minister for Youth, Family and Health in June 1982, MP Schachtschabel asked about the number of UC members in Germany, to what extent the 'brainwashing' allegation applied to the UC, and what measures the Government would take to prevent such practices, if their use were proven. The Ministry responded in late June 1982. In August 1982, the Government replied to a question submitted by MP Kroll-Schlüter and the conservative parties (CDU/CSU) regarding nationwide information, controversies regarding the UC, the effect of membership, recruitment techniques, charitable status, criminal offences, and deprogramming (Deutscher Bundestag, 9. Wahlperiode, Drucksache 9/1932/1895, 23.08.1982). In March 1988, the Government responded to a question by MP Kappes (Deutscher Bundestag, Drucksache 11/2061, 18.03.1988) and in May 1989, it answered a question (Deutscher Bundestag, 11. Wahlperiode, Drucksache 11/4195) from MP Daniels and the Greens on the State's neutrality in religious matters (Deutscher Bundestag, 11. Wahlperiode, Drucksache 11/4533, 11.05.1989).

In October 1990, MP Geiger asked the Government whether Scientology was a religious community and should enjoy the protection of the constitution and whether the Government would investigate and consider banning it. The Government replied that Scientology should not be considered a religious community, this question was disputed in court, it had so far not considered a ban, and information was an effective way to warn of possible dangers. In March 1996, the Federal Ministry for the Family, Senior Citizens, Women, and Youth responded to a question submitted by Conservative (CDU/CSU) and Liberal (FDP) MPs about measures to inform the public about 'youth sects' and 'therapy cults' (Deutscher Bundestag, 13. Wahlperiode, Drucksache 13/3712; Drucksache 13/4132, 15.03.1996).

In January 1997, the provinces of Bavaria and Baden-Württemberg initiated a debate on Scientology in the *Bundesrat*, which referred the appurtenant discussion paper to relevant committees (EZW, 1997). In June 1981, MP Büssow (SPD) of Westphalia raised a question about Scientology's aims, recruitment methods, and other activities in the province and the government's current and future measures. In July 1981, the minister for work, health and social affairs provided a detailed answer (Landtag Nordrhein-Westfalen, 9. Wahlperiode, Drucksache 9/812, 16.06.1981; Drucksache 9/922, 27.07.1981). In August 1982, MP Dehn (SPD) of Lower Saxony addressed a question about the UC's activities in Germany, to which the

minister for economy and traffic replied in November 1982 (Nieder-
sächsischer Landtag, 10. Wahlperiode, Drucksache 10/394). In December
1982, MP Schneider (FDP) asked about the possible dangers of 'youth sects'
in Lower Saxony and enquired how many were active, whether the government could help concerned parents, and what measures were or would
be taken to provide information in schools and youth organizations. The
minister for culture gave a detailed reply.

In 1984, a group of conservative MPs (CSU) in Bavaria introduced a
number of motions regarding support of organizations campaigning against
'youth sects', provision of information, charitable status, and the protection
of personal rights (Bayerischer Landtag, 10. Wahlperiode, Drucksache 10/
2533, 05.01.1984; Drucksache 10/2532, 05.01.1984; Drucksache 10/
2658, 19.01.1984; Drucksache 10/2657, 19.01.1984). In September 1990,
MP Kern (SPD) asked the Westphalia government about its intended
measures against Scientology, which he considered the most dangerous
pseudo-religious group in Germany. The government replied that it could
only provide information for those concerned, although it shared the view of
the court in Düsseldorf that Scientology was a business. In July 1992, the
Liberal Democratic Party (FDP) asked the Westphalia government whether
Scientology was socially damaging and pursued commercial interests, to
which the government replied in April 1993 (Landtag Nordrhein-Westfalen,
Drucksache 11/4104, 20.07.1992; Drucksache 11/5275, 02.04.1993). The
question also led to a parliamentary discussion in May 1993.

In 1995, a motion of the conservative party (CDU) in Westphalia wanted
a possible ban on Scientology and its observation by the *Verfassungsschutz*
examined. The motion was debated in November 1995 and referred to the
committees for interior affairs and for children, youth and family
(Innenministerium des Landes Nordrhein-Westfalen, 1996).

Committee hearing

In October 1991, the Committee for Women and Youth of the *Bundestag*
heard experts on 'youth sects'. The hearing was not open to the public, but
proceedings were made public. Experts (R. Abel, H. Baer, J. Eiben, T.
Gandow, H. Hemminger, J. Keltsch, R.-D. Mucha, N. Nedopil, N. Potthoff)
were invited to submit statements and speak at the hearing. They focused
on seven areas: (1) structures and strategies of new religious movements,
'therapy cults', and other movements; (2) social conditions in which such
religious movements form; (3) infiltration of social structures by 'therapy
cults'; (4) the State's tasks and possible ways of dealing with 'therapy cults';
(5) medical experience and assessment of psycho-somatic consequences and
dangers for those affected; (6) legal aspects; (7) tasks for political action
(Deutscher Bundestag (Ausschuss für Frauen und Jugend), 1991). The
Minister for the Family and Senior Citizens, Hannelore Rönsch, reportedly
stated that the hearing underlined the urgency in taking measures against

'therapy cults', especially Scientology. The Committee was unanimous that an independent centre for documentation was needed to report on activities of 'youth sects' to administrative and legal institutions. Scientology featured large in the experts' statements. They also pointed out that Scientology was particularly successful in eastern Germany because people lacked orientation in the wake of reunification.

Conclusions

This section showed how the first parents' initiative in Germany, *Elternini-tiative zur Hilfe gegen seelische Abhängigkeit und religiösen Extremismus e.V.*, constituted itself in the mid-1970s under the direction of Pastor Haack. He was instrumental in the group's foundation and formation of its aims and direction. Haack's connections with similar organizations in the US, Britain, and France had inspired *Ei*'s foundation and they provided the blueprint for *Ei*'s organization. Parents' groups arose primarily from *parental* concerns about 'cult' membership and its effects on families and individuals. These concerns extended to the perceived threat from the recruitment and activities of 'cults' to society. Parents feared that more and more people would be drawn to them and believed that they undermined society by injecting their teachings into social institutions, the economy, and politics, without, however, revealing who they really are. The term often used in this context is *Unterwanderung* (infiltration) (e.g. Flöther and Haack, 1985). These concerns compelled parents' organizations to campaign against 'cults' and educate the public and public authorities about them.

The perspectives and approaches of FAIR and *Ei* overlap in a number of areas. Both see 'cult' members as victims who need help, aim to provide support and information for parents, and want to educate the public. Both call on politicians and public authorities to curb the influence of 'cults' in society. Both are engaged in gathering and disseminating information and lobbying MPs in European, national, and provincial governments.

However, while FAIR arose from parental concerns addressed to an MP (Paul Rose), *Ei* arose from pastoral care which parents sought from the churches, in particular Pastor Haack, the first full-time *Sektenbeauftragte*. British parents appealed to their *political* representatives, while German parents turned to *pastors* and *priests*. This suggests that parents in Britain saw the 'cult' problem primarily in social and political terms, while parents in Germany saw it primarily in religious terms. Although British parents, too, sought advice and help from local clergy and often received both (comments in FAIR newsletters point to good relationships between some local clergy and parents), church organizations took time to find an official voice – the Church of England Synod report was not published until 1989. In Germany, help and advice for parents did not just depend on *local* clergy, as both Roman Catholic and Protestant Churches installed a network of 'sect experts', who did not just take a theological or pastoral stance. Some became engaged in the campaign to address wider social and political issues. Thus, German parents received practical help and advice *and* won the churches for their cause. Parents in Britain did not find that alliance with the churches and thus sought help from political agents and agencies – their local MPs and government bodies.

Since *Ei*'s creation, other organizations formed in Germany, some in conjunction with *Sektenexperten*. This created a network of information and assistance between churches and parents' organizations, a symbiotic, mutually beneficial relationship. In this aspect, *Ei* differs from FAIR. Another difference is the relatively minor role which German parents appear to have played in founding parents' organizations. While parents were looking and asking for help, they were apparently not prepared to set up formal structures to fight 'cults', although they joined these, once they were in place. Parents may simply have been too fearful to campaign openly. At the time, the idea of self-help groups was not common, although *Bürgerinitiativen* (single-issue campaigns) had began to form (mainly for environmental issues). These realized how powerful a voice they could have in local decisions. In contrast, Britain has a tradition of associations for political causes or medical conditions, which seek political action or provide mutual support. Beckford (1983b) therefore speaks of a 'voluntaristic' response to the 'cult problem' in the UK (and US).

While the churches' co-operation with parents' groups in Germany has been beneficial overall, it has also had drawbacks. While parents' groups were backed by powerful institutions which could advance social and theological arguments against 'cults', had ready-made communication networks and a voice in society, they appeared to be the churches' 'appendices' or 'servants', instead of independent organizations. Also, they tended to adopt the *theological* perspective which *Sektenbeauftragte* took by virtue of their office. Although *Ei* and FAIR share concerns about a wide range of religious groups and organizations, the reasons prompting these concerns differ. While FAIR's concerns relate primarily to groups which elicit its attention because of the problems they cause, *Ei* tends to include any religious groups outside the churches in its remit. Therefore, non-mainstream religious groups are 'sects' – the very approach theologians take. Haack, for example, collected and published information about non-mainstream groups and movements, such as non-conformist churches (Haack, 1980f), secret orders (Haack, 1980c), and Freemasons (Haack, 1988e). Information distributed by the Roman Catholic *Sektenbeauftragte* in Saxony covers all non-mainstream groups, but defines those outside the categories 'sects' and 'therapy cults' as 'not dangerous'.

Ei followed Haack's terminology and definition of *Jugendreligionen, Psychomutation*, and *Seelenwäsche* as a framework within which to explain and understand 'cults' and 'cult' membership. This model is very similar to FAIR's and to current thought in North American 'cult-monitoring' groups. This model leaves little, if any, place for social scientific thinking. Haack's influence on *Ei* also shaped parents' views of social scientific work – he was dismissive of social scientific studies of *Jugendreligionen* and warned parents against co-operating with any 'scientific' surveys.

FAIR and *Ei* have used the medical perspective to explain 'cult' membership. While FAIR is still pursuing this angle, *Ei* (and other groups) seem to have moved away from the 'medicalization' of the 'cult' phenomenon. While conferences and seminars (co-)organized by parents' groups in the late 1970s and early 1980s included professors of medicine and psychiatry and health-care professionals (Evangelische Akademie Tutzing, 1980; Müller-Küppers and Specht, 1979; Karbe and Müller-Küppers, 1983) from Germany and the US (J. Clark, M. Singer, J. West), the focus seems to have shifted to general information, possible legal instruments, co-ordination of institutions, and clarification of constitutional questions, such as the boundaries between religious freedom and 'democratic' behaviour.

Ei and other parents' groups have lobbied and used contacts with politicians and parliamentarians to further their cause and bring about legal and political action. As a result, government bodies have deliberated and published reports about 'cults'. Compared to FAIR, *Ei* and related groups seem to have been far more successful in mobilizing support from public authorities: they received moral support, because politicians and MPs attended their conferences, political support, because action has been taken, and financial support, because they were subsidized. Evidence that public authorities took the issue seriously can be seen in the number of official reports, parliamentary questions, debates in political parties, and discussions in other public bodies, in the significant number of politicians attending conferences organized by parents' groups, in the funding and material support of parents' groups and projects. By contrast, the only government official attending a FAIR conference was Tom Sackville at the FAIR meeting in 1996, when he was an MP. Also, FAIR's applications for Government funds have so far been refused.

Several reasons account for the success of parents' organizations. First, personal circumstances involved some politicians and government officials at the very beginning. Some, like Karbe (in the Federal Ministry of Finance), were affected parents. They knew the 'system' and had connections. They also had enough social standing for their concerns not to be ignored.

Second, despite the separation of Church and State, the State could not ignore that the churches had taken up the issue and raised their voices for affected parents. Beckford points out that Germany has been characterized by a stable equilibrium between the two churches and a high degree of moral consensus. Therefore, the phenomenon of young people joining 'cults' has been perceived as disaffection with prevailing values, on a par with the 1960s student rebellion and political terrorism (Beckford, 1983b: 208–209). This still applies to some extent, considering frequent references in the literature to parallels between the appeal of terrorism and the appeal of 'cults' and to the need for providing young people with meaning and values.

Third, the State's constitutional duties require the protection of the personal rights of citizens, including young people. These rights revolve around issues regarding human dignity and health. The State thus has to at least hear evidence, consult with experts, and give the matter due consideration. Parents and *Sektenexperten* supplied evidence in letters and reports. For example, in preparation for the Hanover conference, AGPF (1978) submitted a dossier of cases to illustrate the effects of 'cult' membership on parents and members. Haack encouraged parents to write to politicians and ministers. The State's duty to inform and educate the public thus explains the number of official reports.

The difference in the approaches is related to the religious cultures in Germany and Britain. Germany's written constitution arose from the Weimar Republic and the lessons drawn from the Nazi regime. It is therefore deeply committed to enshrining and protecting religious freedom, freedom of conscience, and freedom of speech as basic rights so that they can never be taken away again by any political regime. The constitution's design also seeks to prevent totalitarian groups of whatever political colour from undermining the State or even gaining influence or political power. Therefore, the State has to be vigilant to recognize any indication of such developments and nip them in the bud. Vigilance is also the official task of the *Verfassungsschutz*, the body which observes the activities of potentially unconstitutional political parties or organizations. Regarding the 'cult' issue, constitutional commitments conflict with one another. While *bona fide* religious organizations should be protected by the constitution, those perceived as incipiently totalitarian and extremist groups pose a threat to society and must not be allowed to operate under the protection of the constitution. This is the background against which the decision to place Scientology under the observation of the *Verfassungsschutz* needs to be seen.

Fourth, Germany's federal system combines central Government with provincial governments, the structure of the latter mirroring that of the former, so that procedures and modes of operation are largely the same in both. While the *Länder* have a great deal of autonomy, political mechanisms, such as regular ministerial meetings, allow them to consult with one another to co-ordinate and harmonize regulations. The hierarchical layers of political and bureaucratic bodies provide each authority with a distinct brief and referral system. This principle of subsidiarity allows for matters to be passed to appropriate and, if necessary, higher authorities. Beckford (1983b) speaks of a reticular system in Germany.[94] This system is well illustrated by the way *Jugendschutz* is organized: public and private sector rely on one another and need to co-operate effectively to ensure the protection of young people. Parents' organizations have been successful in joining forces with these institutions. Shupe *et al.*'s (1983: 187–190) comparison of 'anti-cult movements' in the US and West Germany cites three factors which explain the greater official response to 'cults' in Germany: the religious (ecclesiastical) tradition, Church–State relations (relative co-operation), and low tolerance for young people engaging in alternative lifestyles.

Fifth, State funding of day-to-day running costs and staff of parents' organizations was crucial for furthering their cause (until it was declared 'unlawful' by the courts): this provided material means to operate and recognition of their work, because – unlike in Britain – receiving funds from a state authority is a stamp of approval.

Sixth, Scientology's activities in the 1990s confirmed the perceived threat parents' organizations warned against. In a number of *Länder*, the courts declared Scientology a business. Scientology was shown to use 'front' organizations for business management courses and real estate offices. Scientology used lawsuits to silence critics and sought to portray the campaign against it as religious persecution similar to the persecution of the Jews under Nazism – a strategy which could not fail to provoke outrage: hence the official reports which focused on Scientology and whether it should come under closer scrutiny; hence a substantial number of publications on Scientology, which is why Behnk spoke of Scientology as the 'cult' *par excellence* in Germany. These developments reinforced the perception of the threat of 'cults' to society and State, which parents' groups and *Sektenbeauftragte* had repeatedly spelt out.

Finally, very few, if any, academics were called upon to appear as experts in political hearings and official reports included little, if any, academic literature. By the time *Religionswissenschaftler* started to examine the phenomenon, the debate had progressed so far that the cult-monitoring groups' explanatory model was well established and instituted in parents' organizations, the *Sektenbeauftragte*, and public authorities. Kehrer's (1981a) volume on the UC was the first major academic publication. Shupe *et al.* (1983: 186, 190) also note that social scientists in Germany 'have shown a surprising lack of interest' in the phenomenon of new religions. However, the *Enquête-Kommission* is significant, as its panel of experts included students of *Religionswissenschaft* and social science.

Notes

1 References to FAIR's newsletter in this section vary due to name changes: it was *F.A.I.R. NEWSLETTER* (until February 1980), then became *NEWSLETTER* (until October 1982), reverted to *F.A.I.R. NEWSLETTER* for one edition (February 1982), before changing to *FAIR NEWS* (from June 1982 to date).

2 This meeting celebrated FAIR's 20th anniversary. The speakers included past and present chairpersons. As Rose could not attend in the end, a message was read instead. Summaries of the addresses appeared in *FAIR NEWS* (Autumn 1996: 2–3).

3 Deo Gloria Trust was founded in 1977 by Kenneth Frampton, a wealthy businessman with strong Christian convictions. His two adult sons were involved with the Children of God (COG, now The Family) for some time. Until the late 1990s, Deo Gloria had a permanent office in South London. It was concerned

with 'religious error and abuse' regarding evangelical Christian teachings. After an initially high-profile campaign against 'cults', Deo Gloria scaled down its operations, responding to enquiries for information, but referring requests for counselling (Beckford, 1985: 227). Kenneth Frampton died in 1988. In 2000, Deo Gloria helped Dialog Centre UK to establish offices, which were opened in April 2002.

4 FAIR and Deo Gloria had a very close and mutually beneficial relationship, despite distinct differences in their aims and practices. Deo Gloria was stronger as an organization in the early 1980s (in terms of material and human resources), but FAIR regained its former prevalent position by 1984, after persuading Deo Gloria members to join its membership. McCann dismissed the suggestion of FAIR's closer contact with evangelical groups as 'poppycock', but according to Rose (1981a: 186–187), FAIR was working 'closely with evangelical Christians in the Deo Gloria Trust' and had 'close contacts with the Church of England Enquiry Centre and the Evangelical Alliance'. *FAIR NEWS* of October 1982 warmly welcomed new subscribers recommended by Deo Gloria, but pointed out that Deo Gloria had neither folded, nor had FAIR made a take-over bid. My fieldwork also corroborates close links.

5 The 17-page October 1982 edition of *FAIR NEWS* includes 3.5 pages of UC-related items, undoubtedly connected with the *Daily Mail* libel case. Some movements (Scientology, COG, Rajneesh Foundation, etc.) take up about a page, and others (DLM, Emin, Exegesis, etc.) a mere paragraph. From April 1983, groups appeared in alphabetical order, with the UC still occupying more space than other groups.

6 According to the *Los Angeles Times*, 'The challenge is not to the [Unification] church's teachings or to the vitality of the religious conversion. The challenge is to the church's practice of misrepresenting or concealing its identity to bring unsuspecting outsiders into its highly structured environment.' (*FAIR NEWS*, Winter 1989/90: 11–12).

7 Rose made this point in his address to the 1996 Meeting and Freeland, in his address, drew parallels between the regimes in 'cults' and under Hitler, a parallel often drawn by 'radical' 'anti-cult' circles. Ironically, some 'cults' draw comparisons between the Hitler regime and (perceived) persecution by State and public authorities. In *Hate and Propaganda*, the Church of Scientology (1993) maintained that the measures taken against it in Germany amounted to the Jews' persecution in the Third Reich. A ban by the German authorities stopped this publication's circulation.

8 The February 1982 newsletter stated (p. 10): 'This organisation [Opus Dei] ought to be mentioned in a category of its own as it is neither a cult nor a sect, rather a movement within the Roman Catholic Church, approved by the Vatican and respected by Roman Catholics throughout the world. But a long article in *The Times* in January 1981 gave a disturbing report on what appeared to amount to cult-like features of the movement. The article was followed by a flood of readers' letters, both for and against Opus Dei. FAIR received enquiries regarding the group'.

9 For example, *FAIR NEWS* of January 1985 lists five groups under 'miscellaneous' and reminds readers that: they are new to FAIR's files, they reflect the kind of enquiries FAIR receives apart from those on the 'major cults', FAIR has little information on them and would appreciate details from readers.

10 In 1985, a group of 'hardliners' broke away from FAIR and formed Cultists Anonymous (CA) to help families and individuals caught up in 'cults'. It did not last very long, because its 24-hour helpline ran out of money. It claimed to be non-political and non-religious (McCann, 1986: 7; Storm, 1989; Doyle, 1989). FAIR invited CA members back, but very few rejoined.

11 The context for this comment is an article in *Medina Rajneesh* magazine (May–September 1983), which claimed that press reports are mainly based on 'inaccurate and inflammatory information released by anti-cult organisations like FAIR, EMERGE and DEO'. Another article in the magazine attacks Richard Cottrell, FAIR, and Pete Broadbent. *FAIR NEWS* (July 1983: 7) commented that 'The article is subjective and full of inaccuracies and seems to have been created in the same mould the Moonies have used in the past when trying to discredit critics'. The editorial of *Rajneesh Times* (June 1984) also attacked FAIR, stating that FAIR is 'an insidious anti-religious movement . . . spreading hysteria and distress, wreaking havoc in many innocent families. Masquerading as a fact-finding bureau, this seemingly innocent group of pious do-gooders has done more to destroy family relations than any other single movement.'

12 'Love bombing' has been reported mainly in connection with UC's recruitment strategies, but came to describe general 'cult' practice. It involves constant attention by existing members to potential recruits. They are never left alone, not even to go to the loo, treated in an extremely friendly way, and told repeatedly how welcome they are.

13 Alland (1962) showed how manipulation of sensory factors induces trance-like states and mystical experiences. Suedfield (1975) concluded that extreme forms of sensory deprivation lead to decreased intellectual functioning and mood shifts, even hallucinations.

14 Lifton's *Chinese Thought Reform and the Psychology of Totalism* – considered central to the literature on 'cults' and totalism in general (especially Chapter 22) – is a study of Westerners and Chinese intellectuals who had been subjected to 'thought reform' in China. Schein *et al.*'s *Coercive Persuasion* is, with Lifton's book, an important early study of 'brainwashing'. It deals with American civilians imprisoned by the Chinese Communists in 1950–1956. Many made confessions of a politically damaging nature, some appeared converted to Communism, even on repatriation. Schein examined the pressures designed to change beliefs, attitudes, and values, discusses psychological theories which explain the process of change, and draws attention to similar phenomena within American society. The issue of 'brainwashed' POWs became topical again after seven allied airmen who had been captured during the Gulf War were paraded in front of TV cameras to denounce the 'war against peaceful Iraq'. McGurvey's (1992) article quotes Philip Zimbardo, a Stanford University Professor of Psychology: 'Effective mind control exists in the most mundane aspects of human existence: the inner pressure to be bonded to other people; the power of group norms to influence behaviour, and the force of social rewards . . . It is people in convincing social situations, not gadgets or gimmicks that control the minds of other people.' Zimbardo has also contributed to AFF's *Cultic Studies* (Anderson and Zimbardo, 1984; Zimbardo and Hartley, 1985; Zimbardo, 2002). The topic of brainwashing featured in the BBC Radio 4's 'Start the Week' programme of 4 April 2005, during which Catherine Taylor, a research scientist at Oxford, discussed the background, without reference to 'cults' – this connection was mentioned in passing by Andrew Marr who presents the programme.

15 For example, in October 1985, *FAIR NEWS* drew attention to a report in *The New Pacific* (MacIntyre, 1985) on a Japanese management school which teaches assertiveness in a 'training course in hell': its first step consists in 'brainwashing', followed by lessons in yelling, chanting, memorizing useless information, and round-the-clock activities. *FAIR NEWS* commented (pp. 18–19) that 'If it exists in the realm of business, why is the presence of mind control – even in a much more refined and less obvious form – in the cult context so hotly denied by some?'

16 This group had primarily political, not religious, motives and promoted violence. Patricia Hearst was imprisoned for actions she committed as an SLA member, until President Carter commuted her sentence. Her story is in an auto-biographical book co-authored with Alvin Moscov (1983) and a film (Pearce, 1989). Her case regained publicity recently in connection with trials of former SLA members.

17 FAIR shares its rejection with its German counterparts: *FAIR NEWS* of January 1983 (pp. 4–5) included the full text of a press release on deprogramming by the parents' initiative in Munich '[a]s it largely corresponds with the views of FAIR'. The January 1988 edition summarized the views of Haack, who also opposed the practice.

18 At FAIR's 1981 Open Forum, some parents and ex-members seemed to be in favour of deprogramming, but FAIR's chairman stuck to the policy of counsel-ling only those willing, while pointing out that FAIR's role was to advise parents and decisions were up to them (*NEWSLETTER*, October 1981: 4). FAIR's official policy was upheld after a meeting in March 1982 (*FAIR NEWS*, June 1982: 3).

19 An attempt to extricate a UC member failed (*FAIR NEWS*, October 1982: 8). Another UC member, Nicola Raine, had mysteriously disappeared (*FAIR NEWS*, June 1982: 6), but had actually rejoined the UC. Her case featured in a BBC1 programme on deprogramming (22 April 1983). The mother of an ISKCON member, Bernadette Bradfield, failed to get her daughter out (*FAIR NEWS*, April 1983: 4–5). Two attempts occurred in New Zealand, one success-ful, the other not, both involving UC members. One was counselled during a surprise home visit; the other was kidnapped and deprogrammed (*FAIR NEWS*, October 1983: 11). The husband of a Faith Assembly member organized coercive deprogramming (*FAIR NEWS*, January 1984: 7). Another attempt involved a UC member in New Zealand (*FAIR NEWS*, April 1985: 8). After Andrew Dobie had spent £100,000 on Scientology books and courses, his family arranged deprogramming (*FAIR NEWS*, January 1986: 9). After an unsuccessful attempt to extricate a Swedish UC member, Britta Adolfsson (aka Britta Hitchler), the deprogrammers were charged with kidnapping and con-spiracy, but the jury decided the defendants should be acquitted on the 'choice of evils' defence (*FAIR NEWS*, Winter 1989: 12). This defence had also been used in Daniel Leitner's trial in 1981 (*NEWSLETTER*, October 1981: 6). In 1991, failed deprogramming was reported regarding Viscount Reidhaven who had become a follower of Muhammad Ali of the Naqshbandi (*FAIR NEWS*, Winter 1991/92: 14; October 1994: 11). In 1993, a young woman who had joined the Central London Church of Christ (CLCC) was reportedly depro-grammed. Her mother recommended parents not to follow her example (*FAIR NEWS*, Spring 1993: 5). The case also featured in a Cook Report on the CLCC of 6 August 1990.

20 One of the known deprogrammers is Martin Faiers, a former high-ranking UC member, who apparently runs or used to run COMA (Council on Mind Abuse). He is said to live in the south of France and work for the Spanish 'market'. There is apparently no connection with a Canadian group of the same name (Christ, 1989; Storm, 1989). Faiers was involved in an ISKCON member's (Sandro Passera's) attempted deprogramming in the Ticino, Switzerland, in March 1989. However, the police arrested Faiers and his team, which included Passera's parents (Christ, 1989). The case was tried in 1990 (*Tribune de Genève*, 26 novembre 1990). Faiers took part in the previously mentioned BBC1 programme on deprogramming (22 April 1983). Cultists Anonymous apparently endorsed deprogramming and acted as an agency (Storm, 1989: 6; McCann, 1986: 7).

21 The Minutes recorded the attendance of: Centre for New Religious Movements (represented by myself, as an observer), Cultists Anonymous, Cult Education, Cult Information Centre, Deo Gloria Outreach, Dialog Centre UK, Ex-Cult Members Support Group, FAIR, FAIR International, Family Support Group, Student Pastoral Ministries.

22 Ian Haworth set up Cult Information Centre (CIC) in 1987 (www.-cultinformation.org.uk), after he had run COMA in Canada. It became a registered charity in 1992. Its aim has been to provide, from a secular perspective (CIC claimed to be the first organization to do so), an information service on 'cults' and 'cult' activity. Haworth described his work as an 'immunization programme' which he takes to universities and youth groups (Doyle, 1989). He and an associate reportedly lost a court case brought by Werner Erhard against COMA and Haworth allegedly fled Canada to avoid payment (Victor, 1994). Haworth was also said to have gone bankrupt because of this case.

23 The Reachout Trust, based in Richmond, Surrey, began in 1982; its director is Doug Harris (www.reachouttrust.org). A charity since 1986, it describes its work as 'an international Christian ministry that upholds biblical truth and builds bridges to people in cults, occult and new age'.

24 CONCERN was set up to support parents of COG members and former members. With a strong Christian outlook, it concentrated on counselling and published a newsletter of the same name.

25 Housetop is a Roman Catholic missionary team which included research of new religious movements in its tasks. Its director, Hans Wijngaards, had worked in India and FAIR appreciated his knowledge of Eastern mysticism. FAIR's close contact with Housetop became problematic when Wijngaards became an INFORM governor. Housetop's 'vision combines Christian commitment to wholehearted acceptance of technology' and specializes in video courses and TV programmes (www.housetop.com).

26 The Dialogue Centre in Dublin consists of Mike Garde (fieldworker) and Fr Martin Tierney (chairperson). It is supported by the Church of Ireland and the Presbyterian Churches.

27 The Irish Family Foundation (IFF) formed in 1982. Although it was active for a while, it soon folded.

28 EMERGE developed within FAIR during 1980 and was initially its 'newly established youth branch', but wanted to be recognized as a group in its own right. It consisted of ex-members (a core of 25–30) who offered assistance to those toying with 'cult' membership and to parents seeking better understanding of their 'cult'-involved children. By April 1981, EMERGE had a 'statement of position' and held monthly meetings in the London area, with plans to create regional branches. By October 1982, EMERGE ran into difficulties and by 1986, it was no longer active.

29 T.O.LC. formed in the early 1990s and was originally a group of CLCC ex-members whose spokesman was Ayman Akshar (he died in early 2002). It published a newsletter, Close to the Edge. Its focus is now on the International Churches of Christ (www.tolc.org).

30 Catalyst is run by Graham Baldwin as a sanctuary for ex-members who need help (Doyle, 1989). It was started in late 1993, engages in 'exit counselling', and supports former 'cult' members and their families (Victor, 1994; MacDonald, 1989; www.catalyst-uk.freeserve.co.uk).

31 The Panhellenic Parents Union for the Protection of Greek Orthodoxy, the Family and the Individual (PPU) was founded by (the late) Father Alevisopoulos, Secretary of the Greek Church Synod with special responsibility for monitoring sects and 'para-religions'.

32 CAN described itself as 'a national non-profit organization founded to educate

the public about the harmful effects of mind control as used by destructive cults. CAN confines its concerns to unethical or illegal practices including coercive persuasion or mind control; and does not judge doctrine or beliefs.' Daphne Vane described CAN as a national family support organization which had grown out of small grassroots groups across the US (*FAIR NEWS*, July 1987: 2). In late 1995/early 1996, CAN was forced to file for bankruptcy after a jury had awarded Jason Scott US$1,087,500 in damages in September 1995. CAN was accused of having conspired to have Scott kidnapped and deprogrammed. In November, the judge denied CAN's post-trial motion. In October 1995, when Scott moved to collect his award, CAN filed for protection under Chapter 11 of the United States Bankruptcy Code and discontinued its Internet activities. In October 1996, the law firm Bowles and Hayes acquired CAN's legal name and logo. Timothy Bowles had been part of Bowles and Moxton, a law firm acting on behalf of Scientology. Fears that Scientology might use CAN's name to cause confusion materialized with the establishment of New CAN (www.cultawarenessnetwork.org). In 1996, when CAN's future was uncertain, Margaret Singer announced the Singer Foundation, which planned to make court records and documentation on 'cults' available on the Internet.

33 AFF describes itself as 'a tax-exempt research center and educational organisation founded in 1979 to assist ex-cult members and their families. AFF studies cultic groups and psychological manipulation and abuse. AFF disseminates its findings through conferences and . . . reports, information packs, books and periodicals.' AFF's three programmes are research, education, ICEP (International Cult Education Program), and Victim and Family Assistance. AFF published (1984–2001) *Cultic Studies Journal* and *Cult Observer*, publishes *Cultic Studies Review*, and maintains an extensive web site (http://csj.org). In late 2004, AFF changed its name to International Cultic Studies Association (ICSA) 'to better reflect the organization's focus and increasingly international and scholarly dimensions' (ICSA leaflet).

34 For example, conferences of CFF (Washington DC, 1982); AGPF (Bonn, 1984), AFF and CAN (1987), Asociación Pro Juventud (Spain, 1987), and Panhellenic Parents Union (Greece, 1993).

35 Cult Project, founded in 1980, is based in Montreal, with Mike Kropveld as Executive Director. It is an education and resource centre on 'cultism' and its objectives are prevention, education, and exposure. In 1990, the name was changed to Info-Cult (*info secte* in French); it describes itself as independent, bilingual, non-denominational (www.infocult.org).

36 This was established in 1984 as a non-denominational parents' support group. In 1986, it decided to merge with the Cult Project.

37 This support group for COG ex-members was started by David and Mary Hiebert, themselves COG members between 1971 and 1986. It is based in Richmond, BC, Canada, and publishes a newsletter under the same name.

38 Concerned Christians Growth Ministries publishes a bi-monthly magazine, *Take a Closer Look*. Van Leen published on Rajneesh (1983) and Fringe Christian groups (1990).

39 No figures are available for 1989/90, except that enquiries covered 138 'cults' and fringe groups, 77 of which were very obscure. In 1990/91, 1,700 letters were recorded, 1,200 phone calls, and 250 calls to the helpline. The number of groups enquired about reached 148. The figures were similar for 1991/92, but the groups enquired about increased to 171.

40 *Est* is subsumed under 'other self-improvement groups'. The latter probably comprise groups for which Paul Heelas coined the term 'self-religions': groups which offer techniques and practices which encourage experience and perfection of the self (Heelas, 1982; 1984; 1988).

41 Cottrell's report underwent various draft stages, described by David Wilshire (1984; 1990), then head of Cottrell's private office. The preliminary report was delivered in late January 1983 and debated in the European Parliament's Committee for Youth, Culture, Education, and Sport in March 1983. The full report was submitted in late January 1984. The Committee accepted Cottrell's guidelines and draft proposals in March 1984. In May 1984, the European Parliament voted on Cottrell's resolution, which required ratification by member countries to have validity across the European Community. Cottrell investigated 'cult' activities across Europe and proposed a code of conduct which was welcomed by cult-monitoring groups, but met with scepticism, if not rejection, by established churches and denominations.

42 David Alton referred to the lobby when he proposed his Private Member's Bill in October 1984, stating that FAIR had organized it (*Hansard*, 24.10.1984: 708).

43 Parents representing Cultists Anonymous delivered a letter to the Prime Minister at Downing Street. It suggested that Parliamentary Acts relating to hypnosis, trade description, anti-slavery, and mental health could be extended to clamp down on 'cult' recruitment. In October 1988, the Advertising Standards Authority (ASA) confirmed that it was investigating complaints regarding Scientology's advertising material, in particular its personality test.

44 The January 1985 edition of *FAIR NEWS* reported the press reception of *The Making of a Moonie*. While the *Spectator* criticized it as 'too detached and too sociological', *The Times Literary Supplement* stated that now, 'there are no grounds for resenting your offspring joining the UC, provided he/she made use of Moon's "free choice" to do so'. *THES* expressed relief and believed 'things are not really so bad', a view *The Times* echoed, adding that opposition to the UC was religious intolerance. Wallis commented in *New Society* that parental worries were exaggerated. *The Tablet* and *The Catholic Herald* felt the author was too sympathetic towards the UC and by leaving out hard evidence, the book created dangerous complacency.

45 More than 50 relatives, mostly 'cult' members' parents, attended. The academics present included Peter Clarke (King's College London), Eileen Barker (LSE), Kim Knott (University of Leeds), Paul Heelas (Lancaster University), and Judith Coney (*FAIR NEWS*, July 1985: 3).

46 Reviews by academics were also critical, as, for example, Peter Clarke's in *Religion Today* (1 (1), 1984), but perhaps unsurprisingly, their points of criticism differed from those raised by McCann.

47 'We are taken on a tour of "anti-cult" (rather dated phrase) demonology, taking in brainwashing (which Dr Mullan should define before he starts to write [sic]. . . . FAIR predictably receives a sideswipe (why?) and predictably too the reader is referred to 'New Vigilantes' which is a reasonably good (but highly inaccurate) study of anti-cult groups in America. But FAIR is not anti-cult . . . We are not cult bashers, and if Bob Mullan had tackled his task in a more even-handed fashion he could have been fairer to FAIR. This constant packaging in the rhetoric of the New Vigilantes is unacceptable and unprofessional' (*FAIR NEWS*, January 1984: 13).

48 *Unification News* even stated that the author 'temporarily joined the UC to make this report', but *FAIR NEWS* (January 1986: 14) doubted this: 'We have always understood that Eileen Barker has never at any time been a member and feel that the statement may not be correct'. Because of his role as editor of *The World and I*, a UC-related publication, Morton Kaplan (University of Chicago, now Professor Emeritus) has been considered close to the UC.

49 The MP for Gravesend, T. Brinton, raised the question in the House of Commons and asked participants to put the problems of British members and

their families to UC leaders. While some academics reportedly considered Brinton's motion a 'rather crude attempt at intimidation', others apprised the UC of academics' reluctance to attend in future, unless British parents' concerns were addressed. Before the conference, McCann had written to all likely participants urging them not to take part (*NEWSLETTER*, October 1981: 6). *FAIR NEWS* of April 1987 (p. 13) stated that FAIR had the list of participants of the 15th ICUS conference of November 1986, among them 23 British academics whom the newsletter named. The argument that the conference is a chance to meet fellow academics from across the world is countered by the question whether any thought is given to how the UC raises money and whether 'anything but hostility' can be expected 'from parents whose intelligent youngsters gave up a promising future in order to be exploited' (ibid.). In connection with two meetings organized by the ICF (International Cultural Foundation, another UC branch) in Edinburgh in 1991, *FAIR NEWS* (Autumn 1991: 13) commented that few participants realize that 'their names may be used not only to attract other academics but also to gain young recruits . . . and reassuring doubters in the UC ranks. Lending respectability by association to the UC can inadvertently lead to becoming responsible for much heartbreak.' However, an academic at the University of Aberdeen withdrew from ICUS conferences after receiving complaints from parents (*F.A.I.R. NEWSLETTER*, February 1980: 2).

50 In 1991, PWPA offered Bridgeport substantial sums to boost the university's ailing funds. After initial refusal, the Board of Trustees accepted, despite protests from staff and students. In August 1992, PWPA effectively gained control, when 16 members joined the Board. In early May 1993, the *New York Times* reported that opponents to the University's affiliation with PWPA filed a suit challenging the agreement. Around 1980, the UC apparently offered money to the Divinity Faculty at Cambridge, but G. Lampe, then Regius Professor of Divinity, stated that the university would not accept UC money.

51 INFORM also attracted critical media interest. For example, in *Reporting London* (ITV, 3 July 1989), Barker responded to criticism from a former UC member, members' relatives, and Lord Rawlinson. John Waite's *Face the Facts* programme (BBC Radio 4, 25 May 1989) was very critical.

52 Richard Cottrell was a guest speaker at FAIR's AGM in 1984 and 'assured us of his intention to continue the fight against the destructive element in the cults' (*FAIR NEWS*, October 1984: 2). 'Cult-monitoring' groups welcomed the Cottrell Report. The 1987 conference in Spain (Asociación Pro Juventud, 1988) commended the European Parliament for Cottrell's proposals and called on governments to ratify them and initiate a European code.

53 Exegesis was run by Robert d'Aubigny and operated a Standard Seminar or Programme under the name of 'Infinity Trainings' between 1976 and 1984. It offered 'enlightenment' to its 'graduates' as the reward for their expenses. Heelas (1987) includes it in his category of 'self-religions'. Later, Exegesis became known as Programmes Ltd., which is now transformed again. Exegesis regained publicity in 2002, when it was revealed that Cherie Blair employed a former member (Carole Caplin) as a 'lifestyle guru'.

54 Alton, MP for Liverpool, Mossley Hill, chaired an all-party group pressing for a voluntary code of practice for 'cults' and thus welcomed Cottrell's code (*Hansard*, 24.10.1984: 708). He is a committed Christian known for his pro-life campaign and abortion bill.

55 However, it was reported in March 1985 that the French Assembly prepared a bill to enable police and magistrates to investigate 'cult' membership. Police were to be empowered to enter centres to find out whether individuals were held against their will.

56 Other speakers included Lord Houghton of Sowerby, Lord Hampton, Lord

Sandys, Lord Thurlow, Baroness Macleod of Borve, Baroness Lane-Fox, Lord Craigmyle, Baroness Ewart-Biggs, Earl Ferrers for the Home Office, and the Bishop of Chelmsford.

57 So far as I am aware, only *Elterninitiative zur Wahrung der Geistigen Freiheit e.V. Leverkusen* (founded in 1984 because of parental concerns about ISKCON) has a newsletter, *EL-Mitteilungen*. It was at first a monthly and became a quarterly in 1990. It mainly contains material from publications by 'sister' organizations, such as *FAIR NEWS, BULLES, Cult Observer*, and includes press reports and book extracts, such as *Monkey on a Stick* (Hubner and Gruson, 1988) or *Combatting Cult Mind Control* (Hassan, 1988). AGPF members receive *AGPF Aktuell*, a quarterly 'information service'. Some church organizations have newsletters, such as *Bischöfliches Jugendamt Münster* and *Arbeitskreis 'Jugendreligionen' Münster* in Münster, Westphalia, who publish *Forum Jugendreligionen*. *Arbeitsgemeinschaft 'Neue religiöse Gruppen' e.V.* in Frankfurt (part of the Lutheran Church), publishes *Forum* occasionally. The Roman Catholic *Sektenbeauftragte* in Saxony provides a quarterly 'information service' to a selected readership.

58 'Cult(s)' is used here in a generic sense to describe groups which have caused controversy and problems for relatives, to avoid listing the terms current in the German literature every time. The terminology of parents' initiatives is discussed below.

59 The translation of quotations from German sources are my own, unless otherwise stated.

60 Haack actually uses the term 'anti-cult' (*Antikult*) here, although it is generally not used in the German literature. Parents' initiatives use *Sektenkritiker* (critics of sects) and 'sect experts' to describe themselves. Thiel (1986) uses *Anti-'Sekten'-Kampagne* (anti-sect campaign).

61 This booklet provides fact-sheet type descriptions of *Jugendreligionen, Psychogruppen*, 'guru movements', and groups which offer new revelations (*Neuoffenbarungsbewegungen*, a term also used by Pastoralamt in Vienna – Kommer, 1993), with a brief introduction to *Ei*, and addresses for help and advice.

62 Schneider's (1995) contribution to *Ei's* twentieth anniversary volume is primarily concerned with the topic of 'cults' in the RE curriculum and the way 'cults' have used schools for recruitment purposes. He argues that teachers are not sufficiently informed and that RE does thus not provide 'preventative information'.

63 Westhoven (1995: 212) mentions Canesius Reichhold as a founding and, 'until recently', a committee member, but provides no further details.

64 Haack (1986c: 60) concedes that a pastor (Thomas Gandow) initiated the creation of *Eltern- und Betroffeneninitiative gegen psychische Abhängigkeit – für geistige Freiheit Berlin e.V. (EBI)* in Berlin and that an employee of the *Stadtjugendamt* (local authority for the concerns of youth) and educators started *Aktion Psychokultgefahren* in Düsseldorf. *Arbeitskreis Sekten* in Herford was organized by a member of a political women's group, *Arbeitskreis Jugendsekten* in Essen was begun by a Roman Catholic, and the parents' group in Hamburg arose from the pastoral work of the local *Sektenbeauftragte*. However, *Initiative Jugendschutz e.V.* in Bremen and *Niedersächsische Elterninitiative gegen Mißbrauch der Religion e.V.* resulted directly from the concerns of affected parents.

65 Haack (1986c: 80–85) discusses possible projects and suggests how to make rehabilitation effective. Höft (1996), Mamay (1980), and Karbe (1980: 34) comment on the lack of suitable programmes, while Sieber (1980) argues the relative lack of demand for counselling by former members. In the mid-1980s (1984–1987), the Johanneshof near Bonn offered rehabilitation, as did the later

Odenwälder Wohnhof in Leibenstadt (2000–2003), now succeeded by a smaller scheme of Wohnhof e.V. The Federal Ministry for the Family commissioned a three-year (2000–2003) 'model project' to improve care and counselling in advice centres. The final reports are posted on the Ministry's web site (www.bmfsfj.de/Kategorien/Forschungsnetz/forschungsberichte,did=15890. html).

66 Two letters from parents, which Röder quoted in his opening address to *Ei*'s twentieth anniversary conference, illustrate this. The first was written 15 years ago, the second had been received a few weeks before the conference. Yet the contents of both letters were almost identical and attested that parents' concerns and the causes of these concerns had not changed (Elterninitiative, 1996: 15).

67 EAP is a branch of USLP (US Labor Party), an organization led by Lyndon H. LaRouche who was a presidential candidate in the 1979 elections in the US. In 1980, LaRouche's wife, Helga Zepp-LaRouche, was the EAP candidate in the German parliamentary elections (Haack, 1980a: 125–140; *Der Spiegel* 39, 1980; King, 1984; Ralfs-Horeis, 1991; Beyes-Corleis, 1994).

68 Other publications on 'therapy cults' include Sieper (1986), Hemminger (1990), and Haack (1991a).

69 The text of the statement, signed by M. Ach, C. Reichhold, and F.-W. Haack, is included in Haack (1986b: 105–106) and in the appendix of Elterninitiative (1995).

70 Mucha (1988: 68), (then) chairman of *Aktion Psychokultgefahren e.V.* in Düsseldorf, also warns parents against deprogramming – on similar grounds: it is not a suitable way for 'sect' members to leave, it is costly, it is carried out by foreigners, it is unlawful, it causes misery and suffering for everyone involved, it is as inhuman a practice as that used by 'sects'.

71 Its chairperson is Solveig Prass and its *c.*50 members meet regularly. EBI Leipzig's annual report for 1995 refers to 130 projects (meetings, talks, etc.) organized that year. In March 1996, it hosted a conference for those working in the 'cult-monitoring' field (MacKenzie, 1996).

72 This *Elterninitiative* started in 1978 as a group of relatives affected by COG. Nußbaum's (1996) contribution is a mother's account of her daughter's involvement with COG, which also highlights the problems related to children in *Jugendreligionen*.

73 The proceedings include statements and short essays: F.-W. Haack on the characteristics of *Jugendreligionen*, A. Schöll of *Interessengemeinschaft Jugendschutz e.V.* on TM, K. Thomas, a medical practitioner, on *Psychomutation*, Professor Langen, Director of the Clinic for Psychotherapy at the University of Mainz, on vulnerability and 'thought reform', Professor Müller-Küppers, Director of the Psychiatric Clinic of the University of Heidelberg, on *Jugendreligionen* as a new way of young people rejecting the establishment, F. Valentin, *Pastoralamt* in Vienna, on new religiosity in Austria, Professor Spiel, a consultant for child and youth psychiatry, on alternative religious life and group dependency, I. Mamay, a former COG member, on rehabilitation and COG membership, R. Diethelm-Thenisch, a medical doctor, on TM in Switzerland, K. Karbe on a concerned parent's experience, and O. von Hammerstein, a former UC member, on UC membership.

74 Bötsch (1986) examines how politicians can support the work of parents' initiatives by strengthening the legal and social framework, especially in areas concerning young people.

75 Glück (1986) deals with the State's constitutional and welfare duties regarding young people.

76 Bocklet (1986) provides some background to the Cottrell Report and the European Parliament's resolution.

77 Götzer (1986) explores legal areas which allow the State to act against *Jugend-religionen*. He (1985) also contributed to AGPF's 1984 European Congress in Bonn, which was sponsored by the Federal Ministry for Youth, Family and Health. AGPF's (then) chairman, Eckart Flöther (1985), edited the proceedings.

78 Caberta's particular concern is Scientology (e.g. Caberta, 1994). She attended EBI Leipzig's conference in March 1996 (MacKenzie, 1996), served as an 'expert' for the *Enquête-Kommission*, and heads the task force on Scientology in Hamburg.

79 Kränzle's (1996) paper examines the range of possible State action against 'cult' activities.

80 In 1995, the *Oberverwaltungsgericht* (upper administrative court) in Berlin ruled that Jehovah's Witnesses should be recognized as a corporation under public law (*Status einer Körperschaft des öffentlichen Rechts*), but was over-ruled in 1997 by the Federal Administrative Court (*Bundesverwaltungsgericht*).

81 The *Bundesrat* is the second chamber of the German Parliament, whose members represent the provinces and are elected indirectly. The *Bundestag* is the assembly of directly elected MPs.

82 Unlike other provinces (*Länder*), the 'free state' of Bavaria has its own constitution.

83 This includes papers of a seminar held in October 1982 in Boppard. Among the contributors are H. Waldenfels, W. Kuner, R. Oerter, and F. Merkel, with papers by Scientology and UC members and a paper on TM.

84 *Sekten-Info Essen* was registered as an association in March 1984 and recognized as an independent provider of *Jugendhilfe* in August 1984. From April 1984, the city of Essen provided office space and maintenance and money for materials. The province of North-Rhine-Westphalia covered staff costs from 1 January 1985. The city of Bochum granted an annual subsidy from 1985. The rest of the budget came from membership fees and donations (Sekten-Info Essen e.V., n.d.: 5).

85 The only academic work which seems to have received such support is a bibliography on *Jugendreligionen* by the University of Tübingen (Universität Tübingen, 1981).

86 In his discussion of current legal thinking, Behnk (1996a: 84–85) argues that were *Universelles Leben*'s case brought to court now, the licence would not be granted. In 1990, Scientology's plans to transform a former children's home in Hoisdorf, near Hamburg, into a boarding school were thwarted by a local parents' initiative which was formed specifically to fight these plans (*Bürgerinitiative besorgter Eltern e.V.*). In Switzerland, conflicting decisions emerged from two education authorities in 2003: Zurich granted two licences for Scientology-run schools (despite a report in 1995 stating the opposite), while Lucerne did not grant such a licence.

87 In this case, a former Scientology member had sued for 'proper' wages. The defendant (Scientology) could not prove to the court that the plaintiff was only employed for religious purposes. The judge stated that a work contract could not simply be re-labelled and that Scientology had to respect German industrial law (Kränzle, 1996: 60).

88 Schuster (1995: 199) mentions Otto Wiesheu, who became minister for economic affairs in Bavaria, Alfred Sauter, later under-secretary in the interior ministry of Bavaria, and F.-C. Zeitler, later deputy federal chairman and under-secretary in the Federal Ministry of Finance.

89 It was published by ARW and includes descriptions of the major *Jugendsekten* and 'therapy cults' in Germany. It wants to engage readers (teachers, parents, people involved in parish work and politics, the caring professions) in a critical discussion.

90   For example, in May 1989, the political party of the conservative party (CSU) in Baden-Württemberg submitted a motion asking for information about the activities of occult movements and 'destructive cults' in the province. In April 1994, the Bavarian parliament adopted a motion proposed by three *Landtag* members to report on *Universelles Leben*.

91   The speakers included R. Rennebach, O. Schily (then deputy chairman of SPD's parliamentary party), I. Heinemann (AGPF), H. Hemminger (EZW, Stuttgart), A. Christ (chair of SINUS e.V.), W. Gross (speaker for the Association of German Psychologists), B. Dewald-Koch (official of Rhineland-Palatinate), K.-H. Eimuth (Office for Questions of Religion and *Weltanschauung* of the Lutheran Church, Frankfurt), U. Caberta (Working Party on Scientology in Hamburg). No university researchers seem to have been present.

92   According to the statutes of the *Bundestag*, an *Enquête-Kommission*'s task is to investigate 'complex and important matters' in preparation of decisions in Parliament. A quarter of *Bundestag* members need to support an application. An *Enquête-Kommission* is normally composed of parliamentarians and 'experts' and has no legal authority to summon individuals to give evidence or provide material.

93   Yonan (1996) links the application for the *Enquête-Kommission* with the publication of Eimuth's book (1996a) on children in 'sects' and argues that the churches, especially the Lutheran Church, are the Government's main advisors in 'sect' matters.

94   Beckford's (1983b) comparison of ways of conceptualizing the 'cult problem' in five countries (US, UK, France, Germany, Japan) suggests that the UK and US represent a voluntaristic response, while France and Japan have an organicist and Germany a reticular response. Germany's reticular system has made the lobbying of parents more effective.

6 The response of the mainstream churches

Introduction

This section examines the Church of England's response to NRMs and shows how it developed in the 1980s. This process is followed through the considerations and reflections in the structures of the Church, the General Synod, and relevant committees. The question raised in the Synod in November 1983 marks the starting-point and results in deliberations by the Board for Mission and Unity and House of Bishops. Their considerations are contained in the Report for the General Synod of June 1989 and in the Synod's motion of November 1989. They are reinforced by speeches in the House of Lords by the Bishop of Chelmsford (February 1988) and the Bishop of Chester (November 1989). Finally, Colin Slee's (1995; 1999) contribution to the topic is examined. These are the available documents which provide insight into the Church's stance.

Although the Church of England is a state church established by law and although establishment links it closely to Parliament, its affairs are largely managed by the General Synod. This is composed of three houses: Bishops, Clergy, and Laity (Linzey, 1996: 3–5). The Synod's constitution lays down all the aspects of its functions (ibid.: 9–12). Motions are carried when the majority of members in each House present and voting give their assent, unless the chair and Synod decide otherwise. The constitution describes the Synod's functions as follows:

(a) to consider matters concerning the Church of England and to make provision in respect thereof [. . .]
(b) to consider and express their opinion on any other matters of religious or public interest.

(ibid.: 10)

The latter (point b) makes the Synod the appropriate forum for discussing NRMs within the Church. The Synod's committees and commissions, composed of *ex-officio*, appointed, and elected members as well as (assistant) secretaries include advisory committees, such as the Board of Mission, the Council for Christian Unity, and the Board for Social Responsibility (ibid.: 6–9).[1] These committees, especially the (then) Board for Mission and Unity, were involved in formulating the Church's response.

The question in the Synod

The first time NRMs were addressed in the General Synod was in its November 1983 session, when the (then) Archbishop of Canterbury, Dr Robert Runcie, answered a question in the House of Bishops. This had been raised by the (then) Dean of St Albans, the Very Revd P. C. Moore:

> Will the House of Bishops put in hand a consideration of the influence of so-called 'new religious movements' in this country and invite the Board for Mission and Unity, and the Board for Social Responsibility in consultation with other appropriate bodies, (e.g. BCC [British Council of Churches], the Centre for the Study of New Religions at King's College London, FAIR etc) to examine the teachings propounded and report to Synod advising the clergy and people of the Church of England how to respond to help those who are damaged, and to teach the faith more clearly in order to remedy the influence of such movements, particularly with regard to (1) those who claim membership is not in conflict with holding Christian faith, and (2) those which do not specifically claim compatibility with Christian faith but use holy scripture and church property in their activities?
>
> (Board for Mission and Unity, 1983)

The Archbishop answered that 'This is a matter which I am prepared to raise with the Standing Committee of the House of Bishops' (ibid.). Canon Alan Freeman (St Albans) then asked whether it would not be useful to have more information about the School of Economic Science (SES),[2] EMIN, and the COG. He was concerned 'that the majority of the trustees of one of the organisations listed in the Church of England Yearbook are [SES] members' (ibid.). The Archbishop replied that he would seek advice from the Board for Mission and Unity.[3]

The question in the board

With the matter handed to the Board for Mission and Unity, Canon Martin Reardon,[4] at the time the Board's general secretary, wrote, in December 1983, to Peter Clarke at the Centre for New Religions at King's College London regarding a consultative meeting. Due to press coverage of the Synod, both the SES and EMIN had approached the Board directly (Board for Mission and Unity, 1984: 2). The Board had already had contact with the Centre earlier that year. The meeting took place on 13 December 1983,[5] before the Board's meeting on 14 December, which discussed the question asked in the Synod and considered whether to conduct a survey of about 40 movements or to restrict research to the three groups mentioned and whether the survey should be confidential or more widely available. No decisions were reached. The Board recognized, however, the validity of objective accounts of new religions, while addressing aspects, such as proselytism, compatibility with the Church's beliefs, tolerance, freedom of expression, and effects on family life.

Canon Reardon asked Clarke to prepare factsheet-type descriptions of EMIN and the COG, which had already been done for the SES. Also, Clarke was to indicate issues which should be included in a paper for the House of Bishops. He provided the requested summaries and raised issues which he hoped the Bishops would consider: reasons why new religions emerge, the kind of people they attract,[6] their impact, their methods of conversion and proclamation of faith. He further stated the need for 'guidelines on methods of evangelization in the modern world'.[7]

The meeting of the Board's Executive Committee on 18 January 1984 discussed NRMs. According to the minutes, the Board's Secretary introduced Clarke's outlines of the SES, EMIN, and the COG and the Committee considered three options suggested by him: (a) the Church should take no further action; (b) the Board for Mission and Unity should prepare a brief report which focuses on the Church's values, such as Christian orthodoxy, rationality in religious belief, tolerance and freedom of religious expression, rejection of undue pressure on (prospective) followers. The report could examine some new religions from this perspective. Clarke would assist in drawing up the report; (c) the Board would proceed as in point (b), but include a wider range of movements, again with Clarke's assistance.

The Board's Executive Committee considered the options which the House of Bishops would have after deliberating any report submitted by the Board. Again, three options emerged: (1) to do nothing; (2) to issue pastoral guidelines to clergy in confidence; (3) to issue guidelines publicly. The Committee felt, however, that were the Bishops to adopt options 2 or 3, the guidelines should be accompanied by a background paper from the Board.

The Committee recognized the advantages and disadvantages of the options. There was agreement that information on new religions was desirable and that the Board for Mission and Unity could act as a channel for gathering such information, while also counting on assistance from the Centre for New Religions. According to Canon Reardon, a meeting in 1984, attended by himself, the Archbishop, Professor S. Sutherland, and Peter Clarke, discussed the establishment of a centre which could provide factual information about NRMs. However, Clarke apparently did not want to get too involved in this matter. From the Church's point of view, the creation of a centre under its own aegis would have been perceived as a rival, non-independent organization. The Committee realized that some of the criticism levelled at NRMs regarding methods of proselytism could equally be levelled at some orthodox Christian groups, a point reinforced by the Chaplain of St John's College: 'far more important numerically in my ministry are those damaged by main-line Christian denominations . . . What is of far more concern than the growth of the cults is the world-wide increase of intolerant fundamentalism in the three monotheistic faiths of Christianity, Judaism and Islam' (*The Times*, 13.9.84: 11).

While Committee members acknowledged the need for guidance on the question whether NRM membership was compatible with Church membership, they were uncertain whether it was proper or wise to enter into direct criticism of the content of their teachings. This ties in with the attitude of 'cult-monitoring' groups who do not criticize 'cults' for their beliefs, but for the way they proselytize and treat members and for their attitudes to society. The Church's reluctance to engage with NRMs' teachings is somewhat surprising, as one would expect it to be concerned with truth claims – its own and those of other religions. However, the Church's cautious approach explains this reluctance: unwanted publicity or even litigation, which – it was thought – could result from public critiques of NRM teachings, should be avoided. Indeed, the Committee advocated extreme caution to avoid that danger but expressed the need for guidelines and brief factual information.

The question with the bishops

Neither the House of Bishops nor its Standing Committee were able to attend to the question of NRMs, when they held their respective meetings in late January 1984. The matter was probably not considered sufficiently urgent and was therefore deferred until the next meeting, scheduled for June 1984.

The question back in the board

NRMs were again on the agenda of the Board for Mission and Unity's meeting on 14 March 1984. Half an hour of the three-hour meeting was set aside and Peter Clarke had been invited for that period. In May 1984, the Board summarized the deliberations in a document (Board for Mission and Unity, 1984), which reconsiders the Dean of St Albans's question of November 1983 in the light of discussions and meetings since then. It takes up two aspects of the Dean's question: information (regarding NRMs' influence and teachings) and guidelines (regarding pastoral care and the Church's theological standpoint). The first part of the document refers to documentation available at the Centre for New Religions and the difficulty of defining NRMs. It states that it would be a difficult and enormous task for the Church to produce comprehensive information on all movements, especially as this would soon be out of date and might have to be produced in conjunction with NRMs to avoid litigation. Existing literature is cited, such as a leaflet on the UC by the BCC's Youth Unit of 1979, a short document on the UC prepared by Kinchin Smith for the Church of England Enquiry Centre (a part of the Church's communications section which deals with enquiries from the public), and Annett's (1976) *The Many Ways of Being*. In its initial stages, FAIR had connections with the Enquiry Centre, as Pete Broadbent, FAIR's chairman at the time, knew staff there. Enquiries addressed to the Centre were referred to FAIR, because, as Broadbent later stated, there was no-one else (General Synod, 1990: 1284). The Enquiry Centre still holds files on NRMs from that time, but special permission is needed to consult them. The Enquiry Centre's role in the early 1980s shows that the Church dealt with NRMs in a pragmatic way and did not formulate a 'general strategy' or theological concept for its approach until the mid-1980s. Just as some parish clergy dealt with the matter as part of their day-to-day pastoral duties, Church House 'dealt' with it by default: through an established in-house facility, the Enquiry Centre, the first point of contact for public enquiries.

The Board's document endorsed the need for factual information about NRMs, which experts, such as Harold Turner, or institutions, such as the Centre for New Religions, might provide (Board for Mission and Unity, 1984: 2). The question was whether the House of Bishops wanted to pursue the idea of using the Centre for New Religions.

The second part of the document states that correspondence received by Lambeth Palace and the Board highlighted the need for pastoral guidance for those affected by some NRMs. The correspondence also indicated strong views, even among Anglicans, both in favour and critical of some NRMs. As to compatibility of NRM beliefs with Christianity, possible incompatibilities, such as belief in reincarnation, could be pointed out, but the Board judged it unwise to compare too closely specific NRM teachings with the Christian faith, for two reasons: first, NRM teachings were seen to be still developing and second, there was the risk of being accused of misrepresentation or, as the document puts it, 'the scope for charges of misrepresentation would be endless' (ibid.: 3). The core of Christian orthodoxy should be pointed to, for example, the doctrine of the Trinity and the uniqueness of the Christian revelation. These could be criteria for assessing compatibility between NRMs and Christianity.

The document further suggests guidelines for 'the place of rationality in religious belief, the desirability of tolerance and freedom of religious expression, the rejection of improper methods of conversion and undue pressure upon adherents' (ibid.). However, such guidelines would apply to *all* religious movements – Christian or non-Christian, old or new. Some Christian groups have used 'methods of persuasion at least as bad as those' for which some NRMs are criticized. The question arose whether the House of Bishops or the BCC should draw up guidelines.

The third part of the document is concerned with action taken by government and legislation regarding NRMs, including Richard Cottrell's draft report to the European Parliament. Cottrell's report had identified pertinent and controversial features of NRMs, recommended a voluntary code of behaviour, and requested harmonization of tax and charity laws within the European Community, a Community Register of Charities, together with increased co-operation between member states regarding information, missing persons, entry regulations, and social problems arising from third country relations. After considering the report, the BCC's Executive Committee wrote to MEPs asking them to reject it. The Committee rejected the report's approach, even after Richard Cottrell had attended one of its meetings. One of the reservations was that the report did not adequately define the term 'modern religious movement'. This, the Committee felt, clashed with the report's clause that 'such movements must inform the competent authorities on request of the address or whereabouts of individual members' (ibid.: 3). In May 1984, the BCC's General Secretary set out the Committee's position in a letter to the British MEPs in the light of its discussions with Mr Cottrell.

The Committee further objected to the clause that 'persons under the age of majority should not be induced on becoming a member of a movement to make a solemn long-term commitment that will determine the course of their lives' (ibid.). This objection relates to discrimination: religious liberty is indivisible and governments should not apply some rules or laws to some religious movements and not to others (ibid.: 3–4).[8] Cottrell argued, however, that existing laws in European countries were inadequate to deal with abuses by some NRMs.[9] The question was whether the Board for Social Responsibility and/or the BCC's Division of Community Affairs should examine existing laws to establish whether UK citizens were sufficiently protected against NRMs.

Finally, the document presents the Board's recommendations:

1 that an independent agency (perhaps the Centre for New Religious Movements at King's) be approached about the possibility of providing information about at least some new religious movements;
2 that some general pastoral guidelines should be drawn up on issues raised in the debate about these movements;
3 that the Board for Social Responsibility be invited to consider whether it or the B.C.C. might examine British law to discover its adequacy to deal with the kind of abuses attributed to some N.R.M.s.
(ibid.: 4)

The question back with the bishops

In early June 1984, the House of Bishops devoted almost an hour to NRMs. Discussions were based on the Board's document (Board for Mission and Unity, 1984) and a letter from FAIR. The bishops took up the suggestion to seek further information from the Centre for New Religions because it wanted the Board to explore this possibility further. They also asked the

Board to continue work on pastoral guidelines for clergy and lay people, possibly in consultation with the BCC. Both requests were accompanied by expressions of great caution, as bishops had voiced many differing views and some wished to guard against over-reaction to what they considered the media's exaggeration of the subject's importance. The Board's Executive Committee considered the matter again on 4 July 1984.

The formulation of an approach

The Church of England was faced with conflicting considerations: there was general consent that information about NRMs was expedient, but there was recognition that some allegations levelled against NRMs, especially regarding proselytism, could be levelled at some mainstream Christian groups. The need for pastoral guidance was acknowledged, but it seemed advisable not to engage in open criticism of NRM teachings: hence the bishops' decision to proceed with extreme caution. The Church was also wary of the consequences of possible legislation by European agencies, for example the European Parliament, especially in the light of the BCC's stance regarding the Cottrell resolution.

By then (1984), the Board for Mission and Unity's discussions had resulted in the proposal of a three-pronged approach: information, pastoral guidelines, legal provisions. An independent agency might be approached for the provision of information on a continual basis, general pastoral guidelines should be drawn up, and the law examined as to whether it was adequate to safeguard against abuses. The House of Bishops did not, however, want the third avenue explored. This was because of the Cottrell Report, which was also the reason why the bishops preferred to see existing legislation tightened.

While the Board continued work on information and guidelines, there were other developments: in April 1986, the BCC held a conference on NRMs to facilitate general consultation and discussion of case studies, attended by representatives of churches and denominations. A report of the proceedings was distributed to participants, but not made public because of the inclusion of individual cases. The conference took place in the aftermath of the Cottrell Report, following the general interest in NRMs in the 1980s, and continued the Board for Mission and Unity's work in the Church. After the conference, the BCC's Executive Committee asked Canon Reardon to represent it, as the Church of England's approach towards NRMs was in full agreement with that of the BCC executive.

The idea of INFORM was taking shape in late 1986, so that INFORM was ready to cover the first part of the Church's approach and act as the independent information centre. The Church stated its intention to work with INFORM in the Bishop of Chelmsford's speech in the House of Lords in February 1988 (*Hansard*, 10.02.1988: cols. 247–275) – with Earl Ferrers presenting the Government's position and commenting on possible legislation, the establishment of INFORM, and charitable status (ibid.: cols. 269–275) – and reinforced it in the Synod Report of 1989. According to Canon Reardon, from the Church's point of view, the academic approach to NRMs assisted the theological perspective. The Church did not want to play a prominent role in INFORM for the same reason for which it did not want its own centre. It was thus anxious not to have too many clergy on INFORM's Board of Governors.

Further, in early 1988, the (then) Attorney General announced that the investigation into the UC's charitable status would be abandoned (*Hansard*, 03.02.1988: col. 978), while a general reform of the law governing charities would be prepared – the subsequent White Paper *Charities: A Framework for the Future* (HMSO, 1989). The announcement sparked a private member's motion in the General Synod by John Saxbee (then Prebendary in Exeter) which in turn sparked the Synod Report of June 1989. However, although Saxbee's motion was submitted on 5 February 1988 (just two days after the Attorney General's statement), the Synod did not discuss it until November 1989 (General Synod, 1990: 1275–1279). The motion wanted the Synod to support legislation which would deprive the UC of charitable status. The Archdeacon of Croydon, the Venerable Frederick Hazell, proposed an amendment to the motion, which explained the Board for Mission and Unity's standpoint towards NRMs (ibid.: 1279–1282) and the Revd Peter Broadbent tabled an amendment to the amendment (ibid.: 1282–1284).

When the House of Lords debated the White Paper on *Charities* (HMSO, 1989) in late November 1989 (*Hansard*, 30.11.1989: cols. 526–590), the Bishop of Chester restated the Church's position towards NRMs (ibid.: cols. 542–546), repeating – in substance – the points made by the Bishop of Chelmsford (*Hansard*, 10.2.1988: cols. 247–275), the Synod Report (General Synod, 1989), and the Archdeacon of Croydon (General Synod, 1990). The Bishop of Chelmsford's speech and the Synod Report are summarized and discussed in further detail, as are the proceedings of John Saxbee's motion (General Synod, 1990).

The bishop's speech

On 10 February 1988, 'pseudo-religious cults' were debated in the House of Lords (*Hansard*, 10.02.1988: cols. 247–275), a debate initiated by Lord Rodney in the wake of the Attorney General's withdrawal of the case against the UC. On this occasion, the Bishop of Chelmsford gave his maiden speech, which gave insight into the perspective from which the Church of England and the churches in general viewed this topic.

The speech acknowledges the importance of the NRM problem, commenting that most members of the Lords are aware of the 'deep pain and sorrow [which] have been caused through the activities of some of those cults'.[10] The Bishop refers to personal experience 'of speaking with distraught parents, as well as with the devastated spouse of someone who disappeared from the family scene as a result of being brought under the evil influence of one of the most notorious of those cults, which rejoices in the name of The Children of God' (ibid.: col. 255). Given the effects of 'cults', it is not surprising that politicians and clergy are 'besieged' to act and 'that we feel the urge to respond' (ibid.: col. 256). Yet, before addressing what can be done, two other questions need to be examined: what this phenomenon is and why it happened.

Some 500 new movements have sprung up in Britain, 'which may with varying accuracy be referred to as "religious" '. As to their origins, most are derived from Eastern religions or Christianity and some have linked these with modern philosophy, psychology, or therapy. Some 'are genuine religious movements' which offer valuable insights and spiritual practices, others are 'superficial' or 'dangerous in their teaching, using dubious, not to say illegal, methods of attracting adherents'. Regarding their relationship with the outside, some are open and free, with 'an infectious joy about them', others 'are secretive and tyrannical, dividing families and causing deep pain' (ibid.).

The Bishop pointed out that 'probably fewer than 15,000 people belong to such groups in the United Kingdom' and conceded that this 'is not a menacingly large number'. However, he stressed 'that the teaching and methods of some of those movements are a shame to those who perpetrate them and cause distress out of all proportion to the numbers involved' (ibid.).

Historically speaking, we should not be surprised about the phenomenon, as it happened before, particularly at times of social and cultural upheaval. Yet, regarding the reasons why people are attracted to such movements, the evidence suggests that the teachings are not the prime motive for joining, but the offer of a purpose in life, an enthusiastic commitment to a cause, and warm, supportive groups. The appeal of NRMs is to young and middle-aged people alike: the young seek a cause for their idealism and an alternative community, the middle-aged seek to offset years they spent leading what they have come to view as a pointless life.

As to action to be taken, the practice of 'deprogramming' is a desperate remedy arising from a desperate situation, yet impracticable, because 'Whatever the rights or the outcome of such action, surely we cannot see in that an answer which can be of general application'. As to possible legislation against NRMs, the Bishop states that other Lords are 'better qualified than I to pass judgement on the practicability of such a course of action', but refers to the BCC's reservations. It saw 'huge problems' in any attempt to legislate against NRMs, even when orthodox churches consider them 'in grave error' and society considers them 'either potty or dangerous, or both'. Moves towards such legislation would have immediate implications for the Universal Declaration of Human Rights, which would have wide-ranging consequences, because '[o]ne could be in danger of playing into the hands of those atheistic regimes in Eastern Europe which are seeking to justify their suppression of religious freedom' (ibid.). Therefore, the answer must lie in applying existing laws firmly, in ensuring that they are not contravened and the rights of others not infringed. Further, existing laws could be tightened and made more effective for activities, such as soliciting money in public. New legislation may be needed here.

An area of law in need of 'some drastic action' is the charity law (as it stood at the time). The churches would co-operate with the Government, with the proviso that 'we must note and accept that such legislation must apply equally to all, whatever their religious beliefs' (ibid.: col. 257). The Bishop refers to a private member's motion submitted to the Synod – undoubtedly Saxbee's motion – which deplored the UC's charitable status.

Yet, the ultimate answer to NRMs is not legislation, but 'a revitalising of society and a renewing of the Christian Church and the other older movements' (a conclusion similar to that reached by the Roman Catholic Church). NRM followers are disillusioned not only with 'a materialistic, self-seeking and individualistic society', but also with 'a Church which appears to be at odds with itself and lukewarm in its commitment', a point also made by Canon Slee, in commenting that the Church has failed NRM members by not responding adequately to their needs. NRMs would have limited scope in an 'enthusiastic and idealistic church made up of supportive groups of Christians' – a comment which echoes the RCC's 'base' or 'ecclesial communities', strong, active, local groups. According to the Bishop, this kind of renewal is already happening. Yet, everyone needs to contribute towards 'a society which is not about the pursuit of an arid materialism but is a society in which ideas and ideals can flourish' (ibid.).

The Bishop concludes by reporting the appointment of diocesan advisers, who 'will provide clear information and advice on all matters arising from these movements' and 'will be ready to put those who need counsel in touch with those who can counsel them'. While this initiative is inter-denominational and ecumenical, it is assisted by 'a unique experiment', the 'coming together of academics, voluntary agencies, the churches and Government to establish an independent body'. This body is INFORM whose task 'will be to provide objective information on the teaching and practice of these movements and about available counselling'. While the Bishop is aware of trenchant media coverage of INFORM, he comments that 'I am reliably informed that much press criticism is largely due to a misunderstanding of the role of INFORM or a misguided desire to undermine its work' (ibid.). The churches 'intend to work with this body and continue to contribute to its work their own experience and insights' (ibid.: col. 258) and commend the Home Office for supporting it financially.

Regarding other organizations which collect NRM data – the Centre at Selly Oak Colleges, the Centre for New Religions, Housetop, and FAIR – the Bishop states that 'we wish them well'. The debate in the Lords will, he hopes, result in 'a strengthened resolution to seek to bring to light hidden things of darkness and to offer hope and practical help to those who find themselves caught up in what can prove for them an experience of confusion, pain and grief'. There is an urgency in this matter which 'demands the best endeavours of us all' (ibid.).

The bishop's speech in perspective

The Bishop of Chelmsford's speech uses strong language when it speaks of the 'deep pain and sorrow' caused by 'cults' and 'the *evil* influence of one of the *most notorious cults*, which *rejoices* in the name of The Children of God' (emphasis added). This kind of language may stem from direct contact with concerned parents or 'anti-cult groups'. Different language is used in the comments about the NRM phenomenon – descriptive, analytical, non-emotional. Despite dealing with the topic in general terms, there are no stereotypical or simplistic generalizations – the picture described is fair and balanced. This also applies to the section about the reasons why people join. These passages could have come from an academically constructed brief. The circumstances which led to the Bishop's speech provide some indication about possible (co)authorship: at least one bishop is present in the House of Lords every day to fill the prayer rota. When matters of great importance to the Church are on the agenda, the bishop who is expert in the matter makes the presentation. As there is no NRM expert, the Board for Mission and Unity asked the bishop on the prayer rota to deliver the speech – this happened to be the Bishop of Chelmsford.

While conceding that the number of NRM members is small, some practices need to be counteracted on moral and humanitarian grounds, because 'the teaching and methods . . . are a shame to those who perpetrate them and cause distress out of all proportion'. Looking at possible action, deprogramming is mentioned first: it is not openly condemned, but deemed impracticable or generally inapplicable. As to legislation, the speech refers to the BCC's views: the churches were extremely wary of legislation which could affect themselves, their related institutions, and freedom of religion. There is a hint at more far-reaching implications: legislation might undermine human rights and their safeguard in Eastern European countries then still under Communist rule. Instead, the tightening and firm application of existing laws are recommended, except for the charity law where the churches' willingness is signalled to support the Government in introducing changes. However, legislation apart, effective counter-action is seen in a renewal of the churches and society. Both have failed NRM members in their quest for community and spirituality.

On a more practical level, the collaboration is announced between appointed diocesan advisers and the recently created INFORM. This would combine the provision of information and counselling. The Home Office is commended for granting funds to, and taking a continued interest in, INFORM. Regarding the criticism levelled at INFORM, its role is misunderstood and there is a 'misguided desire to undermine its work' (ibid.:

col. 257), but there are no details about the criticism or who is motivated by 'misguided desire'.

The Bishop's speech confirms the churches' cautious stance on new legislation against NRMs, which guided the deliberations in the House of Bishops. However, mention of diocesan advisers and collaboration with INFORM anticipates the main points of the Synod Report. The reference to possible changes in the charity law explains the inclusion of (uncommented) parts of the White Paper in the Report's appendix.

The Bishop of Chelmsford's speech – which is understood to speak for *all* mainstream churches – illustrates, indirectly, the churches' dilemma vis-à-vis NRMs, as Colin Slee also apprehends. The churches recognize and acknowledge the problems which NRMs create on a personal level (for individuals and families), but they do not want to engage in 'anti-cult' activities, such as active campaigns ('cult-bashing') or 'deprogramming'. They realize that NRMs present a threat, because they entice church members away. The churches do not favour dual membership. Therefore, they wish to distinguish themselves clearly from NRMs, while remaining open towards, and even establishing dialogue with, them. They recognize that both society and they themselves have in some ways failed those who feel drawn towards NRMs. They respond by strengthening church structures to make churches more attractive and encourage wider society to nurture positive values and lifestyles. Beyond that, the churches seek to co-operate with secular bodies and organizations, such as INFORM. While they would like to see action taken, they adopt a guarded stance towards legislation, arguing the sufficiency of existing laws, if properly applied, and pointing to wider implications relating to basic rights and charitable law.

The Synod Report

On 19 June 1989, Keith Lichfield, (then) chairman of the Board for Mission and Unity, presented a report on NRMs to the General Synod (General Synod, 1989).[11] This document is in two parts: the Report by the Board's chairman (ibid.: 1–11) and the appendix, the sections of the White Paper on *Charities* relevant to charitable status and religion (ibid.: 13–24). The first part has three sections: the recommendations of the House of Bishops (ibid.: 1–6), the Church's general attitude towards NRMs (ibid.: 6–9), and a draft code of practice (ibid.: 9–11).

The bishops' recommendations

The first section states the Report's purpose and intention, which is 'to inform members of the General Synod what work has been done and is proceeding' on NRMs. It refers again to the Dean of St Albans's question in November 1983 and states that the Bishops adopted two recommendations suggested by the paper which the Board for Mission and Unity had submitted to them on 7 June 1984:

(i)   That there should be an *independent agency*, not simply an agency of the Church, which should try *to provide objective information* about the new religious movements.

(ii) That some general *pastoral guidelines* should be drawn up on issues raised in the debate about these movements.

(ibid.: 1–2; emphasis in original)

The Bishops had not adopted the Board's third recommendation – that the Board for Social Responsibility 'should keep a watching brief on the law as it affected New Religious Movements'. The Board's paper had suggested the BCC for this task, but the Bishops had expressed the hope that the Board 'would work in close conjunction with the British Council of Churches' (ibid.: 2).

INFORM

The Report then addresses the need for an independent agency (ibid.: 2–4). The Board had approached the Centre for New Religions, the Centre at Selly Oak, the Housetop Centre, and FAIR. However, although these organizations were extremely helpful, 'it became clear that something else was necessary', because none of them combined expertise and availability to enquirers. Yet, exactly this combination was to be offered by INFORM which

> would liaise with other centres which were willing to co-operate with it and have access to acknowledged experts in this field. It would seek the support of leading academics, the traditional Christian Churches and other bodies. It would seek to provide as objective information as possible, and would be willing to pass enquirers on to networks of counselling and advice, some secular, some Christian, according as the enquirers requested.

(ibid.: 2)

With the support of the Archbishop of Canterbury, Cardinal Hume, the Moderator of the Free Church Federal Council (the Archbishop, the Moderator and the RC Bishop John Crowley became INFORM's initial patrons) and with a grant from the Home Office,[12] INFORM started to operate in January 1988. When the Synod Report was prepared, INFORM was in the process of being established as 'a research and educational charitable company limited by guarantee', a status which it still has.[13]

The Report provides INFORM's contact details at the time (it subsequently moved a couple of times) and describes what kind of material it holds and how material is recorded and accessed. The Report briefly describes the contents and aims of Eileen Barker's (1989a) *New Religious Movements: A Practical Introduction*, published in 1989. The Report finally summarizes INFORM's activities, including seminars, talks, and enquiries from the public (ibid.: 3–4).

Pastoral guidelines

The Report turns to the second recommendation adopted by the Bishops: to set up pastoral guidelines. After a meeting of the Bishops in 1984, the Board for Mission and Unity drew up guidelines, which the BCC's Day Consultation on NRMs in April 1986 considered. The report resulting from the Consultation was sent to the Board and BCC's Executive Committee. However, the Synod Report states that 'it became clear that written guidelines in themselves were not enough' and a 'church network of advisers' was needed (ibid.: 4–5).

On 2 October 1986, the BCC's Executive Committee asked the Church of England 'to consider whether it would be possible through the Board for Mission and Unity ... to prepare guidelines and initiate a network of advisers based upon dioceses' (ibid.: 5) and based on ecumenical co-operation. On 6 January 1988, the Committee decided that a nationwide inter-denominational network of advisers and counsellors should be set up and the Anglican bishops should take the initiative for England, while respective councils should follow suit in Ireland, Scotland, and Wales. The Board for Mission and Unity, assisted by the Board for Social Responsibility and INFORM, produced another set of draft guidelines. These included: (1) an outline for existing resources (agencies, bibliography, addresses), (2) a general description of NRMs, with an estimate of their size and impact in the UK, (3) an outline of principles of religious liberty as relevant to NRMs, (4) an outline of suggested principles for relations between churches and NRMs, (5) an outline of what attracts people to NRMs, what Christians may find lacking in the Church, (6) points of doctrine and ethics which allow discrimination between some NRMs and orthodox Christian churches, (7) advice for relatives and friends (ibid.: 5–6).

In May 1988, the guidelines were sent to the Bishops, with the request to appoint – after consultation with other churches – diocesan advisers. The other churches in England were informed. By the time the Synod Report was written, half the dioceses had either appointed advisers or indicated they would do so shortly. In his capacity as INFORM's vice-chairman, Canon Reardon wrote to the Anglican bishops in 1988, asking them to name those willing to join INFORM's network of advisers. The names were to be chosen in consultation with other mainstream churches in the dioceses (INFORM Annual Report, 1988: 3).

The Church's attitude

The second section states that 'it has become apparent that many people are unclear about the Church's attitude to New Religious Movements' and affirms that 'Christians believe in the uniqueness of God's revelation in Jesus Christ as set out in the Holy Scriptures and affirmed in the Catholic Creeds'. While Christians can learn from other religions, they cannot accept what is incompatible with God's revelation. Due to the variety of NRMs, the teachings of each need to be considered separately. Some are still in a state of flux. Therefore, literature becomes quickly out of date, but the positive aspect is that 'the leaders of some New Religious Movements are still open to the influence of dialogue with the Christian Churches'. Some NRMs are secretive about their teachings, even possibly to new followers (General Synod, 1989: 6–7).

There are, however, 'some key areas of Christian doctrine' which should be considered when NRMs are compared with Christianity, in particular the doctrines of Christ and God: 'Very few New Religious Movements profess an orthodox understanding of the Trinity. Very few, when pressed, would accept the uniqueness and divinity of Jesus Christ.' Other areas concern notions of sin and evil, which are 'not taken as seriously as Christians believe necessary', and the doctrine of justification by faith. This is due to 'an over-sanguine belief in the capabilities of men and women to work for their own perfection'. This means that the idea of the grace of God is not as central in NRMs as it is in orthodox Christianity; it is replaced by belief in the power of auto-suggestion and positive group thinking or in salvation by good works. The belief in reincarnation goes against the Christian understanding of resurrection. Ideas about salvation and the end of world, found in millenarian, utopian, or messianic NRM teachings, require careful study (ibid.: 7–8).

The Report also addresses the question of moral behaviour which results from some NRM teachings. That a movement encourages mass suicide (an allusion to the deaths of The People's Temple members in Jonestown in 1978) and sexual favours by female members to potential converts ('flirty fishing', a former practice in the COG) or condones deception for soliciting money is 'unacceptable to Christians' (ibid.). Also, 'spiritual exercises, such as forms of meditation, are not necessarily 'neutral'. Particular meditation techniques have developed within religious traditions and 'an unwary person' acquires elements of these while learning such techniques. They have their uses, but they should be learnt with 'experienced Christian guidance' to avoid the 'risk of unrecognised syncretism' (ibid.). (Some of these arguments reflect the RCC's position on this point.) On a practical level, the Report recommends caution before churches allow such movements to use their premises, especially if is not clear under whose auspices events are held (ibid.: 8–9). The Report identifies 'another cause of confusion': NRMs which regard themselves as part of the Christian tradition or claim to be philosophies rather than religions. In these cases, 'the unwary Christian' may think it possible to belong to both the NRM and the Church, but 'as a general rule we have found that this is not possible'. The commitment demanded by NRMs ultimately forces individuals to choose (ibid.: 9).

Draft code

The third section proposes a code of practice to which all religions should adhere (ibid.: 9–11), suggested as a discussion document. The code seeks to counter the controversies over some NRMs' behaviour and aims to be applicable to all religions. It has two parts: the first addresses grievances which have emanated from NRMs, the second addresses practices associated with the 'anti-cult movement'. Both have the heading 'the Board [for Mission and Unity] deplores . . .'. The first part comprises nine points, which include the following issues: inviting people to an event under false pretences, raising money under false pretences, hiding the true identity of fundraisers or recruiters, unfair or immoral means of persuasion, concealing from prospective adherents implications and consequences of membership, discussion with minors without knowledge of their carers, hindering access to (prospective) adherents, offering financial gain as inducement, failure of public accountability for finance, irresponsibility in employment (ibid.: 9–10). The second part comprises four points, which address forcible 'deprogramming', declaring illegal or withdrawing rights from NRMs without evidence, lack of concern for the truth, misinformation, denial of individuals' right to choose their religious beliefs (ibid.: 10–11).[14]

The second part is an appendix with (uncommented) sections from the White Paper on proposals to reform the charity law.

Saxbee's motion

The Synod Report had been brought about by John Saxbee's private member's motion to the Synod in February 1988. Saxbee had personal experience of NRMs in his parish, of the UC in particular – hence the mention of the UC in the motion. Saxbee felt that restrictions for this group would have implications for others (General Synod, 1990: 1275–1276). The motion was finally discussed in the Synod's November 1989 session (ibid.: 1275–1279).[15]

The motion proposed 'That this Synod supports the introduction of legislation to exclude the Unification Church (known as the "Moonies") from any presumption of charitable status given to religion by English law'. Saxbee explicitly pointed out that the motion was not about UC's leader, individual UC members, UC beliefs, or INFORM, nor an attack on religious freedom, but about unacceptable methods and behaviour. While he welcomed the White Paper, he found its conclusions too tentative. He also welcomed the Synod Report's draft code and concluded that legislators determined to re-establish the credibility of charity law could do so, without threat to religious freedom or civil liberties. However, they would need the Church's encouragement and expertise and Synod members could further this by endorsing the motion (ibid.: 1278–1279).

The Archdeacon of Croydon, the Venerable Frederick Hazell, proposed an amendment on behalf of the Board for Mission and Unity (ibid.: 1279–1282).[16] It argued that the motion should not be supported, because the Synod would appear to ask for a bill which would single out one movement and deny it charitable status. In light of insufficient evidence to support such action in court, this would be a first step towards discriminating against a religion, which certainly contravenes the UN's Declaration on Human Rights (ibid.: 1279).

Outright rejection of the motion would, however, signal the Synod's lack of concern about the UC or could signal support for the UC. Yet, the White Paper did not single out any religious group, but tackled the problem in general – the very problem the motion addresses. The charity law had Christianity in mind when it speaks of 'religion' and thus makes certain assumptions: that charitable purposes are for the public benefit, the advancement of religion is to be for public benefit, and trusts for the furtherance of religion are understood to be charitable. In modern multicultural and multi-faith society, a variety of Christian and other groups have obtained charitable status. The question is whether the positive assumptions about religion – in the words of Justice Cross, 'As between religions the law stands neutral, but it assumes that any religion is at least likely to be better than none' – can be upheld, given NRMs' 'deplorable' activities, such as deception, unfair means of persuasion, and the destruction of families.

While the Government was sympathetic to those who expressed anxiety about existing charitable law, it decided against removing religion as a ground for charitable status or making this status dependent on a test of positive worth; it proposed instead to warn charities to change or remove them from the register of charities, if their behaviour was shown to be against the public good. The Board for Mission and Unity considered this 'the right way forward', which is why it produced the Synod Report. Contravention of its proposed code of practice could be considered evidence that a charitable organization acted against the public good. The Board considered this 'a more constructive and wide-reaching way forward' than that proposed by the motion, because it avoided discriminating against any religion on the grounds of its beliefs and preserved the essential basis of religious liberty – a wiser and more effective way of combating harmful and destructive behaviour in all religious movements in the long run.

The amended motion proposed to welcome the White Paper on charities and to encourage the Government 'to make explicit, and if necessary to strengthen', the Charity Commissioners' powers to remove a charity from the register where evidence existed that it was acting in ways which are not for the public benefit' and commended the Synod Report's draft code whose contravention might constitute such evidence (ibid.: 1281–1282).

Although Saxbee still wanted to see the UC mentioned in the motion and thought that the White Paper did not go far enough, he declared himself 'happy to accept the Archdeacon's amendment'. The Revd Peter Broadbent then tabled an amendment to the amendment (ibid.: 1282–1284), suggesting an insertion commending the Synod Report, especially pertinent paragraphs, as a statement of the Church's doctrinal position regarding NRMs (ibid.: 1282–1283).

Peter Broadbent referred to his chairmanship of FAIR, although he did not speak on FAIR's behalf, but from his own experience. The reason for the insertion was the specific need to spell out theological differences between NRM and mainstream Christian beliefs. In his response, the Archdeacon acknowledged this need, but rejected the amendment because it deflected from the main purpose of his amendment, which was to use NRM activities and behaviour as main criteria. Broadbent's amendment was voted against, but the Archdeacon's amendment and thus the amended motion were carried (ibid.: 1286–1288).

The Bishop of Chester's speech in the House of Lords in November 1989 (during the debate on the White Paper) reiterated the points made by the Archdeacon, the Synod Report, and the Bishop of Chelmsford: the Synod Report outlined the Church's attitude towards NRMs; the Archbishop of Canterbury was one of INFORM's patrons, and INFORM worked closely with the Church's advisers. The Bishop quoted the Synod motion of 1989 and repeated the arguments advanced by the Archdeacon of Croydon regarding NRMs' beliefs and activities (*Hansard*, 30.11.1989: cols. 544–546).

Reflections on the Synod Report

The Church of England considered questions and problems arising from the emergence of NRMs in Britain earlier than the RCC. The impetus for discussions and consultation between the Church's various bodies was the question to the General Synod in 1983. The timing of the question needs to be seen in the context of van Driel and Richardson's (1985) survey findings regarding print coverage of NRMs in the US between 1972 and 1984. While the press generally adopted a predominantly negative attitude towards NRMs, a peak in negative coverage occurred in the late 1970s, coinciding with the Jonestown events, with an ebb following in the early 1980s. Beckford and Cole (1988) showed a similar process in Britain.

However, as in the RCC's case, the urgency in addressing the issue came from the Church's grassroots, from clergy 'on the ground', such as Colin Slee, who encountered NRM activities and effects of NRM membership day to day. Some parents and relatives turned to them for advice and help. Slee, at the time chaplain at King's College London, where he dealt with SES members, was instrumental in bringing the question before the General Synod. With the impulse given, the Board for Mission and Unity had the task of exploring the matter, consulting with appropriate bodies – both academic and 'cult-monitoring'. During the mid-1980s, it gathered material and discussed possible action, which the House of Bishops in turn considered.

The Bishops recognized the need for guidelines and more information. They recognized the similarity in behaviour between orthodox Christian groups and NRMs. While they wanted clear distinction between NRM and Christian teachings, they did not want too precise a comparison. They pointed to the continuous development of NRM teachings, but were afraid of being accused of misrepresenting these. Despite their recommendation to draw up guidelines, they were mindful that these had to apply to any religion or religious group.

Overall, the House of Bishops and the Board for Mission and Unity took a very cautious approach towards action regarding NRMs. Several reasons account for this: first, they feared that legislation or drastic measures would backfire and damage 'orthodox' religion – hence the BCC's objections to Cottrell's code of practice. Second, they felt that the media had blown the importance of NRMs out of proportion. Third, they were concerned that NRMs would take the Church to court for 'misrepresenting' them.

A further reason for the cautious approach is that the Church did not want to act on its own – it wanted to co-operate with other agencies and act in consultation with the umbrella organization for Christian Churches in Britain, the (then) BCC. It was the latter which the House of Bishops recommended to track British legislation aimed at NRMs, not the Church's Board for Social Responsibility. Further, given the religious culture in Britain and the Church's role, it would have been 'out of character' for the Church to act in isolation or take an overly critical or competitive stance towards NRMs.

By the time the Synod Report was prepared in 1989, the situation had changed. The role which the Centre at King's College London could or might have played was assigned to the (then) newly formed INFORM. For the Church, INFORM seemed ideal, because it offered what was deemed necessary, but not available elsewhere: the combination of information and counselling. This was to be complemented by diocesan advisers, appointed on an ecumenical basis, in conjunction with other denominations. Advisers would specialize in NRMs and be involved in INFORM's emerging network. (They are comparable to the German *Sektenbeauftragte* who liaise with one another, although their network is not quite comparable to INFORM's.) For the Church, this seemed the right kind of action: it was an inclusive approach which promised to be effective and positive, while remaining low key. Further, together with the BCC, guidelines were drafted to underpin the network of advisers and a code of practice applicable to *all* religions was devised.

The code's first part reflects, to some extent, allegations levelled against NRMs by the ACM, including all kinds of deception (invitations and fund-raising under false pretences or for undeclared purposes, recruitment without revealing movements' identity or the level of commitment required) and immoral persuasion techniques (sleep or food deprivation, hypnosis or

forms of 'blackmail', etc.). The code can be said to be influenced by considerations which the ACM brought to the Church's attention. There was
indeed contact between Church bodies and 'cult-monitoring' groups.

The code's second part addresses issues practised by some ACM groups,
such as 'forcible deprogramming', which the code does not endorse. It
affirms the right of individuals to choose freely their religious beliefs. It does
not want to see rights declared illegal or withdrawn from any NRM without
justifiable evidence or truth disregarded or misinformation spread. This part
of the code can be read as a veiled message to some ACM quarters that they
cannot expect the Church to co-operate in or condone such actions.

As to the Church's general attitude, the Synod Report comments mainly
from a theological perspective. In this respect, it shares the approach of the
RCC and EZW. However, as the rejection of Peter Broadbent's amendment
shows, the Church did not want to emphasize theological differences too
much. While it points out that NRM teachings need to be considered case by
case, it affirms that some teachings are incompatible with the Christian faith
and these aspects need to be studied and clarified. The Report criticizes some
NRMs' moral behaviour, such as encouraging suicide, using sexual favour
for recruitment or soliciting money. These are glaring examples of NRMs
behaving badly – one need not be a Christian to reject them. However, the
more recent cases of the Solar Temple and Aum Shinrikyo suggest that the
People's Temple was not as exceptional a case as once thought.

The Synod Report also takes a very cautious attitude towards spiritual
exercises from other traditions. The arguments against these are very similar
to those advanced by the RCC. Churches should not allow their premises to
be used for such exercises, without knowing exactly who offers them. The
Report considers dual membership impossible, even when NRMs present
themselves as part of Christianity or as philosophies – the latter a reference
to the SES.

Finally, the Synod's interest in the Government's White Paper on charities
was understandable, since any changes in charitable law would affect all
religious organizations. The Church was bound to keep a watchful eye on
proposed changes to make sure they did not affect its own structures
adversely. The beginning of the Bishop of Chester's contribution to the
debate on the White Paper in the Lords was concerned with possible consequences for contemplative religious communities in the Church of England
and the RCC (*Hansard*, 30.11.1989: cols. 542–543).

Colin Slee's paper

In April 1995, the Institute of Oriental Philosophy's European Centre at
Taplow Court, near Maidenhead in Berkshire, held a symposium on 'New
religious movements: Challenge and Response'. Colin Slee, Provost of South-
wark Cathedral and INFORM governor since October 1994, presented a
paper on 'New religious movements and Church Responses' (Slee, 1995),

subsequently published (Slee, 1999) in the conference proceedings (Wilson and Cresswell, 1999). Slee's paper examines the mutual responses of established churches and NRMs. He argues that the churches have, overall, failed in communicating their doctrines and that their hostile stance towards NRMs arose from ignorance and insecurity. He identifies shared and distinguishing features of churches and NRMs and explores areas for common ground and dialogue.

Slee uses a personal encounter with a fundamentalist Christian to illustrate the kind of conversation and emotional reaction which typically occurs between NRM members and church representatives. He felt challenged about the Church and Christianity to the point of losing his temper. He felt threatened and insulted, because, for his interlocutor, Jesus was the answer to everything.

NRMs are nothing new – Christianity itself started as a new religious movement, as Stark (1996a) also discusses. New or syncretistic movements within Christianity are not recent phenomena, as the early Church fathers testify who often wrote against heresy rather than about faith. However, it is worth exploring whether 'we are witnessing an explosion of NRMs in the last few years', especially considering issues such as globalization, international communications, and high literacy.

While admitting that it is difficult to define NRMs, Slee suggests two theological tests: the test of Gamaliel and the 'test from Tradition'. The former (Acts 5, 34–42: 'For if this idea of theirs or its execution is of human origin it will collapse; but if it is from God you will never be able to put them down, and you risk finding yourselves at war with God.') takes the long view and requires patience, time, and tolerance, but NRM activities have raised great concern and some teachings are clearly outside Christian theology. The second test refers to the continuity of tradition within the churches which – despite disputes and debates – is accepted as rooted in the Gospel, received through the Apostles, and conveyed in a succession of leadership and distilled understanding. While Christian churches value tradition as a treasure and resource, NRMs disregard or see it as an impediment. On an institutional level, this test relates to church bodies where membership is contingent on doctrinal issues.

Slee concedes the complexity of theology: Christian truth is open to new revelation, but new truth needs to be tested. Openness to new revelation cannot mean acceptance of *any* new idea and testing involves hostility and trial by fire. The churches need to strike a balance between closing doors to movements whose ideas go beyond traditional teachings and welcoming those which merely claim adherence to church precepts. Slee considers NRMs to pose threats in three other respects, apart from the theological: NRMs criticize churches for not teaching the truth about God (adequately); they threaten membership and bring religion into disrepute, which jeopardizes its place in the wider culture and undermines freedom of expression, including their own.

According to Slee, in general, authors using 'cult' and 'sect' take a hostile stance towards NRMs. Their hostility is not so much based on NRMs' teachings as on a perceived threat to their monopoly claim to truth. Hostility may be perceived or real, have good reason or just be a 'knee jerk' reaction. Authors using 'NRM' are consistent in their efforts to adopt a neutral or academic stance.

Slee's active part in submitting the NRM question to the General Synod in 1983 arose from his view that the Church's stance was somewhat patronizing and ostrich-like. As university chaplain, he observed the SES's effect on undergraduates and was refused a meeting with SES leaders. As Dean of St Albans, he found three SES members in his congregation (hence the mention of the SES in the Synod question). The Synod 'expressed the wish that the Church should take unspecified action' and detailed considerations were passed to the House of Bishops. The Bishops' deliberations are confidential, but Slee believes that they were split between a strong response to NRMs and fear of court action. They passed the matter, deemed to be of an ecumenical nature, to the BCC, which recognized the problem, but stressed the importance of freedom of expression and religious freedom. Any proscriptive action initiated by the churches might be interpreted as censorship or a way to counteract empty pews. Such action might also affect religious privilege in general (the very reason the BCC did not accept the Cottrell Report). Instead, the BCC encouraged the creation of INFORM and appointed a permanent member of staff to observe NRMs and relations with them.[17] Slee considers this response positive, albeit not media effective, as it conveys a cautious, academic, and non-confrontational approach. His own attitude developed over time: it changed from qualifying SES a 'cult' – he was quite happy to see the term used in Hounan and Hogg's (1985) book, on which he collaborated – to seeing it as an NRM; instead of thinking of it as 'the enemy', he came to a see it as 'strangely misguided and potential[ly] harmful, but not necessarily so'. The imperial view of a confirmed liberal theologian gave way to a willingness to examine why people joined.

Many people join and remain members because they are sincere and because the churches have somehow failed them. This failure mainly concerns teaching and information: people are not taught enough to be able to question NRM doctrines and to identify inconsistencies or errors in scriptural interpretation. (The RCC also makes this point.) The Church also failed in informing people about what it can offer. Young people interested in exploring community and contemplative life are not encouraged to do this within the Church's framework. Disillusioned, they go elsewhere – to NRMs. Another possible failure is the churches' insufficient demand on members. Some are attracted to NRMs because these require great commitment. Also, the churches have no novelty value, because they are historic. Finally, the Church has failed in the way it conveys answers. Most members are seeking 'Truth' which NRMs offer with simple messages and lifestyles. However, the search for truth should engage with and acknowledge complexity. Typical answers from Anglican quarters are phrased too equivocally and are not satisfactory or helpful to those who want clear solutions and simple lives rather than intense debates and constant decision-making.

Slee compares the behaviour of some church sections with that of some NRMs. He sees, for example, strong parallels between NRMs and evangelical circles, which condemn NRMs as manifestations of the 'Anti-Christ', or the Christian Union's (CU's) practices, comparable to NRMs' 'love-bombing' techniques. Yet Slee identifies areas where churches and NRMs differ markedly, such as transparency regarding teachings, financial matters, and identity, although some NRMs have made connections between various organizations more obvious.

Change in the churches parallels changes in interfaith dialogue with increasing exchange and conversation between churches and the main NRMs. Discussions between the world religions are fruitful for the churches' understanding of NRMs' attraction and teachings, as some reflect Hindu and Buddhist approaches. Understanding these allows for indirect insight into the way NRMs address certain issues.

In conclusion, relations between churches and NRMs would be enhanced 'by a large dose of humility on both sides' and by the acceptance by both that no-one can truthfully claim a monopoly on revelation. The churches also need to acknowledge malpractices which they condemn in other religious groups, while NRMs need to 'emerge from their Laager mentality and be less paranoid'. They need to realize that transparency in teachings, publicity, and administration will reduce suspicion and hostility, which will in turn reduce their sense of persecution. Lessons learnt from interfaith dialogue can be applied to dialogue between churches and NRMs. The theological critique of NRMs has mainly come from evangelical quarters, but there should be serious study from the central or radical parts of the churches (a point which Michael Fuss also makes).

Reflections

Colin Slee supplements available information and considerations in the Church. His comments are important because they are grounded in personal pastoral experience. While he does not systematically discuss NRM-related issues, he addresses some questions which are important to the churches and shows their difficulty and dilemma. One major difficulty is the question what a 'new religion' is. Mindful of Christianity's beginnings as a 'new religion' and the need to take the revelation of new truth seriously, Slee proposes two tests (Gamaliel and Tradition), but neither is ideal – the first requiring the long view, the second requiring consensus within orthodox Christian churches. Therefore, they need to strike a balance between closing their doors to innovative religion and opening the floodgates to novel religion.

Slee also discusses NRMs as a (perceived) threat to mainstream churches. Some church sections feel their monopoly of 'Truth' threatened by NRMs and assume a hostile stance, while the Synod and BCC have taken a positive and non-confrontational, if cautious, approach. Slee's important point is that his own attitude evolved over time from a somewhat combative, campaigning crusade against 'cults' to a willingness to examine 'NRMs' and their members closely and acknowledge the positive in them.[18] His perspective changed from 'cults' as a form of 'bad religion', unworthy of theological attention, to 'new religions' as legitimate forms of innovative religion. Saliba (1995: 106) draws attention to this very point.

In Slee's view, the churches have failed their members in four areas. First, they have not taught them enough to evaluate NRM doctrines appropriately. Second, they have not told them about the range of spiritual lifestyles within their structures. People's spiritual or other needs could be met, if they knew what is on offer. Those young people who wished to explore communal life were not directed to the right places. Third, the churches may have failed in not requiring greater commitment; the cost of membership is too low – a point which Stark (1996b) discusses regarding NRMs' success or failure. Fourth, the churches have not provided straightforward answers to those who seek a simple life. While Slee acknowledges that Truth is complex, especially in a (post-)modern society, the churches need to articulate the contradiction between ready-made answers and the need to address complicated issues.

Slee sees parallels and differences between the way sections of the churches and some NRMs operate. The parallels relate to 'love-bombing' techniques, Bible study, approach to Scriptures and acceptance of other groups, while important differences relate to transparency, particularly regarding 'front' organizations and accountability. Yet, noting recent changes in NRMs and the churches, Slee is optimistic about better understanding on both sides. While the churches have opened up to interfaith dialogue, some NRMs have changed their approach to publicity.

Slee concludes that generalizations should be guarded against, that 'a good dose of humility' should be administered, that both sides need to accept that no-one has a monopoly on truth and need to put their respective houses in order, and that interfaith dialogue can be used as a model for dialogue between churches and NRMs. (Some Roman Catholic theologians have also explored this approach.) Yet Slee's conclusions rest on an important premise: both sides need to relinquish the idea of holding the Truth and the claim to absolute truth.

Parallels in behaviour and perception between NRMs and evangelical circles point to different interests *within* the Church, with evangelical and liberal wings bound to differ in perceptions and interests. This would account for differences in approach: while there may be an implicit alliance between evangelical circles and 'cult-monitoring' groups, the liberal wing would incline towards academic perspectives. Slee may be a case in point: his former role as a university chaplain and his churchmanship as a provost would place him in the liberal camp and close to the academic position. The internal variety of interests and approaches may have made it impossible for the Church to be more explicit about NRMs and their teachings than it has been, for example, in the Synod Report. Handing the issue to an organization outside its structures, INFORM which operates on an academic footing, could be an endorsement of the position which clergy such as Slee have taken. However, apart from the Church's internal concerns, its role and status as the established Church have had a crucial impact on its approach to NRMs. This role and status include speaking for religion in general and on behalf of all religions so that the Church has always shown tolerance towards other religions and pursued an inclusive approach.

THE RESPONSE OF THE PROTESTANT CHURCH IN GERMANY

EVANGELISCHE ZENTRALSTELLE FÜR WELTANSCHAUUNGSFRAGEN (*EZW*)

Introduction

This section describes the work of the *Evangelische Zentralstelle für Weltanschauungsfragen* (EZW) in Germany, literally, the Protestant Church's centre for questions of *Weltanschauung*.[19] It focuses in particular on the conception of this work as shaped by Dr Reinhart Hummel during his 14-year directorship of the EZW (1981–1995). Therefore, his publications and an in-depth interview with him largely inform this section. The EZW is also placed within the wider context of the responses of the churches and other social institutions in Germany.

The EZW within the EKD

The EZW is an institution of the *Evangelische Kirche in Deutschland* (EKD), the Protestant Church of Germany,[20] the umbrella organization for, and a union of, 21 Lutheran (*lutherische*), Reformed (*reformiert* – Protestantism largely based on Zwingli and Calvin), and Unified (*uniert*)[21] *Landeskirchen* or *Gliedkirchen* (member churches). Eight member churches form the *Vereinigte Ev.-Luth. Kirche Deutschlands* (VELKD), the unified Protestant-Lutheran Church in Germany. Church structures changed in 1989 after the fall of the Berlin Wall with an expansion of the EKD to include the churches in eastern Germany.

Like the *Länder*, the *Landeskirchen* are largely independent. For example, ministers (male and female) are trained and ordained within their *Landeskirche* which has its own rules and regulations concerning clergy, although transfer is possible. *Landeskirchen* have their own synods, elected by parish councils. The EKD is thus invested with relatively few powers, as all matters of faith and belief are the preserve of member churches. Its main tasks are to promote co-operation between *Landeskirchen* and speak for them in relation to state or public authorities. It also plays a role in promoting ecumenism.

The EKD and its member churches see themselves as a *Volkskirche*, a church of the people, to which people belong mainly because of background and convention.[22] For individuals, membership is related to residence and baptism. Baptism involves 'automatic' membership of the respective *Landeskirche*, which is transferred in case of relocation.[23] The EKD's three bodies are the *Rat der EKD* (the council), Synod, and *Kirchenkonferenz* (church conference). The *Rat* is the executive arm and consists of 15 members elected by Synod and church conference. Its tasks are to manage EKD affairs and represent it.[24] The Synod – composed of members elected by the synods of the *Landeskirchen* and the EKD's council – has legislative powers and issues statements on social and church matters. The church conference – composed of member church leaders – considers matters relating to the EKD's work and submits proposals to Synod and council. It plays a part in the election of council members and in legislation.

The EZW's tasks

The EZW was established in 1960. Until 1997, its seat was in Stuttgart, in the south-west, but the wake of reunification brought plans to transfer it to Berlin. The EZW had a precursor, the *Apologetische Centrale* or Centre for Apologetics, established in 1919 during the Weimar Constitution (*Weimarer Reichsverfassung*) and forced to close in 1937 under National Socialism. The EZW sees its work as a continuation of the *Centrale*'s.[25] It also builds on the work of Kurt Hutten, a theologian and early apologist, whose *Sekten, Grübler, Enthusiasten* has become a classic.[26] The EZW is relatively independent, although it is placed under the supervision of the *Kuratorium*, a board of trustees. The board's two functions are to appoint theologians who work in the EZW and to mediate between the EZW and EKD council. The EZW's mandate is laid down in its *Ordnung* or *Satzung* (statutes):

> [the EZW] has the task to *observe* religious currents and currents of *Weltanschauung* of the time and to promote the analysis of contemporary spiritual matters by the Church.
>
> (emphasis added)

This gives the EZW great latitude, as it is not specified how or indeed which currents are to be observed. Its introductory leaflet (EZW, n.d.) 'Im Gespräch mit der Zeit' (in discussion with contemporary matters) elucidates its aims further:

> The EZW has the task to observe contemporary religious and spiritual currents as well as currents of *Weltanschauung*; seeks to offer help for a

Christian answer to, and for an appropriate dialogue with, believers of another faith or non-believers; is prepared, as much as is possible, to supply information or to give advice, and to work with other organizations with regard to publications, conferences and seminars.

Given this conception, the EZW takes a special position among other information centres – there is no comparable institution in Germany.

EZW staff

The EZW consists of theologians who have a *Referat*, a particular remit, and are supported by secretarial staff. The contours of the remits can change: in 1995, they comprised religion in eastern Germany; science and psychology; charismatic renewal groups; contemporary secular and religious currents; New Age, para-psychology, and occultism; Scientology, 'traditional sects', and esoteric movements, and in 1998, they comprised contemporary secular and religious currents, fundamental questions; non-Christian religions, especially Eastern religiosity and spirituality; Christian *Sondergemeinschaften*, Scientology; Pentecostal and charismatic groups and movements, fundamentalism; esoterism, occultism, spiritualism; religious aspects in schools of psychology, aspects of *Weltanschauung* in science and technology. One of the *Referenten*, appointed by the *Kuratorium*, acts as director – until 31 January 1995, Dr Reinhart Hummel. who reflected on his 14 years in the EZW in an interview with one of his colleagues (EZW, 1995b). In July 1995, Dr Michael Nüchtern became director, followed by Dr Reinhard Hempelmann in January 1999.

The mandate of the *Referenten* covers two aspects: first, dissemination through publications and public presentations, with publications aimed at individuals and centres for redistribution, for example *Sektenbeauftragte*, teachers or advice centres.[27] Second, responding to enquiries. Lehmann's (1994) survey of enquiries underscores the EZW's special position. Although a substantial part of Lehmann's sample (27 per cent) came from church-related quarters, a far greater proportion (*c*.60 per cent) did not. The sample comprised 775 written enquiries received during 1993 and lodged in EZW's archives, around 15 per cent of *all* written enquiries that year.[28] About half were not motivated by personal interest, but by professional necessity, arising, for example, from pastoral care, the media, or academic interest. However, co-operation with state bodies dealing with religious phenomena appeared to be low, with only 5 per cent of enquiries originating from these. This figure might imply differences unrelated to EZW's remit and point to neglect of this field by the State. Enquiries also ranged widely, regarding both topic and geography,[29] and, in Lehmann's view, can be considered 'typical' for Germany (Lehmann, 1994: 196–197).

The two-fold mandate strikes a balance between theoretical and practical concerns, two aspects which inform and correct one another. According to

Hummel, dealing with enquiries and counselling requires staff to keep their feet firmly on the ground, because these convey problems which arise from encounters with religion and inter-religious encounters. However, problems and conflicts are but one aspect and EZW staff need to see them in perspective so that they do not focus exclusively on potential conflict in religious pluralism (EZW, 1995b: 135).

EZW's purview

Even a cursory glance at EZW's publications shows how wide its purview is. EZW's very name, *Zentralstelle für Weltanschauungsfragen*, indicates that its work encompasses a great variety of groups and movements which express *Weltanschauungen*[30] which differ distinctly from the Protestant Church's. In my interview with Hummel, he pointed to the wide spectrum of groups with which the EZW deals, including traditional sects, *Sondergemeinschaften*, and NRMs. 'Sect' (*Sekte*) here describes religious groups which resulted from schisms within mainstream or world religions. They are defined by differences in relation to the religions from which they broke away. From Christianity's point of view, sects are different from NRMs (*Jugendreligionen*) and using the term need not connote value judgement. Yet, in popular parlance, especially in the media, 'sects' denote religious groups which deviate from mainstream social ethos and are associated with negative values. Hansjörg Hemminger (1995) remarks that the term 'sect' has 'undergone a process of secularization'. The term 'traditional sects' largely covers groups which formed in the nineteenth century, such as Mormons, Jehovah's Witnesses, Seventh-Day-Adventists, etc. *Sondergemeinschaften* is a term which Hummel described as 'first of all, a friendlier word for "sects" and it is also a designation for groups which do not have such an exclusive claim to absolute truth as to refuse ecumenical contact'. The term *Sondergemeinschaften* thus describes groups in relation to the mainstream churches. It is used within them and from their viewpoint, as the titles of major publications by Protestant and Roman Catholic theologians indicate (Gasper *et al.*, 1990; Eggenberger, 1990; Hutten, 1984; Pastoralamt der Erzdiözese Wien, 1982a; Reller, 1985).

Sources of information

The EZW gathers information 'through established channels and within established structures', which operate on various levels: (1) individuals, some of whom are involved with groups or movements; (2) the press and media; (3) parents' initiatives; (4) the movements themselves; (5) existing literature, e.g. the *Encyclopedia of American Religion* (Melton, 1978); (6) the clergy network in the *Landeskirchen* – the *Sektenbeauftragten*; (7) international contacts, such as comparable institutions in Austria, for example, *Pastoralamt der Erzdiözese Wien* (Pastoral Office of the Archdiocese of

Vienna, which was until July 1999 under the direction of Dr Friederike Valentin), and Switzerland, for example, *Arbeitsgruppe 'Neue Religiöse Bewegungen in der Schweiz'* (Working Group on Religious Movements), a joint initiative of the Roman Catholic and Protestant Churches in Switzerland (*Schweizerische Bischofskonferenz* and *Schweizerischer Evangelischer Kirchenbund*).

The EZW's material on groups and movements is brought up to date in the light of new developments. Research is sometimes prompted by enquiries, when available information is insufficient or when no information is on file at all. This is the case for movements which are relatively new to Germany, for example Mahikari or the Church of Christ. In such cases, EZW taps into the wider network.

Collecting data in the field or through participant observation is not considered a viable option, although Hummel visited the headquarters of some movements while preparing his postdoctoral thesis. He travelled, for example, to Seelisberg, the seat of the World Government of Spiritual Regeneration Movement, to converse with 'ministers of the world government'. He openly stated the purpose of his visit and the nature of his work.[31] Hummel believes that university affiliation afforded him greater access to movements than the directorship of the EZW would have. Other reasons why EZW *Referenten* do not engage in fieldwork is lack of time and lack of training in fieldwork or participant observation. Also, as Hummel stated, 'participant observation requires a degree of neutrality and readiness to let oneself be compromised, if need be, which I can ill afford'. This suggests that, as theologians working for the EZW and the Church, *Referenten* cannot be *seen* to fraternize with members and leaders of religious groups which are considered rivals. The interpretation which may arise from such associations could undermine, even compromise the Church. Therefore, *Referenten* cannot take part in NRM-sponsored events, such as conferences.

EZW's approach

The EZW does, however, maintain direct contact with some movements. Some supply information for the archives and with some the EZW is on speaking terms, as Hummel put it, although *Referenten* do not visit their centres. He pointed out that some groups are well versed in relating to outside institutions, which – to some extent – facilitates relations with them. However, it is important to note that there is no uniform approach to the way EZW relates to movements:

> the way we deal with our *clientèle* [groups and movements] varies within the sections . . . if the question is, what is the overall approach of the EZW, then it is difficult to express it in one formula.

Whether *Referenten* deal with scientific topics, ISKCON, charismatic renewal movements or Mormonism, they need to find an *appropriate* way to deal with each:

> One cannot apply one and the same schema . . . but one has to find an appropriate way of how things should be dealt with, depending on each case, on the particular area and on the particular phenomenon.

Thus the subject matter and not the person dealing with it determines the approach. EZW *Referenten* share common principles in the way they carry out their work. They apply 'scientific' methods and aim to be fair and object-ive, but they work within the framework of the Church, or, in Hummel's words, *in kirchlicher Verantwortung*, with a sense of responsibility towards the Church. EZW *Referenten* know they are in the Church's employ and this affords them freedom or independence from other claims: 'by tying our-selves to the Church, we free ourselves from other predicated patterns, assertions, etc.'

The Church does not interfere with what the EZW does or says, *unless* political events stir it into action – 'political' understood here in the wider sense – which has on the whole not happened. From the Church's point of view, the EZW can be left to its own devices, as long as it fulfils its task, which is to look after an area which is not in the limelight of the Church's attention. This has brought a great degree of continuity to the EZW, with a widening and greater specialization of sections over the years. Work on charismatic groups is, for example, a relatively recent addition to the EZW's core subjects (interview with R. Hummel).

EZW's freedom questioned

Despite the EZW's great freedom over the years, there are two instances in which the Church administration severely undermined this freedom and called the EZW's independence into question. The first arose in connection with a controversial movement, *Verein zur Förderung der Psychologischen Menschenkenntnis* or VPM (Association for Promoting the Psychological Knowledge of Man), the second in connection with EZW's transfer to Berlin. Each case will be dealt with in turn.

The case of VPM

In 1991, the EZW published a statement about VPM, which had been pre-pared by one of its *Referenten*, Hansjörg Hemminger (1991), and resulted from previous reports on the movement. Founded in Zurich in 1986, VPM was based on the work of the late (he died in 1982) Friedrich Liebling, a pupil of Freud and Adler, who had laid the foundations in the 1950s. The organization, also known as the *Züricher Schule*, pursued various activities in Switzerland, Austria, and Germany, including drugs and AIDS programmes, counselling, learning aids, and holidays for children and adults. (In March 2002, it announced that it was officially dissolved – ostensibly a tactical measure, as some activities continue.) The practice of VPM teachings provoked controversy and legal proceedings. The EZW's statement described Liebling's ideas and showed how a 'sectarian' group developed around his *Weltanschauung*. VPM became particularly known by the way it dealt with critics, often involving lengthy libel cases. Hemminger concurred with other psychologists in his conclusion that VPM induced dependency, with a strict hierarchy of control and neutralization of internal criticism. The statement's final section commented on the response of the church and its organizations.[32]

The EZW's previous reports about VPM had resulted in attempts to suppress any statements about it. Therefore, when Hemminger's statement was published, VPM threatened legal action, sent letters of protest to national and local sections of the Church administration, and made personal representations to church leaders. In early 1991, VPM had filed suit against Hemminger and the publisher (Herder-Verlag) of *Lexikon der Sekten, Sondergruppen und Weltanschauungen* (Gasper *et al.*, 1990) regarding a brief description of VPM (ibid.: cols. 1039–1040). The case was, however, thrown out by the appeal court (Hemminger, 1992: 361). In the meantime, the EZW's *Kuratorium* and the Church administration had commissioned Hemminger to write a more detailed account of VPM. Before this was published, VPM sought to delete some of the contents through an injunction. The court recognized, however, that VPM had gained access to Hemminger's unpublished manuscript by using 'immoral methods', namely 'under false pretences', and did not grant the injunction, even after VPM had brought another lawsuit. By then, VPM had started a defamation campaign against Hemminger, the EZW, other *Sektenbeauftragte* and critics, accusing them to be 'on the extreme left, without conscience, criminal, and damaging to the Church'. EZW's press statement of 10 October 1991 prompted VPM to apply for another injunction, which was not granted either. An attempt to prevent the publication of a talk by Hemminger was equally unsuccessful (Hemminger, 1992: 361–362).[33] VPM's failure to obtain injunctions or verdicts against the EZW's statements or publications meant that these stood and could be reproduced.[34] The courts upheld the *Grundrecht der Meinungsfreiheit*, the fundamental freedom of expression, as a constitutional right.

The important point about the proceedings is this: VPM's protests and presentations, although directed to the EZW and Hemminger, threw the EZW into the limelight of the Church's attention, which stirred the Church administration into action. To stem the pressure of protest, the Church hierarchy requested that the EZW publish a *Gegendarstellung* or correction to satisfy VPM's demands. The EZW refused, on the grounds that this was undue interference in its work and unacceptable condescension. A noticeable gap appeared between the perspectives of the Church administration and the EZW. From the Church's viewpoint, a critical situation had arisen which put pressure on all levels of its hierarchy: VPM had lodged its protest with officials of the Bavarian member church; the bishop of Bavaria then made representations to the Church administration which in turn sought to solve the matter by putting pressure on the EZW. The Church's strategy aimed at avoiding legal proceedings, a strategy which was as understandable as it was convenient. The publication of a correction would have meant compliance with the letter of the law and VPM would have backed down.

From the EZW's viewpoint, the Church administration's action was not founded in judiciousness or insight into the matter, but in political considerations. The Church used its authority to impose its will on one of the institutions which it technically controls. After years of enjoying the freedom to do its work quietly, the EZW felt undermined by being ordered to publish a correction; this feeling was all the more acute, as the EZW had not been consulted. The EZW *Referenten* were convinced that they had done their work properly and that the statements about VPM stood up to scrutiny. The gap between the two perspectives arose therefore from a distinct clash of interests. The Church administration's interest lay in avoiding conflict. The EZW's interest was to uphold the contents and veracity of its statements and to preserve its independence.

This case provoked an important discussion of the independence – or the lack of independence – of the EZW. The incident tested the limits of the EZW's freedom. It also demonstrated the limits of the *Kuratorium*'s influence on the Church administration and of its mediating role. There was talk about changing the EZW's statutes with a view to emphasizing its status as a *kirchliche Dienststelle*, a Church office. This seemed to imply the Church administration's intention to keep tighter control over the EZW and its work.

The move to Berlin

The second instance in which the EZW felt the Church's reins to a greater degree than before concerned the transfer to Berlin. The November 1993 edition of *Materialdienst* contained the first report (EZW, 1993a),[35] stating that EZW *Referenten* and associated colleagues learnt about the plans through the press and hearsay. The *Frankfurter Allgemeine Zeitung* (FAZ) of 8 July 1993 had reported that the EKD intended to buy the former headquarters of the CDU's (Christian Democratic Party's) eastern branch (Christian Democratic Party) in central Berlin from the *Treuhand-Anstalt* (the agency established after the fall of the Berlin Wall to deal with property in eastern Germany). These premises would be the seat for the official representation of the EKD council to the government (which was to move from Bonn to Berlin) and house other EKD institutions, among them the EZW. While the FAZ had reported *plans* to relocate the EZW, *Materialdienst* pointed out that the relocation was already decided. In fact, the EKD's *Rat* had determined the EZW's move in late June 1993.[36]

What caused great consternation among the EZW *Referenten* was being confronted with a *fait accompli*, as neither consultation nor opinion-forming processes had taken place. Not even the *Kuratorium* had been involved in any discussion or decision. In their letter to the *Kuratorium* of 5 July 1993, EZW staff expressed bewilderment at the lack of consultation. The body representing theologians associated with the EZW also wrote to the EKD administration's president.[37] While *Referenten* and associated colleagues felt their trust in the EKD shaken, they still hoped for constructive discussions with relevant church bodies. It is, however, clear from the statement in *Materialdienst* that the EZW considered its relocation unnecessary and damaging.

The advertisement for the EZW's directorship in February 1994 stated that the vacancy was due to the present director's retirement and briefly explained the work of the EZW, together with all the usual details about employment procedures. The advertisement also noted that 'The [EZW's] seat is in Stuttgart (a possible transfer to Berlin is conceivable)'. At that stage, it was apparently still open whether the EZW should indeed move to Berlin. However, by August 1994, the die was cast: *Materialdienst* announced the relocation to Berlin by 1997. The EKD's *Rat* had decided in May 1994 that the EZW's work in Stuttgart would be suspended and resumed in Berlin, either with existing or new *Referenten*, by February 1997 at the latest. The move was intended as a gesture towards Eastern Germany where the EKD wished to be represented. However, as *Materialdienst* comments,[38] this motive was given precedence over the concern about the continuity and quality of the EZW's work in Stuttgart, despite representations by the EZW and concerned sympathizers. Much would depend on the way the transfer would proceed, but in the meantime, the EZW would endeavour not to let the impending move affect its work. There was an intimation of the hurt inflicted: 'That the uprooting from the south of Germany and the transplantation to Berlin have caused many a wound and pain, needs no further elaboration' (*Materialdienst* 57 (8), 1994: 247).

In July 1995, Michael Nüchtern, already located in Berlin, became the EZW's director. (An advertisement for a *Referent* in April 1995 had given Berlin as *Dienststelle* or place of work.) Nüchtern's departure in October 1998 made his directorship, compared to Hummel's, rather short.

As in the case of the statements about VPM, both the EZW and the *Kuratorium* saw themselves powerless in relation to the Church authorities. The only concessions which could be extracted from them concerned the timetable for the move, but this seemed insignificant in view of the EKD's far-reaching decisions.

Apologetics and dialogue

As the EZW does not have a uniform approach to the groups and movements with which it is concerned, the way *Referenten* deal with their subject areas is closely linked with particular phenomena and issues. This is reflected in the publications which show a mix of historical, theological, sociological, and apologetic concepts. The reason for this multifaceted approach lies in the EZW's statutes which do not stipulate a particular approach. While the EZW is an observation point for the Church, which allows it to follow developments within non-Christian religious groups and thus makes it better equipped for dealing with these, the statutes make no mention that the work needs to be within a theological framework. The absence of references to theology has given rise to the reproach that the EZW is simply a *Kulturinstitut* or cultural institute. However, the EZW does assess non-Christian groups to a considerable extent, but not exclusively, from a theological perspective. The guiding principle is the concept of *theologische Apologetik* (theological apologetics). The late Hans-Diether Reimer, a long-standing *Referent*, took the view that the intention of establishing the EZW was to have an institute of apologetics in the Church, although there is no mention of apologetics in the EZW's constitutional documents (Reimer, 1991). Hummel refers to *theologische Apologetik* also as *apologetischer Dialog* (apologetic dialogue) or *Apologetik im Dialog* (apologetics in dialogue) or *verstehende Apologetik* (empathic apologetics). The latter is reminiscent of Weber's concept of *verstehen*, which Hummel did, however, not cite.

In *Begegnung und Auseinandersetzung* (Hummel *et al.*, 1994), three EZW *Referenten*, Hummel (1994a), Gottfried Küenzlen (1994), and Hemminger (1994b), reflect on the fundamentals of the EZW's work in discussing their approach to apologetics. They see their reflections as a continuation and extension of concepts formulated by earlier *Referenten* (Aichelin *et al.*, 1976), in the light of changes in Church and culture. The essays evolved from discussions among EZW *Referenten* and *Kuratorium* members, but are not intended as a comprehensive portrayal of EZW thinking.

The notion of apologetics has undergone changes, evolving from the idea of anxious defence of faith to the description of the work undertaken by experts on sects and *Weltanschauung*, including the EZW. Within this context, apologetics is now understood as:

> providing answers to the questions which a pluralistic, religious or a-religious world addresses to the Church, whether they are questions emanating from currents of *Weltanschauung* of our culture or questions emanating from small, isolated communities.
>
> (Hummel *et al.*, 1994: 2)

Some EZW *Referenten* addressed apologetics in this sense and sought to explicate it, such as Reimer (1986) and Thiede (1992a).[39] The contents of the three essays on apologetics are examined in more detail.

Hummel's models

The contemporary context is an increasing pluralism of religion and the EZW's task is therefore to provide 'a Christian orientation' (Hummel, 1994a: 3). Pluralism has three aspects:

> first of all the factual plurality (that other gods are 'socially at hand' . . .), further, the resulting relativization on a social and also on a theological level, and finally losing the possibility to use control or sanctions which secured the dominant position of the Churches in the past.
>
> (ibid.)

Christianity – both contemporary and early – has a missionary intention: it testifies to reconciliation and extends the invitation to follow Jesus. However, the Christian faith needs to be justified by the Scriptures and accepted forms of interpreting these. Interpretation is not only about issues of dogma, but also about questions of conduct. Apologetics plays an important role here, because 'One's own faith unfolds in the discussion with other positions; it must allow itself to be questioned by these and in its turn questions them' (ibid.).

Hummel distinguishes three 'ideal types': *traditionsorientierte Abgrenzungsapologetik* (traditional apologetics), *apokalyptische Apologetik* (apocalyptic apologetics), and *dialogische Apologetik* (dialogical apologetics) (ibid.: 5–6). He first identified these in the New Testament and then translated them into the contemporary context (ibid.: 3–8). Traditional apologetics is mindful of Church tradition and defines as heretical what goes against apostolic faith or biblical canon. This type of apologetics is directed towards the pluralism within the Christian faith and is mainly practised by Lutheran churches. It has two weaknesses: first, it is effective *within* the Church where scripture and testimony are accepted. What distinguishes religious pluralism from the pluralism within Christianity is the lack of generally accepted norms. These can, if at all, be established by dialogue. Second, the tendency of traditional apologetics towards traditionalism and anti-modernism precludes discussion of and with contemporary religions.

Apocalyptic apologetics, practised by some sections of the evangelical movement, seeks to defend Christianity against clearly perceived opponents, in an end-time scenario. Dialogical apologetics involves distinction of Christianity from other faiths, with a clear line between them, yet also involves openness and willingness towards integration. The EZW pursues this, but does not claim to have a monopoly. However, dialogical apologetics cannot mean that: Christianity simply accepts propositions of another faith without careful examination; it is motivated by the quest for enemies in order to define itself; it seeks harmonization or assimilation. Further, dialogical apologetics must not be tempted to make inappropriate concessions, because it then ceases to be properly understood. The 1980s and 1990s saw growing uncertainty of faith and a growing need for Christian orientation and affirmation. Dialogical apologetics has a pragmatic side, as it helps to overcome prejudices and preconceived ideas. Dialogue promotes better understanding of, and respect for, those who think and believe differently. It is important that *people* are involved in dialogue, not only ideas; pertinent questions must be heard and solidarity demonstrated with those who seek and question, even if this puts apologists in opposition to their own church, because 'The apologist is not only the advocate of the gospel, but also the advocate of Man in search of the way, the truth and the life' (ibid.: 10).

Within the wider theological context, Hummel sees apologetic dialogue as an aspect of *theologica viatorum*: the Church's need of inculturation, learning, change, self-correction. The difficulty with contemporary pluralism is the need to conduct a pluralism of dialogues, shaped to other religions or *Weltanschauungen*. Dialogue is also plural regarding the levels on which it is conducted with a given group to find common ground. Yet there is need for fine balance:

> Christian Apologetics must withstand the natural need to both distinguish itself from and to embrace [the other], and be able to define both, the shared and the divisive, in relation to religions and *Weltanschauung*.
>
> (ibid.: 11)

There is also the need to address the wider social and cultural environment, which – having cast off essential Christian aspects (or being largely secularized) – has post-Christian character. Apologetics needs to direct attention towards cultural developments when these compete with Christianity and cannot be reconciled with Christian ideas or ethics. Here, too, apologetics needs to be able to distinguish – in Christian terms – the acceptable from the unacceptable, without passing blanket judgements. However, 'Apologetics is not the extended arm of a society striving for consensus' (ibid.: 12). Society can be measured by its tolerance of different, even radical, forms of religious (particularly Christian) commitment. It cannot be the task of Christian apologetics to defend such commitment against the claim to exclusivity in a technological civilization and its purpose-oriented rationality.[40]

The recognition that other faiths or religious movements may have genuinely religious or spiritual aspects has earned Hummel and his colleagues criticism from within the Church.

Küenzlen's apologetics in contemporary culture

In Küenzlen's (1994) view, the notion of apologetics seems to be losing its original significance within the Protestant Churches. It has become associated with the Church's need to demarcate its territory and with its inability to conduct dialogue. However, apologetics is one of the Church's fundamental tasks and cannot be the concern of specialized 'defence experts'. In contemporary society, the Church needs to reconsider and re-define its apologetic task. Apologists employed by the church need to draw attention to the current spiritual and cultural situation so that the Church recognizes how urgent this reconsideration is.

Given spiritual currents which challenge Christianity and Church, apolo-getics involves differentiation and orientation. Modernity is marked by uncertainty. Belief in progress, science, and politics has withered; there is a maze of contemporaneous secular and religious propositions, compounded by obsolescence which dates everything prematurely. The *Zeitgeist* is ephemeral. The loss and corrosion of traditions, together with weakening institutions, have made religion a matter of personal choice. The churches, which have traditionally preserved, tended, and transmitted religion, are increasingly criticized, because religious subjectivism can dispense with institutions. Religion is undergoing de-institutionalization: it has become subjective in the pluralism of lifestyles.

Internationalization and globalization have brought nations closer, to the point where exchanging ideas is instant and matter of fact.[41] Secular or religious teachings are thus universally present and can be experienced or followed by whoever chooses to do so. However, as teachings are detached from their national and cultural origins, they undergo changes and appear in new syncretistic forms. Two other disparate, yet dominant contemporary currents constitute forces which compel the Church to reconsider its apologetic task: secularization and religious revival.

For Küenzlen, secularization is a process of increasing this-worldliness, in the Weberian sense: 'The *material* goods of this world are gaining inescap-able power over people' (ibid.: 17, emphasis in original). Secularism has neutralized creeds and credos, religious and secular, resulting in hedonistic gratification and eliminating questions of transcendence. The reunification of Germany might reinforce this process. Secularization is accompanied by aggressive criticism of Church and Christianity. Not only humanists and atheists display their 'new hatred', but also the media and other public opinion-forming agencies. The extreme right – so far presenting 'only' potential protest against social and political matters – might adopt a *Welt-anschauung* of salvation which goes beyond right-wing ideas current in neo-pagan groups.[42] Such groups might gravitate towards extreme national-ism – a form of secular religion.

Despite secularization and secularism, there is renewed interest in religion, with new forms of spirituality and religiosity emerging. Despite talk about an 'age without religion', religion is alive and well, albeit *outside* the churches. There is a religious marketplace where a host of groups set out their wares: sects, *Sondergemeinschaften*, *Weltanschauungsgemeinschaften*, NRMs, 'vagrant religion',[43] neo-Pentecostalism, charismatic renewal groups, evangelical groups (some at the fringes of, others outside, the mainstream churches), fundamentalism, and the world religions. This plurality has undermined the position of the Christian churches. They, like other religions, now just occupy a stall in the marketplace. In postmodern thinking, Truth is dissolved into truths and cultural pluralism celebrates the multiplicity of values.

Given secularism and religious plurality, apologetics must be dialogic to fulfil three tasks: *verstehen* from the inside (*inneres Verstehen*), questioning and being questioned, discernment. *Inneres Verstehen* is, for Küenzlen, the pastoral aspect of church apologetics: followers of other religious groups should be regarded as individuals who are seeking certainty in a brittle and confusing world. Considered judgement is necessary, because 'Anticipated judgement or even hasty condemnation are not the way of church apologetics' (ibid.: 20). This requires accurate information about the 'other' religions' teachings, practices, and claims, an 'ethos of factual diligence' to ensure that groups are not pressed into one mould of apologetic assessment. Küenzlen subscribes to Julius Kaftan's (1848–1926) statement that:

> Whoever wishes to criticize must first of all assume the opposite position and bring it to mind, as the representative of this position wishes to see it understood and believes it substantiated. Only the reasons brought against it will then decide the matter – to kill the caricatures which we ourselves have invented is child's play compared to that.

Regarding the second task, to question and allow for the possibility of being questioned, the encounter with other faiths entails questioning one's own faith. This raises topics for the Church and for Christians, which have often been set or left aside. It may be worth exploring these, not least to understand the trend towards religious experience outside the Church.

Regarding discernment, Church and Christianity cannot always wish to compete with religious aspirations which other groups promote. The *Zeitgeist* produces ideas which are irreconcilable with Christianity. Here, apologetics must define positions clearly. Yet, apologetics is a tool for the Church: it can assist the Church to find its role in a multi-religious culture, to facilitate and prepare dialogue which, given prevailing developments, will become more and more important.

Hemminger's apologetics

Hemminger's (1994b) essay is concerned with methodological and practical aspects of apologetics. He identifies three theological methods which find application in apologetics. First, in assessing the statements of other religious groups apologetics uses principles of interpretation current in the theology of history and systematic theology. It is less important to reconstruct how statements came to be made than to examine how claims to truth and validity are expressed and justified. Second, methods and insights from pastoral care can be applied in cases where individuals from other religions seek advice. There should be co-operation with parishes, church advice centres, etc. Third, methods of *Religionswissenschaft* and missiology can be employed when describing and evaluating groups with an Eastern background. However, the application of these methods focuses on communication and encounter, which need to be examined carefully.

Applied apologetics (*praktische Apologetik*) requires reliable information on religious groups and movements. This is the first and foremost 'service' which the EZW and other *Sektenbeauftragte* offer. Information is gathered in meetings with representatives of groups and during some of their events and by talking to former members, parents, and relatives. Information gathered in this way, however, does not lead to 'objective' accounts, if 'objective' means not stating one's own position clearly. There is objectivity in the sense that accounts are not coloured by personal wishes or anxieties and that they include all the essential information.

Descriptions of groups should be such that they can be justified to groups (as partners in dialogue), to members, critics, and parents. This is a difficult task and, in the case of controversial groups, well-nigh impossible. Yet, such descriptions find a varied audience, inside *and* outside the Church. The interests of the audience vary according to the way such material is evaluated or used. However, an apologetic approach which seeks to take responsibility for the Christian faith in the encounter with other faiths needs to be accountable for what it says about them. This does not mean that other faiths need to approve what church apologists write about them or that apologists should take their cue from them. Nor is it appropriate for apologists to over-emphasize negative aspects in order to bring parents or critics over to the church's side. Yet negative aspects cannot be ignored for the sake of dialogue.

All parties concerned, including the churches, need to acknowledge that the view from without results in perceptions which differ from the view from within. If religious groups do not acknowledge this, they preclude encounter in the stricter sense, because they can then only be explored from the outside. Groups are characterized as 'radical' or 'extreme' when they reject the view from outside or fiercely dispute it.

The methods to formulate the view from outside vary: in some cases, a comparative approach may be appropriate, in others, a historical approach may be more useful or even a combination of both. A number of tools in the academic disciplines (history, natural science, sociology, psychology, *Religionswissenschaft*, etc.) can be of assistance to describe and inform. Applied apologetics endeavours to capture the whole picture of a phenomenon in its respective contexts:

> For example, it is not sufficient to simply state the existence of a particular idea. We need to know its importance in the respective 'hierarchy of truths', its importance for the ethics of the group, and of course the way

the idea is put into practice – together with the often highly practical experience of those outside.

(ibid.: 27)

Understanding the 'other side' is closely linked with understanding one's own side, both often going hand in hand. Genuine encounter between faiths requires realistic expectations, neither too much fear nor too much hope. Apologetics must therefore be based on a 'realistic anthropology of encounter', because encounter does not take place in a vacuum. Other faiths have their identity and their views about Christianity, seeing Christians as individuals with a particular worldview and as representatives of the Church. Preconceived definitions are thus inevitable, as are tensions between views from within and views from without. Encounters have a constructive outcome when prejudices and tensions can be dealt with successfully. This is possible when both sides keep an open mind about their assumptions, although it does not mean simply adopting what the other party says about itself. Listening attentively to a New Ager, for example, is a process of learning about New Age. Only then is there a chance that the New Ager may be ready to hear what Christianity is about. Stubborn rigidity in patterns of perception precludes openness in groups professing 'radical' religions or ideologies. Dialogue in such cases consists in 'attention, encouragement, and listening' and collecting information from without.

Communication also requires clear discrimination between the view from without and the view from within. Tensions between them can be a topic for discussion in dialogue. For example, the picture one draws of 'therapy cult' members who consult their 'therapists' before making any decisions will depend on which view one takes: from outside, such behaviour looks like subordination, from inside, it is considered a token of trust. In encountering such individuals, Christians could explain that they would not endow anyone with so much power or reverence and thus convey the view from without – the perception of subordination – even if it is not accepted.

However, the confusing array of religions impairs communication. While religiosity appears in many different *milieus* and forms, there is increasing ignorance of religious concepts and rituals, which renders people unable to integrate or interpret religious experience arising from existential crises and emergencies. This explains why 'sects' or 'therapy cults' draw people: they provide answers, solutions, and recipes for living. Apologetics must therefore take the form of pastoral care and show alternative ways of understanding and coping. Despite endeavouring to understand other faiths, apologetics cannot just describe them and strive towards harmonious coexistence. Encounter with them includes taking a position, for questions of truth and ethics.

Apologetics needs a theological basis which informs the evaluation of other faiths. Kurt Hutten developed the *evangelische Rechtfertigungslehre* (Protestant teaching of justification) which is still valid regarding traditional sects and groups claiming new revelation, but not applicable to the contemporary spectrum of *Weltanschauung*, given dual membership (Christians who profess, for example, sympathies with esoteric teachings or New Age) and de-Christianization in eastern Germany. A binary approach is needed: secular contexts or foreign faiths require a position based on elementary Bible teachings, while groups with a Christian background require a position grounded in the gospel, with guidance from Hutten's *Rechtfertigungslehre*.

Agreement is needed regarding the theological basis, but the churches themselves experience the ripple of contemporary currents. They tend to make the battles of secular culture their own, which blends Christian and secular identities. The Church's liberal, progressive wing inclines towards utopian secular positions and friendliness for esoterism, while the conservative wing tends to criticize all these. Taking sides for reasons of church politics is antipathetic to Christian apologetics, which seeks to evaluate other religious groups on the basis of the gospel. Apologetics may not become an instrument for church politics and thus merely be a defence mechanism. While the basic notions of the *Rechtfertigungslehre* were still dominant and undisputed in Hutten's work, today the central perspective of a Christian understanding of the World, Man, and God needs sound foundations so that assessment criteria can be derived from them. This task should not remain in the hands of specialists, but become the concern of theology and the whole Church.

Evaluating the EZW's approach

Although the essays address different issues and approach them from different angles, they share common themes. Apologetics should not be the domain of specialists, but the task of the whole Church. Apologetics needs to be directed towards dialogue, hence *dialogical apologetics*. Apologetics is a way of dealing with pluralism in the postmodern world, not only regarding the multiplicity of other religions, but also regarding secular developments in society. Apologetics has the task of differentiating, providing orientation for Christians, and exploring potential for dialogue. Apologetics requires openness towards the 'other', but also openness about Christianity itself, the willingness to question and be questioned. Apologetics must be founded on accurate information, compiled with Küenzlen's 'ethos of factual diligence'. Information is used to describe other religions and various methods are applied for this purpose from academic disciplines, not just theology. The clear distinction between the view from without (*Außenansicht*) and the view from within (*Innenansicht*) is important.

Apologetics has a wider political dimension for the Church, but this should not be the overriding concern. The main concern is *people*, of whatever faith; their quest must be taken seriously, their questions on the transcendent must be heard and addressed, even when genuine dialogue is not possible. This concern emphasizes the pastoral aspect of apologetics (*inneres Verstehen*). Apologetics has a clear missiological dimension: the Christian faith needs to be professed where possible and necessary.[44] Apologetics is, however, independent of social and cultural forces and cannot be instrumentalized for wider social and political issues. The idea that apologetics and its practitioners might become an extended arm of society is unacceptable (also Hummel, 1995b).

My interview with Hummel included a discussion of Wallis's (1984) model of approaches to the study of NRMs, which distinguishes between 'external' and 'internal' perspectives and between 'hostile' and 'non-hostile' attitudes. The EZW approaches NRMs and marginal religions from an external point of view by taking the *Außenansicht*. For Hummel, it is important to make clear which view is taken and not to have too wide a gap between the two views. A group must make sure that its understanding (*Selbstverständnis*) and presentation of itself (*Selbstdarstellung*) are not too far apart; yet the view from without should not be taken without empathy (*empathische Berührung*). The two views will thus not be totally congruent, but each side can understand the other's language and recognize aspects of itself.

For Hummel, the terms 'hostile' and 'non-hostile' need careful interpretation. However, considering the three levels of encounter (dialogue, co-existence, mission), it can be said that Christianity's stance towards other religions is non-hostile. However, the EZW's dealings with NRMs require a more qualified stance. It is generally assumed within the Church that the EZW and *Sektenbeauftragte* deal with the controversial aspects of inter-religious dialogue, while the Church leadership can attend to relations with the world religions. The EZW resists this assumption by keeping its purview wide, hence repeated references to not relegating apologetics to the domain of specialists.

For Hummel, the decision to assume a 'hostile' or 'non-hostile' attitude is a research *outcome*:

> whether I am 'hostile', that is the result of my work, although one can, of course, say that someone approaches everything with a preconceived opinion, and there are *the* cults and an overall negative or positive attitude towards them.

Differentiation between NRMs is needed and perhaps categories such as 'cult' should no longer be used. Perhaps general religious phenomena should be the focus, some of which may – for particular reasons – appear in particular movements with noticeable frequency. When everything is examined, one could end up being 'hostile' towards a particular group, for example, Scientology. It is important to recognize the differences between movements, which is why the response to them must be differentiated, as one cannot simply take an overall negative attitude.

A different perspective on this issue assumes three circles regarding 'cults': first, individuals on a quest (*suchende Menschen*); second, what 'cults' offer (*Angebote*: teachings and practices); and third, the movements' organization (*Vertrieb*). This three-tier model reflects the principles of the market: demand, supply, distribution. Individuals, whether seekers or members, cannot be met with hostility. They need pastoral care, someone listening to their problems. The teachings, often based on 'old' ideas, need to be classified and put in historical context. Above all, one's own position needs to be conveyed – questions of belief and faith. Finally, the way ideas are 'marketed' needs to be examined. Where the three circles intersect, movements have potential for conflict (*konfliktträchtig*). One can thus speak of *konfliktträchtige* or *konfliktreiche Bewegungen*: movements 'tending towards' or 'rich in' conflict.[45] The degree of conflict can increase or decrease over time, leading to sectarianization (*Versektung*) and de-sectarianization (*Entsektung*) (also Hummel, 1985; 1994b). In summary, although the EZW takes the view from without or Wallis's external approach, it resists reducing its approach to a formula of 'hostile' or 'non-hostile', because the phenomena are too varied to fit into neat categories. Not only is there variety among the groups, there is also variety in the aspects of the groups, regarding the model of the three circles.

The EZW in the German context

The EZW and other Sektenbeauftragte

The EZW's approach to apologetics is not necessarily shared by other representatives of the Protestant Church (*Sektenbeauftragte*), as an article on apologetics, entitled 'Apologetics: Harmful Affirmation or Necessary Diaconate?' by Pastor Thomas Gandow demonstrates. Gandow, *Sektenbeauftragter* in Berlin, responded to Hummel's (1994a) essay in the EZW's publication on apologetics (Hummel *et al.*, 1994) summarized above (Hummel, 1995b). Hummel's statements that 'apologetics is not in the service of a society striving for consensus' and that 'critical solidarity with one's own culture and life world' and 'critical distance with one's own culture' are needed meet Gandow's criticism – he interprets them as 'a withdrawal from confrontation into an apologetic ivory tower'.

The irritation underlying such a response relates to the way apologetics is practised, understood, and interpreted. Hummel affirms that apologetics is 'necessary diaconate', a labour of love for society and a service *for* society, but not *in* society's service. There are things apologetics must *not* do: it must not join in any wave of 'sect' hysteria and echo unqualified blanket judgements. It must not transgress the line between criticizing 'sects' and criticizing religion, because this contributes to 'self-secularization'. It must not appeal to social defence mechanisms directed against minority groups. It must not be used or mis-used, for example, by providing ammunition for someone else's weapons. It must not jeopardize peace between religions unnecessarily.

Those concerned with 'sects' and NRMs know the areas of potential conflict; for example, requests for affidavits regarding social or personal controversies; attempts to instrumentalize apologetics and apologists to assist in decisions, such as planning permission for mosques, stupas, or NRM centres; over-generalized comments about charismatic groups. In such instances, society resorts to defence mechanisms to preserve consensus. Yet, apologists cannot join in, if they are to act in Christian responsibility and maintain Christian standards. Sometimes apologists work with, sometimes they work in opposition to, parents, but they often act as intermediaries and brokers. Apologetics occurs in the context of pluralism and is thus a balancing act (*Gratwanderung*) which cannot be thought about and discussed enough in public. Apologists may neither indulge in meditative contemplation in ivory towers nor look out for foes from the crenellations of their citadels.

Pastor Gandow is perceived to have taken on the mantle of Pastor Haack, the late *Beauftragte für Weltanschauungsfragen* of the Bavarian *Landeskirche* in Munich, as his approach to new religions and *Sondergemeinschaften* is similar to Haack's. (Haack's successor is Wolfgang Behnk (e.g. 1994a) whose approach seems somewhat different from Haack's.) For Hummel, this kind of approach is 'militant apologetics', which is part of the 'field of tension' for those concerned with non-mainstream religions. As the EZW's director, he sought to steer a course which preserved the EZW's independence and autonomy *and* maximized co-operation with all parties concerned – the *Sektenbeauftragte* in the Protestant and Roman Catholic Church, parents' groups, and institutions which take the approach of *Religionswissenschaft*. It is recognized that this integrative endeavour advanced the respect for the EZW's work (EZW, 1995b: 130, 133).

Hummel's remarks on 'militant apologetics' reflect his disposition towards integration, an apologetics which is outspokenly critical and clearly outlines the apologist's stance. For Hummel, it has a place and it has merit: it has purchase and an impact in public and it is an appropriate way of dealing with *some* groups. The EZW has, however, resisted this kind of approach because other groups require a more differentiated approach. Also, 'militant apologetics' cannot claim a monopoly position within the Church. The EZW's approach is characterized by an effort to be fair and objective.

Fairness and objectivity imply multiple perspectives. In the case of NRMs, this means taking into account the view from within (*Innenperspektive*), but some *Sektenbeauftragte* and parents frown on this. Some have reproached Hummel for including the view from within in his descriptions of NRMs: 'You always think of the NRM members themselves – what about us and your readers?' Being prepared to see matters from the vantage point of the other side is, to some extent, a reason to be disqualified, because it implies an act of taking the other seriously, and some think that this should not be done.[46]

Regarding other centres, institutes, and individuals concerned with 'sects' and new religions, the EZW is faced with a *Gratwanderung* or treading a thin line between positions which it cannot or will not adopt, but with which it wishes to be in dialogue. This *Gratwanderung* is similar to the one involved in the dialogue with the religions themselves.

EZW and Religionswissenschaft

REMID (*Religionswissenschaftlicher Medien- und Informationsdienst*), created in the late 1980s, is probably the most prominent of the institutes referred to earlier as *religionswissenschaftlich orientierte Stellen* and another factor in the 'field of tension'. According to Hummel, organizations, such as REMID (which he did not specifically mention), play into the hands of the 'anything goes mentality' of postmodern pluralism, given that 'pure' *Religionswissenschaft* does not apply values or make value judgements, which involves making clear distinctions or drawing clear lines. It puts forward the *Absolutheitsanspruch des Dialogs* (the claim that dialogue is absolute) which the EZW resists.

The detached view and the descriptive approach of *Religionswissenschaft* preclude taking sides or condemning religious phenomena. Although there is not enough work based on such an approach in Germany, Dr Hummel regrets that *Religionswissenschaftler* feel the need to raise their profile by taking a stance against Church representatives (*Sektenbeauftragte*). This has led them to speak up for organizations, such as Scientology (an allusion to REMID's *Thesenpapier* or position paper on Scientology). A division of labour would be useful, with *Religionswissenschaft* assisting in achieving an objective view and theology providing the criteria for a Christian evaluation (EZW, 1995b: 133–134).

REMID's *Thesenpapier* of 1990 is a five-page document entitled 'Statement regarding the current discussion of the Church of Scientology'. Although intended as general information for enquirers, the statement was widely circulated between autumn 1990 and late 1991. Significantly, the Church of Scientology had appropriated the document for circulation. It even found its way on to the agenda of the CDU's national party conference in Dresden in December 1991, which debated a motion on incompatible dual membership of CDU and Scientology (Thiede, 1992b: 149).

The *Thesenpapier* has to be seen against the background of widespread criticism of Scientology in Germany, from former members, *Sektenbeauftragte*, and the media.[47] The brochure 'Hate and propaganda' (Church of Scientology, 1993), banned soon after its publication, drew parallels between Scientology's perceived persecution in Germany and the suffering of the Jewish people during Nazism. It was also distributed to participants in the conference on 'New religions and the new Europe', held in 1993 in London, and H. Jentzsch, international head of Scientology, displayed the contents on big placards in a session dedicated to presentations by NRM representatives.[48] Since the ban on 'Hate and propaganda', Scientology has continued to present itself as a persecuted religious minority (hence the US State Department's criticism of Germany in recent years in its annual human rights reports) and argued that it should enjoy constitutionally guaranteed religious freedom. However, some *Länder* authorities have maintained that Scientology's business activities need to be declared, licensed, and taxed (e.g. EZW, 1995c; 1995d).

REMID's *Thesenpapier* raised the suspicion that REMID might be a 'front organization' for Scientology. The EZW received enquiries which suggested this, although it did not harbour this suspicion itself (Thiede, 1992b: 151). However, the EZW criticized REMID's aims and statements in the paper (Thiede, 1992b). The points of criticism can be placed under three headings: REMID and *Religionswissenschaft*, REMID and 'sects', REMID and NRM practices.

Regarding the first, REMID aims to take a neutral stance towards NRMs and provide factual information about religious groups and related issues. It speaks of a 'value neutral approach' and of 'reliable information about religious groups, topics, and developments' and wants information presented without bias regarding religious convictions. Thiede, at the time EZW *Referent*, counters such statements by quoting Fritz Stolz who declared that 'The postulate of an "non-partisan", "objective" approach to religion is sheer naivety'. Given REMID's emphasis on *verstehen*, this hermeneutic recognition should not be ignored (ibid.: 150).

Thiede sees an inherent contradiction in REMID's avowed neutrality, when it states that 'Information from Church offices are on the whole coloured by apologetics and often present matters in a distorted way'. This is a blanket judgement of *Sektenbeauftragte* and demonstrates a lack of reflection on the notion of apologetics. It implies that there are *Religionswissenschaftler* and experts of *Weltanschauung* who have no denominational affiliations or religious convictions. REMID's emphasis on neutrality is also contradicted by the advertisement of an NRM in *spirita*, a journal for *Religionswissenschaft*, edited and published by two REMID members.[49] The first two *spirita* issues in 1991 included the advertisement, which shared space in the second issue with a report of a successful court case regarding that very group (ibid.: 151).

However, REMID had a point in seeking to counterbalance what it perceived as the 'stigmatization'[50] of NRMs in Germany. Admittedly, Haack's terms *Jugendreligion* and *Jugendsekte* are 'coloured with criticism', and in the case of Scientology, no monographs exist which provide a balanced viewpoint, either from the perspective of theology or *Religionswissenschaft* (ibid.: 152).[51]

Regarding REMID and 'sects', REMID's understanding of 'sect' is another point of criticism: it implies the opposition between ideal or 'right' religion and negative or 'wrong' religion. Using the term in this way is 'ideological' and 'non-scientific' (*nicht religionswissenschaftlich*). The notion of 'sect' has outgrown its original theological usage to describe a religious group emanating from schism with the mother church. The term's new 'colouring' has extended its meaning so that 'sect' applies not only to religion, but also to secular aspects: sectarian behaviour (as, for example, described in Kakuska, 1991: 173) implies narrow-minded or totalitarian teachings and practices. In that sense, it is a critical assessment of religious groups or movements (ibid.: 153).

Thiede takes issue with REMID's contention that religious groups must decide for themselves whether they are 'churches' or 'religious communities' and that there is a good reason why the *Bundesverfassungsgericht* does not assume an ideal 'religion' or 'church'. The court's previous rulings show that it relies on a general understanding of 'religion' and 'religious community', despite the State's neutrality in religious matters. The State thus relies on what is commonly recognized as religion, when required to grant the status of religion. If religious groups claim religious freedom under the constitution, they must satisfy certain criteria. Whether Scientology can be considered a 'church' or 'religious community' is an intensely disputed question in Germany. Thiede criticizes the REMID paper for lacking awareness of such problematic aspects (ibid.: 154).

Regarding REMID and NRM practices, a further criticism is the *Thesenpapier*'s assessment of the *e-meter* (an instrument used in Scientology for *auditing* sessions – basically, a device consisting of two tin cans wired to a gauge; auditing is to identify and eliminate individuals' *engrams*, unconscious memories which prevent progress). Although it may be questionable whether the *e-meter* can indeed measure currents of consciousness, as Scientology claims, the *Thesenpapier* argues that even if the *e-meter* were to be shown ineffectual, it would still be of central importance to Scientologists, like the consecrated wafer is to Christians. Thiede disputes that like is compared with like (and suspects inspiration by Omar Garrison's book of 1980), because for Christians, there are non-verifiable matters of faith, but a technical instrument, such as the *e-meter*, lies within the realm of verification. *Religionswissenschaftler* have the right, even the duty, to point out problematic aspects by taking a discriminating and evaluative approach (ibid.: 155).

REMID cannot claim to be 'neutral' in appearing to be sympathetic to Scientology's extremely expensive courses. REMID points out that as Scientology cannot rely on church tax, it brings business activities to the fore and charges for services. Thiede thinks that *Religionswissenchaftler* should point out that Scientology courses are very costly and often lead followers into debt, as Scientology's enterprises are generally considered to be driven by pecuniary motives. Hubbard's statement that money and the sale of services are the organization's *raison d'être* is often quoted, but this overlooks spiritual aspects. Scientology believes in self-realization through 'total freedom' which is reflected in followers' ambitions for power and success, but based on Hubbard's *Weltanschauung*. Thiede agrees with REMID that a comprehensive discussion of this worldview within the framework of *Religionswissenschaft* and theology is still outstanding (ibid.: 156).[52]

EZW and the State

Lehmann's survey of enquiries showed that the EZW co-operates with the State and State authorities, but that this is not a substantial part of its work. Only 5 per cent of enquiries came from such authorities. In 1994, a new office (*Bundesverwaltungsamtsstelle*) for NRMs was set up in Cologne under the directorship of Dr Jutta Wettengel to gather information about new religions and similar groups.[53] Because of issues relating to data protection (what kind of information could be stored and recorded), the office got off to a slow start. It was initially not clear, for example, whether press cuttings which mention Scientology could be stored. Also, the constitutional separation between State and religion – the State's obligation to be neutral – was relevant, as it includes not only how the State treats religions, but also how it observes, gathers data about them, etc. This ties the hands of the State at times, which is why the churches are called upon to act in its place. However, this creates situations which leave the churches sitting between two stools.[54]

Before the *Bundesverwaltungsamtsstelle* was set up, new religions fell under the remit of the ministry for the family. During that time, the ministry was apparently not able to set up any archives on NRMs. Some state authorities have suggested a ban on Scientology, which – in Hummel's view – is an unrealistic proposition. It is, however, impossible for the EZW to comply with matters which should be dealt with by the State:

> For example, if a company tells us they are suspected of being a front for Scientology and could we give them a certificate which says they are not, we cannot do that. That is something society has to sort out itself, otherwise we are in conflict with our own tasks and do become an instrument of the State.
>
> (interview with Hummel)[55]

The problem is that the constitution does not stipulate a total separation of Church and State. Further, past court rulings (for example, regarding public subsidies for parents' groups) deter the State from getting involved in matters relating to any organization which can be defined in terms of religion or *Weltanschauung* and claims the protection afforded by Article 4 (ibid.).

EZW and NRMs

Some NRMs supply the EZW with information, which maintains contact with their spokespersons and participates in some of their events. However, participation in UC-organized conferences is not acceptable to the EZW or the *Sektenbeauftragte*. Hummel voiced strong opposition to such associations, also to attendance by professors of theology,[56] on theological grounds, because participants at UC conferences take part in the messianic plan which is central to UC teachings. The professed aim of the conferences is to further unification between religion and culture, Christianity and religions. According to Hummel, theologians cannot contribute to the UC's monocentric ecumenism, which is its messianic programme. If they do, they get involved with the view from within.

In his paper on Church apologetics, *Oberkirchenrat* Karl Dienst (1993) states that theologians who lecture at universities undermine the Church when they take an NRM's side.[57] This involves opposite positions in the same *milieu* and leads to 'frustrations'. Commenting on the conference on 'A New Vision for World Peace', organized by the UC in 1990, Eimuth (1990b) refers to Professor Schwarz's participation. He had declared that he would not 'advertise' for the UC, but speak wherever his opinion and expertise were wanted.[58] Eimuth, considers Schwarz's participation a 'misuse' of his reputation and criticizes his nonchalant comment that those who question his participation do not appreciate the meaning of pluralism. Schwarz reportedly welcomed the UC's invitation, stating that other new religions would not do this.[59] The provost of Frankfurt disapproved of a theologian speaking at a UC-sponsored conference and the *Landeskirchenrat* of the Protestant Church in Bavaria hoped Schwarz would not do this again. Eimuth concludes that although *Religionswissenschaftler* need to seek dialogue with religions, they must not allow themselves to be harnessed for their purposes (ibid.: 46–47).

Eimuth (1992a; 1992b) also expressed criticism, as did a number of Synod members, when Edmund Weber, professor of theology at Frankfurt, was called to the Synod of the Church in Hessen and Nassau, while ostensibly co-operating with a UC branch.[60] The UC likes to surround itself with 'unsuspecting partners in dialogue' to underline its inter-disciplinary and ecumenical approach and to improve its 'dented image'. In 1991, Haack had declared that such conferences were an opportunity for the UC to gain influence. Church officials took exception to Weber speaking at the conferences, but the fact that he chaired on one occasion weighed even heavier. This form of participation could not be justified in terms of inter-religious dialogue.

Like Schwarz, Weber was perceived as lending the UC his reputation and authority and as being 'harnessed' for its purposes. His unconcern about the possible effect of his participation drew further criticism. No critical comments about the UC could be found in his contributions to *Forum und Weltgestaltung* and this was perceived as damaging inter-religious dialogue. While Eimuth emphasized the importance of dialogue, he drew a clear line between the search for truth in dialogue and advertising for new religions. He (1992b: 239) cited a passage from Hans Küng's *Projekt Weltethos* (The Project of a Universal Ethos):

Even a Christian does not have a monopoly on truth, nor the right to renounce the testimony of faith within a libertarian pluralism. No, dialogue and testimony are not mutually exclusive. The testimony of faith includes the courage to recognize untruth and to address it.

This quotation ties in with earlier comments about apologetics in dialogue. For Eimuth, Weber transgressed the boundaries of religious tolerance by allowing a controversial organization to use him. Weber's call to the Synod was an affront to those in the Church who are concerned with *Weltanschauung*. (Weber resigned from this post in 1996.)

Against this background, the conference of the *Sektenbeauftragte* in May 1992, organized by the EZW, expressed disapproval of Protestant theologians who take part in events organized by the UC for promoting its objectives. In a press release, the EZW stated that increasing pluralism cannot not be dealt with by 'softening Christian identity'. Dialogue is necessary, yet in conducting dialogue with religions and *Weltanschauung* of an 'extreme' kind, the Christian claim to truth may not be surrendered. Dialogue with NRMs which differ greatly from one another should not be conducted without responsibility towards the churches, parents, and relatives. The conference called on the churches to recognize the serious challenge of increasing religious and cultural multiplicity and welcomed efforts of the *Landeskirchen* to take more account of it in their educational programmes (EZW, 1992b: 236–237).

The press release was accompanied by a 'statement regarding the participation at conferences organized by S. M. Moon's "Unification Church" ', which set out the reasons for non-participation in greater detail (ibid.: 237–238; also Hummel, 1990). As the number of UC members and scientists is low, non-UC participants are needed to fill the large-scale conferences. Therefore, theologians and members of Christian churches are invited who often do not know what they are letting themselves in for, but should guard against being 'used'. The statement would like to see six aspects considered: (1) Participants should not undermine their integrity and independence by accepting financial benefits, such as generous expenses, and be in a position to express criticism of the UC. (2) It should be transparent how the conferences are financed: through fundraising by grassroots members or with income from industrial enterprises, such as arms manufacture. (3) Participants' names should not be used for UC purposes, especially considering that its fundamental beliefs stand in opposition to those of the Christian churches. (4) Participants should be clear about the conferences' 'hidden agenda': unification of religions, ideologies, and sciences and ultimate victory over Communism are part of the 'messianic timetable' of Moon's 'design of history' and intended to confirm Moon as the returning messiah. (5) Organizations, such as the World Conference of Religions for Peace, are more appropriate for inter-religious activities than UC-sponsored conferences. The latter are not neutral forums where different schools of thought and belief meet, but means to spread Moon's ideology and to expand its sphere of influence. (6) Many NRMs, including the UC, are controversial and thus severely criticized by former members and relatives, especially for their 'questionable' methods of recruitment and manipulation. Dialogue with such movements requires particular differentiation and sensitivity and is more problematic than dialogue with traditional religions. Those wishing to engage in such dialogue must do this with responsibility towards relatives and, in the case of Christian theologians, the Church, hence the disapproval of the *Sektenbeauftragte* of theologians participating in UC conferences.

Some of the arguments cited here are very similar to those advanced against sociologists and scientists who participated in UC conferences; for example, that generous expenses threaten participants' integrity and independence, that the UC 'used' participants to gain legitimization, and that conferences are ultimately financed by 'exploiting' grassroots members (Arweck, 1994a; 1994b). However, the statement included important theological considerations which addressed theologians' participation in particular, such as Moon's messianic programme, the existence of more appropriate arenas for conducting dialogue, and how to conduct dialogue on UC's terms while bearing in mind the concern of the Church and relatives.

Concluding remarks

Among the institutions concerned with NRMs, sects, *Sondergemeinschaften*, and questions of *Weltanschauung*, the EZW has a particular position. Its purview of topics and approaches is wide. It has established a wide network of information and expertise. This provides advantages regarding contact with individuals and institutions working in different fields, but sometimes requires a *Gratwanderung*. This means that the EZW has sought to steer clear of falling or being drawn into particular camps. It has consistently pursued a policy of integration and co-operation with the various 'players in the field', such as other wings in the Church, *Sektenbeauftragte*, the State and public authorities, parents and parents' groups, and religious groups. It has done this, without – on the whole – compromising its stance which is, as Hummel said, guided by the principles of objectivity and fairness. This policy has had the imprint of the EZW's former long-standing director, Dr Hummel. The circulation of REMID's *Thesenpapier* and the subsequent discussions demonstrated that the EZW does not run the risk of being misinterpreted or 'used' by groups or movements, because its status as a Christian institute leaves no doubt about its stance.

The EZW has moved to Berlin and is now under the directorship of Dr Reinhard Hempelmann. Its work seems to continue as before, but it will need further research to examine whether changes have ensued and whether the events surrounding the VPM case and the relocation to Berlin have indeed had repercussions on the EZW's freedom in relation to the Church authorities.

PASTOR FRIEDRICH-WILHELM HAACK AND ARBEITSGEMEINSCHAFT FÜR RELIGIONS- UND WELTANSCHAUUNGSFRAGEN

Introduction

This section assesses the work of Pastor Friedrich-Wilhelm Haack in relation to the churches' response in Germany by providing an overview of Haack's wider context and publications and by describing the aims of the *Arbeitsgemeinschaft für Religions- und Weltanschauungsfragen* (ARW). Haack's approach to *Jugendreligionen*, his position within the Lutheran Church, and his views of the Church's approach are discussed. Haack's concepts of religion and *Jugendreligionen* are outlined, together with his explanation for their success and his views on religious freedom. These ideas are related to Haack's thought about the State's role and the contribution of *Religionswissenschaft*. The section also shows how Haack's close links with parents' organizations moulded his approach to apologetics.

The context

In 1969, Friedrich-Wilhelm Haack was appointed *Beauftragter für Sekten- und Weltanschauungsfragen* (expert on sects and questions of *Weltanschauung*) of the Protestant Church of Bavaria, a post especially created for him. Until his death in March 1991, Haack was one of the most, if not *the* most, prominent representatives of the Church to speak out against 'cults'. He became well known for his often unreserved animosity towards them, which he promulgated in the media, public addresses, and numerous publications. By 1987, he had published 40 books and sold about 700,000 copies. Haack wrote articles for newspapers and magazines,[61] appeared on radio and television, and contributed to seminars and books (e.g Haack, 1982a; 1988d; Flöther and Haack, 1985).

Haack forged close links with parents' organizations, particularly with the group in Munich, *Elterninitiative zur Hilfe gegen seelische Abhängigkeit und religiösen Extremismus e.V.* or *Ei* on whose executive board he served from its inception in 1975. In 1986, he became *erster Vorsitzender* (chairman) so that he could represent *Ei* in a court action brought by Scientology. Haack worked closely with the *Sektenbeauftragten* in Germany, Austria, and Switzerland. There were regular exchanges of information and twice yearly conferences presented opportunities to reinforce personal connections. Haack circulated a *Persönlicher Informationsbrief* (personal letter for information) marked 'strictly confidential'.

Haack was well known in Europe and the US, where he had links with parents' organizations and 'cult experts' – with FAIR in Britain, ADFI in France, the Dialog Center in Aarhus, the Panhellenic Parents' Organization in Greece, and AFF in the US. Continuous exchange of information was complemented by visits, joint trips, and conferences. In 1988, Haack addressed the FAIR Annual Meeting. In August 1984, a delegation of *Ei*, which included Haack and Madame Champollion of ADFI, visited the Panhellenic Parents' Organization, with further visits planned for 1985 and 1987 (Haack, 1992: 37, 62). In 1987, Haack attended the conference on 'Sects and Society' in Barcelona (Asociación Pro Juventud, 1988).

Haack's publications: an overview

Haack's first book appeared as early as 1973, followed by a string of publications. These were (some still are) continually updated and revised, often reprinted and brought up to date in many editions. Yet only one book was translated into another language: an early publication (1979a) appeared in French (1980b). The groups and movements described in Haack's work range widely: spiritualism (1973), secret orders (1980c), *Jugendreligionen* (1974; 1979b; 1980d; 1982d; 1983a), witchcraft and superstition (1982e), Germanic folk religion (1983b; 1981b), Freemasonry (1988e), parapsychology (1983c), gnostic movements (1985a), occultism (1989c), traditional sects (1980e), non-conformist churches (1980f), satanism (1987). Haack also covered related aspects, such as *Psychomutation* (1978), legal matters (1981c), advice for parents (1979c; 1988a), theology (1980g; 1980e), apologetics (1988f). Often, the description of movements and discussion of particular topics were combined, such as 'guruism' and 'guru movements' (1982f) or shepherding and disciplining (1988g).

Haack sought to systematize information in dictionary-type books, such as *Findungshilfe Religion 2000* (1990a), a thesaurus of movements and related organizations; *Unification Church Connections* for UC-related organizations and topics (1989d); cross-references regarding *Jugendreligionen*, 'guru movements', and 'therapy cults' (1985b), and a reference book on Scientology (1990b). Haack wanted his publications to be accessible to the general reader, including young people, and used for religious education in schools or similar. Hence his sets of slides (n.d./a; n.d./b) and overhead transparencies (n.d./c; n.d./d), succinct descriptions (1979a; 1981d; 1981e) and practical information about help and advice (e.g. 1979a; 1983d). Some publications were written jointly, with Manfred Ach (Haack, Schuster and Ach, 1986), his daughter Annette (Haack and Haack, 1989), and Pastor Gandow (Haack and Gandow, 1991), who updated some publications (e.g. Haack, 1979d; 1985c).

Arbeitsgemeinschaft für Religions- und Weltanschauungsfragen

One channel for disseminating these publications has been the *Arbeitsgemeinschaft für Religions- und Weltanschauungsfragen* or ARW (Association for the Study of Questions of Religion and *Weltanschauung*), which Haack founded in 1965 – well before NRMs emerged in Germany. Its task was to build bridges between the Lutheran Church and other faith communities and to provide information and advice for parishes. ARW's archives should assemble materials about contemporary religious movements and organizations and make them available to the public. ARW was to reduce antagonism between religions, while mapping differences between them – it was to have an apologetic agenda (Ach, 1995b: 5–6).

While ARW initially consisted only of Haack,[62] others joined over the years. Its publishing section became *Verlag der ARW*, a non-profit enterprise, in January 1976, staffed (on a part-time and voluntary basis) by Haack's wife and Ach, who both had some experience in publishing. With Haack's death, the archives ceased to function. Haack effectively ran the archives and played a pivotal role in the network. Only ARW's publishing section has survived.

Around the time of ARW's creation, other organizations sprang up with similar aims: *Arbeitsgemeinschaft für religiöse und weltanschauliche Begegnung* (Association for the Study of Religious Encounter) was founded in 1968 and *Arbeitskreis für Religion und Weltanschauung* (Association for the Study of Religion and *Weltanschauung*) in 1969. Other *Sektenbeauftragte* started resource centres and archives. These centres complemented Haack's work to some extent, so that the discontinued ARW archives did not leave a gaping hole. Although Haack's post was filled again, it is Pastor Thomas Gandow, *Sektenbeauftragter* in Berlin, who gradually assumed Haack's mantle of outspoken 'cult' critic. Gandow and Johannes Aagaard of the Dialog Center in Aarhus created *Berliner Dialog*, an apologetic magazine, similar to the Dialog Center's periodical, *Update & Dialog*.

ARW's brief, which Haack, his wife, and Ach devised in late 1975, was to publish information about contemporary trends in religion and *Weltanschauung*. The target audience, understood to be small, were people with an interest in religion. *Verlag der ARW* arose because in the 'supermarket of truths', there was a need for 'consumer protection'. The criteria for assessing information were to be derived from Western Christianity and humanitarianism. A special series was to reprint rare and inaccessible manuscripts to facilitate research, especially on popular religion.

ARW was suspected to be a 'front' for the Lutheran Church, but its aims were inter-denominational. ARW was also suspected to be a 'front' for Freemasonry, Gnosticism, or magic circles. Haack's award of the *Bernhard Beyer Medaille* (Bernard Beyer Medal) by the *Vereinigten Großlogen von Deutschland* (United Grand Lodges of Germany) in 1982 may account for the imputed masonic connection.[63] ARW's opponents apparently promoted such rumours and the absence of information about ARW in public records (*Verlag der ARW* was not officially registered) fed them.

By the late 1980s, ARW had created six publications series[64] and distributed books for other publishers. Intended projects, such as *ARW-Archivdienst* (archive service) or a series of readers, never got beyond the planning stage and neither did the idea of reprinting rare manuscripts, due to lack of interest. ARW also abandoned a joint venture with the *Institut für Eidologie und Symbolforschung* (Institute for the Research of Symbols), which was to issue a limited edition of rare masonic emblems.

From pastor to 'sect expert'

Haack's appointment as *Sektenbeauftragter* seemed to 'just happen'. Haack could not explain exactly why he became a *Sektenpfarrer* (pastor for sects) nor did he believe that people made landmark decisions and programmatic resolutions: 'I am inclined to believe that things just happen. Call it providence, if you will' (Wartmann and Madaj, 1987: 109). His interest in other religions began when he read theology at Heidelberg: he was one of the few who attended lectures on the topic. His interest intensified in the early 1960s when his daily walk to a preacher seminar took him past the meeting places of non-mainstream religions; within a week, he counted over 60 groups. In fulfilling his parish duties Haack realized that although people attended services and listened to sermons, the place where they decided about their religion was at their front door. He resolved to tell churchgoers why they should not become Jehovah's Witnesses and started to gather material and write about the Mormons, Rosicrucians, the Neo-Apostolic Church, and others. This is how Haack's collection began. When journalists visited the ARW's offices in 1987, there was hardly any wall space, with files piled from floor to ceiling. Haack's office was also littered with an astonishing array of religious objects, which reminded them of an inquisitor's treasure house. Haack had amassed esoteric and ritual objects – ritual swords, I Ging coins, macumba dolls, Grail crosses, tarot cards, etc. – and symbols of occult orders, lodges, and magic circles. He apparently even experimented with magic formulas (Wartmann and Madaj, 1987).

Ritual objects and experiments were part of Haack's hands-on approach. Whenever possible, Haack corresponded or met with representatives of 'sects' and *Jugendreligionen*. Some welcomed him, others had strained relations with him, yet others did not want any contact at all. Haack was, for example, on friendly terms with local Buddhist groups, but his relations with the Brahma Kumaris were, as he put it, 'not always easy'. When he planned to attend a pagan festival, the organizers declared that his presence would be like the devil's presence at a church service. Similarly, *Universelles Leben* did not want anything to do with him,[65] nor did *Deutsche Kulturstiftung* (German Cultural Foundation), which he considered a 'front' for TM.

Where he was not known, Haack went unnoticed, for example at a service of *St. Michaelisgemeinde* in Dozwil, near Lake Constance.[66] He visited the UC's most revered site in Korea, the memorial of the hut in Pusan where Unificationism is said to have begun. The line between fieldwork and sightseeing seems to have been blurred at times. Haack travelled across Germany and the globe, trips which were often combined with conferences and talks. He went to countries where some religious phenomena originated – Brazil,

Japan, Ireland, Uruguay, Korea – stating that 'If I want to know about a new guru cult, I go to India and have a look'.[67] Sometimes, the 'need' for information seemed to justify, if not excuse, such expeditions: a lawsuit by the UC prompted Haack to journey to Korea to gather further evidence. His own funds, royalties from his publications, and fees received for speaking engagements and providing expert opinion paid for these trips, the same resources which maintained the archives.

Haack's increasingly full-time occupation with unorthodox religion turned his workplace into an emporium. When information could not be found in the archives or supplied through the network, Haack applied 'journalistic zeal and detective instinct' (Wartman and Madaj, 1987). This suggests that this work became Haack's passion, perhaps even an obsession. When asked whether he ever needed time off, he said: 'You know, when a gravedigger looks at people, he thinks of their funeral. When I am on holiday, I am bound to discover the poster of an interesting group at the next street corner' (ibid.). Haack's occupation merged personal interest with professional assignment. Some thought that he often seemed to pursue things as if something was pursuing him.

Haack collected and collated information so that he could provide it to those variously affected by unorthodox religious groups. The enquiries he received are familiar to any institution offering advice in this field: husbands whose wives join yoga classes and want to donate property to the group; parents whose children disappear, most likely to join some group; criminal investigators who examine satanic circles, etc. Haack used his store of information and the network to refer enquirers to lawyers, psychologists, and parents' groups. Haack found his pastoral duty to strict confidentiality helpful, but did not consider it his duty to return lost sheep to the fold of the Church. Religion was a personal matter: 'I have always thought that everyone must find their own way to God' (ibid.). When asked what he would do to bring young people back into the Church, he said: 'I would refuse to get involved in a campaign which would have two powerful institutions fighting for the poor soul – on the one hand the sect, on the other the anti-sect, both tugging at either end. What I, the Church, and the parents' organization in Munich offer people is help to help themselves' (Mittler, 1984).

Controversy in the church

Haack's enthusiasm for field research and his directness did not win him universal approval, not least among his colleagues and church leaders. Some suspected that his passion had got the better of him, that he had 'gone native' or 'toppled into the other camp' (Wartmann and Madaj, 1987). When asked whether in his 20 years of researching religion he had encountered any which fascinated him and questioned his faith, he answered:

If you are hit on both cheeks, you are likely to remain upright. This means that I examine a particular group intensely and the correction does not come from this particular group itself, but from dealing with another one which shows me where the first one's flaw is.

(ibid.)

When Haack became *Sektenbeauftragter*, a colleague in the Catholic Church referred to him mockingly as *Geisterpfarrer* or pastor for the spirits.[68] By the late 1980s, good-humoured banter had turned to acrimonious irritation: Haack had become a troublesome spirit which some – both within and outside the Church – would have liked to see gone. It was probably Haack's plain speaking which made enemies in his own ranks and provoked criticism from the Church leadership, just as it did among 'cults'.

Some in the Church said that Haack was more Lutheran than Luther, after they had experienced his apologetic fervour against those he considered heretics in his own camp. Haack upbraided a young vicar who took part in 'occult therapies' (the vicar had been granted a year's leave by the bishop after he had joined the Rajneesh movement, see Küpper, 1983; Haack, 1992: 31), a theology professor who was a part-time astrologer, and theologians who participated in UC conferences. Haack criticized the naivety of comments about NRMs in church periodicals, such as a review of a book by Sri Chinmoy in *Deutsches Pfarrerblatt* (Heymel, 1984). This prompted Haack to say that

> In some Christian circles, there is increasing concern about whether the official church is moving outside the circle which, from the viewpoint of the New Testament, can still be considered 'biblical' and thus 'Christian' (there is no such thing as a non-biblical Christianity, let alone a non-biblical Christian belief).

Haack's candid criticism was bound to create animosity, especially when he berated the charismatic renewal movement which swept through the churches in the late 1970s emphasizing the workings of the Holy Spirit, with speaking in tongues, spiritual baptism, and prophetism. Haack commented critically when Hans-Diether Reimer, then EZW *Referent*, stated that pastor Kopfermann had not 'really' left the Church when he established his own church.[69] Haack (1992: 73–74) also criticized 'unreflective New Age thinking in the Church'. When voices in the Church leadership demanded that he should go, the threat of losing his job did not seem to trouble him; he indicated that his work would continue (Wartmann and Madaj, 1987).

Haack's high profile in public risked creating the impression that he was speaking for the whole Church. Thus, *Oberkirchenrat* Michael Mildenberger (1982a) – a former EZW *Referent* for Asian religions – pointed out in *Evangelische Kommentare* that the print-run of certain publications did not indicate a uniform attitude in the Church regarding a particular subject.

This was understood to be a clear indication that not everyone in the Church agreed with Haack's views of new religions (Feldmann, 1982: 32). Mildenberger's comments responded to a previous article (Eberlein, 1982) in *Evangelische Kommentare*, which had asked critical questions about the churches' negative stance towards NRMs.

The unease between some Church quarters and Haack was mutual. Journalists observed that when speaking at Church-related events, Haack never stayed longer than strictly necessary, thus precluding any rapport (Wartmann and Madaj, 1987). Haack was disappointed about some Church representatives – there were, for example, critical reactions from the Church leadership, triggered by an 'unfortunate article' on Haack by the Protestant press agency (Haack, 1992: 54) – but this did not stop him from defending his faith with vehemence and affirming it as 'the indispensable foundation for my work'.

His view of the way in which the Church dealt with *Jugendreligionen* and the work of the *Sektenbeauftragte* seemed to oscillate between criticism and praise. At times, he complained that the Church did not do enough:

> Sometimes, one has the feeling that the established churches wish they could free themselves of all the problems [regarding *Jugendreligionen*] by looking the other way, . . . that the instalment of *Sektenbeauftragte* can become a fig leaf for continued lack of action. . . . A well-worn argument against further action are 'the bad times', the alleged lack of money, etc.
>
> (ibid.: 31)

And then he could be full of praise, as this passage in his 1979 Christmas circular illustrates:

> As I am in the process of thanking people, I also want to thank my Church. There is so much to do these days, but the possibilities (and resources) are limited. In the Lutheran churches in Germany, the work [regarding *Jugendreligionen*] is almost exemplary. [. . .] The study group on the free churches and sects, the *Sektenbeauftragte*, the Lutheran World Federation in Geneva, and the Theological Faculty in Aarhus are dedicated to work on the problems of youth religions, sects, and groups with a particular *Weltanschauung*.
>
> (ibid.: 9)

This is echoed in his 1981 Christmas circular: 'I have found great understanding and also exceptional support in my *Landeskirche*. For this last, I have good reason to be especially thankful.' (ibid.: 20). Haack was very pleased about the creation of another post in the Bavarian *Landeskirche* in 1985, the post of *Beauftragter für religiöse und geistige Strömungen* (expert for religious and spiritual currents), which was to reinforce and complement his work (ibid.: 54, 75).

Jugendreligionen respond

Haack's practical approach brought him in contact with many groups and movements, but his relations with them were mixed. Haack's bluntness and caustic remarks must have been a deciding factor in shaping relations. What Haack wrote decided some: *Universelles Leben*, for example, found its beliefs distorted, while the Freemasons did not. Some movements felt misrepresented by or aggrieved about Haack's statements, but took no action beyond severing contact and belittling him. In their view, he was misguided, as the comment of *Universelles Leben* shows, a paraphrase of a Bible verse: 'Lord, we have forgiven, forgive him for he does not know what he is doing' (Wartmann and Madaj, 1987). Other movements resorted to lawsuits against anyone who, in their view, spread falsehoods about them. In 1981, Scientology, for example, took the Federal Government to court. Although other *Sektenbeauftragte* were faced with such suits, Haack probably fought the greatest number of court cases because of his prominent position. Movements, perceived to be powerful, such as Scientology, the UC, and TM, proved increasingly litigious.

By 1987, Haack claimed to have fought 58 cases and reported proudly that he had lost only one, with two others settled out of court. Most charges against Haack (which often included *Ei*) related to allegations of *Volksverhetzung*[70] and defamation or libel. In 1981, the UC brought a libel case after Haack (1979b) published *Jugendreligionen – Ursachen, Trends, Reaktionen*. The case was initially thought to repeat the UC's libel case against the *Daily Mail*. Unlike his colleagues, Haack did not shy away from court cases and was able to mobilize the support of parents and parents' groups. However, such cases are serious matters, as defeat jeopardizes the position of *Sektenbeauftragte*. They generally have to fight on their own account, without the support of the Church. In some cases, Haack's defence consisted in taking the plaintiffs to court, returning the charges of libel and defamation.[71]

Action against Haack consisted sometimes of personal threats: in the early 1970s, a man barged into Haack's office swinging a hammer 'to put an end to it all'. There was an attempt to push him in front of an underground train. Haack became *blasé* about death threats on the telephone, telling callers they had to submit the purpose of their call in writing. He was also the butt of macabre jokes: a funeral director called at his house 'to pick up the deceased'. But Haack could give as good as he got: after a whole summer of being watched by a private detective, Haack quietly slipped out of his house one night and caught the detective unawares.

There were campaigns aimed at undermining Haack's reputation. *Freiheitsspiegel*, a newspaper published by Scientology, claimed, for example, that Haack had taken 'a rather young girl' to see a pornographic film. Haack fought back, took the paper to court, and won. The *Freiheitsspiegel* was legally required to withdraw the allegation, but Scientology circumvented this by discontinuing the paper. Haack successfully sued a

Scientology member for 'slander', after defamatory pamphlets had been distributed to participants of a conference which Haack addressed.

Another campaign which aimed at character assassination went undetected for some time: an individual impersonating Haack made nuisance calls to Haack's colleagues. This is an instance of what Haack called 'disinformation tactics'. He was only too aware that such campaigns were effective. In his 1984 Christmas circular, Haack (1992: 41) declared, tongue in cheek, an amnesty for all those who spread rumours about him. He also pointed out that people like him paid a high price:

> Those committed to this work on *Jugendreligionen*, . . . put their good name under a shower of dirt. They put their reputation on the line and perhaps – if they are not sufficiently backed – also their job and quiet family life.

Letters to editors, pamphlets, and articles sought to taint Haack's character. In 1984, an article in *Wie es ist*, a magazine published by ISKCON, claimed that Haack made a mint out of publications, TV appearances, fees for conference papers and talks, suggesting that he gained financially from the controversy over 'sects' (ibid.). In 1987, Scientology distributed a pamphlet which portrayed Haack as a modern 'inquisitor', 'inexorable opponent of religious freedom', and 'self-styled expert', whose views were disputed within the Church and among academics (ibid.: 66–67).

While Haack often shrugged such 'disinformation tactics' off or made light of them, he was also deeply hurt. When asked how he coped with having enemies, Haack answered: 'Oh, quite well. One just lives by the grace of God and sees to it that one has no more to do with them than necessary' (Mittler, 1984). But he was wounded by vicious comments, such as those in a retired colonel's letter sent after one of Haack's TV appearances: 'Your unkempt hair, your hairy arms, and especially your big belly made you conspicuous among the panel in the most unpleasant way; you looked disgusting' (Wartmann and Madaj, 1987). A journalist of *Stuttgarter Zeitung* was equally personal in reporting one of Haack's talks in 1987:

> Then a bull-necked man gets up, he is probably a two and a half hundred-weight, but his hands betray the intellectual. . . . The highest inquisitor of the Lutheran Church in Bavaria leans leisurely over the rostrum and tells the members of . . . parish what is threatening the Occident today.
>
> (Haack, 1992: 67)

A week later, members of *Universelles Leben* distributed the same report in the town where Haack was to speak. In his 1981 Christmas circular, Haack mentioned the difficult and troublesome aspects of his job for which he needed the support of his family (ibid.: 20).

Haack's seminal publications

Haack's major publications, five volumes entitled *Die neuen Jugendreligionen*, contain his core concepts and ideas. The series was an important vehicle for disseminating information. The first volume appeared as early as 1974, initially a booklet of about 80 pages which was repeatedly revised and re-issued – the twenty-fourth edition dates from 1988. It was seminal, not least because it introduced the term *Jugendreligionen*. Haack initially subsumed five organizations under this heading (UC, Scientology, COG, DLM, ISK-CON) and added TM in the tenth edition (1977). Haack described the groups' beliefs and practices and assessed them from a Christian perspective. The brief introduction outlines common features – Haack's notions of *Rettendes Rezept, Gerettete Familie*, and *Heiliger Meister* – and examines whether all 'sects' originated in the US, why young people in particular join them (in Haack's view, they offer a way out for the discontented), and whether one could argue that Jesus, too, was radical. Haack offers advice to Christians (how they could respond), to young people who consider joining, and to parents. Addresses of *Sektenbeauftragte* and parents' groups are listed for those seeking further advice. Subsequent editions include new prefaces (1979, nineteenth edition), continuously extended address lists (ibid.; 1983, twenty-second edition; 1988, twenty-fourth edition), and a checklist for common features of *Jugendreligionen* (1983).

The sequel, *Die neuen Jugendreligionen. Teil 2. Dokumente und Erläuterungen* (Part 2. Documents and Explanations, 1984b, sixth edition), is divided into three sections: Part 1 describes *Jugendreligionen* as alternatives to society, discusses the loss of a sense of future, belonging, and meaning in a technological society, how young people are recruited, and what *Jugendreligionen* offer (again the three concepts of *rettendes Rezept, gerettete Familie*, and *heiliger Meister*). Part 2 discusses Haack's concept of *Seelenwäsche* or 'brainwashing' and his views of deprogramming, looks at social and legal problems, and describes 'legitimization efforts'. There is also an introduction to the parents' group in Munich. Part 3 consists of original documents by ISKCON, the UC, Scientology, and the COG.

The preface of the third volume, *Die neuen Jugendreligionen. Teil 3. Berichte und Analysen* (Part 3. Documents and Analyses, 1985d, first edition), points out that the term 'new' in the title was retained for the sake of continuity – there was a ten-year gap between this volume and the first. The purpose of this publication was to provide further information. Again, the contents are in three parts: the first includes Küenzlen's (1985) comments on the crisis in Western societies and what *Jugendreligionen* offer. Other sections deal with the dangers of 'guruism' in the West, children in *Jugendreligionen*, and financial activities, with particular reference to the UC's 'economic empire'. Part 2 includes documents: a mother's report of a Divine Light festival, an interview with an ex-member of the COG, a description of *est*, extracts from Scientology literature, letters from UC and ISKCON members, and Flöther's ten steps out of 'spiritual dependency'. Part 3 presents extracts from court verdicts regarding Scientology, the UC, and ISKCON and looks at the approach of political bodies.

The fourth volume, *Die neuen Jugendreligionen. Teil 4: Aktionen, Hilfen, Initiativen* (Part 4: Action, Help, Initiatives), is edited jointly with Manfred Ach and Udo Schuster (Haack *et al.*, 1986). The contents document the tenth annual meeting of *Elterninitiative* and reflect the views and activities of parents' groups and political institutions regarding *Jugendreligionen*.

The final volume, *Die neuen Jugendreligionen. Teil 5. Gurubewegungen und Psychokulte. Durchblicke und Informationen* (Part 5: Guru Movements and Therapy Cults – Insight and Information, 1991a), is a booklet of some 100 pages with (then) recent information and thoughts about *Jugendreligionen*, 'guru movements', and therapy cults. It deals with the 'new' ethical code and 'crimogeneity' of these movements, looks at areas where they clash with families, the wider economy, and business behaviour, and discusses what Haack called 'guru corporations'. For the first time, estimates of movements' numerical strength are included. The list of internationally active 'anti-cult movements' and parents' initiatives is updated.

Haack and religion

Haack did not agree with the prediction of the mid-1950s that the post-religious age was imminent. He argued that even when the sense of belonging disappeared, the future was devalued, and the quest for meaning had become meaningless, the demand for religion was great. He saw this confirmed in the wide-ranging contemporary religious organizations (Haack, 1978: 436). Haack did not object to the multiplicity of religions and religious communities, but compared it to the abundance of herbs on the wayside – one could nibble at all of them, but this was not advisable. People needed to be prevented from 'nibbling' at too many religions and this was to be achieved by protective mechanisms. Just as commercial goods were regulated to ensure they were safe and fit for the purpose, similar regulations should protect against 'unsafe' religion. This idea is further reflected in Haack's view of religion: it can create the most positive and the most negative states in human beings. Therefore, the criteria applied to the release of medicines are appropriate for assessing religion. Medicines can only be sold if proven not to have too many negative side-effects. Thus, only those religions should be allowed to operate which do not have 'negative side-effects' for their followers. Haack conceded that his position was influenced by his particular experiences – he was dealing exclusively with religions' negative aspects.

One such aspect was religious fraud. Haack had a section in his archives headed *Sandmännchen* (literally 'sandmen'), charlatans who throw dust in people's eyes. Following the adage that *mundus vult decipi* (the world wants to be deceived), Haack said, they sell objects with alleged occult or magical powers. One sold expensive 'cosmic crosses' which were just pebbles cast in copper (Haack, 1981a). Another was a self-styled priest who blessed the water tap in his house, because he was tired of blessing water in the usual way. Haack knew very well that such cases could only be brought to court if there was proof of fraudulent intent.

For Haack, the way organizations and movements treated individuals was dangerous: 'Religion can certainly . . . be destructive; even where it wants the best and makes the most pious claims, it can be an instrument of evil' (Haack, 1992: 46). Religion was not necessarily a good thing, did not have a 'guarantee of spirituality'; it could give life, but it could also take life; it could involve heroic devotion, but also cruel disdain for people.

'Sects' and *Jugendreligionen*

Haack thought that the terminology of the nineteenth century was superseded and the notion of *Sekten an sich* (sects *per se*) did not fit contemporary groups. Instead, he spoke of *Sekten von* (sects of) something or someone. In his essay on the challenge of *Jugendreligionen* for society, State, and churches, Haack (1979e: 11; also 1978) expounded:

> Regarding these new [religious] movements, it seems wrong to me to speak of 'sects'. A sect is always a group which is in relation to something. There are thus philosophical sects – in relation to certain schools – Christian sects, Buddhist sects, Islamic sects, but there are not just 'sects *per se*'. Therefore, this term should be avoided, because it is not helpful and evokes the wrong associations.[72]

Nor did Haack consider 'destructive cults' appropriate, because it too evoked the wrong associations: the immediate indication is that groups are evil, bad, negative. Haack argued for a term which was neither negative nor charged, namely *Jugendreligionen* because it was sufficiently neutral. Any negative connotations that it acquired were down to the groups themselves:

> I believe that using unclear or incriminating notions is damaging for both those criticised and those criticizing. The term *Jugendreligionen* contains the necessary neutrality, unless – and this does happen – it becomes burdened with certain associations, which is due to the bad behaviour of the groups. But this has nothing to do with the term, it has to do with the particular [religious] groups.
>
> (ibid.)

Haack also argued against *Neureligion* (new religion) and *neureligiöse Bewegungen* (new religious movements) as being too broad and too general. Every religious movement was a new movement at some point and the use of these terms would mean that the Mormons or the Baha'i would be under the same heading as the Family of Love and the UC.[73]

For Haack, the term *Jugendreligionen* describes the phenomenon of new religiosity adequately[74] and refers to a specific kind of religious group or movement. *Jugendreligionen* share common features and structures: *das rettende Rezept* or *Weltrezept* (the world-saving formula), *der heilige Meister* (the holy master), and *die gerettete Familie* (the saved family). To these, Haack added hierarchy of information and internationality. *Jugendreligionen* also share a particular way of indoctrinating members, which Haack called *Seelenwäsche* (literally 'soulwashing'), the result of which is *Psychomutation*. A closer examination of these concepts follows.

Das rettende Rezept

According to Haack, *Jugendreligionen* believe and claim that they possess a method or formula which solves the problems faced by individuals and the whole world and engenders a 'positive state' unattainable by any other means. This knowledge or mastery allows groups to repair and revitalize a world which, in their view, is in decline. The promise of the 'positive state' is expressed in slogans about 'total freedom', 'absolute bliss' or 'a world without hatred or crime' – universal concepts which draw wide appeal. TM, for example, promises that only 1 per cent of the population using its method (meditation practice) is needed to decrease the proportion of prevailing 'negativity'. Haack calls this knowledge *das rettende Rezept*, the world-saving formula, or *Weltrezept*, world formula: it confers on *Jugendreligionen* authority or power of attorney because this is the means by which they alone can save the world. When asked to name one shared trait in the kaleidoscope of ideas among *Jugendreligionen*, Haack answered that there was one notion none of groups likes to hear: you are one among thousands. Every group sees itself at the centre of world events.

The assumed authority justifies the demand for total commitment from those who are initiated into the special knowledge. While 'traditional sects' had a millenarian perspective to which they committed their lives (the expectation of an apocalypse or Last Judgement before the arrival of the Kingdom of God), the prevalent view of *Jugendreligionen* is that 'We are saving the world here and now or nobody else will do it after us'. They are offering the *last* opportunity to save the world and some predict when this is to happen.

Those opposed to the world-saving formula are enemies, because they impede the future of mankind. Enemies must be criminals, as it says in a pamphlet: 'We have yet to meet a critic of our group who is not a criminal.' In Haack's view, the idea of a world-transforming formula appeals to young people, because they are in transition – between learning and applying learning, between home and independence from home – a time when they are critical of their parents, full of ideals, and questioning their childhood religion.

Der heilige Meister

Haack calls the person who created or found the formula *der heilige Meister*, the holy master. He 'has made it'; he is said to have searched until he received answers to all the questions; he is sent directly from God. In her book, *Miracles for Breakfast*, Ruth Minshull wrote, for example, that L. R. Hubbard, the founder of Scientology, 'is the only man in our civilization who has had the courage to keep searching until he learned the truth about the human person'. The holy master is the undisputed leader, sometimes called 'his divine grace' or 'his holiness', often 'father'. The leader of COG, David Moses Berg, claimed to be God's only prophet. Jim Jones, the leader of the People's Temple, was called 'father'. In the UC, Sun Myung Moon and his wife are considered to be the 'true parents'. Followers relate to leaders as children relate to a father, but absolute obedience can lead to disasters.

As leaders cannot be in several places at once, they sanction a hierarchy of sub-leaders. Hence a pyramid structure in *Jugendreligionen* with group leaders and national leaders; some groups, such as the COG, have a more intricate hierarchy (Haack, 1988g: 8–13). Individuals in the hierarchy behave towards those beneath them like the holy master behaves towards the group as a whole. Obedience determines the structure.

Die gerettete Familie

Followers at the bottom of the pyramid are the chosen or saved. Haack called them *die gerettete Familie* or the saved family. They see themselves as an alternative society and are somewhat economical with the truth towards outsiders, an attitude also known as 'heavenly deception'.[75] The rationale is that the world-saving formula must be promoted at any cost and by any means so that the new society can come about (Haack, 1979e: 17; 1978: 439–440; 1992: 49).

Information and internationality

Haack identified two other features of *Jugendreligionen*: a hierarchy of information and internationality. The letters of the COG illustrate the first well. They are marked according to recipients: 'GP' for the public, 'DFO' for friends and followers, 'DO' for members only; some are for leaders only. Another example is Scientology's system of courses. This hierarchy, Haack argued, is a way to preclude criticism, as critics would be told they did not understand sufficiently about the group until they reached the next stage of instruction.

As to internationality, Haack thought that groups restricted to a region or locality could not be *Jugendreligionen*. They might be called groups similar to *Jugendreligionen*, for example the People's Temple; this group had emigrated to Guyana and lived in isolation. For Haack, *Jugendreligionen* had an international network and organizational structures for managing this network.

Indoctrination and Psychomutation

Haack shaped a terminology to describe techniques which *Jugendreligionen* reportedly use to recruit and retain members. Instead of 'brainwashing', he spoke of *Seelenwäsche* (soul washing). The former involves breaking an individual's will, while the latter works with the individual's consent. 'Brainwashing' uses the very energies which individuals develop to fight it, while *Seelenwäsche* is used for those who co-operate willingly. Careful observation of the way fundraising or recruiting members approach people in pedestrian zones, Haack said, shows that they ask confident and self-assured young people for a donation, but invite those apparently unsure and vulnerable to come to their centres.

The result of *Seelenwäsche* is *Psychomutation*. For Haack, this was an 'unheard-of concept of indoctrination' which took individuals away from their familiar surroundings, families, religion, and friends. It means surrendering their attitude towards the world, personal well-being, the well-being of their families and friends. Training individuals to serve the group's aims and demanding great sacrifices was total re-education. Haack did not agree with the idea that recruitment and membership can be explained in terms of *Sucht* – dependency or addiction – as Gascard (1984) suggested.

Haack cited the practice of 'flirty fishing' in the COG[76] as an example of how radical a change *Psychomutation* could effect. Young women of a middle-class background did not join the group because they were curious about sexuality, but because they wanted to do something for God. Yet, they accepted 'flirty fishing'. Ananda Marga members took their own lives through self-immolation in the late 1970s.[77] According to Haack, they were told in training camps that 'the body is nothing but a machine' and that 'those who give their bodies to the movement's mission, receive more and more grace'.

Psychomutation also results in 'de-personalization', because members surrender entirely, including their hopes and ambitions, to the leader and the group. This is coupled with immunization against criticism, which is perceived as coming from Satan who is in turn believed to seek the destruction of the group's mission. Haack used the example of a young man who attended a UC workshop; his mother's alarm about this induced a vision in him: he saw Satan standing behind her stretching out his claws. The young man concluded that he really had to join the UC so that they would both be saved.

In an early essay, Haack (1978) describes *Psychomutation* as a psychological change of personality to which the concept of conversion did not adequately apply. *Psychomutation* involved a set of distinctive features: (1) complete re-orientation of life according to hitherto unknown or unapplied principles; (2) total alteration of behaviour towards the world which is perceived and treated as hostile and in need of change; (3) radicalization in all areas of life; (4) total subordination to authority; (5) a kind of siege mentality, which includes the wish to associate only with fellow members; (6) close ties with, if not dependence on, the leader whose worldview is adopted and whose example is followed; (7) the short duration of the process.

Psychomutation had three stages: fascination, destruction of self-confidence, and construction of a new identity or indoctrination. Young people are fascinated by organizations which appear self-confident, successful, and efficient and offer a clear and positive message. Fascination is also created by 'star witnesses', endorsements by film or rock stars or connections with established institutions or personalities.[78] For newcomers, the fascination stage is coupled with the impression that they stand in negative contrast to the group, as deficient individuals who need help. Scientology, for example, achieves this with the evaluation of the personality test. Help is offered in exchange for commitment to the group's cause and the abandonment of former ties (ibid.: 443–445).

New members thus become detached from previous commitments, not only from family and friends, but also from their language structures. Members learn group-specific, internal language.[79] Haack (1980a: 179) pointed to the power of language in stating that 'Those who let themselves in for a strange, new language will become dependent on interpretations which others give to words'. To illustrate he referred to happiness:

> For example, the notion of happiness is associated with certain experiences. If our experiences are taken away, we become dependent on someone who tells us what happiness is, namely happiness is to march somewhere in formation, behind the banner of some political or religious leader.
>
> (ibid.)

Haack believed that the process of intertwining language, experience, and behaviour had the effect of mental chains which keep members totally focused on the group. Orwell's *1984* was a graphic description of what happens when words and concepts are distorted and how control of language features in dictatorships. For Haack, this implied that *Jugendreligionen* are of a dictatorial nature, because they share this feature.

In Haack's thought, the construction of new identity is the longest phase in the process of *Psychomutation*. It involves 'constant indoctrination', with little time to think and a rigorous timetable. Haack speaks of regression to childhood in this phase, often reflected in the use of language and behaviour.[80] If members leave, they are no longer able to relate to the world outside, not least because they no longer behave like people outside. For many, Haack claimed, the only way out was self-inflicted injury, if not

suicide (Haack, 1980a: 179; 1978: 445–447). One such casualty is mentioned in a Christmas circular (Haack, 1992: 32), but Haack never provided
any detailed statistics.

Haack's notions and terminology were not generally accepted within the
Church. Mildenberger (1982a), for example, rejected the term *Jugendsekten*
as a 'textbook example of undifferentiated argumentation' and objected to
Psychomutation to explain the changes observed in NRM followers. He
urged the churches to change their attitude towards those with different
religious views and towards non-Church or non-Christian groups. As to
how the Church should deal with NRMs, Mildenberger advocated neutrality and the role of church counsellors as honest brokers or mediators for
NRM members and their families (Mildenberger and Klaes, 1982; Schreiner
and Mildenberger, 1980). Theologians should review the social causes and
implications of NRMs so that the churches can, if necessary, correct their
course (Mildenberger, 1977; 1982b; EZW, 1982c).

The success of *Jugendreligionen*

For Haack, the reasons why *Jugendreligionen* are successful in recruiting
young people are closely linked to modernity and the modern way of life.
While technical civilization has improved social conditions and provides all
sorts of amenities, it has also created massive conurbations, centres of high-
performance production, which have a great impact on people's *Lebensge-
fühl* (sense of life). Modernity and progress have exacted a high price:
Geborgenheitsverlust (loss of a sense of belonging), *Zukunftsverlust* (loss of
a sense of the future), and *Sinnverlust* (loss of meaning). Haack explained
these in greater detail (Haack, 1979e: 23; 1978: 440; 1984b: 9–12, 12–14).

As to *Geborgenheitsverlust*, children cannot have a sense of belonging in a
world where space is at a premium. Playgrounds are too small and living
space is expensive. There cannot be a sense of belonging in complex and
confusing city-scapes which dwarf individuals, make them feel expendable,
and offer no continuity in individuals' lives. The sense of belonging is also
undermined when traditional villages lose their autonomy: incorporation in
large administrative units has taken away direct control of local affairs
(Haack, 1979e: 24, 1980a: 167–168; 1981a).

As to *Zukunftsverlust*, Haack argued that the notion of future is of little
value in a technical civilization. We witness the destruction of nature and the
extinction of species. The education system fosters ambitions and offers
opportunities, but these do not materialize, because of incommensurate job
availability; a carpenter with a university degree is bound to be less happy
than one who went through apprenticeship. The computer age has effaced
what used to offset age: experience. Middle-aged employees, hitherto the
backbone of industry, are no longer wanted (Haack, 1979e: 24–25; 1978:
441; 1980a: 168–169).

As to *Sinnverlust*, it is modernity which has deprived us of meaning; one can ask questions about anything, except about the meaning of it all. Traditional institutions, such as universities and churches, are no longer able to provide meaning. We have settled for *Zustandsfrömmigkeit* or piety for the status quo which only asks for the good life. No wonder that young people are attracted to those who say that the world is upside-down, that they have the solution to everything, and that they can offer a future and a meaningful life (Haack, 1978: 440–441; 1979e: 26; 1980a: 169). For Haack, modern society is in a state of crisis which plays into the hands of *Jugendreligionen*:

> At the moment, our whole culture is stuck in a general crisis. There are the great themes: anxiety, desires, hopes. And the sects play on these in a mendacious way and with incredible arrogance. They use the anxieties of others for their own purposes. They say, 'You haven't developed your full potential. We make you completely new.' And people give themselves over to them, unprepared.
>
> (Mittler, 1984)

While young people no longer believe they have a stake in the future, they are afraid of alternatives, for fear of spoiling whatever chances they might have. Young people from the middle classes are especially insecure, yet have high ideals regarding society and religion. They would easily agree with anyone who suggested that 'we are for a better tomorrow and against the bad yesterday', even if they do not know how to achieve 'the better tomorrow' (Haack, 1978: 440; 1980a: 175, 177–178).[81]

Religion as a front

Haack pointed to political parties which behaved like religions, such as *Europäische Arbeiterpartei* (EAP), to 'therapy cults' which presented themselves as therapies, such as *est* (Erhard Seminar Training),[82] and to businesses, such as Amway,[83] which turn the visit to company headquarters into a journey to the promised land. Business empires organized like a set of Russian dolls are behind some groups which claim to be religions.[84] In one of his books, Haack (1980a) focused on the political aspects of some groups, such as the UC, Scientology, TM, Ananda Marga, and EAP. He described them as 'totalitarian movements' which are dressed up as therapy and self-realization courses, yoga training, and self-help groups and uncovered 'the fascist structures' of *Jugendreligionen* to show that they are socially and politically dangerous. Haack (1992: 62–63, 73) also pointed to TM seminars for business employees and the activities of WISE (World Institute of Scientology Enterprises) in business.

Haack (1980a: 154–160) refuted the argument that criticizing *Jugendreligionen* is 'anti-religious' because religious groups and organizations are protected by the constitution. Some groups use this argument, such as the *Gesellschaft zur Förderung religiöser Toleranz und zwischenmenschlicher*

Beziehungen (Society for the Promotion of Religious Tolerance and Human Relations) – organized, according to Haack (1981a), by the Church of Scientology – which speaks of the 'social murder of religious minorities' and calls upon the Government to distance itself from any such criticism. One strategy which *Jugendreligionen* have used to avoid criticism is to appear in new guises and to re-name branches. In the late 1970s, the UC offered its services to the CDU/CSU parties during the election campaign as *Gesellschaft zur Vereinigung des Weltchristentums* (Society for the Unification of World Christianity), the COG changed to Family of Love, and DLM has at times called itself Divine Light Organizations. In this context, Haack also referred to camouflage and infiltration (Haack, 1979e: 22; 1992: 67).

Haack did not accept TM's claim that it is not a religion, but a technique to expand consciousness free of mythology or ideology.[85] For Haack, TM was a *Jugendreligion*, by far the biggest in Germany, even bigger than the UC and Scientology – regardless of TM's view of itself, regardless of any court verdicts. The *Oberverwaltungsgericht*[86] in Münster (Westphalia) found in TM's favour when it decided that the Federal Government, represented by the Minister for Youth, Family, and Health, should withdraw four statements: TM was part of the religious movements generally described as *Jugendsekten* or *Jugendreligionen*; TM was taught by insufficiently qualified instructors; TM followers risked psychological problems or the destruction of the personality; and TM's financial activities were unsound. However, an appeal to the *Bundesverwaltungsgericht* in Berlin reversed this verdict in May 1989: the Federal Government had indeed been right to warn against the dangers of TM practices and count TM among *Jugendreligionen*. In the mid-1990s, the *Oberwaltungsgericht* in Münster upheld and confirmed this ruling.[87]

Jugendreligionen and religious freedom

Citing Art. 4 of the *Grundgesetz*, Haack (1980a: 157; 1979e: 21) conceded that the constitution grants many freedoms and rights to religious organizations and groups of a particular *Weltanschauung*.[88] Art. 140 guarantees freedom of association and grants religious organizations the freedom to conduct their affairs 'within the boundaries of generally applicable law' (*innerhalb der Schranken des für alle geltenden Gesetzes*) and to administer their affairs without interference from the State or other public authorities. Haack (1979e: 21) underlined that religious freedom and freedom of association relate to *individuals* rather than organizations. The latter enjoy other freedoms, such as freedom of assembly (*Vereinigungsfreiheit*). He emphasized the need to operate 'within the boundaries of generally applicable law' because this imposes certain restrictions on religious organizations: they are placed within State control and are accountable to State and society. While the State cannot make decisions about the religious nature of organizations, there are serious implications when groups, such as Scientology (Haack considered it 'a trade and a money spinning organization'), turn religion into a product.[89] In such cases, the State authorities ensure that groups respect the law and operate within it (Haack, 1980a: 158–159). Haack was well aware that no group could be banned for calling itself a 'religion' or 'church' or for considering itself 'religious', but he thought that 'religion' could be used in a way which was outside the constitutional understanding of religion. He questioned whether organizations which did not behave like, but claimed to be, religions should be granted the constitutional benefits reserved for *bona fide* religions. Haack wanted legal provision for preventing abuse of religious freedom.[90]

Haack believed that criticizing *Jugendreligionen* was the only way to enable members to exercise religious freedom. This, he argued, included the freedom to agree or disagree with beliefs, the freedom to say 'yes' or 'no' (the sub-title of one of his books – Haack, 1981), 'the right to express criticism' – as inviolable a right as religious freedom. Yet *Jugendreligionen* preclude internal criticism. Due to *Psychomutation*, members are locked so firmly into the group that they have neither time nor mental space to formulate critical thoughts or verify the group's claims. They are told that critics tell lies or exploit those who turn to them for help. For Haack, criticizing *Jugendreligionen* in public was thus criticism by proxy, a means to give members the chance to see the group in a different light. Haack thought that *Jugendreligionen* could not have it both ways. If the right to criticize is part of religious freedom, they and related organizations, such as *Gesellschaft zur Förderung religiöser Toleranz und zwischenmenschlicher Beziehungen*, could not claim that criticism infringed religious freedom, especially as they themselves sharply criticized society, the churches, and political parties (Haack, 1979e: 21–22).

The dangers of *Jugendreligionen*

Haack's interest in anything religious induced him to collect material and comment on a wide range of groups, small or big, of international or local import. While not legitimate forms of religion or religiousness, some were more harmful than others, in accordance with Haack's idea of 'consumer protection'. Total submission to leaders and hierarchies was far more dangerous in his view than a group of spiritualists meeting for coffee and communion with 'spirits from the beyond'. He declared *Jugendreligionen* to be 'eminently dangerous'. The notion of 'danger' or 'threat' to state and society runs through Haack's writings like a red thread. The cover of his first book on *Jugendreligionen* displays the sign *Danger – Keep Out*. It puts Haack's assessment of *Jugendreligionen* and his intention to warn against them in a nutshell. Two interrelated aspects make them dangerous: how they recruit young people and use them for their purposes and how they relate to society. These two aspects are closely linked to Haack's censure of deceptive practices in *Jugendreligionen*, namely concealing political and business activities behind a religious front.

Regarding recruitment, Haack observed that in the late 1970s and early 1980s, *Jugendreligionen* switched from approaching young people in the streets to advertising courses or activities in ostensibly unrelated organizations. He noted the increasing influence of *Jugendreligionen* in schools of further education where members offered courses without declaring their adherence (Haack, 1988f: 107–117). Haack mentioned the UC's neighbourhood help scheme which was a way to present the UC as a 'positive Christian group'. Scientology created an educational project, ZIEL or *Zielzentrum für individuelles und effektives Lernen* (Centre for Individual and Effective Learning). TM began presenting itself as a 'health programme' and engaged in drug and prison rehabilitation. Haack saw such projects as 'harmful camouflage' and whitewash (Haack, 1980a: 175). Again, criticism of camouflage is closely linked to criticism of religion serving as façade or front.

Haack believed that *Jugendreligionen* were exploiting the general feeling of insecurity, widespread anxieties about the future, and young people's lack of trust in institutions. This background was the recruitment ground for religious groups. While the world-saving formula promises the liberation of the self, it requires not only total submission, but also turning away from the world. Once people have joined, they are no longer interested in wider society or politics. Membership is dangerous enough, but members' passive attitude towards society harbours dangers for the future.

Regarding the stance of *Jugendreligionen* towards society, Haack considered them agencies which operate outside, but seek influence in, established political and social institutions: 'The political opposition outside Parliament was once said to have engaged in a malicious march through the institutions. This very thing has happened with the sects' (ibid.). With the world-saving formula the only admissible method, 'sects' will not co-operate with society. This makes them dangerous. Haack claimed that core members were 'highly active cadre groups who could be deployed, even at the risk of their lives'. He was convinced that *Jugendreligionen* could only effect destruction. Jonestown demonstrated how much power leaders can have. It would not remain an isolated case.

Haack (1980a: 176–177) counted over 500 'sects' in Germany; of these, he considered about 20 to be 'really dangerous'. Overall, they had about 20,000 core members. They radiated more widely, as Haack put it, including around 300,000 sympathizers – people who take part in courses, feel some affinity with the groups, and are willing to participate to some extent. However, Haack conceded the lack of confirmed statistics, because groups often manipulated membership figures. He said he was more interested in qualitative rather than quantitative analysis of religious groups and pointed to the financial power of *Jugendreligionen*. New members brought possessions and inheritances and provided cheap labour. Long working-hours and avoidance of social security contributions built up large reservoirs of wealth. The businesses and companies of *Jugendreligionen* were part of the wider economy (some offering management training and consultancy), often run in disguise, because registered in members' names. For Haack (1992: 50), similar to Hummel's third level of NRM organization, such groups were not genuine religious communities, but 'distribution systems whose goods look like, among other things, a religion or *Weltanschauung*'. Profits were used to further 'irrational' aims. The UC, for example, spent huge sums to print leaflets for the election campaign. Given the capital and ideology of *Jugendreligionen*, Haack believed that they could become extremely dangerous; after all, one of these groups, the UC, owned a weapons business (Haack, 1980a: 179, 180).

Haack pointed to the way in which *Jugendreligionen* involved themselves in politics. The UC (known for its anti-communist stance) sought to influence the German election campaign by offering its services to the conservative parties. It distributed pamphlets and magazines to influence public opinion, for example *Der Report* which was given to passengers on Pan Am planes (Haack, 1979e: 23; EZW, 1983a). These were 'textbook examples of vitiating the political atmosphere'. Haack's disapproval was about the lack of transparency: the connection between the publications and the UC was not explicit (Haack, 1979e: 22–23).[91]

The Church and *Jugendreligionen*

Despite the dangers which *Jugendreligionen* presented to society, Haack did not regard them as serious competition for the Church, especially in view of the numbers involved: 'It ought to be pointed out that given millions of Protestant Christians, even hundreds of thousands of people joining sects would not provoke action aimed at driving away competition' (Haack, 1992: 9). However, in 1984, prompted by intense recruitment efforts by 'sects', the Church in Bavaria decided to examine non-Christian groups in the Munich area. When asked why it had taken so long to take action, Haack pointed out that the Church in Bavaria had been active for a long time – it was after all the first *Landeskirche* to appoint a 'sect' expert. Pastors and church leaders had too many other things to do. Haack was, however, not entirely convinced that a new study was needed, although its merit lay in looking at the situation 'in the Church's own backyard'. He wanted to see 'sect'-related issues included in the Church's theological training programmes.

Haack dealt with desperate parents trying to find out why their children had joined. Sometimes it became clear that *Jugendreligionen* addressed their spiritual interests or needs. Like Slee, Haack argued that the Church could offer a spiritual home, as in the case of a young woman who was very disturbed by her mother's illness and wanted to become more involved in church activities. The local minister invited her to join the church choir. Haack urged local congregations to think about ways of involving people more. Haack wanted a clear dividing-line between the Church and

Jugendreligionen, hence his denunciation of the minister who became involved with the Rajneesh movement and of ministers participating in *est* seminars or practising TM meditation. Such fraternization undermined the Church.

Before the UC mass weddings in New York and Seoul in 1982, Haack warned that couples were told to repeat the wedding ceremony in their home parishes. They should be refused, Haack recommended, otherwise the Church would support Moon's ideology of creating a new race. Refusing such couples was also a pastoral act, because the Church would make it clear to members that it did not want ecumenical links with the UC. Haack also urged clergy to refuse UC members' help in local parishes.

Like the EZW, Haack objected to the participation, especially of Lutheran theologians, at conferences sponsored or organized by *Jugendreligionen* and used arguments similar to those advanced by the EZW. He (1992: 38) criticized Hans Schwarz, (then) professor of theology at the University of Regensburg, for taking part at UC-sponsored conferences and contributing to UC newsletters: 'If a professor of theology attends such a (New ERA) conference at the Moonies' expense, he won't make it any better by putting an article in a Moonie publication. The New Testament has a rather harsh word for such behaviour.' These contributions put Schwarz's work in the UC's service. Haack drew parallels with apartheid in South Africa and the Mafia: why should association with the UC be 'any less momentous?' Would a scientist be happy to be invited to conferences organized by the Mafia? Referring to reports that the UC joined forces with extreme right-wing groups in Bolivia to plot a putsch, Haack compared association with the UC to church leaders associating with the NS regime. Those connected with the UC had no right to criticize theologians who countenanced Nazism (Haack referred to *Deutsche Christen* who adopted aspects of Nazi ideology, see Bergen, 1995; Künneth, 1979) – they must know the consequences of this approach for church history.

Haack's objection is not just about theologians associating with *Jugendreligionen*; he warns against any all-expenses-paid UC conferences, such as the 'Youth Seminar on World Religions'. In 1982, this seminar offered 140 young people a round-the-world 'pilgrimage' to learn about the world religions, with Professor H. Richardson as director of programme and other academics participating. The beginning of the seminar was to coincide with the mass wedding in New York. Haack's reasons were both practical and ethical: participants had to give written consent that they could be sent home at any time, and as the UC did not belong to any ecumenical bodies, it was implausible that an 'ecumenical research association' sponsored the seminar – Haack thus implied deception. The seminar could also be a means for recruitment 'by the back door', like the invitation to a CARP (Collegiate Association for the Research of Principles, a UC branch active at universities) seminar in Switzerland in 1982, advertised as an introduction to the Association. The money for such events came from young UC members' fund-raising, Haack argued. Potential participants should remember that UC practices were often criticized and ask themselves whether they wanted to benefit from an organization whose members suffered great hardship and were sometimes driven to desperate acts (meaning suicide).

Most of these objections also applied to academics taking part in sponsored conferences. In Haack's eyes, such academics were discredited. He countered the argument that participation was about 'academic freedom': 'Since when is the acceptance of material benefits a question of academic freedom? To have travel expenses and accommodation paid for can be many things (also very convenient), but the freedom of academic work has nothing to do with it' (Haack, 1992: 19). For Haack, it had to do with weapons and other business behind organizations such as PWPA (Professors' World Peace Academy). Nor did Haack accept the argument that such conferences were opportunities to gather valuable information:

> If others . . . justify this by the need to gather information, not even this argument spares them embarrassment. Neither journalistic duty to accuracy nor theological or sociological research requires expensive and long journeys at the expense of a system, such as Mr Moon's.
>
> (ibid.: 38)

Haack pointed to an EZW *Referent* who attended a UC conference to gather information, but paid his own expenses. In Haack's view, the UC used the conferences to expand its sphere of influence and expected participants to give something in return. There were those who attended once and those who attended regularly. The former might not have been aware of the identity of the organizers before attending, while the latter were willing to act as advisers or editorial board members.

Anyone who associated with the UC, and by implication with *Jugendreligionen* in general, was regarded with suspicion. When Haack saw Kurt Becker and Hans-Peter Schreiner – they had edited the proceedings of a symposium on the UC (Becker and Schreiner, 1982)[92] – on the list of participants of CAUSA's Sixth World Media Conference (Cartagena, Colombia, September 1983), they had moved 'into the UC's sphere of influence'. CAUSA (Confederation of the Associations for the Unification of the Societies of America) is a political arm of the UC which aims to counteract communism in Latin America. In discussing the 1986 Consultation on New Religious Movements in Amsterdam (Brockway and Rajashekar, 1987), Haack (1988f: 31) pointed out that nine out of 36 participants had taken part in UC conferences and trips.

What the State should do

Haack stated that despite agreement among Christians, humanists, and political parties about the need for action regarding the serious social and political problem of *Jugendreligionen*, there was little agreement about how this should be done. Although he often appealed to Government and Parliament to act, Haack rejected a ban or police intervention. Instead, he (1980a: 162–170) proposed three ways in which the problem could be tackled: criticism, legal provision, prevention.

Haack thought it was necessary to criticize *Jugendreligionen* so that members could reflect on the group's claims and see the group from another perspective. His publications served this purpose. They sought to point out what was wrong. Criticism could consist in revealing internal documents (hence the inclusion of primary sources or insider material in Haack's publications), non-public events, the inconsistency between ideas or activities, and the groups' public statements. Criticism was 'destructive', because it demolished 'the pious and false pretence', and it could effect change, often because the groups wanted to avoid further criticism. Haack had no time for 'ill-informed church people' and 'wishy-washy politicians' who saw positive aspects in *Jugendreligionen*. This was 'hogwash'. Do we make excuses for terrorists, he asked, because they are nice to song birds? Yet, criticism should not resort to fraudulent or unlawful means, because that would mean using the 'mud-slinging and deceitful' kind of criticism which *Jugendreligionen* employ.

Haack (1980a: 164–166; 1984b: 38–41) wanted some aspects regulated by law, but such provision had to apply to *all* religious groups. These aspects included a 'cooling off' period for withdrawing gifts or property (a suggestion inspired by consumer protection for door-to-door sales), requiring groups to pay social security contributions, a period for reclaiming payments for courses, legally required disclaimers for quasi-therapeutic treatments, examination of special diets or dietary supplements by health authorities, obliging *Jugendreligionen* to repay public money (e.g. grants) for members who discontinue their education, making *Jugendreligionen* legally liable for interfering in members' private affairs (divorce, discontinuation of education), declaring fundraising in public a violation of trade regulations, and classifying exploitative working requirements as illegal.

Some aspects relate particularly to parents, who, in Haack's view, faced a 'devilish' situation. They had both too many duties and too few rights. Although the law gives young people full powers when they reach majority, parents become responsible for their children the moment these are a burden to the State. Parents have a legal duty to support their children, even when they are members of *Jugendreligionen* and leave or lose their jobs. Yet parents have no rights – a gap in the legislation which Haack wanted closed. Haack saw two contradictory tendencies and urged political institutions to address these: to reduce the age of majority as much as possible, which allows young people to make their own decisions, and to extend the penal code for young people to age 25, because they cannot be held responsible.

However, criticism and legal regulations amounted to closing the door after the horse had bolted. Given the reasons why people join, prevention would include improving quality of life, by creating better living spaces or facilitating family life, building a future for young people in which they have a stake, and addressing young people's questions. Political action could offset loss of belonging and meaning by creating humane townscapes, avoiding conurbations and concentrated administration, providing affordable living space, allowing self-contained village life, reducing stress in the education system, and offering worthwhile careers. Young people's sense of disillusion needed to be addressed by encouraging them to make a world which was worth living in. They needed to be motivated to get involved in the political and religious associations which shape society. This would contribute towards creating a human(e) world and counter tendencies towards impersonal 'systems' (Haack, 1980a: 167–182; Hanns-Seidel-Stiftung 1979: 62).

More should be done about informing young people in schools and about political opinion forming, hence Haack's materials for use in schools. His 'checklist', a catalogue of questions to 'test' whether a group shows features associated with *Jugendreligionen* (Haack, 1974: 77–79; 1980a: 171–174), was a way to increase awareness. Thus, if Scientology applied to operate a kindergarten, people would realize what that involved. *Jugendreligionen* which tried to enter the education or health system or businesses had their own agenda, a view which again ties in with Haack's ideas of using religion as a front and infiltrating society. Haack cited a case in France: TM wanted to acquire a company which had gone into liquidation, but required half the workforce to become TM members. Trade unions would have no place in such companies, nor would democracy. Haack wanted more discussion about such matters and more action from the authorities, such as a separate political body to deal with the issues involved (Haack, 1980a: 181).

When asked whether he saw himself as the lonely voice in the wilderness and whether State and society recognized the challenge of *Jugendreligionen*, Haack considered such questions a 'very ambivalent matter'. While numerous people, especially in the churches, realized the need for action, others thought *Jugendreligionen* should be tolerated, even if they were not tolerant themselves. Haack could see little positive about them, given the deaths in Jonestown and, in his view, the increasing suicide rate related to *Jugendreligionen*. While there was understanding in political parties (in 1983, Haack commended *Junge Union Bayern*, the CSU's youth organization, for adopting a catalogue of demands, which focused on a review of charitable status for *Jugendreligionen*, and for submitting it to the CSU party conference) and the Ministry for Youth distributed information (in 1981, Haack praised it for steering a 'sensible course' between warning against the negative consequences of 'sect' membership and safeguarding religious freedom and democracy), Haack wondered how wholehearted this was. *Jugendreligionen* were obviously considered a marginal problem, to be left to the churches. Haack spoke of tokenism, because authorities were *seen* to do something when they published information, while they remained unconvinced of the matter's urgency. He himself was convinced that *Jugendreligionen* were a danger to society, even if this was not obvious. Religion had a political and socio-political effect and *Jugendreligionen* were social factors which needed to be taken seriously. Shock events, such as Jonestown, would make people realize this. Yet Haack did not want *Jugendreligionen* to become a party political issue or a weapon for politicians to blame one other. The issue was a task for society as a whole. It could not be solved by passing the buck (Haack, 1980a: 180–181). He was willing to co-operate with political parties or institutes, such as Hanns-Seidel-Stiftung (Haack, 1979e), PDI – Pressedienst Demokratische Initiative (Haack, 1980a) – and *Junge Union* (e.g. Junge Union Bayern, n.d.).

Haack and *Religionswissenschaft*

Regarding academic work, Haack rejected the term 'NRMs' and criticized academic methods and results. In the early 1980s, Haack recommended, for example, that parents should not take part in any surveys involving questionnaires, because the motives for these were often left unclear or those doing 'scientific' or 'helpful' work wanted to join the debate. Further, *Jugendreligionen* might be behind such surveys and questionnaires could never be entirely anonymous. As Haack ruled out positive aspects in *Jugendreligionen*, this criticism is unsurprising.

Discussing Kehrer's (1981a) volume on the UC,[93] Haack stated that 'the book was of interest to the expert because of its tendentiousness'. The contributions by UC members discredited the publication. This indicates that he did not want NRMs to have a voice. He contested NRM members' right to have a voice at all or to 'talk back', which is precisely what academics have done. Haack probably believed that a volume like Kehrer's could not present an 'objective' point of view. (The list of authors does not mention Feige's or Lindner's UC membership, but Kehrer justifies their contributions in the preface.) Another contributor, Heinz Röhr (then a professor of theology at Frankfurt), was reprimanded for connecting mystic elements in Unificationism with Angelus Silesius: as Röhr 'seems to know only extracts of both', he misinterprets. Commenting on Kehrer's essay, Haack picked on the footnote about the impartial use of 'church' and 'sect'. Haack questioned the impartiality of the whole essay, as the author appeared to be only familiar with UC material published for public consumption. If Kehrer had internal material, but chose not to use it, he should be considered an 'ingratiating scribbler'. Haack's other points include Kehrer's dismissal of Lofland (1980) and reprimand that the UC had become too denominationalized. Haack's criticism is beside the point: it picks out minor details and ignores substantive aspects and arguments, but is typical of Haack's critical method. Yet he considered the essays by Feige, Lindner, and Hardin and Kuner worth reading, although the third lacked facts known to 'experts'.

Haack found fault with the contribution by Barker, whom he described as 'the long-standing participant of and contributor to ICUS'; he said it was only worth reading for what it revealed about the author. He took issue with statements on the back cover which read:

> The media treat 'youth religions', which have emerged outside the churches, in a rough and polemical manner. This book is a first attempt to provide an objective description of one new religion, the Unification Church. It contributes towards an explanation of a novel religious phenomenon and towards religious tolerance.

The novel religious phenomenon might well be true, Haack commented, namely the phenomenon of 'scientists sitting on the fence'; also, there were already 'umpteen first attempts' to provide an 'objective description', but this one had not got beyond being an attempt either. Haack wished for 'thorough *Religionswissenschaft* regarding primary sources and interpretations'. Haack referred to Kehrer's and Röhr's essays as 'opinionated' and 'non-scientific' and called the authors 'established critics of critics', because they only criticized those critical of *Jugendreligionen*, namely the *Sektenbeauftragte*.[94]

Haack made similar remarks about Kuner's empirical study of 1980, which examined the 'psychological state' of German members of the UC, COG, and Ananda Marga. A representative sample revealed psychological profiles within the range of what would be expected from a sample of the general population. Kuner's findings did not support the thesis that UC membership entailed psychological damage (also Kuner, 1982; 1983b). Haack stated that the UC seemed to be heading for a favourable press, as

> We shall soon hear from Tübingen ... that young UC members have particularly valuable and strong personalities, and that 'sect experts' (Kuner always puts this word in quotes, probably for scientific reasons) and parents' organizations are to blame for everything.

Without addressing Kuner's key findings, Haack declared the results as not really revealing anything new:

> Yet it is cheap to find out that followers of *Jugendreligionen* are mainly serious, moral, and interested young people who have a positive attitude towards social, political, and religious matters. Members of rocker gangs don't join *Jugendreligionen*.

Haack (1992: 10) criticized the wording of the results and denied that Kuner's study did not indicate any cases where UC membership had been harmful: he might as well have said that UC members cannot contract cholera, because he had not discovered such cases. Haack questioned the study's credibility: 'so *sociologists* are assessing "psychological states" these days', but clinical psycho-pathology used to be the reserve of medical professionals. But Haack (ibid.: 11) also took issue with Sieber's (1980) study – which *is* psychological – whose findings echo Kuner's.

Another study which *Sektenbeauftragte* criticized was the *Wiener Studie* or Vienna Study, undertaken by the European Centre for Social Welfare and Research in Vienna (Berger and Hexel, 1981a; 1981b), with financial support from the German Federal Ministry for Youth, Family, and Health. The study examined the causes and consequences of young people's social dissension in western Germany, with particular reference to *Jugendreligionen*, taking into account the point of view of members, parents, friends, and ex-members. The study aimed to identify relevant currents and provide preliminary answers. Field research among Ananda Marga, DLM, Scientology, and the UC included interviews, psychological tests, questionnaires, participant observation, group discussions, and videos. In a press statement of May 1982, the conference of the *Sektenbeauftragte* criticized the *Wiener Studie* for 'tendencies to minimize *Jugendreligionen* while claiming to use scientific methods' and 'blanket reproaches against information and counselling services which the Church provides in this problematic area'. There were also 'serious reservations about the study's underlying ideological approach'. An article in *Materialdienst* (EZW, 1982b) referred to the press statement and added further criticism, although the first report of the study in *Materialdienst* (EZW, 1982a: 160–161) had also indicated positive aspects. In a later article in *Materialdienst*, Reimer and Hummel (1984: 104) saw the study as an example of interpreting *Jugendreligionen* within a Marxist framework: the new interest in religion and the 'inner world', which had emerged in the 1970s and included *Jugendreligionen*, fitted into the Marxist theory of compensation (religion compensates for the lack of this-worldly fulfilment) and constitutes a potential for political protest. This fed into the wrong channels, because it helped stabilize the existing order.

The *Elterninitiative* in Munich was equally critical of the *Wiener Studie*. Its statement of 1982 objected to the 'incorrect and tendentious interpretations of the survey results' and cited reasons similar to those of the *Sektenbeauftragte*: the study's authors attribute widespread poverty and threat to peace to capitalism's irrational systems of production and distribution, consider membership in *Jugendreligionen* a protest against prevailing social forces and institutions, and minimize the threat of *Jugendreligionen* to society and young people. *Ei* therefore called for countering such false statements which *Jugendreligionen* may use as advertisements – Scientology and the UC in fact used the study as proof that the allegations against them were unfounded (Minhoff, 1982) – and for an assessment of the interview material by independent experts. Another bone of contention for *Sektenbeauftragte* and *Elterninitiative* was the ministry's financial support of the study (see e.g. ibid.).

Sektenbeauftragte criticized Professor Rainer Flasche at the University of Marburg. In July 1984, the UC organized a conference in Frankfurt to mark the beginning of Sun Myung Moon's imprisonment in the US – the 1982 verdict by a New York jury, which had found him guilty of tax evasion, was upheld after appeal proceedings (EZW, 1983b; 1984a) – and the European Parliament's resolution on NRMs (Eimuth, 1984). In his presentation to the conference, Flasche juxtaposed extracts from the resolution with regulations and prohibitions regarding religious groups under the Nazi regime,[95] commenting that 'the parallels are shattering, especially between the reasons given for the motion for the resolution and the "guidelines for the control of sects" in the instructions of the *Reichsführer SS* of 15 February 1938' (ibid.: 315).[96]

According to Haack (1992: 19), this was not Flasche's first 'well-meaning, but ultimately foolish action'. In November 1981, he had circulated 'Statements regarding Religious Freedom in Germany' with a view to collecting supporting signatures:

> Religious freedom which is constitutionally guaranteed also applies to the so-called *Jugendreligionen*. The right to express one's religion freely is an inalienable human right, closely connected with man's humanity. Hostility towards and fight against those of different faiths, even within a family, not only contradicts the right to religious freedom, but also goes against the German constitution. Therefore, any forms of so-called deprogramming should be immediately rejected in order to quell this practice from the very beginning.
>
> (ibid.: 20–21)

The covering letter spoke of the 'need to prevent the beginnings of religious persecution' and 'a holocaust' against religious minorities. While Haack recognized Flasche's good intentions, Flasche had 'put himself, unprotected, into the wake of the UC' (ibid.: 19).

The champion of parents

Haack's close connection with parents' organizations went beyond his involvement in the creation and operation of *Elterninitiative* in Munich. He was one of its most active protagonists. Haack and the parents' initiatives shared mutual solidarity: they agreed on the causes of membership in *Jugendreligionen*, on their nature and aims, and their effect on young people. They also agreed on the means with which to counteract and oppose them. So much common ground engendered a symbiotic relationship: the parents looked to Haack (and his like-minded colleagues) for help, advice, moral support, guidance, and information, while Haack received first-hand information from parents. Like self-help organizations whose members feel helped by the sheer fact of knowing they are not alone with their problem and the opportunity to exchange information and experience, the network of parents and Haack (and other *Sektenbeauftragte*) supplied information, solidarity, and mutual support for one another.

The network was maintained by continuous mailings, regular meetings (the *Elterninitiative* meets annually), and Haack's Christmas circular (1979–1990). At times, Haack used the mailings to brace parents against future events. In the early 1980s, for example, he expressed unease about the UC's plans, after it had announced 'spectacular events', once the three times seven years after Moon's last marriage in the 1960s had elapsed. Although Haack was on the whole well informed, he put out hostages to fortune by speculating, for example, in 1983 that Scientology would soon go bankrupt and that the Rajneesh movement might follow the People's Temple. Haack saw the work of parents' organizations as complementary to, if not actually integral to, the Church's apologetic work: 'The parents' initiatives till, to a considerable extent, "the field of the churches", because they conduct the churches' apologetic business, even if this is often not noticed or acknowledged' (Haack, 1992: 64).

The network's importance was highlighted by a straw poll among parents who attended *Ei*'s annual meeting in 1983. About 30 responded how helpful personal contact with other parents and access to accurate information was and how important they found the chance to ask for advice and help from experts, such as Haack. Respondents also wanted to see public authorities do more to inform about, and counteract, *Jugendreligionen*.

Haack could mobilize parental support for court cases. Parents supplied sworn affidavits as evidence in court (and for lobbying purposes). There was legal support for parents or those affected by membership: in 1981, *Elterninitiative* set up a legal fund, financed by donations, of which Haack was, however, not a beneficiary. In 1983, the fund was used to cover a former Scientology member's social security payments for the time he worked for the organization. The fund also helped an ex-member to annul her marriage.

Another important aspect in the relationship between Haack and parents' organizations was that Haack's thinking and writing are easily accessible to the general public. His thinking is straightforward, the descriptions are clear, and the arguments are unambiguous. Haack wrote as he spoke, used every-day language and vocabulary, avoided technical terms and abstract concepts. And he had a sense of humour to cheer things up. Thus one of Haack's strengths was the pastoral care for parents: he addressed their practical, everyday problems. His advice was down-to-earth and answered day-to-day questions. They felt there was someone on their side, unequivocally, a parent who understood their parental and personal concerns, a pastor who understood religion and spiritual matters, an outspoken public figure, a well-informed, knowledgeable expert – in short, a true champion of their cause.

Haack did not blame parents. They often question whether they are responsible for their children joining NRMs, just like parents of drug addicts or criminals do. For Haack, the reverse was true: it is because parents instilled certain values in their children that *Jugendreligionen* successfully recruit them. So the blame lay squarely with the movements. Haack advised parents to ignore the question of blame and concentrate on the future, but not to pander to any demands from their member-children, for fear of losing contact. Parents drew comfort and confidence when told that although they *were* sometimes over-protective and *did* make mistakes, they would be reproached anyway. Haack called this 'making mistakes with dignity' and recommended that parents rely on the forgiveness of the Christian faith.

Haack's advice was straightforward and clear – it said what to do and what not to do. It was often very practical: keep a dossier of all the information related to a particular group and the involvement of your son/daughter, do not send money to members. Haack's publications include help and advice sections for parents and young people, with address lists for *Sekten-beauftragte* and parents' organizations, the checklist, guidelines for specific problems (how Christians should behave towards *Jugendreligionen* or what to do when a family member has joined), etc. An early advice booklet (Haack, 1979c), which was issued in five editions, arose from parents' and relatives' need for help in a new and threatening situation and was intended as a form of pastoral care. The topics covered range widely, from legal aspects, inheritance, relations between parents and member-children, the need to be informed about beliefs, advisers, and ex-members, etc., summarized in a 12-point programme.

Regarding deprogramming, Haack suggested his objection when speaking about a campaign to reclaim young people from *Jugendreligionen*. He (1979c: 60–63) defined it as 'wiping out a programme – in this case the programme with which *Jugendreligionen* or sects have programmed their members' so that any attempt to free members from the groups' ideas could be called 'deprogramming'. However, in the US and UK, deprogramming has a more specific sense: either a court injunction to place members under guardianship or kidnapping. As the *Handbook of Deprogramming* was circulated by a *Jugendreligion*, it had given rise to 'considerable lies' about the practice. Deprogrammers were taken to court for unlawful abduction and holding individuals against their will. One such case was brought in Austria in 1988 (Haack, 1992: 73). Some deprogrammed members were grateful for it, but, Haack pointed out, organizations, such as ADFI and *Elterninitiative*, rejected the practice, for moral and legal reasons. Deprogramming played into the hands of the very organizations they sought to counteract, the *Jugendreligionen*. To illustrate this, Haack cited the deprogramming of Barbara Sch., a Scientology member, in November 1987, which involved, he suspected, Scientology itself (ibid.: 69–70). In October 1982, *Elterninitiative* released a press statement which rejected deprogramming and warned that its consequences might make matters worse for individuals. Haack rejected it because it used the principle of 'might is right' – a point of criticism regarding *Jugendreligionen*. At the same time, parents should not be condemned for resorting to it, a view echoed in *Ei*'s statement and FAIR's stance.

Haack (1992: 68) had reservations about the words 'programming' and 'deprogramming', because an individual could not be compared with a disk to store or erase information at will. He inverted this notion:

The *Jugendreligionen* are actually the deprogrammers. They erase the programme for life, which responsible parents have offered their children ... They erase it and replace it with a 'continuous tape' which is full of someone else's views. A number of suicides have shown how truly life-threatening this is.

(ibid.: 19)

Again, *Ei*'s statement repeats this view, stating that the recruitment methods of *Jugendreligionen* are dangerous forms of deprogramming and 'brainwashing'.

Haack was in favour of 'exit counselling', which he called 'liberating conversations'. These took place at members' request, often at the behest of their families or friends. They were forms of pastoral care or therapy and might involve former members. As long as they were voluntary, they were the only expedient form of counselling.

Haack and apologetics

Haack defined apologetics as

the defence of the Christian faith, i.e. the encounter with the perspectives of other religions and *Weltanschauungen*. Apologetics ... must, however, make clear where the boundaries are of what cannot be reconciled with the Christian faith, such as the Church testifies to it.

(Haack, 1992: 76)

He considered apologetics 'fundamental' and 'legitimate', primarily a parish matter, but church leadership had to take responsibility for it. Apologetics was as much part of the Church as liturgy, charitable work, and pastoral care – a church without apologetics would be a 'non-church'. However, 'too many believe that apologetics is the private playground for some specialists and interested individuals' and some people felt uneasy about drawing boundaries. Some even spoke of a 'drawer mentality', but drawers were useful for creating order.

Haack's (1988f) book on apologetics is not a systematic presentation of his views on the topic, but a collection of writings which allow insight into his views. He commented, for example, that

an increasing number of voices have gathered under the banner of 'dialogue', who reject a critical discussion – and apologetics can be only that – when criticism entails drawing boundaries or clear rejection, perhaps the need to warn against other groups, movements or communities.

(ibid.: 30)

Such voices could be heard at the Amsterdam Consultation on New

Religious Movements in 1986. For Haack, apologetics was a 'given of theology' which derived from the Bible (Matthew 28: 19–20, 1 Peter 3: 15). Haack followed Kurt Aland, a German theologian well known for his contributions to New Testament exegesis and church history, for whom apologetics is 'an indispensable sign that the Christian Church is alive', because a church without apologetics is dead and apologetics involves defending one's faith and attacking the beliefs of others. Some notable institutions which take an apologetic approach notwithstanding, apologetics had become a 'waning art' in the churches (ibid.: 33–34; 41–42).

Haack (ibid.; 1985e) propounded five theses: (1) apologetics is action which makes the Church's confession of faith more explicit. Therefore, apologetics cannot refer to general scientific knowledge, but only to the Church's confession. (2) The confession of faith requires the churches to take apologetic action. The Church needs to draw boundaries against those within or outside it, whose teachings go against its faith. (3) The Church's apologetic action helps its members, because it supports their faith. (4) Apologetics is an act of assessment by the Church, because the Church appraises the testimony of faith in its historic and contemporary dimension. The idea that theology should be value-free and descriptive is rejected. (5) The Church's apologetic action must be consistent. It must be defended in a credible way, despite possible consequences.

Haack argued that *Abgrenzung* (boundaries) or even *Ausgrenzung* (rejection) did not preclude, but create the foundation for dialogue. Dialogue 'can only be conducted in recognition of the differences'. It requires the confidence that partners in dialogue take one another seriously and this involves clear boundaries. Dialogue has no place in counselling and pastoral care which address individuals' personal suffering and painful experience.

For Haack, drawing boundaries did not violate religious freedom, because criticism, especially criticism of religious communities' teachings and behaviour, was a 'basic condition' of religious freedom. 'Freedom without criticism – including constructive criticism – is unthinkable'. Haack (1988f: 36) agreed with Agehananda Bharati, a student of *Religionswissenschaft* and a Hindu monk of Austrian origin:

> The idea that there should be 'constructive criticism' is one created by laymen. Criticism derives from Greek *krinein*, which means to cut apart and to analyse. The job of the social critic is not necessarily to improve the society he writes about, since analysis does not imply recommendations.[97]

For Haack, 'constructive criticism' is a form of advertising or complicity. There was an 'apologetic frontline' both in relation to the new religions and within the churches. While apologetic debates within the Church were common, Haack went against those whom Rüdiger Hauth (after Haack, the second longest serving *Sektenbeauftragter*) called the 'Second Front' – those in the churches 'who pursue the sects' cause', motivated by 'well-meaning foolishness' or benefits, such as all-expenses-paid trips, or the wish to raise their personal profile. Theologians who become involved with new religions, for example by participating at conferences, neglect or even forget the apologetic dimension of theology. As some insisted that apologetics should also recognize what was positive in other faiths, Haack (1992: 62–63) declared – tongue in cheek – that his positive contribution to the debate was to award a prize to one of the movements. TM was to receive 'the 1986 Golden Master Key to Article 4 of the Constitution' for making a lot of money while maintaining charitable status.

Haack (1988f: 74, 38–39) felt that the 'the gift of discernment' had never been more important. Discernment had been particularly important under the Third Reich. This gift, he explained, was one of the charisms of the New Testament, the 'gift of guidance'. It was given to the community of the faithful, but it could manifest in individuals, albeit only temporarily. It was a gift of the Holy Spirit.

According to Haack's definition, 'applied or official apologetics' is carried out by church organizations or individuals, such as *Sektenbeauftragte*, commissioned by the Church leadership to fulfil this task. The commissioning institution decides whether this apologetics is 'orthodox' or conforms to its kind of apologetics. Practitioners of 'applied apologetics' are accountable to four groups of people: to the Church leadership who has expectations, some of a contractual nature, others related to groups and currents within the church, such as the charismatic renewal movement; to parishioners who are often grateful, not least because they receive counselling and pastoral care; to the public whose opinion is, on the whole, divided. Agreement about the idea of 'sects' (shaped by the media) entails rejection of sectarianism and support for preventative action. However, if apologists cannot meet the public's expectations, support is withheld or withdrawn. Sections of the public, which are critical of the Church and see themselves as 'alternatives', respond negatively with criticism and insults and finally, to religious groups or individuals at whom apologetics is directed. This area is bounded in four directions: inward (sectarian developments within the Church), outward (the interface between religious and worldly matters, for example management or consultancy courses with an underlying religious content), downward (the line between acceptable and doubtful methods of investigation), and upward (how apologists use information and knowledge) (ibid.: 47–52).

The Church's confession determines at which groups apologetics is directed, not personal relationships or ambitions, ideas of power, Church politics, etc. Apologists take great risks when they criticize interest groups in the Church or allies of such groups outside it. Yet, apologists would jeopardize their morality and theological authority if they allowed their task to be restricted or their assessment predetermined. Applied apologetics may cause a stir within the Church, but its purpose is not to justify peace and complacency – it includes internal criticism and criticism of groups outside

(ibid.: 56). Apologetics also involves information, often corrective information, to counterbalance the self-representations of religious groups. These
obviously seek to display themselves in the best light, but factually accurate
information is needed for a balanced assessment (ibid.: 63).

Haack (ibid.: 66–69) saw apologetic work hampered, even threatened, by
intrigues, jealousies, and unease *within* the Church. These arose when the
need for apologetic work was not recognized and when ignorance about the
problems involved in apologetic work gave rise to doubts about methods, as
the closure of a Roman Catholic advice centre in Lucerne, Switzerland,
demonstrated. Dialogue should not be given priority over counselling and
pastoral care. Apologetic work was also hampered by the activities of the
Jugendreligionen which brand criticism as religious persecution and violation of religious freedom. Some created organizations, such as *Gesellschaft
für religiöse Toleranz und zwischenmenschliche Beziehungen*, which lobby
members of regional and national parliaments. Some used disinformation,
even unlawful means, to undermine apologists (ibid.: 70–73). Haack called
upon the Church leadership to protect apologists against disinformation
campaigns and verify facts before drawing conclusions.

Conclusions

Haack did not treat *Jugendreligionen* as legitimate forms of religion or legitimate expressions of religiousness, but as a danger and threat to individuals,
families, and society. They were the 'dark side' of religion – harmful and
destructive. This view is reflected in Haack's terminology. He opted for the
terms *Jugendreligionen* or *Jugendsekten*, but rejected 'NRMs' or 'new religions'. He also rejected 'destructive cults', but his concept of *Jugendreligionen*
is close to this: groups and organizations which claim to be religious, while
pursuing economic and political aims, whose recruitment methods are
doubtful, if not reprehensible, which exploit members and undermine social
institutions. Haack's perception of how *Jugendreligionen* recruit and
indoctrinate new members – the application of *Seelenwäsche* and *Psychomutation* – is close to the 'brainwashing' thesis. Saliba's (1990d: 133) observation applies regarding the link between terminology and underlying
assumptions about NRMs:

> While most social scientists and historians of religion have opted for
> terms like 'new religious movements', 'new religions', . . . popular and
> news media reports . . . have opted for terms like 'cults' and 'destructive
> cultism'. The former titles designate a neutral classification of these new
> entities, but in the process end up treating them as religious options on a
> par, in many respects, with traditional religions. The latter labels, on the
> contrary, imply that contemporary cults are unique organizations that
> cannot, and should not, be compared with the major religious traditions
> of the world, and that they are, moreover, evil in nature.

Haack's assumption that *Jugendreligionen* are not legitimate forms of religiousness determined his approach. They are groups and organizations which use religion as a façade and violate the principle of religious freedom – they have to be shown to do this and counteracted wherever possible. Three areas require counteraction: individuals and their families, the Church, and the State or politics. The first emphasizes pastoral care, namely moral support and practical help for potential and existing members and their families, particularly parents. Counselling and information are very important, as are advice and assistance in day-to-day matters, hence Haack's close links with parents' organizations. He provided them with a model explaining 'cult' membership and with strategies to cope with the problems.

Regarding the Church, Haack argued for 'applied apologetics', the defence of the orthodox faith, with clear boundaries between what is part of the Church's *Bekenntnis* and what is irreconcilable with Church doctrine. The decision on where to draw the line is based on discernment, a gift of the holy spirit to the Church. Discernment involves critical judgement, criticism, and condemnation of what is unacceptable to the Church's *Bekenntnis*. Saliba (1995: 176) calls this 'negative apologetics' because it only points to what is negative in NRMs and attacks beliefs by underlining weaknesses and inconsistencies. Such defence of Christianity has at times degenerated into shouting matches between members of different religions and the common currency in such encounters are diatribe and abuse instead of dialogue and bridge-building. For Saliba (1995: 180), this is 'the heart of the confrontational approach of negative apologetics' whose 'most forceful line of argumentation has been an attempt to show that the new religions are the work of Satan himself'. Although Haack was outspoken about *Jugendreligionen* and considered them evil, he did not subscribe to the satanic conspiracy theory common among some evangelicals. Haack's 'applied apologetics' included concern with new currents within the Church. It was an uncompromising attitude towards novel forms of religiosity, because it did not engage in dialogue. For Haack, dialogue implied obfuscation of the 'real' issues and 'foul' compromises – useless to those affected.

Haack's concept of apologetics explains his ambivalence towards the Church, particularly Church leadership. When he felt there was agreement with, and support for, his course of action, he was full of praise and approval. However, when he perceived the Church as engaging in 'unhealthy dialogue' with, or being too tolerant towards, currents and groups (without or within it), he thought the Church was misguided or pursued aims which undermined it. This made him critical of the Church, outspokenly so, as he was never one to shy away from controversy.

The third area to counteract *Jugendreligionen* included wider society and social institutions – politics, the law, the State. Here, Haack thought, everything had to be done to make existing legislation watertight, to close gaps in the legislation to prevent *Jugendreligionen* from exploiting loopholes. There was room for complementary legislation, but Haack did not envisage radical solutions, such as a general ban. Another task for the State and its political institutions was prevention: the dissemination of information, safeguarding existing law, and vigilance.

In Haack's view, academic research could not make any viable contribution to the debate of *Jugendreligionen* or the problems they created. Haack criticized academic research methods and considered academics – including theologians – discredited if they even as much as appeared to have connections with *Jugendreligionen*. Not being negative or finding something positive about them indicated connivance or allegiance; this deserved nothing but scorn and disdain. This view explains the approach of Haack's criticism: he frequently missed the point or picked out irrelevant details. If academics did not condemn *Jugendreligionen* as he did, there seemed no need to argue with or criticize the substance of their work: it was self-evident that their statements should not be taken seriously.

Haack's role in dealing with NRMs in the Church was complementary to the EZW's role. His closeness to parents and relatives emphasized his strength in pastoral care and shaped the way in which he related to *Jugendreligionen*: he was prejudiced against them and therefore all groups were of same type; differences between them were differences in appearance only. Haack's forthright stance was very media effective and he cut a high profile in public. This created the impression at times that he spoke for the whole Church, but this made him a controversial figure in the Church. Haack can be described as a moral entrepreneur: the personal mingled with the professional, the professional providing justification for the personal. He stood, however, with both feet in the Church and in Christianity, in the knowledge that this commitment was firm ground on which to operate.

Haack was a valuable link in the network of *Sektenexperten*: he gathered and distributed information and mobilized resources and support when needed. Haack's apologetics is, in Hummel's terms, 'militant apologetics', appropriate and effective with regard to *some* NRMs. While the EZW maintained links with Haack and parents' initiatives, its approach is distinct from Haack's, oriented towards *Religionswissenschaft* and theology. Some *Referenten* held university posts prior to joining the EZW and some resumed these instead of moving to Berlin. Although concerned with pastoral issues related to NRMs, the EZW has had a much broader remit to address wider social, religious, and theological questions. The EZW's apologetic approach seeks to explain and defend Christianity in a social and religious context which is increasingly pluralistic. Its academic approach examines religious beliefs and behaviour *before* assessing these theologically. The merits of groups and movements are explored and there is careful differentiation between movements to identify those which are (potentially) *konfliktträchtig* or *konfliktreich*. The deliberate attachment to the Church grounds the EZW's work, a commitment which it shares with Haack, even if it translates differently into their respective stances.

The EZW takes account of academic work about NRMs, including British and American social scientific studies, to derive theoretical models and theological responses. This approach has placed it at some distance from parents' organizations. While acknowledging problems which *Jugendreligionen* have created for families, the EZW has not catered for parental needs as much as Haack did. It takes (at least some) NRMs seriously enough to explore their teachings and the possibility of dialogue. The EZW's public profile has not matched Haack's; in fact, the EZW has never sought a high profile. It has created an academic and theological knowledge paradigm within and for the Church, building on the *Apologetische Centrale* and Kurt Hutten's work, while upholding the conviction that it should not ignore wider issues pertinent to the Church's concerns or be confined to specializing in apologetics to deal with delicate or difficult areas of interreligious dialogue. These issues have involved exacting balancing acts regarding: the Church leadership and the Church overall, who want to delegate apologetic specialism to the EZW to relieve the Church of apologetic responsibilities; 'militant apologists', including parents' initiatives, who are wary of the EZW's differentiated approach because it precludes blanket condemnation; the NRMs, which should be taken seriously, but have to be examined carefully; the academic community, which questions the EZW's theological and apologetic agenda; the State, which would like to instrumentalize the EZW for its own purposes.

Haack combined 'homegrown' ideas with ideas from other sources. When his interest in 'sects' and *Sondergemeinschaften* began in the 1960s, NRMs were hardly present in Germany. By the mid-1970s, he had made contact with 'cult-watching' organizations in the US and France and co-founded *Elterninitiative* in Munich. In the US, the 'anti-cult' paradigm or 'brainwashing thesis' was in place by then. Haack adopted its ideas, but adapted the 'brainwashing thesis' to the German context by developing separate terminology and concepts, which were informed and motivated by his theological perspective.

It is highly significant that the sensibilities about Germany's Nazi past should emerge on both sides of the NRM argument and in relation to the State's response. Scientology's case exemplifies these sensibilities very accurately and keenly. Voices like Haack's see totalitarian traits in NRMs, which if unchecked and allowed to claim full constitutional rights, will grow out of control. On the other side are voices, illustrated by Flasche's campaign, for whom the parallels between NRMs and potential extreme right-wing tendencies represent an attempt to control NRMs legally. State authorities are painfully aware of the (seemingly harmless) beginnings of Nazism and therefore committed to vigilance and prompt action to curtail any such tendencies. Hence the willingness to place Scientology under the observation of the *Verfassungsschutz* – whose very purpose is to keep a watchful eye on potentially harmful (political) groups. Hence the painstaking legal scrutiny of Scientology's claim to be a genuine religion, because no organization should enjoy constitutional freedoms under false pretences and thus become a (potential) threat to the democratic order. Scientology's (1993) *Hate and Propaganda* brochure stirred these sensibilities in any German, regardless of his/her attitude towards NRMs. Comparing the persecution of the Jews in the Third Reich with the 'persecution' of NRMs (as 'religious minorities') mobilizes such sensibilities, creates alliances, and activates loyalties which might otherwise not emanate, resulting in the very opposite effect to what is intended.

Given their respective positions in the *Kirchenkampf*, the two main churches have particular sensibilities regarding the Third Reich. The churches' role as important pillars of social and cultural life, their influence in the social institutions (through the *Proporzsystem*), and the principle of subsidiarity make them the State authorities' natural allies, especially as new legislation could never be a realistic option. The State has co-operated with the churches to fulfil its obligations towards young people (*Jugendschutz*) and the public in general (*Aufklärung*). The State, however, did not immediately take up the issue of *Jugendreligionen* and related problems, but once it had, it provided funds for parents' initiatives and their activities, until NRMs challenged this support in the courts. Representatives of political parties, parliamentarians, and ministerial officials have been far more sympathetic and supportive than their British and American counterparts, as their presence at conferences organized by parents' initiatives attests.

Unlike the Church of England, the churches in Germany became involved in the NRM issue right from the start and in shaping the knowledge paradigm. They have been close to parents' initiatives, joined the network of information and support channels, and mobilized public and state authorities. However, the churches' response has not been uniform, with differences in approach, exemplified by Pastor Haack and the EZW and resulting tensions within and outside the Protestant Church. In Britain, the Church of England, as an institution, did not become involved in the NRM debate until this debate was well under way. Although individual clergy provided pastoral care locally, the Church was activated only when requested to take an interest through the question in the Synod. It then began to examine the issue, but proceeded with great caution, as it had to consider the internal situation (the spectrum of doctrinal positions ranging from evangelical to conservative) and its position as the Established Church. It also realized that some criticism levelled at NRMs regarding beliefs and practices could be attributed to itself. As the Established Church, the Church of England was accustomed to a pluralistic society and to low attendance and membership; it also considered itself the guardian of religion and its representative in relation to the State. The Church was therefore reluctant to create any agencies which might have suggested rivalry with NRMs. Instead, the Church looked *outside* its structures – to the academic community and the State, while in Germany, the Protestant Church had *internal* structures in place, *Sektenbeauftragte* and the EZW, *before* NRMs appeared.

THE RESPONSE OF THE ROMAN CATHOLIC CHURCH

This section looks at the Roman Catholic Church's (RCC's) approach to NRMs. Some of the key documents published by the Vatican are examined, such as *The Attitude of the Church Towards the Followers of Other Religions* (1984), *Sects and New Religious Movements: Pastoral Challenge* (1986), the encyclical *Redemptoris Missio* (1991), and *Dialogue and Proclamation* (1991). It will show that the F.I.U.C. project and the *Fourth Extraordinary Consistory* of April 1991 continued the process started by the Vatican Report. The response to the Report by an NRM representative (the only one of this kind), Steven J. Gelberg (Subhananda dasa) from ISKCON, is examined. The Plenary Assembly of the Pontifical Council for Inter-religious Dialogue is discussed regarding its contribution to dialogue with NRMs. The comments of various Vatican representatives on NRMs are explored, among them Michael Fitzgerald, Michael-Paul Gallagher, Teresa Gonçalves, and Elisabeth Peter, to show their interpretation of Vatican documents. Three Catholic theologians – Michael Fuss, Hans Gasper, and John Saliba – provide both insider and outsider perspectives. The documents and commentaries appear in chronological sequence, illustrated by a synoptic summary, to draw out the progression in the RCC's considerations and thought.

Introduction

The phenomenon of NRMs was noted and dealt with on the RCC's grass-roots level, by priests in local parishes. This experience was shared by clergy of all churches; in Germany, the clergy of the Protestant Church were the first port of call for parents, but as described earlier, the creation of a network of information and expertise occurred much sooner. Also, the *Evangelische Zentralstelle für Weltanschauungsfragen* (EZW) was in place to observe non-mainstream religious groups and movements and there was a model for dealing with these in pastoral terms, namely through *Sektenbeauftragte*.

By contrast, the RCC had no such mechanisms in place. Its structures are arranged within a centralized system: orders pass from the centre through hierarchical channels to grassroots clergy and the centre takes time to address and assess issues in light of sanctioned doctrine. The exigency for a strategy regarding NRMs came from the grassroots, as the daily encounter with religious pluralism pressed local clergy to find a footing for relating to other religions. The RCC thus entered the NRM debate when this debate was well under way – the Vatican Report of 1986 was triggered by the Episcopal Conferences' concern regarding NRMs – because of three reasons.

First, the Secretariat for Non-Christians (now Pontifical Council for Inter-religious Dialogue), established by the Vatican in 1964, was concerned with the way the Church could or should relate to believers of other faiths. Its document, *The Attitude of the Church Towards the Followers of Other Religions* (Secretariatus pro non Christianis, 1984) speaks of other religions in *general* terms – there is no mention of *new* religions. However, one might extrapolate from it the RCC's attitude towards NRMs. The document has to be seen against the background of Vatican II, as a translation of the reforming spirit into concrete terms.

Second, doctrinal contingencies have played a major role. As the RCC upholds an absolute claim to Truth and sees itself as the 'true' apostolic church, it could not acknowledge 'truth' in other religions or consider them other, yet valid 'paths up the mountain'. It took Vatican II to usher in a process of weakening this claim. This process opened avenues which have allowed the RCC to respect other religions in their own right and have dealings with them.

Third, the RCC has realized that rapid social changes and developments in the modern world compel it to take note of, and recognize, the existence of other religions, beyond established ecumenical channels. This situation has been particularly acute in Latin America where the rise of Pentecostalism has become a serious threat.

Inter-religious dialogue

Since its establishment, the Secretariat for Non-Christians has explored dialogue between the RCC and other religions. *The Attitude of the Church Towards the Followers of Other Religions* acknowledges that the Secretariat's work came in the wake and spirit of Vatican II. The Secretariat was established as an institutional token for the desire to meet and relate to followers of other world traditions and as a response to the climate of Vatican II. Its tasks are laid down in the constitution *Regimini Ecclesiae*: 'to search for methods and ways of opening a suitable dialogue with non-Christians' (quoted ibid.: 8). Possible levels of dialogue are probed in light of the Bible, papal encyclicals, and Conciliar documents. Yet, dialogue is predicated upon mission and evangelization, which shows that the RCC has not entirely relinquished its claim to being the 'true church'.[98] A summary of the Secretariat's document follows.

The Attitude of the Church Towards the Followers of Other Religions contains the Pope's address to the Secretariat's Plenary Assembly in early 1984. The Assembly had been convened to formulate a document regarding dialogue and mission. The Pope refers to the encyclical *Ecclesiam Suam* (its publication in 1964 coincided with the Secretariat's foundation) which is considered to be 'the *magna carta* of dialogue in its various forms' (ibid.: 3). The Pope recognizes the enormous work already accomplished to open appropriate dialogue with non-Christians and the necessity of dialogue between religions; he stresses, in reference to previous encyclicals, the central role of dialogue for the RCC and affirms the values on which dialogue is predicated: respect and love, the freedom to practise one's faith fully and compare it with other faiths.

The Pope notes the Secretariat's instrumental role in encouraging local churches to establish constructive relationships with believers of other faiths and charges it to 'continue to specify and examine an appropriate apostolate for relations with non-Christians' (ibid.: 4). While local churches must be committed to such relations and promote respect for the values, traditions, and convictions of other believers, they must also promote a 'solid and suitable religious education of the Christians themselves, so that they know how to give a convinced witness of the great gift of faith' (ibid.). Dialogue can be conducted on doctrinal questions, in daily relationships and inter-monastic contacts. While all Christians are called to dialogue, some bring useful expertise or special gifts. Dialogue with non-Christians is conducive to realizing unity and collaboration among Christian Churches.

Although dialogue includes the risk that religion be used for division or polarization, it 'means learning to forgive, since all the religious communities can point to possible wrongs suffered through the centuries' (ibid.: 5). It requires commitment to try to 'understand the heart of others' (ibid.), even in the absence of agreement. Dialogue has a place in the RCC's 'salvific mission' for which 'exclusivism and dichotomies' (ibid.: 6) should be avoided. 'Authentic dialogue becomes witness and true evangelization is accomplished by respecting and listening to one another (*Redemptor Hominis*, 12)' (ibid.). Prudence and discernment teach what is appropriate in any given situation, whether collaboration, witness, listening or exchange of values.

The second part of *The Attitude of the Church Towards the Followers of Other Religions* provides details about conducting dialogue. Vatican II was a landmark, with *Nostra Aetate*, a Conciliar document, dedicated entirely to relations with non-Christian religions. *Nostra Aetate*, the *Church's Declaration on the Relationship of the Church to Non-Christian Religions*, has been influential for Catholic statements on other religions. It was intended to lay out the RCC's relations with world religions, but the question is whether it can be extended to tribal religions and NRMs (Saliba, 1992: 15, notes 56, 57). Vatican II ushered in a new attitude in the face of rapid changes in the world and 'the deeper consideration of the church as "the universal sacrament of salvation" (*Lumen Gentium* 48)' (Secretariatus pro non Christianis, 1984: 7). The new attitude is dialogue, understood as norm and ideal, propagated by *Ecclesiam Suam*. Dialogue is 'not only discussion, but also includes all positive and constructive interreligious relations with individuals and communities of other faiths which are directed at mutual understanding and enrichment' (ibid.).

The Secretariat's Assembly in 1984 evaluated existing dialogue, reflected on the RCC's attitude towards other believers, and examined dialogue and mission. While it thought further in-depth theological study necessary and outstanding, it considered *The Attitude of the Church Towards the Followers of Other Religions* to be of a pastoral nature. It was to help Christian communities and leaders to follow Vatican II's directives and overcome difficulties arising from evangelization and dialogue and to help members of other religions understand the RCC's perspective. The document was issued in an ecumenical spirit, given that the World Council of Churches was similarly concerned with dialogue with 'People of Living Faiths and Ideologies'.

The Secretariat affirmed the central role of love: the RCC is its 'living sign' and 'each aspect and activity of the church's mission must therefore be imbued with the spirit of love' (ibid.: 9). For every Christian, 'the missionary duty is the normal expression of his lived faith' (ibid.) – evangelizing and founding churches among people(s) where the RCC has not yet taken root – but is exercised according to conditions. *Redemptoris Missio* states that mission is an issue of faith and that every Church member must bear witness to the Christian faith and life (Catholic Truth Society, 1991: 9). Vatican II, other ecclesiastical teachings, papal addresses, and episcopal conferences addressed the various aspects of mission: commitment to social justice, liberty, the rights of man, and the reform of unjust social structures (Secretariatus pro non Christianis, 1984: 10).

Mission finds many expressions, ranging from the presence and witness of Christian life, to service of mankind, liturgical life, convent life, catechesis, dialogue and co-operation with believers of other faiths. As Vatican II stated, mission must always respect the other's freedom and reject any form of coercion. The reason for dialogue is twofold: the RCC recognizes that every person aspires to being considered responsible and able to act as such. Dialogue shows individuals their limitations and how these can be overcome. The RCC also recognizes that modernity's social conditions make dialogue urgent for people to co-exist peacefully.

The RCC acknowledges that non-Christian traditions contain ' "elements which are true and good" (*OT* 16), "precious things, both religious and human" (*GS* 92), "rays of the truth which illumines all mankind" (*NA* 2)' (ibid.: 16; 21) and that their spiritual heritage is an invitation to dialogue. Dialogue is 'a manner of acting, an attitude and a spirit which guides one's conduct' (ibid.: 17) and 'implies concern, respect, and hospitality towards the other . . . [but] leaves room for the other person's identity, his modes of expression, and his values' (ibid.). Dialogue includes collaboration, often international, towards humanitarian, social, economic, or political goals, and forgetting the past.

Dialogue among specialists is of particular interest, to explore respective religions or to apply specialist expertise to global problems. Pluralistic societies are more conducive to such dialogue. It furthers mutual understanding and appreciation of spiritual values and cultural categories. Dialogue of religious experience can, despite profound differences between religions, lead to enriching and preserving 'the highest values and spiritual ideals of man' and Christians can offer non-Christians the possibility of experimenting 'in an existential way with the values of the Gospel' (ibid.: 19).

Dialogue and mission have several aspects. The aim of mission is conversion, but no-one must be constrained to act against his/her conscience. The missionary intention of other religions is recognized. As 'God has a loving plan for every nation (*Acts* 17: 26–27)' (ibid.: 21), the RCC wishes to work with other nations and religions. Dialogue excludes no-one, is guided by the Holy Spirit, yet is subject to God's mysterious patience.

The Vatican Report

In May 1986, four Vatican offices (dicasteries), the Secretariat for Promoting Christian Unity, the Secretariat for Non-Christians, the Secretariat for Non-Believers, and the Pontifical Council for Culture, jointly published a report on *Sects and New Religious Movements: Pastoral Challenge*, known as the Vatican Report (Secretariat for Promoting Christian Unity *et al.*, 1986).[99] It was a 'response to the concern expressed by Episcopal Conferences throughout the world' about the presence and activity of 'sects, new religious movements, cults' (ibid.: 1) and presented the initial results of a study. A questionnaire had been distributed in February 1984 to gather 'reliable information and indications for pastoral action' (ibid.) and explore what other research should be carried out. By October 1985, the four Secretariats had received sufficient material (questionnaire responses and documents) from 75 Episcopal Conferences and regional episcopal bodies to present an overall picture.

The Report's introductory section briefly discusses the terms 'sect' and 'cult', the emergence of NRMs, pastoral problems, groups most affected, reasons why NRMs are successful, and the RCC's general attitude to this phenomenon. The Report points to 'difficulties in concepts, definitions and terminology' (ibid.: 3), with 'sect' and 'cult' being 'somewhat derogatory' and 'imply[ing] negative value judgment' (ibid.). Therefore, 'more neutral terms such as *new religious movements, new religious groups*' (ibid.) may be preferred. The Report uses 'new religious movements', 'pseudo-religious movements', 'cults', and 'sects', but states that defining movements which are distinct from '*church* or *legitimate movements within the church* is a contentious matter' (ibid., emphasis in original). Groups of Christian origins need to be distinguished from those of other origins, but 'sectarian mentalities and attitudes, i.e. attitudes of intolerance and aggressive proselytism, do not necessarily constitute a sect, nor do they suffice to characterize a sect' (ibid.), because these can be found in groups within the churches and ecclesial communities.

The Report distinguishes 'sects' of Christian origin from 'churches and ecclesial communities' by looking at their teachings: sects have, apart from the Bible, other revealed books or prophetic messages or are groups which exclude certain protocanonical books from the Bible or radically change their content. A passage from a questionnaire explicates 'sects' and 'cults':

a cult or sect is sometimes defined as 'any religious group with a distinctive world view of its own derived from, but not identical with, the teachings of a major world religion'. As we are speaking here of special groups which usually pose a threat to peoples' [sic] freedom and to society in general, cults and sects have also been characterized as possessing a number of distinctive features. These often are that they are authoritarian in structure, that they exercise forms of brainwashing and mind control, that they cultivate group pressure and instil feelings of guilt and fear, etc. The basic work on these characteristic marks was published by an American, Dave Breese, *Know the Marks of Cults*.

(ibid.: 3)

The Report notes a 'serious lack of understanding and knowledge of other Christian churches and ecclesial communities' (ibid.: 4), as some which are not in full communion with the RCC were included in the category 'sect', as were followers of major world religions (Hinduism, Buddhism).

There was virtual unanimity among local church respondents in observing the emergence and proliferation of *new* religious movements, groups, and practices and considering this phenomenon as serious, if not alarming. Only in some countries for example, predominantly Islamic ones, are such developments not pertinent. New religions appear within mainline churches (sects), outside the churches (independent or free churches, prophetic or messianic movements) or 'against the churches (sects, cults)' (ibid.). The last assume churchlike patterns, but 'not all are religious in their real content or ultimate purpose' (ibid.).[100]

NRMs raise pastoral problems, the most immediate is what to do when a family member has joined. Parish priests or local pastoral advisers usually deal with parents and relatives, as there is often only indirect contact with the newly recruited member. Where direct contact is possible and where ex-members need help to reintegrate into society, priests or advisers need psychological skills and expertise. The Report points to vulnerable groups apparently most likely to join: young people from a well-to-do and well-educated background (university campuses are favoured recruitment grounds), although some NRMs target middle-aged people. '[D]ifficult relations with the Church or an irregular marriage situation' are also conducive to NRM membership. NRMs generally attract 'good people'. The reasons for NRMs' success are varied, but they are primarily related to unmet needs and aspirations and NRMs' recruitment strategies, but also to other factors, such as economic advantages, political interest, etc.

While the particular context in which NRMs operate is important, they are symptomatic of the 'depersonalizing structures' of contemporary Western society, which create 'crisis situations' for both individual and wider social contexts. These provoke needs and questions which require psychological and spiritual responses. NRMs claim to have answers, but often respond 'to the affective needs in a way that deadens the cognitive faculties' (ibid.: 5).

Needs and aspirations are expressions of man's quest for wholeness and harmony, participation and realization, truth and meaning, but these are eroded in times of rapid change or acute stress.

While NRMs are perceived as a threat, they are primarily a pastoral challenge. This requires a balance between personal integrity, each religion's right to profess its faith, and believers' right to live according to their conscience. Questionnaire respondents expressed loyalty to dialogue as posited by Conciliar and other Church documents and emphasized general openness and understanding, but pointed to the need for information, education of believers, and a 'renewed pastoral approach'.

In describing the reasons why NRMs have spread widely the Report revisits, but maps in more detail the factors which account for their success. The focus is on individuals' needs and aspirations in modern society, what NRMs offer and their (alleged) recruitment techniques and 'indoctrination procedures'. The crisis situations which raise cognitive and affective needs are characterized as relational, in terms of the individual and society, culture, and the transcendent. Nine categories of needs are identified: quest for belonging/sense of community, quest for answers, longing to be whole, search for cultural identity, need to be appreciated/feel special, quest for spirituality, need for spiritual guidance, need for a vision, need to be involved/participate. Terms are listed which commonly express these needs, together with the ideas or values which NRMs 'appear to offer' (a recurrent phrase, as also noted by other commentators, e.g. Saliba, 1992). Regarding spirituality, people are often not aware of what the Church offers or they are repelled by perceived one-sided emphasis on morality or institutional aspects. One respondent pointed out that individuals feel constrained in discussing religious experience with those in established religion – a serious shortcoming of the RCC.

NRMs' recruitment techniques also account for their success. These are 'often staged' and 'contrived conversion' methods of 'social and psychological manipulation', but those attracted are unaware of this. While NRMs 'often impose their own norms of thinking, feeling and behaving', the RCC's approach 'implies full-capacity informed consent'. NRMs' methods are also 'a combination of *affection* and *deception* (cf. the *love-bombing*, the *personality test* or the *surrender*)' and, although they 'proceed from a positive approach', they 'gradually achieve a type of mind control through the use of abusive behavior modification techniques' (ibid.: 11). Further elements include a subtle introduction process and converts' gradual discovery of their hosts' identity, 'flirty-fishing', free meals, ready-made answers, flattery, isolation (control of rational thinking, elimination of the outside world), continual activity, focus on strong leader.

The section 'Pastoral Challenges and Approaches' deals with 'the symptoms of pathology' in many societies and their impact. Industrialization, urbanization, social upheavals, technocracy, and globalization induce confusion, uprootedness, insecurity, vulnerability. This leaves individuals' aspirations unrealized and real questions unanswered. There 'is a vacuum crying out to be filled', with questionnaire replies pointing to 'many deficiencies and inadequacies in the actual behavior of the Church which can facilitate the success of sects' (ibid.: 13). Respondents' suggested six positive pastoral approaches: first, a rethinking of traditional parish structures to create a greater sense of community; second, greater openness in the Church and better use of the mass media to address the need for evangelization, catechesis, and education for lay people and clergy; third, a personal and holistic approach – people should know they are unique and loved by a personal God – with particular emphasis on the experiential dimension and the healing ministry; fourth, the need for 'inculturation', a topic especially relevant in Africa, to tailor worship and ministry to the cultural environment; fifth, a review of traditional liturgical patterns of prayer and worship to include creativity and celebration: preaching should be centred on the Bible and people rather than theorizing or moralizing; sixth, greater involvement of lay leaders, given increasing shortages of priests and religious vocations, and a softening of the strict hierarchy.

The Report concludes with an outline of the RCC's attitude to NRMs. There is diversity regarding movements and situations. The Church cannot be 'naively irenical', as some NRMs 'can be destructive to personalities, disruptive of families and society, and their tenets far removed from the teachings of Christ and his Church' (ibid.: 15). The Report even states that

> In many countries we suspect, and in some cases know, that powerful ideological forces as well as economic and political interests are at work through the sects which are totally foreign to a genuine concern for the *human* and are using the human for inhumane purposes.
>
> (ibid.: 15–16)

Therefore, 'the faithful', especially young people, have to be informed and 'put on their guard'. Professional help is needed for counselling or legal matters and to support 'appropriate measures on the part of the state'. However, given the beliefs and principles which the Church upholds (respect for individual rights and freedom), it 'cannot simply be satisfied with condemning or combating "sects", with seeing them perhaps outlawed or expelled, and individuals *deprogrammed* against their will' (ibid.: 16, emphasis in original). In the Church's experience, little or no dialogue has been possible with NRMs and they have hindered ecumenical links. The challenge of NRMs stimulates the Church towards greater pastoral efficacy. While trying to understand what they are, the Church must remain faithful to 'the true teaching of Christ' (ibid.) and not allow the preoccupation with NRMs to interfere with ecumenical activities.

The first of the Report's two appendices reproduces extracts from the *Final Report* of the 1985 Extraordinary Synod which called for an assessment and promotion of Vatican II and gave orientations for the Church's renewal. These both addressed the Church's general needs and the needs and aspirations which some seek in NRMs as part of a wider trend towards the return to the sacred. The Synod reiterated statements made in *The Attitude of the Church Towards the Followers of Other Religions*, such as truth in other religions, the commitment to evangelization and catechesis, the centrality of the Bible, the promotion of dialogue and various forms of spiritual life.

The second appendix includes questions for further study, which 'should be undertaken in ecumenical cooperation' (ibid.: 18), such as theological aspects, interdisciplinary projects, psychological and pastoral concerns, NRMs and the family, acculturation and inculturation of NRMs, youth movements, religious freedom in NRMs, and public opinion.

Careful reading of the Report reveals that Roman Catholic clergy and parents' groups share perceptions about what NRMs are, what they do, and why they are successful. They target vulnerable people and fill a vacuum in individuals' lives which is largely created by modernity. They are destructive for individuals, families, and society. They are para-religious groups, sometimes appearing to be religious, while not being religious in content or ultimate purpose. NRMs' success can also be attributed to their recruitment and indoctrination methods, described as 'contrived conversion and training', 'social and psychological manipulation, and 'affection and deception', all objectionable by implication.

Roman Catholic clergy and parents' groups also share the vocabulary which expresses these perceptions: 'deception', 'mind control', 'behaviour modification techniques', 'unconditional surrender', 'consciousness altering methods', etc. And just like parents' groups, the RCC wishes to see the State take appropriate measures. Although, as the Report states, the RCC is prepared to 'recognize, and even support' such measures, it does not clarify what *kind* of measures. Shared perceptions and objectives have facilitated co-operation between clergy and parents' groups, especially locally in parishes regarding pastoral care, and raised the question whether the Report is an 'anti-cult' statement (see Saliba, 1992). However, the Church does not adopt the full 'anti-cult' agenda in rejecting 'deprogramming'. The Church's adherence to religious freedom and individual rights forbids such action. The same principles prohibit the Church to be 'satisfied with condemning or combating' NRMs or 'seeing them outlawed or expelled'.

As the RCC perceives the emergence of NRMs mainly in terms of the failures in mainstream churches, it feels challenged to alter its approach, particularly in parishes. The existence of successful rivals urges the Church to question itself, examine its shortcomings, and devise strategies to counter 'competition'. This entails research into the reasons for the failures, especially regarding young people, and research of NRMs: what they are, what they teach, and how they practise their teachings, hence the study questions at the end of the Report. If NRMs prosper because of deficiencies in the mainstream churches, the RCC is in the same boat as other churches and therefore seeks to activate solidarity and a sense of a common cause through ecumenical channels.

While the RCC recognizes the diversity of NRMs and the contexts in which they operate, it appears to view them as a somewhat sinister phenomenon, as expressed in the suspicion of conspiratorial forces. And although the RCC states commitment to dialogue with other religions, as laid out in *The Attitude of the Church Towards the Followers of Other Religions*, the Report sees few openings for dialogue. It speaks of the experience of generally little or no possibility of dialogue with NRMs and even declares them 'closed to dialogue'.

An NRM response

The only NRM response to the Report is by Steven J. Gelberg (Subhananda dasa), then ISKCON's Director for Interreligious Affairs. His paper on 'The Catholic Church and the Hare Krishna Movement: An Invitation to Dialogue' (Subhananda dasa, 1986b) welcomes the Report as a sign of 'interest and concern about new religions hitherto not in evidence' in the RCC and hopes that the Secretariat for Non-Christians 'will expand its existing boundaries of interreligious fellowship to include members of new and alternative religious organizations' (ibid.: 1). Despite its preliminary nature, the Report 'essays a fair and reasoned critique of the subject' (ibid.). Gelberg offers neither formal critique of, nor formal response to, the Report. His paper was in fact largely completed *before* the Report: it had been prepared for discussions with Roman Catholic educators, clergy, and religious in Ireland in 1983. However, Gelberg responds to the RCC's call for new increased mutual understanding and invites the Church to serious dialogue with ISKCON.

Gelberg is surprised to find statements about 'little or no possibility of dialogue' with NRMs and NRMs being 'closed to dialogue', as ISKCON's founder, Swami Prabhupada, met with Church representatives at various levels and ISKCON members have continually sought contact and dialogue with the Church. (Gelberg may, however, mistake informal dialogue for official Vatican policy.) ISKCON 'is quite open to', and an appropriate partner for, dialogue, both as an NRM and as a representative of 'mainline Hindu tradition' (ibid.: 2). It has sought dialogue with other religions, organizing, for example, a conference with representatives of the Christian tradition in early 1996 to discuss similarities and diverging aspects (see D'Costa, 1996).

Gelberg also addresses wider issues regarding religious pluralism, interfaith encounter, and new religions. He does, however, not wish to 'mount a general defence' of NRMs or 'cults', because they should neither be attacked *en masse* nor defended *en masse*. Each must be studied and experienced in its own right. Vatican II was a watershed for the RCC's attitude towards non-Christian religions by setting 'a new tone of respect' and introducing a less exclusivistic view and new stress on dialogue and greater openness towards the world. Vatican II was also a turning-point for relations between the Church and Hinduism, with some priests and theologians, such as Bede Griffiths, having deepened their insights through travel, study, and residence in India. Gelberg draws parallels between the concept of *bhakti* (selfless surrender and devotion to God) and key Christian concepts, as noted by Western writers, such as Rudolph Otto, Thomas Merton, and Fr Dhavamony. The *Bhagavad-gita* and the *Bhagavata Purana* are fundamental texts in Vaisnavite Hinduism (they elaborate the theology and practice of *bhakti*) and are thus important for Hindu–Christian dialogue.

In sketching the historical background to Vaisnava Hinduism, Gelberg places ISKCON in the tradition of Sri Caitanya, a Vaisnative from Bengal (1486–1534), whose *bhakti* has been a major influence in India. Swami Prabhupada was a 'Caitanyite monk, scholar and religious leader' and ISKCON's 'solid roots in India's devotional heritage have been affirmed by numerous scholars and religious authorities throughout the world' (Subhananda dasa, 1986b: 11). ISKCON is therefore an authentic movement which deserves to be taken seriously as part of the West's changing religious landscape.

Gelberg states that 'anti-cultists' claim that NRM *practices* rather than *beliefs* are objectionable.[101] ISKCON's 'apparent radical otherworldliness, its religious intensity, and its asceticism' (ibid.: 14) have provoked 'anti-cultist' charges of 'brainwashing' and 'mind control'. Yet such allegations can be levelled at any monastic tradition. Gelberg examines ten common allegations against ISKCON and relates them to the RCC's monastic or ascetic traditions, showing that ISKCON's practices are very similar to Christian practices.[102] Also, religion – whether established or new – is subject to psychiatric bias which 'approaches the study of religious persons and religious experience with a reductionist, debunking motive' (ibid.: 24). The 'anti-cult movement' (ACM) applies this approach to NRMs and legitimizes its views and activities by relying on psychiatrists who equate NRM practices as 'manifestations of psychological, even medical, pathology' (ibid.: 25), hence Robbins and Anthony's (1982) concept of 'medicalization'. Gelberg points to the flaws of psychiatric studies (they only involve former NRM members) and to studies which found ISKCON members psychologically healthy.[103]

As to the argument that ISKCON's activities are behind a religious front, its authenticity should be judged 'by the fruits it bears', a biblical criterion (Matt. 7.20), and by first-hand knowledge. The ACM's 'excessive hostility' arises from 'religious prejudice and bigotry' (Melton and Moore, 1982) for which there are historical examples. 'Anti-cultism' is 'essentially antireligious in ideology' (Subhananda dasa, 1986b: 29) which can also be directed against Catholicism (Ted Patrick reportedly 'deprogrammed' converts to Catholicism), but there are reasons why the Catholic monastic tradition has not been targeted by the ACM: the Church is well established in Western society, it is a powerful institution, it is not in the media limelight, Catholic religious are less visible, and monasteries are less likely to cause friction with families, because they do not actively recruit members. The emergence of NRMs has been mainly a media event: they have exaggerated NRMs' characteristics, size, activities, and influence and sensationalized associated issues. Also, 'misinformation and propaganda about ISKCON passed off as authoritative information by sensation- and novelty-seeking journalists' and there were 'libellous press accounts' (ibid.: 37–38).

The RCC has three options for its response to NRMs: a reactive and persecutory stance; relative indifference or aloofness; protagonist for inter-religious understanding and education. The first harbours problems. Given the Report's statements about the necessity to inform young people and support State measures, such an approach could legitimate 'propagandistic, coercive, or repressive' measures. These could backfire, because they could be interpreted as a form of holy war against rivals and invalidate the Church's 'self-declared role as enlightened and impartial advocate of truth and human welfare'. Warning young people with 'hard-core anticult' materials could have a 'boomerang effect' by stirring rather than restraining interest. The Report's commitment to respect religious freedom and its rejection of condemning NRMs and deprogramming are heartening, as this points to a 'reasoned and moderate stance' (ibid.: 30–31). The second option leaves important questions about the RCC's role in religious pluralism, its relationship with religious movements, and its pastoral responsibilities unanswered. 'Anti-cultist' or repressive forces may take the Church's silence as tacit approval. The Church would then fail to uphold the principles of religious freedom and human rights. The third option is the most desirable. Although the Report seems ambivalent about whether the Church should take NRMs seriously, its professed concern with 'the action of the Spirit which is working in unfathomable ways for the accomplishment of God's loving will for all humankind' should compel an approach which regards NRMs as a spiritual concern requiring a theological response.

ISKCON admittedly presents a particular challenge to the Church, because, as a 'foreign' religion in the West, its appeal lies in its specifically Eastern ideas and practices. Yet, just as Christianity points to Christians in the East as evidence for its universality, Eastern spirituality may do likewise in pointing to followers in the West. Contact with ISKCON members allows insight into the appeal of Eastern spirituality. Explaining this appeal as a sociological, psychological or pathological phenomenon leaves out the spiritual dimension, as does the interpretation of NRMs' success in terms of failure in the mainstream churches. RCC and NRMs can co-exist. A 'more theologically sensitive (and spiritually open) approach' is a solution to 'religious and pastoral problems that have arisen' in relation to NRMs (ibid.: 34), an argument advanced by Saliba (1981: 472; cited ibid.):

> A more positive understanding of the new religious movements will be theologically and pastorally more in tune with the Christian spirit and

more suitable for handling the problems which participation in the cults has brought. A Christian reaction which does not contribute to the theological understanding of the cults and to a solution of the pastoral issues they have given rise to is a sterile response.

For Gelberg, this approach is the only possible foundation for dialogue between ISKCON and the Church, a view endorsed, for example, by John Saliba, Paul Mojzes, Gordon Melton and Robert Moore.[104]

The Report speaks about the attitude required for dialogue: respect for the individual and openness and understanding towards sincere believers. There is substantial literature on inter-religious dialogue to guide dialogue between the RCC and NRMs, such as Fr Fallon's article 'For a True Dialogue between Christians and Hindus'. However, the Church needs to overcome prejudice and remain unbiased, particularly in view of 'various channels of public information' having been 'flooded with superficial, sensational, and biased accounts' of NRMs. Openness includes the wish to know the other faith, an attitude which Catholicism has yet to learn, as John Moffitt and Fr Dhavamony have pointed out. The World Council of Churches' *Guidelines on Dialogue* echo this, as does Cardinal Marella's foreword to *Dialogue with Hinduism*.[105] In overcoming prejudice and ignorance, Christians 'should resist the tendency to lump ISKCON together' (ibid.: 38) with groups commonly tagged as 'cults'.[106] Accurate information is required to distinguish authentic from pseudo-religious groups. The Secretariat for Non-Christians' advice that dialogue with non-Christians (for Gelberg, ISKCON is in this category) should judge the 'other' as individuals (rather than representatives of organizations or traditions) is to be endorsed.

Several benefits result from genuine dialogue between the RCC and ISKCON: first, it contributes to dialogue between the Church and Hinduism, because ISKCON offers direct contact with an Eastern religion within the Hindu family. Catholicism itself is influenced by Eastern religion, with retreat programmes incorporating elements of Eastern spirituality. ISKCON is thus a dialogue partner both as an NRM and as a contemporary representative of a long-standing Indian tradition. Second, ISKCON represents a strand of Hinduism which is very close to Christianity and thus a good starting point for Christian–Hindu dialogue. Third, dialogue with NRMs may contribute to the Church's spiritual and ecclesial renewal, as indicated by the Report.[107] The Church can learn from movements like ISKCON; for example, attention for, and commitment to, spiritual life; personal spiritual discipline; experiential and transformational dimensions of spiritual life; inspiration for Christian theology through Vaisnavite philosophy and theology (also Rose, 1986); review of materialism and return to a simpler life.

In turn dialogue will benefit ISKCON. Just as Catholics tend to construct superficial and negative views of ISKCON, ISKCON members tend to do this with regard to Catholics. Also, ISKCON can learn from an institution which has weathered many controversies in its history. NRMs could benefit from constructive criticism and advice to correct shortcomings and mistakes and the RCC's monastic tradition and experience with contemplative life could be helpful for ISKCON members' devotional life.

In conclusion, Gelberg hopes for efforts towards dialogue, especially as it is endorsed by voices within and outside the Church. Those weary of lending 'credibility' or 'respectability' to NRMs by engaging in dialogue should be mindful that 'public relations points' (ibid.: 49) do not make movements succeed or fail. ISKCON's existence does not depend on dialogue with the RCC, but there is genuine change in the Church's motives and approach towards NRMs. Gelberg offers an 'affirmative response' to dialogue and invites anyone concerned – ecclesial, lay or academic – to respond.

Gelberg responds to the Vatican Report on ISKCON's behalf. He welcomes the RCC's call for better mutual understanding and extends ISKCON's invitation to serious dialogue. He examines the Catholic views of Hindu traditions and Vaisnava *bhakti*, discusses implications of 'anti-cult' allegations for the ascetical and monastic traditions within Catholicism, and outlines the benefits of dialogue for both sides. For Gelberg, the Report is an overall positive document which can lead to fruitful dialogue with NRMs and ISKCON. He distances ISKCON from the 'cult' image by rejecting the 'cult' label and refuting criticism from the ACM and media. He seeks to show that ISKCON is part of the great traditions of India by charting ISKCON's emergence from Vaisnavism.

Despite ambivalent and vague passages, Gelberg finds the Report a platform for dialogue. He argues that dialogue with ISKCON is not restricted, that it fits into RCC's dialogue with Hinduism, into inter-religious dialogue, which is far more developed and established than dialogue with NRMs and forms a framework which can accommodate dialogue with ISKCON. Gelberg also seeks to show how much theological ground and devotional practices ISKCON and the RCC share, which could be used for wider discussion. Theologians, such as Moffitt, Dhavamony, and Saliba, are cited to underline the validity of this view and to stress both challenge and benefit of dialogue with NRMs. As dialogue also benefits ISKCON, it is of mutual interest.

Gelberg's essay is a good example of NRMs 'talking back' using language and discourse equal to those of the churches and academics. This is one of the most persuasive features of his claim to be taken seriously as a participant in the debate.

The F.I.U.C. project

F.I.U.C's (*Fédération Internationale des Universités Catholiques*, International Federation of Catholic Universities) Center for Coordination of Research in Rome undertook further in-depth study of NRMs, a need which had been pointed out by the Vatican Report. The same four dicasteries of the Roman Curia which had co-operated for the Report established the 'Research Project on the Phenomenon of Sects, Cults, New Religious

Movements Today' and implemented it in five stages. The project leader was first Fr Remi Hoeckman, OP, then Dr Michael Fuss. Staff of member universities and other experts in the field were invited to co-operate. The project's stated aim was to reach 'a better understanding of the dynamics and content of this phenomenon [NRMs], as well as its implications and consequences for the lives of many people, and therefore for the pastoral ministry of the Church'. Although the project had a more theoretical basis in academic and theological expertise, its underlying concern was still pastoral.

The project outline underscored the project's importance for the Church and its impact on the international community. Global and potentially damaging aspects of the NRM phenomenon were stressed, together with economic, social, cultural, and political aspects which had also featured in both the Vatican and Cottrell Reports. The project's five phases consisted of, first, the information or orientation phase (until late 1988), which created a network of information and communication among around 50 experts. Actual research and preparation of reports took place in phase two (1989), followed by a 'phase of discernment' (until August 1990), which envisaged participating experts receiving reports and identifying specific questions for further study. Phase four (autumn 1990–spring 1991) consisted of five regional seminars with selected experts, local church leaders, etc., to discuss results. The final phase envisaged the publication of reports.

In early 1990, the contributions of experts (members of Catholic Universities across the continents) were circulated in a *Dossier* (Fuss, 1990a). This concluded the orientation phase. The dossier was meant for internal study in participating institutions. It includes 27 papers (an additional paper on new movements within the Churches had to be withdrawn 'due to a problem of co-ordination') in three sections: NRMs as a global phenomenon, continental surveys, and the Christian Church and NRMs. The contributors cover Latin America, North America, Africa, Europe, and the Far East and a wide range of aspects, including conversion and recruitment, social and emotional aspects of NRM membership, Jehovah's Witnesses and the Bible, NRMs' religious nature, UC theology, syncretism, sects in African cities, mission and new religions, etc. The term 'new religious movements' is used as an umbrella for 'sects' (e.g. Pentecostalism, Jehovah's Witnesses), African movements, popular religion, and NRMs (e.g. the UC). The papers not only deal with the emergence of new religions and related phenomena in the West, but also with new forms of religion across the globe and the particular features they have engendered in specific regions and localities.

The first regional seminar was an international meeting at Creighton University, Omaha, USA (May 1991). The second was the European symposium on 'Religious Renewal in Europe: Towards a "Dialogue in Truth" (Dignitate humanae, 3) with New Religious Movements' in Vienna (late October 1991). The Latin American symposium was held in Quito, Ecuador (June 1992); it attended to religious pluralism and apologetic dialogue, a sociological and theological discussion of NRMs, and pastoral concerns.

The Africa seminar took place in Kinshasa, Democratic Republic of the Congo, formerly Zaire (November 1992), and the seminar for Asia and Oceania took place in Manila, the Philippines (February 1993). Publications resulting from the project comprise the proceedings of the last three conferences (Pontificia Universidad Católica del Ecuador – F.I.U.C., 1993; Centre d'Études des Religions Africaine, 1994; Salazar, 1994) and *Rethinking New Religious Movements* (Fuss, 1998) which includes papers written over almost seven years, several of which had been in the *Dossier*.

The pastoral concern of the Church in Europe

Hans Gasper's (1990) 'The Pastoral Concern of the Church in Continental Europe, Especially in German-Speaking Countries' is a F.I.U.C. *Dossier* paper. It describes the new religiosity in Germany and the RCC's position. The paper is discussed here to show, first, the kind of information and thinking gathered in the *Dossier*, and second, the relevance of its perspective to the German context. According to Gasper, the sciences have not fulfilled the hope of replacing religion and human vulnerability, highlighted by industrial and post-industrial society, which makes us realize how 'incurably religious' we are. The burdens created by science and progress (weapons of mass destruction, environmental disasters, etc.) have thrown belief in science into crisis. This has, in turn, led to the rediscovery of religion at a time marked by Habermas's *neue Unübersichtlichkeit* (new opaqueness): deep scepticism and great fear of the future, but also confidence about mastering the problems of the modern world.

Yet, the new religiosity is just another 'product' in the supermarket of transcendental offers – 'esoteric consumerism', syncretistic, merging archaic with magical elements, and motivated by an 'irrational quest for alternatives'. Esoterism, some of it classified as 'New Age', promises advice on life's problems and a more enjoyable life. Is the quest for religious alternatives really a fundamental re-orientation or merely the instrumentalization of religion? Gasper perceives two tendencies in New Age: a gnostic aspiration to raise oneself through knowledge of the divine self and the desire to progress through an inward course. The individual is central in redeeming him/herself through spiritual and esoteric knowledge. There are also 'youth religions', 'offshoots of the westward movement of eastern religiosity' (ibid.: 679), evangelical and pentecostal groups, and traditional sects (Mormons, Jehovah's Witnesses, etc). The new religiosity has virtually bypassed the mainstream churches. Spiritual revivals within them have only addressed committed members, although 'awakening' these is important for evangelization. The new religiosity revitalizes the question of man's origins and the purpose of human existence. 'Selection mentality' encourages random choices in the religious supermarket, because all religious messages are perceived to be similar.

Drawing on Luckmann (1980), Gasper describes threatened identity as a

fundamental problem in contemporary society. It is expressed in the contrast between pluralization and atomization of all spheres and confuses
those unable to cope with life. It is also reflected in syncretism and selection
mentality (in 'post-modern' religiosity or 'city religion') and 'repressive,
fundamentalist anti-cultures' (e.g. *Jugendreligionen*, Jehovah's Witnesses,
etc.), both offering escape. ('Fundamentalist' here means based on a set of
beliefs which are 'fundamentals' for the groups in question – for Gasper,
both NRMs and traditional sects, some of which have political, social, and
economic interests. He points to dualism regarding doctrine and social
relations: highly regulated social contacts and rigid hierarchy.) The Vatican
Report spoke of 'depersonalizing social structures' which deprive individuals
of a sense of belonging and identity.

The term *Jugendreligionen* is now established in German-speaking countries, commonly used with 'so-called' and quotation marks: *sogenannte
'Jugendreligionen'*. They are characterized by: quest for religion and meaning; firm convictions, idealism, commitment; sense of belonging and community; enthusiastic and unquestioning devotion to a master, including
acceptance of change; 'questionable' forms of meditation and therapy;
'repressive' group discipline; economic dependence; 'dishonest' recruitment;
economic and political goals. *Jugendreligionen* are new in the West, offer
Eastern, esoteric or Western secular ideas, and appeal mainly to the post-
1960s generation. The terms 'destructive cults' and 'new religious movements outside the churches' are also in use. (Gasper does not indicate which
terms are appropriate.) *Jugendreligionen* combine a 'volatile mixture' of
features which are not new in themselves. Although the 'brainwashing' concept explains followers' dependence, it simplifies a more complex process.
Following Luckmann, Gasper sees this process as regressive identity formation, identity borrowed from a strong personality or overpowering group.
The disproportionate number of women in *Jugendreligionen* 'calls for
reflection', especially as women want to be more involved in Church
matters.

Charting loss of identity and break with tradition Zsifkovits (1990)
suggests that, in the late 1960s and early 1970s, Germany experienced a
more radical break with tradition than other countries, creating a wide generation gap regarding attitudes towards institutions and values. This gap
explains the significant number of church leavers, increasing numbers of
unmarried couples, and decline in baptism. Gasper sets this against the
background of National Socialism and its aftermath, including the geographical reorganization in the postwar period. Economic prosperity, technological progress, and radical social change have favoured materialism.
Yet, the current post-materialist outlook – with some renunciation of
materialism – rarely leads to re-orientation towards the churches or
Christianity. Eastern Germany is further evidence for the break with tradition: 40 years of atheistic State policy have created conditions which the
churches need to address (disrupted ties with the churches and a strong

demand for consumer goods). Churches must recover from their 'ghetto situation' and lack of information. They played an important role in the liberation process and new religions have become very active.

Role and status of the established churches are twofold: they have the character of *Volkskirche* (they are part of cultural and social identity, provide rites of passage, and contribute to marking significant events, thus functioning as 'civil religion') and they are moving towards free church status, a development which is *de facto* rather than *de jure*. Therefore, individuals relate to them in different ways: some leave and do not want their children baptized; some leave to join other groups; some hold dual membership (the most common position); some remain committed. Diversity of membership reflects perceptions of the churches and Christianity: aberrations and disasters throughout history are laid at the Church's doorstep, as is the 'trauma' of a Christian upbringing. As new Christian movements have no past, they find followers among church opponents. The RCC also faces 'cognitive dissonance' from within, often about sexual morality and authority, which weakens it in relation to innovative groups. Yet, Germans still look towards the churches for guidance on important issues and this should be harnessed.

Six areas give rise to 'exceptional' pastoral difficulties: lack of religious socialization at home, with repercussions for religious education at school; tensions in the RCC about sexual morality; divorcées feeling excluded from the sacraments on re-marriage; impact of high divorce rate on children; women's aspirations to be involved on all levels of social and church hierarchy; significant effects of modern life's pressures on individuals. Four areas present problems for teaching the faith: experience and belief, the path of faith and completeness, orthopraxy and orthodoxy, politics and mysticism. Faith is holistic and oriented towards the centre: the self-revelation of the trinitarian God in Jesus; pastoral work should focus on this centre by devising strategies, such as developing new ways of induction, evangelization, renewal of baptism and faith, seminars on faith; making the path of faith a staged journey; presenting the link between experience and faith; relating belief, prayer, and liturgy to body and emotions; leading others to this experience; renewing and creating opportunities for learning about the faith (families, parishes, spiritual movements); providing spiritual companionship to counter individuals' isolation; counteracting the image of a fearful God and tackling the Church's image; exploring the Trinity and the role of Jesus; exploring 'forgotten truths' (eschatology, healing, angels, demons); strengthening the affiliation of those (still) linked to the Church through its commitment to peace, justice, and the preservation of Creation. In the face of individualism and pluralism, a main objective of the Church's pastoral work is to 'regain permanency and commitment'.

Religious themes in NRMs

John Saliba's (1990d) extensive contribution to the F.I.U.C. *Dossier* ' "Religious" Themes in the New Religious Movements' tackles several issues: three major positions on NRMs' religious nature and factors questioning it, two specific instances (TM, Scientology) which illustrate the problems of designating 'cults' as 'religious' institutions, five major themes which are applicable to NRMs, and the evaluation of NRMs' 'religiousness' or 'spirituality'. Saliba's paper is important because it draws both on academic work on NRMs and Catholic theology, a feature found also in Michael Fuss's paper (see below).

Regarding terminology, social scientists and historians of religion use 'new religious movements', 'new religions', 'fringe religions', 'marginal religious groups', and 'alternative spiritual groups', with detailed discussions in D. Martin (1983) and Ellwood (1986). These terms attempt to find a neutral classification for these groups, but treat them as equal to traditional religions. Popular works, the media, and some psychologists and psychiatrists (e.g. Clark *et al.*, 1981; Langone, 1982) use 'cults' and 'destructive cultism'.[108] They imply that such groups should not be compared with the world religions and that they are evil, because they divert people from genuine religion and cause behaviour which is morally wrong and/or detrimental to members' psychological and social welfare. Like Gasper, Saliba does not state which term(s) to use. He speaks of 'so-called cults' and then mainly of 'cults' (without qualification). Yet, he says, the terminology debate focuses on how to define religion. Saliba identifies three standpoints regarding the religious nature of 'cults', which see them as: pseudo-religious organizations (mainly the ACM's stance), unorthodox religious groups (often the stance among Christian fundamentalists and evangelicals),[109] and genuine religious movements (generally the stance of the social sciences and academic study of religion). The cases of TM and Scientology illustrate NRMs' 'religiousness' (also Saliba, 1995: 167–197). While TM insists it is not a religion, the court in New Jersey ruled in the late 1970s that it is (also Spiritual Counterfeits Project, 1978; Maarbjerg, 1978; Baird, 1982). Scientology's case is the reverse: it claims to be a religion, but the US Internal Revenue Service contested this and did not grant tax exempt status between 1970 and 1972.

Most NRMs, even those whose religious character has been questioned, share five religious features: concept of God or ultimate reality (cosmology), view of human nature (metaphysics), belief in the afterlife (eschatology), ethical norms (morality), and spirituality. Saliba describes each feature, provides an example of its appearance in an NRM, and compares this with mainstream theological concepts.

First, the concept of God, considered central to religion, gives meaning to the universe and human life. Religion is a quest for meaning, which accounts for the success of new religions; 'religious seekers' (Lofland and Stark, 1965) leave their childhood religion to embark on a journey of spiritual discovery.

New religions provide alternative ways of understanding and experiencing the sacred, often in contradiction to the mainline churches' position, as the idea of God in The Way International illustrates. Second, religions share the conviction that something is wrong with the present human condition; a remedy is needed. Salvation is deliverance from what ails the individual and mankind, from affliction and destructive forces. It is also the promise of newness of life, a life free from sin, sickness, and ignorance. It is attained by personal effort or divine intervention. The leaders of Heaven's Gate (Balch and Taylor, 1978) constructed such a path to salvation. Third, belief in an afterlife, also central to religion, is highlighted in spiritualism and channelling. For Spiritualists, the soul survives beyond death and contact with the dead is possible through mediums or channelling. Channelling involves paranormal sources (spirits of the dead, angels, ascended masters) or the 'channel's' divine dimension, from which humans receive or communicate information. Fourth, religion links religious goals and human behaviour considered conducive to attaining such goals. In Christianity, the ten commandments provide rules for moral behaviour. Most new religions have moral codes, even if followers do not always respect them. The UC and ISKCON, for example, have conservative and restrictive rules. Fifth, the appeal of NRMs lies in the promise of a unique and transforming religious or mystical experience. Methods to induce such experience include yoga, meditation, and speaking in tongues. The Vatican Report identified this appeal in needs and aspirations which motivate membership. Its recommendations – to strengthen parish communities and stress evangelization, catechism, and religious education (reiterated again by the Pope in March 2004 while presiding at a Mass in Vatican City – indirectly recognize NRMs' religious and spiritual benefits.

For Saliba, five areas have attracted controversy and criticism regarding NRMs and undermined NRMs' claims to authentic spirituality: sexuality, money, health, social consciousness, and deception. Some NRMs have restrictive codes, but others have promoted sexual practices which counter Christian morality, for example the COG's 'flirty fishing', inappropriate behaviour of some gurus (sexual contact with disciples, see Saliba, 1990d: 182–183; Bancroft, 1993), and Tantric practices in some yoga groups. These have contributed to the negative image of 'cults', but also highlighted an issue largely neglected in the West: the relationship between religion and sexuality. Second, some NRMs' finances have been widely criticized by ACM groups and social scientists (e.g. Harris, 1981), for fraud, exploitation, materialism, power hunger, accumulation of wealth, and tax evasion.[110] While NRMs need strategies to manage finances, their methods to raise funds differ.[111] Saliba considers two issues, which NRMs have not addressed sufficiently: the legal aspect, what is legitimate and illegitimate practice (potential friction with the State may come to the fore, especially when courts need to pronounce on this aspect – see Robbins *et al.*, 1985; Kelley, 1982), and reconciling wealth with spiritual goals and moral demands. Third, NRM members' mental health has been a contested issue, with allegations that rigid lifestyles and indoctrination techniques cause physical, mental, and psychological problems (see Richardson, 1980; Saliba, 1987). Alternative perspectives (e.g. Kilbourne, 1985; Richardson, 1985b) counter this view, arguing that NRM membership is a way of coping with life crises (e.g. Levine, 1984; Galanter, 1989) or a rite of passage (e.g. Melton and Moore, 1982), and thus attribute NRMs a useful function in Western society. Other aspects have caused concern, such as their disdain for orthodox medicine, fasting, chastity and celibacy, long hours of prayer. Although these are recognized 'religious' practices, the health issue in 'cults' persists. Fourth, many NRMs are perceived to lack social consciousness and direct individuals to focus on their godly potential in a narcissistic way, despite claims about improving the human condition and building ideal societies. Bird (1986) shows NRMs' general indifference to issues of social justice and Saliba shows this in DLM (Elan Vital). This apolitical stance contrasts with the Christian stress on social justice as an expression of faith and could be evidence for NRM's para-religious nature, but comparison with the monastic tradition controverts this. Finally, 'cults' have been accused of deception – recruitment and fundraising under false pretences – which cannot be reconciled with any ethical standards. Another aspect of deception is equally serious, yet rarely considered: dual membership.[112] Some groups, including Scientology, TM, and DLM, stress that members do not have to relinquish their previous faith, in most cases Christianity. Yet, differences in theology and practice preclude double commitment.

Although most 'cults' are expressions of genuine religion, they are not 'perfect embodiments' of mankind's spiritual longing. While offering alternative theologies, they do not necessarily have more cogent answers to existential questions or better ways of achieving happiness or union with the divine. Therefore, NRMs need to be assessed. Rapid changes in some groups over the last 20 years suggest distinction between those which promote spiritual growth and those who stunt it. Three approaches can achieve assessment: first, basing evaluation on the match between an NRM's activities and its stated aims, as Deikman (1983) proposes; second, using Welwood's (1983) criteria for discriminating between real and fake spiritual authority, which distinguish 'mindful surrender' from 'mindless submission'; third, applying Anthony, Ecker, and Wilber's (1987) five confusions in new religions: between spiritual perfection and worldly skill, ordinary and transcendent types of non-rational experience or transcendence and regression, transcendence of good and evil and antinomianism, detachment and dissociation and repression, detachment and potent or effective attachment. Some of the 'more balanced writers' admit that not all alternative groups are authentic paths to personal transformation, which is not an 'indirect attack against the cults'. It is 'cautionary advice' which helps young adults to make important decisions about their future and the Church to stimulate 'renewal for greater pastoral efficacy', as the Vatican Report suggested.

Redemptoris Missio

In 1990, Pope John Paul II issued the encyclical *Redemptoris Missio* on the permanent validity of the Church's missionary mandate (Catholic Truth Society, 1991). As the title suggests, it affirms the Church's missionary duty and impresses its urgency on Church members, but enlarges on most topics and aspects addressed in *The Attitude of the Church Towards the Followers of Other Religions*. Were it not for the fact that the encyclical is an important reference point for Vatican officials and commentators in discussing dialogue with NRMs, there would be no need to mention it here.

Redemptoris Missio invites the Church to renew her missionary commitment and clarifies 'doubts and ambiguities regarding missionary activity'. Mission is not replaced by dialogue, but respects freedom of conscience and religious freedom. Mission is an issue of faith and every Church member must bear witness to the Christian faith and life. The encyclical charts 'paths of mission', which are evangelization, proclamation, conversion, forming local churches, ecclesial basic communities, inculturation, inter-religious dialogue forming people's conscience, and charitable works.

Dialogue with other religions is 'a method and means of mutual knowledge and enrichment' and thus not in opposition to mission. The Church sees no conflict between proclamation and dialogue, but they are separate approaches. Dialogue should be 'conducted and implemented with the conviction that *the Church is the ordinary means of salvation* and that *she alone* possesses the fulness of the means of salvation' and 'does not originate from tactical concerns or self-interest' (emphasis in original). It is a means 'to uncover "the seeds of the Word", "a ray of that truth which enlightens all men" ' and other religions stimulate the Church to examine her own identity more deeply (ibid.: 39). Those engaged in dialogue must be open to understanding 'without pretence or close-mindedness', there must be 'mutual advancement on the road of religious inquiry and experience', and 'dialogue leads to inner purification and conversion'. Dialogue happens at various levels, for example between experts or official representatives, but contributions from the laity are indispensable.

Redemptoris Missio does not address any specific issues regarding NRMs, but refers to them in general terms: contemporary religious and social upheavals, including the 'proliferation of messianic cults and religious sects' (ibid.: 23), have created a 'vast horizon of mission', 'Christian and para-Christian sects are sowing confusion', and the 'expansion of these sects represents a threat' for the Church (ibid.: 36).

Dialogue and Proclamation

Another Vatican document, *Dialogue and Proclamation: Reflections and Orientations on Interreligious Dialogue and the Proclamation of the Gospel of Jesus Christ* (Arinze and Tomko, 1991),[113] outlines the RCC's attitude towards other religions and the basis on which to conduct dialogue with them. The authors, Cardinal Francis Arinze, President of the Pontifical Council for Interreligious Dialogue (PCID; formerly Secretariat for Non-Christians), and Cardinal Jozef Tomko, Prefect of the Congregation for the Evangelization of Peoples (CEP), describe possible forms of dialogue, the dispositions required, and potential obstacles. While stressing the importance of proclaiming the gospel, they examine how to reconcile it with dialogue. The reference to 'other religions' suggests that attitudes towards NRMs might be extrapolated from this document.

Dialogue and Proclamation was a joint project of the PCID and CEP, two dicasteries of the Roman Curia, which are concerned with the Church's role in non-Christian countries. The document went through careful preparation before publication and developed alongside *Redemptoris Missio* to complement it. Both texts address similar topics and, although different in authority, style, and scope, 'they are alike in the spirit which influences them' (ibid.: 205). The main questions in *Dialogue and Proclamation* are: how do dialogue (as part of the Church's mission of evangelization) and proclamation relate to one another? Are they mutually exclusive? How can they be reconciled? The document's purpose is to provide clarification and pastoral orientation for those with 'a leadership role in the community' or those 'engaged in formation work', underpinned by references to Vatican II and *Evangelii nuntiandi*, Pope Paul VI's Apostolic Exhortation.

In *The Attitude of the Catholic Church to the Followers of Other Religions*, the PCID viewed dialogue and proclamation as 'component elements and authentic forms of the one evangelizing mission of the Church', an aspect which *Dialogue and Proclamation* considers further. Three reasons make dialogue and proclamation relevant: first, there is new awareness of religious plurality in today's world. Religions 'continue to inspire and influence the lives of millions' (ibid.: 211) who cannot be ignored. Second, understanding of inter-religious dialogue is gradual, its practice hesitant in some places, and situations differ according to cultural, social, and political factors. Third, dialogue raises problems: some think it should replace proclamation, some think it of no value at all, some question which should take priority. This points to the need for doctrinal and pastoral guidance. Inter-religious dialogue and proclamation play a dual role, as affirmed by John Paul II on World Day of Prayer for Peace in Assisi (October 1986) and in his address to the PCID's Plenary Assembly in 1987. This affirmation encouraged the PCID to explore this dual role further.

Dialogue and Proclamation defines 'dialogue', 'religion', and 'religious traditions'. It points to several meanings of dialogue: reciprocal communication, attitude of respect and friendship, and, in religious pluralism, witness and exploration of religious convictions, including 'all positive and constructive interreligious relations with individuals and communities of other faiths which are directed at mutual understanding and enrichment' (ibid.: 214). The latter is the one used in the document. The terms 'religions' and 'religious traditions' 'are used here in a generic and analogical sense' (ibid.: 215), but do *not* include NRMs: *Dialogue and Proclamation* 'will not treat of dialogue with the followers of "New Religious Movements" due to the diversity of situations which these movements present and the need for discernment on the human and religious values which each contains' (ibid.: 215–216). A footnote refers to the Vatican Report.

An overall appraisal of *Dialogue and Proclamation* reveals its reaffirmation of positive values in believers of other religions and traditions as a sound basis for dialogue. The document also reaffirms the RCC's commitment to dialogue with non-Christians, as promulgated by relevant Vatican II documents and *Redemptoris Missio*. However, in defining 'religions' and 'religious traditions' – terms which *prima facie* include NRMs – *Dialogue and Proclamation* explicitly *excludes* these from considerations on dialogue, because they are a separate issue which requires particular attention and treatment. Therefore, this document contributes nothing towards determining the RCC's attitude towards NRMs. An initially promising avenue of extrapolating from *general* comments the *specific* treatment of NRMs has led into a blind alley. The remainder of *Dialogue and Proclamation* is thus of no further consequence here.

The above leads one to conclude that Vatican thinking on inter-religious dialogue develops in parallel to thinking on dealing with NRMs. This is supported by lack of evidence that findings from the F.I.U.C. project fed into the Vatican process at this point. It is, however, confusing to an outsider that Vatican representatives frequently refer to documentation about inter-religious dialogue, when they make statements about NRMs, because this creates the impression that guidelines for inter-religious dialogue inform the Church's approach to NRMs. This is exactly what NRMs, such as ISKCON, want: embedding dialogue within established channels of dialogue with the world religions, as Steven Gelberg's paper shows. It seems, however, that for the Vatican, dialogue with 'other religions' does not automatically include dialogue with NRMs. Exploration of other documents will elucidate these points.

Response to NRMs in progress

At the International Seminar on 'New Religious Movements: The European Situation' in April 1990 (organized jointly by CESNUR and the Swiss National Fund for Scientific Research and sponsored by the (then) Bishop of Lugano, Mgr Eugenio Correcco), Dr Teresa Gonçalves (1990), a PCID representative, introduced her paper on 'The Church and New Religious Movements' with two quotations from John Paul II's address to the European Bishops' VII Symposium of 1989. The first endorsed the duty of mission, the second pointed to the spiritual decay in Europe. Both suggest a crisis of understanding and ignorance of the Catholic faith, a crisis linked to the emergence of NRMs in the West. (Gonçalves uses 'NRMs' and 'sects' interchangeably, without qualification.) The Vatican Report had mainly analysed the causes for NRMs' emergence in Western society, explaining their success in terms of needs and aspirations. The Report's description of these needs as 'so many expressions of the human search for wholeness and harmony, participation and experience: as so many attempts to meet the human quest for truth and meaning of existence' relates to general questions of religion and 'implies a positive evaluation of the causes'. The Church perceives NRMs as a problem, but also as a challenge because many people have not received the 'authentic Gospel message' to fill the void in their lives. However, internal causes are combined with external causes, such as increased mobility, growing interdependence, and powerful communications which assist the spread of NRMs. The proceedings of the WCC's conference in Amsterdam in 1986 contained useful information about the latter, showing that NRMs are largely of American origin. The F.I.U.C. project would shed more light on this aspect.

The Church has examined NRMs from various angles and within different contexts, such as new evangelization, training priests, the situation of local churches, etc. 'Even when not explicitly referred to we find light on these realities [NRMs] in many pontifical documents and at meetings promoted by the Holy See' (ibid.),[114] including, first, the Church's reflections on ecclesial movements, whose formation was recommended by the Vatican Report. The 1987 Synod on the Laity saw them as 'one of many signs of the Spirit' which 'continues to renew the youth of the Church' and 'to inspire . . . holiness and solidarity'. NRMs are such a sign: they question the Church, but will stir it to find answers 'in the form of new-style communities and spiritual experiences' (ibid.: 3). There are analogies between NRMs and ecclesial movements, but the latter are characterized by communion of faith and charity. John Paul II's *Pontifical Exhortation* stated five criteria for ecclesiality: primacy to the call to sanctity for every Christian, responsibility to confess the Catholic faith, testimony to a strong filial communion with Pope and bishops, collaboration with other forms of the Church's apostolate, commitment to be present in society. The ecclesial movements' role consists in lay people testifying to their faith, concern for people at the margins, attitude of dialogue and collaboration, and closeness to 'the man in the street'. This role was highlighted by the ecclesial movements' contribution to the 1989 plenary of the Pontifical Council for the Pastoral Care of Migrants and Itinerant People which deliberated on the 'Spread of the Sects'. Second, the letter of the Congregation for the Doctrine of Faith (1989) on Christian meditation 'does not question authentic inter-religious dialogue', but warns against 'the danger of syncretism, when superficial and scantily formed Christians seek spiritual experiences' through methods used by NRMs. There is danger in 'a spiritual privatism which is incapable of a free openness to the transcendental God' (Gonçalves, 1990: 4). Third, the European bishops' March 1990 meeting in Fatima discussed the role of social communications and mass media, with particular reference to a united Europe, the fall of Communism, and open borders to the East – opportunities for both Church and NRMs. Fourth, the African Synod and the fifth centenary of the evangelization of America gave the Church occasion to reflect on its mission, inculturation, and religious pluralism. Fifth, the topic of inter-religious dialogue, an essential element of mission, was expounded in various documents, such as *The Attitude of the Church Towards the Followers of Other Religions, Dialogue and Proclamation*, the 1986 meeting for peace in Assisi, and the Pope's subsequent address to the Roman Curia.

Yet, despite all the thought and deliberation about NRMs, the Church 'has taken no official position on dialogue with NRM[s]'. Gonçalves suggests that 'perhaps there cannot be an all-inclusive position' so that 'each NRM has to be taken on its own and the way it develops [has to] be observed'. She interprets two kinds of movements in the Pope's post-Assisi address in this light: those which 'reflect the genius and the spiritual "riches" which God has given to the people' and those 'in which are revealed the limitation, the evolutions and the falls of the human spirit which is undermined by the spirit of evil in history' (ibid.: 5). This distinction points to discerning the authentic values in any expression of religiosity.

Dialogue with NRMs on a personal level (as opposed to NRMs as organizations) is possible and not limited, regardless of origins. The encyclical *Ecclesiam Suam* provides the basis: 'Wherever men are trying to understand themselves and the world, we can communicate with them . . . If there exists in men a soul naturally christian [sic], we desire to show it our respect and to enter in conversation with it.' It refers specifically to dialogue where 'one discovers how different the ways are which lead to the light of faith, and it is possible to make them converge on the same goal. Even if our ways are divergent, they can become complementary by forcing our reasoning process out of the worn paths and by obliging it to deepen its research to find fresh expressions' (ibid.: 5, 6).

In summary, Teresa Gonçalves refers to existing Vatican initiatives concerned with the analysis and study of NRMs: the Vatican Report and F.I.U.C. project. Both demonstrate that the RCC takes NRMs seriously. Both attempt to evaluate causes and conditions which allow NRMs to emerge and spread globally. The Report identified 'internal' (psychological) and 'external' (social, cultural) conditions to explain NRMs' success. In assessing the phenomenon, the Church welcomes meetings such as the Amsterdam consultation and the Lugano seminar. However, at that point, the Church had no official position regarding NRMs. Whatever stance had developed was extrapolated from Vatican initiatives and sources, including the importance ascribed to ecclesial communities, the letter on Christian meditation, various synods and bishops' meetings, *The Attitude of the Church Towards the Followers of Different Religions*, papal addresses, and encyclicals. It is important, however, that this extrapolation needs to be done by those conversant in the language and spirit of these documents, namely Vatican 'insiders'. Gonçalves shows that there is overall willingness for dialogue with NRMs as organizations, which derives from the Church's belief that God's plan embraces all people in various ways. However, given differences between religions 'of God' and religions 'of the devil', the Church needs discernment – a recurrent statement. Further, the willingness for dialogue with individual NRM members is unreserved, because, as *Ecclesiam Suam* states, the Church wishes to engage with anything 'naturally Christian' in man.

The view of the Pontifical Council for Dialogue with non-Believers

At the Lugano seminar, Elisabeth Peter (1990) of *The Pontifical Council for Dialogue with non-Believers* reported on the Council's survey on the search for happiness and Christian faith. Drawing on 135 responses to questionnaires sent to bishops' conferences, Catholic universities, theology departments, conferences of male and female religious, and 'unbelievers' interested in dialogue with the Church, Peter examined the link between NRMs and abandonment of the Christian faith in Europe. The survey showed that people need something beyond material well-being to make their lives meaningful and happy. The quest for happiness or this 'inborn metaphysical need' is reflected in the pursuit of new religiosity, a religion without belief in a personal god and without the demand for great commitment. The New Age movement provides such a religion. Its influence has grown in Europe, because, unlike other alternative movements, it presents an optimistic vision: it promotes the power of consciousness, a holistic world vision, an impersonal god, and the process of evolution. It offers an umbrella for a wide spectrum of doctrines and practices and attracts Christians who experience problems with the Church, its doctrines or representatives. This applies all the more when they are not well educated and not required to relinquish their former faith. Elements in New Age thinking echo Christian concepts, such as the 'coming age' and concern for the environment.

NRMs incorporate elements from Eastern religions, sometimes appropriating Eastern techniques improperly. Although some Christians have been working towards integrating Christian and Oriental spirituality, the 'undiscerning introduction of methods of spirituality linked to a completely different cultural background' is bound to 'create numerous problems for European Christians' and becomes 'a danger for their faith' (ibid.: 6). The letter on Christian meditation is concerned with Christians' interest in Eastern forms of meditation, which is an attempt to fuse Christian meditation with something non-Christian, although, the letter concedes, one can take from oriental traditions what is useful, 'as long as the Christian conception of prayer, its logic and requirements, are never obscured' (ibid.: 8). It calls upon Catholics to practise discernment, because 'spiritual well-being' induced by physical posture and breathing should not be mistaken for the 'authentic consolations of the Holy Spirit' (ibid.). If individuals' moral constitution cannot absorb such experience, it can lead to psychological disorders or moral deviations.

NRMs' practices are often 'deformations and misuse of authentic non-Christian spirituality' (ibid.: 9) and, if applied in an undiscerning way, endanger the faith of Christians. NRMs present a challenge to Christian churches: why do Christians look elsewhere for what is available in their own tradition? The need for spirituality will not be met by a religion which is only administrative, social, or purely rational. The Church needs to help Christians understand and live its spirituality and convey to them that this spirituality is also demanding.

In summary, although based on a survey, Elisabeth Peter's paper does not provide any of the questions asked nor gives details about the survey method. The respondents do not appear to be representative of society as a whole. The findings are used to discuss the link between NRMs' success and defection from Christianity. Man has an inherent longing for the transcendent, which material affluence cannot compensate. Europeans are turning towards non-Christian religiosity, especially New Age, to satisfy this longing. The methods of New Age groups and NRMs are mainly derived from Eastern religions. They are attractive because they are new and exotic. Although some Christians have sought to integrate Christianity with Eastern spirituality, improper application of such techniques is detrimental. They should therefore not be mixed with Christian practices. Meditation might tempt Christians to include Eastern elements, but they need to be discerning about authentic Eastern practices. The Church is challenged by NRMs: Christians are turning away from their faith and cannot see that it can meet their spiritual needs. The Church must assist Christians in understanding the richness of the faith and living it fully. Again, the key concepts in this paper are *challenge* and *discernment*.

The Fourth Extraordinary Consistory

In April 1991, John Paul II assembled the Consistory (plenary of the cardinals)[115] to discuss two main themes: 'the Church and the threat to human life' and 'the proclamation of Christ [...] and the challenge of the sects' (Vandrisse, 1991). Discussions of the second topic were based on the report by the Nigerian Cardinal Arinze, president of the Council for the Dialogue with Religions. The Latin American bishops had reported an 'alarming proliferation' of 'sects', with an estimated following of 30 million. Cardinal Poupard observed that 'the Churches seem to be beaten on their own territory, as the soil on which the sects thrive is destined to receive the seed of the Gospel' (ibid.) and questioned why Catholics look elsewhere for what they should discover and live in the Church.

Cardinal Jozef Tomko (1991), the CEP's Prefect, addressed the Consistory on the challenge of 'sects' against the background of *Redemptoris Missio*.

(He does not specify 'sect', but it appears to encompass any new religious group or movement outside the Church. The cited figure for Latin America suggests new Pentecostal groups.) The challenge has pastoral and theological implications and doctrinal confusion promotes sects' proliferation and justification and lack of commitment in pastoral care and proclamation. 'Gnostic relativism' and theological misunderstanding level religions, religious experiences and beliefs. Such theories 'deform the revealed mystery of the Word incarnate in Jesus Christ' and 'construct the divine mystery' in various religious types. Put into pastoral practice, these theories 'eliminate missionary involvement and weaken Christian identity itself'. *Redemptoris Missio* clarifies and corrects such theological tendencies. It also counters 'unacceptable and destructive doctrines' developed by theologians to promote inter-religious dialogue, including inadmissible reinterpretations of Christ, the Spirit, and the Kingdom. They have consequences for the Church's mission, because they reduce and distort 'the scope of evangelization', lead to dialogue 'of the social type', to economic and social advancement, and to 'liberation'. The encyclical is a timely reconfirmation of the 'Church's faith in truths' (ibid.: 4).

The report of the PCID's Prefect, Cardinal Arinze (1991), to the Consistory intended 'to stimulate reflection and pastoral planning' and addressed six topics: terminology, typology of NRMs, origins and reasons for their spread, problems for the Church, general and specific pastoral responses. The emergence of NRMs is a 'marked phenomenon in the religious history of our times' and NRMs are syncretistic in nature. Often, lack of adequate information leads to pastoral inaction or overreaction. As there is great variation in new religions, 'there is as yet no agreed name for them all'. The term 'sect' refers to groups breaking away from major religions, usually Christianity, but in Latin America, all non-Catholic groups tend to be called 'sects', especially those perceived as extremist or aggressive. While 'sect' has negative connotations in Western Europe, this is not the case in Japan. The term 'NRMs' is more neutral, with 'new' referring to both the emergence of their present forms after the Second World War and their self-presentation as alternatives to existing religions and prevailing culture. They are 'religious' because they offer visions of a sacred world or transcendental knowledge, spiritual illumination or self-realization or answers to fundamental questions. Other terms are used, such as 'new' or 'fringe religions', 'free' or 'alternative religious movements', 'marginal groups', and 'cults', but an 'effort should be made to adopt a term which is as fair and precise as possible'. This term is 'NRMs' because 'it is neutral' and serves as an umbrella term for 'movements of Protestant origin, the sects of Christian background, new Oriental or African movements and those of the gnostic or esoteric type' (ibid.: 5).

There are two broad types of NRMs: those referring to Christianity and those referring to 'knowledge'. The first type includes: NRMs arising from the Protestant reform (these pursue aggressive proselytism which 'denigrates the Church', have expansionist programmes, and use the mass media in a way which commercializes religion); sects with Christian roots, but significant doctrinal differences; groups derived from other religions; human potential groups (New Age, therapeutic cults); 'divine potential' groups derived from Oriental traditions; groups arising from contact between universal religions and primal religions. The second type has four sub-types: Christian derived groups; groups derived from other world religions; pagan movements; gnostic movements.

NRMs have been described as 'religious groups with a distinctive world-view [. . .] derived from, but not identical with, the teachings of a major world religion', but this description does not include humanistic, pagan, or gnostic movements nor does it make any value judgement about teachings, moral behaviour or relationship with society. NRMs in traditionally Christian areas reject four aspects of Christianity: the Church, Christ, the role of God, the role of religion. The societal response to NRMs relates to their behaviour rather than their doctrines. Cardinal Arinze warns against 'blanket condemnation or generalization' and judging NRMs incapable of change for the better. NRMs pose a pastoral problem, because 'the faithful' are vulnerable to proposals 'which are contrary to the formation [education] they have received' (ibid.).

There are six reasons why NRMs find followers. First, the Church and other religious institutions have not perceived or succeeded in meeting spiritual needs. Second, in times of cultural change, people feel lost and search for meaning. Third, NRMs provide clear answers and religious rituals and practices. Fourth, NRMs tackle existential problems. Fifth, NRMs 'exploit' the Church's pastoral weakness: for example, where priests are scarce, NRMs provide leaders and evangelists; where Catholics are 'rather ignorant' in doctrine, NRMs use 'aggressive biblical fundamentalism'; where Catholics are lukewarm and indifferent, NRMs bring 'infectious dynamism and commitment', etc. While the Church might learn from such methods, it cannot adopt methods which breach the spirit of the gospel. Here, information and help are needed. Finally, NRMs may result from the action of the devil, 'the enemy who sows darnel among the wheat when the people are asleep' (ibid.).

NRMs' origins and breeding ground are in the United States and they have spread from there. They are mostly of Protestant, but also of Oriental origin or result from fusions between religion and psychology. NRMs in Latin America and the Philippines are mainly of Christian origin, 'generally aggressive and negative towards the Catholic Church', while in Africa, they arise from the postcolonial crisis situation, inculturation processes, and the quest for healing and solving everyday problems. In Asia, NRMs do not threaten minority Christian communities, but when exported to Europe and the Americas, 'they attract people, including intellectuals, with their syncretic and esoteric offers of relaxation, peace and illumination' (ibid.). Due to its 'highly secularized technology society', cultural fragmentation, and lack of shared values and beliefs, Europe is receptive to NRMs from the US and Asia.

NRMs pose problems and challenges for the Church: they 'pull Catholics away from the unity and communion of the Church'. A clear line needs to be drawn between sects/NRMs and churches/ecclesial communities to distinguish ecumenical relations from dealings with sects/NRMs. 'Sects' which 'propose a man-made religious community rather than the Church instituted by the Son of God' undermine or deny the Church's articles of faith. Groups which practise neo-paganism (placing the self at the centre of worship and claiming superior knowledge), occultism, magic, spiritualism, or devil worship entice Christians away from their faith. Some NRMs pave the way to atheism. NRMs' methods violate religious freedom, for example by spreading falsehoods about the Church, luring vulnerable people with material goods, and exerting psychological pressures. In some countries, notably Latin America and the Philippines, NRMs target Catholics and 'misinterpret' the Catholic mission among the poor as communism or subversion. NRMs' recruitment and training methods and harsh regimes have caused individuals 'psychological harm'. Some NRMs' stance towards society has created problems for society or government, regarding 'their failure to teach their members to be concerned citizens' and 'the social disorientation of their followers' (ibid.: 6). Therefore, the NRM phenomenon and related problems must be taken seriously.

Regarding the Church's pastoral response to NRMs, it should be neither attack nor negative action, although the Church must defend itself against unjust attacks. Individual NRM members are 'people redeemed by Christ who are now in error', but 'with whom the Church wants to share the light and love of Christ' (ibid.). NRMs are a sign of the times which compels the Church to ask why people join NRMs, what their legitimate needs are which it is not addressing, what other reasons there are for the rise of NRMs, and what God's will is for the Church in relation to NRMs.

Like Cardinal Tomko, Cardinal Arinze refers to the Vatican Report and its reception within the Catholic Church where it promoted greater communication between dioceses, bishops' conferences, and the Holy See. It also led to study centres, commissions, and books on NRMs and initiated information and training of pastoral workers. Although the F.I.U.C. project continued the Report's work, the question of NRMs needs careful research and study to find a 'well-founded and lasting pastoral approach' (ibid.).

As to dialogue with NRMs, the Church is open to dialogue with individuals and groups which are 'of the style of the Church's apostolate'. While Vatican II called for dialogue with Christians *and* other believers, the difficulty regarding dialogue with NRMs is the question of conducting it 'with due prudence and discernment'. Given their nature and manner of operation, dialogue with NRMs is 'particularly problematic', because priests have a duty to 'defend the Catholic faithful from erroneous or dangerous associations' (ibid.). Yet, there is no room for blanket condemnation.

Instead, there should be careful and continuous study and recognition of what is 'good or noble' and of what facilitates collaboration. NRMs with an aggressive strategy against the Church need special attention.

Specific pastoral measures can be taken in nine areas. First, where Catholics are lured away because they are confused about doctrinal matters, bishops need to be particularly attentive 'preachers of faith'. Second, effective catechesis and Bible instruction can counteract NRMs which exploit people's ignorance. Third, proper understanding of the Church's liturgical and devotional tradition will not attract those wishing for 'satisfying prayer and worship' to NRMs. Fourth, NRMs' promises of wisdom, peace, harmony, and self-realization should be offset by presenting Christianity as 'good news', 'divine wisdom', 'unity and harmony with God and all creation', 'happiness which is the earthly preparation for heavenly bliss', and 'peace which the world cannot give' (ibid.). Religious experience is also emphasized. Fifth, NRMs' emphasis on emotional elements can be counteracted by taking 'more notice of the body, gestures, and material things in liturgical celebrations and popular devotions'. Sixth, sense of community and belonging needs to be taken to heart in large parishes where it attracts people to NRMs. Seventh, more lay people should take leadership roles to diminish the perception that the Church is 'run by ordained bureaucratic functionaries'. Eighth, while people may find greater depth in their religious lives by joining NRMs, this is short lived and conducive to confusion. Here, pastors and people need guidance. Finally, each diocese should examine 'searching questions': Which NRMs and sects are present? How do they operate? Which of the Church's weaknesses do they exploit? What practical and spiritual help is available for the faithful? What information do people receive from the mass media? What action can the bishop take? Cardinal Arinze concludes that the Church cannot ignore NRMs: they present both challenge and opportunity. The Church has the resources for both. Quoting from the papal address to the Mexican bishops (May 1990), he points out that NRMs give the Church reason to examine local ministerial life and combine this with a quest for answers and guidelines. Developing pastoral options is not just responding to the immediate challenge, but creating new channels for evangelization.

In summary, Cardinal Arinze reaffirms the Vatican Report's views about NRMs. He repeats the RCC's perception of NRMs and 'sects': they are a global phenomenon and a threat. He reiterates the reasons why people join and the potential harm of their practices. NRMs are competition for the Church, because they entice the faithful away from the faith. Some of the NRMs' success can be attributed to the Church's failure, which makes NRMs indeed a challenge and opportunity.

As to pastoral responses to NRMs, Cardinal Arinze goes further than the Vatican Report. While the latter was mainly concerned with general approaches, he addresses particular areas which demonstrate the Church's shortcomings. Measures to overcome these arise from questions, such as what NRMs do or offer which the Church does not and how the Church can 'match' such offers, hence encouragement to involve more lay people in leadership, the recommendation to emphasize parish community, and guidelines for worship and prayer, etc. Overall, Cardinal Arinze conveys the impression that the Church takes a *reactive* rather than pro-*active* stance, which is reflected in the recommendation to ask 'searching questions', in the encouragement to study and examine NRMs carefully, the willingness to conduct dialogue with NRMs (if such dialogue is possible), the emphasis on defending the Church against attacks and falsehoods, and the reminder to bishops and priests about pastoral duties. In all this, the Church is, as repeatedly validated in Vatican documents and addresses, deeply committed to evangelization and proclamation.

The Consistory also heard reports on NRMs on the five continents, prepared by the respective archbishops (Ahumada *et al.*, 1991). No definition of 'sect' is provided in them nor is its use explained. After referring to the Vatican Report regarding general aspects of NRMs, Cardinal Ahumada's report on North America focuses on 'sects' spreading in Mexico, Central America, the Caribbean, and the United States. As Protestantism is their 'immediate antecedent', Christian 'sects' predominate – Pentecostal, Baptist, Adventist, and independent (most of them call themselves 'evangelical'), with some 'pseudo-Christian sects' (Jehovah's Witnesses, Mormons), while groups of Eastern origin (Hare Krishnas, Buddhism, Zen, Mahikari) are less widespread. Scientology/Dianetics, 'nature cults', gnostic groups, and cultural organizations are classed as 'societies of a sectarian nature'. 'Sects' offer community, participatory worship, Bible teaching, direct forgiveness of sins, no complication about birth control or abortion, and regularization of second marriages. They also convey ideological and political messages. In the US, they make successful use of the mass media and target ethnic groups. Since 1960, the number of 'sects' has increased greatly. Church guidelines to regional pastors recommend lively and community-based evangelization, revitalization of parishes, training lay people, active liturgical celebrations, and effective use of the media.

Cardinal do Nascimento's report on Africa states that 'sects, religious movements and "independent Churches" ' did not multiply before the end of the nineteenth century. Although number and membership of those of African origin are difficult to assess, estimates speak of thousands and millions. Two main questions arise: why so many 'sects' in sub-Saharan Africa? Do 'sects' not show that the RCC has to question its evangelization? The latter is all the more important given indications that Catholics abandon their faith because of 'defective' catechesis. Two points are stressed: the background to 'sects' is colonialism (see the rise of Rastafarianism and Ethiopian churches) and the emergence of 'pneumatic sects' which promise cures, consolation, and contact with the beyond. There are more charismatic–Pentecostal than political 'sects', but both are rooted in traditional African culture. The Church in Africa cannot be indifferent and needs to take inculturation seriously. Inculturation has to be accompanied by discernment so that it smacks of neither folklore nor archaeology. The true causes for this phenomenon need to be identified.

Cardinal Bravo's report on Latin America states that the many terms make it difficult to describe 'the religious phenomenon'. In Latin America, 'sects' are seen as separatist groups – exclusive, excessively reliant on the Bible, oriented towards psychological certainties, moralistic, aggressively anti-Catholic, and intent on expansion and proselytization. Evidence suggests that 'sects' are promoted by outside interests (a view also voiced in the Vatican Report). Given increasing numbers, the phenomenon is established. Aspects which attract people include sense of community, attention, religious experience, solutions to personal problems, participation, and spiritual guidance. Areas where the Church's pastoral care fails include lack of missionary fervour, weak evangelization, routine liturgy, and lack of priests. The Church has seven pastoral options: active commitment to evangelization, creation of genuine base communities, commitment to the poor and marginalized, sound catechesis, apostolate for the family and young people, renewal of popular devotion, and using the media for evangelization.

Cardinal Goicoechea's report on Europe looks at the proliferation of 'sects' and 'new religious movements'. They are syncretistic and draw almost 6 per cent of the population. Complex causes and conditions account for the phenomenon. Psychological causes include insecurity and fear created by the crisis of values and rapid social change, lack of guidance and leadership, indecision and confusion. Among the social factors, the crisis of the family stands out. There is also a manifest lack of religion. If the gospel continues to be reduced to concern for the temporal, people will search for the sacred outside the Church. The Church should offer them the 'divine' and 'mystery'. Its response must be 'realistic' and 'lively'. The renewal ushered in by Vatican II must be deepened in the local churches where participation and the experience of Christian fraternity are needed. Knowledge of the scripture and exegesis should be promoted and the Church needs to show it is both active and contemplative.

Cardinal Vidal's report on Asia covers only the Philippines. The renewal envisioned by the Philippines' Plenary Council was precipitated by the rapid proliferation of fundamentalist and evangelical groups, especially their inroads in traditionally Catholic families and institutions. These groups make massive use of the media, launch direct attacks against the Catholic Church and faith. Their appeal is due to the skills of preachers, well-advertised healing, and particular interpretations of the Bible, furthered by prevailing economic, sociological, and religious conditions. Fundamentalist groups are well funded. The paucity of Catholic priests plays into their hands and they recruit those most vulnerable: the young and poor. This 'challenge' should be counteracted by more Bible study, more catechesis, involving the marginalized, warmer and more lively church services and prayer meetings, training lay people to evangelize, and creating base communities.

In summary, the regional reports reflect the concerns and considerations of Cardinal Arinze's report. Despite regional variations and peculiarities, the cardinals agree on the causes and effects of 'sects' which the Church encounters in various parts of the world. They are rivals and a serious threat, because they use the weaknesses of social structures and local churches. Therefore, the Church's pastoral response must be twofold: analysing the Church's local and regional weaknesses and finding solutions to them. Some solutions consist of taking aboard or imitating NRM practices or addressing the causes which underlie NRMs' success. The cardinals agree that liturgical celebrations ought to be more lively, lay members should be more involved, the faithful need better instruction, the Church needs to use the media, ministry for the poor and socially marginalized is needed, 'sects' need to be studied closely, and more effort must be made for evangelization. What is notable about these reports is that all except one are dominated by the concern about 'sects', largely Pentecostal and 'acculturated' Protestant groups. Only the report on Europe deals with NRMs. Therefore the continued tendency to lump 'sects' and NRMs together is most striking.

Sects and NRMs and the Church's teaching

The paper of PCID member Mgr Michael L. Fitzgerald on 'Sects and New Religious Movements in the Light of the Recent Magisterium of the Church' (Fitzgerald, 1991; 1992) to the F.I.U.C. seminar in Vienna comments on the emergence and spread of NRMs and the increasing appeal of prophetic voices at the approach of the millennium. Fitzgerald refers to 'sects and other religious movements' to begin with, but uses 'NRM' for convenience, without intending 'to prejudge terminology to be discussed in this meeting'. He draws attention to the global nature of the phenomenon and the diversity in NRMs' origins. He quotes *Redemptoris Missio* regarding material prosperity and quest for meaning and an inner life. What some NRMs offer to Western societies is 'essentially therapeutic', oriented towards the *individual*, not the common weal. Others are more universalistic, aiming at world unity, celebrated as Mother Earth or Gaia, to be brought about through awakening the planet to a new consciousness. The Church feels challenged and needs to address how the message of salvation can be conveyed today. Fitzgerald describes what the Church has done so far. 'The need to discern what the Spirit is saying to the Churches today' (Fitzgerald, 1992: 210) motivated the consultation which led to the Vatican Report. He discusses other Vatican documents offered for reflection on this matter and appends a list of further documentation to his paper.

The Consistory's consideration of theological and pastoral dimensions was another step 'in this process of discernment'. Cardinal Tomko (1991) warned against relativistic tendencies and doctrinal confusion. Cardinal Arinze (1991) addressed the pastoral dimension of NRMs. The cardinals called for evangelization to 'correspond to the needs of the times' (Fitzgerald,

1992: 211), for promoting greater familiarity with the Scriptures, to be rooted in tradition and to 'nourish personal prayer' and 'authentic spirituality', and for creating 'true Christian communities' for people to feel welcome, involved, and respected. While the Vatican Report identified aspirations to which NRMs respond, the Consistory underlined 'the need for desire itself to be evangelized, for these religious aspirations to be purified'. NRMs would thus not challenge the Church and stimulate renewal. The Church would challenge NRMs. Regarding evangelization of the quest for happiness in the religious supermarket, Fitzgerald refers to the 'ideal' of 'living as children of God in freedom', as proposed in the Pope's address to the Sixth World Youth Day. This 'includes liberation from evil, the root of all human enslavement' and, because it is '[b]ased on respect for the truth about human nature and creation, it leads to commitment and service' (ibid.).

The Pope addressed Christianity and happiness in another speech:[116] 'True happiness comes from encountering Christ . . . and allowing oneself to be changed so that the fruits of the encounter become evident in daily life' (quoted ibid.: 212). Regarding religious pluralism and the proliferation of NRMs, the Pope referred to Vatican II in declaring the Holy Spirit 'active outside the visible boundaries of the Church' (ibid.). The fruits of the Spirit ought to be recognized in the lives of members of other religions and to lead to sincere and respectful dialogue with them. Yet, 'only in Christ is to be found the fulness of Truth' (ibid.). The encyclical *Centesimus Annus* rejects relativism and fundamentalist fanaticism, because the Church upholds respect for freedom. Freedom 'attains its full development only in accepting the truth . . . The Christian upholds freedom and serves it, constantly offering to others the truth which he has known, in accordance with the missionary nature of his vocation' (quoted ibid.).

Although *Dialogue and Proclamation* expresses similar ideas, it does not address dialogue with NRMs, 'due to the diversity of situations' and 'the need for discernment on the human and religious values'. This points to the controversies surrounding some NRMs and invites 'prudent discernment'. *Dialogue and Proclamation* adds that some NRMs use methods which affect human dignity and freedom, while others pursue ideologies or economic and political motives which are not in humanity's best interest. Fitzgerald reinforces this point by affirming religious liberty which *Dignitatis Humanae*, a Vatican Council document, declares to comprise freedom to search for truth and adherence to it. Yet, many thorny questions which some NRMs raise have less to do with matters of belief than with psychological pressure exerted on members, restrictions imposed on their movements and contacts with their families and society at large. As Cardinal Arinze's report warned against generalizations and indiscriminate condemnation, NRMs should be observed carefully and their positive elements be used as foundations for dialogue. NRMs are a challenge for the Church, but in turn the Church is a challenge to NRMs, because it offers criteria for discerning false and true promises: true faith in the transcendent God safeguards human liberty and frees from narcissistic tendencies; love and power-seeking do not go together; suffering and death can be overcome by transfiguring love. But the Church can only respond to a challenge when it knows its dimensions. To explore these, the F.I.U.C. project was launched.

In summary, Mgr Fitzgerald's paper follows a pattern common to most Vatican documents: it draws pertinent points from encyclicals, papal addresses, and documents of Pontifical Councils. Key issues recur, such the explanation of NRMs in the West in reference to modern and postmodern culture (materialism, consumerism, religious pluralism, secularization, urbanization, etc.) and the human quest for religion and spirituality. Like the regional reports to the Consistory, comments refer to both 'sects' and NRMs. Other recurring themes are the Church's resistance against relativism, its continuous mission and evangelization, religious freedom, and willingness to engage in dialogue with *all* religions. Dialogue and proclamation are repeatedly affirmed as the twin approach to dealing with NRMs. Yet dialogue with NRMs is separate from dialogue with other religions, because NRMs present obstacles: they are controversial because of their methods (such as psychological pressure) which violate religious liberty, a principle the Church endorses and upholds, and they pursue economic and political aims and embrace objectionable ideology, aims which run counter to mankind's best interests. The solution is to practise, and develop criteria for, discernment. False promises must be discriminated from true promises or, by implication, 'good' NRMs from 'bad' or 'harmful' NRMs. Discernment rests on theological arguments: 'true' religion upholds religious freedom, is community oriented and motivated by love, and has no place for narcissism or power.

A critical encounter with NRMs

Dr Michael Fuss's (1992a; also 1990b; 1992b; 1993b) 'critical encounter' with NRMs examines possibilities for dialogue with NRMs. While *Dialogue and Proclamation* explicitly excludes such dialogue, *Redemptoris Missio* places the response to NRMs within ecumenical dialogue. According to Vatican II, the Church is in dialogue with all mankind about existential questions and Fuss explores how this dialogue can be conducted with NRMs. He seeks to define the phenomenon and offer criteria for dialogue in the pluralism of religions and *Weltanschauungen*, summarized in six points. First, a 'dialogue of truth' requires thorough examination of NRMs' origins. Second, evaluation of NRMs should be influenced less by differences in history, institutions or beliefs than by the distinction between 'autonomous' and 'dialogical' religions.[117] Third, dialogue requires willingness and genuine honesty on both sides and includes steadfastness and, if necessary, protest. Fourth, depending on 'autonomous' and 'dialogical' religions, dialogue can be inter-cultural, inter-religious or ecumenical. Each level of encounter requires an appropriate method which the dialogue partners need to choose. Fifth, dialogue presupposes a shared assumption about the experience of transcendence. This informs mutual confidence and listening to one another. The question of 'truth' and 'fulness of life' is essential here. Sixth, guidelines for dialogue arise from mutual respect and the wish for better understanding. Inter-religious dialogue is grounded in the 'seeds of Truth' found in all traditions. Ecumenical dialogue is based on baptism and has important theological motives.

Before Fuss expounds these criteria further, he carefully examines 'sect', 'cult', and 'new religious movement'. He sets sects in the Church context and derives the psychoanalytic idea of the 'shadow' from Schluckebier's model of sect development:[118] Judaic-Christian religion is 'shadowed' by 'the vital, elementary powers'.[119] Negative connotations are associated with 'sect',[120] which is – with reference to Troeltsch's model – characterized as voluntaristic and dependent on the Church for recruitment, also as ecclesiological-ecumenical, biblical, social, and missionary. Fuss concludes that the sect concept is not useful to discuss NRMs, because they go far beyond the antithetical, addressing modern man's psycho-mental and therapeutic aspiration, and are – except neo-Pentecostal and evangelical groups – generally new and autonomous.

Becker (von Wiese and Becker, 1932) extended Troeltsch's model by adding the concept of 'cult', defined as a loose, ephemeral, amorphous group with a charismatic leader, a description echoed in Yinger (1957) and Kolb (1964). Stark and Bainbridge's (1985) typology ('audience cult', 'client cult', 'cult movement') describes progressive degrees of organization, with the first type being the loosest and the third the most organized.[121] For Fuss, this typology and Luckmann's (1967) of transcendental experiences are very similar: the typology reveals the social concretization of experiences of transcendence. The ethnological and anthropological definition of 'cult' describes either a system of cosmic religion or a particular aspect within a religion. 'Crisis cults', for example 'cargo cults', arise from creative transformation caused by the acculturation of Western goods and the return to traditional values. While 'sect' is associated with the religion in relation to which it is heretical, 'cult' refers to an independent, non-schismatic movement which is imported from another cultural context (Eister, 1972) or arises as an innovative religious movement. While 'sects' aim to restore 'authentic' faith and a reformed church, 'cults' are original new developments based on traditional host religions, which create new syncretism from various traditions.

'New religious movement' was introduced by H. Turner (1977b) who used it for new groups emerging from the impact of European culture in other parts of the world. NRMs are a global phenomenon. They result from the interaction between imported and traditional religions. This also applies to Europe where the idea of interaction is equally significant, even if it is triggered by the need of liberating the self and by subjective religiosity. After looking at Barker's (1989a: 145) definition of NRMs, Haack's *Jugendreligionen*, and Heelas's (1988) 'self-religions', Fuss concludes that a typology of NRMs can be based on the way they express genuine experiences of transcendence rather than on their teachings or organizational structures. Nelson (1987) emphasizes the innovative aspect of NRMs and considers them the result of a creative process.

Fuss's important contribution is the distinction between 'autonomous' and 'dialogical' religion. In the former, magic and rational revelation co-exist, while the latter offers the liberating dimension of a transcendental mystery.[122] Autonomous religion can mature into dialogical religion, moving from egotistic self-realization to altruism and self-lessness. The process is like a spectrum which ranges from 'distorted forms' to forms of mature inculturation. NRMs are in this spectrum, described as an 'arch of tension'. To identify where exactly a given NRM is in the spectrum, the discernment of spirits is needed and openness to dialogue needs to be assessed.

Fuss follows Waldenfels's (1990) preference for 'encounter' (*Begegnung*) rather than 'dialogue' and looks at Swidler's (1987) hierarchy of (sub-)levels of encounter, each level having specific goals and prerequisites. Fuss recommends Swidler's approach for dialogue with NRMs (also EZW, 1992c), which requires above all willingness and total honesty and openness, as stated in *Redemptoris Missio*. NRMs should be questioned about their openness to the unspeakable experience of transcendence. The encyclical *Centesimus Annus* provides an important reference point for encounter: the attitude towards the greatest mystery: the mystery of God. National cultures are basically different ways of asking about the meaning of life.

Three types of dialogue are discussed in Vatican II documents: ecumenical, inter-religious, and cultural dialogue. NRMs are part of the pluralism of religions, a plurality of sub-cultures where religious elements are linked with lifestyle. In contemporary, permissive society, individuals can draw orientation at leisure from the pluralism of cultural niches and sub-cultures. Guardini (1956) sees 'autonomous man' as *homo faber* for whom the world is like a Meccano set and Fuss sees NRM religiosity as a DIY construct or *bricolage* and concerned only with realizing the self. Yet, such *Ersatz* religion is an expression of man's quest for meaning, although it can only be the starting-point for genuine religious experience and full dialogue with church religion.[123] Thus, dialogue with NRMs begins with cultural dialogue, until the elements of religious transcendence are sufficiently uncovered. Then the principles of inter-religious or ecumenical dialogue can be applied, as documented in *Dialogue and Proclamation*.

Three theological questions are relevant for dialogue with NRMs, contained in St John's gospel: 'I am the way, the truth and the life'. They refer to the utility of religion, Truth, and 'fullness of life'. Utility is relevant in autonomous religion because it employs utilitarian magic which is expected to 'work'. Salvation and healing coincide and – as such religion revolves around the self – wholeness must be experienced. Often, the key to dealing with the present is sought in historic or mythical cultures. The longing for harmony is satisfied in an ideal mythical past. The romantic dream of the 'noble savage' is realized in psychological dimensions. Utility is also relevant regarding the functionalist approach in the social sciences. However, reducing religion thus is limiting its scope: true religion is the experience of ultimate truth and the transformation of the human condition. True religion confronts man with the Truth, but claims to truth from competing religions and NRMs are not equally valid, although they have equal value and are within 'the family of truth'. The Church is the advocate of religious freedom and guardian of a genuine link with Truth, legitimated by the Church's fundamental duty to Truth. Faced with an irenic and relativizing *Religionswissenchaft*, which postulates scientific objectivity, and NRMs' request not to be interfered with, truth legitimizes a 'properly understood apologetics': an apologetics for the sake of truth.

Dual membership is ruled out because Christian conversion is not transformation of consciousness, but acceptance of divine revelation. The question of truth is decided by NRMs' position towards Jesus: if the identity of the God-man and the tension between cosmic master and historical Jesus are dissolved, there can be no common ground. Christology is closely linked with ecclesiology, the theological opposition between Church and sect. Religious pluralism cannot be the co-existence of different, yet equal, religious institutions, because that betrays the Church's spiritual dimension as the 'mystical body of Christ' and sign of God's Kingdom.

Finally, the question of truth is related to 'fullness of life': religions must prove themselves in social activities by facing challenges for survival, crisis in meaning, poverty, justice, etc. NRMs' active response to the world's challenges is a criterion for their viability, unless they dismiss these as 'chaos', 'system', or 'outgoing era'. Man's attitude towards himself, his fellow men, the world, and God are reference points for his quest for salvation. The Christian Trinity is a model for giving oneself to creation, for Man to experience himself as loved, personally addressed, and called to responsibility. The concern with self-realization is suspended and Man becomes his own partner in dialogue. Religion is then pure relation based on the suspension of self. Inter-religious dialogue must be grounded in this depth. Without this shared ground, dialogue with NRMs will be superficial. Christianity's religious structure is dialogical, both in form and content. The relationship of Jesus with God the Father and Mankind needs a 'pure heart', transparent openness, suspension of self for the 'dialogue of salvation' to unfold. This 'invisible piety' is the source for inter-religious encounter and reveals the dialogical character of Christian religiosity.

In summary, Fuss follows other Vatican theologians and representatives in referring to Vatican documents which have featured repeatedly in this section: *Dialogue and Proclamation*, *Redemptoris Missio*, and Vatican II documents. Although none of these contain anything about dialogue with

NRMs – as we have seen, *Dialogue and Proclamation* even expressly excludes this topic – Fuss's starting-point for exploring this dialogue is the stated willingness to inter-religious dialogue. Its framework can accommodate dialogue with NRMs. Fuss employs *sociological* categories to discuss concepts and definitions regarding 'sect', 'cult', and 'NRMs', but harnesses *theological* criteria to discuss dialogue with NRMs. However, sociological categories (belief content and organization) are not useful for developing a typology of NRMs so that Fuss's criterion is NRMs' expression of 'genuine experiences of transcendence'. This is another *theological* category, which requires further theological criteria: discernment is needed to distinguish between genuine and fake. In setting out levels of dialogue and encounter, Fuss follows Waldenfels's and Swidler's theological propositions and Vatican II documents which frame dialogue with the modern world. He also posits NRMs' attitude towards Jesus as the crucial criterion for dialogue with them.

Regarding the use of religion, Truth, and 'fullness of life', Fuss argues from the perspective of a Roman Catholic theologian. His considerations revolve around the claim to truth/Truth, which places the perspectives of NRMs and the Church in opposition to one another. With the process of maturation in mind, Fuss argues that 'autonomous' religion (NRMs) is a 'distorted form' of mature, 'dialogical' religion (RCC religion). This view presents religion within an evolutionary progression (a theme prevalent in traditional approaches of *Religionswissenschaft*) in which NRMs represent an earlier ('immature') form, while Church religion represents a 'mature' form, a kind of *Hochreligion*. Although NRMs offer beneficial and positive aspects, which they share with 'true religion', they are deficient in the ultimate religious experience: divine revelation. Levels of dialogue test how much ground NRMs share with genuine religion, with Christology the main criterion. Fuss sees less need for an apologetic defence than for a clear explanation of the Church's beliefs, particularly its interpretation of Jesus as the 'ultimate revelation of God'. While NRMs aim at self-realization, Christianity aims at suspending, or giving of, the self for the 'dialogue of salvation' to unfold. This 'invisible piety' underlies inter-religious encounter and reveals Christianity's dialogical nature.

Assessing the Vatican's response

Saliba (1992), too, reflects on Vatican documents and statements which we have visited before: the Vatican Report, the letter on Christian meditation, the statements by Cardinals Arinze and Tomko. He adds Remi Hoeckman's interpretation of the Report and two contrasting examples of academic critique. Saliba examines whether the Report is an 'anti-cult' statement, reactions to the letter, and future prospects. His comments are of interest here because his perspectives make him a valuable 'voice': he has observed Christian responses to NRMs since the early 1980s. Grounded in Catholic theological thought through his membership of the Society of Jesus, he is likely to have insight into the way Vatican offices develop doctrine and deal with important issues and is therefore in a better position than an outsider to interpret Vatican statements, identify areas of particular emphasis, and assess the weight documents carry. As a member of a religious studies department, Saliba is well grounded in academic discourse and sociological research on NRMs and he was involved in the F.I.U.C. project.

For Saliba, the Vatican Report indicated that the 'highest levels of authority in the Catholic Church' (ibid.: 3) were concerned about the impact of NRMs[124] on the faithful, especially young adults, and that NRMs needed to be addressed, after the US Bishops had highlighted the success of evangelical sects among Latin American Catholics.[125] Although the Report was provisional, to be followed up by the F.I.U.C. project, it allows insight into the Church's general attitude and response to NRMs.[126] While the F.I.U.C. project was in progress, Vatican offices issued two major documents: the letter on Christian meditation by the Congregation for the Doctrine of Faith (1989), which Saliba considers the most authoritative,[127] and the addresses by Cardinals Arinze and Tomko to the Consistory.

For Saliba, the Vatican Report is a unique document because it resulted from the co-operation of four Vatican offices, but does not claim to be authoritative on doctrinal matters. As it does not contain specific teachings, moral directives, or pastoral injunctions it lends itself to interpretation. It does not attempt to assess NRMs theologically, judge defecting Catholics or find a way of relating to NRMs. Instead, it 'admits' that definite proposals or an official response need more research.[128] It is not 'a policy statement', but 'an informative and comprehensive narrative of what was reported by the hierarchy about the NRMs in different parts of the world'. Saliba detects 'conflicting views of what the "cults" are and apparently irreconcilable opinions about the attitude and response the Church should adopt towards them'. The Report should be read with care, as omissions are as significant as actual statements.

According to Saliba, Hoeckman played a major role in composing the Report. Hoeckman's paper to the Ecumenical Conference on New Religious Movements at the Catholic University of America[129] indicates how to read the Report: it is a progress report, a first step towards gathering information, concerned with pastoral issues and challenges. These call for self-examination and renewal in the Church. It is not an 'anti-cult' statement, as its 'underlying concern and approach have nothing to do with an anti-cult crusade mentality' so that those who expected 'official fundamentalist anti-cult literature' would be 'disappointed'. Nor is the Report an attempt to solve the NRM debate or provide a 'cult catechism'. It must be read as a whole and its generalizations are an inherent limitation of documents of this kind. It is a prudent statement about issues which have raised concern in the Catholic community.

The Church does not consider dialogue with NRMs to be of the ecumenical and inter-religious kind, although such dialogue is not ruled out at the local level, 'between sincere individual believers'. NRMs present particular difficulties, not least because their claims are met with suspicion. There is doubt about the authenticity of some NRMs' spirituality. The Report does not distinguish religious from pseudo-religious groups because this requires further study. The Amsterdam consultation complements the Report.

Saliba considers Hoeckman's paper 'carefully worded'. The Report is 'ambivalent', but Hoeckman provides guidelines for reading it. He takes a balanced approach: there can be neither blanket approval of NRMs' belief systems and activities (a veiled reference to American Catholic priests involved in 'anti-cult' activities) nor a response resembling a crusade. The Report calls upon Catholics to live their faith more deeply and renew parish life and thus render NRM activities ineffective.

Saliba then considers the critiques by William Dinges (1986) and Walter Debold (1987), two academics who present opposing viewpoints. Dinges's reservations are representative of some social scientists' views. Although he thinks the Report's call for further study and self-examination is positive, he finds fault with three aspects: the definition of 'sects' or 'cults' is muddled and derogatory and confirms popular, negative views. Second, explaining the emergence of NRMs with deprivation theory and focusing on recruitment and indoctrination is reductionist. Third, the Report tends towards superficiality, because a 'realistic appraisal of the pastoral challenge' requires 'fundamental structural alterations' in the Church. 'Trying to out-evangelize' NRMs or 'intensify Catholic identity' cannot arrest their growth. The emphasis on inculturation is a 'fundamental' question.

Debold's analysis relies entirely on 'anti-cult' perspectives. He criticizes Catholic periodicals for including 'sympathetic' material on 'cults', which, Saliba suspects, means anything that does not condemn them outright. Debold focuses on two aspects: 'cults' meeting genuine human needs and their manipulative practices. He reads support of the 'brainwashing' theory into the Report and takes deprivation theory to support his view that NRMs exploit legitimate human needs to entice individuals by screening political and economic goals with religion. There is no place for a link between a theology of religion and a theology of 'cults' or the possibility of constructive dialogue with NRMs.

Saliba then looks at negative interpretations of the Report. Some 'anti-cult' circles distributed it because they believed it supported their perspective. The commentary which accompanied the English version in *Origins* arguably supported a negative interpretation, because it included the reaction of Father LeBar, a popular 'cult' expert in the US, who considered the Report helpful because it explains why people join and why 'cults' are successful. LeBar included the Report in his book (LeBar, 1989), although uncommented. He misunderstands, Saliba observes, the Report's 'generally mild, tolerant, and understanding tone' and mistakes its call for education for a call to warn about the danger and deceptive methods of 'cults'. LeBar does not approve of dialogue with them and construes Hoeckman's participation at the ecumenical conference as an attempt by the conference organizers to lend credence to their project. Saliba notes that LeBar is probably not familiar with Hoeckman's paper.

Cardinal König's (1986; extracts from König, 1985) commentary in *Origins* is about dialogue: he speaks of obstacles in Catholic evangelization, refers to some types of NRMs, and subscribes to the deprivation theory. Addressing the Church's response, the question is whether a particular defence is needed or whether human contact, dialogue, and personal action can bring them the authentic message. These comments suggest that Cardinal König argues for a more confrontational approach (see also König, 1991).

A third commentary is an extract from an address by Rabbi Tucker (1984) of the Jewish Theological Seminary of America, who recalls the Jonestown tragedy, in his view not an isolated event. 'Cults' are 'less extreme manifestations' of the same phenomenon. Those who join merit more attention than those who just leave their faith. This statement, Saliba (1992: 12–13; also 1986a, 1989) comments, should be seen against the background of disproportionate numbers of Jews in NRMs, but Israel (1980) showed that more young adult Jews committed suicide than joined ISKCON. Tucker's approach is confrontational, thus leaves no room for dialogue or understanding. For Saliba, the juxtaposition of a Jewish anti-cultist's unofficial comments and the Vatican Report indicates that the editors of *Origins* were leaning towards a negative interpretation of the Report. Yet how can a negative reading be accounted for, given that Hoeckman's analysis does not endorse it? Some passages appear to point towards a negative stance and Saliba deals with four of these.

First, despite stressing difficulties with definitions, the introduction seemingly condones a negative definition of 'sect' or 'cult' by quoting from Breese's popular *Know the Marks of Cults*, the response of an Evangelical Christian. While common among Protestant fundamentalists, it has no standing in the academic community. The quotation reproduces 'anti-cult' notions and can be interpreted as lending them credence. Breese's approach can and should not be taken as representative of the Vatican stance, but illustrates the kind of response NRMs have elicited. Second, the recurrence of 'seem' or 'appear to offer' reinforces the 'tacit allegation' that NRMs do not really offer viable answers to spiritual questions. Concepts, such as 'deception', 'love-bombing', 'mind control', and 'abusive behaviour modification techniques', are unmistakably recognizable as 'anti-cultist'. Third, the conclusion speaks of NRM attitudes and methods which 'can be destructive to personalities, disruptive to families and society' and 'their tenets' are 'far removed from the teachings of Christ and his Church'. It refers to 'powerful ideological forces as well as economic and political interests foreign to genuine concern for the person'. Such comments are 'misleading because they confuse moral and theological with social and psychological evaluations'.

They can also be construed as blanket condemnation of NRMs, despite the reference to *Nostra Aetate* to indicate that the Church does not refuse anything 'true and holy in non-Christian religions'. Fourth, those who do not advocate dialogue with NRMs will find support in the statement that there is 'generally little or no possibility of dialogue' with NRMs, that they are 'closed to dialogue' and 'a serious obstacle to ecumenical education and effort'. Therefore, a negative evaluation of NRMs is not based on occasional references in the Report, yet other sections 'portray a balanced and responsible overview of an admittedly complex phenomenon' and the overall tone does not confirm negative opinions. To reach a more comprehensive understanding, there is need for 'reflective examination of what the document attempts to do' (Saliba, 1992: 12–16) and to what extent it succeeds in its aims. Saliba sets this out in six points.

First, he looks at the way the Report was produced. In 1983, seven questions were drafted to consult national and regional bishops' conferences.[130] How they dealt with the questionnaire is not known. Presumably, local 'experts' formulated the answers, but neither their identities nor qualifications are disclosed.[131] The replies include theological, psychological, and sociological interpretations. The communiqué accompanying the Report stated that it was 'based on the pastoral letters, articles, and other publications received from various dioceses' and that 'the help of specialists enabled us to create a synthesis'. No names are mentioned, but the F.I.U.C. *Dossier* lists 33 contributing authors and 26 other participants, with Fr LeBar a notable omission. The Report thus appears to recognize the necessity to consult more experts, before a comprehensive approach to NRMs can be reached. Hence the last question in the questionnaire. It is not known whether academic experts were consulted. Some shortcomings could have been remedied, if they had been consulted. While contradictory views about NRMs are not surprising – the 25-year long debate has still not produced unanimous conclusions – the representativeness of the Report's statements lacks support. There is no indication whether replies reflect a majority view or what criteria guided the selection or omission of statements. Second, regarding the atmosphere which the Report creates and the attitudes it promotes, again, omissions are as important as inclusions. NRMs are perceived as a challenge, not a threat.[132] Instead of a confrontational approach to, or crusade against, NRMs, there is a call for self-improvement and institutional reform. NRMs' success teaches the Church that it has a long way to go before it can meet people's legitimate spiritual needs. (see also Saliba, 1986b) Third, there is no fear of 'cults', although the Report is concerned about those who abandon the Catholic faith. While NRMs are generally considered a serious, even an alarming, matter, the reader's apprehension is not increased by emotive language. Nor are there 'vapid denunciations, condemnations or tirades', 'hyperbolic adjectives' or 'hysterical pronouncements on the evils of cultism', nor is the Jonestown tragedy used as a 'cult' paradigm (Saliba, 1992: 18). The Report's message is optimistic hope that the presence of NRMs will lead the Church to renewal and reform. Fourth, there is no apologetic argument: neither is the Catholic faith defended nor are NRM beliefs attacked. The Report is 'an exercise in self-examination' reflecting critically on the Church's pastoral ministry. It ties in with its approach to dialogue with other churches and world religions. (This point contradicts Hoeckman and the document on inter-religious dialogue – both pointed to special difficulties with NRMs – but it ties in with Fuss's assessment.) Fifth, there is more stress on preventing young Catholics from joining than bringing NRM members back to the fold. The Report says nothing about evangelizing 'cults' or former Catholic 'cult' members, because the Church might be reproached to practise what it condemns in others, which may entail fruitless debates. The Report therefore avoids aggravating the 'hostile relationship' between many NRMs and the Christian faith.[133] Sixth, NRMs' global view is a strong point, which hints at radical 'restructuring' in religious awareness and the way religion is expressed. The global perspective highlights the Church as an institution and the broader view of the universal Church addresses the role of all Catholics in Church life. Saliba concludes that the Report is 'carefully worded' and has a 'mild and tolerant' tone. It admits indirectly that sweeping generalizations on the nature, intentions, and effects of NRMs are premature, improper, and imprudent and recommends further research and study.

For Saliba, the *Letter* on Christian meditation (Congregation of Faith, 1989)[134] is 'probably the most important' Vatican response to NRMs, 'because it is both instructional and directive' (Saliba, 1992: 19). (This is somewhat surprising, as the *Letter* is hardly mentioned by Vatican commentators, with only Peter and Fuss referring to it. It was not among the documents sent by the PCID, when I asked for information on the Church's response to NRMs, but *Redemptoris Missio* was.) The *Letter* explains the nature of Christian prayer and offers a critique of Eastern meditation methods and a theology of religions. It assumes that there are enough existing studies to warrant definitive guidance for Catholics on Eastern meditation. Despite extensive footnotes, Saliba notes critically, the *Letter* makes no reference to literature on NRMs or Christian Zen or Yoga. It is not intended for lay people, for it requires familiarity with traditional theology to understand Christian prayer and its relation to Catholic doctrine (revelation and the Trinity). Saliba summarizes the seven sections which expound the compatibility of meditation and prayer (ibid.: 19–20). Interpretations of the *Letter* range from criticism or blanket condemnation of Eastern meditation techniques to their acceptance as long as they can be reconciled with Christian theology and spirituality. Commentaries in the (Catholic and general) press adopt the former stance: Eastern techniques should be approached with caution and not be encouraged. The US Hindu and Buddhist communities interpret the *Letter* as condemning Eastern meditation. Official Vatican publications expressed approval, but Catholics involved in inter-religious dialogue found its understanding of Christian prayer or treatment of other faiths unsatisfactory. Basil Pennington's (1990) review acknowledged that the time was opportune to address Christian meditation and agreed with the *Letter*'s theology, but expressed disappointment about how life and prayer in the contemplative monastic tradition (of which he is a member) were treated. Ama Samy (1990; 1991), an Indian Jesuit Zen Master, also saw positive elements, but found the *Letter* wanting in several respects, above all in its ethnocentric perspective.

The *Letter* stirred 'heated debates' within and outside Catholic circles. Saliba offers four reflections towards 'a better understanding of its meanings and significance'. Its main concern is to clarify Christian meditation, not attack Hinduism or Buddhism. It does disapprove of, and denigrate, Eastern meditation techniques indirectly and, at best, ascribes them a secondary role regarding traditional forms of Christian prayer. Yet, while not excluding Eastern practices from Christian spirituality, the *Letter* cautions against unwitting adoption of particular worldviews and/or theologies, as does other literature on the subject. It raises, but does not address, disputed questions, for example, to what extent Eastern techniques can be acceptable methods of Christian prayer, whether Christian theology can be 'inculturated' into Eastern practices, and whether aspects of Eastern spirituality can be included in Christianity (also Saliba, 1995: 170–173). Second, although the *Letter*'s theology is in agreement with the PCID, it seems ignorant about recent thought on the relationship between Christianity and other world religions, as expounded by Knitter, Küng and Moltmann or Amaldoss. Third, Saliba sees the *Letter* in line with *Nostra Aetate* which affirms that the 'Church rejects nothing of what is true' in non-Christian religions, thus does not rule out Eastern techniques and admits shared elements. Finally, the Congregation for the Doctrine of Faith, which issued the letter, exists to maintain boundaries, hence its emphasis on differences rather than similarities and the tendency to create barriers rather than build bridges for co-operation. The *Letter* therefore warns against syncretism and highlights how Eastern meditation differs from Christian prayer. Clarification on this point was sorely needed, as Catholic retreat centres and theologians adopted Yoga and Zen and Catholic periodicals included heated debates about the use of TM.

Overall, while the cautious approach may be justified, the *Letter* suffers from deficiencies which foster rather than dispel confusion, including a narrow theological view of (non-)Christian mysticism, scant knowledge of Eastern techniques, and 'a suspicious attitude to some forms of Christian mysticism' (ibid.: 26). These are obstacles to genuine inter- and intra-religious dialogue, because the focus is on one aspect of Catholic life (spirituality). The letter seems to address ecclesiastics with a limited interest in, or knowledge of, developments in the theology of religions since Vatican II and presents a view of meditation and contemplation suitable for monastic institutions rather than everyday life.

Saliba then examines the Fourth Extraordinary Consistory of April 1991, the 'third major event marking the Vatican's increased concern about the NRMs' (ibid.: 28). However, the summary of the deliberations adds little to the Vatican Report. It speaks of the emergence of NRMs as 'a changing phenomenon of alarming proportions', 'one of the greatest challenges the Church must face with evangelical charity and courage'. It stresses internal evangelization – Bible study and ecclesial communities, so that Catholics 'rediscover their identity as well as the riches of their faith in Christ'. Liturgy and popular devotions should be adapted to the cultural context, 'cults' studied continuously, a 'healthy theology' promoted, and an adequate pastoral strategy sought. In accounting of the numbers of NRMs and their influence, the regional reports agree that NRMs' activities have intensified and that Catholics should be prevented from leaving the Church. The recommendations in the Vatican Report are repeated, such as the need for religious education, inculturation, and ecclesial communities.

Saliba considers Cardinal Arinze's address a 'well-prepared and elaborate analysis', which is both similar to and fundamentally different from the Vatican Report. Cardinal Arinze's use of 'NRMs' is different – it is neutral and inclusive, as is the recognition of NRMs as religious entities. Second, he indicates that dialogue with NRM members is possible, because the question is 'how to conduct dialogue with due prudence and discernment', adding that dialogue is easier with pastors and 'persons well trained theologically', as it might be useless or harmful for those 'not well prepared to confront the forceful proselytizing of some NRMs'. In Saliba's view, this remark could be interpreted as patronizing. (Interestingly, it is not in the version published in *L'Osservatore Romano*.) Third, it is significant that Cardinal Arinze explicitly rejects overall condemnation of NRMs. The Church's pastoral response should not be an attack on NRM members, although the Church may need to be defended against unjust attacks. Fourth, one of the explanations for the rise of NRMs is the 'action of the devil'. Fifth, Saliba thinks that Cardinal Arinze leans heavily towards the need for drastic structural changes to make the Church's ministry effective. This would involve minimizing hierarchical distinctions between clerics and laity. Overall, Cardinal Arinze's address is consistent with the Vatican Report, but goes beyond it by showing increased understanding of NRMs.

Nonetheless, Saliba detects 'ambiguities'. Cardinal Arinze questions whether contemporary paganism can be considered a religion. His typology includes sects which show 'signs of decomposing the genuine idea of religion and a return of paganism'. Movements, Saliba points out, which are said to promote neo-paganism, place self at the centre of worship, and claim extraordinary knowledge are lumped together with occultism, magic, spiritism, and even devil worship, as are NRMs and traditional sects. Also, despite avoiding over-generalizations, Cardinal Arinze could be interpreted as saying that most NRMs cause the problems mentioned. To state that 'many NRMs use methods that violate the rights of other believers or religious bodies to religious freedom' is too vague. Finally, Saliba finds evidence of influence from 'anti-cult' propaganda, particularly in the sections on pros-elytization, NRMs' combative attitude towards the Church, psychological harm to individuals, and problems which NRMs create for society. Some statements equally apply to the Church, such as control over members' finances and the tension between State and religion.

For Saliba, the question whether NRM practices are detrimental to indi-viduals' psychological well-being must be settled by psychiatrists, not by theologians and evangelizers. Yet the Vatican Report and Cardinal Arinze's address convey the impression that they subscribe to the view that NRM membership causes psychological harm. Both fail to mention research which contradicts this view. The reference to Jonestown could be perceived as endorsement of the 'anti-cult' view that 'cults' are 'embryonic replicas of the People's Temple', although Cardinal Arinze refers to it as 'an extreme case'. For Saliba, extreme cases should not be included in the discussion of widespread phenomena.

In Saliba's view, Cardinal Tomko's address to the Consistory contrasts sharply with Cardinal Arinze's, because it only refers to sects, 'cults' or NRMs to show that their emergence is linked to insufficient instruction in the Catholic faith. While Cardinal Tomko commends theologians who have been working towards inter-religious dialogue, he chides 'some' for having developed 'unacceptable and destructive doctrine', without saying who they are. He describes doctrinal distortions which are made in the name of dia-logue, but have 'devastating consequences'. Saliba reads Cardinal Tomko's address as a reflection of the Asian perspective, because it deals with mission rather than with NRMs' effects in the West. However, Cardinal Tomko renews attention to issues raised in the Vatican Report, such as the need for evangelization, catechesis, and education, and underlines the tension between evangelization and dialogue. Comparing the cardinals' addresses, Saliba finds both common features and differences. Neither attacks NRMs. Both identify the Church's shortcomings as reasons why NRMs have spread so fast. Both agree that the Catholic community must be led out of doctrinal disorientation and confusion. While Cardinal Arinze sees the need for reform in the Church's structures, Cardinal Tomko sees the need for better education of Catholics in traditional dogma.

In drawing all these sources together, Saliba thinks that the publication of major official documents by the Vatican within five years (1986–1991) reveals an 'intensified concern about the presence and success of NRMs'. The 'nagging question' is *why* the sudden interest – NRMs have been present in the last 20 years and concern about them dates from the mid-1970s. Saliba sees the Vatican documents as a belated reaction to public concern. They may point towards more fundamental religious changes, 'not unrelated to the growth of NRMs', which affect the Church globally. These are two-fold: first, the Church is losing young adults who take their allegiance elsewhere, although they do not leave altogether. Hence the preoccupation with spiritual needs, which reflects the difficulty in retaining members. The reasons for this cannot be ascribed to NRMs or society alone; they may also lie in the Church itself. Second, there is growing evidence that the Church is losing influence in traditionally Catholic countries, especially in Latin America. (See e.g Freston (1996). There is also evidence (e.g. Borowik, 1996) that self-proclaimed Catholics adopt a 'pick and choose' attitude towards the Church's teachings.) Having lost its monopoly position, the Church is forced to compete in a world where religious freedom is highly prized, to rethink its customary forms of organization, evangelization, and ministry, and to explore new ways of being 'religious' and a 'church'. In the light of global changes, the Church cannot respond to NRMs in the traditional way. It is, however, not quite ready either for a universal policy, as *Dialogue and Proclamation* excluded NRMs and Cardinal Arinze stated that there was no 'quick and easy solution'.

For Saliba, the Vatican documents share four features which suggest that the Church will not embrace 'anti-cultism': they acknowledge the diversity of causes for the emergence of NRMs, do not engage in diatribes against NRMs, are not apologetic in tone, and do not attempt to refute NRMs' tenets. The Vatican documents cannot be confused with, or quoted as, 'anti-cult' statements, especially as they implicitly recognize that treating NRMs and their members in an unjust or uncharitable way would be counter-productive. Instead, the recommendation for informal dialogue with willing NRMs would be more in line with the work of the Pontifical Council for Promoting Christian Unity and the PCID. Three NRMs – the UC, ISKCON, and Scientology – already conduct unofficial dialogue with the mainstream churches.

The framework for dialogue set by Vatican II and *Ecclesiam Suam* should be wide enough to include dialogue with NRMs, even if such dialogue proves difficult. Saliba notes the stress on dialogue with the world and various religions in John Paul II's 1991 address[135] for the convocation of the African Bishops: dialogue is a formidable exercise which requires listening to the other with respect, charity, and patience. The Church will continue to perceive NRMs as a challenge and opportunity rather than a threat. Even where 'threat' is used, Saliba states, it is clear from the context that a fearful and desperate reaction to NRMs is not contemplated. On the contrary, *Redemptoris Missio* encourages Christians to 'discover and acknowledge the sign of God's presence' in other religions and adopt an ecumenical response to para-Christian sects whose activities 'are sowing confusion'.

The variety of NRMs and cultural environments might lead to different approaches. For example, established dialogue with Pentecostal churches could be expanded to newer Pentecostal groups. The Charismatic Movement has been instrumental in establishing this dialogue. In 1991, a Catholic–Buddhist dialogue group in America met for the first time, with a similar project underway for the Hindu community. Interestingly, Saliba thinks NRMs which align themselves with a major religion in the East could be included in inter-religious encounters. This supports ISKCON's stance. Yet the Church will continue its emphasis on ministering to the spiritual needs of the faithful, as set out in the Vatican Report's section on pastoral renewal, both through instruction programmes and the development of spiritual opportunities. The Church will, however, not engage in evangelization campaigns, as these create rather than solve problems and tensions.

Saliba also discusses the stated need for ecclesial communities or 'base', 'basic' or 'small Christian communities'. As these are designed for faith-sharing, 'the most concrete pastoral response' to NRMs 'will be the restructuring of the traditional parish'. Strengthening the devotional and sacramental life of the faithful and creating better opportunities for instruction will not be enough. A more radical approach is needed, which, as Dinges suggested, addresses the viability of traditional ecclesial structures. Cardinal Arinze grasped this need, but it remains to be seen whether ecclesial communities will be universally established and whether they will be the most effective pastoral response to NRMs. They could transform the roles of clergy and lay members, because they introduce novel ways of ministry and offer ecclesiology more suited to changing social structures. If such communities were officially sanctioned and encouraged, NRMs might eventually be considered to have been a blessing in disguise. If the challenge of new spiritualities and religions is not met, an opportunity would be missed to recognize the 'signs of the times'[136] and respond to a call to reform and renewal, 'integral elements of Christian faith and life'.

In summary, Saliba's paper is notable for its synoptic critique and evaluation of Vatican documents from academic and theological perspectives. He considers, for example, the *Letter to the Bishops on Christian Meditation* 'probably the most important' Vatican response to NRMs, an importance which I could not detect in the documentation. Significantly, as Saliba points out, the letter is not intended for the lay person and might therefore be classed an 'internal' document for Church theologians. Saliba's paper is also notable for its publication date (1992): by then, the RCC's response had progressed sufficiently to allow for a comparative assessment of Vatican documents as components in a progressive chain of thought, which could also be assessed in the light of the F.I.U.C. findings.

Saliba's paper is further notable for its publication in *Theological Studies* which has a theological rather than academic readership. It is worth noting that the responses his paper considers were either published in theological periodicals (*Origins*, *Pastoral Life*, *Inculturation*, *Review for Religious*), whose audience mainly consists of theologians or ecclesiastics, or in periodicals not widely read by, or readily accessible to, theologians or academics (*America*, *Journal of Dharma*).

Like Fuss, Saliba examines whether dialogue is possible with NRMs and what form such dialogue should take. Like Fuss, Saliba considers the framework set by Vatican II documents and their subsequent interpretations as wide enough to accommodate dialogue with NRMs, but realizes that Vatican offices have not yet reached this conclusion. Saliba anticipates that the Church will have to distinguish between the various 'sects' and NRMs and develop a differentiated approach to dialogue. The Church will thus have to conduct a plurality of dialogues, or, in Fuss's words, conduct dialogue on various levels, as and how these are appropriate, while at the same time work towards pastoral and spiritual renewal. Saliba believes that ecclesial communities would achieve this, although it remains to be seen whether these would be universally established.

Dialogue with religions and NRMs

In November 1992, the PCID's Plenary Assembly discussed the state of dialogue in the respective countries and sought to evaluate the Council's activities in the light of its future tasks. Apart from the PCID's general activities, the Assembly considered the document *Dialogue and Proclamation*, dialogue with Muslims, Buddhists, Hindus and followers of other Indian religions, relations with the traditional religions, and the challenge of 'sects' and 'new religious currents' (see *Bulletin* 82, 1993: 1).

In his address to the Assembly, Pope John Paul II describes inter-religious dialogue as a 'dialogue of salvation, because it seeks to discover, clarify and understand better the signs of the age-long dialogue which God maintains with mankind' (ibid.: 6). Referring to *Dialogue and Proclamation* (which addresses the Church's mission and basis for dialogue in detail), he affirms these two aspects to be 'intimately related but not interchangeable' (ibid.). The encyclical *Redemptoris Missio* further affirms these aspects in calling Catholics and other Christians to 'practise dialogue, although not always to the same degree or in the same way' (ibid.: 7). Dialogue is particularly important to eliminate intolerance and misunderstanding. A spirit of mutual respect and co-operation fosters attention to what people have in common and what promotes fellowship. 'A wise exchange between Catholics and the followers of other traditions can help in discerning points of contact in the spiritual life and in the expression of religious beliefs, without ignoring the differences' (ibid.: 8). Such discernment is all the more urgent where people turn to new religious movements. The Pope emphasizes the importance of theological considerations on the doctrinal foundations of inter-religious dialogue and encourages Catholic universities and seminaries to train people for dialogue. He concludes, similar to his *Message for the World Day of Peace* of January 1992, that inter-religious contacts and ecumenical dialogue are obligatory paths to avoid painful wounds and heal old ones.

In his report on the PCID's general activities,[137] Cardinal Arinze recalls the tasks assigned to this dicastery in *Pastor Bonus*: to promote dialogue with followers of other religions, to spearhead studies and meetings to favour mutual understanding and joint efforts to promote human dignity and other social benefits, and to contribute to the formation of those engaged in inter-religious dialogue. The PCID is active within the Church, for example it collaborates with other dicasteries, such as the Pontifical

Council for Promoting Christian Unity and the Pontifical Council for Dialogue with Non-Believers and for Culture on the question of 'sects' and 'new religious movements'. The PCID engages in ecumenical activities, especially with the World Council of Churches in Geneva, participates in multireligious encounters, 'when discretion so advises', and plans theological meetings.[138]

Mgr Fitzgerald's presentation to the Assembly is only indirectly relevant to dialogue with NRMs and is therefore summarized here. He explains the conception and drafting of *Dialogue and Proclamation*, which was jointly produced by the PCID and the Congregation for the Evangelization of Peoples (CEP) and focuses on the reactions to the document (ibid.: 24–33). These have generally been favourable, with a number of positive aspects noted, among them the document's limitation to religions in general and exclusion of dialogue with new religions. It is thought wise that the document remains at the general level. There were also critical comments and reactions from non-Catholics were mixed. Suggestions to improve the document included clarification of some points and clearer indication of how the document ties in with previous documents. Mgr Fitzgerald describes the use which has been made of the document and mentions various articles which comment on it.

The report by Fr Thomas Michel, SJ, Head of PCID's Office for Islam, on activities (April 1990–November 1992) regarding the dialogue with Muslims (ibid.: 34–45) contains nothing relevant to NRMs and is thus of no concern here. However, the report by the PCID's under-secretary, Fr John Masayuki Shirieda, SDB, on Christian–Buddhist dialogue (ibid.: 46–63) is relevant, as dialogue with new Buddhist groups and movements, such as Rissho-Koseikai, a Japanese 'new religion', and the new Buddhist movements in Europe, is included.[139] In his introduction, Fr Shirieda points out that 'Buddhism is not a solid block' and that 'there is no such thing as "the Buddhist position" on this or that question' (ibid.: 46). Dialogue with Buddhism thus needs to take account of the great variety of currents and schools.

In describing the state of dialogue with Buddhism in the respective countries, Fr Shirieda highlights two pastoral concerns: dual membership – 'Buddhist Christians' or 'Catholic Zennists' – and reincarnation. While Buddhist methods of introspection can be useful and effective, 'indiscriminate use of them may lead to confusion in faith and a danger of syncretism' (an echo of the arguments advanced in the *Letter on Meditation*). As to reincarnation, two documents provide guidance: the International Theological Commission's 'Some Actual Questions Concerning Eschatology' (see *La Civiltà Cattolica*, 7 March 1992: 486–489) and the *Letter to the Bishops on Meditation*. Other measures include greater study of meditation, developing criteria for discerning authentic meditation practices, and detailed examination of whether a Buddhist form of meditation can or should be adapted to Christian spiritual life.

The brief report by Fr George Koovackal, CMI, responsible for Asia, describes the state of dialogue with Hindus, Sikhs, Jains, and Zoroastrians (ibid.: 64–66). By implication, only the 'mainstream strands' are dealt with. Unlike new Buddhist groups, the new religious movements of the 'Hindu family' are not included here. The report considers dialogue and related questions considering the situation in India and refers to the presence of Indian religions in other countries as the religions of immigrants. The Plenary discussion declared that dialogue should first of all take place in India. 'When dialogue is organized elsewhere, there should always be consultation of the Indian Bishops' Conference' (ibid.: 69).

The report on dialogue with traditional religion by Fr François-Marie Gapi and Fr Maria Laura Marazzi, respectively responsible for Africa and Latin America (ibid.: 70–76; 77–79), yields nothing for the study of the Church's stance regarding NRMs.

Sects and new religious movements

The final report to the Plenary by Dr Teresa Gonçalves, responsible for new religious movements in the PCID (ibid.: 80–88), explains the progression from the document on 'sects' to the creation of a new post. Dr Gonçalves also refers to PCID's mandate in *Pastor Bonus* (June 1988):

> to favour and regulate the relations with members and groups of religions which are not designated as 'Christian', and also with those which are, in whatever manner, endowed with a sense of the religious.
> (art. 159, quoted ibid.: 80, my translation from the French original)

This sets the framework within which PCID operates: it is not limited to traditional religion, but potentially open to all expressions of religiosity.

Since the 1970s, the PCID, like other Vatican dicasteries, has been concerned with the emergence of 'sects' and new religious movements in the West and elsewhere. This led to the survey of the bishops' conferences of 1984 by four pontifical councils, published in 1986 as the Vatican Report. The very choice of these four councils for this task shows the Church's willingness to understand the underlying reasons for the phenomenon, its nature and causes, so that appropriate pastoral approaches can be found. The Vatican Report encouraged the whole Church to join in this endeavour. It was received favourably within and outside the Church. Local churches are taking action in the form of pastoral letters, study centres, books, and training of pastoral workers. They are also feeding information back to the PCID, which provides criteria for discernment and pastoral responses beyond the Report's general reflections.

The co-operation between the four councils continues, through the material provided by local Churches, consultation in inter-dicasterial meetings, and attendance at international seminars. As it became obvious that the co-ordination of these activities should be assigned to one person, the State Secretary authorized the creation of a new post in the PCID, responsibility for NRMs, which is held by Dr Gonçalves. It involves collating information from the bishops' conferences, study centres, and NRMs themselves, preparing summaries for other dicasteries, taking part in relevant academic or pastoral conferences, and proposing pastoral reflections in collaboration with other dicasteries. However, the new post interferes in no way with other dicasteries' work on NRMs.

The second section of Dr Gonçalves's report describes the convocation of the Extraordinary Consistory of 1991, for which 'sects' were a main theme. The discussion of this topic in this forum marked an important stepping stone in the considerations of the collegiate of the Church's pastors and encouraged local Churches to pay more attention to this subject. The Consistory looked at 'sects' and NRMs from doctrinal and pastoral perspectives. While Cardinal Tomko reaffirmed the importance of proclamation, Cardinal Arinze underlined the urgency for a more incisive pastoral response. Dr Gonçalves considers Cardinal Arinze's address important, because it expands on points on which the Vatican Report hardly touched. It avoids false generalizations and recognizes not only faults, but also potential religious values of the various movements. Such an attitude is indispensable for understanding the real reasons for NRMs' success and deciding how pastoral care should be renewed.

The third section discusses inter-disciplinary research and conferences, to which the Vatican Report had pointed with its list of issues for study. The F.I.U.C. project was launched in 1988 for this very purpose. The contributions of about 100 specialists were discussed in three international seminars, collaboratively organized by F.I.U.C. and the PCID, with PCID representatives (among them Dr Gonçalves) attending the meetings. (Mgr Fitzgerald's paper to the Vienna seminar on 'Sects and New Religious Movements in the Light of the Recent Magisterium of the Church', which is discussed above (Fitzgerald, 1991), was published in *Bulletin* 27 (2), 1992: 209–216.) The F.I.U.C. project's final phase will produce material for further pastoral reflection. Dr Gonçalves attended other conferences, including those organized by CESNUR[140] and GRIS (*Groupe de Recherche et d'Informations sur les Sectes*) in Bologna, Italy, which is recognized by the Italian Bishops' Conference.

The fourth section describes the problems which NRMs raise for dialogue. The question of how the PCID should contribute towards a 'correct' attitude towards 'sects' and NRMs raises the need to identify the main problems. Despite general willingness to look for the positive and religious in these movements and treat followers of other religions with respect, as set out in the encyclical *Ecclesiam Suam*, there are problems on the practical level.

The great variety of movements and situations makes it well-nigh impossible to develop exact terminology, a scientific typology or reliable statistics.

While terminology may appear to be of negligible importance, it is a way of expressing a complex reality. For example, in Latin America, the term 'sect' is negative and describes any non-Catholic denomination, from the traditional Protestant churches to neo-Pentecostal groups, from Oriental religions to new syncretistic movements. The terms 'pseudo-Christian' or 'pseudo-religious' often have little meaning and are simply dissuasive. Cardinal Arinze suggested using the term 'new religious movements', for its neutrality and use in the sociology of religion. However, some Cardinals reject it because it could be confused with 'new ecclesial movements', and 'new alternative movements' is rejected as being equivocal. In France, 'new religious currents' describes ill-defined and syncretistic forms of new religions which cannot be qualified as 'sects'.

Further problems concern discernment: which NRMs should be chosen for dialogue? Pastoral sensibility is required here, which led the authors of *Dialogue and Proclamation* to exclude NRMs from their considerations. There are also problems related to NRMs' attitudes towards the Church and dialogue. Some exclude all dialogue and adopt an aggressive stance towards the Church, while others – those of a syncretistic tendency – are more inclusive and facilitate dual membership and aim towards the unification or convergence of all religions. A third group are highly contentious, not only vis-à-vis other religions, but also vis-à-vis society; they use psychological pressure and deceit for recruitment and combine the religious with economic and political ends.

However, no movement can be denied the possibility of positive change (as also noted by Cardinal Arinze). Some NRMs pursue a sincere and genuine dialogue which benefits peace and harmony among mankind, while others tend to 'exploit' any contact to promote their image in public and use it for propaganda purposes (a concern also voiced in the context of academics participating in conferences organized by new religions). This is relevant for Catholics participating in conferences which gather representatives of mainstream religions and NRMs, notably in meetings on the New Age movement where the concept of religion is slipping towards notions of spiritual quest and away from any affirmation of monotheistic religion.

The final section of Dr Gonçalves's report looks briefly at problems specific to the respective continents. In North America, there is a strong opposition between those who attack 'cults' and those who defend them, on the social and legal level, among sociologists of religion, and on the theological and pastoral level. In Latin America, the Church is faced with an immense number of neo-Pentecostal and fundamentalist Christian groups and syncretistic Afro-American and new Buddhist groups. In Europe, as Cardinal Arinze stated, secularization and the crisis of values promote NRMs, with very active New Age groups. In the former Communist countries, the increasing presence of NRMs is fostered by the new religious freedom and the spiritual void. The European Council's deliberations on NRMs' impact on the social order stressed the need to fight the secrecy of some NRMs and to guard against crimes. It also proposed to deepen ethical concerns in inter-religious relations. Africa poses different problems for dialogue and pastoral care, with movements from abroad, which have financial support, and independent churches, some of which are open to ecumenical dialogue. Inculturation is a serious question for the Church, as is the vulnerability of the faithful vis-à-vis prophets and healers. In Asia, fundamentalist and syncretistic imports from Europe and North America cause problems and some Hindu and Buddhist groups are proving attractive, mainly in the West.

In conclusion, Dr Gonçalves states that both the positive challenges of these newly fermenting forms of religion – the thirst for spirituality, harmony, and unity – and the negative aspects must be recognized, which prevent spiritual liberation and genuine religious identity. However, a number of questions remain unanswered: what criteria for discernment can the Church offer those on a quest? What are the possibilities and limits of dialogue with NRMs? What contribution can the PCID offer? Which problems should be given priority? The Plenary's discussion of this report did not allow for all the questions to be addressed properly. The questions of terminology and which forums could address the NRM problem adequately remain unresolved. The Plenary affirmed that the attitude towards NRMs must safeguard the right to religious freedom and observe appropriate distinction between movements. Genuine spiritual leaders should be encouraged rather than movements' authenticity be discussed. The response to more extreme religious forms must be positive and found in prayer. The faithful need to be instructed to pray, study the Bible, and build lively communities. The opportunity for inter-dicasterial co-operation was underlined, with particular attention to proclamation in the postmodern culture where there is a return to non-Christian – polytheistic and pantheistic – religions.

In summary, Dr Gonçalves's report reiterates some of the points already encountered in Vatican documents. It refers to the Vatican Report and to the F.I.U.C project as important Church initiatives to understand the NRM phenomenon, which is again treated in a global context, with differences and variations underlined. Further underscored is the importance of co-operation between the four Pontifical dicasteries.

It is interesting to note that difficulties with terminology have not been resolved. As Dr Gonçalves quite rightly points out, appropriate terminology allows for a grip on a reality in finding correct words to describe a phenomenon. It is important that the Vatican dicasteries see dialogue with NRMs as *separate* from dialogue with other religions, such as Hinduism, Buddhism, and Islam. Yet in the case of Buddhism, some new centres and movements are included, such as Rissho Koseikai. This may be explained by the way these groups are perceived: not as NRMs, but as part of 'mainstream' Buddhism. As mentioned, some NRMs, like ISKCON, want to be seen as part of a world religion and strive for dialogue on that basis.

This brings us back to the difficulty with terminology, the precise definition of 'new religious movement'. The Vatican Report's use of this term is not identical with its use in the sociology of NRMs, even if it is used in the wider sense. As pointed out earlier, for academic usage, 'NRMs' includes religious groups and movements which arose in the West since the Second World War, where they emerged as a new phenomenon, even if their roots reached further back in history or if their dates of foundation lay before 1945. Thus new religions arising in Latin America, Africa, and Asia are treated differently. However, the Vatican documents regard any religious group outside the Catholic purview as a 'sect' or a 'new religious movement', including neo-Pentecostal groups, evangelical movements, African forms (such as Umbanda, Candomblé), etc.

Notable in Vatican documents of this nature is the recurring concept of 'discernment'. This term is nowhere explained, but Dr Gonçalves again points to the need for criteria for discernment.

The creation of a post solely for the co-ordination and collation of material on NRMs is a recent development and marks another important step by the Church towards formulating a policy on NRMs. It is part of a process of building institutions and structures within the Vatican and the Church designed to deal with this particular issue. It is likely to help focus the study of NRMs by centralizing information on this topic and allowing one person to attend relevant conferences and seminars. The new post may also provide NRMs with a direct link to the Vatican.

Discernment

In March 1993, Dr Michael-Paul Gallagher, SJ – like Elisabeth Peter a representative of the Pontifical Council for Dialogue with Non-Believers – addressed the concept of discernment at the conference on 'New Religions and the New Europe'. The conference took place in London and was organized jointly by INFORM (Information Network Focus on Religious Movements), CESNUR (Center for the Study of New Religions), and ISAR (Institute for the Study of American Religions). Gallagher's paper was entitled 'Traditions of Spiritual Discernment as relevant to NRM's [sic] in Europe' (Gallagher, 1993; 1994). Although it was in a session on the response of the churches, its purpose was not to outline the Roman Catholic responses to NRMs, but refers to the relevant documents, such as the Vatican Report and the reports to the Extraordinary Consistory of 1991 and to Saliba's article of 1992 (Gallagher, 1993: 1). Gallagher focuses on discernment and its applications to new religions. My impression is that he sought to do this independently of 'official' Vatican thinking.

Gallagher states that discernment is an 'ancient skill' which is relevant in the contemporary spiritual crisis, particularly evident in Europe after the demise of Communism, with a great deal of spiritual vulnerability on either side of the former divide. For different reasons, Europe's inherited religion – Christianity – faces new pressures and challenges. Gallagher's central thesis is 'that unless discernment is known and practised, the danger is that people, within a period of such spiritual-cultural confusion, fall into accepting short-term answers to deep human hungers' (ibid.: 2).

Starting with the concept of *discretio* in medieval philosophy, 'a capacity to examine situations to reach a good decision', Gallagher sees discernment as a 'spiritual development of *discretio*', which 'involves a process of making choices in the light of faith, which pays special attention to what are called the *movements of the Spirit* within a person's experience and within the signs of the times' (emphasis added). This process 'specializes in unmasking illusion and in offering skills for a deeper wisdom in decision-making'. Discernment is thus a 'practical skill of sifting genuine from deceptive in spiritual experiences' and offers 'criteria for judging how a person or community can truly claim to be guided by God's Spirit'. Discernment 'in the Christian understanding . . . seeks to unite the Revelation of God in Christ with the here-and-now options of one's life and history' and this method provides the practical wisdom needed to see through the deceptions in the spiritual supermarket and find a path towards 'mature religious faith' (ibid.: 3–4).

The concept appears in the New Testament (Cor. and 1 John) as the 'discernment of spirits' (as we have seen, it is also a core concept in the EZW's approach where it appears as *Scheidung der Geister* and *Unterscheidung*) which indicates that it is not for beginners in spiritual life. Discernment is also expounded in Ignatius of Loyola's *Spiritual Exercises*, whose initial prerequisite is an individual's inward freedom. A person must be 'in consolation' to make decisions. Freedom and consolation are vulnerable, they can *seem*, but may not *be* genuine. Loyola recommends attention to one's spiritual movements to test whether they last and lead in the right direction. Subtle deception betrays itself in disquiet. Applied to NRMs, these considerations draw attention to signals of danger, e.g. rigidity, not listening to advice, impulsiveness, inability to engage in dialogue or discern, etc. The last is 'the most characteristic and dangerous by-product of some of the NRM's [sic] in practice' and 'they offer short-term good which in time reveals itself as long-term destructiveness' (ibid.: 7–8).

Gallagher cites the case of a young man who felt drawn to spiritual life. Given the confusion in his life at the time, he could have easily joined an NRM. Fragmentation marked both his personal life and his cultural environment, a situation when spiritual quests 'become more dangerous' (ibid.: 10) because there is no anchor in community, tradition, family or religion and there is disenchantment with everyday life. Discernment skills are then crucial to uncover potential self-deception.

Gallagher derives three criteria of discernment from St Paul: the outcome should build up the church community; at its core should be the recognition of Jesus as Lord; genuine fruits are marked by love, joy, peace, and similar unfakeable qualities of spirit and everyday living. Some NRMs are in danger of being sectarian and separatist; they break away from the Church and eventually narrow into a ghetto of righteousness without compassion or grace. Questions are recommended as 'tools for discernment' (taken from a publication by the Pontifical Council for Dialogue with non-Believers) such as is this experience leading to compassion, gentleness and self-giving or to self-concern and even pride? Is this leading to a stronger sense of Jesus as Lord and Saviour? Is it causing a certain vagueness about God? Is prayer rooted in a sense of reverence for God or is it content with ways of meditation that remain with a world of self-silence? Have these approaches any place for a personal Saviour or do they tend to self-pedal the reality of sin and evil? (See Poupard and Gallagher, 1992: 96–97; quoted in Gallagher, 1993: 11.)

In conclusion, Gallagher repeats the great relevance of discernment, the practice of 'practical wisdom and self-questioning' (ibid.: 11), for the pastoral care of those in danger of joining NRMs. Three core ideas underlie the process: good decisions come from the true self, while bad decisions are the result of pressures and panics of the false self; decisions should therefore not be made in periods of feeling 'down'. Second, spiritual experiences are not necessarily genuine; therefore, questions need to be asked, such as: Do experiences of peace and freedom last? What fruits do they bear in the long run? Where are they leading? Finally, fear of exploring such questions with people outside one's immediate circle is a sign of potential danger and deception. Gallagher comments that his thoughts are more relevant to those advising potential NRM members rather than addressing current members directly. People would not be attracted to 'deceptive forms of religiousness' (ibid.: 12) if they attained spiritual discernment through self-awareness and inner freedom. As this demanding skill is often out of their reach, it is vital for advisers and counsellors.

In summary, Dr Gallagher's paper is important because it sheds light on a concept which has repeatedly appeared in the documents reviewed above and need for 'discernment' is continuously emphasized. Although Mgr Fitzgerald presented some criteria, only Gallagher presents a detailed exposition of this concept. He places it in a wider context and explains its anchorage in Gospel and Church canon. Discernment is seen as a spiritual development of the medieval practice of *discretio* and consists of a dual approach: recognition and removal of obstacles towards making a genuine choice on the one hand and engagement in the search for the good on the other hand. Gallagher cites the Scriptures where spiritual discernment is embedded in the 'discernment of the spirits', one of the cornerstones of the approach which the EZW has taken towards NRMs. Gallagher shows that the New Testament texts contain an underlying assumption of potential deception through which discernment has to see in order to allow a 'godly choice' to be made. The idea of deceptive spiritual experiences is addressed more explicitly in the writings of Ignatius of Loyola who speaks of consolation as coming from God and of desolation as coming from the 'bad spirit'. Yet Loyola recognizes that consolation is not infallible; hence the need for discernment to distinguish between genuine and deceptive signs of consolation.

Gallagher's three criteria from St Paul have fed into the 'tools of discernment' which a publication by the Pontifical Council for Dialogue recommended with special reference to movements within the New Age spectrum. Gallagher expands them for general application and argues that potential NRM members are those who have lost the capacity to discern and are deceived by the short-term good which NRMs offer. This is why advisers and counsellors need the skill of discernment in the pastoral care of such people.

Conclusion

As mentioned in the introduction to this section, clergy in the parishes were the first to experience and deal with the phenomenon of NRMs. They were faced with pastoral problems brought to them by parents and relatives. Clergy of all the churches shared this experience. The status and presence of the Roman Catholic Church (RCC) show marked differences between Britain and Germany. In Germany, both mainstream churches found themselves in a similar situation, as described in Chapter 4. Given their role in German society and the understanding between them, they joined forces and developed a network of specialists (*Sektenbeauftragte*) and exchange of information. However, the problems which Catholic clergy faced in dealing with NRMs raised wider pastoral and theological problems which they wanted to see addressed, as they were unlikely to find guidance in existing documents on doctrine and inter-religious relations. The request from the grassroots – the Episcopal Conferences – eventually led to the Vatican Report. In Britain, the Roman Catholic Church is a minority religion. Although it has gained a sizeable membership (10 per cent), it, too, felt the attrition in membership at the time when NRMs began to emerge. However, the numbers involved have not been as dramatic as they have been for the Catholic Church in Germany and therefore, an initiative like Housetop may have been considered sufficient to counteract the trend.

However, what has been the most acute problem for the Catholic Church has been the emergence of 'sects' in Latin America, Asia and Africa, syncretic groups and movements which combine elements of indigenous religiosity, such as spirit possession, with Pentecostal Protestantism. They have posed a serious threat to Catholic membership and raised important questions for the Church regarding inculturation or acculturation. It is this worldwide phenomenon which really set the Vatican process in motion to assess the situation and find appropriate remedies for it. As we have seen in various Vatican documents and the papers of some Vatican representatives, the Vatican position towards NRMs is one which has so far failed to disentangle NRMs from 'sects' in the developing world. This is complicated by the twin approach of mission and dialogue, the express commitment to mission and evangelization on the one hand and the commitment to dialogue with other religions on the other hand. Vatican documents have stated repeatedly that the two elements of this approach can be reconciled with one another and that they are complementary to each other. However, when the Church speaks of dialogue, it means ecumenical dialogue and inter-religious dialogue – frameworks for dialogue from which NRMs are explicitly excluded.

However, some NRMs, such as ISKCON, believe that the dialogue with the Church should or could be conducted within the framework of inter-religious dialogue, given that ISKCON is part of a strand in mainstream Hinduism, as S. Gelberg (Subhananda dasa) argues in his response to the Vatican Report. Theologians, such as Fuss and Saliba, maintain that dialogue with NRMs can be developed within the framework of inter-religious dialogue, once they have been found to fulfil the necessary criteria. The discrepancy between these contrasting views could be explained in three ways: first, they illustrate the internal debate within the Catholic Church, where there may, as yet, not be any consensus about how to deal with NRMs. Second, commentators, such as Hoeckman, may be closer to Vatican thinking than theologians, such as Fuss or Saliba, who may argue from a perspective which combines theological and academic discussions. Third, the time differential between the various publications – for example, Hoeckman's paper dates from 1987 and Fuss's and Saliba's papers from 1992 – may indicate a development in Vatican/Catholic thinking. It is, however, significant that theologians, such as Fuss and Saliba – who have both been involved in the F.I.U.C. project – have gone further in their argument than the Vatican: Fuss shows that dialogue with NRMs can occur on different levels and Saliba points to a differentiated approach which takes into account the various types of religious groups and movements.

Chronology of Vatican and related documents

1984	*The Attitude of the Church towards Followers of Other Religions*, published by the Secretariat for Non-Christians
1986	Vatican Report: *Sects and New Religious Movements: Pastoral Challenge*, published by four Vatican Secretariats
1986	S. Gelberg's Response to the Vatican Report
1988–1994	F.I.U.C. Project
1990	H. Gasper's paper 'The Pastoral Concern of the Church in Continental Europe' (included in F.I.U.C. *Dossier*)
1990	J. Saliba's paper's ' "Religious" Themes in the New Religious Movements' (included in F.I.U.C. *Dossier*)
1990/91	Encyclical *Redemptoris Missio* (issued in 1990, published in 1991)
1991	*Dialogue and Proclamation* by Cardinals Arinze and Tomko
1990	Paper by T. Gonçalves in Lugano on 'New Religious Movements: The European Situation'
1990	Paper by E. Peter in Lugano on 'New Religious Movements in Europe and the Loss of Christian Faith'
1991	Fourth Extraordinary Consistory Address by Cardinal Tomko on the 'Challenge of Sects', Report by Cardinal Arinze, Regional reports

1991/92	Mgr Fitzgerald's paper 'Sects and New Religious Movements in the Light of the Recent Magisterium of the Church' held in Vienna in 1991, published in 1992
1992	M. Fuss's paper 'A Critical Encounter with NRMs'
1992	J. Saliba's paper 'Vatican Response to the New Religious Movements'
1992/93	Plenary Assembly of Pontifical Council for Interreligious Dialogue (PCID), held in 1992, proceedings published in 1993 Report by T. Gonçalves
1993/94	Gallagher's paper 'Traditions of Spiritual Discernment' presented at Conference in London in 1993, published in 1994

Note: The documents are not arranged in *strict* chronological order. Some developed contemporaneously to one another and some were available *before* they were published. The logical sequence of argument and thought overrode chronology where appropriate.

Notes

1 The Board for Social Responsibility was set up by resolution of the Church Assembly in 1958 and became an Advisory Committee of the General Synod in 1971. Its constitution requires it to 'promote and co-ordinate the thought and action of the Church in matters affecting the lives of all in society' (Linzey, 1996: 30).

2 The reference to the SES needs to be seen in the context of disquiet about this group at the time, which culminated in Hounan and Hogg's (1985) *Secret Cult*. The authors, reporters with *The Standard*, based the book on research carried out for a series of articles, interviews with ex-members, church leaders critical of the SES and its practices, and leading SES representatives, and written testimonies from former members.

3 The Board for Mission and Unity's responsibilities are now divided between the Board of Mission and the Council for Christian Unity. The latter 'was established as an advisory committee of the General Synod on 1 April 1991 to continue and develop the ecumenical work formerly undertaken by the Board for Mission and Unity' (Linzey, 1996: 29–30, 33–34).

4 Canon Reardon served in this capacity 1978–1989. He now works for Churches Together in England, an association of member churches and bodies in Britain in Ireland. Together with similar bodies in Wales, Scotland, and Ireland, they are co-ordinated by the Council of Churches for Britain and Ireland (CCBI), an Associated Council of the Church of the World Council of Churches and Conference of European Churches (Linzey, 1996: 335–337; CCBI, 1995). CCBI (1995) is 'a fellowship of churches in the United Kingdom of Great Britain and Northern Ireland which recognize the Lord Jesus Christ as God and Saviour and seek to fulfil their common calling to the glory of one God, Father, Son and Holy Spirit'. Its purpose is 'to encourage and enable the churches themselves to grow together and take action together in a co-ordinated way'.

5 It is not clear whether this is the same meeting attended by Barry Morrison (former co-chairman of FAIR), some clergy, and others already involved in the study of, and in dealing with, 'cults', the first attempt to set things in motion. A proposal was discussed to set up a centre for co-ordinating and researching 'cults' and NRMs.

6 In a letter to *The Times*, 13 September 1984 (p. 11), Anthony Phillips, then Chaplain of St John's College, Oxford, voiced his view: 'As an Oxbridge chaplain for 15 years, I have encountered those young adults who have been caught

up in the cults to the concern and hurt of their families. But it is my experience that the reason for their absorption into the cult (as also with suicide or attempted suicide) has been their inability, rightly or wrongly, to find love and acceptance within their family.'

7 In December 1986, the Centre for New Religions conference explored new religions' methods of evangelization (Clarke, 1987a).

8 This difficulty – setting up legal provisions to apply to some religious groups, but not to others – has so far blighted most attempts to introduce new laws against NRMs. The Chaplain of St John's College did not think that legislation was the way forward: 'The proper defence against the misuse of religion is not legislation but theology – the Cinderella subject of British education.' His remedy was proper theological education: 'Schools would best prepare their children for the undoubted pressures to which their pupils will be subjected by ensuring its proper teaching on a non-confessional basis' (*The Times*, 13.9.1984: 11).

9 Yet, the Vivien Report (Vivien, 1985), the Guyard report (Guyard, 1996), and various reports published by provincial and national governments in Germany repeatedly stressed the adequacy of existing laws and argued that they have not been fully enforced. This is, of course, countermanded by the recent About-Picard Law in France.

10 The Bishop used 'cults', 'pseudo-religious cults', and 'new movements' interchangeably. 'NRMs' will be used here.

11 The General Synod has two kinds of reports: 'GS' and 'GS MISC', the latter indicating that reports are not meant for debate, but as background information for Synod members. The NRM Report is of the second kind, marked 'GS MISC 317'.

12 According to INFORM's audited accounts for 1/10/1987–31/3/1988, INFORM received £25,000 from the Home Office and £500 from the Board for Mission and Unity (INFORM Annual Report, 1988: 10). The Home Office agreed to pay a grant of £120,000 over a three-year period (INFORM Annual Report, 1989: 14). Altogether, INFORM received core funding for six years until 1993, when the Home Office felt it was no longer appropriate to provide money for any 'cult-monitoring' group. In 1995, a consultancy fee started for INFORM's services to the Home Office. This fee stopped in autumn 1996 and resumed in late 1997.

13 In its Annual Report of 1988 (p. 1), INFORM is described as a 'Private Limited Company, with three mainstream Churches and two professional organisations nominating five of the members of the Board of Governors'. The nominating churches are the Free Church Federal Council, the Church of England (Archbishop of Canterbury), and the Westminster Roman Catholic Diocese Trustee; the nominating professional organizations are the British Sociological Association Sociology of Religion Study Group and the British Association for Counselling.

14 *FAIR News* of Winter 1989/90 (p. 3) includes the draft code, with the comment that it is similar to that proposed by Richard Cottrell, although 'at the time, the British Council of Churches criticised the Cottrell proposals. It is encouraging to see that now the Church of England has produced its own version of a code of conduct.'

15 The number of signatures attached to motions determines whether they are debated in a given session. Motions with the most signatures take precedence. It is therefore never quite certain which motion is debated in which set of sessions. One reason why Saxbee's motion had to wait may have been the topicality of women's ordination, which was also on the agenda for the Synod's November 1989 sessions (General Synod, 1990).

16 The Archdeacon mentioned that he was brought up in 'an extreme religious sect' which 'destroyed the life of my family' because he joined the Church of England (General Synod, 1990: 1279). The sect in question is the Exclusive Brethren, as it turned out, when in March 1992, the Archdeacon took part in a panel discussion at the INFORM Seminar on 'Children in New Religious Movements'.

17 I have not been able to ascertain whether such staff exist. Enquiries from the Council for Churches in Britain and Ireland were unsuccessful.

18 It is interesting that the change of vocabulary is accompanied by a change in attitude and that vocabulary indicates stance, as Slee comments: use of 'cult' signifies hostility, while use of 'NRM' signifies a more detached view. Teresa Gonçalves, who deals with NRMs in the Vatican, points out that having the right words for phenomena helps us understand them.

19 The translation of all German names are mine, unless stated otherwise.

20 I avoid the term 'evangelical' deliberately, because it is not equivalent to *evangelisch*. In German, 'evangelical' is *evangelikal*. To avoid confusion 'Protestant' or 'Lutheran' Church is used here for *Evangelische Kirche*. *Evangelikal* designates a theological school within Protestantism, especially within the Anglican Church, which takes a fundamental stance in referring to the New Testament as unconditionally authoritative, while *evangelisch* can be used in two ways: in a general sense to indicate reference to the Christian gospel (*Evangelium*) and in a denominational sense, to distinguish churches resulting from the Reformation (Protestant churches) and from Roman Catholicism.

21 *Uniert* refers to the *Evangelische Kirche der Union* (Protestant Church of the Union) which resulted from the *Evangelische Kirche der altpreußischen Union* (Protestant Church of the Old Prussian Union), a union of Lutheran and Reformed Churches in Prussia (1817).

22 An issue which has greatly exercised the churches is the question whether the *Volkskirchen* could still claim to represent the whole of society and to what extent they have the power to promote integration and the ability to provide meaning (Feldmann, 1982: 32).

23 The number of those opting out of church membership is increasing, mainly because people feel that the churches have nothing to offer beyond rites of passage and because they object to paying church tax. Opting out involves explicit renunciation of membership. Nominal membership (sometimes for political and social reasons) has always been accepted. It would, for example, not befit members of political parties professing Christian values to relinquish church membership.

24 The *Rat* appoints 20 members to the Synod and is advised by committees (*Kammern*) and commissions (*Kommissionen*) consisting of experts in church matters.

25 The *Centrale*'s task was to 'bring order' into the relationship between Church and nation (the Weimar Constitution separated State and Church) and to provide orientation in the politico-religious conditions of the time. The State police closed the *Centrale*, after its director, Walter Künneth, had rejected that the Church could 'serve' National Socialist aims (Slenczka, 1995; Künneth, 1979; Pöhlmann, 1998; 2000) – one component of the years of the *Kirchenkampf* (e.g. Schmidt, 1995). Interestingly, Kupisch's (1966) detailed historical review of the Church only refers briefly to Künneth (ibid.: R143). The *Walter-Künneth-Institut*, founded in 1994 with a narrower brief than the EZW's, sees itself as the *Centrale*'s heir, with Adolf Künneth, Walter Künneth's son, as its president. The EZW considers the *Institut* politically conservative and opposed to its position. Also, the *Institut*'s existence reinforces the trend towards splinter groups and factions *within* the Church. Ironically, the institute on (anti-)fascism in

Bonn (*Bonner Institut für Faschismusforschung und Antifaschistische Aktion*, BIFF) suspects the EZW of being fascist, while conservative church circles suspect it of being left-wing (EZW, 1995a).

26 Hutten laid the foundation for 'modern' apologetics in the postwar period. His handbook, originally published in 1950, was the first to take a factual approach in describing groups and movements outside the churches. Updated editions followed (e.g. Hutten, 1958), the most recent published in 1984.

27 The EZW offers a range of publications, for use in pastoral work, religious education (RE) in schools (RE is mainly provided by clergy), church academies, etc. Series include *Informationen* (information about contemporary religion and spirituality), *Impulse* (impulses for topical issues), *Arbeitstexte* (selected documents on a given issue), and *Orientierungen und Berichte* (orientation and reports on particular subjects). They are written by EZW *Referenten* or other theologians. Topics range widely, from New Age, conscientious objection, spiritualism and mediumship, fundamentalism to liberation theology, death, charismatic movements, superstition, a range also reflected in books and book series (some written with Catholic colleagues). A monthly, *Materialdienst*, includes articles on current events, recent developments, and book reviews. The overall aim is to inform and provide signposts in the religious 'marketplace'.

28 Due to the method of selecting enquiries for the archives, the requirements of an unrestricted random sample were not met. Overall, the EZW receives about 3,000 enquiries by telephone a year and around 8,000 enquiries which do not enter the archives. Lehmann (1994: 193–196) speculates that *Sektenbeauftragte* and parents' groups must deal with even more enquiries. To my knowledge, no national statistics exist, except for annual reports of some groups, such as *Sekten-Info Essen*, which registered 1,885 enquiries during its financial year of 1988–1989 (Sekten-Info Essen, [1989]: 9–10), 1,484 for 2002, and 1,160 for 2003 (Sekten-Info website, accessed 20/2/04 and 17/3/04).

29 This is not the case for *Sekten-Info Essen*: most enquiries came largely from or around the city of Essen and concerned 149 groups and movements for 1988/89 (Sekten-Info Essen, [1989]: 9–10), 407 for 2002, and 402 for 2003 (Sekten-Info website, accessed 20/2/04 and 17/3/04).

30 It is significant that *Weltanschauung* has no adequate translation in English. It is defined as a 'set of ideas or views, which explain the world and man's place within it' and 'general, pre-scientific or philosophical view of the world and man, which intends to direct behaviour'. The notions of cosmology may come closest, understood, as 'a set of principles intended to explain the origin and arrangement of the universe'. *Weltanschauung* is often translated as 'worldview', a word which is, interestingly, not listed in *The Shorter Oxford English Dictionary*.

31 I only know of one *Sektenbeauftragter* who engaged in covert participation by registering under an assumed name at the UC's theological seminary in Barrytown to discover 'what really went on' in this movement.

32 Hemminger's book on VPM (1994a) is an extension of the statement. Further accounts of VPM are in Sorg, 1991; Stamm, 1993; and Vontobel *et al.*, 1992: 159–178. A collaborator of Liebling's and VPM co-founder, Josef Rattner, had left in the early 1960s (Rattner, 1986). A group of former VPM members formed *Psychostroika* (Ritzmann and Meier, 1990; Ritzmann, 1990).

33 In early January 1992, a press statement appeared, allegedly issued by the EZW. It purported that the EZW had disavowed Hemminger because of his 'illegal and un-Christian conduct' and that disciplinary action against him was pending. Wording and contents strongly suggested VPM or VPM-related quarters as the source.

34 However, in late 1991, VPM *was* granted an injunction against Hemminger's

(1991) account of VPM published by *Pastoralamt Wien* in Austria, but there was no verdict until December 1992. Until then, the injunction was not in force. While the case was pending, VPM claimed that it was in force and that it also applied in Germany. In contradiction to the latter claim (the injunction's validity in Germany), VPM brought another lawsuit against Hemminger in the summer of 1992 in Hanover (Hemminger, 1992: 363). By early 1998, VPM had lost both cases (EZW, 1998). Other church institutions and individuals, the *Protestantische Kirchenbund der Schweiz* (Switzerland's Union of Protestant Churches), church officials, and *Sektenbeauftragte* faced legal proceedings brought by VPM. It also sued the *Berufsverband Deutscher Psychologen* (German Association of Psychologists), journalists, and others. After VPM attacked Hemminger in its *Studie zu modernen Formen der Inquisition* (Study of Modern Forms of Inquisition), he sued VPM, with the support of the EKD. Hemminger's other legal proceedings against VPM were abandoned for technical reasons (Hemminger, 1991: 363–364).

35 Reports about EZW's internal matters appear under the heading *In eigener Sache* (concerning ourselves). Previous *Materialdienst* editions suggest that such reports have never been controversial or critical of other Church institutions. Announcements usually referred to retiring or new EZW *Referenten*, changes in editorial arrangements, obituaries, or corrections when the EZW's position was thought to have been misrepresented in the media.

36 In late 1992, the EZW had established a branch in Berlin and appointed a *Referent* knowledgeable about the situation of religion in eastern Germany. The new job had been advertised in December 1991. EZW's offshoot in Berlin probably arose from the great concern in the aftermath of reunification about the impact of NRMs in eastern Germany.

37 The communication of the *Mitarbeitervertretung* or MVG (representation of associated members) to the EKD administration referred to the MVG's guidelines, pointing out that the MVG had a consultative role 'when church offices or substantial parts of them are dissolved, scaled down, *relocated* or merged' (EZW, 1993a: 342–343; emphasis in original).

38 EZW *Referenten* used not to put their full names to brief reports in *Materialdienst*, although they could be identified by their initials. The reports regarding the move to Berlin were written by Dr Hummel.

39 Further discussion of church apologetics and the EZW's role can be found in Hemminger (1995) and Reimer (1991). Apologetics in the relationship between Church and State is examined by Slenczka (1995), (then) chair of the EZW *Kuratorium*. Problems regarding the reception of apologetics are raised in Dienst (1993). Since 1989, *Materialdienst* has included articles on apologetics and related questions. The articles mentioned here form part of the series and include Thiede (1992a) and Küenzlen (1989).

40 Further explication of Hummel's apologetics are in Hummel, 1993a; 1994b; 1995a. The latter is from the last chapter of Hummel's (1994b) book (see also EZW, 1995b).

41 The idea of the 'global village' has become commonplace, where 'the medium is the message', to paraphrase McLuhan and Fiore (1967).

42 This comment refers to assertions that neo-paganism and New Age embrace ideas contiguous to extreme right-wing ideology, as expressed in fascism, anti-Semitism, racism, etc. (e.g. Müller, 1989; Kalman and Murray, 1995; Poewe, 1999).

43 'Vagrant religion', sometimes called 'city religion' (Küenzlen, 1994: 19; Höhn, 1990), comprises forms of religion which are diffuse, syncretic, eclectic, and based on subjective experience, for example New Age thought.

44 Some aspects of dialogical apologetics discussed here overlap with the

guidelines of Johannes Aagaard of the Dialog Centre International in Aarhus, Denmark (e.g. Aagaard, 1992a; 1992b).

45 This terminology has to some extent been adopted in German-speaking countries, for example by Pastoralamt Wien and the *Enquête-Kommission*'s report (Deutscher Bundestag, 1998).

46 Some *Sektenbeauftragte*, like Pastor Haack, have worked very closely with parents' groups (e.g. Haack, 1992) and benefit from this close co-operation by receiving important information. However, such close links may entail some obligation regarding what can or cannot be said in public. In that sense, some *Sektenbeauftragte* may be tied, others may find that their stance coincides with that of parents' groups.

47 See Hartwig, 1994a; 1994b; Haack 1983e; 1982d; EZW, 1995c; 1993b; 1992a; Hummel, 1993b; Valentin and Knaup, 1992; Pastoralamt der Erzdiözese Wien, 1983; Thiede, 1991; Bendrath, 1991; Voltz, 1995; von Billerbeck and Nordhausen, 1993; Herrmann, 1992; Stamm, 1982.

48 Hummel (1993b; also EZW, 1993b) commented critically on this presentation.

49 The NRM is *Universelles Leben*, also *Heimholungswerk Jesu Christi*, founded in the early 1980s by Gabriele Wittek who proclaims a 'new' way of following Jesus by listening to the 'word within'. Her teachings are based on revelations from 'Brother Emmanuel' (e.g. Mirbach, 1994; Mayer, 1989; Reimer, 1988; Enz, 1986; Haack, 1986a; 1985c; Pastoralamt der Erzdiözese Wien, 1982b).

50 For a detailed discussion of this topic, see Usarski, 1999; 1995; 1992; 1990a; 1990b; 1988.

51 Haack's (1982d) book on Scientology is very informative, but does not explain 'religion' or 'magic' (Thiede, 1992b: 152) – hence Thiede's (1992c) own book on Scientology.

52 In an interview with *spirita*, Flasche comments on the question of approaching NRMs from the perspective of *Religionswissenschaft* or apologetics (Rink and Schweer, 1993). For REMID's view of the aftermath of the *Thesenpapier* and Thiede's critique, see Schweer, 1993.

53 The *Bundesverwaltungsamtsstelle* supports the Government regarding 'So-Called Youth Sects and Therapy Cults'. Its remit includes provision of documentation, information, reports, and analyses which form the basis for legal initiatives, statements, and Government reports. The office co-ordinates the *Bund-Länder-Gesprächskreis* (national-regional discussion group) on the topic and manages the 'permanent inter-ministerial working group for the co-ordination and gathering of activities on national and regional level regarding Scientology' (written communication of 8 April 2004; http://www.bva.de/aufgaben/jugendsekten psychogruppen/index.html, access date 18/3/04).

54 Kurt-Helmuth Eimuth (1990a) of the *Ev. Arbeitsstelle für Religions- und Weltanschauungsfragen* (Protestant Office for Questions of Religion and *Weltanschauung*) in Frankfurt a.M. discusses whether the *Sektenbeauftragten* act as guardians of the constitution or counsellors for consumers.

55 In Germany and Switzerland, some consultancy firms have been shown to have close links with Scientology (e.g. le Bé, 1994; von Somm, 1992).

56 For example, Hans Schwarz, Professor of Protestant Theology at the University of Regensburg, attended conferences organized by the Religious Freedom Foundation in Germany, a UC branch. His contributions are published in *Forum und Weltgestaltung*, a periodical published by the UC in Frankfurt (e.g. Schwarz, 1990; 1988). Schwarz (1984) also contributed to the newsletter of the New Ecumenical Research Association *New Era*.

57 The title *Kirchenrat* is used in some *Landeskirchen* for pastors working full-time for the church administration. *Oberkirchenrat* indicates a senior position.

58 In an interview, Schwarz said enthusiastically that the 'Moonies' were open to

dialogue and committed people who wanted 'to live like the early Christians'; their commitment could give the churches fruitful impulses. After returning from an international seminar in Portugal, Schwarz stated that instead of 'demonizing' and spreading 'unproven' claims about the UC, Christians ought to take up its offer of dialogue. Allegations of 'brainwashing' and 'psychological terror', which allegedly ensure absolute obedience, could only apply to 'individual cases'; such allegations were exaggerations, if not 'malicious falsehoods'. After all, members' intense focus on the group and isolation from the world outside are common for novices in Roman Catholic orders. The kidnapping methods of desperate parents were far 'more horrendous'. Although Schwarz conceded that Unificationism had nothing to offer to theological debates, Christians could learn from the 'Moonies' about commitment and human relationships. For example, marriage, still largely neglected in the churches, had a new value in the UC. Marriages involving the choice of partners based on Sun Myung Moon's objective advice rather than subjective impressions stood a better chance of survival (Feldmann, 1982: 31).

59 Wilson (1983: 184–185) makes a similar point: some 'sects' and NRMs have shown far greater willingness to co-operate with researchers than might have been expected and have shown remarkable tolerance and openness towards sociological enquirers.

60 Weber took part in conferences organized by the Religious Freedom Foundation and papers appeared in *Forum und Weltgestaltung* (e.g. Weber, 1988; 1989; 1990). He was involved in the German translation (Weber, 1985) of Gelberg (Subhananda dasa)'s *Hare Krishna, Hare Krishna* (Gelberg, 1983).

61 A selection of these articles (1967–1981) are in Haack, 1981a. See also Haack, 1978; 1982a; 1982b; 1982c; 1984a; 1988b; 1988c; 1989a; 1989b.

62 Although a Lutheran pastor, Haack's full-time work as *Sektenbeauftragter* made him a 'shepherd without a flock', because instead of doing parish work, he looked after the 'exotic flowers in the wild garden of the irrational and magic'. He exchanged dog collar and vestments for telephone, dictaphone, and intercom (Wartmann and Madaj, 1987).

63 Haack accepted the award, interpreting it as appreciation of his publication on Freemasonry (Haack, 1988e). However, Haack's (1981b) publication which linked popular religion and extreme right-wing political activism was not well received by the Ludendorff group.

64 *Material-Edition* for miscellaneous material; *Moonchild-Edition* for documents on magic and ritual, especially reprints; *Nada-Edition* for publications on mysticism and spiritualism; *Irmin-Edition* for Ariosophy and popular beliefs; *Hiram-Edition* for orders, lodges, and secret societies; *Dokumentations-Edition* for reports and conference proceedings. Ach (1995b: 8–84) includes a complete list of ARW publications between 1976 and 1995.

65 The animosity of *Universelles Leben* was undoubtedly due to Haack's (1985c; 1986a) critical exposition of the group. He described it, for example, as 'a backroom association of a spiritualist make-up' which had graduated to 'a multi-million religious syndicate' (Wartmann and Madaj, 1987; Haack, 1986a: 4).

66 Müller (1990) provides details about *St. Michaelisgemeinde*.

67 In 1981, Haack visited India, in 1984, Japan and Korea, and in 1986, South America (Haack, 1992: 20, 37–38, 60).

68 Given his sense of humour, Haack probably appreciated the joke. He could be quite self-deprecating: when one of his colleagues commented on the threat of the New Age to the Church saying 'We cannot but fold our hands [to pray])', Haack replied 'Yes, around our own necks' (Wartmann and Madaj, 1987).

69 Kopfermann was a leading figure in the *Geistlichen Gemeinde-Erneuerung in*

der Evang. Kirche (spiritual renewal movement in the Protestant Church), until he left to create the *Anskar Kirche* in Hamburg.

70 *Volksverhetzung* is 'a punishable act committed by whosoever attacks the dignity of others in a way which disturbs the peace, by inciting to hatred against parts of the population, instigating violent or arbitrary measures against these, or maligning them, maliciously deriding or defaming them. The punishment is a three month to five years' prison sentence (§130 of the penal code).

71 One such case involved an organization which campaigned against drug use. It claimed that Haack had indicated connections with Scientology, which is known to support Narconon, a drug rehabilitation programme (e.g. Church of Scientology, 1992: 407–417; Maes, 1977; Atack, 1993; Schmidt, 1993). Although Haack obtained an injunction against the organization (its president agreed not to repeat the allegation), he successfully sued for damages. However, as it turned out later, the organization had connections with a 'political sect', namely *Europäische Arbeiterpartei* (EAP).

72 This definition approaches the definition of 'sect' derived from Troeltsch's tripartite typology. However, for Haack and his colleagues, *Jugendsekten* and *Jugendreligionen* are often interchangeable, probably because 'traditional sects' are included in the debate on *Jugendreligionen* and because popular literature, including the print media and publications by parents' groups, uses 'sect' generically for non-mainstream religion, just as 'cult' is used in the UK and US.

73 This argument is somewhat tortuous, as 'traditional sects' tend to be included in the debate on *Jugendreligionen*. Haack also seemed unaware or chose to ignore that in sociological usage, 'NRMs' does *not* include 'traditional sects' and is used precisely because it is perceived to be neutral. Interestingly, in Haack's essay of 1978, translated into English by the WCC's Language Service, *Jugendreligionen* is rendered as NRMs. A footnote states that 'The term "new youth religions" is widely used in Germany to refer to the phenomena we have called "new religious movements" in this issue' (Haack, 1978: 436).

74 However, Haack was well aware that the term was not acceptable to everyone, especially not to the groups themselves. Haack (1979e: 11–12) refers to *Gesellschaft zur Förderung religiöser Toleranz und zwischenmenschlicher Beziehungen* (Society for the Promotion of Religious Tolerance and Human Relationships) which argued that not all members were young people and all the criticism of *Jugendreligionen* came from a handful of 'fanatical agitators', like Haack. Writers, such as R. Lenz (1978; 1982), criticize the term precisely for what Haack claimed it not to be: charged with certain connotations. Finally, people in the churches would prefer the term 'religion' not be used in relation to *Jugendreligionen*, but for Haack, they did present new religiosity in many guises.

75 'Heavenly deception' is a term initially used within the UC and became a generic feature of 'cults'. While fundraising, for example, UC members would ask for a donation for a 'Christian organisation' (Barker, 1984: 174; 1989b: 49–51). The titles of two books by UC ex-members include 'heavenly deception' (Elkins, 1980; Brooks, 1985).

76 'Flirty Fishing', also known as 'FFing', was a controversial practice in the COG or, in Wallis's words, a 'sophisticated prostitution business'. It was an evangelizing technique in the late 1970s (Wallis, 1978a; 1978b; 1979c; Wangerin, 1984; Wikström, 1977), from which the COG have since distanced themselves.

77 In 1978, two Ananda Marga members died as living torches in front of the *Gedächtniskirche* in Berlin, a third in Manila, a fourth in Geneva. The self-immolations were acts of protest against the imprisonment of Ananda Marga's leader, S. S. Anandamurti, in India.

78 Haack (1978: 444) mentioned John Travolta's membership of Scientology and the papal audience granted to COG members, among them Berg's daughter

Faithy. Other examples include the Beatles meeting the Maharishi, the Scientology membership of Priscilla Presley, Tom Cruise and others, and Shirley MacLaine's adoption of New Age ideas. Haack (1984b: 41–44) also discussed the use of endorsement and expert opinion. The association with well-known individuals or institutions which are respected by 'mainstream' society can be seen as means of legitimization, a technique which is, of course, not unique to NRMs. Enroth and Duddy (1983) discuss the way in which the UC and Scientology sought to become more acceptable to society and legitimate themselves.

79 The glossaries in some of Haack's books are attempts to capture internal language or specific uses of language, such as overlaying everyday words with particular meanings. Little academic work exists in this area. Some studies deal with religion and language in general. Baker (1978), for example, looks at allegorical structures and symbolic interpretation in religion. Zaretzky and Leone (1974 : 56, 58) look at speech as ritual. Arweck (1985: 164–168) examines language in NRMs generally.

80 To underline the processes involved in *Seelenwäsche* and *Psychomutation*, Haack (1980a: 182–190) complemented his statements with testimonies from parents and a former member, which are extracts from AGPF (1978). Another detailed account of *Psychomutation* is Thomas (1980).

81 Haack is not alone in explaining the success of *Jugendreligionen* by the 'crisis of modernity' (see Hummel, 1982; Küenzlen, 1985; Schorsch, 1989; Schulze-Berndt, 1981b; Wittman, 1982).

82 See Baer and Stolz, 1978; Bartley, 1978; Bry, 1976; Erhard and Gioscia, 1979; Fenwick, 1976; Greene, 1976; Hann, 1982; Hoffman, 1977; Nachtigall, 1984; Pastoralamt der Erzdiözese Wien, 1984; Pelletier, 1986.

83 Amway, a business without traditional retail channels, uses 'pyramid selling' or 'pyramid marketing' techniques. These involve 'Tupperware parties' in self-employed people's front rooms. Similar businesses appeared in the 1990s, ranging from water filters to jewellery, but those in the pyramid with negative experiences criticized the schemes (Popham, 1992; *Time Out*, 1994; Mitchison, 1991). FAIR reported 56 enquiries regarding Amway in the first nine months of 1995 (*FAIR News*, Summer 1995: 7; also *Berliner Dialog* 3: 26). The Department of Trade and Industry issued information about legislation relating to multi-level selling schemes. In Germany, they became illegal. A recent variant are *Schenkkreise* or 'gift circles'.

84 For Behnk (1996b; 1994b), *Universelles Leben* is such a case. In 1983, *Materialdienst* (EZW, 1983a) reported an increasing interlacing of religion, business, and politics in the UC's activities in Germany.

85 Whether TM is to be considered a *bona fide* religion or not is disputed. In its case against TM, the Spiritual Counterfeits Project (SCP), an evangelical Christian counter-cult organization in California, argued that TM teaching in five New Jersey high schools violated the first amendment of the US Constitution. SCP wanted the court to pronounce on the religious nature of the TM textbook and *puja* ceremony used for the course. TM claimed to be scientific and secular. The court concluded that 'no inference was possible except that the teaching of SCI/TM and the puja are religious in nature' (Spiritual Counterfeits Project, 1978).

86 The administrative courts (*Verwaltungsgerichte*) deal with 'public disputes of a non-constitutional nature' not expressly allocated to any other courts (those dealing with constitutional, labour, social, disciplinary, etc. matters). The *Oberverwaltungsgericht* is the highest such court in a *Land* and the *Bundesverwaltungsgericht* is the highest instance on the national level.

87 In June 1996, the court in Münster passed a similar verdict regarding Scientology: the (then) Federal Minister Norbert Blüm could refer to Scientology as 'a con-

sortium of suppression which despises people' (*menschenverachtendes Kartell der Unterdrückung*) and a 'giant octopus' (*Riesenkrake*) which propagates a 'deluded ideology' (*verblendete Ideologie*) and say that Scientology members were 'brainwashed'.

88 Religious freedom is, according to Art. 4, freedom of belief and conscience (*Glaubens- und Gewissensfreiheit*) which guarantees, in matters of belief and *Weltanschauung* and for decisions of conscience (*innere Gewissensentscheidungen*), freedom from state coercion (*staatlicher Zwang*). This is complemented by the freedom to proclaim one's religion or *Weltanschauung* (*Bekenntnisfreiheit*), the right to exercise one's religion freely in private and public (*Kultusfreiheit*), and the right to form religious associations or communities of *Weltanschauung*. Religious freedom protects both religious and irreligious beliefs, it grants the right to voice, or remain silent about, personal beliefs or disbeliefs (*negative Glaubens- und Gewissensfreiheit*). Religious freedom further includes the right to proselytize and convert, but excludes inadmissible methods (*unlautere Methoden*) or immoral means. Art. 4 expressly grants the right to conscientious objection.

89 The Church of Scientology lost charitable status in some *Länder*, after this very argument was decided in court. In March 1996, the Conference of the Heads of the Provincial Governments in Germany (*Konferenz der Ministerpräsidenten der deutschen Bundesländer*) decided to tighten regulations relating to Scientology and its activities. However, the ruling of the *Verwaltungsgerichtshof* Baden-Württemberg (in Mannheim) of December 2003 (that Scientology is an *Idealverein* and not commercially active, a confirmation of the verdict of the *Bundesverwaltungsgericht* of 1997) paved the way for the Scientology branch in Düsseldorf to become a registered association (*eingetragener Verein*) in March 2004.

90 The *Elterninitiative* in Munich shares this view. A press release in July 1983 urged the Government to ensure 'that the constitutional freedom to exercise one's religion is not abused by extreme religious groups, sects, *Jugendreligionen*, and therapy groups to the detriment of German citizens'. A statement on 21 June 1982 (issued before the UC mass wedding in July in New York) had made a similar appeal: 'It is the view of the *Elterninitiative* that this procedure [the mass wedding] violates the constitutional protection of the dignity of man. Churches and politicians should do everything in their power to prevent a further proliferation of such religious dictatorships, protect the basic human rights guaranteed by the constitution and UN charter, and safeguard these against abuse in the name of religion.'

91 Regarding the involvement of *Jugendreligionen* in politics, the activities of EAP have already been mentioned. TM has set up the Natural Law Party, with candidates taking part in parliamentary elections in France and Britain. The Humanist Party has taken part in provincial elections in Bavaria.

92 The symposium became known as the *Frankenthaler Gespräche* (Frankenthal Talks), because the *Pegulan-Werke* in Frankenthal had organized it. Haack apparently presented a paper, but it is not in the proceedings. Some, for example Pfeiffer (1982), considered the participation of academics as a UC whitewash, but Pfeiffer is also critical of the *Sektenbeauftragte*.

93 This is a collection of essays, with chapters on ethics and behaviour in the UC (Kehrer, 1981c), the methodological stranger (Barker, 1981b; also 1980b), the dynamic between ideology and social organization in Unificationism (Bromley and Shupe, 1981b), key elements of Unification theology (Flasche, 1981), UC's history in Germany (Hardin and Kuner, 1981), mystical elements of Unificationism (Röhr, 1981), 'youth religions' in religious education (Tworuschka, 1981),

belief and practice in the UC by a former member (Lindner, 1981), and UC's view of family and society by a member (Feige, 1981).

94 Organizations which are against 'cult-monitoring groups' (Haack's critics of critics) or the 'anti-anti-cult movement' include organizations created by NRMs themselves.

95 The comparison of the persecution of the Jews in the Third Reich with the 'persecution' of NRMs as 'religious minorities' in contemporary Germany has been made repeatedly, for example, by the Church of Scientology (1993) and *Universelles Leben* (Haack, 1992: 67).

96 Dr Alfred Weil, spokesperson for two German MEPs, Heidi Wiezorek-Zeul and Rudi Arndt, thought the comparison 'monstrous' and that Flasche wanted to 'conjure up ghosts'. (Eimuth, 1984: 315)

97 The Greek–English Lexicon (1957: 452–453) gives a number of meanings for *krinein*: (1) separate, distinguish, (2) judge, think, consider, (3) reach a decision, decide, propose, (4) (legal) judge, decide, (5) see that justice is done, (6) criticize, find fault with. In speaking of cutting criticism, Agehananda Bharati may refer to Hebrew 4: 12: 'For the word of God is quick, and powerful, and sharper than any two-edged sword, piercing even to the dividing asunder of soul and spirit, and of the joints and marrow, and is a discerner of the thoughts and intents of the heart.'

98 Mission is also a significant factor in dialogue for the Protestant Church, in particular the EZW. Yet, the Church wishes to engage in dialogue first and in mission only if there is an opening. The missionary endeavour is thus not the first priority in dialogue.

99 The Report appeared in various versions and translations. The French original, 'Les "Sectes" ou "Mouvements Religieux": Défi Pastoral', was issued in *Documentation Catholique* (69, June 1, 1986: 547–554). The official English translation in *L'Osservatore Romano* (19, 19 May 1986: 5–8) was entitled 'Sects or New Religious Movements: Pastoral Challenge'. Other versions appeared in *Origins* (16, 22 May 1986: 1–9) as 'Vatican Report on Sects, Cults, and New Religious Movements' and in *The Pope Speaks* (31, 1986: 270–283) as 'Challenge of New Religious Movements (Sects or Cults)'. The Report was reprinted in Brockway and Rajashekar (1987: 180–197) under the title used in *L'Osservatore Romano* and was published as a booklet (Secretariat for Promoting Christian Unity *et al.*, 1986). The *Werkmappe Sekten, religiöse Sondergemeinschaften, Weltanschauungen* included a German translation (Pastoralamt der Erzdiözese Wien, 1986) and a summary appeared in *Origins* (NC Documentary Service) (Vatican, 1986). Vernette (1986) provides a French translation and discusses it. Another discussion is in *Materialdienst* (Reimer, 1987). A response by an NRM is in Subhananda dasa, 1986b.

100 'Cult-monitoring' circles often argue that some 'cults' only *look like* religions. Scientology, for example, is said to hide a business behind the mask of religion. Saliba (1990d) discusses whether NRMs are genuinely religious.

101 Gelberg wants differentiation in the approach to NRMs – they should not be attacked *en masse* – yet uses the blanket term 'anti-cult movement' (ACM) without any qualification, thus attacking the ACM *en masse*.

102 Parallels include: turning away from, and minimizing contact with, the world, leaving families and making spiritual life the first priority, submitting to a spiritual superior, renouncing material possessions, leading an austere and spiritually intense life, repeating God's name, meditating, praying, observing celibacy or marital chastity, following dietary rules, changing name, dress, and hairstyle (Subhananda dasa, 1986b: 15–24).

103 Gelberg makes extensive use of social-scientific literature to support his arguments. This endorses my argument that social scientists are *perceived* to be

sympathetic towards NRMs, not only by the ACM, the media, and the public, but also by NRMs themselves.

104 Saliba (1981: 470, cited in Subhananda dasa, 1986b: 34) argues that 'The Christian response to the cults should stem from a prolonged, and maybe painful, dialogue with members of new religious groups . . . Christianity has often taken the initiative in starting intensive dialogue with the other great religions, and there seems to be no reason for excluding the new religious movements in this truly Christian enterprise.' Mojzes (1981: 476, 477; cited ibid.: 34–35), managing editor of the *Journal of Ecumenical Studies*, points out that two decades ago, Protestants and Catholics undertook a process of learning and evaluating one another and overcoming initial distrust. Such an approach should be taken to NRMs, because 'dialogue yields much better results and helps move both partners to new levels of understanding and common cooperation'. Melton and Moore (1982: 111; quoted ibid.: 35) see dialogue as a means for better understanding, an opportunity to 'influence the practices that trouble us', as 'facilitating reconciliation within families', and 'challenging those patterns and practices on both sides which heighten paranoia and hysteria and which feed destructive interactions'.

105 The guidelines (World Council of Churches, 1979: 18, cited in Subhananda dasa, 1986b: 37) emphasize the need to listen 'carefully to the neighbours' self-understanding' which 'enables Christians better to obey the commandment not to bear false witness against their neighbours, whether those neighbours be of long established religions, cultural or ideological traditions or members of new religious groups'. Cardinal Marella (1971: 5; cited ibid.) states that 'no one can enter into a fruitful dialogue . . . with another without a more than superficial grasp of his spiritual aspirations and his habits of thought and action. And the picture he has formed of his interlocutor must be so faithful as to permit the latter to recognize himself'. These principles can also be detected in the EZW's approach.

106 In 'Please Don't Lump Us In: A Request to the Media', Gelberg (Subhananda das, 1978) had attempted to distance ISKCON from the 'cult' designation.

107 Saliba (1981: 473; cited in Subhananda dasa, 1986b: 44), too, sees NRMs' 'contribution to Christianity's self-understanding and development in the changing religious scene of our time'. In a later article, Saliba (1982: 483; cited ibid.) gives this idea wider scope: 'The new religious movements can be looked upon as an educative tool in the hands of Christianity. They provide a mechanism for the Church to examine itself, to study her tradition at greater depth, and to evaluate her effectiveness as a sign of God's presence in the world. The cults can indirectly teach us that Christian life and practice are in constant need of critical reflection. They point to where the Church has failed in her ministry. They furnish Christians with a learning experience which can contribute to the vitality of the Church in our times.' Harvey Cox (1977: 6; cited ibid.: 45) also considers NRMs as forces of cultural renewal, interprets them as 'symptoms of a hunger seemingly too deep for our existing religious institutions to feed', and speculates that spiritual seekers will pass through them before they return to neglected Western traditions.

108 Publications whose titles use 'destructive cults' or 'destructive cultism' include Flöther, 1985; Hassan, 1988; Karbe and Müller-Küppers, 1983; Landesregierung Rheinland-Pfalz, 1979; McManus and Cooper, 1984; Obst, 1984; Rodriguez, 1988; Ross and Langone, 1988; Shapiro, 1977.

109 In his paper 'Christian and Jewish Responses to ISKCON', Saliba (1986a) examines the response of those who are looking for a theological explanation for NRMs' presence and success and the 'typical' Christian and Jewish responses to 'cults' in general and ISKCON in particular.

110 The most prominent court case involving tax evasion was Sun Myung Moon's, but Scientology and other groups have also faced such charges (Robbins, 1988c). Emory and Zelenak (1985) discuss legal implications for tax-exempt status for both new and established religions.

111 Richardson (1988) provides insights into the way NRMs generate and manage money and Valentin and Knaup (1992) discuss money matters in Scientology.

112 Concern about dual membership is addressed in other Catholic documents, e.g. in the Vatican Report, and by Elisabeth Peter, Michael Fuss, and Hans Gasper.

113 The document was published in the *Bulletin* of the Pontifical Council for Interreligious Dialogue (77, 1991: 201–250) and is available as an offprint.

114 This statement led me to believe that the Church's stance towards NRMs could be extrapolated from documents like *Redemptoris Missio* and *Dialogue and Proclamation*.

115 This is the official governing body which deals with Church business. Up to 120 cardinals under the age of 80 form the conclave for the election of the Pope. They also act as counsellors, comparable to a senate.

116 It was prepared for his visit to Vicenza, but not delivered in favour of an address *ex tempore* (Fitzgerald, 1992: 212).

117 'Dialogical religions' is a term used by Dr Hummel and the EZW. Hummel remarked that Roman Catholic theologians seem to have adopted it from his writings.

118 Schluckebier developed six models in 1964: docetism, gnosticism, libertinistic aspirations for freedom, Judaic legalism, religio-politico messianism, nature religion and divinization of nature (Fuss, 1992a: 356).

119 In 'New Age and Europe', Fuss (1990b) explains this idea in greater detail: cosmic religiosity, a fundamental current of any universal religion, has – like a 'shadow' – accompanied the official, institutionalized religious bodies of the Jewish-Christian tradition from its beginning, sometimes secretly, sometimes openly visible. 'Similar to a second self within the invisible vital forces of the "anima" which have to be balanced by the intellectual activity of reason, and which are often eliminated as "heretic", "magic", etc. because of their dark and elementary power. Its main characteristic is the experience of the awe-inspiring, dark profundity of the cosmos from where the higher forces originate and exercise their influence on man. Still within the limits of this world although complementary to its visible appearance, is an experience of "transcendence within immanence" ' (ibid.: 640–641) Also, 'Cosmic religiosity is ecclectic [sic], it does not pose the question of truth, and expresses its vitality indiscriminately by using all cultural patterns which eventually fit into its syncretism' (ibid.: 641; 1993a: 9; 1993b: 8). Fuss (1990b: 640, 666) uses 'cosmic religiosity' as an alternative to 'primitive' religion: 'in order to avoid any disparaging judgement on this most elementary form of religious expression which historians of religion so far had described in primal societies, we prefer the term "cosmic religiosity" '.

120 These are linked with the 'theory of decline': the sect sees itself as the 'true church' and a return to the original community. This overlooks that the original community found its apostolic norm within the surrounding religiosity. The theory of decline applies to reforming sects, while prophetic sects proclaim new revelation and oppose the 'orthodox' church's 'superficial' interpretation of the Bible. In the Reformation, 'sect' became a negative label, because groups outside the main churches had no legal legitimization (Fuss, 1992a: 357).

121 'Client cult' members are interested in 'applied magic' (*Gebrauchsmagie*) and the promise of immediate healing. They wish for continuous self-realization and use pseudo-scientific and superstitious practices which provide meaning, but do not require moral commitment (Fuss, 1992a: 361). Clients and therapists

have no communal ties, because, as Durkheim (1976: 44) states, '*there is no Church of magic*'. 'Cult movements' are communities of *Weltanschauung*: 'fully-fledged religious organizations that attempt to satisfy all the religious needs of converts' and do not tolerate dual membership (Stark and Bainbridge, 1985: 29). Conflict with other religious groups or churches arises from the transition of 'client cult' to 'cult movement', as partial claim to truth turns to absolute claim, which involves social control. Hummel defines NRMs as *konfliktreiche religiöse Bewegungen* (religious movements rich in conflict) (Fuss, 1992a: 362, note 23).

122 In his article on paganism, Fuss (1993a: 8) postulates Christianity as 'dialogic': 'If somebody would [sic] attempt to define Christianity just by one term, one might call it "dialogic": in its Trinitarian mystery, in its salvation history, in its witness to the world.' 'Dialogic' is opposed to 'autonomous' religion: 'Two types of religious experience appears [sic] complementary yet strongly opposed to each other, which I identify as "autonomous" and "dialogic", or self-affirming and self-transcending religiousness' (ibid.). Elsewhere, Fuss (1993b: 8) states that in the NRM case, 'one should speak of "autonomous religions"', because the inherent structure of religious experience remains ultimately in autonomous self-realization (in meditation or psycho-hygiene) or in the absolu-tization of established values (persons, doctrines, communities), without tran-scending oneself to a gratifying and demanding mystery and thus being truly liberated towards a "dialogic religion" in all dimensions of life (relating to God, to his neighbour, to himself).'

123 This view recurs in Fuss's (1993a: 8) article on paganism: in general, NRMs cannot be disqualified as heretical or pathological on the level of organization or teaching, but 'they reflect pre-religious experiences which constitute an inherent polarity of every religious act. Hence their ambivalence: they express on the one hand a serious response to the religious quest of individuals, and reveal on the other hand new aspects of a free-thinking critique of religion which initiates from the inner structure of the religious itself.' Because 'When-ever a pre-personal, "autonomous" religiousness is transferred into a personal, "dialogic" openness towards a gratifying and demanding mystery, one can speak of a truly religious experience' (ibid.: 9).

124 Saliba (1992: 3) points out that 'cults' and 'new' do not appear in the French title. In the relevant French literature, *sectes* generally describes movements outside the mainstream churches. 'Nouveaux movements religieux' has slowly entered the vocabulary, often in inverted commas, to indicate that it is bor-rowed from Anglo-Saxon terminology. Saliba also points out that the Vatican Report adopted the term 'NRMs'. Although it has become the 'most commonly used term in academic circles', 'it is not completely adequate', but Saliba does not say why. Also, in academic literature, 'cult' is often used interchangeably with 'NRMs'.

125 See the Pastoral Letter of the US Bishops, 'The Hispanic Presence: Challenge and Commitment', *Origins* 13, 1984: 529–541.

126 The Report had called national bishops' conferences to assess the local situation and give pastoral guidance in letters to parishes. Therefore, Cardinal Danneels (1991), Archbishop of Malines-Brussels, addressed the New Age Movement in his 'Le Christ ou le Verseau' (Saliba, 1992: 4, note 6). The Pope's speech to the Mexican Bishops in May 1990 also addressed pastoral issues related to NRMs (*L'Osservatore Romano* 23, 12 May 1990: 1–2).

127 The letter exists in Latin as *Ad totius catholicae ecclesiae episcopos: de quibusdam rationibus christianae meditationis*, in *Acta Apostolicae Sedis* 82, 1990: 362–379. The English text is in *Origins* 19, December 28, 189: 492–498. The letter is signed by Cardinal J. Ratzinger and Archbishop Bovone,

respectively President and Secretary of the Congregation for the Doctrine of Faith (Saliba, 1992: 4, note 7).

128 One could argue that this cautious stance is consistent with Vatican policy of taking things slowly and only responding after lengthy deliberation and consultation, that the Church has ignored or neglected the presence of NRMs for a long time, considering them perhaps too ephemeral to merit attention, but is now waking up to the 'threat' of losing members. Thus the need for information and assessment precludes rash pronouncements. Further, the Vatican views 'sects' and NRMs as a global phenomenon. While this makes sense overall, it is bound to produce a mixed picture. The geographical reports to the Consistory show parallels, but also significant differences in the emergence and impact of new religions – a difficulty for devising a 'global' strategy. The Church recognizes this indirectly by calling on the bishops to guide the faithful and on local parishes to make parish life more appealing and lively.

129 Hoeckman (initially in charge of the F.I.U.C. project) sought to update the Vatican's position on NRMs and summarize the results of the Amsterdam consultation. The paper was published in *Origins* (17, 30 July 1987: 136–143). The conference was organized by the American Conference on Religious Movements of Rockville, MD, attended by clergy from various denominations (some with experience in counselling NRM members and their families), and some NRM members (Saliba, 1992: 6, 11, note 40).

130 These are, in abbreviated form: (1) To what extent and in what way is the problem of sects present in your country or region? (2) What are the principal pastoral problems posed by this phenomenon? (3) What action has the Church in your country been able to take concerning this problem? (4) What seem to be the reasons for the success of sects among Catholics? (5) What attitude does the Gospel require us to take regarding this situation? (6) What significant documents or books have been published in your country or region? (7) Are there people with special competence in this matter who could take part, at a later stage, in carrying this consultation further? (Saliba, 1992: 16, note 58) The questions are listed in an appendix to the Report and reproduced in *Origins* 22 (May 22), 1986: 3 (see ibid.), but my edition of the Report does not include them.

131 *Origins* (22, 16 May 1986: 4–5) mentions informal consultation with Fr LeBar, without indication of time or topic (Saliba, 1992: 16).

132 'Challenge' occurs frequently in Vatican documents: NRMs are a challenge for the Church and vice versa. One could argue that the term has become a euphemism for threat, as its use in the world of commerce suggests: rivals or competitors are a 'challenge' to market share.

133 Some NRMs are (now) willing to exchange views with Christians. In January 1996, ISKCON organized a conference on 'The Nature of the Self' to explore common ground with strands of the Christian faith (see e.g. D'Costa, 1996). ISKCON has realized that Christianity is not a uniform bloc of beliefs and that it must explore dialogue with the willing parts.

134 The letter is dated 15 October 1989, but was not released until 14 December 1989. Its main author was the late Swiss theologian Hans Urs von Balthasar who must have written it over a year before, as he died in June 1988 (Saliba, 1992: 19, note 66).

135 'The Church in Africa and Her Evangelizing Mission toward the Year 2000: "You Shall be My Witnesses" ', published in instalments in *L'Osservatore Romano* (24, 7, 14, 21 January 1991). This document is another example of extrapolating from Vatican statements which do not refer explicitly to NRMs or dialogue with NRMs.

136 This phrase recurs, e.g. in Fuss's article and Cardinal Ahumada's report. Saliba

(1992: 39, note 121) traces it to *Gaudium et spes*, the Vatican II document, *Pastoral Constitution on the Church in the Modern World*. Saliba's (1995: 167–197) theological perspective concludes that NRMs are 'signs of the times' and an opportunity for reform and renewal: 'New religions are indicators of genuine religious needs and aspirations at a time in history when spiritual yearnings are either being downplayed or ignored. They offer an excellent opportunity for the Christian Church to better understand and execute its mission, to adapt and react more meaningfully and relevantly to the changing needs, problems, and conditions of the modern age, and to reform, re-evaluate and renew itself in the spirit of the Gospel' (ibid.: 192).

137 As mentioned, Pope Paul VI established the PCID in 1964 as the Secretariat for non-Christians.

138 The acts of one such theological colloquium on 'Jesus Christ, Lord and Saviour, and the Encounter with Religions', held in Pune, India, in August 1993 (*Bulletin* 82, 1993: 21–22), are in a special *Bulletin* issue (85–86, 1994). The contributions and discussion groups are concerned with inter-religious dialogue, but do *not* include dialogue with NRMs.

139 A number of meetings with Rissho-Koseikai and other Buddhist groups took place in the period covered by Fr Shirieda's report (April 1990–November 1992). Two visits, organized jointly by WCRP (World Conference on Religion and Peace)/Japan and Rissho-Koseikai, were concerned with co-ordinating humanitarian aid for Gulf War victims. Female Rissho-Koseikai members visited PCID in July 1990. Two further Rissho-Koseikai delegations were received in September 1991 and June 1992. WCRP/Japan and Rissho-Koseikai organized a meeting in Tokyo and Kyoto on justice and peace in the Middle East, bringing together Jews, Christians, and Muslims. A PCID representative participated (see *Bulletin* 82, 1993: 47–49). In June 1993, a meeting with Rissho-Koseikai members, including N. Niwano, Rissho-Koseikai's President, took place in Rome (see *Bulletin* 84, 1993: 314–315).

140 CESNUR is described as consisting of an international and ecumenical scientific committee which organizes annual sociology of religion conferences under the presidency of Mgr G. Casale, Archbishop of Foggia-Bovino, and under the directorship of Massimo Introvigne (*Bulletin* 82, 1993: 83).

7 Conclusions

The previous chapters examined and reviewed institutional responses to NRMs and the way in which they have interacted with one another. Although I have dealt with a selection of institutional responses, my objective has been to place these in the contexts in which they unfolded and to show how academic, 'anti-cult', and theological responses have evolved as the NRM debate progressed over time. The chronology of the institutions is bound up with a sequence of events which developed from the interaction of the different parties involved, but is also bound up with the sheer accident of particular people and institutions being present in a particular place at a particular time. The element of 'accident' has also been present in the course which my own research has taken, with the discovery of contacts and material at times contingent on particular moments in time and place.

My major concern has been the intrinsic content of what institutions have said and done. I also wanted to show how they have interacted with, and influenced, one another in the development of their respective responses. Establishing the chronological sequence of the various responses allows for a better understanding of how they 'fit' into the development of arguments and counter-arguments over time and for tracing the sources which informed the reasoning and rationalization. My work seeks to provide a clearer idea of the history of responses to NRMs and a clearer sense of who is indebted to whom regarding use of language, construction of knowledge paradigms, and shifts in knowledge paradigms. I also indicated to what extent NRMs themselves played a role in the interaction of the various voices. Their participation involved – like that of the other voices – gradual changes over time: NRMs have, to some extent, modified their behaviour and strategies and they have become voices in their own right, by 'talking back' and claiming the 'right to reply'. This occurred regarding accounts about them, with NRMs at times even claiming the right to negotiate such accounts, as for example, in the case of Wallis's publication on Scientology. While the academic community has taken cognisance of these claims and accommodated them in their study and research of NRMs, albeit to varying degrees, the 'cult-monitoring' groups have not conceded NRMs the right to 'talk back' or 'negotiate' accounts about them. The churches have not really considered this right or claims to it as a central issue, although their willing-ness to conduct dialogue on some level signals implicitly that the voice(s) of NRMs should be heard. The EZW, for example, is aware of the difference between accounts from outside and accounts from within groups and con-siders it desirable not to have too wide a gap between the two. However, the EZW is well aware that the two viewpoints can never be identical and there-fore strives to narrow the gap between them as much as possible, without, however, blurring the boundaries. To achieve this, the EZW believes that the gap between *Selbstverständnis* (the way a group sees itself) and *Selbst-darstellung* (the way a group represents itself towards the outside) should not be too wide.

Unless we have a clear idea of the chronology of the NRM debate regard-ing the voices and arguments involved and their adaptations and changes over time (a process which is ongoing), it is not possible to detect patterns of mutual influence. I have treated statements by the 'ACM' and the churches as being of the same credence value. I wanted to situate available documents in the chronology – without commenting too extensively – to show what happened, so far as my material allowed. My aim was to weave the story out of strands which the material yielded. With this approach, I have followed the traditional, largely text-oriented approach of *Religionswissenschaft*. However, the very fact of having selected and de-selected from the documen-tation represents some form of comment. I have sought to balance this by pointing to the importance of particular documents in the chronological sequence, as it became apparent in the course of reviewing the material. I avoided speculation, basing comments and analysis on documents, and indi-cated the lack or absence of evidence where applicable. Overall, I confined myself to what can be said, given available documentary data, although, where possible, I sought to support insights gained from the documents with fieldwork data, such as interviews and conversations with relevant inform-ants and attendance at relevant events. Analysis consists mainly in the juxtaposition of the histories of various responses and the way particular institutions have created knowledge and interacted with one another. It is not a question of whether one source is more credible than others, but a question of creating a coherent map of responses and chronological order.

I charted the chronology of the NRM debate in Britain and Germany to gain insight into the similarities and differences between the two countries. The comparison reveals both parallels and differences, which is unsurprising in itself, but where the parallels and differences lie exactly is the surprise and challenge.

In Britain, a 'cult-monitoring' group was the first institution to concern itself with the topic. This group – FAIR – resulted (in the mid-1970s) from the 'joint venture' of a parliamentarian, concerned parents, journalists, and clergymen (most likely of the evangelical persuasion) – people who had a personal and/or professional interest in NRMs. FAIR looked towards the United States to formulate its knowledge paradigm, as the phenomenon had made its presence felt earlier there (I have spoken of the ripple effect: NRMs started to emerge in the United States, from where they spread to Britain and from there to Continental Europe) and US psychiatrists and psychologists had developed the first elements of a paradigm. This was based on academic research in psychiatry and psychology and informed by findings from studies of 'brainwashing' regarding prisoners of war and political re-education programmes in Communist China. The atmosphere of the Cold War was a defining element for the 'mind set' within which this paradigm was located.

By the time social scientists began to take an interest in the subject, this 'territory' was 'occupied' – the 'ACM' paradigm was established. Academics began to construct an alternative paradigm, which – at least initially – worked on refuting the 'ACM' paradigm. Academics also started to establish institutional structures within which the alternative paradigm could be developed. Like the 'cult-monitoring' groups, social scientists in Britain looked towards the United States, where research and study of NRMs had got underway earlier than in Britain, for theoretical frameworks within which the topic could be placed and explored. The interesting point is that academics – just like the 'ACM' – relied on an *existing* knowledge paradigm within which to accommodate the phenomenon. Their paradigm came from a different academic discipline – the social sciences – and consisted in functionalist and Marxist approaches to deprivation. This paradigm was applied to NRMs, until it was realized that it did not quite 'fit' and needed adjustment.

Another important point is that the 'ACM' and social scientific paradigms have been competing with one another, so some of the NRM controversy can be explained in terms of competition. It is closely linked to the different – and to some extent irreconcilable – approaches which the two paradigms have taken: one is focused on the *individual*, the other on *general* patterns of social behaviour, yet both claim scientific status and use scientific language.

As to the Church of England, it joined the debate at a late stage. Given its role and status as the established church, it first took a 'pragmatic' approach (an approach which developed 'by default' rather than by deliberate policy) leaving it to individual parish clergy to deal with pastoral problems regarding NRMs and how they arose. When the Church was called upon to formulate a policy, it approached the topic with great caution, by activating its internal structures and commissioning one of its bodies – the (then) Board for Mission and Unity – to look into the matter. However, the Church looked towards academics to inform its stance and contribute towards a 'solution' to the problem. This is why INFORM appeared as the 'ideal' and 'arms-length' solution. In view of the Church's established status and concomitant links with the Government, the Home Office's involvement in the creation of INFORM was consonant with the Church's overall attitude and policy. The Church as part of the Establishment would have regarded the universities – such as King's College London – and the State as natural allies. It did, however, not want to get embroiled in apologetics or legal reforms, because either would have opened up divisions in the Church itself – between conservatives and liberals and between Evangelicals and Catholics, divisions which it could ill afford, given, for example, the controversy over women's ordination. This would also have affected the Church's position as the voice for *all* 'legitimate' religions in Britain.

In Germany – as in Britain – a 'cult-monitoring' group, the *Elterninitiative* in Munich, formed quite early in the chronology of events (in the mid-1970s, like FAIR) as a response to NRMs making their presence felt. However, unlike the British case, the creation of *Elterninitiative* was due to the active involvement of a clergyman of the Lutheran Church, Pastor Haack, who had taken a keen interest in non-mainstream religion since the mid-1960s, well *before* NRMs had appeared on the scene. Haack's *Landeskirche* had created a post for this interest in the late 1960s and it served as a model for the other *Landeskirchen* and for the Catholic Church. Thus, in Germany, the 'ACM' paradigm is closely linked with the Churches, because of the significant influence Haack had on *Elterninitiative* and because of the influence which *Elterninitiative* had on other parents' groups. The 'ACM' paradigm in Germany is, however, also closely linked with the 'ACM' knowledge paradigm which formed in the United States and Britain, which is due to Haack's contacts in these countries. Haack adapted this paradigm to the German context by creating his own language and ideas around the 'brainwashing thesis', partly informed by theological concepts and motivated by an underlying apologetic agenda. Haack coined the term *Jugendreligionen*, spoke of 'soulwashing' (*Seelenwäsche*) instead of 'brainwashing', called the result of the indoctrination process *Psychomutation*, etc. The 'ACM' paradigm in Germany has also been influenced by the experience of Nazism – hence the references to totalitarian traits in NRMs and, initially at least, the emphasis on *young* people being drawn to them. It may be significant that Haack 'happened' to be in the capital of Bavaria, the very place which is closely linked to early Nazism. However, his thought on urbanization and the effects of modernity are undoubtedly linked to the rural background of his parish in Hof, which he later exchanged for a modern urban environment.

Another important link in the chain of chronology is the creation of the *Evangelische Zentralstelle für Weltanschauungsfragen* (EZW) which the Lutheran Church had established in 1960, again well *before* the appearance of NRMs. The EZW was set the task of observing non-mainstream religions and *Weltanschauungen*. NRMs easily fitted in EZW's brief, once they became an issue. Thus, the Lutheran Church had a 'ready-made' solution which was in place *before* NRMs became part of the religious landscape. It was a solution which addressed both practical and theoretical aspects of the NRM problem: the post of *Sektenbeauftragte* served as a national model and this led to a network of specialists who could take care of pastoral problems and act as observers in the field, while the EZW was set up as an 'observation point' for religions outside the churches with a mixed approach combining theology, history, and *Religionswissenschaft*. In its way, the EZW has built up an academic knowledge paradigm in its own right, one which is informed by, and reconciled with, theological/exegetical and apologetic considerations.

The academic community in Germany, unlike that in Britain, entered the debate on NRMs at a stage when this debate was well underway and they, too, found the territory occupied. The late entry of academic voices was due to Germany's academic culture, where *Religionswissenschaft* has dominated the study of religion and sociology of religion is considered a sub-discipline or an auxiliary discipline to *Religionswissenschaft* and thus has a tenuous institutional foothold in the overall academic setting. Traditionally, *Religionswissenschaft* has concerned itself with the history of religion rather than with 'living religion', unless such religion could be found in a (non-indigenous) anthropological context. Further, when a handful of academics did tackle the issue and began to develop an academic knowledge paradigm, they, too, were faced with the 'gap' between their paradigm and the 'ACM' paradigm which they found allied with the power and standing of the churches. They, too, were faced with the controversy arising from competing paradigms. Given the disproportion between the number of academics and 'cult-monitoring' groups and *Sektenbeauftragte*, it was difficult for the academic community to contend with the controversy and compete with the 'other' paradigm successfully. Some academics did not relish controversy and left the field. It may be that ethical and political issues, tangled as they were with the aftermath of Nazi history, were just too intense for a profession which had for so long been shielded, in particular from media controversy, by its tradition of 'ivory tower' and 'a-political' assumptions. The EZW had similar problems, as my interview with Dr Hummel highlighted. This may have been a factor in Dr Nüchtern's relatively short directorship.

In their attempts to develop an alternative paradigm, German academics looked towards Britain and the United States, which was also due to the lack of suitable frameworks in *Religionswissenschaft*. Although the academic community found it difficult to make its voice heard in the NRM debate, the creation of REMID sought to act as a counterbalance. It is further significant that a student of *Religionswissenschaft*, Hubert Seiwert, acted as an expert for the *Enquête-Kommission*, although, or maybe because, his expertise lies in ancient Chinese religion rather than NRMs.

The Roman Catholic Church also entered the debate at a late stage and with great caution. On the practical level, it 'dealt' with the problem by teaming up with other institutions. However, the differences between Britain and Germany are very important: in Britain, the Church did not feel the 'threat' of NRMs so acutely, as it is a minority religion; Housetop, later in conjunction with INFORM, could take care of whatever problems needed to be dealt with. In Germany, the Church plays an important pillar role and found itself in the same situation as the Lutheran Church, regarding pastoral problems and threat to membership. However, it 'imitated' the Lutheran Church by installing in each diocese designated 'experts', who have worked closely with their Lutheran counterparts. On the international level, the situation has been altogether different and required due care and consideration. When the Vatican started to concern itself with the issue in response to demands for guidance from the 'grassroots', it had no structures in place whose remit would encompass this issue. Therefore, the co-operation and co-ordination of four separate dicastaries were enlisted for the Vatican Report, the result of a 'fact-finding' and survey exercise for which responses to a questionnaire from local bishops' conferences were collated. These responses made clear that the phenomenon involved both pastoral and theological issues and prompted the Vatican to create structures for exploring these issues. The F.I.U.C. project was set in motion as a follow-up to the Vatican Report and eventually a 'chair' for NRMs was created in one of the Vatican offices, the Pontifical Council for Interreligious Dialogue, so that one person would co-ordinate relevant studies and materials.

Like the Anglican Church, the Roman Catholic Church looked towards the academic community for developing its own knowledge paradigm: it launched the F.I.U.C. project with a view to gathering knowledge from theologians at Catholic universities and other academics. At the same time, Vatican offices started to explore the possibility of dialogue with NRMs by studying existing Vatican documents, including papal encyclicals and addresses as well as pronouncements on inter-religious dialogue resulting from Vatican II. Despite Vatican officials looking for guidance in such documents, the Church has so far declared dialogue with NRMs to be distinct from inter-religious dialogue. For someone extraneous to Vatican thinking, there is a puzzling contradiction. The documents to which repeated references are made regarding possible dialogue with NRMs deal with dialogue *in general terms* – ecumenical and inter-religious dialogue, but they do not address NRMs at all or mention them only in passing as a modern phenomenon which the Church needs to take into account. One of these documents, *Dialogue and Proclamation*, actually deals with dialogue with NRMs, but only to *exclude* them from its considerations. While one might conclude that statements about inter-religious dialogue could be applied to NRMs, especially because Vatican officials and theological commentators so often refer to them, this is thwarted by the equally frequent statement that NRMs are unlike other religions and can thus not be treated within the framework formulated for inter-religious dialogue. This apparent contradiction – the examination of documents on inter-religious dialogue and the insistence that dialogue with NRMs requires special treatment – seems to indicate that the Church is still in the process of formulating its stance towards NRMs, in particular regarding the question of whether, and if so how, dialogue should be conducted with them. Yet some theologians, such as Michael Fuss, have already 'decided' that dialogue with NRMs is possible and developed the theological groundwork for the way in which such dialogue should or could be conducted. At the same time, some NRMs, such as ISKCON, are pressing for recognition as part of 'other religions' or the 'world religions', a recognition which would 'automatically' place them within the framework of inter-religious dialogue and thus eliminate the question how the dialogue with NRMs should be shaped.

In examining selected institutions involved in the NRM debate, I have, in some instances, referred to the role of other institutions and 'voices'. The media have played a central role, but I have only touched on this issue, as it would require a study in its own right. This is a difficult area, because the material is far more diffuse. I had originally envisaged focusing on the media, but realized that it is virtually impossible to assess their role without a clear idea of the chronology of responses to NRMs. My research then became an exercise in situating different discourses from different interest bases and tracing the interaction among them. What has been said about the media also applies to the assessment of the responses of governments and state authorities, although some material about this is included here.

Another underlying concern in my research has been the question of methodology. The introductory chapter mentioned some of the problems I encountered. While exploring different institutional responses, I have been running into methodological problems and found a minefield in the arbitrary heuristic separation of the description of institutions and what they themselves have said. Initially, I perceived these methodological problems as acute ethical problems: they concern the question of how and for what purpose information is created, how and to which institutions it is distributed. These are questions with which the sociology and philosophy of knowledge are concerned.

When I realized that the *provenance* of information was an important factor in evaluating information, I started with the notion of 'contamination'. This notion conveys the sense that the *provenance* affects the 'moral' as well as 'scientific' value of the information. It does, however, not address the real issue, which is the purpose for which information is created and distributed. Nor does it bring the debate forward, because it involves an element of judgmental righteousness. There is nothing intrinsically wrong in information being created and distributed for a particular purpose. One can, of course, question the validity and 'morality' of a given purpose, but that is a separate question. The notion of 'contamination' could, however, be useful, if understood in connection with Berger's concept of 'cultural contamination', which is based on the idea that in a pluralistic world, plausibility structures are only temporary; 'cultural contamination takes place, when we are exposed to other cultures or communities. In this sense, the notion of 'contamination' could be helpful in exploring the extent to which accounts are 'negotiated' between the various voices in the NRM debate.

The problems, which I encountered during my research and sought to explore in interviews with some academics, seemed to be 'ethical' problems.

Perhaps they should be considered methodological problems with an ethical dimension, for example, attending NRM-sponsored conferences, accepting NRM research funding, acting on behalf of NRMs in the sense of 'speaking out' in their defence. Homan (1991: 1) perceives a distinction between morality and ethics in social research: 'morality is often thought of as being exogenous, whereas ethics refers to the standard established within the profession for the conduct of its members'. Homan quotes B. Häring, for whom the ethos of a profession consists of the 'distinctive attitudes which characterize the culture of a professional group' (ibid.) and ethics are the attempt to express and elaborate this ethos. Homan argues that ethics consist now in recognizing consensual standards according to which social research is judged. In this sense, some of the problems I encountered are of an 'ethical' nature. However, it is my impression that the academic community concerned with the study of NRMs has not come to a consensus on some of the issues involved. The debate on these issues is problematic in itself, because it can so easily glide into personal attacks and *ad hominem* arguments. However, I do believe that such issues can be and should be debated on questions of principle, not least to give 'younger' researchers guidance or make them aware of potential conflicts and dilemmas. Homan (ibid.: 25) would like to see ethical principles included in social science courses, both at under- and postgraduate level. This would also serve as an induction into relevant professional associations. 'The appreciation of professional standards is an aspect of professional socialisation which is seriously neglected in the social sciences when compared with other fields such as medicine and law' (ibid.: 26; also 183).

Homan's discussion of ethics and morality concludes that instead of ethics in social research, there should be a professional morality, located between public and private morality. However, social research is problematic when it involves tension between personal moral standards and professional ethics. Such tension arises from the fact that professional ethics are largely based on professional self-interest which turns into ethical guidelines what are otherwise considered moral ends in themselves. For example, open procedures for social research are recommended not only because people have a right to know, but also because their use furthers the reputation of the research community or the quality of the research results. To illustrate, Homan quotes the Market Research Society's *Code of Conduct* and researchers who combine ethical considerations with methodological considerations (ibid.: 3–4). However, compared with medicine, moral principles applied to social science are poorly developed and ethical guidelines 'invite professionals to play their own system' (ibid.: 181). Homan finds an explanation for these inadequacies: ethical principles have been fuelled by professional self-interest rather than moral convictions. Ethical behaviour is recommended only because unethical practice results in unwanted consequences – it stems from expediency rather than principled professional attitude. The literature which deals with the ethics of social research hardly mentions morality, except in terms of values and dispositions which the researcher brings to the research situation. These are perceived as separate from the professionally agreed ethics. However, '[p]rofessionals can undercut one another with their moralities as they can with their ethics' (ibid.: 182), if one researcher will not accept a contract because he/she has moral scruples, another will because he/she does not share such scruples. There is a need for a professional morality in view of researchers trading and offering the reputation and integrity of the profession – in some cases irredeemably so.

Again, I believe further exploration is needed regarding the study of NRMs. There are, for example, various roles which researchers may combine in relation to research subjects. A researcher may have a role in the private life of subjects and thus gain access to data which would be inaccessible for other researchers. There is the question whether – or to what extent – insiders can carry out research on their own organization from within the conceptual framework of social science. Homan (1991: 62) describes the case of Samuel Heilman, a sociologist, who was offered a grant to study the Orthodox Jewish community of which he was a long-standing member. He had qualms about using his friends as informants and his privileged access for research purposes. His research had serious consequences for his membership and his work was discredited by the fact that he was an insider. To my knowledge, this has not happened in NRM research or research in the Anglican Church.

As to other methodological problems – how to conduct research, how to apply the concept of *verstehen*, how to 'bracket off' personal preconceptions and preconceived ideas – it seems that some researchers 'solve' these by using a 'positivistic' approach or viewing such problems as not overly significant. For others, the idea of researchers stepping back as persons while doing research is an ideal at best, an impossibility at worst. They believe that one can but apply available techniques to reduce personal feelings and preconceptions, including de-roling exercises, organizing research in stages to defer exposure to 'biased' opinion, postponing discussion of research data until subjects have had a fair hearing, etc., but academics are people after all, people with opinions and views which influence and shape the selection of data and the conclusions drawn from the data, people with varying degrees of awareness regarding their opinions and views. Moreover, 'postmodern' social theory insists on the inescapable 'positionality' of the observer, which bedevils further an already delicate problem. At the same time this implicitly or explicitly acknowledges the validity or in any case the incommensurability of various discourses and thus gives rise to relativism.

An important aspect of all these considerations is that the study of NRMs is a highly sensitive area because of the potential for controversy and contest. The clash of interests between the various participants in the debate are connected to the different agendas which each party pursues. Reconciling research interests with one set of participants may alienate another set and thus preclude research in that area. What paralysed me in my own research at some points were areas where methodological and ethical considerations were closely intertwined and where relative lack of experience and status affected the situation.

These issues cannot be separated or understood without the processes involved in the creation and exchange of knowledge, again, because knowledge is created and exchanged for particular purposes. There is miscommunication, ambiguity, competition, and disagreement about what is and what is not. While a definitive version is neither possible nor intended, the main threads can be traced and the issues raised to a different level of discussion. Taking the approach of sociology of knowledge may allow for a fuller analysis of the material, for which this book may provide the basis. *Religionswissenschaft* or the theologies of the different movements could also yield useful analyses, as might other conceptual approaches, such as rational choice theory.

Bibliography

Aagaard, Johannes. 'Dialog and Apologetics.' *Update & Dialog*, 1992a: 12–14.

Aagaard, Johannes. 'Zehn Leitsätze für einen relevanten Dialog zwischen Religionen.' *Materialdienst* 55 (10), 1992b: 296–297. (First published in *Update & Dialog* 1 (June), 1992.)

Abel, Ralf, *et al*. *Die Rechtssprechung zu Neueren Glaubensgemeinschaften: Ein systematischer Überblick*. Krefeld: Dokumentations- und Informationszentrum Jugendsekten/Psychokulte, 1991.

Ach, Manfred. 'Das geht nicht spurlos an einem vorüber: Rückblick auf einen Lebensabschnitt.' In *20 Jahre Elterninitiative*. Elterninitiative zur Hilfe gegen seelische Abhängigkeit und religiösen Extremismus e.V., Ed. Munich: Elterninitiative zur Hilfe gegen seelische Abhängigkeit und religiösen Extremismus, 1995a: 25–32.

Ach, Manfred. *Under Cover: 20 Jahre ARW*. Munich: Arbeitsgemeinschaft für Religions- und Weltanschauungsfragen (ARW), 1995b.

AGPF (Aktion für geistige und psychische Freiheit – Arbeitsgemeinschaft der Elterninitiativen e.V.), Ed. *Dokumentation über die Auswirkung der Jugendreligionen auf Jugendliche in Einzelfällen*. Bonn-Bad Godesberg: AGPF, 1978.

AGPF (Aktion für geistige und psychische Freiheit – Arbeitsgemeinschaft der Elterninitiativen e.V.). *Stellungnahme der 'Arbeitsgemeinschaft der Elterninitiativen e.V.' zum Bericht der Bundesregierung vom 21. Dezember 1979*. Bonn: AGPF, 1980.

Ahlstrom, Sydney E. 'The Traumatic Years: American Religion and Culture in the '60s and '70s.' *Theology Today* 36, 1980: 504–522.

Ahumada, Ernesto Corripio, 'Fourth Extraordinary Consistory: Regional Reports on Sects.' *L'Osservatore Romano* 15 (15 April), 1991: 7–9.

Aichelin, Helmut, Michael Mildenberger, Wilhelm Quenzer, Hans-Diether Reimer, and Hannelore Schilling. *Im Gespräch mit der Zeit*. Impulse, Vol. 10 III. Stuttgart: Evangelische Zentralstelle für Weltanschauungsfragen (EZW), 1976.

Aktion Bildungsinformation e.V. *Die Scientology-Sekte und ihre Tarnorganisationen. Informationen über die Größte der neuen Sekten*. Stuttgart: Aktion Bildungsinformation e.V., 1979.

Aktion Jugendschutz. *Destruktive Kulte. Neue Heilslehren, Jugendsekten, Psychokulte. Gefahr und Herausforderung. Eine Information*. Stuttgart: Aktion Jugendschutz, n.d.

Aktion Jugendschutz – Kath. Landesarbeitsstelle Rheinland-Pfalz e.V., Ed. *Neue religiöse Organisationen/Jugendreligionen – Informationen, Dokumente, Meinungen*,

Fakten. Pirmasens: Aktion Jugendschutz, 1978 (1982). Schriftenreihe Beiträge zum Jugendschutz.

Aktion Jugendschutz – Kath. Landesarbeitsstelle Rheinland-Pfalz e.V., *Neue religiöse Organisationen – Glück oder Gefahr?* Pirmasens: Aktion Jugendschutz, 1983.

Aktion Jugendschutz Nordrhein-Westfalen. *Die Regenmacher. Informations- und Werkheft zu den sogenannten Jugendreligionen, Psychokulten und Meditationssekten.* Köln: Moekerdruck, 1980.

Alevisopoulos, Antonios. 'Skafidia.' In *20 Jahre Elterninitiative.* Elterninitiative zur Hilfe gegen seelische Abhängigkeit und religiösen Extremismus e.V., Ed. Munich: Elterninitiative zur Hilfe gegen seelische Abhängigkeit und religiösen Extremismus, 1995: 33–58.

Alland, A. 'Possession in Revivalist Negro Church.' *Journal for the Scientific Study of Religion* 1, 1962: 204–213.

Ammerman, Nancy T. Report to the Justice and Treasury Departments Regarding Law Enforcement Interaction with the Branch Davidians in Waco, Texas. 3 September, 1993.

Ammerman, Nancy T. 'Waco, Federal Law Enforcement, and Scholars of Religion.' In *Armageddon in Waco: Critical Perspectives on the Branch Davidian Conflict.* S. A. Wright, Ed. Chicago: University of Chicago Press, 1995: 282–296.

Andersen, S. and Philip G. Zimbardo 'On Resisting Social Influence.' *Cultic Studies Journal* 1 (2), 1984.

Annett, Stephen, Ed. *The Many Ways of Being: A Guide to Spiritual Groups and Growth Centres in Britain.* London: Abacus and Turnstone, 1976 (London: Sphere, 1979).

Anthony, Dick, and Thomas Robbins. 'The Meher Baba Movement: Its Effects on Post-Adolescent Youthful Alienation.' In *Religious Movements in Contemporary America.* I. Zaretzky and M. Leone, Eds. Princeton, NJ: Princeton U. P., 1974: 479–511.

Anthony, Dick, Thomas Robbins and Paul Schwartz. 'Contemporary Religious Movements and the Secularization Premise.' In *New Religious Movements.* J. Coleman and G. Baum, Eds. New York: Seabury, 1983: 1–8.

Anthony, Dick, Bruce Ecker, and Ken Wilber. *Spiritual Choices: The Problem of Recognizing Authentic Paths to Inner Transformation.* New York: Paragon, 1987.

Arbeitsgemeinschaft (AG) der Evangelischen Jugend in der BRD und Berlin West e.V. *Erfahrungen mit Jugendreligionen, Bericht von Jugendlichen, Eltern und Beratern mit Werkmappe 'Jugendreligionen'.* Stuttgart: AG, 1978a.

Arbeitsgemeinschaft (AG) der Evangelischen Jugend in der Bundesrepublik Deutschland und Berlin West e.V., Ed. *Guru Maharaj Ji: Reine und vollkommene Liebe.* Stuttgart: AG, 1978b.

Arbeitsgemeinschaft (AG) der Evangelischen Jugend in der Bundesrepublik Deutschland und Berlin West e.V., Ed. *Die neue Religiosität. Anfragen an die Praxis evangelischer Jugendarbeit.* Stuttgart: AG, 1978c.

Arbeitsgemeinschaft Kinder- und Jugendschutz (AJS) and Ministerium für Arbeit/ Gesundheit und Soziales des Landes Nordrhein-Westfalen, Eds. *Sogenannte neuere Glaubensgemeinschaften unter besonderer Berücksichtigung der Scientology Kirche. Bericht des Ministeriums für Arbeit, Gesundheit und Soziales des Landes Nordrhein-Westfalen.* Essen: Drei-W-Verlag, 1993 (1st edn; 1994, 2nd edn). AJS Forum – Vierteljährlicher Info-Dienst der AJS, Landesstelle NRW e.V., Special Issue.

Arinze, Francis. 'A Pastoral Approach to the Challenge Posed by the New Religious Movements.' *L'Osservatore Romano*, 15 April 1991: 5–6. (Also published in *Catholic International* 2 (13), 1–14 July 1991: 605–618.)

Arinze, Francis and Jozef Tomko, 'Dialogue and Proclamation: Reflections and Orientations on Interreligious Dialogue and the Proclamation of the Gospel of Jesus Christ.' *Pontificium Consilium pro Dialogo Inter Religiones Bulletin* XXVI (2), 1991: 201–250.

Arweck, Elisabeth. Die Sekten in Frankreich. Unpublished MA Thesis. Johannes-Gutenberg-Universität Mainz, FB Angewandte Sprachwissenschaft, Germersheim, 1985.

Arweck, Elisabeth. 'Research Note: Sekten in Frankreich.' *Religion Today* 3 (1), 1986: 11–12.

Arweck, Elisabeth. 'The Role of the Sociologist of New Religious Movements: Devil's Advocate or Advocate of the Devil?' Paper presented to the Social Science Seminar at King's College London, 1994a.

Arweck, Elisabeth. 'Advocates of the Devil? The Role of Sociologists of NRMs.' Paper presented to the Sociology of Religion Seminar at London School of Economics, London, 15 June 1994b.

Arweck, Elisabeth and Peter B. Clarke. *New Religious Movements in Western Europe: An Annotated Bibliography*. Westport, CT: Greenwood Press, 1997.

Asch, S. E. *Effects of Group Pressure Upon the Modification and Distortion of Judgement*. New York: Holt, Rhinehart and Winston, 1952.

Asociación Pro Juventud. *Las sectas como problema social. Ponencias presentadas y communicados. Actas del Primer Congreso Internacional sobre Sectas y Societad, November 27–29, 1987*. Barcelona: Asociación Pro Juventud, 1988.

Atack, Jon. 'Scientology Goes East.' *Update & Dialog* 2 (1), 1993: 14–16.

Badham, Paul. 'Religious Studies at Lampeter.' *BASR Bulletin* 79 (November), 1996: 21–23.

Baer, Donald M. and Stephanie B. Stolz. 'A Description of the Erhard Seminars Training (est) in Terms of Behavior Analysis.' *Behaviorism* VI (1), 1978: 45–70.

Bahre, Jens. *Die Sekte*. Bergisch-Gladbach: Bastei-Lübbe, 1995.

Bainbridge, William S. and Rodney Stark. 'Cult Formation: Three Compatible Models.' *Sociological Analysis* 40 (4), 1979: 283–295.

Bainbridge, William S. and Rodney Stark. 'Client and Audience Cults in America.' *Sociological Analysis* 41 (2), 1980: 137–143.

Baird, Robert D. 'Religious or Non-Religious: TM in American Courts.' *The Journal of Dharma* 7 (4), 1982: 391–407.

Baker, Carlos. *Emerson among the Eccentrics: A Group Portrait*. New York: Viking Penguin, 1996.

Baker, George. 'Language and Mind in the Study of New Religious Movements.' In *Understanding the New Religions*. J. Needleman and G. Baker, Eds. New York: Seabury, 1978: 285–298.

Balch, Robert W. 'Looking Behind the Scenes in a Religious Cult: Implications for the Study of Conversion.' *Sociological Analysis* 41 (2), 1980: 137–143.

Balch, Robert W. and David Taylor. 'Seekers and Saucers: The Role of the Cultic Milieu in Joining a UFO Cult.' In *Conversion Careers: In and Out of the New Religions*. J. T. Richardson, Ed. Beverly Hills, CA: Sage, 1978: 43–64. (Also published in *American Behavioral Scientist* 20 (6), 1977: 839–860.)

Bancroft, Anne. 'Women Disciples in Zen Buddhism.' In *Women as Teachers and*

Disciples in Traditional and New Religions. Studies in Women and Religion, Vol. 32, E. Puttick and P. B. Clarke, Eds. Lampeter: Edwin Mellen, 1993: 91–96.

Bankstone, W. B., C. J. Forsyth and H. H. Floyd. 'Toward a General Model of Radical Conversion.' *Qualitative Sociology* 4, 1981: 279–297.

Barker, Eileen. 'Living the Divine Principle: Inside the Reverend Sun Myung Moon's Unification Church in Britain.' *Archives des Sciences Sociales des Religions* 45 (1), 1978: 75–93.

Barker, Eileen. 'Whose Service is Perfect Freedom: The Concept of Spiritual Well-Being in Relation to the Reverend Moon's Unification Church in Britain.' In *Spiritual Well-Being: Sociological Perspectives.* D. O. Moberg, Ed. Washington: UP of America, 1979: 153–172.

Barker, Eileen. 'Free to Choose? Some Thoughts on the Unification Church and Other Religious Movements: Parts I and II.' *The Clergy Review* 65 (10, October; 11, November), 1980a: 365–368; 392–398.

Barker, Eileen. 'The Professional Stranger: Some Methodological Problems Encountered in a Study of the Reverend Sun Myung Moon's Unification Church.' In *Open University Course Media Notes for AD207. An Introduction to Sociology.* Milton Keynes: Open University, 1980b: 5–15.

Barker, Eileen. 'Who'd be a Moonie? A Comparative Study of Those Who Join the Unification Church in Britain.' In *The Social Impact of New Religious Movements.* B. R. Wilson, Ed. New York: Rose of Sharon, 1981a: 59–96.

Barker, Eileen. 'Der professionelle Fremde: Erklärung des Unerklärlichen beim Studium einer abweichenden religiösen Gruppe.' In *Das Entstehen einer neuen Religion. Der Fall der Vereinigungskirche.* G. Kehrer, Ed. Munich: Kösel-Verlag, 1981b: 13–40.

Barker, Eileen, Ed. *New Religious Movements: A Perspective for Understanding Society.* New York, Toronto: Edwin Mellen, 1982a.

Barker, Eileen. 'New Religious Movements: A Perspective for Understanding Society.' In *New Religious Movements: A Perspective for Understanding Society.* E. Barker, Ed. New York: Edwin Mellen, 1982b: ix–xxv.

Barker, Eileen. 'Supping with the Devil: How Long a Spoon Does the Sociologist Need?' *Sociological Analysis* 44 (3), 1983a: 197–205.

Barker, Eileen. 'New Religious Movements in Britain: The Context and the Membership.' *Social Compass* 30 (1), 1983b: 33–48.

Barker, Eileen. 'The Ones Who Got Away: People Who Attend Unification Workshops and Do Not Become Moonies.' In *Of Gods and Men: New Religious Movements in the West.* E. Barker, Ed. Macon, GA: Mercer, 1983c: 309–336.

Barker, Eileen. *The Making of a Moonie: Brainwashing or Choice?* Oxford: Blackwell, 1984.

Barker, Eileen. 'New Religious Movements: Yet Another Great Awakening?' In *The Sacred in a Secular Age: Towards Revision in the Scientific Study of Religion.* P. E. Hammond, Ed. Berkeley: University of California Press, 1985a: 36–57.

Barker, Eileen. 'The Conversion of Conversion: A Sociological Anti-Reductionist Perspective.' In *Reductionism in Academic Disciplines.* A. R. Peacocke, Ed. Guildford, Surrey: SHRE and NFER Nelson, 1985b: 58–75.

Barker, Eileen. 'World Congress for the Synthesis of Science and Religion: A Personal Account.' *ISKCON Review* 2, 1986a: 133–147.

Barker, Eileen. 'Religious Movements: Cult and Anti-Cult since Jonestown.' *Annual Review of Sociology* 12, 1986b: 329–346.

Barker, Eileen. 'Freedom to Surrender with Bhagwan.' *Self and Society: European Journal of Humanistic Psychology* 15 (5), 1987a: 209–216.

Barker, Eileen. 'Brahmins Don't Eat Mushrooms.' *LSE Quarterly*, June, 1987b: 127–152.

Barker, Eileen. 'Kingdoms of Heaven and Earth: New Religious Movements and Political Orders.' In *Politics of Religion and Social Change: Religion and the Political Order. Vol. 2.* A. D. Shupe and J. K. Hadden, Eds. New York: Paragon House, 1988: 17–39.

Barker, Eileen. *New Religious Movements: A Practical Introduction.* London: HMSO, 1989a.

Barker, Eileen. 'Tolerant Discrimination: New Religious Movements in Relation to Church, State and Society.' In *Religion, State and Society in Modern Britain.* P. Badham, Ed. Lampeter: Edwin Mellen, 1989b: 185–208.

Barker, Eileen. 'Re-Born or Mis-Used?' *LSE Magazine*, Spring, 1990: 4–7.

Barker, Eileen. 'Charismatization: The Social Production of "an Ethos Propitious to the Mobilisation of Sentiments".' In *Secularization, Rationalism and Sectarianism.* E. Barker, J. Beckford, and K. Dobbelaere, Eds. Oxford: Oxford University Press, 1993: 181–201.

Barker, Eileen. 'Presidential Address: The Scientific Study of Religion? You Must be Joking!' *Journal for the Scientific Study of Religion* 34 (3), 1995: 287–310.

Barker, D., L. Halman and A. Vloet. *The European Values Study 1981–1990: Summary Report.* London: European Values Group, 1993.

Barnes, D. F. 'Charisma and Religious Leadership: An Historical Analysis.' *Journal for the Scientific Study of Religion* 17, 1978: 1–18.

Bartley, W. W. *Werner Erhard: The Transformation of a Man: The Founding of est.* New York: Clarkson N. Potter, 1978.

Baumann, Martin. 'Empirische Untersuchungen in der Religionswissenschaft. Notwendige Anmerkungen zu einem Artikel von M. Pilger in Form eines Literaturberichts.' *spirita* 3 (January), 1989: 19–21.

Baumann, Martin. *Buddhisten in Deutschland. Geschichte und Gemeinschaften.* Marburg: diagonal-Verlag, 1993.

Baumann, Martin. ' "Merkwürdige Bundesgenossen" und "naive Sympathisanten": Die Ausgrenzung der Religionswissenschaft aus der bundesdeutschen Kontroverse um neue Religionen.' *Zeitschrift für Religionswissenschaft* 3 (2), 1995: 111–136.

Beale, Alex and Rosalind Mitchell. 'I Am Not Moonstruck Any More.' *Crusade*, January, 1978: 4.

Bear, David M. and Paul Fedio. 'Quantitative Analysis of Interictal Behavior in Temporal Lobe Epilepsy.' *Archives of Neurology* 34 (August), 1977: 454–467.

Becker, Howard. *Systematic Sociology on the Basis of the Beziehungslehre und Gebildungslehre of Leopold von Wiese.* New York: Wiley; London: Chapman and Hall, 1932.

Becker, Howard. *Outsiders: Studies in the Sociology of Deviance.* New York: Free Press, 1963.

Becker, Kurt E. and Hans-Peter Schreiner, Eds. *Neue Religionen – Heil oder Unheil? Beispiel: Vereinigungskirche Sun Myung Moons.* Landau/Pfalz: Pfälzische Verlagsanstalt, 1982.

Beckford, James A. 'British Moonies on the Wane.' *Psychology Today* (UK Edition) 2 (8), 1976: 22–23.

Beckford, James A. 'Accounting for Conversion.' *British Journal of Sociology* 29 (2), 1978a: 249–262.

Beckford, James A. 'Through the Looking-Glass and Out the Other Side: Withdrawal from the Reverend Moon's Unification Church.' *Les Archives des Sciences Sociales des Religions* 45 (1), 1978b: 95–116.

Beckford, James A. 'Politics and the Anti-Cult Movement.' *Annual Review of the Social Sciences of Religion* 3, 1979: 169–190.

Beckford, James A. 'Functionalism and Ethics in Sociology: The Relationship between "Ought" and "Function".' *Annual Review of the Social Sciences of Religion* 5, 1981a: 101–132.

Beckford, James A. 'Cults, Controversy and Control: A Comparative Analysis of the Problems Posed by New Religious Movements in the Federal Republic of Germany and France.' *Sociological Analysis* 42 (3), 1981b: 249–263.

Beckford, James A. 'Beyond the Pale: Cults, Culture and Conflict.' In *New Religious Movements: A Perspective for Understanding Society.* E. Barker, Ed. New York, Toronto: Edwin Mellen, 1982: 284–301.

Beckford, James A. 'The Public Response to New Religious Movements in Britain.' *Social Compass* 30 (1), 1983a: 49–62.

Beckford, James A. 'The "Cult Problem" in Five Countries: The Social Construction of Religious Controversy.' In *Of Gods and Men: New Religious Movements in the West.* E. Barker, Ed. Macon, GA: Mercer, 1983b: 195–214.

Beckford, James A. 'Some Questions About the Relationship Between Scholars and the New Religious Movements.' *Sociological Analysis* 44 (3), 1983c: 189–195.

Beckford, James A. 'The State and Control of New Religious Movements.' In *Acts of the 17th International Conference for the Sociology of Religion.* Paris: Editions CISR, 1983d: 115–130.

Beckford, James A. ' "Brainwashing" and "Deprogramming" in Britain: The Social Sources of Anti-Cult Sentiment.' In *The Brainwashing and Deprogramming Controversy.* D. G. Bromley and J. T. Richardson, Eds. New York, Toronto: Edwin Mellen, 1983e: 122–138.

Beckford, James A. *Cult Controversies: The Societal Response to the New Religious Movements.* London: Tavistock, 1985.

Beckford, James A., Ed. *New Religious Movements and Rapid Social Change.* London: Sage Publications, 1986.

Beckford, James A. 'New Religions: An Overview.' In *Encyclopedia of Religion.* Vol. 10, M. Eliade, Ed. New York: Macmillan, 1987: 390–394.

Beckford, James A. 'The Literature on Western NRMs Outside the USA and the UK.' In *Cults, Converts and Charisma: The Sociology of New Religious Movements.* T. Robbins, Ed. London, Newbury Park, Beverly Hills: Sage, 1988: 17–23.

Beckford, James A. 'Politics and Religion in England and Wales.' *Daedalus* 120, 1991: 179–201.

Beckford, James A. 'States, Governments and the Management of Controversial New Religious Movements.' In *Secularization, Rationalism and Sectarianism.* E. Barker, J. Beckford, and K. Dobbelaere, Eds. Oxford: Oxford UP, 1993: 125–143.

Beckford, James. 'The Mass Media and New Religious Movements.' *ISKCON Communications Journal* 4 (July–December), 1994: 17–24.

Beckford, James A. and Melanie Cole. 'British and American Responses to

New Religious Movements.' In *Bulletin of the John Rylands University Library of Manchester*. Vol. 70, A. Dyson and E. Barker, Eds. Manchester, 1988: 209–224.

Beckford, James A. and Martine Levasseur. 'New Religious Movements in Western Europe.' In *New Religious Movements and Rapid Social Change*. J. A. Beckford, Ed. London: Sage, 1986: 29–54.

Beckford, James A., and Thomas Luckmann, Eds. *The Changing Face of Religion*. London, Newbury Park, CA: Sage, 1989.

Beckford, James A. and James T. Richardson. 'A Bibliography of Social Scientific Studies of New Religious Movements in the US and Europe.' *Social Compass* 30 (1), 1983: 111–135.

Bednarowski, Mary Farrell. *New Religions and the Theological Imagination of America*. Bloomington, Indianapolis: Indiana UP 1989.

Behnk, Wolfgang. 'Kirche des Evangeliums – Freiheit zur Orientierung. Zur Sinnkrise der Gesellschaft zwischen Verdrossenheit und Sektierertum.' *Materialdienst* 57 (7), 1994a: 185–192.

Behnk, Wolfgang. *Abschied vom 'Urchristentum'? Gabriele Witteks 'Universelles Leben' zwischen Verfolgungswahn und Institutionalisierung*. Munich: Arbeitsgemeinschaft für Religions- und Weltanschauungsfragen (ARW), 1994b.

Behnk, Wolfgang. 'Elterninitiativen aus kirchlicher Sicht.' In *20 Jahre Elterninitiative*. Elterninitiative zur Hilfe gegen seelische Abhängigkeit und religiösen Extremismus e.V., Ed. Munich: Elterninitiative zur Hilfe gegen seelische Abhängigkeit und religiösen Extremismus e.V., 1995: 59–75.

Behnk, Wolfgang. 'Neue Psychogruppen und Sekten – Eine Herausforderung für Gesellschaft, Kirche und Politik.' In *1995 – Und es geht weiter*. I. Kroll, B. Dürholt, im Auftrag der Elterninitiative zur Hilfe gegen seelische Abhängigkeit und religiösen Extremismus e.V., Eds. Munich: Arbeitsgemeinschaft für Religions- und Weltanschauungsfragen (ARW), 1996a: 71–97.

Behnk, Wolfgang. 'Der Artikel 4 des Grundgesetzes und die Frage der staatlichen Neutralitätspflicht, Dargestellt am Beispiel der Organisation "Universelles Leben".' *Materialdienst* 59 (7), 1996b: 204–213.

Bell, Daniel. 'The Return of the Sacred? The Argument on the Future of Religion.' *British Journal of Sociology* 28 (4), 1977: 419–449.

Bellah, Robert N. *The Broken Covenant: American Civil Religion in a Time of Trial*. New York: Seabury, 1975.

Bendrath, Detlef, Ed. *Information und Material zu Scientology/Dianetik*. Lübeck: Nordelbisches Kirchenamt (Kiel), 1991 (2nd revised and expanded edn), Nordelbische Reihe für Weltanschauungsfragen, Vol. 4.

Bennett, Clinton. 'Victory for Religious Freedom.' Address by the Revd Clinton Bennett, Secretary of the Committee for Relations with People of Other Faiths of the British Council of Churches (BCC), to the 'Interfaith Thanksgiving' held at the Unification Church Headquarters, Lancaster Gate, London, on 21 February 1988.

Bergen, Doris L. *Twisted Cross: The German Christian Movement in the Third Reich*. Chapel Hill, NC: University of North Carolina Press, 1995.

Berger, Herbert and Peter Hexel. *Ursachen und Wirkungen gesellschaftlicher Verweigerung junger Menschen unter besonderer Berücksichtigung der 'Jugendreligionen'*. Vienna: European Centre for Social Welfare, Training and Research, 1981a.

Berger, Herbert. and Peter Hexel. 'Zwischenbericht zum Forschungsprojekt "Ursachen und Wirkungen gesellschaftlicher Verweigerung junger Menschen unter besonderer Berücksichtigung der Jugendreligionen" ' *Eurosocial Newsletter* 21, 1981b: 10–12.

Berger, Peter L. *The Social Reality of Religion*. London: Faber, 1969.

Berger, Peter L. *A Rumour of Angels: Modern Society and the Rediscovery of the Supernatural*. Harmondsworth: Penguin Books, 1970.

Berger, Peter L. 'Whatever Happened to Sociology?' *First Things: The Journal of Religion and Public Life* 126, October 2002: 27–29.

Berger, Peter L. and Thomas Luckmann. 'Sociology of Religion and the Sociology of Knowledge.' *Sociology and Social Research* 47, 1963: 417–427. (Reprinted in Robertson, R., Ed. *Sociology of Religion: Selected Readings*. Harmondsworth: Penguin, 1969: 63–64.)

Beyer, Peter. *Religion and Globalisation*. London: Sage, 1994.

Beyes-Corleis, A. *Verirrt. Mein Leben in einer radikalen Politiorganisation*. Freiburg i. Br.: Herder, 1994.

Binning, Sarah. 'Business Profits with Responsibility for the New Age: Depicting Findhorn's Worldview and its Impact upon Current Business.' Paper presented to the Conference on 'New Religious Movements: Work and Business', King's College London, 11 December 1988.

Bird, Frederick. 'The Pursuit of Innocence: New Religious Movements and Moral Accountability.' *Sociological Analysis* 40 (4), 1979a: 335–346.

Bird, Frederick. 'Charismatic Cults: An Examination of the Ritual Practices of Various New Religious Movements.' In *Ritual and Ceremonialism in the Americas*. Vol. 2. N. R. Crumrine, Ed. Greeley, CO: Museum of Anthropology, University of Northern Colorado, 1979b: 214–249.

Bird, Frederick B. 'Theories of Justice in New Religions and Para-Religious Movements.' *Studies in Religion* 15, 1986: 17–28.

Bird, Frederick B. and Frances Westley. 'The Economic Strategies of New Religious Movements.' *Sociological Analysis* 46 (2), 1985: 157–170. (Reprinted in Richardson, J. T. Ed. *Power and Money in the New Religions*. Lewiston, NY: Edwin Mellen, 1988: 45–68.)

Bjorling, Joel. *Mediumship and Channeling: A Bibliography*. New York: Garland, 1990.

Black, Alan W. *Is Scientology a Religion?* Los Angeles: Freedom Publishing, n.d.

Blasi, Anthony J. and Michael W. Cuneo. *Issues in the Sociology of Religion: A Bibliography*. New York: Garland, 1986.

Bloom, William, Ed. *The New Age: An Anthology of Essential Writings*. London: Rider for Channel 4, 1991.

Board for Mission and Unity. 'Document BMU (E) 38/83.' 15 November 1983.

Board for Mission and Unity. 'Document BMU/26/84.' 21 May 1984.

Bochinger, Christoph. *'New Age' und moderne Religion: Religionswissenschaftliche Analysen*. Gütersloh: Gütersloher Verlagshaus, 1995.

Bochinger, Christoph. ' "Kritik an Religionen?" Symposium in Marburg, 24 bis 26 November 1995.' *spirita* 10 (1), 1996: 42–44.

Böckenförde, E.-W. *Religionsfreiheit: Die Kirche in der Modernen Welt*. Schriften zu Staat, Gesellschaft, Kirche, Vol. 3. Freiburg i. Br.: Herder, 1990.

Bocklet, Reinhold. 'Kampf gegen die Jugendsekten auf europäischer Ebene.' In *Die neuen Jugendreligionen. Teil 4: Aktionen, Hilfen, Initiativen*. F.-W. Haack,

U. Schuster and M. Ach, Eds. Munich: Evangelischer Presseverband Bayern, 1986: 14–18.

Borenstein, Eliot. 'Articles of Faith: The Media Response to Maria Devi Khristos.' *Religion* 25 (3), 1995: 249–266.

Borowik, Irena. 'Religion and Sexual Values in Poland.' *Journal of Contemporary Religion* 11 (1), 1996: 89–94.

Bötsch, Wolfgang. 'Eine grundlegende Jugendpolitik als Hilfestellung.' In *Die neuen Jugendreligionen. Teil 4: Aktionen, Hilfen, Initiativen.* F.-W. Haack, U. Schuster and M. Ach, Eds. Munich: Evangelischer Presseverband Bayern, 1986: 9–13.

Boulton, David. *The Making of Tania: The Patty Hearst Story.* London: New English Library, 1975.

Bowart, Walter. *Operation Mind Control.* Glasgow/Douglas, Isle of Man: Fontana/ Collins, 1978.

Bowie, Fiona, Ed. *The Coming Deliverer: Millennial Themes in World Religions.* Cardiff: University of Wales Press, 1997.

Breese, Dave. *Know the Marks of Cults.* Wheaton, Ill.: Victor Books, 1985.

British Council of Churches (BCC). *The Unification Church: A Paper for Those Who Wish to Know More.* London: BCC, 1978.

British Council of Churches – Committee for Relations with People of Other Faiths. *Secretary's Twentieth Informal Report.* September–December, 1985.

Brockway, Allan R. and J. Paul Rajashekar, Eds. *New Religious Movements and the Churches.* Geneva: World Council of Churches Publications, 1987.

Bromley, David G., Ed. *Falling from the Faith: Causes and Consequences of Religious Apostasy.* Beverly Hills, CA, London: Sage, 1988a.

Bromley, David G. 'Hare Krishna and the Anti-Cult Movement.' In *Krishna Consciousness in the West.* D. Bromley and L. Shinn, Eds. Lewisburg, PA: Bucknell U. P., 1988b: 255–292.

Bromley, David G. and Anson D. Shupe. 'The Tnevnoc Cult.' *Sociological Analysis* 40 (4), 1979: 361–366.

Bromley, David G. and Anson D. Shupe. 'Financing the New Religions: A Resource Mobilization Approach.' *Journal for the Scientific Study of Religion* 19 (3), 1980: 227–239.

Bromley, David G., and Anson D. Shupe. *Strange Gods: The Great American Cult Scare.* Boston, NY: Beacon, 1981a.

Bromley, David G. and Anson D. Shupe. 'Dynamik zwischen Ideologie und sozialer Organisation in sozialen Bewegungen: Der Fall der Unifikatorischen Bewegung.' In *Das Entstehen einer neuen Religion: Das Beispiel der Vereinigungskirche.* G. Kehrer, Ed. Munich: Kösel-Verlag, 1981b: 109–127.

Bromley, David G. and Anson Shupe. 'Anti-Cultism in the United States: Origins, Ideology and Organizational Development.' *Social Compass* 42 (2), 1995: 221–236.

Bromley, David, Anson D. Shupe, and Joseph C. Ventimiglia. 'Atrocity Tales, the Unification Church and the Social Construction of Evil.' *Journal of Communication* 29 (Summer), 1979: 42–53.

Bromley, David G., Bruce C. Busching, and Anson D. Shupe. 'The Unification Church and the American Family: Strain, Conflict and Control.' In *New Religious Movements: A Perspective for Understanding Society.* E. Barker, Ed. New York: Edwin Mellen, 1982: 302–311.

Brooks, Maggie. *Heavenly Deception.* London: Chatto and Windus, 1985.

Brown, Callum. *The Death of Christian Britain*. London: Routledge, 2001.

Bruce, Steve S. 'Born Again: Conversion, Crusades and Brainwashing.' *Scottish Journal of Religious Studies* 3 (2), 1982: 107–123.

Bruce, Steve, Ed. *Religion and Modernization: Historians and Sociologists Debate the Secularization Thesis*. Oxford: Oxford UP, 1992.

Bry, Adelaide. *60 Hours That Transform Your Life: est: Erhard Seminar Training*. New York: Avon, Harper and Row, 1976 (London: Turnstone, 1977).

Bulmer, Martin. 'Comment on "The Ethics of Covert Methods".' *British Journal of Sociology* 31, 1980: 59–65.

Bulmer, Martin, Ed. *Social Research Ethics*. London: Macmillan, 1982.

Bundesminister für Jugend, Famile und Gesundheit, Ed. *Jugendreligionen in der Bundesrepublik, Bericht der Bundesregierung an den Petitionsausschuß der Deutschen Bundestages*. Bonn: Bundesminister für Jugend, Famile und Gesundheit, 1980. Berichte und Dokumente der Bundesregierung, Vol. 21.

Bundesministerium für Familie, Senioren, Frauen und Jugend. *Die Scientology-Organisation: Ziele, Praktiken und Gefahren*. Cologne: Bundesverwaltungsamt, 1996.

Byrne, Peter, and Peter Clarke. *Religion Defined and Explained*. Basingstoke: Macmillan, 1992.

Caberta, Ursula. 'Probleme von Scientology-Aussteigern: Nachsorge und Selbsthilfe.' In *Anstösse. Beiträge zur Landespolitik*. SPD Landtagsfraktion Baden-Württemberg, Ed. Stuttgart: SPD Landtagsfraktion Baden-Württemberg, 1994: 22–24.

Campbell, Colin. 'The Cult, the Cultic Milieu, and Secularization.' In *A Sociological Yearbook of Religion in Britain*. M. Hill, Ed. London: SCM Press, 1972: 119–136.

Campbell, Colin. 'The Secret Religion of the Educated Classes.' *Sociological Analysis* 39 (2), 1978: 146–156.

Campiche, Roland. 'Le traitement du religieux par les médias.' *Études théologiques et religieuses* 72 (2), 1997: 267–279.

Carroll, Jackson W. 'Transcendence and Mystery in the Counter-Culture.' *Religion in Life* 42, 1973: 361–375.

Carter, Lewis F. *Charisma and Control in Rajneeshpuram: The Role of Shared Values in the Creation of a Community*. New York: Cambridge UP, 1990.

Cashmore, Ernest. *Rastaman: The Rastafarian Movement in England*. London: George Allen and Unwin, 1983 (first published in 1979).

Cashmore, Ernest E. *The Rastafarians*. London: Minority Rights Group, 1984.

Catholic Truth Society. *Redemptoris Missio: Encyclical Letter of the Supreme Pontiff John Paul II on the Permanent Validity of the Church's Missionary Mandate*. London: Catholic Truth Society, 1991.

Causton, Richard. *Nichiren Shoshu Buddhism: An Introduction*. London: Rider, 1988.

CCBI (The Council of Churches for Britain and Ireland). 'CCBI Brochure.' London: CCBI, 1995.

Centre d'Études des Religions Africaines. *Sectes, Cultures et Sociétés. Les enjeux spirituels du temps présent. Quatrième Colloque International du C.E.R.A. en collaboration avec la Fédération Internationale des Universités catholiques (F.I.U.C.) (Kinshasa 14–21 novembre 1992)*. Kinshasa: Facultés Catholiques de Kinshasa, 1994. (= Cahiers des Religions Africaines 27–28 (53–56), 1993–1994).

Cheal, David. 'Cult Follower.' *She* Magazine, November, 1985.

Chéry, H.-Ch. *L'Offensive des Sectes*. Paris: Le Cerf, 1954 (2nd edn).

Choquette, Diane. *New Religious Movements in the United States and Canada: A Critical Assessment and Annotated Bibliography*. Westport, CT, London: Greenwood Press, 1985.

Christ, Christine. 'L'anguille anglaise.' *Hebdo*, 13 April 1989: 82.

Chryssides, George. 'Religious Syncretism with Specific Reference to the Unification Church.' Paper presented to the BASR Annual Conference on 'Religions in Transformation: Innovation, Adaptation and Syncretism', Winchester, 8–10 September 1992.

Chryssides, George. 'Religious Studies at Wolverhampton.' *BASR Bulletin* 80 (March), 1997: 6–11.

Chryssides, George. 'Britain's Anti-Cult Movement.' In *New Religious Movements: Challenge and Response*. Bryan Wilson and Jamie, Cresswell Eds. London and New York: Routledge, 1999: 257–271.

Church of Scientology. *What is Scientology? The Comprehensive Reference on the World's Fastest Growing Religion*. Los Angeles: Church of Scientology of California, 1992 (first published in 1978).

Church of Scientology. *Hate and Propaganda Sanctioned and Promoted by the German Media and Government*. (no place indicated): Church of Scientology International, 1993.

Clark, E. T. *The Small Sects in America*. New York: Abingdon, 1937.

Clark, John. 'Investigating the Effects of Some Religious Cults on the Health and Welfare of Their Converts.' Testimony to the Special Investigating Committee of the Vermont Senate, 1976.

Clark, John G. 'The Noisy Brain in a Noisy World.' Paper presented to the Association of Psychology of New Jersey, 11 May 1977.

Clark, John G. 'The Manipulation of Madness.' Paper presented to the German Society for Child and Adolescent Psychiatry in Hannover, 24 February 1978a.

Clark, John. 'Problems in Referral of Cult Members.' *Journal of the National Association of Private Psychiatric Hospitals* 9 (4), 1978b: 27–29.

Clark, John G. 'Untersuchungen über die Auswirkungen einiger religiöser Sekten auf Gesundheit und Wohlergehen ihrer Anhänger.' *Praxis der Kinderpsychologie und -psychiatrie* 27 (2), 1978c: 55–60.

Clark, John G. 'Der künstlich gesteuerte Wahnsinn.' In *'Neue Jugendreligionen': Vorträge und Berichte einer Fachtagung über 'Probleme im Zusammenhang mit den sogenannten Jugendreligionen' am 23./24. Februar 1978 in der Medizinischen Hochschule Hannover*. M. Müller-Küppers and F. Specht, Eds. Göttingen: Vandenhoeck and Ruprecht, 1979a: 85–103.

Clark, John. 'Cults.' *Journal of the American Medical Association* 242 (3), 1979b: 279–281.

Clark, John. 'Sudden Personal Change and the Maintenance of Critical Governmental Institutions.' Paper presented to the Annual Meeting of the International Society of Political Psychology, Washington, DC, 1979c.

Clark, John, Michael Langone, Robert Schecter, and Robert Daly. *Destructive Cult Conversion: Theory, Research and Treatment*. Weston, MA: American Family Foundation, 1981.

Clarke, Peter B. *Black Paradise: The Rastafarian Movement*. Wellingborough, Northants: Aquarian Press, 1986.

Clarke, Peter B., Ed. *The New Evangelists: Recruitment, Methods and Aims of New Religious Movements.* London: Ethnographica, 1987a.

Clarke, Peter B. 'New Religions in Britain and Western Europe: In Decline?' In *The New Evangelists: Recruitment, Methods and Aims of New Religious Movements.* P. B. Clarke, Ed. London: Ethnographica, 1987b: 5–15.

Clarke, Peter B. 'New Religious Movements.' In *The World's Religions.* S. Sutherland *et al.*, Eds. London: Routledge, 1988: 905–966.

Clarke, Peter B. 'New Religious Movements.' In *Contemporary Religions: A World Guide.* I. Harris, S. Mews, P. Morris, and J. Shephard, Eds. Harlow, Essex: Longman, 1992: 57–66.

Clarke, Peter B. 'Introduction: Change and Variety in New Religious Movements in Western Europe, *c.*1960 to the Present.' In *New Religious Movements in Western Europe: An Annotated Bibliography.* E. Arweck and P. B. Clarke, Eds. Westport, CT.: Greenwood Press, 1997: xvii–xliii.

Clarke, Peter B. and Jeffrey Somers, Eds. *Japanese New Religions in the West.* Folkestone, Kent: Curzon Press/Japan Library, 1994a.

Clarke, Peter B. and Jeffrey Somers. 'Japanese "New" and "New, New" Religions: An Introduction.' In *Japanese New Religions in the West.* P. B. Clarke and J. Somers, Eds. Folkestone, Kent: Curzon Press/Japan Library, 1994b: 1–14.

Clayton, J. P. 'Religious Studies at Lancaster University.' *BASR Bulletin* 75 (June), 1995: 9–15.

Cohen, Stanley. *Folk Devils and Moral Panics: The Creation of Mods and Rockers.* London: MacGibbon and Kee, 1972.

Colley, Linda. *Britons: Forging the Nation 1707–1837.* London: Pimlico/Random House, 1994. (First published in 1992 by Yale UP.)

Colpe, Carsten. 'Zur Neubegründung einer Phänomenologie der Religionen und der Religion.' In *Religionswissenschaft: Eine Einführung.* H. Zinser, Ed. Berlin: Reimer, 1988: 131–154.

Condon, Richard. *The Manchurian Candidate.* New York, 1958.

Congregation of Faith. *Letter to the Bishops of the Catholic Church on Some Aspects of Christian Meditation.* Vatican: Typis Polyglottis Vaticanis, 15 October 1989.

Conover, Patrick W. 'The Alternate Society: Its Sources and its Future.' *Technological Forecasting and Social Change* 5, 1973: 295–304.

Conway, Flo and Jim Siegelman. *Snapping: America's Epidemic of Sudden Personality Change.* Philadelphia, PA; New York: Lippincott; Dell, 1978.

Conway, Flo and Jim Siegelman. 'Information Disease: Have Cults Created a New Mental Illness?' *Science Digest* 90 (January), 1982: 86–92.

Cornille, Catherine. 'The Phoenix Flies West: The Dynamics of Inculturation – Mahikari in Northern Europe.' Paper presented to the conference on 'New Religions in a Global Perspective', Buellton, California, 1991.

Cornille, Catherine. 'Jesus in Japan: Christian Syncretism in Mahikari.' In *Japanese New Religions in the West.* P. B. Clarke and J. Somers, Eds. Folkestone, Kent: Curzon Press/Japan Library, 1994: 88–102.

Corten, André. 'The Growth of Literature on Afro-American, Latin American and African Pentecostalism.' *Journal of Contemporary Religion* 12 (3), 1997: 311–334.

Cottrell, Richard. 'The Influence of New Religious Movements within the European Parliament.' Draft Working Document for the Committee on Youth

Culture, Education, Information and Sport. Strasbourg: European Parliament, 1983.

Cottrell, Richard. *Report on the Activity of Certain New Religious Movements within the European Community.* PE 82.322/fin. Strasbourg: European Parliament – Committee on Youth, Culture, Education, Information and Sport, 22 March 1984.

Coulter, Carol, Ed. *Are Religious Cults Dangerous?* Dublin: Mercier Press, 1984.

Cowan, Douglas E. 'Religion, Rhetoric, and Scholarship: Managing Vested Interest in E-Space.' In *Religion on the Internet: Research Prospects and Promises.* Jeffrey K. Hadden and Douglas E., Cowan, Eds. New York and Amsterdam: Elsevier Science, 2000: 101–124.

Cowan, Douglas E. 'Exits and Migrations: Foregrounding the Christian Counter-Cult.' *Journal of Contemporary Religion* 17 (3), 2002: 339–354.

Cowan, Douglas E. *Bearing False Witness? An Introduction to the Christian Countercult.* Westport: Praeger, 2003.

Cox, Harvey. 'Playing the Devil's Advocate, As It Were.' *New York Times*, Op-Ed Essay, 16 February 1977.

Cox, Harvey. 'Deep Structures in the Study of New Religions.' In *Understanding the New Religions.* J. Needleman and G. Baker, Eds. New York: Seabury, 1978: 122–130.

Cozin, M. 'A Millenarian Movement in Korea and Great Britain.' In *A Sociological Yearbook of Religion in Britain.* Vol. 6. London: SCM, 1973: 1–36.

Crockford's Clerical Dictionary 1995/96: A Directory of the Clergy of the Church of England, the Church of Wales, the Scottish Episcopal Church, Church of Ireland, 94th edn. London: Published for the Church Commissioners for England and The Central Board of Finance of The Church of England by Church House Publishing, 1995.

Cush, Denise. 'A Concern for Cooperation: A Word from the NATFHE Religious Studies Section.' *BASR Bulletin* 74 (March), 1995: 2–3.

D'Costa, Gavin. 'The Nature of the Self: Report of a Two-Day Christian-Vaishnava Conference, 20–21 January 1996, Buckland, Wales.' *Journal of Contemporary Religion* 11 (3), 1996: 355–356.

Daiber, Karl-Fritz. 'Volkskirche: Religionssoziologisch.' In *Evangelisches Kirchenlexikon: Internationale theologische Enzyklopädie.* E. Fahlbusch *et al.*, Eds. Göttingen: Vandenhoeck and Ruprecht, 1996 (3rd edn): cols. 1199–1202.

Daner, Francine J. 'Conversion to Krishna Consciousness: The Transformation from Hippie to Religious Ascetic.' In *Sectarianism: Analyses of Religious and Non-Religious Sects.* R. Wallis, Ed. London: Peter Owen, 1975: 53–69.

Daner, Francine. *The American Children of Krishna: A Study of the Hare Krishna Movement.* New York: Holt, Rhinehart and Winston, 1976.

Danneels, Godfried. 'Le Christ ou le Verseau? A Christmas Message.' *La Documentation Catholique* (Belgium) 73 (2021, 3rd February), 1991: 117ff. (An English translation of the section on New Age appeared as 'Christ or Aquarius?' *Catholic International* 2 (3 May), 1991: 480–488. Published in Italian as 'Cristo o l'Acquario', *Il Regno* 36 (664), 1 July 1991: 415–424.)

Davie, Grace. *Religion in Britain since 1945: Believing Without Belonging.* Oxford: Blackwell, 1994.

Davies, C. 'Religion, Politics and "Permissive" Legislation.' In *Religion, State and Society in Britain.* P. Badham, Ed. Lewiston, Lampeter: Edwin Mellen, 1989: 319–340.

Debold, Walter. 'The New Cults: A Threat to Unity and Authentic Humanity.' *Journal of Dharma* 12, 1987: 63–70.

Deikman, Arthur J. 'The Evaluation of Spiritual and Utopian Groups.' *Journal of Humanistic Psychology* 23 (3), 1983: 8–18.

Demerath, N. J. 'In a Sow's Ear: A Reply to Goode.' *Journal for the Scientific Study of Religion* 6, 1967a: 77–84.

Demerath, N. J. 'Son of Sow's Ear.' *Journal for the Scientific Study of Religion* 6, 1967b: 275–277.

Deutscher Bundestag (Ausschuss für Frauen und Jugend). 'Stenographisches Protokoll über die 13. Sitzung des Ausschusses für Frauen und Jugend: Anhörung "Jugendsekten".' 09.10.1991.

Deutscher Bundestag. 'Antwort der Bundesregierung auf die Kleine Anfrage der Abgeordneten Ortrun Schätzle, Maria Eichhorn und der Fraktion der CDU/CSU sowie der Abgeordneten Heinz Lanfermann, Hildebrecht Braun (Augsburg), Dr Dieter Thomae, Cornelia Schmalz-Jacobsen und der Fraktion der F.D.P.' Drucksache 13/4132, 15.03.1996.

Deutscher Bundestag. 'Zwischenbericht der Enquête-Kommission "Sogenannte Sekten und Psychogruppen".' Drucksache 13/8170, 07.07.1997.

Deutscher Bundestag. 'Endbericht der Enquête-Kommission "Sogenannte Sekten und Psychogruppen".' Drucksache 13/10950, 09.06.1998a.

Deutscher Bundestag, Ed. *Neue religiöse und ideologische Gemeinschaften und Psychogruppen. Forschungsprojekte und Gutachten.* Hamm: Hoheneck-Verlag, 1998b.

Dienst, Karl. 'Akzeptanz-Probleme kirchlicher Apologetik.' *Materialdienst* 56 (12), 1993: pp. 345–355.

Dillon, Jane and James Richardson. 'The "Cult" Concept: A Politics of Representation Analysis.' Manuscript, May 1995.

Dinges, William. 'The Vatican Report on Sects, Cults and New Religious Movements.' *America*, 27 September 1986: 145–147, 154.

Dittes, J. E. 'Typing the Typologies: Some Parallels in the Career of Church–Sect and Extrinsic–Instrinsic.' *Journal for the Scientific Study of Religion* 10 (4), 1971: 375–383.

Dobbelaere, Karel. 'CISR: An Alternative Approach to the Sociology of Religion in Europe: ACSS and CISR Compared.' *Sociological Analysis* 50, 1989: 377–387.

Dornbusch, Sanford N. 'The Military Academy as an Assimilating Institution.' *Social Forces* 33, 1955: 316–321.

Downton, James V. *Sacred Journeys: The Conversion of Young Americans to Divine Light Mission.* New York: Columbia UP, 1979.

Downton, James V. 'An Evolutionary Theory of Spiritual Conversion and Commitment: The Case of Divine Light Mission.' *Journal for the Scientific Study of Religion* 19 (4), 1980: 381–396.

Doyle, Christine. 'Cults: The Mind Drug.' *The Daily Telegraph Student Extra*, Michaelmas, 1989: 7.

Dupertius, Lucy. 'How People Recognize Charisma: The Case of Darshan in Radhasoami and Divine Light Mission.' *Sociological Analysis* 47 (2), 1986: 111–125.

Dürholt, Bernd and Ilse Kroll, Eds. *Streifzug durch den religiösen Supermarkt: Jugendreligionen, Gurubewegungen, Psychokulte, Sekten.* On behalf of the Elterninitiative zur Hilfe gegen seelische Abhängigkeit und religiösen Extremismus e.V. Munich: Arbeitsgemeinschaft für Religions- und Weltanschauungsfragen (ARW), 1994. Junge Münchener Reihe.

Durkheim, Émile. *The Elementary Forms of the Religious Life*. London: George Allen and Unwin, 1976.

Dvorkin, Alexander. 'A Presentation on the Situation in Russia.' The FAIR Lecture, October 1997, Annual Open FAIR Meeting in London, 1997.

Eberlein, Gerald C. 'Angst vor der Konkurrenz? Die Jugendreligionen in der Kritik der Kirchen.' *Evangelische Kommentare* 4 (April), 1982: 187–190.

Edwards, Christopher. *Crazy for God: The Nightmare of Cult Life by an Ex-Moonie Disciple*. Englewood Cliffs, NJ: Prentice-Hall, 1979.

Eggenberger, Oswald. *Die Kirchen, Sondergruppen und religiösen Vereinigungen*. Zurich: Theologischer Verlag, 1990 (4th edn).

Ehrlich, Max. *The Cult*. London: Mayflower, 1978.

Eiben, Jürgen. 'Sekten, Kulte, Kultbewegungen. Formen nichtkirchlicher Religiosität in Deutschland.' Paper presented to the 26. Deutscher Soziologentag, Düsseldorf, 28.9–2.10, 1992.

Eiben, Jürgen. 'Vom Sektenmarkt zum Psychomarkt – wo bleibt die Verantwortung der Wissenschaft? Versagen ihre Instrumentarien?.' In *Vom Sektenmarkt zum Psychomarkt*. Politische Studien: Zweimonatsschrift für Politik und Zeitgeschehen. Vol. 47, Hanns-Seidel-Stiftung e.V., Ed. Munich: Atwerb-Verlag, 1996: 109–121.

Eimuth, K.-H. 'Aktion der Vereinigungskirche "Religionsfreiheit in Gefahr".' *Materialdienst* 47 (10), 1984: 314–315.

Eimuth, Kurt-Helmuth. ' "Der Sektenexperte" als Verfassungsschützer oder Verbraucherberater.' *Forum – Materialien und Beiträge zum religiösen Dialog* 6 (April), 1990a: 23–29.

Eimuth, Kurt-Helmuth. 'Vor den Werbekarren gespannt. Evangelischer Theologe sprach bei Mun-Veranstaltung.' *Forum – Materialien und Beiträge zum religiösen Dialog* 6 (April), 1990b: 46–47.

Eimuth, Kurt-Helmuth. 'Theologieprofessor brüskiert Weltanschauungsbeauftragte.' *Forum – Materialien und Beiträge zum religiösen Dialog* 7 (November), 1992a: 20–23.

Eimuth, Kurt-Helmuth. 'Theologieprofessor brüskiert Weltanschauungsbeauftragte.' *Materialdienst* 55 (8), 1992b: 238–239.

Eimuth, Kurt-Helmuth. *Psychische Kindesmißhandlung. Autoritäre Religionen lassen Kindern keine Chance*. FORUM-Spezial, Vol. 2. Frankfurt a.M.: Arbeitsgemeinschaft neue religiöse Gruppen e.V., 1992c (2nd edn).

Eimuth, Kurt-Helmuth. *Die Sekten-Kinder. Mißbraucht und betrogen – Erfahrungen und Ratschläge*. Freiburg i. Br.: Herder, 1996a.

Eimuth, Kurt-Helmuth. 'Informationen: Bundestag untersucht Sekten – Enquête-Kommission eingesetzt.' *Materialdienst* 59 (6), 1996b: 188–189.

Eister, Alan W. 'Toward a Rational Critique of Church–Sect Typology: Comment of "Some Critical Observations on the Church–Sect Dimension".' *Journal for the Scientific Study of Religion* 6, 1967: 85–90.

Eister, Allan W. 'An Outline of a Structural Theory of Cults.' *Journal for the Scientific Study of Religions* 11 (3), 1972: 319–334.

Elkins, Chris. *Heavenly Deception*. Wheaton, IL: Tyndale Press, 1980.

Ellwood, Robert. 'The Several Meanings of "Cult".' *Thought* 61, 1986: 212–224.

Elterninitiative zur Hilfe gegen seelische Abhängigkeit und religiösen Extremismus e.V. *Jugendreligiöse Institutionen und deren Co-Organisationen. Guruistische*

Bewegungen und Psychokulte. Eine Findungshilfe. Munich: Elterninitiative zur Hilfe gegen seelische Abhängigkeit und religiösen Extremismus, 1985.

Elterninitiative zur Hilfe gegen seelische Abhängigkeit und religiösen Extremismus e.V., Ed. *20 Jahre Elterninitiative.* Munich: Elterninitiative zur Hilfe gegen seelische Abhängigkeit und religiösen Extremismus, 1995.

Elterninitiative zur Hilfe gegen seelische Abhängigkeit und religiösen Extremismus e.V., Ed. *1995 – Und es geht weiter. Dokumentation zur Fachtagung zum 20jährigen Bestehen der Elterninitiative zur Hilfe gegen seelische Abhängigkeit und religiösen Extremismus e.V. am 24. Juni 1995 in der Auferstehungskirche, München.* Munich: Elterninitiative zur Hilfe gegen seelische Abhängigkeit und religiösen Extremismus, 1996.

Emory, Meade and Lawrence Zelenak. 'The Tax Exempt Status of Communitarian Religious Organizations.' In *Cults, Culture and the Law.* T. Robbins, W. Shepherd and J. McBride, Eds. Chico, CA: Scholars, 1985: 177–205.

Engstfeld, Paul A. and Hanns-Seidel-Stiftung/Akademie für Politik und Zeitgeschehen, Eds. *Juristische Probleme im Zusammenhang mit den sogenannten neuen Jugendreligionen.* Munich: C.H. Beck/Olzog Verlag, 1981. Berichte und Studien der Hanns-Seidel-Stiftung e.V. München, Vol. 19.

Enroth, Ronald. *Youth, Brainwashing and the Extremist Cults.* Grand Rapids, MI: Zondervan, 1977.

Enroth, Ronald M. and Neil T. Duddy. 'Legitimation Processes in Some New Religions.' *Update* 7 (3), 1983: 42–54.

Enz, Hans. *Die Prophetin. Wie Gabriele Wittek in ihr Heimholungswerk lockt.* Berlin: Luck, 1986.

Erhard, Werner and Victor Gioscia. '*est*: Communication in a Context of Compassion.' In *Current Psychiatric Therapies*, Vol. XVIII, J. H. Masserman, Ed. New York: Grune and Stratton, 1979: 117–125.

Evangelische Akademie Tutzing, Ed. *Dokumentation zur Expertenkonsultation zum Thema Jugendreligionen. Protokoll einer Tagung in Heilsbronn vom 9.–11.11.1979.* Munich: Arbeitsgemeinschaft für Religions- und Weltanschauungsfragen (ARW), 1980. Material-Edition, Vol. 13.

Evans, Peter. 'Productive Partners: The View from Radio.' In *Social Scientists Meet the Media.* C. Haslam and A. Bryman, Eds. London, New York: Routledge, 1994: 151–164.

Evans, Suzanne. 'NRMs and the Media.' Paper presented to the INFORM Seminar on 'The Media and NRMs', London, November 1997.

EZW. 'Wiener Studie über Jugendliche in "Neuen Religiösen Bewegungen".' *Materialdienst* 45 (6), 1982a: 159–162.

EZW. 'Aufklaricht – Noch einmal: Wiener Studie über Jugendliche in "Neuen Religiösen Bewegungen".' *Materialdienst* 45 (10), 1982b: 297–300.

EZW, Ed. *Neue Jugendreligionen. Ein Spektrum verschiedener Sichtweisen.* Stuttgart: Evangelische Zentralstelle für Weltanschauungsfragen (EZW), 1982c (3rd edn).

EZW. 'Tong-Il Kyo (Vereinigungskirche) – ein wirtschaftlicher Machtkomplex.' *Materialdienst* 43 (1), 1983a: 28–30.

EZW. 'Vereinigungskirche: Gerichtsverfahren und Urteile.' *Materialdienst* 46 (1), 1983b: 26–28.

EZW. 'Ein Urteil, das S. M. Moon den Trumpf in die Hand spielte.' *Materialdienst* 47 (10), 1984a: 311–314.

EZW. 'Religion und Recht: Gratwanderung zwischen Schutz und Verletzung der Bürgerrechte.' *Materialdienst* 47 (8), 1984b: 249–252.

EZW. 'Scientology: Rückschläge in Deutschland.' *Materialdienst* 55 (4), 1992a: 118–120.

EZW. 'Dialog mit der Moon-Bewegung?' *Materialdienst* 55 (8), 1992b: 236–239.

EZW. 'Der Dialog Dekalog L. Swidlers.' *Materialdienst* 55 (8), 1992c: 232–236.

EZW. 'In eigener Sache: "EKD will ehemaliges Gebäude der Ost-CDU in Berlin kaufen".' *Materialdienst* 56 (11), 1993a: 341–343.

EZW. 'Scientology: "Haß und Propaganda"-Broschüre erregt international Aufsehen.' *Materialdienst* 56 (4), 1993b: 111–113.

EZW. 'Walter-Künneth-Institut und EZW.' *Materialdienst* 58 (5), 1995a: 156–157.

EZW. 'Interview with Reinhart Hummel.' *Materialdienst* 58 (5, May), 1995b: 130–139.

EZW. 'Scientology: "Kirche" nur Vorwand – Scientology muß Gewerbe anmelden.' *Materialdienst* 58 (5), 1995c: 154–155.

EZW. 'Scientology: Rechtsfähigkeit in Bremen und Karlsruhe aberkannt.' *Materialdienst* 58 (2), 1995d: 55–56.

EZW. 'Neue Religiöse Bewegungen: Eine Publikation des Berliner Senats und ihr gerichtliches Nachspiel.' *Materialdienst* 58 (7), 1995e: 216–217.

EZW. 'Diskussion im Bundesrat über die Scientology-Organisation.' *Materialdienst* 60 (3), 1997: 86–88.

EZW. 'Verein zur Förderung der Psychologischen Menschenkenntnis (VPM): VPM unterliegt vor Gericht.' *Materialdienst* 61 (5), 1998: 144–145.

EZW. 'Im Gespräch mit der Zeit.' (leaflet). Stuttgart: Evangelische Zentralstelle für Weltanschauungsfragen (EZW), n.d.

FAIR. *Influence and Stress Related Issues*. Proceedings of the Seminar held under the same title at The Royal Society of Medicine, London, 22 March 1993. London: FAIR, 1993.

Falaturi, Abdoldjavad, Michael Klöcker and Udo Tworuschka, Eds. *Religionsgeschichte in der Öffentlichkeit*. Cologne: Böhlau, 1983. Kölner Veröffentlichungen zur Religionsgeschichte, Vol. 1.

Farber, I. E., H. F. Harlow and L. J. West 'Brainwashing, Conditioning and DDD (Debility, Dependency and Dread).' In *Control of Human Behaviour*. R. Ulrich, T. Stachnik, J. Mabry, Eds. London: Glenview, 1966: 322–330. First published in *Sociometry* 20 (December), 1957: 271–285.

Featherstone, Mike, Scott Lash and Roland Robertson, Eds. *Global Modernities*. London: Sage, 1995.

Feige, Franz. 'Die Betrachtung von "innen": Familie und Gesellschaft in der Vereinigungskirche.' In *Das Entstehen einer Neuen Religion: Das Beispiel der Vereinigungskirche*. G. Kehrer, Ed. Munich: Kösel, 1981: 235–247.

Feldmann, Christian. 'Nachdem Jesus mit San Myung Mun gesprochen hatte … Christliche Theologen gehen der "Vereinigungskirche" auf den Leim.' *Publik-Forum* 25/26 (22 December), 1982: 31–32.

Fenn, Richard K. *Liturgies and Trials: The Secularization of Religious Language*. Oxford: Blackwell, 1982.

Fenwick, Sheridan. *Getting It: The Psychology of est*. Philadelphia; New York: J. B. Lippincott; Penguin, 1976.

Festinger, Leon, Henry W. Riecken and Stanley Schacter. *When Prophecy Fails: A*

Social and Psychological Study of a Modern Group that Predicted the Destruction of the World. New York: Harper and Row, 1956.

F.I.U.C. file papers. 'A Collection of materials about the F.I.U.C. project, including correspondence with the project leader, the project outline, and information about F.I.U.C.' Archives of the Centre for New Religious Movements, King's College London, n.d.

Fichter, Joseph H., Ed. *Alternatives to American Mainline Churches*. New York: Rose of Sharon Press, 1983.

Fisher, Humphrey J. 'More Roses than Thorns? A Residential Course for Religious Studies Students.' *BASR Bulletin* 69 (June), 1993: 16–21.

Fitzgerald, Michael L. 'Sects and New Religious Movements in the Light of the Recent Teaching of the Church.' Paper presented to the F.I.U.C. Symposium, Vienna, 1991.

Fitzgerald, Michael L. 'Sects and New Religious Movements in the Light of the Recent Teaching of the Church.' *Bulletin of the Pontificium Consilium pro Dialogo Inter Religiones* 27 (2), 1992: 209–216.

Flasche, Rainer. 'Neue Religionen als Forschungsgegenstand der Religionswissenschaft.' *Zeitschrift für Missions- und Religionswissenschaft* 4, 1978: 164–173.

Flasche, Rainer. 'Hauptelemente der Vereinigungstheologie.' In *Das Entstehen einer neuen Religion. Das Beispiel der Vereinigungskirche*. G. Kehrer, Ed. Munich: Kösel, 1981: 41–77.

Flasche, Rainer. 'Die Lehren der Vereinigungskirche.' In *Neue Religionen – Heil oder Unheil? Beispiel: Vereinigungskirche Sun Myung Moons*. K. E. Becker and H.-P. Schreiner, Eds. Landau: Pfälzische Verlagsanstalt, 1982a: 97–108.

Flasche, Rainer. 'Jugendreligionen zwischen Verunglimpfung und Verfolgung?' *Gewissen und Freiheit* 19, 1982b.

Flasche, Rainer, Ed. *Lebensgeschichte und Lebenslegende einiger Gründer Neuer Religionen*. Marburg: Universität Marburg, 1985.

Flasche, Rainer. 'The Unification Church in the Context of East-Asian Religious Traditions.' In *Acta Comparanda II*. Antwerpen: Faculteit voor Vergelijkende Godsdienstwetenschappen, 1987a: 25–48.

Flasche, Rainer. ' "New Age" – Gegenstand der Religionswissenschaft?' *spirita* 1 (December), 1987b: 39–41.

Flasche, Rainer. 'Religiöse Weltgestaltungen.' *Forum Religion und Weltgestaltung* 1, 1988a: 18–22.

Flasche, Rainer. 'Zum Umgang mit den Jugendreligionen.' *Zeitschrift für Religions- und Geistesgeschichte* 40 (1), 1988b: 44–53.

Flasche, Rainer. 'Religiöse Entwürfe und religiöse Wirkungen von Religionswissenschaftlern.' In *Die Religion von Oberschichten. Religion – Profession – Intellektualismus*. P. Antes and D. Pahnke, Eds. Marburg: diagonal-Verlag, 1989: 203–217.

Fleming, Patricia Ann and Jean Anne Schuler. 'Academics and the Ethics of Sponsorship: The Moonie Case.' *Areopagus* 3 (4), 1990: 13–18.

Flinn, Frank K. *Scientology: The Marks of Religion*. Los Angeles: Freedom Publishing, n.d.

Flöther, Eckart, Ed. *Familie und destruktive Kulte: Menschenwürde, Recht und Freiheit. Dokumentation der Referate des europäischen AGPF-Kongresses vom 28.–30.5.84 in Bonn*. Bonn: Aktion für geistige und psychische Freiheit (AGPF), 1985. AGPF Schriftenreihe, Vol. 1.

Flöther, Eckart and F.-W. Haack. 'Ausblick auf die Sektenscene der nächsten Jahre.' In *Familie und destruktive Kulte*. E. Flöther, Ed. Bonn: Aktion für geistige und psychische Freiheit (AGPF), 1985: 96–117.

Foss, D. and R. Larkin. 'The Roar of the Lemming: Youth, Post-Movement Groups and the Life Construction Crisis.' *Sociological Inquiry* 49 (2–3), 1979: 264–285.

Frank, Thomas, Uli Grandtner, and Stephan Kippes. *Sektenreport: Analysen, Originalmaterial, Hilfestellung*. Dokumentation-Edition, Vol. 24. Munich: Arbeitsgemeinschaft für Religions- und Weltanschauungsfragen (ARW), 1993 (2nd edn).

Freston, Paul. 'The Protestant Eruption into Modern Brazilian Politics.' *Journal of Contemporary Religion* 11 (2), 1996: 147–168.

Frick, Tobias. 'Trennlinien in der Religionswissenschaft: Studentisches Symposion in Marburg zeigte unterschiedliches Selbstverständnis.' *spirita* 9 (1), 1995: 37–38.

Frick, Tobias. 'Methodenlos, strukturlos, nix los? Die religionswissenschaftliche Lehre in Deutschland – Plädoyer für Professionalisierung.' *spirita* 11 (1), 1997: 8–16.

Fuss, Michael, Ed. *Research Project on New Religious Movements: Dossier*. Rome: F.I.U.C., 1990a.

Fuss, Michael. 'New Age and Europe: A Challenge for Theology.' In *Research Project on New Religious Movements: Dossier*. M. Fuss, Ed. Rome: F.I.U.C., 1990b: 637–673.

Fuss, Michael. 'Unsichtbar bleibt ihre Frömmigkeit. Kritische Begegnung mit Neuen Religiösen Bewegungen.' *Studia Missionalia* 41, 1992a: 353–389.

Fuss, Michael. 'Zwischen "autonomer" und "dialogischer" Religion: Eine neue Phase der Religionskritik.' In *Gemeinsam Kirche sein. Theorie und Praxis der Communio. Festschrift der Theologischen Fakultät der Universität Freiburg i. Br. für Erzbischof Dr. Oskar Saier*. G. Biemer, B. Casper, and J. Müller, Eds. Freiburg i. Br.: Herder, 1992b: 162–177.

Fuss, Michael. 'Tomorrow's Paganism: The Role and Mission of the Churches in the European House: Part I.' *Update and Dialog* 2 (1), 1993a: 6–9.

Fuss, Michael. 'Anonymous [sic] and Dialogical Religion: The Role and Mission of the Churches in the European House, Part II.' *Update & Dialog* 3 (October), 1993b: 8–12.

Fuss, Michael A., Ed. *Rethinking New Religious Movements*. Rome: Pontifical Gregorian University, Research Center on Cultures and Religions, 1998.

Gaiman, David. 'Appendix: A Scientologist's Comment.' In *Doing Sociological Research*. C. Bell and H. Newby, Eds. London: Allen and Unwin, 1977: 168–169.

Galanter, Marc. *Cults: Faith, Healing, and Coercion*. New York: Oxford UP, 1989.

Galanter, Marc, Richard Rabkin, Judith Rabkin and Alexander Deutsch. 'The "Moonies": A Psychological Study of Conversion and Membership in a Contemporary Religious Sect.' *American Journal of Psychiatry* 136 (2), 1979: 165–170.

Gallagher, Michael-Paul. 'Traditions of Spiritual Discernment as Relevant to NRM's in Europe.' Paper presented to the Conference on 'New Religions and the New Europe', London, 1993.

Gallagher, Michael-Paul. 'Traditions of Spiritual Discernment.' *Update & Dialog* 4 (May), 1994: 3–7.

Gandow, Thomas. 'Jugendreligionen und neue religiöse Gemeinschaften in Berlin. Herausforderung für Kirchen und Jugendarbeit.' In *Eindeutig zwischen den Stühlen. Zehn Beiträge zur Apologie der Apologetik. F.-W. Haack zum 50. Geburtstag*.

M. Ach, Ed. Munich: Arbeitsgemeinschaft für Religions- und Weltanschauungs-fragen (ARW), 1985: 29–40.

Gandow, Thomas. 'Cults and Religious Movements in the New Europe.' Paper presented to the Annual Open Meeting of FAIR in London, September 1992.

Gantzel, Christine, Wolfgang Kimmeskamp and Ralf Ventur. *Religiöse Gemeinschaften in Essen. Die religiöse Landschaft neben den großen Kirchen*. Marburg: diagonal-Verlag, 1994.

Garrison, Omar V. *Playing Dirty: The Secret War Against Beliefs*. Los Angeles: Rabton-Pilot, 1980.

Gartrell, C. David and Zane K. Shannon. 'Contacts, Cognitions, and Conversion: A Rational Choice Approach.' *Review of Religious Research* 27 (1), 1985: 32–48.

Gascard, Johannes. *Neue Jugendreligionen – zwischen Sehnsucht und Sucht*. Freiburg i. Br.: Herder, 1984.

Gasper, Hans. 'The Pastoral Concern of the Church in Continental Europe, especially in German-Speaking Countries.' In *Research Project on New Religious Movements: Dossier*. M. Fuss, Ed. Rome: F.I.U.C., 1990: 675–700.

Gasper, Hans, Joachim Müller and Friedericke Valentin, Eds. *Lexikon der Sekten, Sondergruppen und Weltanschauungen. Fakten, Hintergründe, Klärungen*. Freiburg i. Br.: Herder, 1990.

Gatto Trocchi, Cecilia. 'Charismatic Feminist Leaders in Magic-Esoteric Groups in Italy.' In *Women as Teachers and Disciples in Traditional and New Religions*. E. Puttick and P. B. Clarke, Eds. New York, Lampeter: Edwin Mellen, 1993: 115–124.

Gelberg, Steven J. (Subhananda dasa), Ed. *Hare Krishna, Hare Krishna: Five Distinguished Scholars on the Krishna Movement in the West*. New York: Grove Press, 1983.

General Synod. *New Religious Movements: A Report by the Board for Mission and Unity*. London: General Synod of the Church of England, 1989.

General Synod. *November Group of Sessions 1989: Report of Proceedings. Vol. 20. No. 3*. London: Church House Publishing, 1990.

Gilliat, Sophie. 'Civic Religion in England: Traditions and Transformations.' *Journal of Contemporary Religion* 14 (2), 1999: 233–244.

Gladigow, Burkhart. 'Religionsgeschichte des Gegenstandes – Gegenstände der Religionsgeschichte.' In *Religionswissenschaft: Eine Einführung*. H. Zinser, Ed. Berlin: Reimer, 1988: 6–37.

Gladigow, Burkhard. 'Naturwissenschaftliche Modellvorstellungen in der Religionswissenschaft in der Zeit zwischen den Weltkriegen.' In *Religionswissenschaft und Kulturkritik: Beiträge zur Konferenz The History of Religions and Critique of Culture in the Days of Gerardus van der Leeuw (1890–1950)*. H. G. Kippenberg and B. Luchesi, Eds. Marburg: diagonal-Verlag, 1991: 177–192.

Glock, Charles Y. 'The Role of Deprivation in the Origin and Evolution of Religious Groups.' In *Religion and Social Conflict*. R. Lee and M. E. Marty, Eds. New York: Oxford UP, 1964: 24–36.

Glock, Charles Y. 'On the Origin and Evolution of Religious Groups.' In *Religion in Sociological Perspective: Essays in the Empirical Study of Religion*. C. Y. Glock, Ed. Belmont, CA: Wadsworth, 1973: 207–220.

Glock, Charles Y. 'Consciousness among Contemporary Youth: An Interpretation.' In *The New Religious Consciousness*. C. Glock and R. Bellah, Eds. Berkeley: University of California Press, 1976: 353–366.

Glock, Charles Y. and Robert N. Bellah, Eds. *The New Religious Consciousness.* Berkeley, Los Angeles: University of California Press, 1976.

Glock, Charles Y. and Rodney Stark. *Religion and Society in Tension.* Chicago: Rand McNally, 1965.

Glück, Gebhard. 'Jugendreligionen – eine Herausforderung für den Sozialstaat.' In *Die neuen Jugendreligionen. Teil 4: Aktionen, Hilfen, Initiativen.* F.-W. Haack, U. Schuster and M. Ach, Eds. Munich: Evangelischer Presseverband Bayern, 1986: 19–28.

Goffman, Erving. *Asylums: Essays on the Social Situation of Mental Patients and Other Inmates.* Harmondsworth: Penguin, 1968.

Goldschmidt, D. and J. Matthes. *Probleme der Religionssoziologie.* Cologne: Westdeutscher Verlag, 1962.

Gonçalves, Teresa. 'The Church and New Religious Movements.' Paper presented to the conference on 'New Religious Movements: The European Situation', Lugano (Switzerland), 20–21 April 1990.

Gonçalves, Teresa. 'Sectes et nouveaux courants religieux.' *Pontificio Consilium pro Dialogo inter Religones Bulletin* 28 (1), 1993: 80–88.

Goode, Erich. 'Some Critical Observations on the Church–Sect Division.' *Journal for the Scientific Study of Religion* 6, 1967a: 69–77.

Goode, Erich. 'Further Reflections on the Church–Sect Typology.' *Journal for the Scientific Study of Religion* 6, 1967b: 270–275.

Götzer, Wolfgang. 'Jugendreligionen – Die Antwort der Politik auf eine Herausforderung.' In *Familie und destruktive Kulte.* E. Flöther, Ed. Bonn: Aktion für geistige und psychische Freiheit (AGPF), Bonn, 1985: 118–131.

Götzer, Wolfgang. 'Keine Chance mehr für Seelenfänger: Politische Initiativen gegen Jugendsekten.' In *Die neuen Jugendreligionen. Teil 4: Aktionen, Hilfen, Initiativen.* F.-W. Haack, U. Schuster and M. Ach, Eds. Munich: Evangelischer Presseverband Bayern, 1986: 29–42.

Greeley, Andrew M. 'Implications for the Sociology of Religion of Occult Behavior in the Youth Culture.' *Youth and Society* 2 (2), 1970: 131–140.

Greene, William. *est: 4 Days to Make Your Life Work.* New York: Simon and Schuster, 1976.

Greil, Arthur L. 'Previous Dispositions and Conversion to Perspectives of Social and Religious Movements.' *Sociological Analysis* 38 (3), 1977: 115–125.

Greil, Arthur L. and David R. Rudy. 'What have We Learned from Process Models of Conversion? An Examination of Ten Studies.' *Sociological Focus* 17 (4), 1984: 305–323.

Greschat, Hans-Jürgen. *Was ist Religionswissenschaft?* Stuttgart: Kohlhammer, 1988.

Guardini, R. *Freiheit, Gnade, Schicksal.* Munich, 1956.

Guest, Tim. *My Life in Orange.* London: Granta Books, 2004.

Gustafson, Paul M. 'UO-US-PS-POI: A Restatement of Troeltsch's Church–Sect Typology.' *Journal for the Scientific Study of Religion* 6, 1967: 64–68.

Guyard, Jacques, Rapporteur. *Assemblée Nationale: Les sectes en France.* Coll. documents d'information de l'Assemblée Française: La Documentation Française, 1996.

Haack, Annette and F.-W. Haack. *Jugendspiritismus und -satanismus. Begriffe, Informationen, Überlegungen.* Munich: Arbeitsgemeinschaft für Religions- und Weltanschauungsfragen (ARW), 1989 (3rd edn).

Haack, F.-W. *Rendezvous mit dem Jenseits. Der moderne Spiritismus/Spiritualismus und die Neuoffenbarungen. Bericht und Analyse.* Munich: Arbeitsgemeinschaft für Religions- und Weltanschauungsfragen (ARW), 1973 (1st edn; 1986, 2nd edn; 1992, 3rd edn).

Haack, F.-W. *Die neuen Jugendreligionen.* Münchner Reihe. Munich: Evangelischer Presseverband für Bayern, Abt. Schriftenmission, 1974 (1977, 10th edn; 1979, 19th edn; 1983, 22nd edn; 1988, 24th edn).

Haack, F.-W. 'New Youth Religions, Psychomutation, and Technological Civilization.' *International Review of Mission* 67, 1978: 436–447.

Haack, F.-W. *Verführte Sehnsucht – die neuen Jugendreligionen.* Junge Münchener Reihe. Munich: Arbeitsgemeinschaft für Religions- und Weltanschauungsfragen (ARW), 1979a (3rd edn; 1984, 4th, newly designed and updated edn).

Haack, F.-W. *Jugendreligionen – Ursachen, Trends, Reaktionen.* Munich: Claudius/Pfeiffer, 1979b.

Haack, F.-W. *Ratschläge. Jugendreligionen, -bewegungen und Sekten. Was können Betroffene und Verantwortliche tun?* Münchener Reihe. Munich: Arbeitsgemeinschaft für Religions- und Weltanschauungsfragen (ARW), 1979c (3rd edn; 1983, 5th edn).

Haack, F.-W. *Transzendentale Organisation. Maharishi Mahesh Yogi – Weltplan – RRA e.V.* Munich: Evangelischer Presseverband für Bayern, 1979d (4th edn; 1992, 6th edn).

Haack, F.-W. 'Die neuen Jugendreligionen – Herausforderung für Gesellschaft, Staat und Kirchen.' In *Die neuen Jugendreligionen – Herausforderung für Gesellschaft, Staat und Kirchen.* Hanns-Seidel-Stiftung e.V., Ed. Munich: Hanns-Seidel-Stiftung e.V., 1979e: 11–27.

Haack, F.-W. *Führer und Verführte. Jugendreligionen und politreligiöse Jugendsekten.* Munich: Pressedienst Demokratische Initiative (PDI), 1980a.

Haack, F.-W. *Des Sectes pour les Jeunes? Fiches d'identité. Approche critique psycho-sociale.* Paris: Mamé, 1980b. François Vial, transl. and ed.

Haack, F.-W. *Die Fraternitas Saturni als Beispiel für einen Arkan-Mystogenen Geheimorden des 20. Jahrhunderts.* Munich: Arbeitsgemeinschaft für Religions- und Weltanschauungsfragen (ARW), 1980c (2nd edn).

Haack, F.-W. *Transzendentale Meditation.* Munich: Arbeitsgemeinschaft für Religions- und Weltanschauungsfragen (ARW), 1980d (5th edn; 1st edn published in 1976).

Haack, F.-W. *Erkaufte Hoffnung – Die christlichen Sekten.* Junge Münchener Reihe. Munich: Arbeitsgemeinschaft für Religions- und Weltanschauungsfragen (ARW), 1980e.

Haack, F.-W. *Die freibischöflichen Kirchen im Deutschsprachigen Raum. Amtsträger und Institutionen.* Munich: Arbeitsgemeinschaft für Religions- und Weltanschauungsfragen (ARW), 1980f.

Haack, F.-W., Ed. *Ein Messias aus Korea? Eine Hilfe zur theologischen Auseinandersetzung mit der Vereinigungskirche und ihren 'Göttlichen Prinzipien'.* Munich: Evangelischer Presseverband für Bayern, 1980g.

Haack, F.-W. *Kein Blatt vor dem Mund. Von der Religions-Freiheit, Ja und Nein zu sagen.* Munich: Arbeitsgemeinschaft für Religions- und Weltanschauungsfragen (ARW), 1981a.

Haack, F.-W. *Wotans Wiederkehr – Blut-, Boden- und Rasse-Religion.* Munich: Claudius-Verlag, 1981b.

Haack, F.-W. *Juristische Probleme im Zusammenhang mit den sogenannten Jugendreligionen.* Munich, 1981c.

Haack, F.-W. *Jesus und/oder San Myung Mun. Begegnung zwischen möglichen Bekenntnisstandpunkten oder status confessionis?* Material-Edition, Vol. 25. Munich: Arbeitsgemeinschaft für Religions- und Weltanschauungsfragen (ARW), 1981d.

Haack, F.-W. 'Jesus Christus und/oder San Myung Moon: Begegung zwischen möglichen Bekenntnisstandpunkten oder status confessionis?' In *Bekennen in der Zeit*. Material-Edition, Vol. 14. W. Metz, Ed. Munich: Arbeitsgemeinschaft für Religions- und Weltanschauungsfragen (ARW), in co-operation with the Evangelischer Presseverband Bayern, 1981e: 151–190.

Haack, F.-W. 'Die Jugendreligionen – Totalitäre Religionsgemeinschaften im Zeitalter der technischen Zivilisation.' In *'Jugendsekten' – Symptome einer gesellschaftlichen Krise?* R. Hummel, Ed. Stuttgart: Evangelische Zentralstelle für Weltanschauungsfragen (EZW), 1982a: 16–20.

Haack, F.-W. 'Jugendreligionen – Die derzeitige Lage.' *Update* 6 (3), 1982b: 67–72.

Haack, F.-W. 'Muns Tong Il-Imperium – Neue Religion oder Machtkonzern?' *Forum – Materialien und Beiträge zum religiösen Dialog* 2 (Juli), 1982c: 27–31.

Haack, F.-W. *Scientology – Magie des 20. Jahrhunderts.* Munich: Claudius-Verlag, 1982d (1st edn; 1991, 2nd edn).

Haack, F.-W. *Hexenwahn und Aberglaube in der Bundesrepublik. Eine Dokumentation.* Munich: Arbeitsgemeinschaft für Religions- und Weltanschauungsfragen (ARW), 1982e (4th edn; 1992, 8th edn).

Haack, F.-W. *Guruismus und Gurubewegungen.* Munich: Arbeitsgemeinschaft für Religions- und Weltanschauungsfragen (ARW), 1982f.

Haack, F.-W. *Die 'Bhagwan'-Rajneesh-Bewegung.* Münchener Reihe. Munich: Arbeitsgemeinschaft für Religions- und Weltanschauungsfragen (ARW), 1983a.

Haack, F.-W. *Blut-Mythos und Rasse-Religion. Neugermanische und deutschvölkische Religiosität.* Munich: Arbeitsgemeinschaft für Religions- und Weltanschauungsfragen (ARW), 1983b.

Haack, F.-W. *Psi/Parapsychologie.* Munich: Evangelischer Presseverband für Bayern, 1983c (4th edn).

Haack, F.-W. *Die neuen Jugendreligionen. Teil 1.* Munich: Evangelischer Presseverband für Bayern, 1983d (23rd edn).

Haack, F.-W. *'Täglich war ich diesem Druck ausgesetzt.' – Erlebnisberichte zu Scientology.* Münchner Texte und Analysen zur religiösen Situation. Munich: Arbeitsgemeinschaft für Religions- und Weltanschauungsfragen (ARW), 1983e (1st edn; 1988, 2nd edn).

Haack, F.-W. 'und morgen die ganze Welt – Die Weltmacht-Pläne des San Myung Moon.' *Deutsche Volkszeitung*, 6 July 1984a.

Haack, F.-W. *Die neuen Jugendreligionen. Teil 2. Dokumente und Erläuterungen.* Münchener Reihe. Munich: Evangelischer Presseverband für Bayern, 1984b (6th edn; 1979, 4th edn).

Haack, F.-W. *Geheimreligion der Wissenden. Neugnostische Bewegungen.* Munich: Arbeitsgemeinschaft für Religions- und Weltanschauungsfragen (ARW), 1985a (6th edn).

Haack, F.-W. *Jugendreligionen, Gurubewegungen, Psychokulte und ihre Tarn- und Unterorganisationen. Hinweise zu Begriffen und Gruppen.* Munich: Arbeitsgemeinschaft für Religions- und Weltanschauungsfragen (ARW), 1985b.

Haack, F.-W. *Das Heimholungswerk der Gabriele Wittek und die Neuof-fenbarungsbewegung.* Munich: Evangelischer Presseverband für Bayern, 1985c (1st edn; 1992, 2nd edn).

Haack, F.-W. *Die neuen Jugendreligionen. Teil 3. Berichte und Analysen.* Munich: Evangelischer Presseverband für Bayern, 1985d.

Haack, F.-W. 'Apologetik und kirchliches Handeln.' In *Grundlagen der Apologetik.* Dokumentations-Edition, Vol. 7. Konsultation Landeskirchlicher Beauftragter (KLB), Ed. Munich: Arbeitsgemeinschaft für Religions- und Weltanschauungsfragen (ARW), 1985e: 19–36.

Haack, F.-W. *Gabriele Witteks 'Universelles Leben'.* Munich: Evangelischer Presseverband für Bayern, 1986a (1st edn; 1992, 2nd edn).

Haack, F.-W. 'Elterninitiativen – Ursachen, Methoden, Ziele. Versuch einer Standortbestimmung und eines Ausblicks.' In *Die neuen Jugendreligionen. Teil 4: Aktionen, Hilfen, Initiativen.* F.-W. Haack, U. Schuster and M. Ach, Eds. Munich: Evangelischer Presseverband Bayern, 1986b: 88–116.

Haack, F.-W. ' "Wenn es nur eine Chance gäbe, wenigstens etwas zu tun" – Die psychomutatorischen Bewegungen und die Arbeit der Elterninitiativen.' In *Die neuen Jugendreligionen. Teil 4: Aktionen, Hilfen, Initiativen.* F.-W. Haack, U. Schuster and M. Ach, Eds. Munich: Evangelischer Presseverband Bayern, 1986c: 53–87.

Haack, F.-W. *Satan – Teufel – Lucifer.* Munich: Arbeitsgemeinschaft für Religions- und Weltanschauungsfragen (ARW), 1987.

Haack, F.-W. *Was können wir tun, wenn . . . <deutsch/englisch>.* Munich: Arbeitsgemeinschaft für Religions- und Weltanschauungsfragen (ARW), 1988a.

Haack, F.-W. 'Geister, Hexen, Satanskult.' *Jugend und Gesellschaft* 4 (August), 1988b.

Haack, F.-W. 'Ein Tag mit der "Royal Family" – Die Kinder Gottes 1988.' *Forum – Materialien und Beiträge zum religiösen Dialog* 5 (May), 1988c: 11–13.

Haack, F.-W. 'Okkultismus.' In *Praktisches Lexikon der Spiritualität.* C. Schütz, Ed. Freiburg i. Br. : Herder, 1988d: 944–947.

Haack, F.-W. *Freimaurer.* Münchener Reihe. Munich: Arbeitsgemeinschaft für Religions- und Weltanschauungsfragen (ARW), 1988e (8th edn).

Haack, F.-W. *Der Weg des Lebens nun ist dieser . . . Apologetik an der Schwelle des 3. Jahrtausends.* Munich: Arbeitsgemeinschaft für Religions- und Weltanschauungsfragen (ARW), 1988f.

Haack, F.-W. *Hirten im eigenen Auftrag. Shepherding – Discipling, Bob Weiner's Maranatha und Kip McKean's Boston Church of Christ.* Dokumentations-Edition, Vol. 17. Munich: Arbeitsgemeinschaft für Religions- und Weltanschauungsfragen (ARW), 1988g.

Haack, F.-W. *Spiritismus.* Munich: Arbeitsgemeinschaft für Religions- und Weltanschauungsfragen (ARW), 1988h (5th edn).

Haack, F.-W. 'What Can We Do?' *Areopagus* 2 (4), 1989a: 11–15.

Haack, F.-W. 'Satanism.' *Areopagus* 2 (4), 1989b: 48–49.

Haack, F.-W. *Bestrafte Neugier. Okkultismus.* Junge Münchener Reihe. Munich: Arbeitsgemeinschaft für Religions- und Weltanschauungsfragen (ARW), 1989c.

Haack, F.-W. *Unification Church Connections. Organisationen, Firmen, Aktivitäten und Begriffe des Mun-Imperiums.* Munich: Arbeitsgemeinschaft für Religions- und Weltanschauungsfragen (ARW), 1989d.

Haack, F.-W. *Findungshilfe Religion 2000 – Apologetisches Lexikon.* Munich: Arbeitsgemeinschaft für Religions- und Weltanschauungsfragen (ARW), 1990a.

Haack, F.-W. *Scientology, Dianetik und andere Hubbardismen.* Munich: Arbeitsgemeinschaft für Religions- und Weltanschauungsfragen (ARW), 1990b (2nd edn; 1993, 3rd edn).

Haack, F.-W. *Die neuen Jugendreligionen. Teil 5. Gurubewegungen und Psychokulte. Durchblicke und Informationen.* Munich: Arbeitsgemeinschaft für Religions- und Weltanschauungsfragen (ARW), 1991a.

Haack, F.-W. *Das Mun-Imperium. Beobachtungen – Informationen – Meinungen.* Munich: Arbeitsgemeinschaft für Religions- und Weltanschauungsfragen (ARW), 1991b.

Haack, F.-W. *Was mir zu denken gibt. Weihnachtsrundbriefe 1979–1990 an die Münchner Elterninitiative.* Munich: Arbeitsgemeinschaft für Religions- und Weltanschauungsfragen (ARW), 1992.

Haack, F.-W. *Lichtbildserie: Sekten.* Munich: Arbeitsgemeinschaft für Religions- und Weltanschauungsfragen (ARW), n.d./a.

Haack, F.-W. *Die neuen Jugendreligionen: Lichtbildserie.* Munich: Arbeitsgemeinschaft für Religions- und Weltanschauungsfragen (ARW), n.d./b (3rd edn).

Haack, F.-W. *Die neuen Jugendreligionen. Unterrichtstransparente für den Religionsunterricht in Hauptschule, Realschule, Gymnasium und im Konfirmandenunterricht.* Munich: Arbeitsgemeinschaft für Religions- und Weltanschauungsfragen (ARW), n.d./c (4th edn).

Haack, F.-W. *Psychomutation – Erzwungene Persönlichkeitsverwandlung. Jugendreligionen – Ideologien – Sekten, Identitätsaustausch durch Lehre und Organisation.* Munich: Arbeitsgemeinschaft für Religions- und Weltanschauungsfragen (ARW), n.d./d (2nd edn).

Haack, F.-W. and Thomas Gandow. *Die neuen Jugendreligionen. Vorbeugen – Hilfe – Auswege.* Weinheim: Beltz Quadriga, 1991.

Haack, F.-W., Udo Schuster and Manfred Ach, Eds. *Die neuen Jugendreligionen. Teil 4: Aktionen, Hilfen, Initiativen: Dokumentation über die 10. Jahrestagung der Elterninitiative zur Hilfe gegen seelische Abhängigkeit und religiösen Extremismus e.V.* Munich: Evangelischer Presseverband Bayern, 1986. Münchner Reihe.

Hadden, Jeffrey K. 'Toward Desacralizing Secularization Theory.' *Social Forces* 65 (3), 1987: 587–611.

Hadden, Jeffrey K. and Douglas E. Cowan, Eds. *Religion on the Internet: Research Prospects and Promises.* New York and Amsterdam: Elsevier Science, 2000.

Hall, John R. 'The Impact of Apostates on the Trajectory of Religious Movements: The Case of People's Temple.' In *Falling from the Faith: Causes and Consequences of Religious Apostasy.* D. G. Bromley, Ed. Beverly Hills, CA: Sage Publications, 1988: 229–250.

Hammond, Phillip E., Ed. *The Sacred in a Secular Age: Toward Revision in the Scientific Study of Religion.* Berkeley: University of California Press, 1985.

Hammond, Phillip E. 'Cultural Consequences of Cults.' In *The Future of New Religious Movements.* D. G. Bromley and P. E. Hammond, Eds. Macon, GA: Mercer UP, 1987: 261–273.

Hampshire, Annette P. and James A. Beckford. 'Religious Sects and the Concept of Deviance: The Moonies and the Mormons.' *British Journal of Sociology* 34 (2), 1983: 208–229.

Hanegraaff, Wouter. *New Age Religion and Western Culture.* Leiden: Brill, 1996.

Hann, Robert R. 'Werner Erhard's *est* – A Religious Movement?' *Quarterly Review* 2 (Fall), 1982: 78–95.

Hanns-Seidel-Stiftung e.V. *Die neuen Jugendreligionen – Herausforderung für Gesellschaft, Staat und Kirchen.* Munich: Hanns-Seidel-Stiftung e.V., 1979.

Hanson, Sharon. 'The Secularisation Thesis: Talking at Cross Purposes.' *Journal of Contemporary Religion* 12 (2), 1997: 159–179.

Hardacre, Helen. *Lay Buddhism in Contemporary Japan: Reyukai Kyodan.* Princeton, NJ: Princeton UP, 1985.

Hardin, Bert and Günter Kehrer. 'Bericht über eine wissenschaftliche Vorstudie im Bereich der "Neuen Jugendreligionen".' Report prepared for the German Federal Ministry for Youth, Family, and Health, Tübingen, Germany, 1978a.

Hardin, Bert and Günter Kehrer. 'Das Phänomen "Jugendreligionen".' *betrifft: erziehung* 11 (12), 1978b: 42, 51–54.

Hardin, Bert and Günter Kehrer. 'West Germany: Identity and Commitment.' In *Identity and Religion: International, Cross-Cultural Approaches.* H. Mol, Ed. Beverly Hills, CA; London: Sage, 1978c: 83–96.

Hardin, Bert and Günter Kehrer. 'Some Social Factors Affecting the Rejection of New Belief Systems.' In *New Religious Movements: A Perspective for Understanding Society.* E. Barker, Ed. New York, Toronto: Edwin Mellen, 1982: 267–283.

Hardin, Bert and Wolfgang Kuner. 'Entstehung und Entwicklung der Vereinigungskirche in der Bundesrepublik Deutschland.' In *Das Entstehen einer neuen Religion. Das Beispiel der Vereinigungskirche.* G. Kehrer, Ed. Munich: Kösel-Verlag, 1981: 129–195.

Hargrove, Barbara. *Religion for a Dislocated Generation: Where Will Those Who Grew Up in the Sixties Find Faith?* Valley Forge, PA: Judson Press, 1980.

Hargrove, Barbara. 'On Studying the "Moonies" as a Political Act.' *Religious Studies Review* 8 (3), 1982a: 209–213.

Hargrove, Barbara. 'New Religious Movements and the End of the Age.' *Iliff Review* 34 (Spring), 1982b: 41–52.

Hargrove, Barbara. 'New Religions and the Search for a Public Morality.' *Nebraska Humanist* 8 (2), 1985: 61–70.

Harris, Marvin. *America Now: The Anthropology of a Changing Culture.* New York: Simon and Schuster, 1981.

Hartman, Patricia A. 'Social Dimensions of Occult Participations: The Gnostica Study.' *British Journal of Sociology* 27, 1976: 169–183.

Hartwig, Renate. *Scientology – Ich klage an.* Augsburg: Pattloch, 1994a.

Hartwig, Renate. *Scientology – Die Zeitbombe in der Wirtschaft.* Pfaffenhofen: Direkt Verlag, 1994b.

Haslam, Cheryl and Alan Bryman, Eds. *Social Scientists Meet the Media.* London, New York: Routledge, 1994.

Hassan, Steven. *Combating Cult Mind Control: Rescue and Recovery from Destructive Cults.* Rochester, VT: Park Street Press, 1988. Published in 1990 in the UK in Glasgow by William Collins.

Hassan, Steven. 'Combating Cult Mind Control.' Paper presented to the Annual Open Meeting of FAIR in London, September 1990.

Hassan, Steven. *Ausbruch aus dem Bann der Sekten. Psychologische Beratung für Betroffene und Angehörige.* Reinbek: rororo, 1993.

Hassan, Steven. *Releasing the Bonds: Empowering People to Think for Themselves.* Freedom of Mind Press, 2000.

Hastings, A. *A History of English Christianity, 1929–1985.* London: Collins, 1986.

Hastings, Adrian. 'Some Thoughts on Research Assessment Exercises.' *BASR Bulletin* 75 (June), 1995: 6–9.

Hauth, R. *Die nach der Seele greifen. Psychokult und Jugendsekten.* Gütersloh: Gütersloher Verlagshaus Gerd Mohn; Siebenstern, 1979 (1st edn; 1985, 2nd edn).

Hauth, Rüdiger. *Jugendsekten und Psychogruppen von A–Z.* Gütersloh: Gütersloher Verlagshaus Gerd Mohn, Siebenstern, 1981.

Hawting, G. R. 'A New Department of Religious Studies at SOAS, University of London.' *BASR Bulletin* 67 (November), 1992: 19–20.

Hearst, Patricia Campbell and Alvin Moscov. *Every Secret Thing.* London: Arrow Books, 1983.

Heelas, Paul. 'Californian Self-Religions and Socializing the Subjective.' In *New Religious Movements: A Perspective for Understanding Society.* E. Barker, Ed. New York: Edwin Mellen Press, 1982: 69–85.

Heelas, Paul. 'Self-Religions in Britain.' *Religion Today* 1 (1), 1984: 4–5.

Heelas, Paul. 'Exegesis: Methods and Aims.' In *The New Evangelists: Recruitment, Methods and Aims of New Religious Movements.* P. B. Clarke, Ed. London: Ethnographica, 1987: 17–41.

Heelas, Paul. 'Western Europe: Self-Religions.' In *The World's Religions.* S. Sutherland *et al.*, Eds. London: Routledge, 1988: 925–931.

Heelas, Paul. 'Experiencing Religious Conversion.' In *Coping With Change. The Marshall Cavendish Encyclopedia of Personal Relationships: Human Behaviour, Vol. 18.* G. M. Breakwell, Ed. New York, London: Marshall Cavendish, 1990a: 2260–2265.

Heelas, Paul. 'The Economics of the New Religious Life.' *Religion* 20, 1990b: 297–302.

Heelas, Paul. 'Cults for Capitalism: Self-Religions, Magic and the Empowerment of Business.' In *Religion and Power: Decline and Growth.* P. Gee and J. Fulton, Eds. London: Chameleon Press, 1991: 28–42.

Heelas, Paul. 'The Sacralization of the Self and New Age Capitalism.' In *Social Change in Contemporary Britain.* N. Abercrombie and A. Warde, Eds. Cambridge: Polity Press, 1992: 139–166.

Heelas, Paul. 'The New Age In Cultural Context: Premodern, the Modern, and the Postmodern.' *Religion* 23 (2), 1993: 103–116.

Heelas, Paul. 'The Limits of Consumption and the Post-Modern "Religion" of the New Age.' In *The Authority of the Consumer.* R. Keat, N. Whiteley, and N. Abercrombie, Eds. London: Routledge, 1994: 102–115.

Heelas, Paul. 'De-Traditionalization of Religion and Self: The New Age and Postmodernity.' In *Postmodernity, Sociology and Religion.* K. Flanagan and P. Jupp, Eds. London: Macmillan, 1995.

Heelas, Paul. *The New Age Movement: The Celebration of the Self and the Sacralization of Modernity.* Oxford: Blackwell, 1996.

Heelas, Paul and Anna Marie Haglund-Heelas. 'The Inadequacy of "Deprivation" as a Theory of Conversion.' In *Vernacular Christianity: Essays in the Social Anthropology of Religion Presented to Godfrey Lienhardt.* Oxford: JASO, 1988: 112–119.

Heinemann, Ingo. *Aus der Schule in die Sekte. Wie die Scientology-Sekte mit Hilfe einer Tarnorganisation um Nachwuchs wirbt.* Stuttgart: ABI-Aktion Bildungsinformation e.V., 1981.

Heinemann, Ingo. *Die Scientology-Sekte und ihre Tarnorganisationen.* Stuttgart: ABI-Aktion Bildungsinformation e.V., n.d.

Heirich, Max. 'Change of Heart: A Test of Some Widely Held Theories about Religious Conversion.' *American Journal of Sociology* 83 (3), 1977: 653–680.

Helsper, Werner. *Okkultismus – die neue Jugendreligion? Die Symbolik des Todes und des Bösen in der Jugendkultur.* Opladen: Leske and Budrich, 1992.

Hemminger, Hansjörg. 'Vom Umgang mit dem Okkultismus – Psychologische und seelsorgerliche Aspekte.' *Materialdienst* 51 (12), 1988: 345–355.

Hemminger, Hansjörg. 'Die alternative Therapieszene und die Psychokulte.' *Materialdienst* 53 (9), 1990: 241–249.

Hemminger, Hansjörg. *Verein zur Förderung der Psychologischen Menschenkenntnis (VPM, IPM, GFPM).* Werkmappe 'Sekten, religiöse Sondergemeinschaften, Weltanschauungen', Vol. 61. Vienna: Referat für Weltanschauungsfragen der Erzdiözöse Wien, 1991.

Hemminger, Hansjörg. 'EZW und *VPM* – Apologetik vor Gericht.' *Materialdienst* 55 (12), 1992: 360–365.

Hemminger, Hansjörg. *VPM. Der Verein zur Förderung der Psychologischen Menschenkenntnis und Friedrich Lieblings 'Zürcher Schule'.* Munich: Evangelischer Presseverband für Bayern, 1994a.

Hemminger, Hansjörg. 'Glauben verantworten: Methodische und Praktische Fragen.' In *Begegnung und Auseinandersetzung: Apologetik in der Arbeit der EZW.* R. Hummel, G. Küenzlen and H. Hemminger, Eds. Stuttgart: EZW, 1994b: 24–35.

Hemminger, Hansjörg. 'Öffentlich über Sekten sprechen. Zum kirchlichen Umgang mit dem Sektenbegriff.' *Materialdienst* 58 (6), 1995: 161–171.

Hemminger, Hansjörg. 'Kein Erdrutsch bei den sogenannten Sekten.' *Materialdienst* 60 (7), 1997: 210–212.

Herrmann, Jörg, Ed. *Mission mit allen Mitteln. Der Scientology-Konzern auf Seelenfang.* Reinbek: Rowohlt, 1992 (3rd edn).

Hexham, Irving and Karla Poewe. *New Religions as Global Cultures.* Boulder, CO, Oxford: Westview Press, 1997.

Heymel, Michael. 'Review of Sri Chinmoy's Das innere Versprechen.' *Deutsches Pfarrerblatt* 11, 1984: 580–581.

Hill, Michael. *A Sociology of Religion.* Hampshire: Avebury, 1973. (Reprinted by Heinemann in 1987.)

Hinnells, John R. *Zoroastrians in Britain.* Oxford: Clarendon Press: 1996.

HMSO (Her Majesty's Stationery Office). *Charities: A Framework for the Future.* London: HMSO, 1989.

Hoeckman, Remi, OP 'The Pastoral Challenge of New Religious Movements.' *Origins* 17 (July 30), 1987: 136–143.

Hoffman, Eva. 'Est: The Magic of Brutality.' *Dissent* 24 (2), 1977: 209–212.

Höft, Ursula. 'Bilanz einer Betroffenen.' In *1995 – Und es geht weiter.* I. Kroll, B. Dürholt, im Auftrag der Elterninitiative zur Hilfe gegen seelische Abhängigkeit und religiösen Extremismus e.V., Eds. Munich: Arbeitsgemeinschaft für Religions- und Weltanschauungsfragen (ARW), 1996: 66–70.

Höhn, Hans Joachim. 'City Religion. Soziologische Glossen zur "neuen" Religiosität.' *Forum – Materialien und Beiträge zum religiösen Dialog* 6 (April), 1990: 4–8.

Holroyd, Stuart. *Psi and the Consciousness Explosion.* London: Bodley Head, 1977.

Homan, Roger. 'The Ethics of Covert Methods.' *British Journal of Sociology* 31, 1980: 46–59.

Homan, Roger. *The Ethics of Social Research.* London, New York: Longman, 1991.

Horowitz, Irving Louis, Ed. *Science, Sin, and Scholarship: The Politics of Reverend Moon and the Unification Church*. Cambridge, MA: MIT Press, 1978.

Horowitz, Irving. 'Universal Standards, Not Uniform Beliefs: Further Reflections on Scientific Method and Religious Sponsors.' *Sociological Analysis* 44 (3), 1983: 179–182.

Hounan, Peter, and Andrew Hogg. *Secret Cult*. Belville, Sydney: Lion, 1985.

Howard, Roland. *The Rise and Fall of Nine O'Clock Service: A Cult within the Church?* London: Cassell, 1996.

Huber, Wolfgang. 'Volkskirche: Theologisch.' In *Evangelisches Kirchenlexikon: Internationale theologische Enzyclopedie*. E. Fahlbusch *et al.*, Eds. Göttingen: Vandenhoeck and Ruprecht, 1996: cols. 1202–1204.

Hubner, John and Lindsey Gruson. *Monkey on a Stick: Murder, Madness, and the Hare Krishna*. New York: Harcourt Brace Jovanovich; Harmondsworth: Penguin, 1988.

Hultkrantz, A. 'Über religionsethnologische Methoden.' In *Selbstverständnis und Wesen der Religionswissenschaft*. G. Lanczkowski, Ed. Darmstadt: Wissenschaftliche Buchgesellschaft, 1972: 360–394.

Hummel, Reinhart, Ed. *Jugendsekten – Symptome einer gesellschaftlichen Krise?* Stuttgart: Evangelische Zentralstelle für Weltanschauungsfragen (EZW), 1982. Arbeitstexte, Vol. 22 (III/82).

Hummel, Reinhart. 'Die sogenannten Jugendreligionen als religiöse und gesellschaftliche Phänomene.' In *Essener Gespräche zum Thema Staat und Kirche*. H. Marré and J. Stüting, Eds. Münster: Aschendorff, 1985: 64–82.

Hummel, Reinhart. 'Religionsfriede statt Dritter Weltkrieg. Sun Myung Moons interreligiöse Aktivitäten.' *Materialdienst* 53 (10), 1990: 291–295.

Hummel, Reinhart. 'Mission, Dialog und Apologetik.' *Zeitschrift für Mission*, 1993a: 211–220.

Hummel, Reinhart. 'Remarks on Heber Jentzsch and Scientology.' *Update & Dialog* 3 (October), 1993b: 7.

Hummel, Reinhart. 'Apologetische Modelle.' In *Begegnung und Auseinandersetzung: Apologetik in der Arbeit der EZW*. R. Hummel, G. Küenzlen and H. Hemminger, Eds. Stuttgart: Evangelische Zentralstelle für Weltanschauungsfragen (EZW), 1994a: 3–13.

Hummel, Reinhart. *Religiöser Pluralismus oder Christliches Abendland? Herausforderung an Kirche und Gesellschaft*. Darmstadt: Wissenschaftliche Buchgesellschaft, 1994b.

Hummel, Reinhart. 'Christliche Orientierung im religiösen Pluralismus.' *Materialdienst* 58 (3), 1995a: 65–73.

Hummel, Reinhart. 'Apologetik: Zur Diskussion über den Apologetik-Text der EZW.' *Materialdienst* 58 (7), 1995b: 215–216.

Hummel, Reinhart, Gottfried Küenzlen and Hansjörg Hemminger. *Begegnung und Auseinandersetzung: Apologetik in der Arbeit der EZW*. Impulse, Vol. 39, ix/1994. Stuttgart: Evangelische Zentralstelle für Weltanschauungsfragen (EZW), 1994.

Hunter, Edward. *Brainwashing in Red China: The Calculated Destruction of Men's Minds*. New York: Vanguard, 1953 (enlarged edn).

Hunter, Edward. *Brainwashing: The Story of the Men who Defied It*. New York: Norton, 1956.

Hutten, Kurt. *Seher, Grübler, Enthusiasten. Sekten und religiöse Sondergemeinschaften der Gegenwart*. Stuttgart: Quell-Verlag der evangelischen Gesellschaft, 1958.

Hutten, Kurt. *Seher – Grübler – Enthusiasten. Das Buch der traditionellen Sekten und religiösen Sonderbewegungen.* Stuttgart: Quell, 1984 (revised and expanded edn).

Innenministerium des Landes Nordrhein-Westfalen, Ed. *Scientology – eine Gefahr für die Demokratie. Eine Aufgabe für den Verfassungsschutz?* Düsseldorf: Innenministerium des Landes Nordrhein-Westfalen, 1996.

Introvigne, Massimo. *Le nuove religioni.* Milan: Sugarco, 1989.

Introvigne, Massimo, Ed. *Il ritorno della magia. Una sfida per la società e per la Chiesa.* Milan: Effedieffe, 1992.

Introvigne, Massimo. 'Strange Bedfellows? Is the Split between the Secular Anti-Cult and the Religious Counter-Cult Movement Bound to Grow into Open Antagonism?' *Update & Dialog* 3 (October), 1993: 13–22.

Introvigne, Massimo. 'The Secular Anti-Cult and the Religious Counter-Cult Movement: Strange Bedfellows or Future Enemies?' In *New Religions and the New Europe.* R. Towler, Ed. Aarhus: Aarhus University Press, 1995: 32–54.

Introvigne, Massimo. 'Of "Cultists" and "Martyrs": The Study of New Religious Movements and the Study of Suicide Terrorism in Conversation.' Paper presented at the 2004 CESNUR conference at Baylor University, Waco, Texas, 18–20 June 2004. Available at http://www.cesnur.org/2004/waco_introvigne.htm, access date: 01/04/05.

ISKCON (Ireland). 'Letters of Representation and a Petition Addressed to an Taoiseach, Dr Fitzgerald Concerning the Removal of ISKCON's Charitable Status in Ireland.' Belfast: ISKCON Ireland, 1984.

Israel, Richard J. 'The Cult Problem is a Fake!' *The National Jewish Monthly* 94 (January), 1980: 34.

Jackson, Robert. 'La Place de la religion dans l'enseignements en Angleterre.' *Revue Internationale d'Éducation* (Sevres) 36, 2004: 37–48.

James, Gene, Ed. *The Family and the Unification Church.* Barrytown, New York: Unification Theological Seminary/Rose of Sharon, 1983.

Janet, P. *The Major Symptoms of Hysteria.* New York: Macmillan, 1929 (2nd edn).

Johnson, Benton. 'A Critical Appraisal of the Church–Sect Typology.' *American Sociological Review* 22, 1957: 88–92.

Johnson, Benton. 'On Church and Sect.' *American Sociological Review* 28, 1963: 539–549.

Johnson, Benson. 'Church and Sect Revisited.' *Journal for the Scientific Study of Religion* 10 (2), 1971: 125–137.

Johnson, Doyle P. 'Dilemmas of Charismatic Leadership: The Case of the People's Temple.' *Sociological Analysis* 40 (4), 1979: 315–323.

Judah, J. Stillson. 'The Hare Krishna Movement.' In *Religious Movements in Contemporary America.* I. I. Zaretzky and M. P. Leone, Eds. Princeton: Princeton UP, 1974a: 463–478.

Judah, J. Stillson. *Hare Krishna and the Counterculture.* New York: Wiley, 1974b.

Junge Union Bayern, Ed. *Jugendsekten – Die Freiheit des einzelnen schützen.* Munich: Erich Wewel, 1985.

Junge Union Bayern, Ed. *Stichwort Jugendsekten: Sonderreport Scientology. Ein Überblick über die zweifelhaften Aktivitäten der Scientology.* Munich: Junge Union Bayern, n.d.

Junge Union Deutschlands, Ed. *Das 1. Wormser Scientology Tribunal, 27–28. November*. Stuttgart: Junge Union Deutschlands, Landesverband Rheinland-Pfalz, 1993.

Junge Union Nordwürttemberg. *Scientology Church. Darstellung der Praktiken einer 'Religionsgemeinschaft'*. Stuttgart: Junge Union Nordwürttemberg, 1992 (2nd, updated edn; first published in 1991).

Junge Union Nordwürttemberg. *Scientology and Dianetik. Dubiose Praktiken unter dem Deckmantel einer 'Religionsgemeinschaft*. Stuttgart: Junge Union Nordwürttemberg, 1995 (4th edn).

Kakuska, R. *Esoterik: Von Abrakadabra bis Zombie*. Basle, Weinheim: Beltz, 1991.

Kalman, Matthew and John Murray. 'New Age Nazism.' *New Statesman and Society*, 23 June 1995: 18–20.

Kaplan, David and Andrew Marshall. *The Cult at the End of the World: The Incredible Story of Aum*. London: Hutchinson, 1996.

Kaplan, Jeffrey. *Radical Religion in America: Millenarian Movements from the Far Right to the Children of Noah*. Syracuse, NY: Syracuse University Press, 1997.

Karbe, Klaus. '[no title].' In *Dokumentation zur Expertenkonsultation zum Thema Jugendreligionen. Protokoll einer Tagung in Heilsbronn vom 9–11.11.1979*. Evangelische Akademie Tutzing, Ed. Munich: Arbeitsgemeinschaft für Religions- und Weltanschauungsfragen (ARW), 1980: 32–34.

Karbe, Klaus G. and Manfred Müller-Küppers, Eds. *Destruktive Kulte – Gesellschaftliche und gesundheitliche Folgen totalitärer pseudoreligiöser Bewegungen*. Göttingen: Verlag für medizinische Psychologie im Verlag Vandenhoeck und Ruprecht, 1983. Beiheft zur 'Praxis der Kinderpsychologie und Kinderpsychiatrie', Vol. 24.

Karow, Yvonne. *Bhagwan-Bewegung und Vereinigungskirche. Religions- und Selbstverständnis der Sannyasins und der Munies*. Stuttgart: Kohlhammer, 1990.

Kehrer, Günter. 'Soziale Bedingungen für nicht-kirchliche religiöse Gruppen in der Bundesrepublik.' In *Zur Religionsgeschichte der Bundesrepublik Deutschland*. G. Kehrer, Ed. Munich: Kösel, 1980a.

Kehrer, Günter, Ed. *Zur Religionsgeschichte der Bundesrepublik Deutschland*. Munich: Kösel, 1980b.

Kehrer, Günter, Ed. *Das Entstehen einer neuen Religion: Das Beispiel der Vereinigungskirche*. Munich: Kösel, 1981a. Forum Religionswissenschaft.

Kehrer, Günter. 'Kirchen, Sekten und der Staat. Zum Problem der religiösen Toleranz.' In *Staat und Religion*. B. Gladigow, Ed. Düsseldorf: Patmos, 1981b: 141–158.

Kehrer, Günter. 'Ethos und Handeln im System der Vereinigungskirche.' In *Das Entstehen einer neuen Religion. Das Beispiel der Vereinigungskirche*. G. Kehrer, Ed. Munich: Kösel, 1981c: 173–187.

Kehrer, Günter. 'Gutachterliche Stellungnahme zur Anwendung der Begriffe "Religion", "Sekte", "Jugendreligion" und "Jugendsekte" auf das Programm der Transzendentalen Meditation (TM). Kurze Geschichte der Verwendung des Begriffs "Jugendreligion/Jugendsekte" in der Polemik und die Rolle des MJFG dabei.' Tübingen: University of Tübingen, 1982.

Kehrer, Günter. ' "Jugendreligionen" in der bundesrepublikanischen Öffentlichkeit.' In *Religionsgeschichte in der Öffentlichkeit*. A. Falaturi *et al*., Eds. Cologne, Vienna: Böhlau, 1983.

Kehrer, Günter. 'Kritische Phasen in der Geschichte neuer Religionen.' In *Der Untergang von Religionen*. H. Zinser, Ed. Berlin: Reimer, 1986: 221–234.

Kehrer, Günter. *Einführung in die Religionssoziologie.* Darmstadt: Wissenschaftliche Buchgesellschaft, 1988.

Kehrer, Günter. 'Tradition und Selbstverständnis der deutschen Religionswissenschaft: ein Hindernis für die Erforschung neuer Religionen?' Paper presented to the Conference on 'Streitfall Neue Religionen: Religionswissenschaftliche Perspektiven im internationalen Vergleich', Marburg, 27–29 March 1998.

Kelley, Dean, Ed. *Government Intervention in Religious Affairs.* New York: Pilgrim, 1982.

Keltsch, Jürgen. 'Reichen die Gesetze aus, um den Konsumenten auf dem Psychomarkt zu schützen?' In *1995 – Und es geht weiter.* I. Kroll, B. Dürholt, im Auftrag der Elterninitiative zur Hilfe gegen seelische Abhängigkeit und religiösen Extremismus e.V., Eds. Munich: Arbeitsgemeinschaft für Religions- und Weltanschauungsfragen (ARW), 1996: 17–38.

Kempcke, Helga. 'Allerliebster Meister.' *Deutsches Allgemeines Sonntagsblatt* 50, 15 December 1985: 16.

Kilbourne, Brock K. 'The Conway and Siegelman Claims Against Religious Cults: An Assessment of their Data.' *Journal for the Scientific Study of Religion* 22 (4), 1983: 380–385.

Kilbourne, Brock, Ed. *Scientific Research and New Religions: Divergent Perspectives. Proceedings of the Annual Meeting of the Pacific Division of the American Association for the Advancement of Science, 59th Meeting of the Rocky Mountain Division.* San Francisco: Pacific Division of the American Association for the Advancement of Science, 1985.

Kilbourne, Brock K. and James T. Richardson. 'Cultphobia.' *Thought* 61 (241), 1986: 258–266.

King, Christine E. *The Nazi State and the New Religions: Five Case Studies in Non-Conformity.* New York: Edwin Mellen, 1982.

King, Dennis. *Nazis ohne Hakenkreuz. Der Lyndon-LaRouche-Kult und sein Kampf gegen die amerikanische Arbeiterschaft.* Dokumentations-Edition, Vol. 6. Munich: Arbeitsgemeinschaft für Religions- und Weltanschauungsfragen (ARW), 1984.

Kippenberg, Hans G. 'Einleitung: Religionswissenschaft und Kukturkritik.' In *Religionswissenschaft und Kulturkritik: Beiträge zur Konferenz The History of Religions and Critique of Culture in the Days of Gerardus van der Leeuw (1890–1950).* H. G. Kippenberg and B. Luchesi, Eds. Marburg: diagonal-Verlag, 1991: 13–28.

Kippenberg, Hans G. and Brigitte Luchesi, Eds. *Religionswissenschaft und Kulturkritik: Beiträge zur Konferenz The History of Religions and Critique of Culture in the Days of Gerardus van der Leeuw (1890–1950).* Marburg: diagonal-Verlag, 1991.

Kirchner, Wolfgang. *Denken heißt zum Teufel beten. Roman über eine Jugendsekte.* Reinbek: Rowohlt, 1981.

Klosinski, Gunther. *Warum Bhagwan? Auf der Suche nach Heimat, Geborgenheit und Liebe.* Munich: Kösel, 1985.

Knott, Kim. *My Sweet Lord: The Hare Krishna Movement.* Wellingborough, Northants.: Aquarian Press, 1986.

Knott, Kim. 'Contemporary Theological Trends in the Hare Krishna Movement: A Theology of Religions.' *Diskus* 1 (1), 1993.

Kolb, W. L. 'Cult.' In *A Dictionary of the Social Sciences.* J. Gould and W. L. Kolb, Eds. London: Tavistock, 1964.

Kommer, Wolfgang and Pastoralamt der Erzdiözese Wien. *Neuoffenbarungen und neue Offenbarungen. Darstellung und Kritik.* Werkmappe der 'Sekten, religiöse Sondergemeinschaften, Weltanschauungen', Vol. 67. Vienna: Referat für Weltanschauungsfragen, Sekten und religiöse Gemeinschaften, 1993.

König, Franz. 'Dialogue: A Demanding Struggle.' *Origins* 14 (April 4), 1985: 692–695.

König, Franz. 'Dialogue: A Demanding Struggle.' *Origins* 16 (May 22), 1986: 5–6.

König, Franz. 'Der religiöse und interreligiöse Dialog im neuen Haus von Europa.' Paper presented to the F.I.U.C. Symposium in Vienna, 1991.

König, René, Ed. *Soziologie.* Frankfurt a. M.: Fischer, 1960.

Kränzle, Bernd. 'Die Frage der Psychogruppen und Sekten aus Politischer Sicht.' In *1995 – Und es geht weiter.* I. Kroll, B. Dürholt, im Auftrag der Elterninitiative zur Hilfe gegen seelische Abhängigkeit und religiösen Extremismus e.V., Eds. Munich: Arbeitsgemeinschaft für Religions- und Weltanschauungsfragen (ARW), 1996: 55–65.

Kuhn, Thomas. *The Structure of Scientific Revolutions.* Chicago: University of Chicago Press, 1962.

Küenzlen, Gottfried. 'Die westliche Orientierungskrise und das Angebot der "Jugendreligionen".' In *Die neuen Jugendreligionen, Teil 3: Analysen und Informationen.* F.-W. Haack, Ed. Munich, 1985: 7–14.

Küenzlen, Gottfried. 'Kirche und Zeitgeist – Überlegungen zu Grundfragen kirchlicher Apologetik.' *Materialdienst* 52 (4), 1989: 99–112.

Küenzlen, Gottfried. 'Kirche und die geistigen Strömungen der Zeit – Grundaufgaben heutiger Apologetik.' In *Begegnung und Auseinandersetzung: Apologetik in der Arbeit der EZW.* R. Hummel, G. Küenzlen and H. Hemminger. Stuttgart: Evangelische Zentralstelle für Weltanschauungsfragen (EZW), 1994: 14–24.

Kuner, Wolfgang. 'You Gotta be a Baby oder Happiness flutsch flutsch. Eine Untersuchung zu Charakter, Genese und gesellschaftlichen Ursachen einer den sogenannten "Jugendreligionen" zugeordneten sozialen Bewegung: der Children of God (Family of Love).' Unpublished MA Thesis, Tübingen, 1979.

Kuner, Wolfgang. ' "Jugendsekten": Ein Sammelbecken für Verrückte?' In *'Jugendsekten' und neue Religiosität: Notwendige Anmerkungen.* H.-W. Baumann *et al.*, Eds. Gelsenkirchen-Buer: Farin und Zwingmann, 1982: 172–196. (First published in *Psychologie Heute* 9, September, 1981: 53–61.)

Kuner, Wolfgang. *Soziogenese der Mitgliedschaft in drei Neuen Religiösen Bewegungen.* Europäische Hochschulschriften, Reihe XXXI, Politikwissenschaft, Vol. 46. Frankfurt, Berne, New York: Peter Lang, 1983a.

Kuner, Wolfgang. 'New Religious Movements and Mental Health.' In *Of Gods and Men: New Religious Movements in the West.* E. Barker, Ed. Macon, GA: Mercer UP, 1983b: 255–263.

Kuner, Wolfgang. 'Skizze zu einer Soziologie der neuen religiösen Gruppen.' In *Neue religiöse Organisationen – Glück oder Gefahr?* Aktion Jugendschutz – Kath. Landesarbeitsstelle Rheinland-Pfalz e.V., Ed. Pirmasens: Aktion Jugendschutz, 1983c: 172–189.

Künneth, Walter. *Lebensführungen: Der Wahrheit verpflichtet.* Wuppertal: Brockhaus, 1979.

Kupisch, Karl. *Die Deutschen Landeskirchen im 19. und 20. Jahrhundert.* Göttingen: Vandenhoeck and Ruprecht, 1966.

Küpper, Otto. 'Für den Guru: Bischof beurlaubt Vikar.' *Express*, 17 November 1983.

Kurtz, Lester. *Gods in the Global Village: The World's Religions in Sociological Perspective*. London: Pine Forge Press, 1995.

La Fontaine, Jean. *(Report on Ritual Satanic Abuse) The Intent and Nature of Organised and Ritual Abuse*. London: HMSO, 1994.

Landesarbeitsgemeinschaft der Freien Wohlfahrtspflege in Niedersachsen – Landesstelle Jugendschutz, Ed. *Jugendsekten – Dargestellt am Beispiel der Vereinigungskirche, der Scientology-Church und der Kinder Gottes*. Hannover: Franz Neuenfeldt, 1979. Jugendschutz, Vol. 1.

Landesregierung Rheinland-Pfalz, Ed. *Jugendliche in destruktiven religiösen Gruppen*. Mainz: Landesregierung Rheinland-Pfalz, 1979.

Landesstelle Jugendschutz Niedersachsen, Landesgemeinschaft Kinder- und Jugendschutz, Aktion Kinder- und Jugendschutz, Schleswig-Holstein, Arbeitsgemeinschaft, Kinder- and Jugendschutz Hamburg, Eds. *Meister und Geister*. Hannover: Landesstelle Jugendschutz Niedersachsen, etc., 1995.

Landtag von Baden-Württemberg. '1. Bericht der "Interministeriellen Arbeitsgruppe für Fragen sog. Jugendsekten und Psychogruppen".' 11. Wahlperiode, Drucksache 11/4643, 21.09.1994.

Landtag von Baden-Württemberg. '2. Bericht der "Interministeriellen Arbeitsgruppe für Fragen sog. Jugendsekten und Psychogruppen".' 11. Wahlperiode, Drucksache 11/6704, 10.11.1995.

Landtag von Baden-Württemberg. '3. Bericht der "Interministeriellen Arbeitsgruppe für Fragen sog. Jugendsekten und Psychogruppen".' 12. Wahlperiode, Drucksache 12/1411, 29.04.1997.

Lang, Bernhard. 'Kleine Soziologie religiöser Rituale.' In *Religionswissenschaft: Eine Einführung*. H. Zinser, Ed. Berlin: Reimer, 1988: 73–95.

Langone, M. D. *Destructive Cultism: Questions and Answers*. Weston, MA: American Family Foundation, 1982.

Langone, M. D., Ed. *Deprogramming: An Analysis of Parental Questionnaires*. Weston, MA: The American Family Foundation, 1984. (Excerpts published under the same title in *Cultic Studies Journal* 1 (1), 1984: 63–78.)

Langone, M. D. and John G. Clark. *New Religions and Public Policy: Research Implications for Social Scientists*. Weston, MA: The American Family Foundation, 1984.

Langone, M. D. and John G. Clark. 'New Religions and Public Policy.' In *Scientific Research of New Religions: Divergent Perspectives*. B. K. Kilbourne, Ed. San Francisco: AAAS, 1985: 90–113.

Larson, Martin. *New Thought or A Modern Religious Approach: The Philosophy of Health, Happiness, and Prosperity*. New York: Philosophical Library, 1985.

LeBar, James J. *Cults, Sects and the New Age*. Huntingdon, Indiana: Our Sunday Visitor, 1989.

le Bé, Philippe. 'Ces étranges conseillers d'entreprises.' *Bilan*, 6 June 1994: 72–84.

Leduc, Jean-Marie and Didier de Plaige. *Les Nouveaux Prophètes*. Paris: Buchet/Castel, 1978.

Leech, Kenneth. *Youthquake: The Growth of a Counter Culture*. London: Sheldon Press, 1973.

Léger, Danièle. 'Charisma, Utopia, and Communal Life: The Case of Neorural Apocalyptic Communes in France.' *Social Compass* 29, 1982: 41–58.

Lehmann, Karsten. 'Konflikte mit "Sekten" und "fremden Religionen". Worauf antwortet die EZW?' *Materialdienst* 57 (7), 1994: 192–197.

Lemke, Waltraud, Imogen Schäfer and Thomas Gandow. 'Fluchtpunkt Berlin: Ein Hilfsangebot für Aussteiger aus destruktiven Kulten, Jugendreligionen, Gurube-wegungen in Berlin.' In *Eindeutig zwischen den Stühlen. Zehn Beiträge zur Apologie der Apologetik*. M. Ach, Ed. Munich: Arbeitsgemeinschaft für Religions- und Weltanschauungsfragen (ARW), 1985: 61–76.

Lenz, Reimar. ' "Jugendreligionen": Notwehr oder Hexenjagd? I + II.' *esotera* 11 and 12 (November and December), 1978: 996–1005; 1123–1128.

Lenz, Reimar. 'Im Protestantismus: Sektenkampagne statt Spiritualität.' In *'Jugendsekten' – Symptome einer gesellschaftlichen Krise?* R. Hummel, Ed. Stuttgart: Evangelische Zentralstelle für Weltanschauungsfragen (EZW), 1982: 20–21.

Levine, Edward M. 'Rural Communes and Religious Cults: Refuges for Middle Class Youth.' *Adolescent Psychiatry* 8, 1980: 138–153.

Levine, Edward M. 'The Case for Deprogramming Religious Cult Members.' *A.F.F. Advisor*, February/March, 1981.

Levine, Saul V. 'Youth and Religious Cults: A Social and Clinical Dilemma.' *Adolescent Psychiatry* 6, 1978: 75–89.

Levine, Saul V. 'Cults and Mental Health: Clinical Conclusions.' *Canadian Journal of Psychiatry* 26 (8), 1981: 534–539.

Levine, Saul V. *Radical Departures: Desperate Detours to Growing Up*. New York: Harcourt Brace Jovanovich, 1984.

Levine, Saul L. and Nancy E. Slater. 'Youth and Contemporary Religious Movements: Psychosocial Findings.' *Canadian Psychiatric Association Journal* 21, 1976: 411–420.

Levitt, Mairi. 'Parental Attitudes to Religion: A Cornish Case Study.' Paper presented to the BSA Sociology of Religion Study Group, St Mary's College, Twickenham, 1992.

Lewin, Kurt. 'Group Dynamics and Social Change.' In *Social Change: Sources, Patterns and Consequences*. A. Etzioni and E. Etzioni-Halevy, Eds. New York: Basic Books, 1973 (2nd edn).

Lewis, James R. *The New Age Movement: A Bibliography of Conservative Christian Literature*. Santa Barbara, CA: Santa Barbara Centre for Humanistic Studies, 1989.

Lewis, James R., Ed. *Magical Religion and Modern Witchcraft*. Albany, NY: State of New York UP, 1996.

Lewis, James R. and J. Gordon Melton, Eds. *Perspectives on the New Age*. Albany: SUNY, 1992.

Lieberman, Seymour. 'The Effects of Changes in Role on the Attitudes of Role Occupants.' *Human Relations* 9, 1956: 385–407.

Lifton, Robert J. 'Thought Reform of Western Civilians in Chinese Communist Prisons.' *Psychiatry* 19 (May), 1956: 385–402.

Lifton, Robert J. *Thought Reform and the Psychology of Totalism: A Study of 'Brainwashing' in China*. London: Gollancz, 1961 (New York: Norton, 1963; Chapel Hill, North Carolina: University of North Carolina Press, 1989).

Lifton, Robert J. 'Thought Reform of Chinese Intellectuals: A Psychiatric Evaluation.' *Journal of Social Issues* 13, 1967: 5–19.

Lifton, Robert J. 'Religiöse Kulte und Totalitarismus.' In *'Neue Jugendreligionen.' Vorträge und Berichte einer Fachtagung über 'Probleme im Zusammenhang mit den sogenannten Jugendreligionen' am 23./24. Februar 1978 in der Medizinischen*

Hochschule Hannover. M. Müller-Küppers and F. Specht, Eds. Göttingen: Vandenhoeck and Ruprecht, 1979: 73–84.

Lindner, Robert. *The Fifty-Minute Hour: A Collection of True Psychoanalytic Tales.* New York: Bantam Books, 1954.

Lindner, Klaus M. 'Kulturelle und semantische Probleme beim Studium einer neuen Religion.' In *Das Entstehen einer Neuen Religion: Das Beispiel der Vereinigungskirche.* G. Kehrer, Ed. Munich: Kösel, 1981: 219–234.

Lindt, Gillian. 'Journeys to Jonestown: Accounts and Interpretations of the Rise and Demise of the People's Temple.' *Union Seminary Quarterly Review* 37 (Fall/Winter), 1981–1982: 159–174.

Linzey, Jo, Ed. *The Church of England Year Book 1996.* London: Church House Publishing, 1996 (112th edn).

Littler, June D. *The Church of Scientology: A Bibliography.* New York: Garland, 1991.

Lofland, John. *Doomsday Cult: A Study of Conversion, Proselytisation and Maintenance of Faith.* New York: Irvington, 1980 (revised edn; originally published in 1966 in Englewood Cliffs, NJ by Prentice-Hall).

Lofland, John and James T. Richardson. 'Religious Movement Organisations: Elemental Forms and Dynamics.' In *Research in Social Movements, Conflicts and Change.* L. Kriesberg, Ed. Greenwich, Conn: JAI Press, 1984: 29–53.

Lofland, John and Norman Skonovd. 'Patterns of Conversion.' In *Of God and Men: New Religious Movements in the West.* E. Barker, Ed. Macon, GA: Mercer, 1983: 1–24.

Lofland, John and Rodney Stark. 'Becoming a World-Saver: A Theory of Conversion to a Deviant Perspective.' *American Sociological Review* 30 (December), 1965: 862–874.

Long, Theodore E. and Jeffrey K. Hadden. 'Religious Conversion and the Concept of Socialization: Integrating the Brainwashing and Drift Models.' *Journal for the Scientific Study of Religion* 22 (1), 1983: 1–14.

Loth, Heinz-Jürgen. *Rastafari: Bibel und afrikanische Spiritualität.* Kölner Veröffentlichungen zur Religionsgeschichte, Vol. 20. Cologne: Böhlau-Verlag, 1991.

Loth, Heinz-Jürgen. 'Rastafari.' In *Religionen der Welt. Grundlagen, Entwicklung und Bedeutung in der Gegenwart.* U. and M. Tworuschka, Eds. Gütersloh, Munich: Bertelsmann, 1992: 399–400.

Lucas, Phillip Charles and Robbins, Thomas, Eds. *New Religious Movements in the 21st Century: Legal, Political, and Social Challenges in Global Perspective.* New York and London: Routledge, 2004.

Luckmann, Thomas. *The Invisible Religion: The Problem of Religion in Modern Society.* New York: Macmillan, 1967.

Luckmann, Thomas. 'Anonymität und persönliche Identität.' In *Christlicher Glaube in moderner Gesellschaft.* T. Luckmann, H. Döring and P. M. Zulehner, Eds. Freiburg i. Br.: Herder, 1980.

Maarbjerg, Peter. 'TM is a Religious Practice, Court Rules.' *Update* 2 (1), 1978: 27–30.

MacDonald, Victoria. ' "Safe" House for Brainwashed Cult Victims.' *The Sunday Telegraph*, 4 June 1989.

MacIntyre, Michael. *The New Pacific.* London: Collins/BBC Publications, 1985.

MacKenzie, Ursula. 'Leipzig Conference, 29.–31.3.1996.' *FAIR NEWS* Summer, 1996: 11.

Maes, Jochen. *Geschäfte mit der Sucht. Von der Droge in die Sekte. Scientology Sekte Narconon e.V. Staatlich bezuschußte Heilslehre.* Berlin: Eine Zitty Dokumentation, 1977.

Mamay, Inge. '[Haus Altenberg].' In *Dokumentation zur Expertenkonsultation zum Thema Jugendreligionen. Protokoll einer Tagung in Heilsbronn vom 9– 11.11.1979.* Evangelische Akademie Tutzing, Ed. Munich: Arbeitsgemeinschaft für Religions- und Weltanschauungsfragen (ARW), 1980: 24–26.

Martin, Bernice. 'Whose Knowledge? Methodological Problems and Procedures Arising from Sociology's Rediscovery of Religion.' In *Youth in Perspective: Methodological Problems and Alternatives in the Study of Youth.* M. Vassallo, Ed. Malta: The Euro-Arab Social Research Group, 1981a: 85–114.

Martin, Bernice. *A Sociology of Contemporary Cultural Change.* Oxford: Blackwell, 1981b.

Martin, David. 'The Denomination.' *British Journal of Sociology* 13 (1), 1962: 1–14.

Martin, David. *A Sociology of English Religion.* New York: Basic Books, 1967.

Martin, David. *A General Theory of Secularization.* Oxford: Blackwell, 1978.

Martin, David. 'A Definition of Cult: Terms and Approaches.' In *Alternatives to American Mainline Churches.* J. H. Fichter, Ed. New York: Rose of Sharon, 1983: 27–42.

Martin, David. 'The Churches: Pink Bishops and the Iron Lady.' In *The Thatcher Effect.* D. Kavanagh and A. Seldon, Eds. Oxford: Clarendon Press, 1989: 330–341.

Martin, David. *Tongues of Fire: The Explosion of Protestantism in Latin America.* Oxford: Blackwell, 1990.

Mayer, Jean-François. *Une honteuse exploitation des esprits et des porte-monnaie? Les polémiques contre l'Armée du Salut en Suisse en 1883 et leurs étranges similitudes avec les arguments utilisés aujourd'hui contre les 'nouvelles sectes'.* Fribourg, Switzerland: Les Trois Nornes, 1985.

Mayer, Jean-François. 'Spiriti e medium nelle nuove religioni.' In *Lo Spiritismo.* M. Introvigne, Ed. Leumann, Turin: Elle Di Ci, 1989: 173–224.

McCann, Casey. 'The British Anti-Cult Movement . . . A View from Within.' *Religion Today* 3 (2), 1986: 6–8.

McGurvey, Robert. 'The Brainwashing Puzzle.' *The American Legion*, 1 April 1992.

McLuhan, Marshall and Quentin Fiore. *The Medium is the Massage: An Inventory of Effects.* Harmondsworth: Penguin, 1967.

McManus, Una and John Cooper. *Dealing with Destructive Cults.* Grand Rapids, MI: Zondervan, 1984.

Meier-Hüsing, Peter. *Religiöse Gemeinschaften in Bremen. Ein Handbuch.* Marburg: diagonal-Verlag, 1990.

Melton, J. Gordon J. *The Encyclopedia of American Religion.* Wilmington, NC: Consortium Books, McGrath, 1978 (1st edn; Detroit, MI: Gale, 1989, 3rd edn).

Melton, J. Gordon. *Magic, Witchcraft and Paganism in America: A Bibliography. Compiled from the Files of The Institute for the Study of American Religion.* New York: Garland, 1982.

Melton, J. Gordon. *Encyclopedic Handbook of Cults in America.* New York, London: Garland, 1986 (1st edn; 1992, revised and updated edn).

Melton, J. Gordon. *Encyclopedia of American Religions: Religious Creeds.* Detroit, MI: Gale, 1988 (1st edn; 1993, 4th edn).

Melton, J. Gordon. 'Al-Qaeda as a New Religious Movement.' Paper presented to the CESNUR 2003 International Conference on 'Religion and Democracy: An Exchange of Experience between East and West', Vilnius, Lithuania, 9–12 April 2003.

Melton, J. Gordon. 'The Fate of NRMs and their Detractors in Twenty-First-Century America.' In *New Religious Movements in the 21st Century: Legal, Political, and Social Challenges in Global Perspective*. P. C. Lucas and T. Robbins, Eds. New York and London: Routledge, 2004: 229–240.

Melton, J. Gordon and Robert L. Moore. *The Cult Experience: Responding to the New Religious Pluralism*. New York: Pilgrim, 1982.

Mikos, Lothar. ' "Jugendsekten" und Subkultur.' In *'Jugendsekten' und neue Religiosität: Notwendige Anmerkungen*. H.-W. Baumann *et al.*, Eds. Gelsenkirchen-Buer: Farin und Zwingmann, 1982: 197–212.

Mildenberger, Michael. 'Auf der Suche nach dem Neuen. Religiöse Erwartung und Erfahrung in der jungen Generation.' *Reformatio* 2, 1976: 82–84. Reprinted in EZW, Ed. *Neue Jugendreligionen. Ein Spektrum verschiedener Sichtweisen*. Stuttgart: Evangelische Zentralstelle für Weltanschauungsfragen (EZW), 1982: 19–25.

Mildenberger, Michael. 'Kritische Seelsorge.' *Evangelische Kommentare* 6, 1977. Reprinted in EZW, Ed. *Neue Jugendreligionen. Ein Spektrum verschiedener Sichtweisen*. Stuttgart: Evangelische Zentralstelle für Weltanschauungsfragen (EZW), 1982: 28.

Mildenberger, Michael. 'Die religiöse Szene-Kirchliche Apologetik als Sündenbock.' *Evangelische Kommentare* 4 (April), 1982a: 190–192.

Mildenberger, Michael. 'Kirchliche Apologetik muß Achtung vor Andersdenkenden haben.' In *'Jugendsekten' – Symptome einer gesellschaftlichen Krise?* R. Hummel, Ed. Stuttgart: Evangelische Zentralstelle für Weltanschauungsfragen (EZW), 1982b: 21–22.

Mildenberger, Michael and Norbert Klaes. 'Modell eines Beratungsgesprächs.' In *'Jugendsekten' – Symptome einer gesellschaftlichen Krise?* R. Hummel, Ed. Stuttgart: Evangelische Zentralstelle für Weltanschauungsfragen (EZW), 1982: 4–7.

Milgram, Stanley. *Obedience to Authority*. New York: Harper and Row, 1974.

Miller, Donald E. 'Deprogramming in Historical Perspective.' In *The Brainwashing/ Deprogramming Controversy: Sociological, Psychological, Legal and Historical Perspectives*. D. G. Bromley and J. T. Richardson, Eds. New York: Edwin Mellen, 1983: 15–28.

Minhoff, Christoph. 'Ein ominöses Papier. Viel Geld für wenig Wissenschaft.' *Bayernkurier*, 24 July 1982.

Minister für Arbeit, Gesundheit und Soziales des Landes NRW. *Sogenannte Jugendsekten in Nordrhein-Westfalen*. Düsseldorf: Minister für Arbeit, Gesundheit und Soziales des Landes NRW, 1979.

Minister für Arbeit, Gesundheit und Soziales des Landes NRW. *Jugendreligionen. 2. Sachstandsbericht der Landesregierung*. Minden: Minister für Arbeit, Gesundheit und Soziales des Landes Nordrhein-Westfalen, 1983.

Ministerium für Kultus und Sport Baden-Württemberg. *Bericht über Aufbau und Tätigkeit der sogenannten Jugendreligionen*. Stuttgart: Ministerium für Kultus und Sport, 1988.

Ministerpräsidentin des Landes Schleswig-Holstein. *Sekten und sektenähnliche Vereinigungen: Rechtliche Aspekte öffentlichen Handelns*. Kiel: Dokumentationsstelle 'Sekten und sektenähnliche Vereinigungen', 1995.

Mirbach, Wolfram. *Universelles Leben: Originalität und Christlichkeit einer*

Neureligion. Erlanger Monographien aus Mission und Ökumene, Vol. 19. Erlangen: Verlag der Evangelisch-Lutherischen Mission, 1994.

Mischo, Johannes. *Okkultpraktiken bei Jugendlichen. Ergebnisse einer empirischen Untersuchung*. Edition Psychologie und Pädagogik. Mainz: Matthias-Grünewald-Verlag, 1991.

Mitchison, Amanda. 'Cleaning Up.' *The Independent Magazine*, 12 October, 1991: 36–39.

Mittler, Dietrich. 'SZ-Kurzinterview. Heute: Friedrich-Wilhelm Haack.' *Süddeutsche Zeitung*, 24–25 March 1984.

Mojzes, Paul. ' "Am I my Brother's and Sister's Keeper?" The Responsibility of Mainline Churches Towards the New Religions.' *Journal of Ecumenical Studies* 18 (3), 1981: 474–477.

Morgan, Peggy. 'Methods and Aims of Evangelisation and Conversion in Buddhism with Particular Reference to Nichiren Shoshu Soka Gakkai.' In *Methods and Aims of Conversion and Evangelisation in New Religious Movements*. P. B. Clarke, Ed. London: Ethnographica, 1986: 113–130.

Mucha, Ralf.-D. 'Jugendliche und junge Erwachsene im Markt der Sinnstiftungsangebote: Überlegungen zum administrativen und praktischen Handeln von Behörden, Institutionen und Initiativen.' In *Europas neue Religiosität. Entwicklung, Ursachen, Folgen*. U. Schuster, Ed. Munich: Arbeitsgemeinschaft für Religions- und Weltanschauungsfragen (ARW), 1988: 50–78.

Mullan, Bob. *Life is Laughter: Following Bhagwan Shree Rajneesh*. London: Routledge and Kegan Paul, 1983.

Müller, Daniel. ' "Das ist im Grunde kein Thema für uns …" Neuheidentum zwischen New Age und Faschismus.' *spirita* 3 (June), 1989: 14–19.

Müller, Joachim. 'Die Michaelisvereinigung in Dozwil.' *Materialdienst* 53 (6), 1990: 166–169.

Müller-Küppers, Manfred and Friedrich Specht, Eds. *'Neue Jugendreligionen.' Vorträge und Berichte einer Fachtagung über 'Probleme im Zusammenhang mit den sogenannten Jugendreligionen' am 23./24. Februar 1978 in der Medizinischen Hochschule Hannover*. Göttingen: Vandenhoeck and Ruprecht, 1979 (2nd edn). Beiheft zur Praxis der Kinderpsychologie und -psychiatrie, Vol. 21.

Musgrove, Frank. *Ecstasy and Holiness: Counterculture and the Open Society*. London: Methuen, 1974 (Bloomington, Indiana: Indiana UP, 1975).

Nachtigall, Flora. 'Est – oder: Wie ich lernte, die schöne neue Welt zu lieben.' *Materialdienst* 47 (3), 1984: 73–78.

Nakano, Tsuyoshi. 'Soka Gakkai and Its Peace Movements: The Making of a Counter Community?' *Religion Today* 7 (2), 1992: 5–8.

Nanko, Ulrich. 'Religionswissenschaft im Banne von Theologie.' *spirita* 5 (October), 1991: 21–27.

Nelson, Geoffrey K. *Cults, New Religions and Religious Creativity*. London: Routledge and Kegan Paul, 1987.

Neumann, Johannes and Michael W. Fischer, Eds. *Toleranz und Repression. Zur Lage religiöser Minderheiten in modernen Gesellschaften*. Frankfurt a. M., New York: Campus, 1987.

Niebuhr, Reinhold. *The Social Sources of Denominationalism*. New York; Hamden, CT: Shoe String Press, 1954 (first published in 1929).

Nüchtern, Michael. 'Zuviel Ehre.' *Materialdienst* 60 (3), 1997: 65.

Nußbaum, Hildegard. 'Der Bericht einer Betroffenen.' In *1995 – Und es geht weiter.* I. Kroll, B. Dürholt, im Auftrag der Elterninitiative zur Hilfe gegen seelische Abhängigkeit und religiösen Extremismus e.V., Eds. Munich: Arbeitsgemeinschaft für Religions- und Weltanschauungsfragen (ARW), 1996: 39–46.

Nye, Malory. 'Department of Theology and Religious Studies, King's College London.' *BASR Bulletin* 68 (March), 1993: 17–18.

Nye, Malory. 'Hare Krishna and Sanatan Dharm in Britain: The Campaign for Bhaktivedanta Manor.' *Journal of Contemporary Religion* 11 (1), 1996: 37–56.

Nye, Malory. *Multiculturalism and Minority Religions in Britain: Krishna Consciousness, Religious Freedom, and the Politics of Location.* Richmond, Surrey: Curzon Press, 2001.

Obst, Helmut. *Neureligionen, Jugendreligionen, destruktive Kulte.* Berlin: Union Verlag (VOB), 1984 (1st edn; 1986).

Ofshe, Richard. 'Beware of Americans Bearing Gifts.' FAIR Lecture presented to the Annual Open Meeting of FAIR in London in October 1994.

Ofshe, Richard and Margaret Thaler Singer. 'Attacks on Peripheral versus Central Elements of Self and the Impact of Thought Reforming Techniques.' *Cultic Studies Journal* 3 (1), 1986: 3–24.

Osborn, Lawrence and Andrew Walker, Eds. *Harmful Religion: An Exploration of Religious Abuse.* London: SPCK, 1997.

Pakleppa, Michael. 'Divine Light Mission: Ein Modellfall.' *Materialdienst* 38, 1975: 82–87, 98–104.

Palmer, Susan J. 'Charisma and Abdication: A Study of the Leadership of Bhagwan Shree Rajneesh.' *Sociological Analysis* 49, 1988: 119–135.

Partridge, Christopher H. 'Truth, Authority and Epistemological Individualism in New Age Thought.' *Journal of Contemporary Religion* 14 (1), 1999: 77–95.

Pastoralamt der Erzdiözese Wien. *Zu religiösen Sondergemeinschaften.* Information, Vol. 1/82. Vienna: Referat für Weltanschauungsfragen, Sekten und religiöse Gemeinschaften, 1982a.

Pastoralamt der Erzdiözese Wien. *Heimholungswerk Jesu Christi. Anspruch – Lehre – Praxis.* Dokumentation, Vol. 3/82. Vienna: Referat für Weltanschauungsfragen, Sekten und religiöse Gemeinschaften, 1982b.

Pastoralamt der Erzdiözese Wien. *Scientologie in Theorie und Praxis.* Dokumentation, Vol. 2/83. Vienna: Referat für Weltanschauungsfragen, Sekten und religiöse Gemeinschaften, 1983.

Pastoralamt der Erzdiözese Wien. *EST.* Information, Vol. 3/84. Vienna: Referat für Weltanschauungsfragen, Sekten und religiöse Gemeinschaften, 1984.

Pastoralamt der Erzdiözese Wien. *Sekten und religiöse Bewegungen – Eine Herausforderung für die Seelsorge.* Dokumentation, Vol. 2/86. Vienna: Referat für Weltanschauungsfragen, 1986.

Patrick, Ted. 'Interview.' *Playboy* 3 (March), 1979: 53–58, 60–88, 220.

Patrick, Ted and Tom Dulak. *Let Our Children Go.* New York: Dutton, 1976.

Pavlos, Andrew J. *The Cult Experience.* Contributions to the Study of Religion, Vol. 6. Westport, London: Greenwood Press, 1982.

Pearce, Garth. 'Patty Hearst: The Mystery Still Remains.' *Best* magazine, 7 April 1989: 66–67.

Pelletier, Pierre. ''est, une nouvelle religion?' *Studies in Religion/Sciences Religieuses* 15 (1), 1986: 3–15.

Pennington, Basil, OSCO. 'Christian Meditation: The Ratzinger Letter.' *Pastoral Life* 39 (December), 1990: 6–10.

Pepinsky, Harold E. 'A Sociologist on Police Patrol.' In *Fieldwork Experience: Qualitative Approaches to Social Research*. W. B. Shaffir, R. A. Stebbins and A. Turowetz, Eds. New York: St. Martin's Press, 1980: 223–234.

Peter, Elisabeth. 'New Religious Movements and the Loss of Christian Faith.' Paper presented to the Conference on 'New Religious Movements: The European Situation', Lugano, Switzerland, 1990.

Pfeiffer, Arnold. 'Eine unaufhaltsame Religion? "Vereinigungskirche" macht von sich reden.' *Forum – Materialien und Beiträge zum religiösen Dialog* 2 (July), 1982: 20–26.

Pilger, Matthias. 'Einheitliche Vielfalt. Bericht über ein religionswissenschaftliches Brachland.' *spirita* 3 (October), 1988: 18–21.

Piryns, Ernst D. 'Japan's New Religions: An Interpretation.' *Update* 8 (3/4), 1984: 43–51.

Poewe, Karla. 'Scientific Neo-Paganism and the Extreme Right Then and Today: From Ludendorff's Gotterkenntnis to Sigrid Hunke's Europas eigene Religion.' *Journal of Contemporary Religion* 14 (3), 1999: 387–400.

Pöhlmann, Matthias. *Kampf der Geister. Die Publizistik der 'Apologetischen Centrale'*. Stuttgart: Kohlhammer Verlag, 1998.

Pöhlmann, Matthias. 'Evangelische Apologetik im Wandel der Zeit: Von der Apologetischen Centrale zur Evangelischen Zentralstelle für Weltanschauungsfragen.' In Pöhlmann, M., Ruppert, H.-J. and Hempelman. *Die EZW im Zug der Zeit. Beiträge zu Geschichte und Auftrag evangelischer Weltanschauungsarbeit*. EZW-Texte 154. Berlin: EZW, 2000: 2–17.

Pontificia Universidad Católica del Ecuador – F.I.U.C.. *Proyecto de Investigación: New Religious Movements – Nouveaux Mouvements religieux – nuevos movimientos religiosos. Informe*. Quito: Pontificia Universidad Católica, 1993.

Popham, Peter. 'What Friends are For.' *The Independent Magazine*, 5 December 1992: 22–28.

Potter, Sarah. 'Religious Studies at West Sussex Institute of Higher Education.' *BASR Bulletin* 69 (June), 1993: 22.

Poupard, Paul and Michael Paul Gallagher. *What Will Give Us Happiness*. Dublin: Veritas, 1992.

Pritchett, W. Douglas. *The Children of God/Family of Love: An Annotated Bibliography*. New York, London: Garland, 1985.

Puttick, Elizabeth and Peter B. Clarke, Eds. *Women as Teachers and Disciples in Traditional and New Religions*. Lewiston, NY; Lampeter: Edwin Mellen, 1993.

Pye, Michael E. 'The Study of Religion as an Autonomous Discipline (review article).' *Religion* 12 (1), 1982: 67–76.

Ralfs-Horeis, Hella. ' "Menschheitsretter" LaRouche – Innenansichten einer totalitären Bewegung.' *Materialdienst* 54 (10), 1991: 296–308.

Rambo, Lewis R. 'Current Research on Religious Conversion: A Bibliography.' *Religious Studies Review* 8, 1982: 146–159.

Rambo, Lewis R. *Understanding Religious Conversion*. New Haven: Yale UP, 1993.

Rattner, Josef. 'Miteinander leben lernen.' *Zeitschrift für Tiefenpsychologie und -therapie* 4, 1986: 24–29.

Reader, Ian. 'Aum Affair Intensifies Japan's Religious Crisis: An Analysis.' *Religion Watch* 10 (9), 1995: 1–2.

Reimer, Hans-Diether. *Apologetik*. Hamm: Hoheneck, 1986.

Reimer, Hans-Diether. 'Der vatikanische Bericht über Sekten.' *Materialdienst* 50 (3), 1987: 80–86.

Reimer, Hans-Diether. *Die 'Prophetin der Jetztzeit' und ihr 'Heimholungswerk'.* Vienna: Referat für Weltanschauungsfragen, 1988.

Reimer, Hans-Diether. 'Kirchliche Apologetik im Rahmen der EKD.' *Materialdienst* 54 (7), 1991: 208–212.

Reimer, Hans-Diether and Reinhart Hummel. 'Jugendreligionen in den 80er Jahren: Eine Bestandsaufnahme.' *Materialdienst* 47 (4), 1984: 92–113.

Reller, Horst. *Handbuch religiöse Gemeinschaften – Freikirchen, Sondergemeinschaften, Sekten, Weltanschauungsgemeinschaften, Neureligionen.* Gütersloh: Gütersloher Verlagshaus Gerd Mohn, 1985 (3rd revised and expanded edn; 1993, 4th edn; 1979, 2nd edn; 1978, 1st edn).

REMID. 'Stellungnahme zur gegenwärtigen Auseinandersetzung um die Scientology-Kirche.' Marburg: REMID, 1990.

Richardson, Herbert, Ed. *New Religions and Mental Health: Understanding the Issues.* New York, Toronto: Edwin Mellen, 1980.

Richardson, James T. 'People's Temple and Jonestown: A Corrective Comparison and Critique.' *Journal for the Scientific Study of Religion* 19 (3), 1980: 239–255.

Richardson, James T. 'Financing the New Religions: A Broader View.' In *Of Gods and Men: New Religious Movements in the West.* E. Barker, Ed. Macon, GA: Mercer UP, 1983: 65–88.

Richardson, James T. 'The Active vs. Passive Convert: Paradigm Conflict in Conversion/Recruitment Research.' *Journal for the Scientific Study of Religion* 24 (2), 1985a: 163–179.

Richardson, James T. 'Psychological and Psychiatric Studies on New Religions.' In *Advances in the Psychology of Religion.* L. B. Brown, Ed. New York: Pergamon, 1985b: 209–223.

Richardson, James T., Ed. *Money and Power in the New Religious Movements.* Lewiston, Lampeter: Edwin Mellen, 1988. Studies in Religion and Society, Vol. 22.

Richardson, James T. 'Journalistic Bias Toward New Religious Movements in Australia.' *Journal of Contemporary Religion* 11 (3), 1996: 289–302.

Richardson, James T. and Barend van Driel. 'Journalists' Attitudes Toward New Religious Movements.' *Review of Religious Research*: Special Issue: Mass Media and Unconventional Religion 39 (2), 1997: 116–136.

Richardson, James T., Jan van der Lans and Franz Derks. 'Leaving and Labeling: Voluntary and Coerced Disaffiliation from Religious Social Movements.' In *Research in Social Movements.* K. Lang, Ed. Greenwich, CT: JAI Press, 1986: 97–126.

Richardson, James T., Joel Best and David Bromley. *The Satanism Scare.* Hawthorne, NY: Aldine de Gruyter, 1991.

Rink, Steffen. 'Einsteiger, Umsteiger, Aussteiger: Gibt es berufliche Perspektiven für Religionswissenschaftler?' *spirita* 11 (1), 1997: 17–24.

Rink, Steffen and Thomas Schweer. 'Sind neue Religionen Sündenböcke? Interview mit Professor Dr Rainer Flasche.' *spirita* 7 (November), 1993: 41–48.

Ritzer, George. *The McDonaldization of Society: An Investigation into the Changing Character of Contemporary Social Life.* London: Pine Forge Press, 1995.

Ritzmann, Iris. *Befreit vom Jenseits, befreit von der Sünde. Lieblinge über Gott und die Welt.* Psychostroika-Dossier, Vol. 2/1990. Zurich: Psychostroika, 1990.

Ritzmann, Iris and Markus Meier. *Warum heulen die Wölfe und geifern die Schakale? Vom Umgang der Lieblinge mit Kritik 1980 und 1990: Ein Vergleich.* Psychostroika-Dossier, Vol. 1/1990. Zurich: Psychostroika, 1990.

Robbers, Gerhard. 'Staatskirchenrecht.' In *Evangelisches Kirchenlexikon: Internationale theologische Enzyclopedie.* E. Fahlbusch *et al.*, Eds. Göttingen: Vandenhoeck and Ruprecht, 1986 (3rd edn): cols 469–472.

Robbins, Harold. *Spellbinder.* London: New English Library, 1982.

Robbins, Keith. 'Religion and Identity in Modern British History.' In *Religion and National Identity.* S. Mews, Ed. Oxford: Blackwell, 1982.

Robbins, Thomas. 'Sociological Studies of New Religious Movements: A Selective Review.' *Religious Studies Review* 9 (3), 1983: 233–239.

Robbins, Thomas. 'Church–State Tensions and Marginal Movements in the United States.' In *Church–State Relations: Tensions and Transitions.* T. Robbins and R. Robertson, Eds. New Brunswick, NJ: Transaction, 1987: 135–149.

Robbins, Thomas. 'The Transformative Impact of the Study of New Religions on the Sociology of Religion.' *Journal for the Scientific Study of Religion* 27 (1), 1988a: 12–31.

Robbins, Thomas. *Cults, Converts and Charisma: The Sociology of New Religious Movements.* London, Beverly Hills: Sage, 1988b.

Robbins, Thomas. 'Profits for Prophets: Legitimate and Illegitimate Economic Practices in New Religious Movements.' In *Money and Power in New Religious Movements.* J. T. Richardson, Ed. New York: Edwin Mellen, 1988c: 70–116.

Robbins, Thomas and Dick Anthony. 'The Sociology of Contemporary Religious Movements.' *Annual Review of Sociology* 5, 1979a: 75–89.

Robbins, Thomas and Dick Anthony. ' "Cults", "Brainwashing", and Counter-Subversion.' *Church and State Issue: The Annals of the American Academy of Political and Social Science* 446 (November), 1979b: 78–90.

Robbins, Thomas and Dick Anthony. 'Deprogramming, Brainwashing and the Medicalization of Deviant Religious Groups.' *Social Problems* 29 (3), 1982: 283–297.

Robbins, Thomas and Susan J. Palmer. *Millennium, Messiahs and Mayhem: Contemporary Apocalyptic Movements.* New York: Routledge, 1997.

Robbins, Thomas, William C. Shepherd and James McBride, Eds. *Cults, Culture and the Law: Perspectives on New Religious Movements.* Chico, CA: Scholars Press, 1985.

Roberts, Richard, Ed. *Religion and the Transformation of Capitalism: Comparative Approaches.* London: Routledge, 1995.

Roberts, Richard. 'Review of *Strategic Church Leadership* by R. Gill and D. Burke (1996).' *Journal of Contemporary Religion* 13 (1), 1998: 106–108.

Robertson, Roland, Ed. *Sociology of Religion: Selected Readings.* Harmondsworth: Penguin, 1969.

Robertson, Roland. *The Sociological Interpretation of Religion.* Oxford: Blackwell, 1970.

Robertson, Roland. 'Scholarship, Sponsorship and "The Moonie Problem": A Comment.' *Sociological Analysis* 46 (2), 1985: 179–184.

Rochford, E. Burke. *Hare Krishna in America.* New Brunswick, NJ: Rutgers UP, 1985.

Rochford, E. Burke. 'Family Structure, Commitment, and Involvement in the Hare Krishna Movement.' *Sociology of Religion* 56 (2), 1995: 153–175.

Röder, Willi. 'Das alte Problem im neuen Gewand: Elterninitiative auf dem Weg in das 2. Jahrtausend.' In *20 Jahre Elterninitiative*. Elterninitiative zur Hilfe gegen seelische Abhängigkeit und religiösen Extremismus e.V., Ed. Munich: Elterninitiative zur Hilfe gegen seelische Abhängigkeit und religiösen Extremismus, 1995: 175–184.

Rodríguez, Pepe. *La conspiración Moon*. Barcelona: Ediciones B, 1988.

Rodríguez, Pepe. 'Jóvenes y menores captados por sectas destructivas.' *Menores* (Madrid: Dirección General de Protección Jurídica del Minor) 9 (May–June), 1988: 14–25.

Rohde, Dieter. 'Statistik zur Konfessionszugehörigkeit und zum kirchlichen Leben.' In *Theologische Realenzyklopedie, Band VIII: Chlodwig-Dionysius Areopagita [Theological Encyclopedia. Vol. VIII]*. G. Krause and G. Müller, Eds. Berlin, New York: Walter de Gruyter, 1981: 599–605.

Röhr, Heinz. 'Mystische Elemente in der Vereinigungstheologie.' In *Das Entstehen einer neuen Religion. Das Beispiel der Vereinigungskirche*. G. Kehrer, Ed. Munich: Kösel, 1981: 79–107.

Rose, Kenneth. 'Has ISKCON Anything to Offer Christianity Theologically?' *ISKCON Review: Academic Perspectives on the Hare Krishna Movement* 2, 1986: 64–75.

Rose, Paul. *Backbenchers' Dilemma*. London: Frederick Muller Ltd., 1981a.

Rose, Paul. 'The Moonies Unmasked.' Unpublished Manuscript, 1981b.

Ross, Joan Carol and Michael Langone. *Cults: What Parents Should Know: A Practical Guide to Help Parents with Children in Destructive Groups*. Weston, MA: The American Family Foundation, 1988.

Roszak, Theodore. *The Making of a Counter-Culture: Reflections on the Technocratic Society and its Youthful Opposition*. London: Faber and Faber, 1968 (New York: Doubleday, 1970).

Rubenstein, Steve. 'Margaret Singer – Expert on Brainwashing.' *San Francisco Chronicle*, 25 November 2003: A-19.

Rudolph, Kurt. 'Das Problem der Autonomie und Integrität der Religionswissenschaft.' *Nederlands Theologisch Tijdschrift* 27, 1973: 105–131.

Rudolph, Kurt. 'Texte als religionswissenschaftliche "Quellen".' In *Religionswissenschaft: Eine Einführung*. H. Zinser, Ed. Berlin: Reimer, 1988: 38–54.

Rudolph, Kurt. 'Die religionkritischen Traditionen in der Religionswissenschaft.' In *Religionswissenschaft und Kulturkritik: Beiträge zur Konferenz The History of Religions and Critique of Culture in the Days of Gerardus van der Leeuw (1890–1950)*. H. G. Kippenberg and B. Luchesi, Eds. Marburg: diagonal-Verlag, 1991: 149–156.

Ruppert, Hans-Jürgen. *Theosophie – unterwegs zum okkulten Übermenschen*. Reihe Apologetische Themen, Vol. 2. Konstanz: F. Bahn Verlag, 1993.

Ruttmann, Hermann. *Religionen – Kirchen – Konfessionen. Glaubensgemeinschaften in Marburg*. Marburg: REMID, 1993.

Salazar, Robert C., Ed. *New Religious Movements in Asia and the Pacific Islands: Implications for Church and Society*. Proceedings of a Conference sponsored by the International Federation of Catholic Universities, Association of Southeast and East Asian Catholic Universities, February 10–13, 1993. Manila, Philippines: De la Salle University, 1994.

Saliba, John A. 'The Christian Response to the New Religions: A Critical Look at the Spiritual Counterfeits Project.' *Journal of Ecumenical Studies* 18 (3), 1981: 451–473.

Saliba, John A. 'The Christian Church and the New Religious Movements: Towards Theological Understanding.' *Theological Studies* 43 (3), 1982: 468–485.

Saliba, John A. 'Christian and Jewish Responses to ISKCON: Dialogue or Diatribe?' In *ISKCON Review: Academic Perspectives on the Hare Krishna Movement.* Vol. 2. Subhananda dasa (Steven J. Gelberg), Ed. Washington, DC: Institute for Vaishnava Studies, 1986a: 76–103. Reprinted in *ISKCON Communications Journal* 3 (2), 1995: 51–71.

Saliba, John A. 'Learning from the New Religious Movements.' *Thought* 61, 1986b: 225–240.

Saliba, John A. *Psychiatry and the Cults: An Annotated Bibliography.* New York, London: Garland, 1987.

Saliba, John A. 'Christian and Jewish Religious Responses to the Hare Krishna Movement in the West.' In *Krishna Consciousness in the West.* D. G. Bromley and L. D. Shinn, Eds. Lewisburg; London: Bucknell UP; Associated UP, 1989: 219–237.

Saliba, John A. 'Introduction: Social Science and the Cults: An Overview and Evaluation.' In *Social Science and the Cults: An Annotated Bibliography.* J. A. Saliba, Ed. New York: Garland, 1990a: xvii–xl.

Saliba, John A. 'Preface: The Nature, Scope, and Limitation of this Bibliography.' In *Social Science and the Cults: An Annotated Bibliography.* J. A. Saliba, Ed. New York: Garland, 1990b: ix–xvi.

Saliba, John A. *Social Science and the Cults: An Annotated Bibliography.* New York: Garland, 1990c.

Saliba, John A. ' "Religious" Themes in the New Religious Movements.' In *Research Project on New Religious Movements: Dossier.* M. Fuss, Ed. Rome: F.I.U.C. (Fédération Internationale des Universités Catholiques), 1990d: 133–187.

Saliba, John A. 'Vatican Response to the New Religious Movements.' *Theological Studies* 53 (1), 1992: 3–39.

Saliba, John A. *Perspectives on New Religious Movements.* London: Geoffrey Chapman, 1995.

Samy, Ama. 'May a Christian Practice Zen or Yoga?' *Inculturation* 5 (1), 1990: 28–32.

Samy, Ama. 'Can a Christian Practice Zen, Yoga or TM?' *Review for Religious* 50, 1991: 535–544.

Sargant, William. *Battle for the Mind: A Physiology of Conversion and Brainwashing.* London: Heinemann, 1957.

Scharf, Betty R. *The Sociological Study of Religion.* London: Hutchinson University Library, 1970.

Scheffler, Albert C. 'Religiöse Minderheiten in der BRD. Vorläufige statistische Angaben.' *spirita* 2 (April), 1988: 43–45.

Scheffler, Albert C. *'Jugendreligionen' in Deutschland. Öffentliche Meinung und Wirklichkeit. Eine religionswissenschaftliche Untersuchung.* Europäische Hochschulschriften, Series 23: Theology, Vol. 360. Frankfurt a. M., New York: P. Lang, 1989.

Scheflin, Alan W. and Edward M. Opton. *The Mind Manipulators.* New York: Paddington, 1978.

Schein, Edgar F. 'The Chinese Indoctrination Program for Prisoners of War.' *Psychiatry* 19 (May), 1956: 149–172.

Schein, Edgar F. 'Reactions and Patterns to Severe, Chronic Stress in American Army Prisoners of War of the Chinese.' *Journal of Social Issues* 13, 1957: 321–330.

Schein, Edgar H. 'The Chinese Indoctrination Program for Prisoners of War: A study of Attempted Brainwashing.' In *Readings in Social Psychology*. E. E. Maccoby, T. M. Newcomb and E. L. Hartley, Eds. London: Methuen, 1959 (3rd edn): 311–334.

Schein, Edgar H., Inge Schneier and Curtis H. Becker. *Coercive Persuasion: A Socio-Psychological Analysis of the 'Brainwashing' of American Civilian Prisoners by the Chinese Communists*. New York: Norton, 1961.

Schipmann, Monika and Berliner Senatsverwaltung für Jugend und Familie. *Informationen über neue religiöse und weltanschauliche Bewegungen und sogenannte Psychogruppen*. Berlin: Berliner Senatsverwaltung für Jugend und Familie, 1994.

Schleswig-Holsteinischer Landtag und Landtag Schleswig-Holstein. 'Bericht der Landesregierung: Bericht über die Aktivitäten von Sekten in Schleswig-Holstein.' Drucksache 13/2630, 21.03.1995.

Schmidt, Markus. *Scientology: Entwicklung – Praxis. Stellungnahme*. Werkmappe 'Sekten, religiöse Sondergemeinschaften, Weltanschauungsfragen', Vol. 66. Vienna: Referat für Weltanschauungsfragen, Sekten und religiöse Sondergemeinschaften, 1993.

Schmidt, Walter. 'Geschichte der Apologetik: Evangelischer Gemeindedienst Württemberg. Zwischen Anpassung und Widerstand im Weltanschauungskampf des Dritten Reichs.' *Materialdienst* 58 (5), 1995: 148–154.

Schneider, Karl H. 'Der pädagogische Bereich als Operationsfeld für Psychokulte.' In *20 Jahre Elterninitiative*. Elterninitiative zur Hilfe gegen seelische Abhängigkeit und religiösen Extremismus e.V., Ed. Munich: Elterninitiative zur Hilfe gegen seelische Abhängigkeit und religiösen Extremismus e.V., 1995: 185–194.

Schorsch, Christof. 'Die Krise der Moderne: Entstehungsbedingungen der New Age-Bewegung.' Aus *Politik und Zeitgeschehen*: Beilage zur Wochenzeitung Das Parlament B 40/89, 29 September 1989: 3–10.

Schreiner, Lothar and Michael Mildenberger, Eds. *Christus und die Gurus. Asiatische religiöse Gruppen im Westen*. Stuttgart, Berlin: Kreuz, 1980.

Schubert, Christoph. 'Nicht Konfession, nicht Sekte – die religiöse Subkultur in Deutschland.' In *'Jugendsekten' und neue Religiosität: Notwendige Anmerkungen*. H.-W. Baumann *et al.*, Eds. Gelsenkirchen-Buer: Farin and Zwingmann, 1982: 224–231.

Schulze-Berndt, Hermann. 'Die neuen Kulte rufen auch zur Selbstkritik auf.' *Forum Jugendreligionen* (Münster) 2, 1981a: 6–7.

Schulze-Berndt, Hermann. *Jugendreligionen – eine Herausforderung. Arbeitsmaterialien für die Sekundarstufe*. Düsseldorf: August Bagel, 1981b.

Schuster, Udo. *Bhagwan, der Rolls-Royce-Guru in Oregon*. Dokumentation. Munich: Junge Union Bayern, 1984.

Schuster, Udo. 'Betroffen sind wir alle.' In *Eindeutig zwischen den Stühlen. Zehn Beiträge zur Apologie der Apologetik*. M. Ach, Ed. Munich: Arbeitsgemeinschaft für Religions- und Weltanschauungsfragen (ARW), 1985: 99–108.

Schuster, Udo. 'Hilfe durch Selbsthilfe.' In *Die neuen Jugendreligionen. Teil 4: Aktionen, Hilfen, Initiativen*. F.-W. Haack, U. Schuster and M. Ach, Eds. Munich: Evangelischer Presseverband Bayern, 1986: 5–8.

Schuster, Udo, Ed. *Europas neue Religiosität. Entwicklung, Ursachen, Folgen*. Munich: Arbeitsgemeinschaft für Religions- und Weltanschauungsfragen (ARW), 1988. Dokumentations-Edition, Vol. 14.

Schuster, Udo. 'Totalitäre Kulte: Herausforderung in Vergangenheit und Zukunft.' In

20 Jahre Elterninitiative. Elterninitiative zur Hilfe gegen seelische Abhängigkeit und religiösen Extremismus e.V., Ed. Munich: Elterninitiative zur Hilfe gegen seelische Abhängigkeit und religiösen Extremismus, 1995: 195–206.

Schuster, Udo and Markus Sackmann. *Argumente für Junge Leute: Sekten – Nein Danke! Geschäftemachern keine Chance, Informationen und Aktionvorschläge*. Munich: Junge Union Bayern, n.d.

Schwarz, Hans. 'Notes from the Present Theological Scene in Germany.' *New Era: A Newsletter of the New Ecumenical Research Foundation* III (6), 1984: 1–3.

Schwarz, Hans. 'Freiheit und Weltverantwortung in lutherischer Sicht.' *Forum Religion und Weltgestaltung* 2/3, 1988: 34–37.

Schwarz, Hans. 'Absolute Werte für die heutige Gesellschaft?' *Forum Religion und Weltgestaltung* 2, 1990: 13–17.

Schweer, Thomas. 'Grober Klotz und grober Keil. Zur Diskussion um die Scientology Kirche.' *spirita* 7 (November), 1993: 26–40.

Schweer, Thomas. 'Sekten und Psychogruppen. Gefahren – Strategien – Antworten. Diskussionsveranstaltung der SPD-Bundestagsfraktion am 13. März 1996 in Bonn.' *spirita* 10 (1), 1996: 45–47.

Scotland, Egon. 'Lehre des Propheten unter deutscher Aufsicht: In Nordrhein-Westfalen wurde ein ausführliches Konzept für islamischen Religionsunterricht entwickelt.' *Süddeutsche Zeitung* 242, 21 October 1987.

Secretariat for Promoting Christian Unity, Secretariat for Non-Christians, Secretariat for Non-Believers, Pontifical Council for Culture. *Sects or New Religious Movements: Pastoral Challenge*. Washington, DC: Publishing and Promotion Services, United States Catholic Conference, 3 May 1986.

Secretariatus pro non Christianis. *The Attitude of the Church Towards the Followers of Other Religions: Reflections and Orientations on Dialogue and Mission*. Città del Vaticano: Secretariatus pro non Christianis, 1984.

Sekten-Info Essen e.V. *Tätigkeitsbericht für den Zeitraum vom 01.07.1988–30.06.1989*. Essen: Sekten-Info Essen e.V., 1989.

Sekten-Info Essen e.V. *Konzeption des Informations- und Beratungszentrums*. Essen: Sekten-Info Essen e.V., n.d.

Senator für Schulwesen, Jugend und Sport, Berlin. '*Jugendsekten' und Psychokulte*. Berlin: Senator für Schulwesen, Jugend und Sport, Berlin, 1983.

Senatsverwaltung für Frauen, Jugend und Familie (Berlin). *Informationen über neue religiöse und weltanschauliche Bewegungen und sogenannte Psychogruppen*. Berlin: Senatsverwaltung für Frauen, Jugend und Familie, Abteilung II, 1988.

Shapiro, Eli. 'Destructive Cultism.' *American Family Physician* 15 (2), 1977: 80–83.

Shepherd, William C. 'Religion and the Counter Culture: A New Religiosity.' In *Religion American Style*. P. McNamara, Ed. New York: Harper and Row, 1974: 348–358.

Shinn, Larry D. *The Dark Lord: Cult Images and the Hare Krishnas in America*. Philadelphia: Westminster, 1987.

Shirieda, John Masayuki, SDB 'Catholic Church and Christian Dialogue.' *Pontificio Consilium pro Dialogo inter Religones Bulletin* 28 (1), 1993: 46–63.

Shupe, Anson D. and David G. Bromley. 'The Moonies and the Anti-Cultists: Movement and Counter-Movement in Conflict.' *Sociological Analysis* 40 (4), 1979: 325–334.

Shupe, Anson D. and David G. Bromley. 'Witches, Moonies and Accusations of Evil.' In *In Gods We Trust: New Patterns of Religious Pluralism in America*.

T. Robbins and D. Anthony, Eds. New Brunswick, NJ: Transaction, 1980a: 247–262.

Shupe, Anson D. and David G. Bromley. *The New Vigilantes: Deprogrammers, Anti-Cultists and the New Religions.* Beverly Hills, CA: Sage, 1980b.

Shupe, Anson D. and David G. Bromley. 'Apostates and Atrocity Stories: Some Parameters in the Dynamics of Deprogramming.' In *The Social Impact of New Religious Movements.* B. R. Wilson, Ed. New York: Rose of Sharon, 1981: 179–215.

Shupe, Anson and David C. Bromley, Eds. *Anti-Cult Movements in Cross Cultural Perspective.* New York: Garland, 1994.

Shupe, Anson D., Bert Hardin and David G. Bromley. 'A Comparison of Anti-Cult Groups in the United States and West Germany.' In *Of Gods and Men: New Religious Movements in the West.* E. Barker, Ed. Macon, GA: Mercer, 1983: 177–193.

Shupe, Anson D., David G. Bromley and Donna L. Oliver. *The Anticult Movement in America: A Bibliography and Historical Survey.* New York: Garland, 1984.

Sieber, Günter. *'Jugendsekten' – Zur Evaluierung des Beratungs- und Rehabilitationsbedarfs Betroffener.* Munich, 1980.

Sieper, Roswitha, Ed. *Psychokulte – Erfahrungsberichte Betroffener.* Munich: Evangelischer Presseverband für Bayern, 1986. Münchner Reihe.

Simmel, Oskar and Rudolf Stählin, Eds. *Christliche Religion.* Frankfurt a. M.: Fischer, 1957.

Singer, Margaret Thaler. 'Cults.' *Baltimore Jewish Times,* 3 June 1977, 14–21, 30–33.

Singer, Margaret Thaler. 'Therapy with Ex-Cult Members.' *Journal of the National Association of Private Psychiatric Hospitals* 9 (4), 1978: 14–18.

Singer, Margaret Thaler. 'Coming Out of the Cults.' *Psychology Today* 12 (8), 1979a: 75–76, 79–80, 82.

Singer, Margaret Thaler. 'Coercive Persuasion und die Probleme der "Ex-Cult-Members".' In *'Neue Jugendreligionen.' Vorträge und Berichte einer Fachtagung über 'Probleme im Zusammenhang mit den sogenannten Jugendreligionen'.* M. Müller-Küppers and F. Specht, Eds. Göttingen: Vandenhoeck and Ruprecht, 1979b (2nd edn): 104–120.

Singer, Margaret Thaler. 'Consultation with Families of Cultists.' In *The Family Therapist as Consultant.* L. C. Wynne, T. Weber and S. McDaniel, Eds. New York: Guildford, 1985.

Singer, Margaret Thaler. 'The Impact of Cults on Individuals and Families.' Paper presented to the Annual Open Meeting of FAIR in London, November 1989.

Singer, Margaret Thaler and Janja Lalich. *Cults in Our Midst.* San Francisco: Jossey-Bass, 1995.

Singer, Margaret Thaler and Janja Lalich. *Crazy Therapies.* San Francisco: Jossey-Bass, 1997.

Singer, Margaret Thaler and Edgar H. Schein. 'Projective Test Responses of Prisoners of War Following Repatriation.' *Psychiatry* 21 (4), 1958: 375–385.

Singer, Margaret Thaler, M. Temerlin and Michael Langone. 'Psychotherapy Cults.' *Cultic Studies Journal* 7 (2), 1990.

Slee, Colin. 'New Religious Movements and Church Responses.' Paper presented to the Conference on 'New Religious Movements: Challenge and Response', Taplow Court, Maidenhead, Berks., 1995.

Slee, Colin. 'New Religious Movements and the Churches.' In *New Religious Movements: Challenge and Response*. B. Wilson and J. Cresswell, Eds. London, New York: Routledge, in association with the Institute of Oriental Philosophy European Centre, 1999: 165–180.

Slenczka, Reinhard. 'Apologetik als Auftrag der Kirche in öffentlicher Verantwortung.' *Materialdienst* 58 (8), 1995: 225–237.

Snow, David Alan. 'The Nichiren Shoshu Buddhist Movement in America: A Sociological Examination of its Value Orientations, Recruitment Effort, and Spread.' PhD dissertation, Los Angeles, University of California, 1976.

Snow, David A. and Richard Machalek. 'The Sociology of Conversion.' *Annual Review of Sociology* 10, 1984: 167–190.

Sorg, Eugen. *Lieblings-Geschichten – Die 'Züricher Schule' oder Innenansichten eines Psycho-Unternehmens*. Zurich: Weltwoche-ABC-Verlag, 1991.

SPCK. *The Story of the SPCK*. London: SPCK Worldwide, n.d.

Der Spiegel. 'Alles umkehrbar.' *Der Spiegel* 34 (26), 23.6.1980: 69–71.

Der Spiegel. 'Sekten: Raub der Kindheit'. *Der Spiegel* 27, 1997: 86–99.

Spinrad, Norman. *Mind Game*. New York: Jove, 1981.

spirita. 'REMID, spirita und die Anzeigen.' *spirita* 6 (1), 1992: 86–87.

Spiritual Counterfeits Project. *TM in Court*. Berkeley, CA: Spiritual Counterfeits Project, 1978.

St John, Warren. 'Vanity's Fare.' *Lingua Franca* September/October, 1993: 1, 22–25, 62.

Stamm, Hugo. *Scientology. Seele im Würgegriff. Übermenschen zwischen Ausbeutung und Psychoterror*. Horgen: Gegenverlag, 1982.

Stamm, Hugo. *Die Seelenfalle: 'Psychologische Menschenkenntnis' als Heilsprogramm*. Zurich: Werd-Verlag, 1993.

Stammler, Eberhard. 'Bundesrepublik Deutschland.' In *Evangelisches Kirchenlexikon: Internationale theologische Enzyklopedie: Erster Band A–F*. E. Fahlbusch *et al.*, Eds. Göttingen: Vandenhoeck and Ruprecht, 1986 (3rd edn): cols. 579–586.

Stark, Rodney, Ed. *Religious Movements: Genesis, Exodus, and Numbers*. New York: Paragon, 1985; Barrytown, NY: Unification Theological Seminary/Rose of Sharon, 1986.

Stark, Rodney. 'How New Religions Succeed: A Theoretical Model.' In *The Future of New Religious Movements*. D. G. Bromley and P. E. Hammond, Eds. Macon, GA: Mercer UP, 1987: 11–29.

Stark, Rodney. *The Rise of Christianity: A Sociologist Reconsiders History*. Princeton: Princeton UP, 1996a.

Stark, Rodney. 'Why Religious Movements Succeed or Fail: A Revised General Model.' *Journal of Contemporary Religion* 11 (2), 1996b: 133–146.

Stark, Rodney. 'The Rise and Fall of Christian Science.' *Journal of Contemporary Religion* 13 (2), 1998: 189–214.

Stark, Rodney. 'Atheism, Faith, and the Social Scientific Study of Religion.' *Journal of Contemporary Religion* 14 (1), 1999: 41–62.

Stark, Rodney and William S. Bainbridge. 'Toward a Theory of Religion: Religious Commitment.' *Journal for the Scientific Study of Religion* 19 (2), 1980a: 114–128.

Stark, Rodney and William S. Bainbridge. 'Secularization, Revival, and Cult Formation.' *Annual Review of the Social Sciences of Religion* 4, 1980b: 85–119.

Stark, Rodney and William S. Bainbridge. 'American-Born Sects: Initial Findings.' *Journal for the Scientific Study of Religion* 20, 1981: 130–149.

Stark, Rodney and William S. Bainbridge. *The Future of Religion: Secularization, Revival, and Cult Formation.* Berkeley, CA: University of California Press; Paragon, 1985.

Stark, Rodney and Laurence R. Iannaccone. 'Why the Jehovah's Witnesses Grow so Rapidly: A Theoretical Application.' *Journal of Contemporary Religion* 12 (2), 1997: 133–157.

Stenger, Horst. *Die soziale Konstruktion okkulter Wirklichkeit – eine Soziologie des New Age.* Opladen: Leske and Budrich, 1993.

Stern, Susan. *Religionsgesellschaften in Deutschland: Die Beziehungen zwischen Kirche und Staat.* Bonn: Inter Nationes, 1998.

Stolz, Fritz. 'Hierarchien der Darstellungsebenen religiöser Botschaft.' In *Religionswissenschaft: Eine Einführung.* H. Zinser, Ed. Berlin: Reimer, 1988a: 55–72.

Stolz, Fritz. *Grundzüge der Religionswissenschaft.* Göttingen: Vandenhoeck and Ruprecht, 1988b.

Storm, Rachel. 'Meet the Cult Busters.' *Bella* magazine 3 (14), 8 April, 1989: 6–7.

Strauss, Roger B. 'Religious Conversion as Personal and Collective Accomplishment.' *Sociological Analysis* 40 (2), 1979: 158–165.

Subhananda dasa and ISKCON. *Please Don't Lump Us In: A Request to the Media.* Los Angeles: ISKCON, 1978.

Subhananda dasa (Steven J. Gelberg) and ISKCON, Eds. *ISKCON Review: Academic Perspectives on the Hare Krishna Movement.* Vol. 2. Washington, DC: The Institute for Vaishnava Studies, 1986a.

Subhananda dasa (Steven J. Gelberg). 'The Catholic Church and the Hare Krishna Movement: An Invitation to Dialogue.' In *ISKCON Review. Academic Perspectives on the Hare Krishna Movement.* Vol. 2, Subhananda dasa (Steven J.Gelberg), Ed. Washington, DC: Institute for Vaishnava Studies, 1986b: 1–63.

Suedfield, P. 'The Benefits of Boredom: Sensory Deprivation Reconsidered.' *American Scientist* 63, 1975: 60–69.

Sundback, S. 'New Religious Movements in Finland.' *Temenos* 16, 1980: 132–139.

Süss, Joachim. *Zur Erleuchtung unterwegs: Neo-Sannyasin in Deutschland und ihre Religion.* Marburger Studien zur Afrika- und Asienkunde: Religionsgeschichte, Vol. 2. Berlin: Dietrich Reimer Verlag, 1994.

Sutcliffe, Steve. *Children of the New Age: A History of Spiritual Practices.* London: Routledge, 2002.

Swatland, Susan and Anne Swatland. *Escape from the Moonies.* London: New English Library (Hodder and Stoughton), 1982.

Swatos, William. 'Weber and Troeltsch? Methodology, Syndrome and the Development of Church Sect Theory.' *Journal for the Scientific Study of Religion* 15 (2), 1976: 129–144.

Swidler, Leonard. *Toward a Universal Theology of Religion.* New York: Orbis, 1987.

Thiede, Werner. 'Scientology im Gegenwind: Wirbel um die "Hamburg Org" ziehen Kreise.' *Materialdienst* 54 (6), 1991: 172–176.

Thiede, Werner. 'Apologetik und Dialog. Plädoyer für eine Synthese.' *Materialdienst* 55 (10), 1992a: 281–296.

Thiede, Werner. 'Scientology und Religionswissenschaft. Zum Thesenpapier des "REMID".' *Materialdienst* 55 (5), 1992b: 149–156.

Thiede, Werner. *Scientology – Religion oder Geistesmagie?* Apologetische Themen, Vol. 1. Konstanz: Bahn, 1992c.

Thiel, Norbert. *Der Kampf gegen neue religiöse Bewegungen. Anti-'Sekten'-*

Kampagne und Religionsfreiheit in der Bundesrepublik Deutschland. Mörfelden-Walldorf: Kando-Verlag, 1986.

Thomas, Klaus. 'Der Begriff der Psychomutation.' In *Dokumentation zur Expertenkonsultation zum Thema Jugendreligionen*. Evangelische Akademie Tutzing, Ed. Munich: Arbeitsgemeinschaft für Religions- und Weltanschauungs-fragen (ARW), 1980: 10–16.

Time Out. 'Preaching Holy War.' *Time Out*, April 11–17, 1975: 5–6.

Tipton, Steven. *Getting Saved from the Sixties: Moral Meaning in Conversion and Cultural Change*. Berkeley, Los Angeles, London: University of California Press, 1984 (first published in 1978).

Tomko, Jozef. 'Proclaiming Christ the World's Only Saviour.' *L'Osservatore Romano* 15 (15 April), 1991: 4.

Towler, Robert, Ed. *New Religions and the New Europe*. Aarhus: Aarhus UP, 1995.

Trevett, Christine. 'Changes at Cardiff, University of Wales.' *BASR Bulletin* 69 (June), 1993: 23–24.

Tribune de Genève. 'Lugano: Jugement des "déprogrammeurs". Briseurs de sectes en sursis.' *Tribune de Genève*, 26 November 1990.

Troeltsch, Ernst. *The Social Teachings of the Christian Churches*. London: Allen and Unwin, 1931.

Tucker, Gordon. 'Youth, Faith and the Quest for Life's Meaning.' *Origins* 14 (14 June), 1984: 75–80.

Turner, Harold W. *Bibliography of New Religious Movements in Primal Societies*. Vol. I: Black Africa. Boston: Hall, 1977a.

Turner, Harold W. 'New Tribal Religious Movements.' In *Encyclopaedia Britannica*, Macropedia. Vol. 18. Chicago, 1977b (15 edn).

Turner, Harold W. *Bibliography of New Religious Movements in Primal Societies*. Vol. II: North America. Boston: Hall, 1978.

Turner, Harold W. *Religious Innovation in Africa: Collected Essays on New Religious Movements*. Boston: Hall, 1979.

Turner, Harold W. 'A Global Phenomenon.' In *New Religious Movements and the Churches*. A. R. Brockway and J. P. Rajashekar, Eds. Geneva: World Council of Churches Publications, 1987: 3–15.

Turner, Harold W. *Religious Movements in Primal Societies*. Indiana: Elkhart, 1989a.

Turner, Harold W. 'Reports on Practical Legislative Applications (International): Great Britain.' *Conscience and Liberty: International Journal of Religious Freedom* 1 (1), 1989b: 67–72.

Tworuschka, Udo. 'Die Vereinigungskirche im Religionsunterricht.' In *Das Entstehen einer Neuen Religion: Das Beispiel der Vereinigungskirche*. G. Kehrer, Ed. Munich: Kösel, 1981: 197–218.

Ungerleider, J. Thomas and David K. Wellisch. 'Coercive Persuasion (Brainwashing), Religious Cults, and Deprogramming.' *American Journal of Psychiatry* 136 (3), 1979: 279–282.

Universität Tübingen, Universitätsbibliothek, Theologische Abteilung, und Bundes-ministerium für Jugend/Familie und Gesundheit. *Neue religiöse Bewegungen ('Jugendreligionen')*. Neuerwerbungen Theologie und Allgemeine Religionswis-senschaft, special volume. Tübingen: Universitätsbibliothek, 1981.

Update and Dialog. 'What the Dialog Center is All About.' *Update & Dialog* 1 (1), 1992: 4–6.

Updike, John. *S.* New York: Fawcett Crest, 1988.

Usarski, Frank. *Die Stigmatisierung neuer spiritueller Bewegungen in der Bundesrepublik Deutschland.* Kölner Veröffentlichungen zur Religionsgeschichte, Vol. 15. Cologne, Vienna: Böhlau, 1988.

Usarski, Frank. 'Das Bekenntnis zum Buddhismus als Bildungsprivileg. Strukturmomente "lebensweltlicher" Theravada-Rezeption in Deutschland während des Zeitraums zwischen 1888 und 1924.' In *Die Religion von Oberschichten.* P. Antes and D. Pahnke, Eds. Marburg: diagonal-Verlag, 1989: 75–86.

Usarski, Frank. 'Zur Rolle kirchlicher Funktionsträger im Kontext der bundesdeutschen "Jugendsekten"-Debatte. Eine wissenschaftshistorische Betrachtung aus religionswissenschaftlicher Sicht.' In *Religion and Environment/Religion und Umwelt: Proceedings of the Symposium of the XVIIIth International Congress of History of Science at Hamburg-Munich, 1–9 August 1989. Vol. II.* M. Büttner, U. Krolzik and H.-J. Waschkies, Eds. Bochum: Universitätsverlag Brockmeyer, 1990a: 287–309.

Usarski, Frank. 'Die Auseinandersetzung mit den sogenannten "Jugendsekten" in der Bundesrepublik Deutschland.' In *Christliches ABC heute und übermorgen. Handbuch für Lebensfragen und Kirchliche Erwachsenenbildung.* Vol. 5. E. Lade, Ed. Bad Homburg: DIE, 1990b: 23–36.

Usarski, Frank. 'Das Stigma "Jugendsekte" als Konstituente einer "verdoppelten Wirklichkeit": Zum typisch (gesamt-)deutschen Umgang mit alternativer Religiosität.' Paper presented to the 26. Soziologentag, Düsseldorf, 28.9.–2.10.1992.

Usarski, Frank. 'The Response to New Religions in Eastern Germany after the Union of the Two Germanies.' Paper presented to the Conference on 'New Religious Movements: Challenge and Response', Taplow Court, Maidenhead, Berks., 1995. Published as 'The Response to New Religious Movements in East Germany after Reunification.' In *New Religious Movements: Challenge and Response.* B. Wilson, and J. Cresswell, Eds. London, New York: Routledge, in association with the Institute of Oriental Philosophy European Centre, 1999: 237–254.

Ussher, Jane. 'Media Representations of Psychology: Denigration and Popularization, or Worthy Dissemination of Knowledge?' In *Social Scientists Meet the Media.* C. Haslam and A. Bryman, Eds. London, New York: Routledge, 1994: 123–137.

Valentin, Friedericke and Horand Knaup, Eds. *Scientology – der Griff nach Macht und Geld. Selbstbefreiung als Geschäft.* Freiburg i. Br.: Herder, 1992.

van Delden, Gisela. *'Jugendreligionen': Neue Religiosität oder Keimzelle neuer Gewalt?* Europäische Hochschulschriften, Series 22: Sociology, Vol. 154. Frankfurt a. M., Berne, New York, Paris: P. Lang, 1988.

van Driel, Barend and James T. Richardson. 'Cults and the Media: A Longitudinal Study.' Paper presented to the 18th International Conference for the Sociology of Religion, Leuven/Louvain, 1985.

van Driel, Barend and James T. Richardson. 'Cults Versus Sect: Categorization of New Religious Movements in the American Print Media.' Paper presented to the Annual Conference of the Association for the Sociology of Religion, 19 August, New York, 1986.

van Driel, Barend and James T. Richardson. 'Print Media and New Religious Movements: A Longitudinal Study.' *Journal of Communication* 38 (3), 1988a: 37–61.

van Driel, Barend and James T. Richardson. 'Research Note: Categorization of New Religious Movements in the American Print Media.' *Sociological Analysis* 49 (2), 1988b: 171–183.

van Leen, Adrian, Ed. *O is for Orange: An Examination of the Rajneesh Religion, Also Known as the Orange People*. Perth, Australia: Concerned Christians Growth Ministries Inc., 1983.

van Leen, Adrian. *The Problems of Extreme Christian Fringe Groups*. Singapore: SKS Marketing Pte Ltd, 1990.

Vandrisse, Joseph. 'Le pape réunit tous les cardinaux: pour contrer les sectes.' *Le Courrier*, 6–7 April 1991.

Vatican. 'Vatican Report on Sects, Cults and New Religious Movements.' *Origins* (NC Documentary Service) 16 (1, 22 May), 1986: 3–10.

Vernette, Jean. *Les sectes et l'Église Catholique. Le document romain*. Documents des Eglises. Paris: Le Cerf, 1986.

Victor, Peter. 'Anti-Cult Groups Riven by Schism and Bitter Feuds.' *The Independent on Sunday*, 9 October 1994: 9.

Vivien, Alain. *Les sectes en France: Expressions de la liberté morale ou facteurs de manipulations? Rapport au Premier Ministre*. Collection des rapports officiels. Paris: La Documentation française, 1985.

Voltz, Tom. *Scientology und (k)ein Ende*. Olten, Düsseldorf: Walter-Verlag, 1995.

von Billerbeck, Liane and Frank Nordhausen. *Der Sekten-Konzern: Scientology auf dem Vormarsch*. Berlin: Ch. Links, 1993 (1994, 5th edn).

von Hammerstein, Oliver. *Ich war ein Munie. Tagebücher und Berichte einer Befreiung aus der Mun-Sekte*. Munich: dtv, 1980 (1st edn; 1981, 3rd edn).

von Schnurbein, Stefanie. *Religion als Kulturkritik. Neugermanisches Heidentum im 20. Jahrhundert*. Skandinavische Arbeiten, Vol. 13. Heidelberg: Carl Winter Universitätsverlag, 1992.

von Somm, Christian. 'Operating Teutons: The Church of Scientology in Germany.' *Religion Today* 7 (2), 1992: 15–16.

von Stietencron, Heinrich. ' "History of Religions" in the Federal Republic of Germany: Heritage, Institutional Setting and Present Issues.' In *Marburg Revisited: Institutions and Strategies in the Study of Religion*. M. Pye, Ed. Marburg: diagonal-Verlag, 1989: 87–96.

von Wiese, Leopold and Howard Becker. *Systematic Sociology*. New York, 1932.

Vontobel, Jacques, Hugo Stamm, Rosemarie Gerber, Kurt-Emil Merki, Klaus J. Beck and Maja Wicki. *Das Paradies kann warten: Gruppierungen mit totalitärer Tendenz*. Zurich: Werd, 1992 (3rd, revised edn).

Waardenburg, Jacques. *Religionen und Religion: Systematische Einführung in die Religionswissenschaft* Berlin: de Gruyter, 1986.

Waardenburg, Jacques. 'Scholarship and Subversion: A Response to Donald Wiebe.' In *Religionswissenschaft und Kulturkritik: Beiträge zur Konferenz The History of Religions and Critique of Culture in the Days of Gerardus van der Leeuw (1890–1950)*. H. G. Kippenberg and B. Luchesi, Eds. Marburg: diagonal-Verlag, 1991a: 87–92.

Waardenburg, Jacques. 'The Problem of Representing Religions and Religion: Phenomenology of Religion in the Netherlands 1918–1939.' In *Religionswissenschaft und Kulturkritik: Beiträge zur Konferenz The History of Religions and Critique of Culture in the Days of Gerardus van der Leeuw (1890–1950)*. H. G. Kippenberg and B. Luchesi, Eds. Marburg: diagonal-Verlag, 1991b: 31–56.

Waardenburg, Jacques. 'Religious Studies Overseas: Report on Research in Europe.' *BASR Bulletin* 84 (June), 1998: 22–23.

Wach, Joachim. *Religionswissenschaft: Prolegomena zu ihrer Grundlegung*. Leipzig, 1924.

Waldenfels, Hans. 'Neue religiöse Bewegungen.' In *Begegnung der Religionen. Theologische Versuche I*. H. Waldenfels, Ed. Bonn: Borengässer, 1990.

Wallis, Roy. 'Ideology, Authority and the Development of Cultic Movements.' *Social Research* 41 (2), 1974: 299–327.

Wallis, Roy. 'Societal Reactions to Scientology: A Study in the Sociology of Deviant Religion.' In *Sectarianism: Analyses of Religious and Non-Religious Sects*. R. Wallis, Ed. London: Peter Owen; New York: Halstead, 1975a: 86–116.

Wallis, Roy. 'The Cult and its Transformation.' In *Sectarianism: Analyses of Religious and Non-Religious Sects*. R. Wallis, Ed. London: Peter Owen; New York: Halstead, 1975b: 35–49.

Wallis, Roy. 'Relative Deprivation and Social Movements: A Cautionary Note.' *British Journal of Sociology* 26 (3), 1975c: 360–363.

Wallis, Roy. *The Road to Total Freedom: A Sociological Analysis of Scientology*. London: Heinemann; 1976a (New York: Columbia UP, 1977).

Wallis, Roy. 'Dianetics: A Marginal Psychotherapy.' In *Marginal Medicine*. R. Wallis and P. Morley, Eds. London: Peter Owen; New York: Free Press, 1976b: 77–109.

Wallis, Roy. 'The Moral Career of the Research Project.' In *Doing Sociological Research*. C. Bell and H. Newby, Eds. London: Allen and Unwin; New York: Free Press, 1977: 149–167.

Wallis, Roy. 'Fishing for Men.' *The Humanist* 38 (1), 1978a: 14–16.

Wallis, Roy. 'Recruiting Christian Manpower.' *Society* 15 (4), 1978b: 72–74.

Wallis, Roy. *The Rebirth of the Gods? Reflections on the New Religions in the West*. Inaugural Lecture Delivered at the Queen's University of Belfast, 3 May 1978. New Lecture Series, Vol. 18. Belfast: The Queen's University, 1978c.

Wallis, Roy. 'Coping with Institutional Fragility: An Analysis of Christian Science and Scientology.' In *Salvation and Protest: Studies of Social and Religious Movements*. R. Wallis, Ed. London: Francis Pinter, 1979a: 25–43.

Wallis, Roy. 'The Elementary Forms of the New Religious Life.' *The Annual Review of the Social Sciences of Religion* 3, 1979b: 191–211.

Wallis, Roy. 'Sex, Marriage and the Children of God.' In *Salvation and Protest: Studies of Social and Religious Movements*. R. Wallis, Ed. London: Frances Pinter, 1979c: 74–90.

Wallis, Roy. 'What's New on the New Religions? A Review of Recent Books.' *The Zetetic Scholar* 6 (July), 1980: 155–169.

Wallis, Roy. 'The New Religions as Social Indicators.' In *New Religious Movements: A Perspective for Understanding Society*. E. Barker, Ed. New York: Edwin Mellen, 1982a: 216–231.

Wallis, Roy. 'Charisma, Commitment and Control in a New Religious Movement.' In *Millennialism and Charisma*. R. Wallis, Ed. Belfast: The Queen's University, 1982b: 73–140.

Wallis, Roy. 'Religion, Reason and Responsibility: A Reply to Professor Horowitz.' *Sociological Analysis* 44 (3), 1983: 215–220.

Wallis, Roy. *The Elementary Forms of the New Religious Life*. London: Routledge and Kegan Paul, 1984.

Wallis, Roy. 'The Sociology of the New Religions.' *Social Studies Review* 1 (1), 1985: 3–7.

Wallis, Roy. 'Sex, Violence, and Religion: Antinomianism and Charisma.' In

Sociological Theory, Religion, and Collective Action. R. Wallis and S. Bruce, Eds. Belfast: Queen's University, 1986: 115–127.

Wallis, Roy and Bruce Steven. 'The Stark–Bainbridge Theory of Religion: A Critical Analysis and Counter-Proposal.' *Sociological Analysis* 45 (1), 1984: 11–27.

Walsh, John. 'High Evangelicalism: Low Evangelicalism – John Wesley as Cultural Broker.' Paper presented to the All Souls Seminar in Oxford, Trinity Term, 10 June 1993.

Wangerin, Ruth Elizabeth. 'Women in the Children of God: "Revolutionary Women" or Mountin' Maids?' In *Women in Search of Utopias*. R. Rohrlich and E. Baruch, Eds. New York: Schocken, 1984: 54–61.

Wartmann, Thomas and Hans Madej. '[Article on F.-W. Haack].' *Geo* magazine 5/87, 1987.

Washington, Peter. *Madame Blavatsky's Baboon: Theosophy and the Emergence of the Western Guru*. London: Secker and Warburg, 1993.

Waßner, Rainer. *Neue Religiöse Bewegungen in Deutschland. Ein soziologischer Bericht*. Information, Vol. 113. Stuttgart: Evangelische Zentralstelle für Weltanschauungsfragen (EZW), 1991.

Weber, Edmund, Ed. *Krishna im Westen*. Frankfurt a. M., Berne, New York: P. Lang, 1985. Studia Irenica, Vol. 30.

Weber, Edmund. 'Vielfalt und Einheit der Religionen.' *Forum Religion und Weltgestaltung* 2/3, 1988: 11–14.

Weber, Edmund. 'Die Religion in der multikulturellen Gesellschaft der Gegenwart: religionstypologische und dogmatische Argumente für eine irenische Kultur.' *Forum Religion und Weltgestaltung* 2, 1989: 11–14.

Weber, Edmund. 'Die Rolle der Religion im zukünftigen Europa.' *Forum Religion und Weltgestaltung* 1, 1990: 4–7.

Welwood, John. 'On Spiritual Authority: Genuine and Counterfeit.' *Journal of Humanistic Psychology* 23 (3), 1983: 42–60.

West, Louis J. 'Dissociative Reactions.' In *Comprehensive Textbook of Psychiatry*. A. M. Freedman and H. I. Kaplan, Eds. Baltimore: Williams and Wilkins, 1967: 885–99.

West, Louis J. 'Contemporary Cults: Utopian Image and Infernal Reality.' *The Center Magazine* 13 (2), 1982: 10–13.

West, Louis J. 'A Public Health Approach to Cults.' In Asociación Pro Juventud, Ed. *1st International Congress on 'Cults and Society: Cults as a Social Problem'*. Barcelona: Asociación Pro Juventud, 1987: 29–40.

West, Louis J. 'Persuasive Techniques in Contemporary Cults: A Public Health Approach.' *Cultic Studies Journal* 7 (2), 1990: 126–49.

West, Louis J. 'A Psychiatric Overview of Cult-Related Phenomena.' *Journal of the American Academy of Psychoanalysis* 21 (1), 1993: 1–19.

West, Louis J. and M. D. Langone 'Cultism: A Conference for Scholars and Policy Makers. Report of Wingspread Conference.' *Cultic Studies Journal* 3 (1), 1986: 117–34.

West, Louis J. and Paul Martin. 'Pseudo-Identity and the Treatment of Personality Change in Victims of Captivity and Cults.' *Cultic Studies Journal* 13 (2), 1996.

West, Louis J. and Margaret Thaler Singer. 'Cults, Quacks and Non-Professional Psychotherapies.' In *Comprehensive Textbook of Psychiatry, III*. H. I. Kaplan, A. M. Freedman and B. J. Sadock, Eds. Baltimore: Williams and Wilkins, 1980: 3245–3258.

Westhoven, Waltraud. 'Betroffen! Was dann?' In *20 Jahre Elterninitiative*. Elternini-
tiative zur Hilfe gegen seelische Abhängigkeit und religiösen Extremismus e.V., Ed.
Munich: Elterninitiative zur Hilfe gegen seelische Abhängigkeit und religiösen
Extremismus, 1995: 207–213.

Wikström, Lester. 'Happy Hookers for Jesus: Children of God's Sex Revolution.'
Update 1 (3–4), 1977: 59–63.

Wilkens, Edwin. 'Zur Situation der Kirchen in der Bundesrepublik Deutschland.' In
Theologische Realenzyklopedie, Band VIII: Chlodwig-Dionysius Areopagita. G.
Krause and G. Müller, Eds. Berlin, New York: Walter de Gruyter, 1981: 593–599.

Wilshire, David. 'The Cottrell Report: A Practical Response to the International Cult
Problem.' Paper presented to the AGPF conference in Bonn, 28 September 1984.

Wilshire, David 'Cults and the European Parliament: A Practical Political Response
to an International Problem.' *Cultic Studies Journal* 7 (1), 1990.

Wilson, Andy. 'The ITC and Guidelines/Regulations.' Talk presented to the
INFORM Seminar on 'New Religious Movements and The Media', London,
29 November 1997.

Wilson, Bryan R. 'An Analysis of Sect Development.' *American Sociological Review*
24 (2), 1959: 3–15.

Wilson, Bryan R. 'A Typology of Sects in Dynamic and Comparative Perspective.'
Archives de Sociologie de Religion 8 (16), 1963: 49–63.

Wilson, Bryan R. 'A Typology of Sects.' In *Sociology of Religion: Selected Readings*.
R. Robertson, Ed. Baltimore: Penguin, 1969: 361–383.

Wilson, Bryan. *Religious Sects: A Sociological Study*. London: Weidenfeld and
Nicolson, 1970a.

Wilson, Bryan. *Les Sectes Religieuses*. Paris: Hachette, 1970b.

Wilson, Bryan R. 'The Debate over Secularization: Religion, Society, and Faith.'
Encounter 45 (4), 1975: 77–83.

Wilson, Bryan. *Contemporary Transformations of Religion*. London, New York:
Oxford UP, 1976.

Wilson, Bryan R. 'The Return of the Sacred.' *Journal for the Scientific Study of
Religion* 18 (3), 1979: 268–280.

Wilson, Bryan R., Ed. *The Social Impact of New Religious Movements*. New York:
Rose of Sharon Press, 1981.

Wilson, Bryan R. 'Sympathetic Detachment and Disinterested Involvement: A Note
on Academic Integrity in Reply to Professor Horowitz.' *Sociological Analysis* 44
(3), 1983: 183–188.

Wilson, Bryan R. 'The Aims and Visions of Soka Gakkai.' *Religion Today* 2 (1),
1985a: 7–8.

Wilson, Bryan R. 'Secularization: The Inherited Model.' In *The Sacred in a
Secular Age: Toward Revision in the Scientific Study of Religion*. P. Hammond, Ed.
Berkeley: University of California Press, 1985b: 9–20.

Wilson, Bryan. ' "Secularization": Religion in the Modern World.' In *The World's
Religions*. S. Sutherland Leslie Houlden, Peter Clark and Friedhelm Hardy, Eds.
London: Routledge, 1988: 953–966.

Wilson, Bryan R. *The Social Dimensions of Sectarianism: Sects and New Religious
Movements in Contemporary Society*. Oxford: Clarendon Press, 1990.

Wilson, Bryan R. 'Reflections on a Many-Sided Controversy.' In *Religion and
Modernization: Sociologists and Historians Debate: The Secularization Issue*.
S. Bruce, Ed. Oxford: Clarendon Press, 1992: 195–210.

Wilson, B. and J. Cresswell, Eds. *New Religious Movements: Challenge and Response*. London, New York: Routledge, in association with the Institute of Oriental Philosophy European Centre, 1999.

Wilson, Bryan R. and Karel Dobbelaere. *A Time to Chant: The Soka Gakkai Buddhists in Britain*. Oxford: Clarendon Press, 1994.

Wittmann, Gerhard. 'Identitätskrise im Jugendalter – ein Grund für den Erfolg von Jugendreligionen?' In *'Jugendreligionen' und neue Religiosität: Notwendige Anmerkungen*. H.-W. Baumann *et al.*, Eds. Gelsenkirchen-Buer: Farin and Zwingmann, 1982: 161–171.

Wolfe, A. 'Sociology as a Vocation.' *American Sociologist* 21 (1), 1990: 136–149.

Woodhall, Ralph. 'PRINERMS and NRMs.' Paper presented to the F.I.U.C. Symposium in Vienna, 1991.

Woodhall, Ralph. 'The Study of New Movements and the Pastoral Concern of the Churches.' *Religion Today* 7 (2), 1992: 17–19.

Woodrow, Alain. *Les Nouvelles Sectes*. Collection Points. Paris: Seuil, 1977 (1st edn), 1981 (2nd edn).

World Council of Churches (WCC). *Guidelines on Dialogue with People of Living Faiths and Ideologies*. Geneva: WCC, 1979.

Wright, Stuart A. 'Post-Involvement Attitudes of Voluntary Defectors from Controversial New Religious Movements.' *Journal for the Scientific Study of Religion* 23 (2), 1984: 172–182.

Wright, Stuart W. *Leaving Cults: The Dynamics of Defection*. Society for the Scientific Study of Religion Monograph Series, Vol. 7. Washington, DC: Society for the Scientific Study of Religion, 1987.

Wroe, Martin. 'A Cult Bestseller . . . and Why You Can't Read It.' *The Observer*, 22 March 1998.

Wuthnow, R. 'World Order and Religious Movements.' In *New Religious Movements: A Perspective for Understanding Society*. Eileen Barker, Ed. New York, Toronto: Edwin Mellen, 1982: 47–65.

Yinger, J. Milton. *Religion, Society and the Individual*. New York, London: Macmillan, 1957.

Yinger, J. Milton. *The Scientific Study of Religion*. London: Collier-Macmillan, 1970.

Yonan, Gabriele. 'Staatliche Kontrolle? Anmerkungen zu einem Buch über "Sekten-Kinder" und die über die SPD eingesetzte "Enquête-Kommission Sog. Sekten und Psychogruppen".' *spirita* 10 (1), 1996: 5–6.

York, Michael. *The Emerging Network: A Sociology of the New Age and Neo-Pagan Movement*. Lanham, MD: Rowman and Littlefield, 1995.

York, Michael and Elisabeth Arweck. 'New Age Dimensions of Goddess Spirituality.' *Religion Today* 6 (2), n.d.: 6–7.

Zaretzky, Irving and Marc P. Leone, Eds. *Religious Movements in Contemporary America*. Princeton, NJ: Princeton UP, 1974.

Zimbardo, Philip G. 'Mind Control: Psychological Reality or Mindless Rhetoric.' *Cultic Studies Review* 1 (3), 2002: 309–311.

Zimbardo, Philip G. and Cynthia F. Hartley. 'Cults Go to High School: A Theoretical and Empirical Analysis of the Initial Stage in the Recruitment Process.' *Cultic Studies Journal* 2 (1), 1985.

Zinser, Hartmut. *Der Untergang von Religionen*. Berlin: Reimer, 1986.

Zinser, Hartmut, Ed. *Religionswissenschaft: Eine Einführung*. Berlin: Reimer, 1988a.

Zinser, Hartmut. 'Einleitung.' In *Religionswissenschaft: Eine Einführung*. H. Zinser, Ed. Berlin: Reimer, 1988b: 1–5.

Zinser, Hartmut. 'Okkultismus unter Berliner Schülern.' *Materialdienst* 53 (10), 1990: 273–290.

Zinser, Hartmut. 'Okkulte Praktiken unter erwachsenen Schülern des zweiten Bildungsweges in Berlin (West).' *Materialdienst* 54 (6), 1991: 176–189.

Zsifkovits, V. 'Wertwandel heute: Eine Herausforderung der Christen in der säkularisierten Gesellschaft.' *Stimmen der Zeit* 115, 1990: 17–29.

Index

New Religious Movements in Global Perspective

Peter B. Clarke

New Religious Movements in Global Perspective is a fresh in-depth account of new religious movements, and of new forms of spirituality from a global vantage point. Ranging from North America and Europe to Japan, Latin America, South Asia, Africa and the Caribbean, this book provides students with a complete introduction to NRMs such as Falun Gong, Aum Shirikyo, the Brahma Kumaris, the Ikhwan or Muslim Brotherhood, Sufism, the Engaged Buddhist and Engaged Hindi movements, Messianic Judaism, and Rastafarianism.

Peter B. Clarke explores the innovative character of new religious movements, charting their cultural significance and global impact, and how various religious traditions are shaping, rather than displacing, each other's understanding of notions such as transcendence and faith, good and evil, of the meaning, purpose and function of religion, and of religious belonging. In addition to exploring the responses of governments, churches, the media and general public to new religious movements, Clarke examines, the reactions to older, increasingly influential religions, such as Buddhism and Islam, in new geographical and cultural contexts. Taking into account the degree of continuity between old and new religions, each chapter contains not only an account of the rise of the NRMs and new forms of spirituality in a particular region, but also an overview of change in the regions' mainstream religions.

Peter B. Clarke is Professor Emeritus of the History and Sociology of Religion at King's College, University of London, and a professional member of Faculty of Theology, University of Oxford. Among his publications are (with Peter Byrne) *Religion Defined and Explained* (1993) and *Japanese New Religions: In Global Perspective* (ed.) (2000). He is the founding editor of the *Journal of Contemporary Religion*.

Hb: 0–415–25747–6
Pb: 0–415–25748–4
Available at all good bookshops
For ordering and further information please visit:
www.routledge.com

New Religions and the Nazis

Karla Poewe

This book highlights an important but neglected part of Nazi history – the contribution of new religions to the emergence of Nazi ideology in 1920s and 1930s Germany. Karla Poewe argues that Nazism was the unique consequence of post-World War I conditions in Germany, a reaction against the decadence of nineteenth-century liberalism, the shameful defeat of World War I, the imposition of an unwanted Weimar democracy, and the post-war punishment of the Treaty of Versailles. Aiming towards national regeneration, leading cultural figures such as Jakob Wilhelm Hauer, Mathilde Ludendorff, Ernst Bergman, Hans Grimm, and Hans F. K. Günther, wanted to shape the cultural milieu of politics, religion, theology, Indo-Aryan metaphysics, literature and Darwinian science into a new genuinely German faith-based political community. Instead what emerged was a totalitarian political regime known as National Socialism, with an anti-Semitic worldview. Looking at modern German paganism as well as the established Church, Poewe reveals that the new religions founded in the pre-Nazi and Nazi years, especially Jakob Hauer's German Faith Movement, would be a model for how German fascism distilled aspects of religious doctrine into political extremism.

New Religions and the Nazis addresses one of the most important questions of the twentieth century – how and why did Germans come to embrace National Socialism? Researched from original documents, letters and unpublished papers, including the SS personnel files held in Berlin's Bundesarchiv, it is an absorbing and fresh approach to the difficulties raised by this deeply significant period of history.

Hb: 0–415–29024–4
Pb: 0–415–29025–2
Available at all good bookshops
For ordering and further information please visit:
www.routledge.com

New Religious Movements in the 21st Century: Legal, Political and Social Challenges in Global Perspective

Edited by Phillip Charles Lucas and Thomas Robbins

New religious movements are proliferating in nearly every region of the world. From new sects within larger global movements such as Islam, Christianity, or Buddhism, to the growth and spread of minority religions (e.g. ISKON, the Unification Church, and Scientology) and the development of completely new religions, the future of these new religious movements will increasingly come to be played out on a political battlefield. Governments in many countries in both the industrialized and the developing worlds have enacted new policies and legislation that dramatically affect not only marginal and minority religious groups but also the broader power relationships between states and the religious freedom of their citizens.

New Religious Movements in the 21st Century is the first volume to examine the urgent and important issues facing new religions in their political, legal, and religious contexts in global perspective. With essays from prominent new religious movement scholars and usefully organized into four regional areas covering Western Europe, Asia, Africa, and Australia, Russia and Eastern Europe, and North and South America, as well as a concluding section on the major themes of globalization and terrorist violence, this book provides invaluable insight into the challenges facing religion in the twenty-first century. An introduction by Tom Robbins provides an overview of the major issues and themes discussed in the book.

Hb: 0–415–96576–4
Pb: 0–415–96577–2
Available at all good bookshops
For ordering and further information please visit:
www.routledge.com